Texas Public School Organization and Administration: 1994

Fourth Edition

edited by
James A. Vornberg
East Texas State University

A Project of Texas Professors of Educational Administration

KENDALL/HUNT PUBLISHING COMPANY
4050 Westmark Drive Dubuque, Iowa 52002

Cover Photos:
A.C.T. Academy
McKinney Independent School District
McKinney, Texas
214/569-6400

A.C.T. Academy is a federally funded demonstration project housing 250 students ages 5-18 in a renovated 50-year-old school building. Its goal is to establish a 21st century school with emphasis on technology as an instructional tool to develop a world class curriculum.

Architect:
The renovation was done by SHW Group, Inc.
Architects, Engineers
4101 McEwen
Suite 300
Dallas, Texas 75244-5039
214/701-0700

Photo Credits:
Jim R. Wilson
Architectural Photography
214/644-1280

Copyright © 1989, 1991, 1993, 1994 by Kendall/Hunt Publishing Company

ISBN 0-8403-9746-1

All rights reserved. No part of this publication may be reproduced, stored in a retrieval system, or transmitted, in any form or by any means, electronic, mechanical, photocopying, recording, or otherwise, without the prior written permission of the copyright owner.

Printed in the United States of America
10 9 8 7 6 5 4 3 2 1

Dedicated

to

those who inspire teachers to
enter the education profession

and

to my mentors

Bob Grant,
M.B. Nelson,
and
Walt St. John

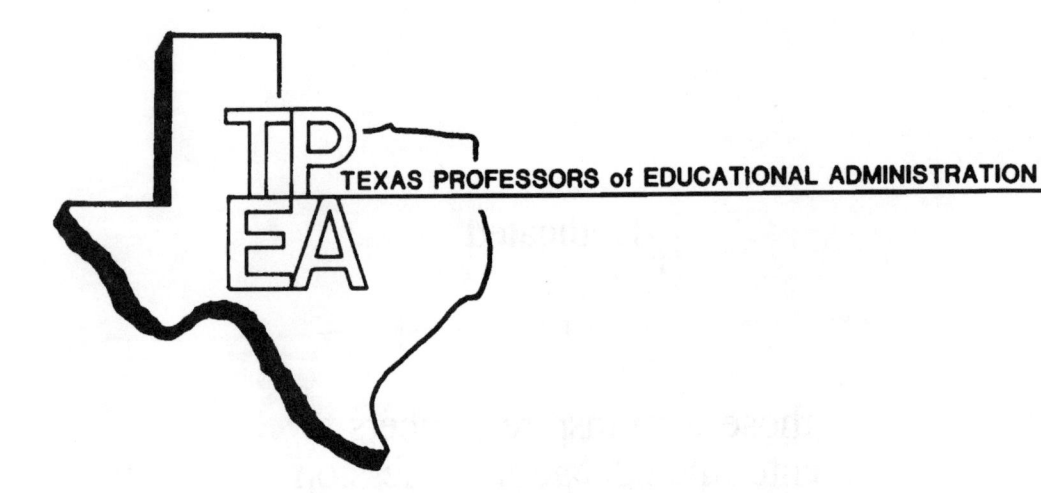

TEXAS PROFESSORS of EDUCATIONAL ADMINISTRATION

Contributors

The Texas Professors of Educational Administration is a professional organization made up of professors who prepare administrators for the schools in Texas. Membership is from thirty-one institutions of higher education, the Texas Education Agency, and the Texas Higher Education Coordinating Board.

James A. Vornberg, editor
Professor of Educational Administration
East Texas State University

Linda Avila
Associate Professor of Educational
  Administration
Texas A&M University--Corpus Christi

Mike Boone
Assistant Professor of Educational
  Administration
Southwest Texas State University

Jo Ann House
Associate Professor of Educational
  Administration
University of Houston at Clear Lake

Max E. Jobe
Professor of Educational Administration
East Texas State University

William D. Alvarez
Associate Professor of Educational
  Administration
Texas A&M University--Corpus Christi

Martha Blake
Assistant Professor of Educational
  Administration
University of Houston at Clear Lake

David W. Gardner
Deputy Assistant Commissioner for
  Research, Planning and Finance
Texas Higher Education Coordinating Record

Tom Huff
Consultant
  Texas Association of School Boards

David T. Kelly
Director of Institutional Certification
Texas Higher Education Coordinating Board

Stephen Knagg
Director of Communications
Garland Independent School District

Frank W. Lutz
Professor of Educational Administration
East Texas State University

Jerry L. Pulley
Professor of Educational
Administration, University
of Texas--Pan American

Ross Sherman
Associate Professor of Educational
Administration, University of Texas at Tyler

Michael P. Stevens
Assistant Professor of Educational
  Administration
West Texas A&M University

Carole Veir
Education Consultant

Clifford L. Whetten
Assistant Professor of Educational
  Administration and Director, Center for
  Community Education
Texas A & M University

William H. Kurtz
Professor of Educational Administration
Southwest Texas State University

Clint Ogilvie
Assistant Professor of Educational
  Administration
Lamar University

Launey F. Roberts, Jr.
Professor of Educational Administration
Texas Southern University

Kip Sullivan
Chairman, Department of Education
Sul Ross State University

Cornell Thomas
Assistant Professor of Educational
  Administration
Texas Christian University

Roosevelt Washington, Jr.
Professor of Educational
  Administration
University of North Texas

Contents

Preface   xv

1. **Organizational structure and Legal Basis of Education in the State of Texas**   1
   Roosevelt Washington, Jr.

   The Development of American Public Schools 2
   Legal Basis for State Control Over Education 3
   The Structure of Government and Sources of Law Relevant to Education 6
   The Study of Case Law 19
   Federal Government Influence Over Education 25
   Summary 28
   References 29

2. **Local School Districts**   31
   Clint Ogilvie

   American School Districts 31
   Texas School Districts 32
   Local School Boards in Texas 34
   The School Superintendent 41
   Challenges/Issues Facing Texas School Districts 44
   Summary 46
   References 46

3. **Regional Educational Service Centers**   47
   Cornell Thomas

   History 47
   Governance 49
   Funding 52
   Services Available 53
   Location of Service Centers
   Current Issues 56
   References 57

4. **The Changing Role of the Central Education Agency**   59
   Martha Blake and Jo Ann House

   Historical Development 60
   State Board 65
   Commissioner of Education 67
   The State Department of Education 69
   Trends 73
   Summary 74
   References 75

5. **Federal Government Involvement in Education**   77
   Roosevelt Washington, Jr.

   Federal Laws and Constitutional Provisions 78
   Federal Legislation Affecting Elementary and Secondary Education 80
   Governmental Commissions 82
   Regulatory Functions of the U.S. Dept of Education 86
   Summary 89
   References 89

6. **Educational Accountability in Texas**   91
   James A. Vornberg

   The Roots of Accountability 92
   The Goals of the Texas System 95
   Managing the Inputs to the System 97
   Monitoring the Process of Education 102
   Assessing the Outputs of the System 104
   Accountability in Texas Reviewed 108
   References 108

7. **Texas Cultural and Ethnic Groups**   111
   Launey F. Roberts, Jr.

   Culture 113
   Cultural Diversity 113
   Racial and Ethnic Groups in Texas: Who Are They? 119
   Educational Equity and Leadership 136
   Urbanization and Population Movement 138
   References 141

8. **The Politics of Education: Texas and the Nation**   **145**
Frank W. Lutz

   Federal Government and School Politics 146
   State Government and School Politics 149
   Politics of Local School Districts 153
   Political Theories of Local School Politics 157
   Education and Politics Revisited 159
   References 160

9. **Texas Public School Personnel**   **161**
Mike Boone

   The Personnel Function 161
   Constitutional Issues Affecting School Personnel Administration 165
   Certification and Contracts 167
   Adverse Actions 171
   Teacher Appraisal 173
   Motivation 174
   Staff Development 177
   Summary 180
   References 181

10. **Financing Schools in Texas**   **183**
William Alvarez

   School Finance and the State 184
   The Evolution of the Equalization Model 185
   Legal Assaults on School Finance 187
   School Finance and the Federal Government 189
   Educational Finance in Texas 190
   Senate Bill 351 Challenged 200
   Elements of Senate Bill 7 206
   Revenue Sources in Texas 206
   Senate Bill 7 Challenged 207
     An Elusive Goal? 208
   References 211
   Suggested Readings 212

11. Curriculum and Instruction in Texas Schools   213
Ross Sherman and Jerry Pulley

   House Bill 246/Chapter 75 214
   Curriculum Guides and Lesson Plans 222
   Textbooks 224
   Standardized Testing 226
   Effective Schools Research 234
   Instructional Models 236
   References 238
   Appendix: TAAS Instructional Targets 240

12. Business Management in Texas Schools   245
Kip Sullivan and Tom Huff

   Educational Planning, Budgeting, Accounting under Bulletin 679 246
   Accounting Code Overview 252
   Purchasing Procedures 263
   Public School Student Transportation 269
   School Food Service 273
   Glossary 275
   References 276

13. Student Discipline   277
William H. Kurtz

   Student Rights and Responsibilities 278
   Enforcing the Student Code of Conduct 279
   Implications for School Administrators 287
   Student Attendance 289
   References 293

14. School Communication and Public Relations   297
Stephen Knagg

   Definition of Educational Public Relations 297
   The Need for a Planned Public Relations Program 298
   Budgeting for the Public Relations Program 299
   The Public Relations Cycle 300
   Written Public Relations Plan 301
   Communicating With a District's Publics 302
   Other Activities of the Public Relations Department 305

Summary 307
References 308

15. Educational Facilities 309
Loren E. Betz and James A. Vornberg

The Texas Situation 309
School District Facility Planning 311
Evaluation of the Existing School Plant 314
Legal Requirements for School Construction 314
Financing School Facilities 315
Opening and Occupying the School Facility 316
Maintenance and Operations 316
Energy Management 321
References 322

16. Dealing with Exceptional Children 323
Linda Avila

Special Education Programs 323
Gifted and Talented Programs 336
References 343

17. The Challenge of Special Population Students 345
Carole Veir

Bilingual Education and English as a Second Language Programs 348
Remedial and Compensatory Instruction Programs 362
Conclusion 378
References 379

18. Vocational, Technical and Career Education 381
Max E. Jobe

Philosophy 381
Historical Development 382
Texas Vocational Education 385
Curriculum 386
Governance 387
Personnel 388
Funding 388
Emerging Trends 389
References 391

19. Community Education   393
Clifford L. Whetton

    Defining and Describing Community Education 394
    The School as a Learning Center for All Ages 396
    Development of Community Education in Texas 397
    Steps for Establishing a Community Education Program 398
    Community Education and the K--12 Program 408
    Summary 410
    References 412

20. Building Level Leadership: The Principalship in Texas   415
Michael P. Stevens

    What is Leadership? 415
    Knowledge and Vision 423
    In Retrospect 425
    References 426

21. Practical Theory in Educational Administration   427
Frank Lutz

    Meaning of Theory 427
    History and Structure of Theory in Educational Administration 428
    The Classical Period (1890-1935) 432
    Humanistic Period (1935-1950) 434
    The Theory Movement (1950-1980) 436
    Post-Positivistic Period (1980-Present) 443
    Suggested Readings 445
    References 446

22. Higher Education in Texas   449
David W. Gardner and David T. Kelly

    Background 449
    Governance 451
    Coordination of Public Higher Education 452
    Financing 454
    Campus Planning 455
    Higher Education and Public Schools 455
    Summary 456
    References 457

Appendixes

A. SBOE Goals and Objectives **459**
B. Field 63: Mid-Management Administrator Objectives **463**
C. Field 64: Superintendent Objectives for the ExCet **471**

Preface

The Texas educational system is a dynamic institution changing as its political, social and economic leaders respond to the demands of the times and the citizens who voice their opinions loud enough to be heard. Even as the finishing touches were being put on the third edition of this book, the Texas legislature was unable to construct a finance plan to overcome the unconstitutional plan designed to respond to the Edgewood v. Kirby case. As the fourth edition was undergoing changes, the legislature and courts still were facing uncertainties in this continuing development. This will be a task worth watching from an educator's viewpoint as well as the average citizen's position. The former will have the parameters of the workplace defined while the latter will be paying the bill and reaping the results in its future leaders and citizens.

The social makeup of Texas is also having to face major changes. A state where the minority is fast becoming the majority in terms of the population makeup, Texas must respond to the educational needs of this new majority in order to maintain its place in the economic picture of the nation. Politicians of all parties must understand the long range impact of their actions with regard to educational programs and remember that education is an investment in the future of our state and of our nation. As important as the immediate economic health of the state is, these policy makers must balance the immediate picture with the long-range picture. What is done in terms of education today will determine the work force which is available to support the economic system in the next generation.

Educational reforms have been prolific over the years. My own generation can remember the postwar baby boom and the scramble to construct enough facilities to house that large group of students; the National Defense Education Act reaction to the Sputnik launch; the Kennedy-Johnson years' goal which brought us the Elementary and Secondary Education Act to displace the educational deprivation of many; and the national response to the *A Nation at Risk* report. This last reform is now characterized as being in its third wave—the first being reforms to change educational priorities focused particularly at the building level; the second restructuring the teaching profession and its role in being accountable for educational results; and the third wave being that of changing the leadership in education by rethinking the preparation of administrators. The quality movement is now impacting the reform activity with an emphasis on making decisions based on actual data as well as building teams to manage and lead at the building level. Texas has responded to all these reforms in a combination of policy changes and procedural initiatives. In fact the changes have occurred at a rate that does not allow for feedback on results of one before another ensues. Through it all, the teachers and their leaders have struggled to maintain their equilibrium and have done a commendable job.

This book helps to describe that system which involves some 261,427 educational professionals, 158,163 classified employees, 7,336 school trustees, and 3,535,742 students. It requires a lot of effort on the part of the authors to develop such a book and maintain it with changes occurring rapidly. Originally seen as a personal writing goal, I quickly realized that it was an impossible task for one person if it was to be current in scope. My colleagues in the Texas Professors of Educational Administration have rallied to make it a reality—now updated in its fourth edition with others planned for every second year. We see it as not only a book for students in educational leadership and policy studies, but one which may be helpful to practicing administrators, school trustees, and for those preparing for their certification examinations (ExCET). This fourth edition adds three new chapters on theory in administration, federal involvement, and leadership at the building level.

Jim Vornberg
East Texas State University

Organizational Structure and Legal Basis of Education in the State of Texas

Roosevelt Washington, Jr.

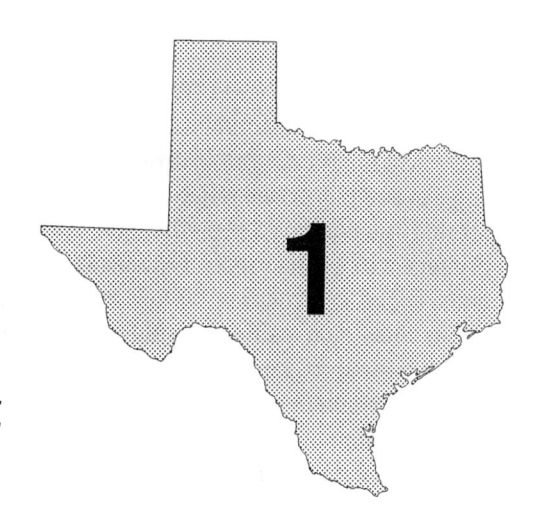

The organization and governance of education in America is unique among the nations of the world. It is a responsibility of the State in which the schools are located; it is given to local decision making; and yet its impact is national and international in scope. No other nation places the responsibility for the education of its citizens at such a grass roots level.

As a function of the State government, education is a major focus of State officials since so many state resources are allocated to advance the development of the young citizen. Texas state government--the administration, the lawmakers, and the court system--is no exception to this focus. Biennially the Texas State Legislature grapples with its financial responsibility for education. Several times in recent years the governor has appointed various committees to explore better ways of administering and improving the schools. The courts in the State of Texas since 1975, also, have been dealing with the problem of how to equitably allocate resources among the districts across the state. Certainly education is a dynamic institution facing a milieu of social problems.

This book depicts the unique and dynamic aspects of the educational system in the State of Texas.

The Development of American Public Schools

The battle in the United States from having only private and parochial schools for the privileged to having free public schools for all, "universal education," was a difficult one and it had different manifestations in different parts of the country, but the battle was finally won. The struggle to develop public school systems in the United States and the respective states that were supported by public monies did not come without bitter battles and controversies. The development of public school systems was promoted and supported, primarily, by middle-class liberals, social and religious reformers, organized labor groups, and the working classes of northern cities. Opposition to public free school schools came primarily from conservatives, southern aristocrats, and certain religious and non-English speaking groups who saw public education movement as a threat by government to grab control over their schools and over the education of their children in their religion and or language.

The primary argument in favor of public schools was that the development and perpetuation of our democratic society and ideals depended upon an educated citizenry. In addition, the argument was made that only through free public secular schools and education that were free from sectarian religious doctrines can the principle of separation of church and state be maintained so as to avoid the problems endemic to most European countries. The basic arguments against free schooling and public control of schools were that private interests and initiative would be undermined by such schools and that the wealth of the privileged should not be taxed to provide an education for the lower classes of the society who could not benefit from education (i.e., education should be reserved only for those who were intellectually able to profit from it and financially able to pay for it). Also, religious groups argued that secular, and therefore "godless" schools, would destroy the religious and moral foundations of the society. In addition, they argued that publicly financed schools would threaten and eventually destroy the financial giving-to and endowments of existing private and religious school systems.

The movement for public education took hold more slowly in the southern states than in other parts of the nation. Before the Civil War, free public education that was provided for the poor and lower class whites and that provided for the land owner, planter, and upper class groups of whites was glaringly disparate; and education for Negroes was nonexistent (in fact, some states had laws prohibiting the education of Negroes in school subjects). However, following the Civil War, free public education, that even included the Negroes, in the southern states was encouraged and supported by various religious and philanthropic groups and the federal government. Despite these efforts, progress in providing free public education for both Negro and poor and lower class white students came slowly.

The development of free public schools in the State of Texas followed much of the same pattern as described above; but the last of the six adopted constitutions in the State in 1876 provided for the development of a system of public free schools. However, McCleskey, Dickens, and Butcher (1975: 290-91) point out in their book that:

> The true beginning of public education in Texas is usually put at 1854, but the painfully slow progress made under the legislation of that year was itself interrupted by the Civil War. During Reconstruction, the Radical Republicans who controlled the state made--to their everlasting credit--a massive assault on the educational problem, but their efforts were so intertwined with the racial question and other political issues of the day that the Democrats, who regained control in 1873, promptly throttled the program. One could without too much injustice say that public education did not finally come of age in Texas until the World War I period, as evidenced by the fact that not until 1915 was there a compulsory school-attendance law, and not until 1918 were free textbooks provided.

Many of the subsequent changes in public education in the State of Texas, as well as in other states, occurred as a result of considerable influence from the federal government, the courts, and public pressure for educational reforms which will be discussed in greater detail throughout this book.

Legal Basis for State Control Over Education

During the colonial period, before the adoption of the United States Constitution, the education of children was a responsibility of the parents. Since the colonial educational system was designed after the English educational system, only the children of the privileged and upper classes received formal education which was provided either by private or religious institutions. The children of the poor and lower classes received little, if any, formal education. For instance, a 1642 Massachusetts law required all parents to educate their own children; and in 1647, the Massachusetts Legislature required towns of 50 families to employ a teacher, and towns of 100 families to establish a Latin Grammar school. In addition, the law permitted taxes to be levied for educational purposes. Despite the presence of these laws, American schools throughout the colonies were essentially private or church-related institutions which were few in number and which had selective enrollments.

Thomas Jefferson was among the first public figures to propose a system of free public education. In a letter to George Wythe in 1786, he wrote in support of a Bill for General Education. He stated that:

> I think by far the most important bill in our whole code is that for the diffusion of knowledge among the people. No other sure foundation can be devised for the preservation of freedom and happiness .... Preach, my dear sir, a crusade against ignorance; establish and improve the law for educating the common people.

Jefferson's plan for education was not passed, but the new philosophy of universal education began to spread and take root. Advocates for state supported education began to emerge and a conflict between church-supported and public-supported developed into bitter struggles in some of the states of our new nation. One of the strongest advocates for state-supported education was Horace Mann who influenced the development of free secular public schools that were supported by both state and local community taxes.

After the adoption of the United States Constitution in 1787, which made no provision for education as a permissible function of the federal government, the legal foundation for education essentially became a State function. The Tenth Amendment to the U.S. Constitution states that "all powers not delegated to the federal government, nor prohibited by it to the states, are reserved to the States or to the people, respectively." Therefore, acting under interpretation of the Tenth Amendment to the U.S. Constitution, all of the States through their constitutions have taken on education as state function. For instance, the Texas Constitution of 1876 established the legal basis the establishment of and control for a public school system in the State of Texas. Article VII, Section 1, of the Texas Constitution reads:

> A general diffusion of knowledge being essential to the preservation of the liberties and rights of the people, it shall be the duty of the Legislature of the State to establish and make suitable provisions for the support and maintenance of an efficient system of public free schools.

It follows, then, that the authority for designating education as a state function is clearly specified in the constitutions of each state which also grants the State Legislature the authority to establish and maintain the system, and to determine its structure and standards by legislative law.

State Legislative Control Over Education

It is clear that education is a state function that is primarily under the plenary control of the State Legislature in the State of Texas as well as in other States. The broad power of the State Legislature, also, extends over public schools as well as over private and parochial schools. In addition, state court decisions have supported the preeminence of plenary State control over education.

Acting under authority of the Texas Constitution, the Texas Legislature has passed laws governing education in the State. The Legislature (TEC §16.001) in its wisdom established the following state policy with regards to education:

(a) It is the policy of the State of Texas that the provision of public education is a state responsibility and that a thorough and efficient system be provided and substantially financed through state revenue sources so that each student enrolled in the public school system shall have access to programs and services that are appropriate to his or her educational needs and that are substantially equal to those available to any similar student, notwithstanding varying local economic factors.

On October 2, 1989, The Texas Supreme Court ruled in *Edgewood Indep. School Dist. v. Kirby,* 777 S.W.2d. 391 (Tex. 1989), that the method of financing education in the State was in violation of Article VII, Section 1, of the State Constitution. In response to this ruling, the Texas Legislature was called into a special (sixth) session by the Governor whereupon it amended this policy to include several provisions concerning the financing of education, in the State. The adopted and signed amendments were as follows:

(b) The public school finance system of the State of Texas shall adhere to a standard of fiscal neutrality which provides for substantially equal access to similar revenue per student at similar tax effort.

(c) The program of state financial support designed and implemented to achieve these policies shall include adherence to the following principles:
  (1) the yield of state and local educational program revenue per pupil per cent of effective tax effort shall not be statistically significantly related to local taxable wealth per student for at least those districts in which 95 percent of students attend school; and
  (2) the level of state and local revenues for which equalization is established shall include funds necessary for the efficient operation and administration of appropriate educational programs and the provisions of financing for adequate facilities and equipment.

(d) Future legislatures are free to use other methods to achieve substantially equal access to similar revenues per student at similar tax effort. These methods may involve minimum tax efforts, redefining the tax base, and other ways to equalize. However, adherence to the state policy described in this section shall be maintained.

State Regulatory Control Over Education

The State Legislature, also, through statutory law created the Central Education Agency (Texas Education Agency) a hierarchical administrative governmental structure to implement, administer, and regulate the state-mandated educational function in the local school districts of the State (see TEC, Title 2, Chapter 11). The primary delegation of authority over education in the state by the Legislature is to the central education agency, called the Texas Education Agency, that consists of a State Board of Education, a Commissioner of Education, and a State Department of Education.

The specific powers and duties of this agency are enumerated and outlined in the Texas Education Code, Title 2, Chapter 11. In addition, this agency also has the authority to make rules and regulations governing education in the state. Those rules and regulations are compiled in the official state publication, *Title 19 Education, Texas Administrative Code.*

As for local school districts, they exist as quasi-municipal corporations—legal extensions (arms or agencies) of the State—whose boards of trustees are considered to be state officials with specific administrative duties and functions mandated by law. The Texas law, §23.25 states that "The board of trustees of an independent school district shall have the powers and duties described in this subchapter, in addition to any other powers and duties granted or imposed by this code or by law." In addition, Texas law §23.26(b) states that "The trustees shall have the exclusive power to manage and govern the public free schools of the district; and in §23.26(d) the trustees are given the authority by law to "adopt such rules, regulations, and by-laws as they may deem proper." Finally, the general duties and authority granted to school superintendents and principals are located in §13.351 and §13.352 of the Texas Education Code.

The Structure of Government and Sources of Law Relevant to Education

In the United States there are two basic structures of government relevant to education, a federal system of government and fifty state systems of government that are highly similar in structure to the federal government, and four basic types or sources of law relevant to education that exist at both the federal and state levels of government which are: (a) constitutional law, (b) statutory or legislative law, (c) administrative (executive) law, and (d) judicial law. A discussion and explanation of each type or source of law at each level of government follows.

Constitutional Law

Constitutional law at the federal level of government, firstly, is composed of provisions that are contained in the U.S. Constitution; it is the basic law of the Nation and it cites our philosophy of government. Secondly, the Constitution defines the structure and specifies the powers and duties of government; however, it provides for a separation of the federal government into three distinct branches of government which in effect defines the other three types of law: Article I creates the legislative branch of government and endows it with the power to make written law; Article II creates the executive (administrative) branch of government and vests it with the power and duty to administer the law and to run the government; and Article III creates the judicial branch of government which is given the power and responsibility of settling controversies arising under the Constitution and Laws of the United States (both statutory and administrative). And, finally, the Constitution defines the rights, privileges, immunities, restrictions, and or guarantees granted to the people and the States of the Nation. Some of the important U.S. Constitutional provisions relevant to education are located in Table 1.1

State Administrative Law

At the State level of government, administrative law is similar to that which exists at the federal level of government. Each state Constitution has created an executive branch of government to enforce the law (both federal and state laws) and run the government. Also each state legislature has created in each State, a state education agency which has been delegated the authority and responsibility to carry out the educational functions of the State as assigned to it by the state law. This agency makes and enforces the rules and, regulations governing education in the state (see Title 19, Education, *The Administrative Code*).

The Governor of the State can issue proclamations and executive orders. The Attorney General of the State can issue his opinions concerning interpretations and issues of law, and the State Education Agency including local school districts have the responsibility of enforcing state laws and making rules, regulations, establishing procedures and guidelines, etc., for implementing the educational function of the state. It is from these departments of state government and its agencies and their officials that administrative law relevant to education at the state level of government exists. Additional information, specifically, about the role and functions of the Texas Governor, Attorney General, and Texas Education Agency follows.

The Office of the Governor The Governor of the State of Texas plays an important administrative law role in the State; especially with regards to state affairs and education. Article IV of the Texas Constitution grants the Governor authority: (1) to address the State Legislature, provide it with information and recommend the enactment of either specific laws or a comprehensive program of legislation; (2) to call special (limited to 30 day) sessions of the Legislature above and beyond the 140 day legislative session that is required every two years to consider matters he deems timely or essential for the conduct of state affairs; (3) to veto laws passed by the Legislature and return them to the Legislature with his objections; (4) to appoint special committees, board members, commissions, and officials of state governmental agencies and departments; and (5) to issue various proclamations and executive orders when deemed necessary. In addition to his constitutionally delegated powers, the Governor has considerable informal power and influence within the state. The fact that the Governor has ready and available access to the media, by virtue of his position as the Chief Executive of the State and leader of his political party, provides him with considerable influence over public affairs and education in the state.

Most recently, however, as a result of a special session of the State Legislature in June 1990, a statute (§11.51a) was passed giving the Governor the authority to appoint the State Commissioner of Education. The law states that

> The State Board of Education shall recommend to the governor a person to be named commissioner of education. The governor shall either reject the recommendation or appoint the person as commissioner of education. The appointment requires the advice and consent of the senate. If the governor rejects the recommendation, the board shall submit further recommendations until one is appointed by the governor and confirmed by the senate.

Also, under this law (11.51b), the State Commissioner serves for a term of four years (expiring on March 1 of the appropriate odd-number year); and "[T]he Governor, with the advice and consent of the senate, may remove the commissioner of education on the petition of two-thirds of the membership of the State Board of Education or may remove for good cause." This law appears to increase the influence and authority of the Governor over education in the State.

The Office of the Attorney General Another functionary exercising an influential administrative law role in the State is the Attorney General. The office of attorney general, which was created by the Texas Constitution, has the following generalized duties and responsibilities as specified by the Texas Constitution and statutory law: (a) to give legal advice to state and local officials in the form of issuing advisory legal opinions (Attorney General's Opinions); (b) to represent the State in civil proceedings as the State's chief legal counsel; the attorney general represents the State and its agencies whenever they are involved in civil litigation; and the attorney general may act independently in initiating a lawsuit on behalf of the State.

Attorney general's advisory opinions can be requested by state agencies or their officials whenever they are confronted with novel or unusually difficult legal questions. The Attorney General's opinions are not legally binding, either on the governmental officials or agencies requesting them or on the courts, but as a practical matter they carry a great deal of influence; especially in those situations in which there is no authoritative interpretation or decision by the courts. However, there is an exception to the advisory (non-legally binding) opinions of the Attorney General with regards to the Texas open records law. The Statute states that if a State governmental body receives a written request for information that it feels is not public (cannot provide) according to the law and there has been no previous determination that the information falls within one of the exceptions specified by law, the government body must within at least ten days request an opinion from the Attorney General to determine whether the information is within that exception. Upon receipt of the request, the attorney general must provide an opinion. However, if a decision is not so requested from the attorney general, the information is presumed to be public information and must be provided. Also, if a governmental body refuses to request an attorney general's opinion or to supply the public information, the attorney general may seek a *writ of mandamus* that compels the government body to make the information available for public inspection. The attorney general's opinion stands as an authoritative and binding interpretation of this legal question facing the State, its agencies and officials.

Texas Education Agency (TEA) The hierarchical structure of the Texas Education Agency consists of the State Board of Education, the Commissioner of Education, and the State Department of Education. The administrative functions of the Texas Education Agency (central education agency) and their administrative offices and officials--including those of local school districts--are divided into two broad categories, ministerial and discretionary functions. Ministerial functions are those required by law; whereas, discretionary functions are those requiring the use of judgment in implementing state law. Ministerial functions includes the right and duty to make policy, rules, regulations, advise, set goals and objectives, establish guidelines and procedures, to supervise, investigate, administer, and coordinate the education function under their jurisdiction. Examples of discretionary functions include quasi-judicial functions such as the settling of disputes between individuals and agencies germane to the state educational function.

It is from the Texas Education Agency and their officials, and the local school districts in the State and their officials, that most of the administrative law relevant to education at the state level of government exists. Many of the published administrative laws, though not as well organized as they are at the federal level of government, can be found in The Administrative Code of the State (Title 19, Education, *Texas Administrative Code*) and in local school district administrative code books. A more thorough discussion and explanation of the roles and functions of the Texas Education Agency, local school districts, and their officials in the State of Texas are provided in subsequent chapters of this book.

Judicial Law

The fourth type or source of law, judicial law, is the law of the courts; i.e., the decisions rendered by the judges of both the federal and state courts. The courts use both the common law and case law in reaching its decisions. Common law is composed of traditions, folkways, and mores which have been handed down primarily from the English legal system, and it derives its authority from "usage and customs of immemorial antiquity (Black, 1979)," and/or judgments rendered by the courts that have recognized such usages and customs. In essence, the common law is based on all the statutory and case law of England and the American colonies before and after the American Revolution. Case law, on the other hand, is the accumulation of law from previous issues or disputes that have been resolved by the contemporary court systems of the United States. A basic principle of case law is the use of precedents by the courts in which they attempt to decide issues on the basis of principles established in previous law cases or disputes of a similar nature. A rule of law that is established in a case for the first time thereafter is considered to be the creation of a precedent. Once a precedent is established, it may serve as an example or authority for resolving cases of a similar nature by a subsequent or lower court. The judges, however, are not bound by precedent, but a precedent is considered to be highly influential in the judicial decision-making process.

Federal Judicial Law

The federal courts operate as the judicial arm of the federal government with jurisdiction, basically, over U.S. constitutional law, federal legislative law, and federal administrative law issues. The federal court system derives its existence and powers from the United States Constitution and subsequent legislation passed by the United States Congress. Article III, Section 1, of the Constitution provides for the establishment of the judicial branch of government through the creation of one supreme court of the United States to which it vests the judicial power of the

United States. Article II, Section 1, states that: "The judicial power of the United States, shall be vested in one supreme court, and in such inferior courts as the Congress may, from time to time, ordain and establish."

Acting within the authority of this constitutional provision, the United States Congress passed the Judiciary Act of 1789 which provided for a supreme court consisting of a Chief Justice and five associate justices. Also, this Act divided the Nation into thirteen judicial districts which were further divided into three circuits, the Southern, Middle and Northern. Subsequent expansion of the Nation from the original thirteen states with the concomitant increased work-load for the judges, Congress authorized the appointment of circuit judges who road the circuit once every two years. In 1891, however, the Congress established nine intermediate appellate courts of appeals which were staffed with their own judges; and in 1911, the Congress enacted the Judicial Code which established a three-level hierarchical system of federal courts. The latest revision of the structure of the federal courts was in 1982 when the Congress authorized the creation of the twelfth circuit court of appeals (a split in the fifth circuit court of appeals). In addition, the Congress has created other specialized courts which have specific functions.

Figure 1.1 depicts the hierarchical structure of our federal court system. At the top is the Supreme Court of the United States which is the court of final jurisdiction. On the next level are the twelve U.S. Courts of Appeals (eleven [11] circuits plus the federal circuit in Washington, D. C.), and on the lowest level are the U.S. District Courts and other specialized courts which are basically courts of original jurisdiction and trial courts.

A person involved in a dispute or controversy involving a constitutional issue or a federal law (statutory or administrative) may seek a resolution through the federal courts. The case will be tried in the federal district court of jurisdiction. Figure 1.2 shows the four federal district courts in the State of Texas. If either the plaintiff or defendant is dissatisfied with the decision of the federal district court, an appeal to the U.S. Court of Appeals in that jurisdiction can be made.

Figure 1.3 shows the jurisdictions of the U.S. Circuit Courts of Appeal and that the State of Texas is in the Fifth Circuit. If the appeal is accepted, i.e., the court grants *certiorari*, the case is reviewed and a decision is reached. Again, if either party, the plaintiff or defendant, in the case is dissatisfied with the decision of the U.S. Appeals Court, an appeal can be made to the U.S. Supreme Court; however, *certiorari*, a successful appeal to the U.S. Supreme Court is rarely granted except in those cases or issues of national significance.

The basic functions of the federal courts are to settle disputes between two or more parties that are permitted by the Constitution and the laws enacted by the Congress. The type of disputes that can be resolved by the federal courts are set forth in Article III, Section, of the U.S. Constitution which states that: "The judicial power [of the federal courts] shall extend to all cases, in law and equity, arising under this Constitution, [and] the laws of the United States. . . to controversies in which the United States shall be a Party; . . .[and] between Citizens of different States. . . the supreme court shall have appellate Jurisdiction both as to law and Fact, with such Exceptions, and under such Regulations as the Congress shall make."

```
            SUPREME COURT
          OF THE UNITED STATES
                   |
     U.S. CIRCUIT COURTS OF APPEALS
          (There are 11 Circuits, plus
           the Federal Circuit in D.C.)
                   |
            U.S. DISTRICT COURTS
             Districts in 50 States
                  Puerto Rico
              District of Columbia
```

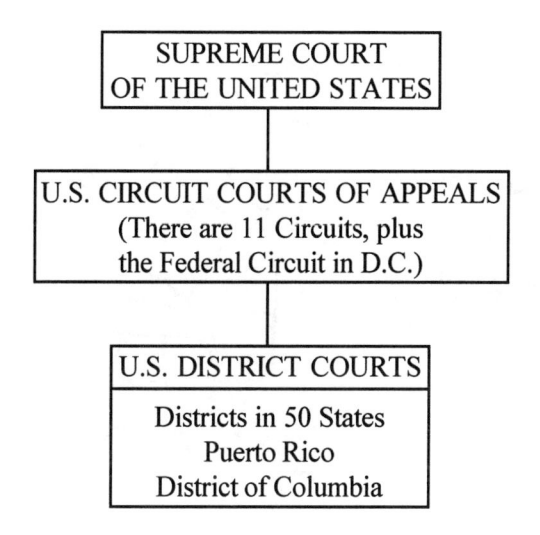

Figure 1.1. The Federal Court System.

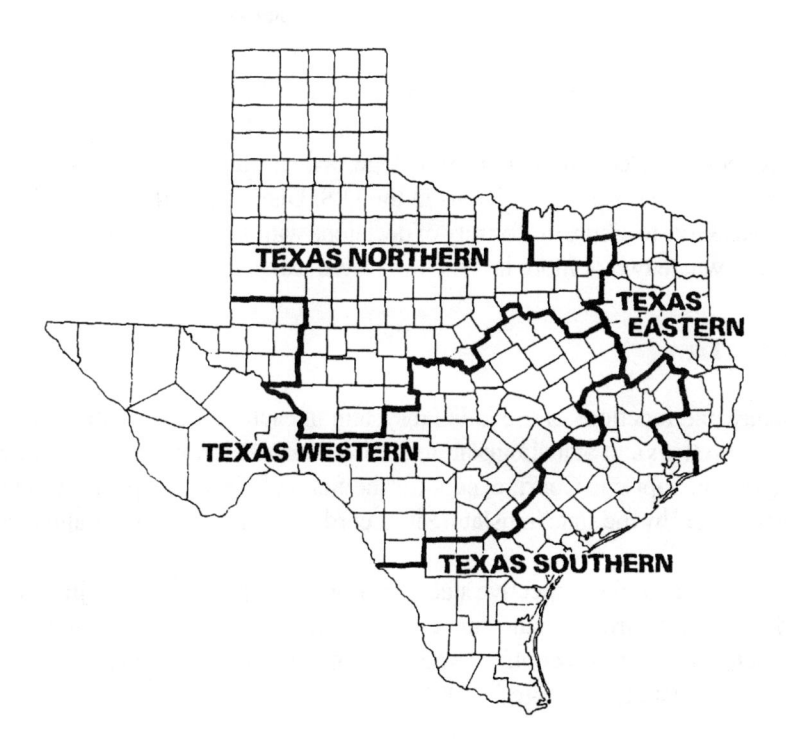

Figure 1.2. Jurisdiction of the U.S. District Courts in the State of Texas.

Figure 1.3. Jurisdiction of the U.S. Circuit Courts of Appeals.

The pyramidal, hierarchical, organizational structure of the federal court system serves two important purposes. First, the U.S. Supreme Court and the U. S. Circuit Courts of Appeals can remedy improper judicial conduct (of the trial judge, lawyers, and jury) and correct judicial errors that have been made in reaching decisions in the U.S. District Courts. Secondly, these higher courts of appeals serve to assure uniformity of decisions within their jurisdiction, respectively, by reviewing cases where two or more lower courts have reached different or conflicting results.

State Judicial Law

The structure and functions of the judicial system in each of the fifty states are provided by their State Constitutions and State Legislatures. All state constitutions provide for a court of final jurisdiction, a State Supreme Court, except for the State of New Hampshire where the highest court was established by the state legislature in accordance with authority granted under its state constitution.

The judicial system of the respective states are not identical, but all state judicial systems are similar in their general structure and functions (in fact, they all resemble the federal judicial system in structure). Figure 1.4 contains a diagram of the court system in the State of Texas was reorganized by the State Legislature in 1981.

Justice of the Peace and Small Claims Courts. The state constitution of Texas provides for the establishment of between four to eight justice of the peace precincts or courts. The justice or judge of which does not have to be an attorney. The justice of the peace (JP) courts have jurisdiction over those misdemeanor violations of the state's criminal laws which are punishable by fines of not more than $200; and the JP cannot confine a person in jail except for contempt of court or to hold a person for further action by a higher court.

With regards to civil matters, the JP courts have jurisdiction over civil disputes and small claims involving up to $1000 (the limit is $2500 for counties with a population exceeding 400,000 people) and other matters not under the jurisdiction of the, county courts and the county courts-at-law such as performing marriages, conducting investigations, and the recording of births and deaths. Civil disputes in the JP courts can be settled without the aid of attorneys, the use of formal judicial procedures, and or the expenses that are usually associated with law suits in higher courts. The Justice of the Peace also has the authority to issue search and arrest warrants, conduct preliminary hearings, and serve as ex-officio notary public. Appeals from this court go the County Court of jurisdiction (Texas Practice, 1989: §23.19).

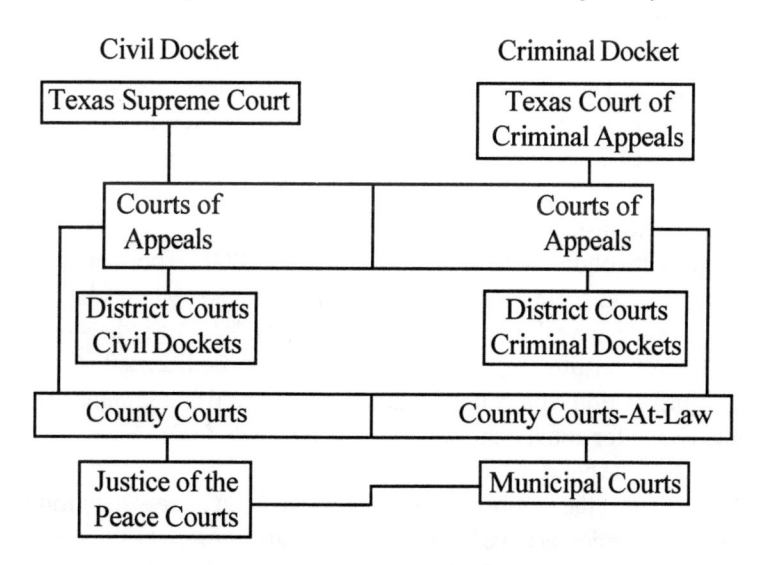

Figure 1.4. State of Texas Court System.

Municipal Courts. A municipal court exists in every incorporated city, town, and village in the state (the mayor acts as the judge if one is not otherwise elected). This court has jurisdiction over all violations of city ordinances which carry punishments of less than $500 and concurrent jurisdiction with the Justice of the Peace Court over misdemeanor violations of state laws involving amounts of less that $500. Also, municipal courts do not have any jurisdiction over civil matters and any appeals from this court goes to the County Court-at-Law of jurisdiction (McCleskey, 1975: 207).

County Courts. The Texas Constitution, Article V, Section 15-18, provides for each county to have a county court, and that the presiding County Judge does not have to be a licensed attorney. At the present time there are 254 county courts. The county judge has jurisdiction over all Class A misdemeanors (violations of law carrying punishments of fines up to $2,000 and/or one year confinement in the county jail) and Class B misdemeanors (fines up to $1,000 and/or confinement in the county jail for up to 180 days). This court, also, has exclusive jurisdiction over civil disputes involving amounts between $200 and $500 and concurrent jurisdiction with the district courts when the amount in controversy is between $500 and $1,000. These courts, also, can hear appeals of decisions from the municipal and justice of the peace courts where the cases are tried *de novo*; i.e., the original case is tried on its merits without any mention of the trial held in the lower court.

There is a special type of county court created by the Legislature that was designed to relieve the county judge of most, if not all, of his/her judicial duties in the more populous counties called a county court-at-law. This court has concurrent jurisdiction with the district court over civil matters involving amounts between $2500 to $50,000 (instead of the $1,000 limit of the constitutional county courts). The judge of the county court-at-law is required by statutory law to be a licensed attorney. Under authority granted by legislation in 1975 and in counties without county courts-at-law, the County Judge may designate a special County Judge (who is a licensed attorney) to act in any criminal or civil matter; however, the elected County Judge is permitted to preside over the county court-at-law if he/she is a licensed attorney (Texas Practice, 1989: §22.5).

District Courts. The district courts are the state's general trial courts and handle criminal cases and civil cases involving a claim of more than $50,000. There are approximately 370 regular district courts, and some of the larger (more populous) counties have such specialized district courts as juvenile and other special jurisdiction courts. The judges of district courts are required by the Texas Constitution, Article V, Section 7, to be licensed attorneys. All district courts share civil jurisdiction with county courts when the punishable sums involved fall within the ranges stated above for county courts (McCleskey, 1975: 209).

Courts of Appeals. The courts of appeals were established by the Texas Constitution, Article V; and, since June of 1981, the number of these courts has been increased to fourteen by the State Legislature. Each of these courts have between three (3) and thirteen (13) judges, but sit in groups of three (3) to hear civil cases by a chief justice and two associate justices. These courts have jurisdiction over all appeals of civil and juvenile cases from the county courts-at-law and district courts in their respective geographic or political regions. Since 1981, these courts have jurisdiction over all criminal appeals except those cases involving the death penalty (McCleskey, 1975: 209).

The Court of Criminal Appeals. Within the State of Texas, this is the court of final jurisdiction for all criminal cases (which in essence is an extension of the court of appeals) unless there is a federal constitutional issue raised whereupon an appeal can be made to the federal court system. The court of criminal appeals is composed of nine (9) judges, one of whom is elected to be the presiding judge; however, for the purposes of hearing appeals, they sit in panels of three (3) members unless there is a successful request by one of the attorneys that the Court sit *En Banc* on a particular appeal (McCleskey, 1975: 209).

The Texas Supreme Court. The Texas Supreme Court is housed in the State Capitol, Austin, Texas, and has a chief justice and eight associate justices. This is the court of final jurisdiction with regards to all civil cases, unless the appellee can successfully raise a federal constitutional issue whereupon an appeal can be made to the federal court system. This court does not review criminal cases (McCleskey, 1975: 209).

The Study of Case Law

A court case is a legal contest or dispute between two parties. It is an adversarial proceeding that takes place in a court of law. In essence, a court case is a civilized method of resolving disputes between two parties. There are two basic types of court cases, criminal and civil, that are litigated in the federal and state courts.

A federal criminal case involves the commission of a wrongful act against the people of the United States; i.e., a violation of the federal constitution or federal law. A state criminal case, on the other hand, involves the commission of a wrongful act against the people of the state; i.e., a violation of the state constitution or state law. When a federal or state crime is committed, it therefore becomes the federal or state government's responsibility to initiate, prosecute, and bear the expense of legal court action against the defendant, the wrongdoer in the federal court.

A federal criminal case, usually, can be distinguished from a federal civil case by its title; e.g., a criminal case cites the People of the United States (as the Plaintiff--the accuser) versus John Doe (the defendant--the accused wrongdoer). A state criminal case, also, is usually distinguished by its title; the People of the State of Texas v. Jane Doe. Successful prosecution of a criminal case can bring penalties of a fine, imprisonment, or both to the adjudged guilty party. Since, in the study of education law, one rarely deals with crimes committed against the federal or state governments, the primary emphasis will be on understanding civil law cases at both levels of government.

A federal civil case involves disputes over one's rights guaranteed by the Constitution of the United States and by federal laws. A state civil case, on the other hand, involves disputes over violations of one's personal rights that are protected under the common law and that State's Constitution and statutory laws. The basic remedies provided by both federal and state courts in civil cases are of the following types:

1. A grant of relief by awarding the aggrieved party compensation, "damages," for the harm or loss suffered by the wrongful acts of another.

2. Commanding the wrongdoer to discontinue the wrongful act(s), in which the court issues a *writ of injunction;* i.e., commanding the person or agency to cease and desist performing the wrongful act or actions. Also, the courts can command a person or agency to act or to perform an act which is to issue a *writ of mandamus.*
3. To restore to the aggrieved person that which was taken or broken (such as to restore one's job, pay, etc.).
4. To declare a federal or state law or an administrative act or action to be in violation of the United States Constitution.
5. To declare a state law or an administrative act or actions to be in violation of the State Constitution.

Role of the Judge and Jury in a Civil Court Case

The role of the judge in a court case is to protect the public interest; i.e., to follow established and acceptable court procedures, to interpret and apply the law, and to provide an answer to the legal question or questions placed before the court that are in accordance with the appropriate and applicable constitutional, statutory, and or common law principles. The jury, on the other hand, if there is one, has the responsibility of making the decision in the case. If there is no jury (i.e., a bench trial--trial by the judge) at the trial court level, then the decision in the case is made by the judge. At the appellate court levels in state courts (as well as in the appellate federal courts), there is no jury or trial; the decision in the case is one for the judge(s) to make.

Role of the Lawyers in a Civil Court Case

Early in American colonial history, courts were established before there were lawyers to practice before them. The judges soon discovered that the issues they were asked to resolve were not clearly understood, and that the people appearing before them were not knowledgeable about the government, law, their rights, or court proceedings, and thus were incapable of effectively asserting or defending their rights. The courts, then, began to authorize men who were well read in government and law to appear in court to represent those persons who appeared before the courts without knowledge and ability. With the adoption of the United States Constitution, lawyers became an essential functionary in the American legal system. The complex nature of our federal and state laws and legal procedures make the use of lawyers in a court case for both the plaintiff and defendant, no matter how trivial the issue before the courts, essential for justice to be served.

The role of the lawyers for both the plaintiff and defendant remain one of defending his or her respective client. Lawyers are commissioned by clients to do everything and anything that is legal, ethical, and moral to advance their particular interests. In any civil court case, both the plaintiff and defendant should have the advice and assistance of a competent lawyer. In a criminal case, the public prosecutor is always the plaintiff's lawyer due the fact that the generalized plaintiff is always the People of the United States or of the State wherein the crime was committed.

Understanding Civil Judicial Procedures

A civil case is initiated by a party who feels aggrieved--feels that his/her personal rights or rights guaranteed by the U.S. Constitution have been violated--or feels that he/she has been wronged by another party and the two parties cannot settle their dispute to the satisfaction of either party. When such an impasse exists, and the aggrieved party has exhausted all reasonable means of resolving the dispute, the issue is usually taken to the courts for resolution. Exhaustion of administrative remedy refers to a situation wherein an individual complains to or about the actions of a government official or a governmental agency (complaints over administrative law), most courts require that the aggrieved party appeal from the lowest administrative level of government to the top of the administrative hierarchy before the issue can be brought to the courts for resolution.

Civil cases that are taken to the federal courts for resolution are bound by the *Rules of Civil Procedures* that have been prescribed by the United States Supreme Court. By an act of Congress in 1934, The Supreme Court of the Unites was authorized to prescribe rules of civil procedures for the United States District Courts and Federal Rules of Appellate Procedures for the United States Courts of Appeals. The law states that:

The Supreme Court shall have the power to prescribe by general rules, the forms of process, writs, pleadings, and motions, and the practice and procedure of the district courts and courts of appeals of the United States in civil actions . . . and for the judicial review of enforcement of orders of administrative agencies, boards, commissions, and officers. Such rules shall not abridge, enlarge or modify any substantive right and shall preserve the right of trial by jury as at common law and as declared by the Seventh Amendment to the Constitution. (20 U.S.C. 2072)

Most state courts have adopted similar rules of civil procedures as mandated for the federal courts by the United States Supreme court. Therefore, is clear that any person has the right, under probable and reasonable cause, to initiate a civil action in the appropriate court, federal or state, to obtain civil redress for grievances.

The task of the courts is to settle specific disputes and issues between parties who are unable to settle their own, controversies. The courts in reaching their decisions must consider only the material facts that are relevant to the case, and when the judge does this, he speaks excathedra, with the full force and authority of the courts and law. However, when the judge departs from the facts or ratio decidendi (reasoning applied by the courts to crucial facts) of the case, he is issuing dicta; i.e., speaking mere words of advice or wisdom that are not binding on anyone, but are words that may be influential in future cases or disputes. The litigation process, the basic outline of how an issue gets to the courts and what the court does to resolve the dispute, is discussed below.

The Litigation Process

Birth of a Lawsuit

Unfortunately, a civil lawsuit begins with a mutually unresolvable complaint between a person or governmental agency and another person or agency over a charge that (1) a state law violates their U.S. or State Constitutional rights, (2) a federal law violates their U.S. Constitutional rights or is in conflict with the U.S. Constitution, (3) an administrative practice or action violates their U.S. or State Constitutional rights, or (4) they have been personally injured as a result of the acts of another or that another's acts or actions of either omission or commission caused their injury. Fortunately, the disputes of the latter two types do not always end up in court; the vast majority of them are either prevented, resolved through administrative remedy, or settled out of court. Moreover, the pressure is growing to minimize the use of the courts to settle such disputes, especially due to the high cost of litigation, both in time and money.

Most lawsuits have their formal beginnings when an aggrieved person seeks out the services of a lawyer concerning an unresolved complaint or problem. At this point, the lawyer either accepts the case or advises the client to either drop the case or to seek the services of another lawyer. If the lawyer accepts the case, the lawyer typically sends a letter or makes a telephone call to the potential defendant threatening legal action unless the client's complaint is resolved satisfactorily. If the lawyer's efforts to settle the dispute are unsuccessful, the situation enters into the arena of the more costly litigation phase.

Selection of a Court

When the decision has been made to have an issue settled in court, the plaintiff's lawyer must select the court having jurisdiction over the subject matter of the complaint. Statutory law usually governs the type of court and place, or venue, when legal action may be brought. Venue is usually dependent upon the residence of the involved parties, the place where the issue developed, or the type of court in which the case will be heard. Most civil cases are filed in state courts; but when the case involves a federal law or a U.S. Constitutional issue, the case could be filed in the federal district courts.

Filing the Complaint

Civil court action is started by the plaintiff's lawyer who files a complaint with the appropriate court; whereupon the defendant must be given a copy of the complaint along with a summons, an order to appear in court. Some states require that the summons be delivered to the defendant in person, while other states permit the delivery of summons to the defendant by registered mail or through published legal notices in local newspapers.

The Pleadings

In the pleadings, the plaintiff alleges that certain facts are true and asks for remedy such as to declare a law or action unconstitutional, impermissible, and/or to seek relief or damages for the wrong or injury received to which the defendant is required by law to state his/her denial or defense against the claim or complaint. If the defendant fails or chooses not to deny the claim(s) within acceptable time limits, under common law principles of pleadings, the alleged materials of fact are usually admitted before the court as presented, which will result more than likely in a victory for the plaintiff by default.

However, the defendant can file a demurrer if he/she believes that the plaintiff's allegations are true, but feels that the defendant failed to state the facts sufficiently to constitute a course of action. Through a demurrer, the defendant alleges that the plaintiff's accusations are not an issue of fact, but an issue of law which must be determined by the court and not by a jury. The judge in the case who conducts the hearing on the demurrer can either sustain or overrule the demurrer. If the demurrer is sustained, judgment will be given to the defendant; and if the demurrer is overruled, judgment will be made in favor of the plaintiff unless either party asks for leave to plead over (which is usually granted by the courts).

Pretrial Discovery

During the pretrial discovery phase, each party in the dispute is given equal access to all of the available facts. Through out-of-court testimony, each party in the dispute, including lawyers and witnesses, engage in exchanging information relevant to the case. Discovery includes dispositions upon written and oral questions, written interrogatories—written questions or requests for information, requests for documents, photos, etc., and requests for permission to enter land or other property for inspection or other relevant purposes, request of physical and/or mental examination if relevant, and requests for admission of facts by both the plaintiff and defendant.

Unless limited by an order of the court, the scope of discovery covers any matter that is relevant to the subject matter involved in the pending action even though it relates to the claim or defense of the party seeking discovery or to the claim or defense of the other party. The object of the discovery phase is to ascertain the truth and to reduce the element of surprise in litigation. Lawyers take the discovery process seriously by turning over evidence and documents that may prove detrimental to their cases; because if they fail to do so, the court may fine or even jail their client for contempt of court. As a result, the discovery process oftentimes promotes out-of-court settlements because it lets each of the parties assess the strengths and weaknesses of their case.

Efforts to Settle the Case Without a Trial

Following the discovery phase of a case, the courts in many states and in the federal courts may order a conference between the plaintiff's and defendant's lawyers to explore the possibility of an out-of-court settlement or reaching an agreement as to what are the important issues or concerns that can simplify and shorten the trial. Also, it has been estimated that about only 10 percent of the cases go to trial. The others are either settled by mutual agreement, dropped, or dismissed by the courts.

The Trial

Each party to the lawsuit has the right to a trial by jury; however, by mutual consent of the parties involved, an action at law may be tried by the judge without a jury. The number of jury members can vary from between six to twelve members, depending upon state law relevant to the issue.

Once the jury members are empaneled, the plaintiff's lawyer presents his/her client's case with each witness being subject to cross examination by the defendant's attorney. The defendant's lawyer then presents his/her clients defense with the plaintiff's being given the same opportunity to cross examine witnesses. After both the plaintiff's and defendant's lawyers present their summation of the case before the court, the judge gives legal instructions to the jury (if there is one) whereupon the case is deliberated and a decision reached.

Unlike in criminal trials, in 31 of the States, the verdict (decision) does not have to be unanimous by the jury; however, in all States, the verdict by the jury must be agreement of at least two-thirds. Also, there are a few infrequent cases in which the judge will overrule the jury or reduce or increase a damage award when it appears that the jury did not reach its decision on the basis of a "preponderance of evidence," the test of conviction applied in civil cases.

The Judgment and Costs

The judgment is the final resolution of the dispute by the court which may include any other orders from the court from which a dissatisfied party can appeal. If the defendant loses the case and refuses to pay the required court ordered damages, the plaintiff may have to get a court order directing the sheriff or other governmental officials to seize the defendant's property and sell it to satisfy the judgment. If the defendant is a governmental agency, the court order will direct the agency to pay.

Common law principles state that the successful party to a lawsuit is ordinarily entitled to costs against the other as a matter of right. If the plaintiff wins, he/she generally recovers a judgment for the amount of the jury's verdict plus litigation costs; and if the defendant wins, he/she can usually recover a judgment for the litigation costs from the plaintiff.

Appellate Review

Following the conclusion of a trial and final judgment, the losing party to the lawsuit, if dissatisfied, has the right to petition a higher court for a review of the case with the hope that the decision will be overturned.

Federal Government Influence Over Education

During the formation of our Nation there was a national interest in education. Under the Continental Congress, the Ordinance of 1785 was enacted. It provided that ". . . there shall be reserved the lot No. 16 of every township for the maintenance of public schools, within said township," in the land of the Northwest Territory later known as the States of Indiana, Illinois, Michigan, Ohio, Wisconsin, and a part of Minnesota. Two years later, the Ordinance of 1787 was passed which provided for the sale of land by federal contract to the Ohio Development Company that reserved a certain township in each territory for the endowment of a university, and expressed the national policy toward education which stated that "Religion, morality and knowledge being necessary to good government shall forever be encouraged."

When the United States Constitution was adopted in 1789, it contained the Tenth Amendment which stated that "The powers not delegated to the United States by the Constitution, nor prohibited by it to the states, are reserved to the States, respectfully, or to the people." This Amendment, thus, defined the American governmental system as one of delegated and implied powers and provided for a division of powers between the federal government and the fifty separate state governments. Even though this division of powers is often wrought with misunderstandings and conflict, by interpretation of the Tenth Amendment, the federal government is prevented from becoming directly involved in education. However, since the founding of our Nation and the adoption of our Constitution, the federal government has sought ways to bring about support for and influence over education in the respective states.

Federal government support and influence over education emanates from the following sources: (a) federal grants to the States and its educational agencies which are provided for under the implied authority given to Congress by the General Welfare Clause of Article 1, Section 8, clause 1, of the United States Constitution, (b) interstate and intrastate standards or regulations that the Congress imposes upon the States under the authority of the Commerce Clause of Article 1, Section 8, clause 3 of the United States Constitution; and (c) federal court judicial review, the right under common law for the federal courts to review state laws and actions which are charged with conflicting with or violating the constitutionally protected rights and freedoms of individuals or States. A brief discussion of each of these powers and sources of federal government influence follows.

Federal Government Influence Through the General Welfare Clause

Article 1, Section 8 (Clause 1) of the Constitution, states that "The Congress shall have Power To lay and collect Taxes...to provide for the common Defence and general Welfare of the United States . . .

" This constitutional provision has served as the legal foundation on which the Congress has relied to pass laws and appropriate federal tax monies to support and influence education within the respective States. The States as a result of this constitutional provision have been able to enter into contract with the federal government and its agencies (most specifically, the Department of Education), for federal funds for specific educational purposes. However, once a State government or any of its agencies accepts federal monies, whether as a grant or as a result of a contract with a federal governmental agency, it is bound by all federal rules, regulations, guidelines, procedures, etc. (i.e., federal administrative laws) associated with the monies as well as with all federal laws.

There have been many unsuccessful challenges to the right of the federal government to provide public tax monies to the States under Article 1, Section 8 (Clause 1) as well as many unsuccessful challenges to the right of the federal government to enforce compliance with federal laws associated with government grants and contracts. These two issues are at the center of most of the conflicts and misunderstandings concerning the federal role and influence over education in the respective States.

Federal Government Influence Through the Commerce Clause

Under the implied powers of the Commerce Clause, Article 1, Section 8 (Clause 3), which states that the Congress shall have the power "To regulate commerce . . . among the several States . . ." The federal government has influenced education in the States through congressional legislation primarily in the areas of employment, labor regulations, and transportation. The broad interpretation concerning the meaning of commerce was explicated by Chief Justice Marshall in *Gibbons v. Ogden*, 9 Wheaton 1; 7 L.Ed 23 (1824), in which he ruled in the majority opinion of the Court that "...Commerce among the states must, of necessity be commerce within the states . . .The power of Congress, then, whatever it may be must be exercised within the territorial jurisdiction of the several states . . . It is the power to regulate; that is, to prescribe the rule by which commerce is to be governed. This power, like all others vested in Congress, is complete in itself, may be exercised to its utmost extent, and acknowledges no limitations other than are prescribed in the Constitution . . ."

In the *National League of Cities v. Usery*, 426 U.S. 833 (1976), a challenge was made concerning the applicability of the 1974 Amendments to the Fair Labor Standards Act to the States which extended wage and hour standards to almost all public employees, including school district employees. The Supreme Court, while admitting that the Amendments were within the scope of the Commerce Clause, held that the Tenth Amendment to the U.S. Constitution was violated. The decision enunciated a restrictive view of the Commerce Clause and interpreted the Tenth Amendment as a clear limiting force upon the power of Congress to regulate activities of a State government or its agencies. However, the ruling in the *National Leaque of Cities v. Usery* was overturned in 1985 by the Supreme court in the *Garcia v. San Antonio Metropolitan Transit Authority*, 471 U.S. 1049 (1985). In this case, the Court ruled that the federal government does have the authority to enforce the Commerce Clause found in Article 1, Section 3, of the U.S. Constitution. The majority opinion delivered by Justice Blackmun stated that:

> Insofar as the present cases are concerned, then, we need go no further than to state that we perceive nothing in the overtime and minimum-wage requirements of the FLSA [Fair Labor Standards Act] as applied to SAMA [San Antonio Metropolitan Transit Authority], that is destructive to state sovereignty or violative of any constitutional provision . . .

Federal Government Influence Through Judicial Review

The third basic source of federal influence over education in the States is through the federal courts. A basic power of the federal courts is the right of judicial review--the power of the courts, and finally the United States Supreme Court, to review and declare both federal and state laws unenforceable for being in violation of the United States Constitution. Also, those individuals who feel that their constitutionally protected rights and freedoms have been violated by a State agency or its officials can seek remedy in federal court in the form of damages under the Civil Rights Act of 1871 (42 U.S.C. 1983) which states that:

> Every person who, under color of any statute, ordinance, regulation, custom, or usage, of any State or Territory, subjects, or causes to be subjected, any citizen of the United States or other person within the jurisdiction thereof to the deprivation of any rights, privileges, or immunities secured by the Constitution and laws, shall be liable to the party injured in an action at law, suit in equity, or other proper proceeding for redress.

The nature of judicial review was explained, eloquently, by Professor Charles L. Black (1960: 12) of the Yale Law School who stated that:

> In the course of a judicial proceeding, it may happen that one of the litigants relies on a statute or other governmental pronouncement which the other litigant contends to be repugnant to some provision of the Constitution. It is the task of the court to determine what the law is. If the constitution is a law of superior status, then the rule of the Constitution, and not the rule of the statute or other governmental pronouncement, is the correct rule of law for application to the case before the court. The Court, under our system, therefore considers itself bound to follow the rule of the Constitution, and so to treat the other rule as a nullity.

The power of judicial review over federal statutes was established by the U.S. Supreme Court in the case of *Marbury v. Madison*, 1 Branch 137 (1803). The Congress passed the Judicial Act of 1801 on February 3 of that year which relieved Supreme Court judges of circuit court duty, increased the number of circuit court judges, and created a number of minor judicial positions. President Adams during his last sixteen days in office proceeded to fill the newly created 67 judgeships with people loyal to his political party. The incensed Jeffersonian party upon taking office repealed the Judiciary Act of 1801 on March 8, 1802. In effect, the Judiciary Act of 1789 was restored whereby the Supreme Court judges were returned to circuit court duty and all of the newly created judgeships and positions were abolished.

When the Supreme Court convened, the case of Marbury v. Madison was on the docket. Marbury was one of the judges appointed by President Adams under the Judiciary Act of 1801 whose commission was not delivered by James Madison, the Secretary of State when Jefferson took office as President of the United States. Marbury filed a suit asking the Supreme Court to issue a writ of mandamus to compel the issuance of his commission as judge. The right to issue such a writ was conferred upon the Supreme Court by the Judiciary Act of 1789. Chief Justice Marshall of the Supreme Court, speaking for the majority of the Court, ruled that, even though the issuance of the writ of mandamus was a proper remedy in this case, the section of the Judiciary Act of 1789 granting the Supreme Court the authority to issue such a writ was void. Thus, the doctrine of judicial review, or the power of the Supreme Court to declare laws of congress unconstitutional, was established. A portion of Chief Justice Marshall's opinion that dealt with the issue concerning the power of the federal courts to invalidate acts of Congress follows:

. . .It is emphatically the province and duty of the judicial department to say what the law is. Those who apply the rule to particular cases, must of necessity expound and interpret that rule. If two laws conflict with each other, the courts must decide on the operation of each. . .

So if a law be in opposition to the Constitution; if both the law and the Constitution apply to a particular case, so that the court must either decide that case conformably to the law, disregarding the constitution, or conformably to the Constitution, disregarding the law, the court must determine which of these conflicting rules governs the case. This is the very essence of judicial duty . . .[1 Cranch 137; 2 L.Ed 60 (1803)].

Summary

This chapter has provided an analysis and discussion how public school education was developed and is organized in the United States and in the State of Texas. In addition, an analysis and discussion has been provided for both the prospective and practitioner school administrator concerning the legal basis of education as a state rather than a federal function; however, it has been emphasized that the federal government has and still continues to exert considerable influence over education in the states through federal programs, federal legislation, and U.S. Constitutional provisions that are enforced through judicial review in the federal courts.

Another important discussion in this chapter that is important to the school administrator is the sections that explain the type or sources of law relevant to education; namely, constitutional, legislative (statutory), administrative, and judicial law. Tables containing some of the important laws of each type at the federal level of government have been provided, and it is recommended that school administrators in the State of Texas become familiar with these laws at the state level of government. The effective administrator needs to know and understand the type of federal and state law that he or she is required to enforce and implement.

References

Black, Charles L. *The People and the Court.* New York: The Macmillan Co., 1960.

Black, Henry Campbell. *Black's Law Dictionary*, Fifth Edition. St. Paul, Minn.: West Publishing Co., 1979.

McCleskey, Clifton, E. Lary Dickens, and Allan K. Butcher. *The Government and Politics of Texas*, Fifth Edition. Boston: Little, Brown and Company, 1975.

Texas Administrative Code, Title 19 Education. St. Paul, Minn.: West Publishing Co. (under authority of the Texas Secretary of State), April 1, 1992.

Texas Education Agency. *Texas School Law Bulletin* (Education Code). Copyright by West Publishing Co.

Texas Legislative Service, Austin, Texas. Senate Bill 1 as Finally Passed and Sent to the Governor (Sixth Called Session), June 1990.

Brooks, David B. *Texas Practice: County and Special District Law,* Vol. 36. St. Paul, Minn.: West Publishing Co., 1989.

Local School Districts

Clint Ogilvie

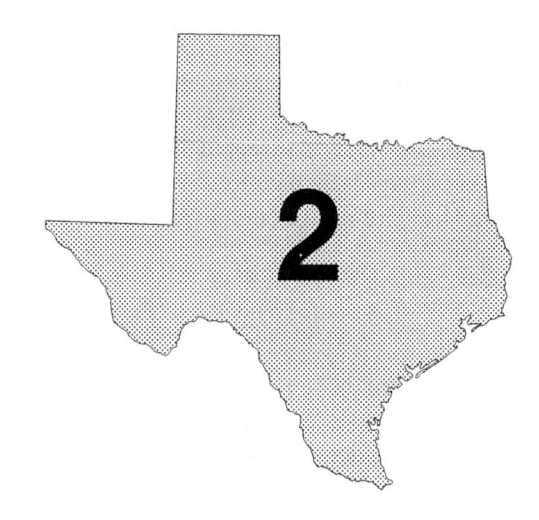

American School Districts

The local school district is a concept originating in America dating back more than 200 years. Education was important to the founding fathers and was critical if the young democracy was to survive. No other country has attempted to educate all its young and to turn over the task of education to its local citizens. This chapter will focus on the major players of local school district governance: the school board and the superintendent.

The basic function of the local school board has been to keep control over education at a point as close to the parent and child as possible. School board members play a major role in the governance of local districts. It is important that board members represent **all** of the citizens of the district and perform their duties in a responsible manner. Local citizens who attempt to gain a position on a school board, motivated by a single issue or other "hidden agenda," do a tremendous disservice to the district and the students of that community. Board members who fail to support and respect the role of the professional staff are compromising the educational program of the school.

The superintendent and other administrators should provide the professional guidance and educational leadership needed to promote excellence in the classroom. These responsibilities require difficult choices and often subject administrators to public criticism. In addition to their instructional leadership, administrators of a school district are responsible for the daily operations of one of the largest "businesses" in the community.

In most areas, *the schools are the largest employer in the community*. The schools have a significant impact on the community's economy. In most cases the school runs the largest transportation system, provides the biggest food service operation, and has an operating budget dwarfing many commercial enterprises in the community.

The framers of the constitution knew that if the democracy was to survive, the masses must be educated. They were opposed to the elitist educational systems of Europe controlled by the ruling class. They also feared putting control of the schools in the hands of central government. By not specifically mentioning education in the federal constitution, it was left as a "state's right." Each state, through its state constitution, has provided for the education of its citizenry.

Texas School Districts

In the State of Texas there are 1,057 school districts and more than 6,700 campuses. These districts are as varied and vast as the state itself. The 212,000 public school educators and 3.4 million students reflect the cultural diversity of the Lone Star State (TEA, 1992).

Six of the 1,057 districts are **common school districts** administered by the county. The remainder are **independent school districts,** including several districts on military bases, all of which are governed by a local school board. Eight districts in the state have over 50,000 students while 598 of the districts have fewer than 1,000 students (TEA,1992).

Due to the large number of smaller districts, school district consolidation has been discussed as a method to reduce educational expenses and provide for more varied educational opportunity. Smaller communities throughout the state make the following arguments against consolidation: loss of local control, loss of community identity, and the student academic success in smaller districts often exceeds that of larger districts.

The 3.4 million Texas students are diverse in terms of ethnicity and educational needs. Forty-nine percent of the students are Anglo, 34% Hispanic, 14% black, with the remainder representing various ethnic groups. Over 40% of the students qualify for free or reduced lunches. In the state there are nearly 450,000 student f.t.e.'s (full time equivalents) enrolled in vocational programs, 300,000 in bilingual programs, 250,000 in gifted and talented programs, and 340,000 in special education programs.

There are over 212,000 teachers in the state, 79% of whom are female and 77% are anglo. There are over 16,000 school administrators and 23,000 other professionals, such as counselors, librarians, etc. These professionals are supported by 33,000 dedicated secretaries and aides and 116,000 auxiliary employees. Education is truly a "labor intensive" operation. Salaries for these 400,000 plus employees and related personnel expenses represent nearly 80% of most school districts' budgets (TEA, 1992).

The average teacher salary for the 1991-92 school year was $27,555 and the average administrator salary equalled $45,941. The state pupil-teacher ratio was 16:1 while the average teacher-administrator ratio was 13:1. The median per pupil expenditure in Texas in 1991-92 was $3,971. Forty-six percent of educational revenue came from the state, 50% from local funds, and 4% from the federal government. Public school education has a tremendous impact upon the lives of the 3.4 million Texas students as well as the Texas economy (TEA, 1992).

The School District Organization Chart (Figure 2.1) is a simplified illustration of school district organization. The solid lines which connect the boxes (positions) indicate a "line," or authority, relationship between the positions while the dotted lines indicate a "staff," or nonsupervisory, relationship.

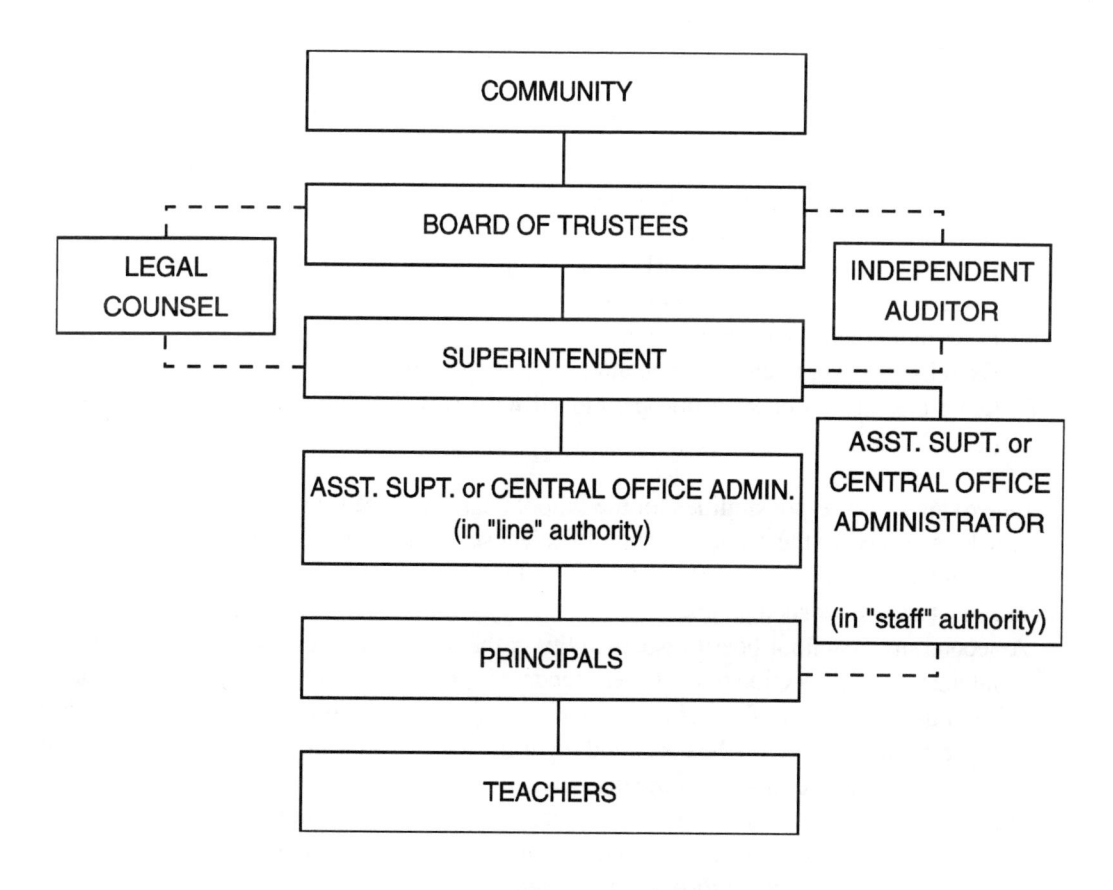

Figure 2.1. School District Organization Chart

Local School Boards in Texas

Powers and Responsibilities of School Boards

The Texas Constitution places the responsibility for public education with the State Legislature. Article VII of the Texas Constitution states: "A general diffusion of knowledge being essential to the preservation of the liberties and rights of the people, it shall be the duty of the Legislature of the State to establish and make suitable provision for the support and maintenance of an efficient system of public free schools." The Texas Legislature has, in turn, delegated to local school boards the authority to carry out this important function. Texas Education Code 23.26 (b) states: "The board shall constitute a body corporate and shall have the exclusive power to manage and govern the public free schools of the district."

As the legal agent of the State of Texas, local school boards have specific statutory powers and duties granted to them by the Texas Legislature. Examples of these statutory powers and duties include:

1. To govern and adopt necessary rules and regulations.
2. To levy, set a tax rate and collect taxes.
3. Have prepared, adopt, and file a district budget annually.
4. Have district funds audited yearly by an independent auditor.
5. Acquire and hold real and personal property in the name of the district.
6. Enter into contracts as may be appropriate.
7. Exercise the right of eminent domain to acquire property.
8. Close the schools or suspend operation if necessary to maintain law, peace and order (TASB,1992).

One of the major responsibilities for the school board is the setting of educational goals and establishing policy for the school system. Efficient school governance requires sound, clearly written, and legally correct school policies. The Texas Association of School Boards provides an excellent source for such policies.

A second major school board responsibility is the selection and evaluation of the school superintendent. The selection of the superintendent is perhaps the most significant decision the board will make in terms of the effect on the educational program of the district. A positive working relationship between the board and superintendent, which will be discussed later in the chapter, is critical to the success of the district.

While the school board has great authority, it should be noted that individual board members have no authorized power outside of school board meetings. *The day to day operation of the school is clearly the responsibility of school administrators and should not be infringed upon by over zealous board members.* "The Board being a body corporate, members can perform no valid act except as a body at meetings properly convened and conducted" (*Buchele v. Woods*, 1975).

Board members must also abide by regulations intended to prevent conflicts of interest. Examples of conflicts of interest include:

1. Contracting with a business entity in which a trustee has a substantial financial interest. (TASB Board Policy ''BBFA'' outlines procedures to be followed in such an instance.)
2. A board member's acceptance of a ''benefit'' in return for a vote or other consideration is construed as bribery (Penal code 36.01).
3. A board member shall not intentionally violate a law relating to the office or misapply anything of value belonging to the district as this is considered a misuse of office.
4. A board member may not occupy two legally incompatible offices, such as teaching and serving on the board in the same district.
5. No person shall be employed in the district who is closely related to a board member. (Nepotism will be further explained in the chapter.)

Eligibility and Qualifications of Board Members

To be eligible for election, a school board candidate must be:

1. A registered voter in the county,
2. A resident in the school district for six months prior to the filing deadline, and
3. A resident of the state for twelve months before the filing deadline.

Beyond statutory requirements, there are personal qualifications a community should look for when selecting their school trustees (board members). A checklist for voters evaluating candidates might include:

1. Does the candidate have the interest of *all* students at heart when making the decision to run for office? (rather than running for personal interests or the interests of only a portion of the community)
2. Does the candidate have the educational background and experience needed to fully understand the issues and make well informed decisions?
3. Does the candidate respect the role of the superintendent and other administrators to manage the district on a day to day basis?
4. Will the candidate be an advocate for educational excellence? (rather than advocating only specific programs or interests, such as ''holding down taxes'')
5. Will the candidate dedicate the time necessary to be an effective school board member?
6. Is the candidate willing to serve without compensation?
7. Will the candidate be willing to make tough decisions even when those decisions may be unpopular in the community?

School board members should adhere to the "School Board Member Code of Ethics." The code, provided below in its entirety (Figure 2.2), requires board members to uphold and enforce state law and State Board of Education rules. Board members should also recognize that decisions are made by the entire board, therefore, a trustee should never make personal promises to constituents. Respecting the confidentiality of information that is privileged should always be honored. The board should vote to appoint the best qualified personnel available only after the superintendent has recommended such personnel.

Board members in Texas serve without compensation. Reimbursement to board members for reasonable travel expenses for attendance at conferences, state meetings, etc., is permissible when attendance at such meetings is deemed desirable in carrying out the educational functions of the district. It is impermissible to reimburse spouse's expenses at such meetings.

School Board Elections

There are three methods of conducting school board elections available to Texas districts: at-large elections, election by position or place, and election by single member districts. Board members normally serve three year terms of office which are staggered to ensure that boards always have experienced members in office and not all members will be up for re-election the same year.

In at-large elections all candidates compete with one another with those candidates receiving the most votes being elected. For example, seven candidates are running for three positions on the board. The three candidates, of the seven, receiving the most votes are elected. Typically, small school districts use the at-large system. The advantage of this system is that only a plurality, rather than a majority, is required for election. This eliminates the need for run off elections except in the unusual case of a tie. The disadvantage of this system is that all candidates, including incumbents, compete against one another.

School board elections may also be by position or place. In this system, designated positions or places, not usually having any relationship with geographic areas, are up for election every three years. Candidates indicate for which position they are running at the time of the filing. In this system a candidate can run against a particular person. Once a district officially adopts this method of electing its trustees, the decision can never be rescinded. The advantage of this system is that it ensures a majority of voters will select the elected members and allows candidates, including incumbents, from competing against all other candidates. The disadvantage is that run off elections are sometimes required to gain a majority of votes needed.

Single member districts are similar to election by place with the exception that in single member districts there are geographical boundaries which determine the place in which you may run. In single member districts, a board can choose to have a small number of board members, less than 30%, elected at large. Single member districts are usually found in larger urban school districts where there is a variety of ethnic groups concentrated in particular areas of the city. The

School Board Member Code of Ethics

As a member of the board, I shall promote the best interests of the school district as a whole, and, to that end, I shall adhere to the following educational and ethical standards:

- Bring about desired changes through legal and ethical procedures, upholding and enforcing all laws, State Board of Education rules, and court orders pertaining to schools;
- Make decisions in terms of the educational welfare of all children in the district, regardless of ability, race, creed, sex, or social standing;
- Recognize that decisions must be made by the board as a whole and make no personal promise or take private action that may compromise the board;
- Focus board action on policy making, goal setting, planning, and evaluation, and insist on regular and impartial evaluation of all staff;
- Support and protect school personnel in the proper performance of their duties;
- Vote to appoint the best qualified personnel available after consideration of recommendations of the superintendent;
- Hold confidential all matters pertaining to school that if disclosed, may needlessly injure individuals or the schools, and respect the confidentiality of information that is privileged under applicable law;
- Attend all regularly scheduled board meetings insofar as possible and become informed concerning the issues to be considered at those meetings;
- Delegate authority for the administration of the school to the superintendent;
- Endeavor to make policy decisions only after full discussion at publicly held board meetings, and render all decisions based on the available facts and refuse to surrender that judgment to individuals or special groups;
- Encourage the free expression of opinion by all board members and seek systematic communications between the board and students, staff, and all elements of the community;
- Communicate to board members and the superintendent at appropriate times expressions of public reaction to board policies and school programs;
- Inform myself about current educational issues by individual study and through participation in programs providing needed information, such as those sponsored by my state and national school board associations;
- Refrain from using my board position for personal or partisan gain;
- Make certain the board remains responsive to the community; and
- Remember always that my first and greatest concern must be the educational welfare of all the students attending the public schools.

Figure 2.2. School Board Member Code of Ethics

advantage of single member districts is to ensure that each geographic area of the city is represented on the school board.

Occasionally a vacancy will occur on a school board due to death, resignation, or removal from office. If a vacancy occurs on the board, the remaining members of the board may fill the vacancy by appointment until the next regular election or may call for a special election to fill the vacancy for the unexpired term. A board member who ceases to reside within the school district vacates his office. A board member may be removed from office for incompetency, as defined by law, official misconduct, or the conviction by jury for a felony.

Most school districts hold regular board elections the first Saturday of May. Alternate dates are available under state election law. School board candidates must file for a place on the ballot at least 45 days prior to election day. There are also various filing requirements for reporting campaign spending. A majority of school boards in Texas are composed of seven members. Districts with more than 64,000 ADA (average daily attendance) are governed by a nine member board.

State nepotism law prohibits a person from being employed in the school district who is related to a member of the board by consanguinity (blood relationship) within the third degree or by affinity (marriage relationship) within the second degree. A chart depicting these relationships is provided in Table 2.1. The exception to this rule is the case in which a person has been employed in the district at least six months prior to the election of the board member relative. The nepotism statute applies only to elected officials. Appointed officials, such as a superintendent or principal, are not subject to the nepotism law.

School Board Training

As of 1984, and the passage of H.B. 72, board members are required to participate in school board training. Within 60 days before or after their election, new board members must participate in a local orientation session. In addition, new members are to earn 20 hours of approved training from the "Statewide Standards on Duties of a Board Member" during their first year in office. In subsequent years, all board members are required to participate in at least six additional hours of training.

The "Statewide Standards on Duties of a Board Member" include:

1. The board member shall uphold the educational and ethical standards that promote the best interest of the district as a whole.
2. The board member shall understand the role and responsibility of the board, board president, and individual members.
3. The board member shall understand and respect the role and responsibility of the superintendent.

TABLE 2.1.
Nepotism Chart

These illustrations depict the relationships that violate the nepotism law.

CONSANGUINITY (Blood Kinship)	Board member is prospective employee's:
First Degree	Parent or Child
Second Degree	Grandparent, Grandchild, Sister, Brother
Third Degree	Great Grandparent, Great Grandchild, Aunt, Uncle, Niece, Nephew
AFFINITY (Marriage Kinship)	Board member's spouse is the prospective employee or Board member's spouse is prospective employee's: or Prospective employee's spouse is the Bd. member's:
First Degree	Parent or Child
Second Degree	Grandparent, Grandchild, Sister, Brother

(Source: TASB, 1992)

4. The board member shall be familiar with the organizational structure of the district and methods of interacting with the community.
5. The board member shall assume an active role in the development of board policy.
6. The board member shall understand the importance of effective planning.
7. The board member shall accept responsibility for the adoption of high quality instructional programs.
8. The board member shall work toward establishing sound business and fiscal practices for the district.
9. The board member shall adhere to legal and ethical constraints and understand the nature of school law.
10. The board member shall understand the board's function relative to district personnel.
11. The board member shall be well versed in board meeting management.
12. The board member shall pursue a course of personal excellence and effectiveness.

School Board Meetings

School boards convene in regular meetings generally once or twice a month and in special meetings as needs dictate. It is important that the community be informed of the business to be conducted in these meetings and have the opportunity to express their wishes to elected officials. Meetings of the school board are open to the general public with the exception of executive sessions, which may only be used in particular circumstances permitted by law. Minutes of board meetings are kept and are also available to the public.

Districts are required to post notice and an agenda of each meeting 72 hours preceding the scheduled time of the meeting. In case of an emergency or urgent public necessity, the notice may be posted two hours before the meeting is scheduled to convene.

Agendas for school board meetings must be sufficiently specific to inform the public of the topics, including any special or unusual matters, to be discussed. A quorum, or majority, of the board must be present to conduct business. No vote of the school board may be taken in executive session or by secret ballot.

Executive sessions, or closed meetings, may be allowed for the following purposes:

1. For private consultation with the board's attorney with respect to pending or contemplated litigation.
2. To discuss the acquisition of real property (land).
3. To discuss personnel matters or to hear charges against an employee, unless that employee requests the hearing be held in open session.
4. In cases involving discipline of a student.
5. In cases where a complaint is brought against an employee by another employee, unless the employee against whom the charge is made has requested the hearing be held in open session.
6. To discuss security personnel or security devices.
7. To discuss individual assessment instruments or achievement tests which are confidential by nature.

It is generally the responsibility of the school superintendent, in consultation with the board president, to set and post the agenda. The board president, or in his absence the vice-president, will preside over the meeting. The secretary of the board is usually responsible for taking board minutes.

Texas Association of School Boards

The Texas Association of School Boards (T.A.S.B.) has provided services to local school districts in Texas for over 40 years. More than 1,000 school districts are members of the state association. T.A.S.B. is a voluntary, nonprofit organization located in Austin.

Services to local districts are financed through membership fees and on a cost basis. Such services include: board policy development, legal services, legislative networking, school board training, risk management, etc. The T.A.S.B. Annual Conference, held in conjunction with the Texas Association of School Administrators, is one of the largest conventions in the state. The conference is usually held in late September.

The School Superintendent

Role and Responsibilities of the Superintendent

The second major player in local school district governance is the school superintendent. The superintendent serves as the educational leader and chief executive officer of the district. The superintendent is appointed to the position by the board of trustees.

Major responsibilities of the school superintendent include:

1. Functions as the advisor to the board of trustees and the chief administrative officer of all divisions and departments of the school system.
2. Administers the development and maintenance of an educational program designed to meet the needs of the community.
3. Recommends the number and types of positions required to provide proper personnel for the operation of the educational program.
4. Recommends policies and procedures on organization, finance, instruction, personnel, school plant, and other functions of the school program.
5. Nominates for appointment, assigns and defines the duties of all personnel.
6. Suspends from duty, subject to confirmation by the board, any teacher or other employee for cause.
7. Supervises the preparation of the annual budget and recommends it to the board of trustees for approval.
8. Keeps the board of trustees continuously informed on the progress and condition of the school system.
9. Attends and participates in all meetings of the board, except when the board is meeting in executive session to discuss the evaluation or contract of the superintendent.
10. Is an ex-officio member of all committees of the board.
11. Conducts a continuous study of the development and needs of the schools and keeps the public informed.
12. Sees that the policies of the local board, rules of the State Board of Education, and applicable laws are observed and executed.

The superintendent, while accountable to the board of trustees, must work as a partner with the board. There is often confusion between the superintendent and board members regarding roles and responsibilities. This confusion, in turn, can result in tension that interferes with the proper governance of the district. Respect for each other's roles and open communication between the superintendent and board are crucial to the success of the district. The following chart delineates some of the major differences in the duties of the superintendent and the school board.

TABLE 2.2.
Selected Duties of the Superintendent and School Board

Function	Duties of the School Board	Duties of the Superintendent
Administration	The board hires the superintendent and delegates responsibility for administrative functions.	The superintendent is responsible for managing day to day operations.
Policymaking	The board establishes policy for the governance of the school district.	The superintendent is responsible for recommending policy to the board and implementing procedures to carry out these policies.
Hiring and Evaluating Personnel	The board employs professional personnel by contract upon recommendations of the superintendent and evaluates only the supt.	The superintendent recommends personnel to be hired, is responsible for evaluation of all employees, and makes other contract recommendations.
Budget	The board communicates the district's priorities to the superintendent through identified goals, reviews the budget, adopts the budget, and sets the tax rate.	The superintendent, or his/her staff, prepares a budget, recommends the budget to the board, makes revisions as requested by the board, and administers the budget.

(Source: TASB 1992)

The superintendency is a very challenging position. The responsibility is significant and the pitfalls are numerous. Politically, a successful superintendent must please his/her seven member board, the community, and the staff. As the educational leader of the district, the superintendent must possess the courage to make tough decisions which will sometimes alienate one of more of these groups. The superintendent deals with controversial issues such as: employment and dismissal of personnel, salary schedules, budgets and tax rates.

In years past, the stereotypical superintendent was seen as a white, male authoritarian figure. Today, a greater number of superintendents' positions are being filled by capable female and minority administrators. With site based management being the focus in Texas schools today, it is important that school superintendents possess a democratic leadership style and serve as a facilitator of group decision making.

The qualifications of a school superintendent include:

1. Masters degree, often a doctorate is preferred
2. Texas Superintendents Certificate
3. Successful administrative and teaching experience
4. Skills in instructional leadership, finance, planning, personnel, school law, communications and public relations

Recruitment and Appointment of the Superintendent

It is the responsibility of the board of trustees to recruit and appoint the superintendent. School boards often times hire consultants to assist with this important function. These consultants, nicknamed "headhunters," may assist the board by advertising the vacancy, actively recruiting qualified administrators, reviewing candidates' resumes, making recommendations regarding the finalists, and assisting with contract negotiations.

Superintendents are usually hired on a multiple year term contract, with a three year contract being most typical. By law, districts with under 5000 ADA can not offer the superintendent a contract longer than three years. Districts exceeding 5000 ADA are limited to no more than a five year contract. It is the practice of many districts to "roll over" the superintendent's contract each year to maintain the length of the multiple year contract. This practice is essential to provide the superintendent the job security and authority needed to be an effective educational leader.

Annual salaries of school superintendents may range from $40,000 in smaller districts to over $100,000 in larger urban districts. While such salaries may seem excessive, they are very reasonable when compared to the salaries of chief executive officers in business and industry with equal responsibility and pressure.

Evaluation of the Superintendent

The school board is responsible for the evaluation of the superintendent. The written evaluation will occur at least yearly and must precede any contract decision. The board shall establish an annual calendar which provides for the following activities:

1. a goal-setting procedure in which expectations and priorities are agreed upon
2. formative conference(s)
3. summative conference(s)

The superintendent shall be involved in the development and selection of the appraisal instrument and process. The summative conference and contract consideration of the superintendent will normally occur in January or February each year.

The criteria used to evaluate the superintendent shall include, but is not limited to, the following (Source: TASB, 1992):

1. Instructional management
2. School/organization climate
3. School/organization improvement
4. Personnel management
5. Administration of fiscal affairs
6. Administration of plant management
7. Student management
8. School/community relations
9. Professional growth and development
10. Board/superintendent relations.

Texas Association of School Administrators

The Texas Association of School Administrators (T.A.S.A.) is a state-wide organization composed of approximately 1,800 superintendents and other school administrators. The organization, which is nearly 70 years old, is headquartered in Austin T.A.S.A. provides superintendents opportunities for professional growth through conferences and training programs. T.A.S.A. is also a strong advocate for Texas school districts with the State Legislature.

Challenges/Issues Facing Texas School Districts

There are many challenges facing Texas school districts today. Those issues often cited by superintendents and school boards include: school finance, problems of governance, politics, and general societal problems. This section will provide a cursory description of these issues.

School Finance

Following the *Edgewood v. Kirby* decision by the Texas Supreme Court, the State Legislature was directed to correct an inequitable system of school finance. Under the pressure of having the entire state school system "shut down," lawmakers in Austin made several attempts to provide such equity only to come up short of the constitutional standard required by the Court.

While some progress was made to enhance funding to property poor schools, these gains created tremendous local property tax increases for nearly all districts. Such tax increases at the local level put many superintendents and school boards at odds with taxpayers in their communities.

State funding for education has been inadequate in recent years to meet the needs of the schools. A growing student population along with increasing state mandates compound the problem. Proration of funding to local districts has been used by the State when shortfalls occurred. Local school districts lost $306 million due to proration in 1991-92 and an estimated $500 million in 1992-93 (Powers, 1992).

These problems of school finance have created tremendous challenges for school boards and superintendents. With the uncertainty of State funding, it is almost impossible for school districts to conduct long range financial planning. Teacher salaries, the replacement of equipment and maintenance of aging school facilities often suffer when districts are forced into budget cuts.

Problems of Governance

One of the major challenges facing school districts today is the problem of school district governance. Governance problems occur when school board members either do not accept or understand their role as a policy making body. Local boards are becoming more involved in the administrative function and day to day operation of the school district although these areas are the domain of school administrators.

This encroachment by misdirected board members creates a tremendous strain on the relationship between the superintendent and school board. In several districts the Texas Education Agency has had to step in to resolve these governance disputes. A school district jeopardizes its accreditation when this occurs.

Politics

Closely associated with governance problems are political problems which arise in the operation of school districts. The influence of politics in educational decision making is a major frustration, yet a normal occurrence, for school administrators. Since school districts are a government entity directed by elected officials, it is quite common for this to occur. It is important that school board members and administrators rise above petty politics and base educational decisions on what is best for all students in the district.

Societal Problems

The schools are confronted with the enormous task of dealing with numerous societal problems. While educators are being held accountable for test scores and other measures of student achievement, the problems in society greatly influence the students taught. The success of students is hindered by poverty, lack of adequate health care, an A.I.D.S. epidemic, gangs, crime, drugs, dysfunctional families and a lack of community support. The expectation that local schools have a responsibility to help solve the problems of society creates pressure for local educators and requires additional resources which are in short supply.

The challenges to local school districts are great. To adequately meet these challenges the schools need administrators, who are outstanding instructional leaders, and school board members dedicated to providing the best educational program possible. School leaders need to be aware of these societal problems and make a commitment to address the needs of all students. Local businesses and school volunteers can be of great assistance in this effort. Bright, energetic school administrators are needed to lead the schools into the twenty-first century.

Summary

The concept of local school districts governed by local citizens originated in America more than 200 years ago. The major players of district governance are the school board and superintendent.

In order for school district governance to function properly it is critical for the superintendent and school board to have a clear understanding of their roles and maintain open communications. The school board is the policy making body for the district while the superintendent is responsible for managing the district on a day to day basis.

The school board and superintendent must work closely together to confront the many challenges facing public schools today. These challenges include school finance, governance, politics, and societal problems.

References

Powers, John (August 30, 1992) "State Trims Aid to Schools." *Beaumont Enterprise*.
Texas Association of School Boards (1992) *1992 Guide for School Board Candidates*. T.A.S.B.
Texas Association of School Boards (1991) *Services and Programs of TASB*. T.A.S.B.
Texas Association of School Boards (July, 1992) *T.A.S.B. Policy Manual*. T.A.S.B.
Texas Education Agency (July, 1992) *Texas Public Schools Statistics for 1991-92*. T.E.A.
Texas Education Agency (1992) *Statewide Standards on Duties of a School Board Member*. T.E.A.
Vornberg, James A. (1991) *Texas Public School Organization and Administration: 1991 Second Edition*. Kendall/Hunt Publishing Co.

Regional Education Service Centers

Cornell Thomas

The Regional Education Service Centers are public institutions charged, by the Texas Legislature, with providing educational services to public school districts on a regional basis. Service centers coordinate educational planning in the region, address the needs of local school districts and serve as a link between the local school districts and the state education department. The following overview delineates the history, governance, funding, available services and a directory of the twenty centers across the state.

History

Before the creation of regional service centers in Texas, small school districts had an extremely difficult time housing adequate media libraries. These districts lacked both the financial and physical capabilities to adequately equip themselves in this area. Although larger independent school districts, colleges, and universities were trying to meet the needs of smaller school districts, the cost and complications, involved with the transport of media software to and from locations was becoming a growing concern across the state. Alternative solutions to this problem were developed. The Texas Legislature, after much input and debate, then took action. This action culminated in the creation of the Regional Educational Service Centers, originally as state-supported, regional media lending libraries and resource centers for instructional materials.

Prior to the creation of the Regional Educational Service Centers and as far back as the mid 1850s, County School Units existed. County School Units were primarily responsible for the construction and maintenance of school buildings and for the hiring of an adequate cadre of teachers and support staff to keep the educational system functioning properly. Each county unit served individual school districts with preset county lines and boundaries.

After the turn of the century, county units began to provide additional services which included bus transportation to the public school children, expanded services for handicapped children, improved bus fleet maintenance, the creation of audio-visual software and hardware, educational consultants and psychologist upon request, and other related services.

State funding for the county units ceased in 1967 with the creation of the twenty Regional Education Service Centers. The legislature, after much controversy and review dating back to the late 1950s, determined that school districts would be better served by the centers.

Only two county units continue to function today—the Dallas and Harris County School Systems. These two systems were supported by voter approved taxing authority prior to the state's decision to discontinue funding. Both units are financially sound at this time and continue to provide and expand services for the public schools they serve.

In 1965 the Legislature authorized the State Board of Education to set up regional media centers by 1967. That same year, the United States Congress passed the Elementary and Secondary Education Act of 1965. The act, under Tittle III, provided funds for supplementary educational centers. As a result, the Texas Education Agency recommended coordination of the state's media centers and the federally-supported service centers. Specifically, Texas Education Code Section 11:32 states: "The State Board of Education shall provide, by rules and regulations, for the establishment and operation of regional education service centers to provide educational services to the school districts and to coordinate educational planning in the region."

Texas is divided into twenty regions, with each region having its own education service center. The centers are service organizations, not regulatory agencies. Participation by districts is voluntary.

In October, 1991, the Commissioner of Education, Lionel R. Meno, presented a plan to reorganize the Texas Education Agency to the State Board of Education. The plan calls for a consolidation and decentralization of various Agency functions in order to improve services to local school districts. The creation of a new Office of Field Services has had the most impact on regional education service centers. This office oversees sixty field service agents who are housed at the regional education service centers. Agents for the Partnership School Initiative, one per center, are also housed at each center.

Another ten Agency positions were transferred from TEA to the regional education service centers in January 1992 to provide regional teacher certification services, with an additional ten positions scheduled to be transferred by January 1993. This position was created to process teaching permits in a timely matter and to provide a direct link between TEA and school districts. Specialists in this position provide the following services:

Teaching Permits
- Process teaching permits to determine eligibility or ineligibility of an applicant
- Technical assistance with teaching permits assignments
- Service on the spot processing permits
- Provide workshop training for teaching permits

Certification
- Information dissemination—requirements for teachers, administrators, and special service positions
- Technical assistance with TEA certification forms
- Consultation of assignments
- Referral to local senior colleges and alternative certification programs

Thirty federally-funded positions in the Child Nutrition Programs division also will be decentralized to the service centers.

To facilitate the personnel transfer and provision of service to local school districts, the plan also moves more than $4.2 million or 17.5 percent of the Agency's general revenue budget to regional education service centers. The transfer of another $1.6 million in dedicated fees and federal funds to the service centers for a total transfer of more than $5.8 million has also been proposed.

Governance

Texas Education Code provides for the authority and responsibilities of service centers. Section 11.32 states that, "The State Board of Education shall provide, by rules and regulations, for the establishment and operation of regional education service centers to provide educational services to the school districts and to coordinate educational planning in the region." Each education service center is governed by a seven-member lay board. Members of the Board of Directors are elected by the region's local school district boards of trustees. In addition, education service centers are directly accountable to the Commissioner of Education and the State Board of Education. Appendix A delineates the performance accountability requirements of Regional Education Service Centers. Members of each Board of Directors are charged with establishing policies that are consistent with state board policy while meeting regional needs. They are responsible for selecting an executive director, in accordance with State Board policy; establishing the salaries for the executive director and all staff members of the service center; developing and approving the annual operating budget for the service center; and approving the appointment and termination of professional personnel upon recommendation by the executive director.

Regional Advisory Committees are required within each Education Service Center. These Committees are formed in order that each school district within the region has an opportunity to participate in and be served by the Center. The Regional Advisory Committee will be advisory to the Center and its Board of Directors and will assist in evaluating the Center's programs and services. A person appointed to the Regional Advisory Committee must hold a certified position with the school district or districts he/she will represent. Each member of the Regional Advisory Committee will serve at the will of the local board of trustees or board of trustees of each institution of higher education that is eligible for membership and will be certified in writing to the Regional Advisory Committee by the president of the local board of trustees or board of trustees of the institution of higher education that is eligible for membership. The statement of membership will become a part of the minutes of the Committee. The role of this committee is to consult and advise with the board of directors on matters concerning educational services provided by the regional education service center, provide information to the executive director regarding school district needs and appropriateness and quality of services provided, and to conduct an annual evaluation and report to the board of directors on the quality of services rendered, the effectiveness of center operations, and the appropriateness of program development efforts.

The Executive Committee will perform as an advisory council to the Regional Advisory Committee. It will perform those other services and duties normally assigned executive committees as the Regional Advisory Committee may wish to delegate. Regional Advisory Committee members from each respective county will elect their representative(s) to the Executive Committee. The college representative will be appointed by the Regional Advisory Committee representatives from the eligible institutions of higher education. Figure 3.1 illustrates the flow of authority in governing service centers.

The system of accountability in the delivery of regional services requires that each regional education service center submit annually a comprehensive application to the Central Education Agency for review and approval. An annual performance report for each of the services specified in the comprehensive application is also required. Management and service audits, along with annual financial audits, are conducted in accordance with section 109.24 of 19 TAC Chapter 53 (the rules and regulations adopted by the State Board of Education for the operation of regional education service centers).

How Are Education Service Centers Governed?

```
State Board of Education
   │
Commissioner of Education
   │
Regional Board of Directors ──Elect Members── Local District Board of Trustees
   │         ┊                                        │
   │         ┊                                        │
Executive    Regional Advisory Committee ──Appoint Members──┤
Director                                                    │
             └──Appoint Members── Institutions of Higher Education
```

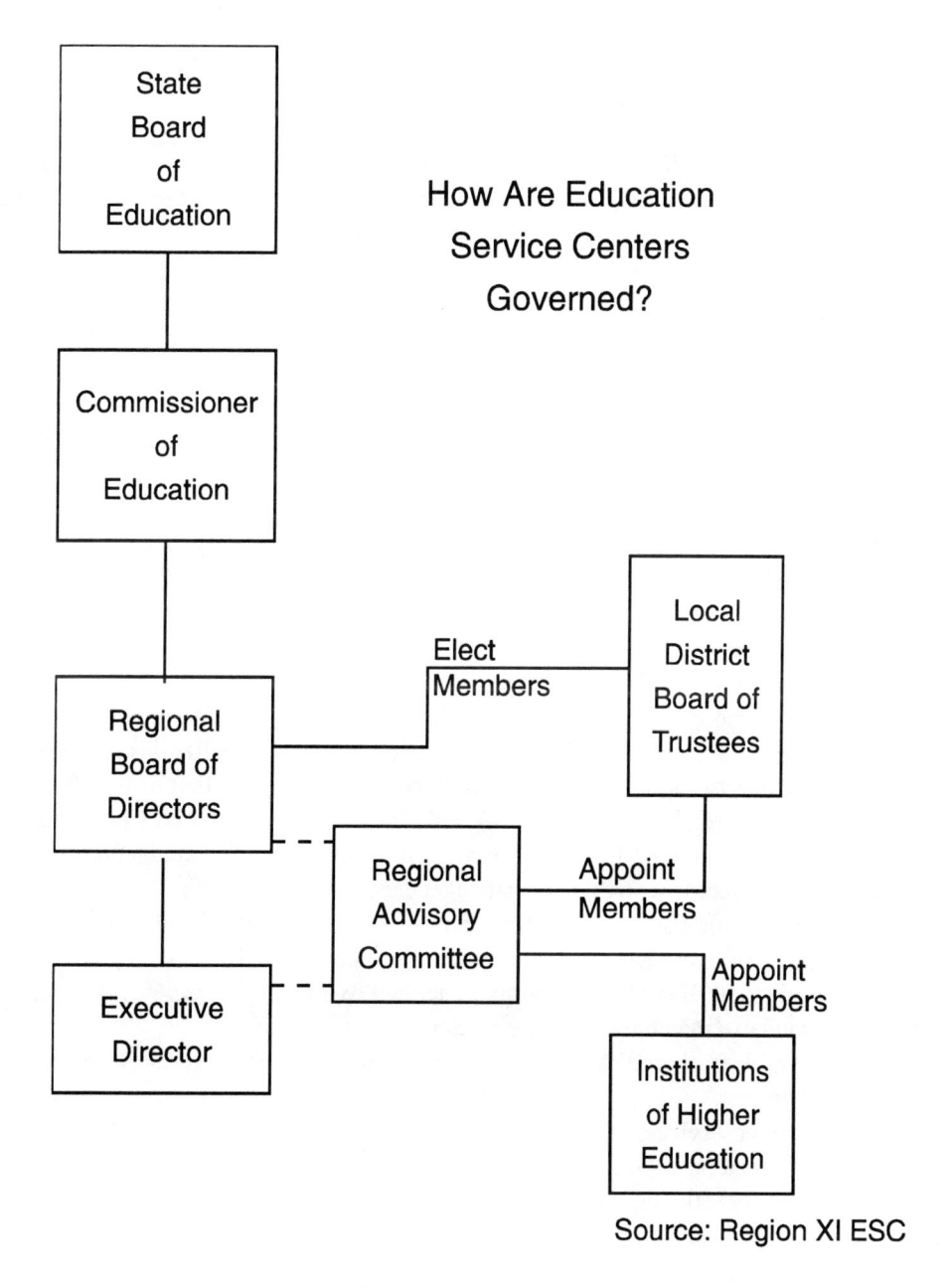

Source: Region XI ESC

Figure 3.1. Regional Education Service Centers' Role and Function.

Funding

Under the legislation which established them, regional education service centers do not possess tax levying or bonding authority. Centers receive funding from:

1. Federal sources which flow through the Texas Education Agency in the form of Title and Chapter funds via "categorical aid." Expenditure of these funds must meet and adhere to very stringent and specific guidelines from the funding law.
   Federal sources are distributed through the comprehensive application based on formulas determined by the commissioner and the State Board of Education. Of the federal fund sources administered by the agency, seven were utilized directly by the centers:
   A. ECIA Chapter 2, Block Grant Programs;
      (Discretionary funds used to provide programs in the areas of gifted and talented, instructional computing, guidance and counseling, pupil transportation, and other such areas).
   B. ECIA Chapter 1, Migrant;
      (Funds used to provide remedial and compensatory instructional programs to "at-risk" students whose parents are classified as migratory agricultural or fishing workers).
   C. IDEA-B Discretionary; Special Education
   D. Carl D. Perkins Vocational Equity;
   E. Drug Free Schools and Communities; and
   F. EHA-B Preschool.
   In addition to these agency administered federal funds, the centers utilize direct federal grant funds and manage, as fiscal agents, federal funds of school district that form cooperatives in such areas as Special Education, EESA Title II Math/Science, ECIA Chapter 2 Block Grants, and ECIA Chapter 1 Regular and Migrant. Centers also operated federally funded programs administered through other state agencies.
2. Local sources which also come in the form of categorical aid. Funds are received as matching funds from the state to support programs of contractual arrangements made with local school districts. Local revenues are generated two ways:
   A. State-mandated matching funds for media services
   B. Fee-for-services charges to school districts and other parties for services rendered which include:
      a. computer services;
      b. staff development training;
      c. bus driver training; and
      d. driver's education.

3. State sources appropriated for approved state programs and are to be used to supplement these programs in order to meet overhead costs. State general revenue funds are received by the centers to support:
   A. Accreditation, Training and Curriculum assistance to school districts;
   B. Certified Appraiser Training;
   C. Public Education Information Management System (PEIMS); and
   D. School Health Services Projects.

Figure 3.2 illustrates funding percentages.

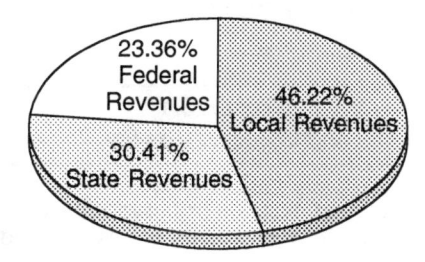

Figure 3.2. 1991-1992 Percent of Funding by Source.

Budgeting, accounting, auditing, and reporting guidelines are spelled out in Bulletin 679, Financial Accounting Manual. While regional education service centers must follow these guidelines by legislative mandate, each individual service center has the authority to establish a system that "expands upon these minimum requirements" as long as the activities do not alter or distort the final financial reports of the fiscal year. The board of directors of each service center is responsible for the development and approval of the center's annual budget. The budget must be in accordance with the Texas Education Code, Section 23.42.

Services Available

Each of the service centers is required, as delineated in the State Plan for Regional Education Service Centers adopted by the State Board of Education, to provide certain core services to districts within the region. Among these core services are: basic instructional media, computer and data processing services, regional assistance with the implementation of the Public Education Information management System (PEIMS), technical assistance to school districts in the areas of school accreditation, curriculum development and revision, administrator, staff and school board member training, and the display of textbooks offered for state adoption. The centers have recently made plans to provide a variety of technology related services at no cost to teachers and administrators. These services will be provided through a Statewide Technology Initiative to be funded by the legislature and the Texas Education Agency. The services will consist of assistance with technology planning, T-Star technical assistance, providing staff development and technical assistance with TENET (Texas Education Network), technical assistance and searches for software evaluation information using TESS (The Educational Software Selector), staff development related to electronic textbooks, cooperative bidding for technology on a limited basis, regional staff development responsive to expressed district needs, a Technology Preview Center, and possibly other services based on forthcoming funding. School district participation in the services of the centers is voluntary.

Regional education service centers support educational excellence by providing a variety of services directly related to State Board of Education's goals for public education. (See Table 3.1 for text of goals and objectives).

TABLE 3.1
State Board of Education's Goals and Objectives as Related to Education Service Centers

Goal 1—Student Learning
- Obtain and/or develop, maintain, and circulate or broadcast student instructional materials
- Provide diagnostic and specialized instructional programs for handicapped and disadvantaged students
- Deliver student instruction through distance learning technology
- Deliver student instruction in driver education and other specialized areas of curriculum
- Deliver student sessions in fine arts
- Support and/or operate pre-kindergarten programs in schools or communities
- Assess handicapped students for Adaptive Assistive Devices

Goal 2—Curriculum and Programs
- Initiate and/or participate in curriculum definition and curriculum guide development
- Develop student assessment materials based on defined curriculum elements
- Coordinate and facilitate curriculum review and revision
- Organize cooperative programs to enhance the utilization of curriculum materials

Goal 3—Personnel
- Design and conduct teacher inservice training in subject content areas, effective teaching practices, collegial coaching, and use of instructional technology
- Develop and install computerized instructional management systems to support teaching tasks
- Provide materials and equipment for preparation of teacher-made instructional materials
- Sponsor alternative certification programs
- Conduct training for administrators in Instructional Leadership Training, Texas Teacher Appraisal System, General Management Training, Administrator Appraisal, and District-Level Decision Making

Goal 4—Organization and Management
- Organize and deliver School Board Member Training
- Conduct accreditation orientation, provide technical assistance, and participate as resource in Texas Education Agency accreditation monitoring visits
- Coordinate state planning through participation on the Commissioner's Advisory Council
- Develop, field-test, and support computer software for instructional management and administrative functions

- Initiate cooperative approaches for addressing local district needs
- Participate in state agency coordination efforts regarding human services

Goal 5—Finance
- Provide training for school personnel in financial accounting, budgeting, and funds management
- Provide regional data processing services via mainframe operations and mini/microcomputer cooperatives
- Serve as fiscal agent for cooperative programs

Goal 6—Parent Responsibility
- Conduct training for parents of handicapped children, school volunteers, and parent advisory committees
- Assist district in developing parental involvement programs

Goal 7—Community and Business Involvement
- Participate in quality work force planning activities
- Provide technical assistance in planning community education programs
- Conduct special events involving students, parents, and community members
- Respond to inquiries about services to handicapped children with referrals and resource information

Goal 8—Research, Development and Evaluation
- Provide technical assistance in the design, implementation, and analysis of community services
- Calculate student enrollment projections
- Design and test innovation approaches for instruction and personnel training
- Provide technical assistance in evaluating local district operations and programs

Goal 9—Communications
- Facilitate information flow and communications among state, regional, and local units
- Assist district in planning, initializing, and maintaining local communications programs
- Maintain active communication linkages with districts regarding center operations and services

---

Location Of Service Centers

The State Board of Education established the initial assignment of the twenty regional education service centers. Initial assignments meet rules outlines in Texas Education Code Section 53.3 which required each geographic area to have 50,000 or more eligible students in average daily attendance, although allowing exemptions in sparsely populated areas. Table 3.2 on the following page provides data for each of the service center regions.

Periodic review of the number, location, and boundaries of each center is required by the Commissioner's Regulations and occurs under the auspices of the State Board of Education. Any changes in the make-up of service center boundaries must be based on demographic or other factors which might warrant making changes to the existing structure as determined by each individual board of directors and with the approval of the State Board of Education

TABLE 3.2.
Regional Education Service Centers

Region	Location	# Counties Served	#Districts Served
1	Edinburg	7	38
2	Corpus Christi	11	44
3	Victoria	11	41
4	Houston	7	56
5	Beaumont	6	29
6	Huntsville	15	59
7	Kilgore	17	98
8	Mt. Pleasant	11	48
9	Wichita Falls	13	41
10	Richardson	8	79
11	Fort Worth	10	78
12	Waco	12	78
13	Austin	15	59
14	Abilene	12	47
15	San Angelo	18	45
16	Amarillo	26	68
17	Lubbock	20	61
18	Midland	19	33
19	El Paso	2	13
20	San Antonio	14	51

Current Issues

The State Plan For Regional Education Service Centers is currently being revised. Major changes are anticipated in the area of governance. Primarily, changes strengthening the authority and role of the commissioner are being considered.

The efforts of the Commissioner of Education to consolidate and decentralize various Agency functions, as a means to improve services to local school districts, will call for many adjustments, as well as generating new ventures at the Regional Education Service Centers. The strength of the Centers will greatly enhance the Texas Education Agency's primary objective for reorganization, to become a positive factor in the improvement of instruction and the educational environment at the classroom, campus, and district levels with the goal of improving student achievement for all the state's students.

References

"A Plan for the Reorganization of the Texas Education Agency." Texas Education Agency, October, 1991.

Edgar, J.W. "Implementing the State Plan for the Establishment of Education Service Centers Including Regional Education Media Centers." Memo to the Presidents of the Board of School Trustees, March 14, 1967.

State Plan For Regional Education Service Centers. June 1988.

Texas Administrative Code and Statutory Citations. Title 19, Part II, Chapter 53, Sub-chapter A. "Regional Education Service Centers," January 14, 1988 (original update).

The Changing Role of the Central Education Agency

Martha Blake
Jo Ann House

In the United States, public policy has held that education is a function of the states. Consequently, Texas, like other states, adopted constitutional provisions citing the importance of public education. The Texas Constitution declares that:

> A general diffusion of knowledge being essential to the preservation of the liberties and rights of the people, it shall be the duty of the Legislature of the State to establish and make suitable provisions for the support and maintenance of an efficient system of public free schools.

Therefore, the progressive evolution of an "efficient system of public free schools" has been through joint legislative action and the Central Education Agency.

The Central Education Agency is an umbrella term covering three divisions: (1) the State Board of Education which includes the State Board of Vocational Education, (2) the Commissioner of Education, (3) and the State Department of Education or the Texas Education Agency. Its purpose is to "exercise general control of public education at the state level" [TEC 1 1.02(a)]. Section 11.021(a) of that same code states that, "It is the policy of the State of Texas that the entire system of education supported with public funds be coordinated to provide the citizens with efficient, effective, and high quality educational services and activities."

The Central Education Agency was created as a result of the Gilmer-Aiken Bills passed by the 51st Legislature in 1949. Prior to the passage of Senate Bill 115, the State Board of Education, the State Department of Education, and the State Superintendent frequently acted independently of each other, connected only by a common vision to improve education In Texas. Yoe (1969) stated that the purpose of Senate Bill 115 was to reorganize the "state administration of education through consolidation and rationalization of existing divisions of the state into one central education agency—the Texas Education Agency." The State Department of Education is commonly referred to as the Texas Education Agency, or TEA, although this name almost never appears in law.

Historical Development

Mirabeau B. Lamar, (1798-1859), frequently called the "Father of Texas Education," called for the establishment of a system of education financed through taxation and the appropriation of land. Eby (1925) suggests, however, that the lawmakers, as well as the citizenry's concept of public education, did not include state supervision of schools.

State supervision came as an aftermath of the Civil War when the Constitution of 1866 "... created the appointive office of State Superintendent of Public Instruction, and required public teachers to obtain certificates..." (T. Thompson, 1986). A new constitution was written in 1869 because the radical reconstructionists who were in office did not consider the constitution an acceptable document. The resultant laws of 1871, which detailed the constitutional provision, included the office of State Superintendent and a State Board of Education composed of the Governor, Attorney General, and Superintendent of Public Instruction.

The office of Superintendent of Public Instruction was abolished in 1873 and replaced by a State Board of Education with the services of a secretary. This Board was frequently referred to as an ex-officio board. Composition of this board was slightly different from the 1870 state board in that its membership included the Governor, the Comptroller, and the Secretary of State. The function of the board included general management of the schools and the protection of the investment of the permanent school fund. The secretary to the board collected reports and dispensed information. Eby (1925) found that the secretary had no allowance for travel across the state nor was money provided for postage. Eleven years later (1884) the secretary's title was again changed to State Superintendent. The change also brought about greater supervisory responsibilities and required that the office of state superintendent be subject to election ever two years.

With time, the State Department of Education grew from a small body of seven clerks in 1907 to a force of nine divisions and 29 professional staff members by 1917. Growth of the department can be attributed to state legislation requiring accreditation, aid to rural schools and federal aid in the form of the Smith-Hughes Act.

S.N.M. Marrs, state superintendent from 1923-1932, proved to be the moving force in guiding the state toward a more professionally managed system of education. Marrs used *The Texas Educational Survey Report* to bring about needed reform. The report, commissioned by the legislature in 1923, cited the State Board of Education for failure to meet due to lack of time and money. Additionally, the report found that:

> The state superintendent's functions were vague and were assigned by the ex-officio board rather than prescribed by law. As the result of changes and reforms, the State Department of Education, consisting of some 56 professional people, had grown too big for the scattered rooms it occupied in the pink granite capital, yet remained too small for the task it was to be doing. (Yoe, 1969)

Following *The Texas Educational Survey Report,* the 1928 legislature passed a constitutional amendment that would create a State Board of Education (SBOE) to replace the ex-officio board of Governor, Attorney General and Secretary of State. The new State Board would consist of nine members appointed by the governor with the approval of the senate. The board's duties, as prescribed by law, included financial oversight of the public schools and higher education institutions. Other legal responsibilities granted were to make budget recommendations, appoint members to the State Textbook Commission, and to regulate teacher certification.

The conflict between an appointed State Board of Education and an elected State Superintendent arose during L.A. Wood's tenure (1932-1948) as state superintendent. As an elected official with public support, Woods frequently found himself facing opposition from both the State Department of Education and the State Board. The Board acted independently of the State Superintendent and the Department of Education. The Board created its own budget, published its own reports, and appointed an executive secretary to head the department of vocational education. As a solution to the dissension, the State Board recommended to the legislature in 1938 that the office of State Superintendent become an appointive office as well.

A remedy was not found until after World War II when the legislature realized that the state had to address a multitude of educational problems. Again, the reform measures were taken from a study committee's report entitled *To Have What We Must.* The Gilmer-Aiken Bills as presented during regular session of the legislature in 1949 called for a complete reorganization of the current system of education, especially the administration of public education and the methods of financing schools.

Committee recommendations made early in 1948 included the consolidation of existing divisions of the State Department of Education, the election of a State Board and the selection of a Commissioner of Education by the elected board. Not surprisingly, board members, the state superintendent, and the affected divisions of the state department of education opposed Senate Bill 115, the legislation supporting the committee's recommendations.

The Gilmer-Aiken Bill (S.B. 115) completely reorganized the entire system of education in Texas as well as the administration of the educational process. The commissioner was to be appointed by an elected State Board of Education, with senate confirmation, to serve for a four year term of office. The Texas Education Agency was restructured in March of 1950. The new organization was made up of four major departments, "school administration and finance, agency administration, instructional services and vocational services" (Yoe, 1969). Each office was headed by either an assistant or deputy commissioner. The agency was to "exercise general control of the system of public education at the state level except higher education" (Evans, 1955).

The duties of the State Board of Education, the State Commissioner of Education, and the Texas Education Agency were so clearly defined by the Gilmer-Aiken Bills that no misunderstanding of responsibilities or overlapping of authority could occur.

The Agency and the State Board continued to expand in number and responsibility over the next thirty-five years. In 1971, "due to reapportionment, the state board increased to 24 members making it the largest such board in the United States" (Gregg, 1982). Three additional members were added after the 1980 census to create a total of 27 members.

Mandated state-wide testing, an increasing number of federal programs, focus on curriculum content and the addition of new services to the state's schools contributed to the Agency's ever increasing size. House Bill 246, which completely revamped curriculum content and the structure of courses in public schools, was passed by statute in 1981. Full implementation was not required until 1984 when it was finally approved by the State Board of Education. Implementation of H.B. 246 coincided with the passage of House Bill 72, which has been described as the second greatest reform measure to affect education in Texas since the passage of the Gilmer-Aiken Bills.

Education by Legislation

Former Commissioner of Education, Bill Kirby, described the political and educational climate of the 80s in the following manner.

> The decade of the 80s in Texas, much like the rest of the country, could be labeled "The Decade of Top-Down Educational Reform" . . . For a state that had long championed "local control of education," Texas abruptly and decisively reversed course and handed down from the legislature through the Central Education Agency massive top-down mandates. The attitude seemed to be if educators haven't fixed education, then the Texas legislature would fix it during the 80's by mandating that it improve (p. 44-45).

How did this occur? What caused these massive reform efforts and the reversal of local control? It should be remembered that the passage of House Bill 72 occurred after the release of a national report entitled, *A Nation at Risk*. The nation and the state were responding to heightened awareness of perceived weaknesses in the educational environment.

Texas began its own reform efforts in 1983 when the governor appointed a Select Committee to study the issues of teacher pay raises and school finance. H. Ross Perot, a Dallas business executive, was appointed chairman of the Select Committee. Characteristic of the outspoken billionaire's leadership style, the scope of the committee's responsibilities was enlarged to include every aspect relating to education in Texas.

Perot believed the key to school reform lay "in the state's existing organizational structure" (Smith, 1984). Perot claimed that the State Board of Education was one of the best kept secrets in the state. Election to the State Board had not been a hotly contested political contest. Members were subsequently reelected with minimum opposition. Perot described the process as "being elected in a vacuum" (Smith, 1984). Long-term board members had been reelected frequently enough to become lobbyists for their own private interest. Perot urged the appointment of a smaller 15-member State Board of Education selected by the governor. The Commissioner would then be selected by the appointed board.

Perot also criticized the Texas Education Agency for failure to pay competitive wages to keep a professional staff. While members of the educational community frequently felt the influence of the Agency, Perot suggested that "very few people even know the Texas Education Agency exists" (Smith, 1984).

Public hearings of the Select Committee were held across the state during the fall of 1983. "The committee's high-profile approach was designed to serve a special purpose-- to galvanize public support and to convince the political leadership that education reform was possible even over the objection of the educational establishment" (D. Thompson, 1986). The committee's recommendations were made public in April of 1984 and a special session was called on June 4, 1984.

Because many of the proposed recommendations were controversial and in many instances revolutionary as far as educational practices in Texas were concerned, Perot and his lobbyists worked to keep the committee's recommendations intact without amendments or changes. The Speaker of the House of Representatives (also a member of the Select Committee) chose to select the issue of an appointed State Board as a trial balloon for the entire package. On June 21, 1984, "by a vote of 97-47, the house voted to change from a 27-member board to a 15-member appointed board." (D.Thompson, 1986). Thompson states that, "after this one vote, the outcome [of H.B. 72] was never in doubt."

As part of a compromise package that emerged between the Senate and House of Representatives, the 15-rnember appointed board would act as a transition board to oversee implementation of House Bill 72 reforms for one four-year term. After the four-year period, the voters of Texas could then decide if they wished to remain with an appointed board or return to an elected board.

The Legislative Education Board, (LEB) created as a part of House Bill 72, presented nominations to the governor for the 15-member board. This highly influential board consisted of the Lieutenant Governor, Speaker of the House of Representatives, chairs of the House and Senate Education Committees, the House Appropriations and Senate Finance chairs, two additional senators and two additional representatives. State Board members also had to have confirmation by the full Senate.

The newly appointed State Board quickly went into action to assist school districts in implementing the major reform measures prescribed by House Bill 72. A chairman of the State Board was selected and a national search was called for the Commissioner of Education. Dr. Bill Kirby (1990), acting interim commissioner, was selected in the fall of 1984. Kirby later recalled that, "by the summer of 1984 statewide reform by the legislature was in full swing and education at the state and local levels were mostly ignored with the passage of H.B. 72" (p. 45).

On November 3, 1987, Texas voters responded to the call for local control and decided by a wide majority to return to an elected board. Accountability to the local constituents was a primary factor in returning to an elected board. The number of elected board members remained at 15, but did not represent congressional districts as had the former elected board. In the general election of 1988, successors to the appointed board were elected to office.

Two years later (1989), the Texas Supreme Court ruled that the method of funding public schools in Texas was neither equitable nor efficient. Lawmakers convened to address the funding issues, and as in the Gilmer-Aiken Bill and in House Bill 72, the legislators took the opportunity to not only reform state funding of schools, but also to reform the governance of the public school system from the top down.

The Central Education Agency's authority was significantly rewritten and reassigned. Senate Bill 1 limited the State Board of Education's rule-making authority by removing section 11.26 (a) from the Texas Education Code. The Commissioner of Education's authority was expanded and the office was given discretionary power. The Legislative Education Board and the governor's office became stronger as the result of this legislation. The impact of these changes will be discussed more fully in the remaining chapter.

Former Commissioner Kirby believed that the legislation written in Senate Bill 1 resulted in some very positive changes for education in the state. He suggests that Senate Bill 1 was the beginning of a return to local control through waivers which would provide relief from legislative mandates. He wrote:

Many of the enactments in 1989 came as suggestions from educators in the field and were fine-tuning adjustments to previous reforms. Most were recommendations endorsed by the Central Education Agency. Perhaps the most noteworthy for its opposite direction to top-down reform was a concept proposed by the Commissioner of Education labeled "flexibility with accountability." The idea was fairly simple--schools with well thought-out plans which were developed at the campus level with extensive teacher and parental input should be given the freedom or flexibility to implement those programs. If regulations or even statues stood in the way of the locally conceived program improvement, then the regulations or statutes would be waived by the state. The waivers could be continued so long as educational improvement was evidenced .... If local innovations were not successful, then the controls would be reinstated. (p 46)

The 72nd Legislative session and the passage of Senate Bill 351 continued to redefine the Central Education Agency. Authority to grant waivers was transferred from the SBOE to the Commissioner. The selection of Texas Successful School Awards was also transferred from the Governor's office to the Commissioner's office.

With the shift in power and a redistribution of responsibilities, it now became possible to make even greater internal reform efforts. The 90s portend to be the beginnings of stability at the Central Education Agency and a refocusing on student learner outcomes.

State Board

The State Board of Education has been an integral part of the public school system in Texas since its inception in 1928. One could arguably go back as far as 1865 when the ex-officio board's original responsibility was the oversight of the public school funds. Regardless of its origins, the Board continues to evolve with greater or lesser authority dependent upon the political climate of the times.

Three very broad functions are assigned to the State Board of Education; (1) implement policy (2) recommend legislation and (3) adopt rules. These functions are determined by the Legislature and the Constitution.

The Texas Constitution gives to the State Board of Education the authority to perform duties assigned by law. These laws change from time to time depending upon legislative involvement. Prior to the passage of Senate Bill 1, the State Board had the authority to be the primary policy-making body of the Central Education Agency. After Senate Bill 1, its authority changed from being the primary policy maker to the implementor of legislative policy. Senator Carl Parker (1990) further described this responsibility as "implementation of educational policy based on the authority of the legislature." As cited earlier, the Constitution provides that the State Board of Education has oversight responsibilities of the permanent school fund.

In an attempt to clarify newly refined roles, the SBOE requested in October of 1991, information from the Commissioner's office to delineate expectations for the State Board of Education and the Commissioner. The report stated that the State Board of Education was to "exercise broad leadership and policy direction for public education; make recommendations for public education legislation; recommend Commissioner of Education nominee to Governor; adopt rules as specifically authorized by statue; review annual program and operating budgets prior to adoption by Commissioner; approve organizational structure of the Agency; adopt request for biennial appropriations; and adopt Long-Range Plan and other Plans" (p. I-49).

The State Board of Education's greatest involvement in public education comes from the authority to adopt rules, approve reports, set standards and/or establish an approval process in many areas affecting education. This authority extends to adult and community education, accreditation, bilingual education, compensatory and remedial education, curriculum, the University Interscholastic League and the Foundation School Program which includes setting standards for facilities. Other rule adoption authority includes: rules regarding bus routes, extracurricular use of buses and driver qualifications; determing the licensing, regulations and fees for proprietary and driver training schools; the establishing and operating of Regional Education Service Centers; contracting and determining standards for criterion-referenced and norm referenced test; developing and maintaining of an electronic information transfer system; the establishing of a center for educational technology; approving of the Master Plan for Vocational Education; setting standards and procedures for approval of teacher education programs; appointing of the Commission on Standards for the Teaching Profession; approves alternative certification programs; and prescribing teacher certification tests. All federal programs must have the SBOE's approval before submission of applications for federal grant funds. Additionally, the SBOE adopts rules and performance standards for accreditation, schedules on-site evaluation visits and reports the state's educational status to the legislature. All of these responsibilities are conducted with the advice and assistance of the Commissioner of Education (p. I-49-53).

Another major responsibility of the State Board of Education is its authority to adopt textbooks for the state. The SBOE appoints the proclamation and adoption advisory committee, adopts the proclamations and subsequent list of textbooks and determines rules for textbook waivers. Because contracts for textbook adoptions for the state of Texas are so lucrative, members are prohibited by law from engaging "in manufacturing, shipping, selling, storing, advertising textbooks . . . or in any other manner connected with the textbook business—to make a financial contribution to or take part in, directly or indirectly, the campaign of any person seeking election to the board. Anyone convicted of violating the provisions of this subsection shall be punished as prescribed by the penal laws of this state" (Sunset Commission, 1987).

For each action that it takes, the State Board of Education must provide legislative authority and must consider comments by the Legislative Education Board (LEB) before taking a final vote. If the State Board of Education is unsure of the legislative intent, it is to request a joint meeting with the LEB for clarification.

Members of the State Board of Education serve on the State Board of Vocational Education. It is to contract with the Texas Higher Education Coordinating Board to "assume leadership and administrative responsibilities relating to technical-vocational programs above the public school level, such as community colleges, public technical institutions and other public post secondary institutions" [TEC 11.24 (b)].

The Board is required by law to hold four meetings per year in Austin on dates determined by the chairman of the State Board of Education. The chairman may also call other meetings as needed. Business sessions are held in the Board Room located at 1701 North Congress Avenue. Each meeting is open to the public except for executive sessions where public access is restricted by law. "Policy decisions must be made by the full board ... much of the detailed preliminary work is completed in open committee sessions held on the Friday preceding each meeting" (Funkhouser, 1986).

Agenda items are made available to the public one week prior to the Board meeting. Topics for discussion are distributed to the 20 regional education service centers, the capital press corp in Austin, the Texas Register, "state headquarters of school-related professional associations, the Governor's Office, Secretary of State, Legislative Budget Board, and other agencies as required by statue or policy" (Funkhouser, 1986).

The State Board of Education is composed of 15 members representing 15 State Board of Education Districts. These districts are compact, contiguous and as equal in population as practical. Districts are redesigned by the legislature after each decennial census.

Board members serve four-year staggered terms with terms of eight of the members expiring on January 1 of one odd numbered year. The remaining seven members' terms expires on January 1 of the next odd-numbered year. After each decennial reapportionment, seven members would again serve two-year terms (*Sunset Commission Report,* 1987).

A Board member must be a resident of the state for one year prior to election, 30 years of age, a citizen of the United States, and a qualified voter of his or her district. Board members may not serve on the board of a state office or any political subdivision of the state. Should a vacancy occur during a member's term of office, the board has the power to fill the vacated office with a "qualified person from the affected district" (TEC, 1988).

The chair of the State Board of Education is appointed by the governor with the advice and consent of the senate. Selection of the chair is made from the 15-member board to serve for a term of two years [TEC 11.23 (b)].

Commissioner of Education

The Commissioner of Education serves as chief executive officer of the Central Education Agency and provides advice and assistance to the *State Board of Education.* The *Texas Education Code* states that the Commissioner must be a citizen of the United States and be a person with broad professional experience. The Commissioner must also have special recognized abilities of the highest order in organizing, directing, coordinating, and administering public schools and public education [TEC 11.51 (c)].

Prior to the passage of Senate Bill 1, the Commissioner served at the pleasure of the State Board of Education. Following the passage of the bill, the State Board of Education was required to submit a recommendation for commissioner to the governor no later than February 1, 1991, and every four years thereafter. The governor could accept or reject the nomination; acceptance requires the advice and consent of the Senate. If the governor rejected the recommendation, the Board must submit further recommendations until one is appointed and confirmed by the Senate [TEC 11.51 (a)].

The Commissioner serves a four-year term of office beginning March 1 following the November gubernatorial election and may serve an unlimited number of consecutive terms. The governor may remove the Commissioner with the advice and consent of the Senate for good cause or upon the petition of two-thirds of the member of the State Board of Education (TEC 11.51 (b)).

The Commissioner's office provides leadership and guidance to the Texas Education Agency and to the public school systems. This includes promoting efficiency and improvement in the public school systems of the state; prescribing the mechanism to secure reports needed from schools; hearing appeals and making decisions concerning those appeals. The Commissioner also transmits information to school districts; convenes advisory groups to share information, ideas and concerns; and makes presentations to schools and public groups on the status of education in Texas.

Other duties include organizing the Agency with the approval of the SBOE; administering programs and monitoring compliance with statutes and SBOE rules; preparing plans and reports; recommending policies, rules and regulations; prescribing a uniform system of forms and reports to obtain district information; reporting to the legislature the condition of public schools; administering funds appropriated to the agency; developing proposed academic excellence indicators, and selecting qualified districts and schools for the Texas Successful Schools Award.

Adult and Community Education come under the Commissioner's administration. Adult literacy programs, the GED, Homeless Assistance and community education are all part of Adult and Community Education. These programs must comply with SBOE rules and federal guidelines and regulations.

The Commissioner may also grant waivers and exemptions from laws and regulations, with exceptions, based on a district's stated achievement objectives. The district must demonstrate that these requirements or prohibitions inhibit student achievement (TEC Section 11.273) (p. I-46).

Senate Bill 1 substantially increased the Commissioner's responsibilities and authority in two areas: budgeting and accreditation. The Commissioner adopts the annual program and operating budgets after submitting them to the SBOE and the Legislative Education Board for review and comment. This budget includes funds to operate the Foundation School Program, the Central Education Agency, and other programs for which the State Board of Education is responsible. Following the adoption by the SBOE and the LEB, the budget is then presented to the governor and the Legislative Budget Board (TEC 11.29).

Previously, school districts bordering on loss of accreditation were threatened with loss of state supported funds, although this rarely occurred. Senate Bill 1 transferred the authority to revoke accreditation from the SBOE to the Commissioner [TEC 21.757 (c)]. Sanctions available to the Commissioner now include the authority to take proper actions against districts not meeting accreditation standards. These actions may include district notification, appointment of a monitor, master, or management team, revocation of accreditation, or the creation of a state-operated school district (TEC 21.757). The Commissioner is also authorized to suspend the powers of district boards of trustees in districts academically unaccredited for a period of one year, remove the local board of trustees, the superintendent, and if necessary replace them with any person of his choice to serve up to a two-year period of time. Other choices include annexation of academically unaccredited schools to neighboring districts and redefining new district boundaries. The Commissioner is to report on the particular districts' progress to the Legislative Education Board.

Organizationally, the Commissioner of Education's office is responsible for and supported by the office of communications, investment office, legal services, internal audit, and the office of the State Board of Education. Associate Commissioners for Field Services, Curriculum and Assessment, Professional Development and the Director of Internal Operations report directly to the Commissioner as well as the offices of the Deputy Commissioners for Program and Instruction, Accountability and School Support Services.

The State Department of Education
(Texas Education Agency)

The State Department of Education is that portion of the Central Education Agency most frequently referred to as TEA or the Texas Education Agency. Confusion over the correct terminology exists due to legal vernacular appearing in law as opposed to the commonly accepted terms used by those familiar with the educational structure. Texas is among six other states (California, Connecticut, Michigan, New Jersey, and New York) that have state departments of education with over 1,000 employees. This number includes the professional, technical, and clerical staff.

The Agency recently has come under public criticism and scrutiny due principally to the Agency's inability to govern itself internally. Senate Bill 1 proved to be the vehicle through which an internal audit would take place. With the election of a new governor in November of 1991 and the resignation of the former Commissioner, the State Board of Education began a national search for a new Commissioner of Education. The SBOE nominated Lionel (Skip) Meno, former Associate Commissioner of New York as their candidate.

Governor Richards and Comptroller John Sharp made it very clear that a fresh new regime was expected. Richards went so far as to say that she expected the new Commissioner to "sweep out the trash [at TEA] . . . and there's an awful lot of trash to sweep out" (Gravois, 1991). Richards noted that "radical" changes were needed in order to bring about major changes at TEA. Early warnings that a change was in order came from an audit of the TEA performed by Price Waterhouse. The report found major shortcomings in policy coordination and communication (Herman, 1991).

Commissioner Meno assumed office July 1, 1991, with a mandate for change. Meno appointed the Texas Education Agency Reorganization Advisory Committee to develop an independent and objective analysis of TEA and to offer direction and guidance for its restructuring (p.1 *Reorganization Report*).

The Committee was given complete freedom to accomplish its charge. It set its own agenda, developed the itinerary, developed the format for the public hearings, and structured the format and content of the final report.

Members of the Committee included three school superintendents, three business people, a classroom teacher, and a university professor. In addition, an Assistant Commissioner from TEA was appointed to serve as a resource person and ex officio member of the committee (p. 1).

Hearings were held across the state and throughout the summer. The final report was written and released less than three months later in September 1991. The Committee's forty-page report was brutally frank and prescriptive in its findings and recommendations. Thirteen areas of concerns and twelve recommendations for improvement were presented as evidence of the much needed reorganization and change at the Agency.

The Committee expressed the belief that "TEA must shift from an educational management system driven by external mandates to one fostering creativity, experimentation, and cooperation" (p. 37). The following is a summary of the Advisory Committee's findings with recommendations that the concerns receive immediate action.

- Decentralize operations and relax regulations to give school districts greater flexibility and authority in local reform efforts.
- Establish a system of communicating with school districts so that districts can receive timely, accurate, consistent, and authoritative answers from Agency personnel.
- Reorganize the structure of TEA to reduce the number of levels for reporting and decision making.
- Revamp completely the accreditation process to place greater emphasis on service.
- Improve the efficiency and accuracy of PEIMS.
- Simplify and clarify certification procedures and regulations.
- Allow more input in the process of development of essential elements and textbook proclamations.
- Reduce the number of plans and reports that must be submitted by school districts to the Agency.
- Give the Commissioner and TEA greater control over education service centers, including the selection, evaluation, and dismissal of ESC executive directors.
- Implement internal staff development programs that emphasize the operation of Texas school districts, the diversity of districts across the state, and the knowledge and skills for each position.
- Establish an objective system of employing and evaluating TEA personnel.
- Establish a competitive salary schedule for TEA staff (p.39-40).

Responding to the Advisory Committee's findings and recommendations, TEA was reorganized into eight major divisions headed by three Deputy Commissioners and eight Associate

Commissioners. The reorganization became effective January 1, 1992. The Agency was immediately reduced by a work force of 87 positions, from 1,266 to 1,179. Reduction of two Deputy Commissioner positions and 4 Assistant Commissioner positions helped to "flatten" the organizational structure and eliminated one to two layers of reporting and decision making (p. 59 *Reorganization Summary*).

Consolidation of offices and the creation of new offices were offered as solutions to make the Agency more responsive to the districts it serves. Decentralization was accomplished through the dispersal of Agency personnel and funds to the twenty Region Service Centers. The intent was to offer better communications response time to district inquiries, and to provide consistent information and interpretation of the Agency's and State Board of Education's rules.

The Agency has been reorganized into the following divisions.

Associate Commissioner for Field Services

This newly created office brings the Educational Service Centers (ESCs) under the direct control and coordination of the Agency. The Field Service office is responsible for Partnership Schools, Education Service Center Support, Small Schools, Waivers and Facilitators at the twenty ESCs across the state.

Associate Commissioner for Curriculum and Assessment

This office was consolidated to "provide for integrated development of student achievement outcomes, curriculum, and assessment methods" (p. 7 *Reorganization Summary*). Three divisions come under this office: General Education, Student Assessment, and Teacher Assessment. The General Education division "researches, develops, and validates the student outcomes and essential elements that combine to establish the state curriculum for general education" (p. 10). Student Assessment researches, develops standards, validates and monitors all phases of student testing and the essential elements. Teacher Assessment administers testing programs that affect teachers or prospective teachers such as the ExCET, TECAT, TASP, TOPT, and the newly developed Texas Master Teacher Examination (TMTE).

Associate Commissioner for Professional Development

This is also another newly created office, which reports directly to the Commissioner. It is responsible for the "comprehensive professional development system, beginning with the support for recruitment of personnel into the profession, continuing with pre-service training, and extending throughout the career of practitioners" (p. 57 *Reorganization Summary*). Staff development for Agency personnel, the Center for Professional Development and Technology and alternative certification are included in this office.

Deputy Commissioner for Programs and Instruction

"The Deputy Commissioner for Program and Instruction directs policy development and supervises activities related to programs serving diverse student population groups and addresses specific educational needs at the elementary, middle, and high school levels" (p. 21 *Reorganization Summary*). This rather large division consolidated multiple offices and programs under three broad subdivisions: Programs, Office of Instruction and Office of Adult and Community Education. An Associate Commissioner heads the Programs department. All three of the subgroups report to the Deputy Commissioner.

The Programs department is responsible for providing services to special populations such as bilingual, special education and services for the deaf. The Office of Instruction has three newly created subgroups which address the needs of elementary, middle, and high school education. Vocational education and gifted and talented education also come under the Office of Instruction. The third department, Adult and Community Education, coordinates instructional programs for a diverse adult population.

Deputy Commissioner for Accountability

The Deputy Commissioner directs policy development and supervises activities related to accreditation, student achievement analysis, compliance analysis, school district governance and special investigations, and institutional development. An Associate Commissioner heads the division of governance and special investigations which includes complaints, civil rights, governance operations, and intervention and oversight.

Deputy Commissioner for School Support Services

The Deputy Commissioner for School Support Services directs policy development and supervises activities related to school support, audits, technology applications, and resource planning. Two Associate Commissioners direct the office of School Support and Technology Application. The Associate Commissioner for School Support supervises the divisions of State Funding and School Facilities, Discretionary Funding and Grants Administration, Child Nutrition Programs, Textbooks, Teacher Records, and Proprietary Schools and Veterans Education. The Associate Commissioner for Technology Applications is the information resources manager for the Agency and supervises the division of information services and technology services.

Office of Internal Operations

The Office of Internal Operations provides general services for all employees and departments across the agency and coordinates interagency administrative functions in the areas of policy planning and evaluation, personnel, budget, accounting, governmental relations, resource center and library, and office services (p. 45 *Reorganization Summary*).

Trends

Further and possibly more sweeping changes are in store for the Central Education Agency. Senate Bill 7 provided for a select committee composed of legislators, educators, business and community representatives to review the mission, organization, size and effectiveness of the Central Education Agency. Among the specific items the committee will address are: (1) the agency's success in addressing national educational goals (2) the effectiveness of programs designed for special populations of students and for teacher and administrator staff development (3) the identification of functions to be performed by the state and those to be performed through regional service centers and (4) the adequacy and effectiveness of assistance provided to site-based management teams. The committee must submit its report and recommendations for statutory changes not later than December 1, 1994.

The implications are clear that the report will be ready in time for the next legislative session. Early indications are that the committee will be looking at every conceivable aspect of the Central Education Agency. Representative Libby Linebarger, co-chair of the Select Committee stated that, "We have an opportunity here to completely revamp the entire system to determine how we're going to best deliver educational services to children in this state ... I hope that our underlying principle will be that business as usual is totally unacceptable to this committee," (*Houston Post*, 1993). Other revisions affecting the Central Education Agency include a planned revision of the Texas Education Code. The intent of the revision is to look at the charter of the Texas Education Code, safety issues, choice, the work force and fiscal accountability.

Major trends reflecting increased state intrusion seems apparent after reviewing legislation of the past ten years. The legislature has taken a more active role in creating and formulating the system of education we now have in Texas. While education is the responsibility of the state, and while the legislature has the responsibility to make laws which support and maintain an efficient system of public schools, it should also be the responsibility of the professional in the field to make recommendations for improvement in education.

Summary

Texas is not unlike other states that have experienced growth efforts relative to the organizational administration of public schools. A national survey conducted in 1983 (Lewis) found that state boards were formed with "often limited ... single program purposes." The primary purpose for organizing the (ex-officio) State Board of Education was to oversee the management of the permanent school funds. From that point forward, the Board has evolved into a sophisticated structure with tremendous responsibilities.

Lewis (1983) found that state departments of education went through three stages of development. The first stage is statistical or data gathering, second is the inspectoral stage and the final stage is one in which the state education agency provides leadership in planning and technical assistance. Texas has experienced similar development, perhaps in response to national trends. Texas may be entering a fourth stage that could be described as quality assurance and accountability.

As of 1987, thirty-four states had state board members appointed by the governor (Ornstein and Lewis, 1989). In Texas, this process has not proved very popular or satisfactory. J.W. Edgar, former Commissioner of Education, stated that "governors of the past [pre 1948] didn't want to be involved with the schools. It was too politically volatile" (Smith, 1986). The last experience with an appointed board (1984-1988) left the populace without access to express state or local concerns through the ballot.

Regardless of the selection process, state boards of education are experiencing a loss of authority and influence in the states' educational processes. Spring (1988) writes that "state legislation and educational interest groups consider state boards of education as having only a minor role in policy making. In fact, very few board members believed they had any meaningful influence on legislative actions." Campbell, et al. (1990) further emphasizes this point by declaring "constitutional and statutory language, court interpretations, and long practice make clear that the legislature of each state is the "big school board."

First and Quaglia (1990) in their analysis of four state boards of education go so far as to suggest that state boards are not really necessary in order for education to go forward. Recent legislative involvement to mandate a "quick fix" assures the rapid demise of the Texas State Board of Education's educational influence. As a consequence, this may be the elimination of any real forum for citizens of the state to have a voice in educational issues.

Texas has gone through all three of the most common methods of selecting a chief administrative office, i.e., (1) election by the people, (2) selection by the state board and (3) appointment by the governor. Twenty-nine states select the chief administrative officer by appointment through the State Board of Education, fourteen by popular election and seven by appointment of the governor (Ornstein and Levine, 1989). Campbell, et al. (1990) cites a major problem in selecting a chief administrator is attracting able people to assume the office. Salaries must be competitive enough to encourage those with "special recognized abilities of the highest order" to seek the position.

Texas will continue to respond to national, state and local education issues as it has in the past. Leadership and innovation rather than a response mechanism is needed to move the state beyond the mediocre national rankings into a position of respectability. The Central Education Agency can and must meet the challenge.

References

Campbell, R.E., Cunningham, L.L., Nystrand, R.D. & Usdan, M.D. (1990). *The organization and control of American schools* (6th ed.) Columbus: Merrill.

Eby, F. (1925). *The development of education in Texas.* New York: MacMillian.

Evan, C.E. (1955). *Story of Texas schools.* Austin: Steck.

First, Patricia F. & Quaglia, Russell J. (1990). *The evolving roles of state boards of education, state education agencies and chief state school officers.* (ERIC Document Reproduction Service No. ED325932)

Funkhouser, C. (1986). *Education in Texas: Policies, practices, and perspectives.* (3rd ed.). Scottsdale: Gorsuch Scarisbrick.

Gregg, E.R. (1982). History of the Texas Association of School Board. Speech presented to the *Texas Association of School Board Conference.* Texarkana, Texas.

Houston Post, "Task Force Questions How to Revamp Educational System," November 5, 1993, Associated Press, Austin.

Kirby, William B. (1990). In Thomas J. Sergiovanni (Ed.), *Target 2000: A compact for excellence in Texas schools.* (pp. 44-46). San Antonio: The Watercress Press. 1990 Yearbook of the Texas Association for Supervision and Curriculum Development.

Lewis, C.J. (1983). *Educational governance in the states: A status report on state boards of education, chief state school officers, and state education agencies.* Washington D.C., Department of Education. (ERIC Document Reproduction Services no. Ed. 234 40.)

Parker, C.A. et al. (1990). Bill analysis (An analysis of Senate Bill 1, addendum to the enacted legislation).

Ornstein, A.C. & Levine, D.U. (1989). *Foundations of Education.* (4th ed.). Boston: Houghton Mifflin.

Spring, J. (1988). *Conflict of interest.* New York: Longman.

Smith, A. (1984). "Perot: 'Local control is solution." *Texas Lone Star.* 4 (2), 22-23.

Texas Education Agency. (1987). *Self-evaluation report to the Texas Sunset Advisory Commission.* Part 1, Austin, Texas.

Texas Education Agency. (1987). *Condition of public education in Texas.* 1986-86, Part 1. Austin: Texas.

Texas Education Agency. (1991). *Reorganization report: A report of the Texas Education Agency Reorganization Advisory Committee.* Austin: Texas.

Texas Education Agency. (1991). *Reorganization summary.* Austin: Texas.

Texas Education Agency. (1991). *Letter from Commissioner to the State Board of Education.* October 12, 1991. Austin: Texas.

Texas Education Agency. (1992). *Letter of information from the Commissioner to administrators addressed.*

Texas Education Code. (1990). *Texas school law bulletin. Texas education code.* Austin: Texas.

Thompson, D. (1986). "How will the history books record House Bill 727." *Texas Lone Star. 4* (2), 17-32.

Thompson, T. (1986). 150 years: They had a dream. *Texas Lone Star. 4* (2), 4-7.

Wilkens, William H. (1981). *The future of state boards of education.* National Association of State Boards of Education, Inc. Washington, D.C.

Yoes, E.D. (1969). "Texas: Texas education agency." In Jim B. Pearson & Edgar Fuller (Eds.), *Education in the states: Historical development and outlook.* Washington D.C.: National Education Association of the United States.

Federal Government Involvement in Education

Roosevelt Washington, Jr

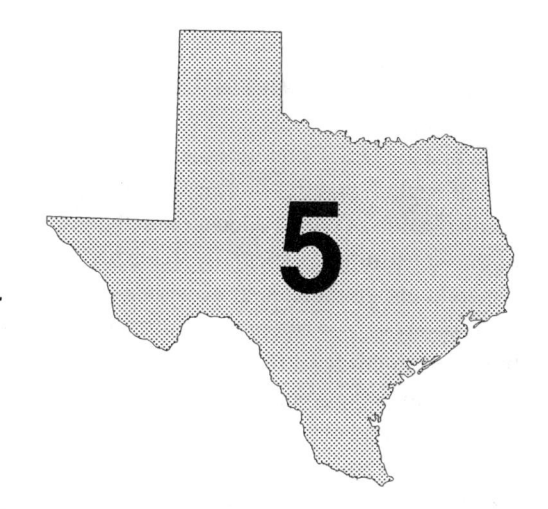

When the United States government was founded, the Constitution that was adopted did not provide for a national system of education such as exists in most other countries. However, in the infancy of the nation, Presidents Jefferson in 1806 and Madison in 1817 urged the adoption of a constitutional amendment granting the federal government control over education in the nation. Such an amendment was never seriously considered or adopted; therefore, by interpretation of the Tenth amendment to the U.S. Constitution, education is solely a state function.

Even though the federal government is precluded from directly participating in or controlling education in the 50 state systems of public education, this does not prevent the national government from becoming involved in education in a variety of ways. It is clear that the federal government has become involved and influential in public education in four distinct and related ways: (1) through the application and guarantees of the U.S. Constitution that are enforced by the courts via judicial review as explained in Chapter 1; (2) by providing federal aid to the States and school districts in a variety of ways. For instance, under the authority of Article 1, Section 8, of the U.S. Constitution, the U.S. Congress can levy taxes to provide for the general welfare and common defense of the United States. Acting under this authority, the Congress has passed a host of legislation that established programs with incentive and categorical grants aimed at influencing the States to develop and implement special educational programs for special populations of students or for other special purposes that serve the national interest; (3) by the studies and reports issued by various federal government commissions on education that are appointed by the president, cabinet members, or congress; and (4), by the administrative and regulatory functions of various agencies of the federal government, such as the U.S. Department of Education, over programs funded by the U.S. Congress.

Federal Laws and Constitutional Provisions

While the U.S. Constitution contains no reference to education, its first ten amendments (The Bill of Rights) and the fourteenth amendment assure control of education by the states and the secularization of public education in the respective states. The First and Fourteenth Amendments of the Constitution, especially, have had a definite impact on education in the states. The First Amendment guarantees to everyone (students and personnel) the right to freedom of religion, expression (speech and press), association (rights to peaceably assemble), and the right to petition the government for a redress of grievances. The Fourteenth Amendment, specifically, defines citizenship in the states and nation, makes the U.S. Constitution (especially the Bill of Rights-- the first ten amendments) applicable to the respective states, and prohibits the states from denying to any person equal protection under the laws and the right to not lose their liberty, life, or property because of government without due process of law. Based upon these two amendments, the federal courts have rendered many decisions that have influenced the direction and implementation of education in the states. The federal courts have decided cases (a) having to do with the rights of parents to send their children to private or parochial schools, (b) clarifying the use of public funds to support private and religious education, and (c) prohibiting the teaching or practice of religion in the public schools.

In *Pierce v. Society of Sisters of the Holy Names of Jesus and Mary,* 268 U.S. 510 (1925), the Supreme Court ruled that the law passed by the legislature of Oregon in 1922 requiring all children to attend public school was unconstitutional. The court reasoned that such a law denied parents the right to control the education of their children; and, that the law, in effect, deprived the private schools their property without due process as guaranteed under the 14th Amendment. As a result of this ruling, children can meet the requirements of compulsory school attendance by attending private schools; and, it was reinforced by this ruling that a state may regulate all schools and require the teaching of specific subjects. Thus, two systems of education, public and private, have continued to coexist in the United States.

There have been numerous cases adjudicated before the federal courts involving the use of public funds to directly or indirectly support private or religious education. Prominent among them are the Cochran and Everson cases. In the *Cochran v. Louisiana State Board of Education*, 281 U.S. 370 (1930) case, the Supreme court held that a state law that provided for furnishing textbooks to children attending parochial schools that was purchased with public monies did not violate the U.S. Constitution. Also, in the *Everson v. Board of Education*, 330 U.S. 1 (1947), the Supreme Court ruled that a New Jersey school district could use locally raised public tax monies to reimburse parents for bus fares expended to transport their children to parochial schools. The rationale of the Court in both of these cases was based on the "Child Benefit Theory" that was developed by the Court which stated that the aid did not benefit the school or religion, but benefited the children. Even though this theory has become an established position of the federal government, some of the states have not accepted this practice or theory. Decisions by the highest courts of Alaska, Wisconsin, Oklahoma, Delaware, and Oregon have struck down laws authorizing either transportation or textbooks for children attending parochial (denominational) schools.

The practice of sectarian religion in the public schools has been dealt with through numerous cases before the Supreme Court of the United States. While the courts have held that bible reading in public schools for academic or literature purposes is constitutional, it has held that it is unconstitutional for religious purposes [*School District of Abington Township v. Schempp and Murray v. Curlett*, 374 U.S. 203 (1963)]. Also, the court has ruled that the recitation of prayers that are demanded, encouraged, or held by school personnel is violative of the Establishment Clause of the First Amendment to the U.S. Constitution. In addition, the court ruled that placing the Ten Commandments in public school classrooms or on the walls in the public schools is unconstitutional (Stone v. Graham, 449 U.S. 39 (1980). The Court has further ruled that releasing children from public school to attend religious exercises is permissible within state laws and school board policies and rules (Zorach v. Clausen, 343 U.S. 306 (1952), but that religious instruction cannot be held on public school property (People ex rel. McCollum v. Board of Education of School District No. 71, Champaign, Illinois, 333 U.S. 68 (1948).

One of the most pertinent uses of the Fourteenth Amendment to the U.S. Constitution were decisions by the Supreme Court in desegregation cases. There were eleven southern states that had statutory laws mandating separation and segregation of the races which is defined as dejure segregation; however, in most of the other states there was evidence of racial separation and segregation of the races called defacto segregation that came about as a result of housing patterns, economic circumstances, religious and other preferences, etc., but not as a direct result of statutory law or administrative. The judicial pronouncement in the Brown case [Brown v. Board of Education of Topeka, Kansas, 347 U.S. 483 (1954)] held that the maintenance of "separate but equal" school for white and black students was unconstitutional and had to be corrected. Furthermore, in its companion case, Brown II, [Brown v. Board of Education of Topeka, Kansas, 349 U.S. 294 (1955)], the court, stated that dejure segregation (segregation by law) had to be corrected with "all deliberate speed." The court, also, placed the desegregation of schools in each community under the jurisdiction of the federal district courts. Judicial decisions with regards to religious freedom and desegregation had legislative power added to their impact on education by the passage of the Civil Rights Act of 1964 by the U.S. Congress.

Federal Legislation Affecting Elementary and Secondary Education

Acting under the authority of Article 1, Section 8, of the U.S. Constitution, Congress has passed legislation that has aided and influenced education in the states. However, the federal government interest and influence in education began before the Constitution was adopted. The Continental Congress passed the Ordinance of 1785 which provided that ". . . there shall be reserved the lot number 16 of every township for the maintenance of public [elementary and secondary] schools in said townships [of the newly developed territories] . . ." In addition, the Congress passed the Ordinance of 1787, commonly known as the Northwest Ordinance, which supported the educational land policy of the Ordinance of 1785, that stated that "religion, morality and knowledge being necessary to good government and happiness of mankind, schools and the means of education shall forever be encouraged." As new states were admitted into the newly formed United States after 1800, each received land grants for schools. These laws and policies, which came without any explicit Constitutional authority to do so, established federal involvement and in public education.

Congress, in response to demands for improved and expanded agricultural, mechanical, and scientific educational programs in the nation's colleges and universities, passed the Morrill Act of 1862. This law granted 30,000 acres of federally owned land to each state for each senator and representative they had in Congress with the provision that the income from the sale or rental of these lands be dedicated to establishing land grant colleges—with specific emphasis on agriculture, mechanical arts, and military science. The Second Morrill Act that was passed in 1890 provided federal funds for these land grant institutions of higher learning.

Since the early 1900's, federal government involvement in education has been for Congress to pass legislation that was aimed at providing incentives (seed money, matching grants, and categorical grants) to the states and local educational systems to provide special programs that met the national interest, goals, and purposes. In 1917, the congress passed the Smith-Hughes Act that' provided grants that were to be matched by state or local governments to provide for the implementation of vocational education, home economics, and agricultural programs. During the Great Depression between 1933 and 1938, a series of legislation was passed and appropriations were made, creating such programs as the Civilian Conservation Corps (CCC), the National Youth Administration (NYA), Federal Emergency Relief Administration (FERA), Public Works Administration (PWA), and the Works Progress Administration (WPA) which provided educational training and work for unemployed youth, adults, and rural teachers and other professionals in addition to providing money for the construction of public and school buildings. These relief agencies were terminated by the mid 1940's when the nation was facing the crisis of World War II.

During World War II the Congress responded to the needs of military personnel and veterans. Congress passed the Lanham Act in 1941 to provide for the construction and maintenance of schools in areas occupied by military personnel, the Occupational Rehabilitation Act of 1943 to provide educational and occupational assistance to disabled veterans, and the Servicemen's Readjustment Act of 1944, called the G.I. Bill of Rights, to provide funds for the education of returning World War II veterans. Many of these benefits, especially the G.I. Bill of Rights, were extended to the veterans of the Korean and Vietnam conflicts.

At the end of World War II and the Korean Conflict, the United States entered into a Cold War with Russia. When the former Soviet Union launched Sputnik in 1957, it was perceived that the nation needed a better educational system to successfully close the scientific gap between these two nations. There was tremendous pressure for the federal government to become more involved in funding education in the states. Congress responded by passing the National Defense Education Act (NDEA) of 1958. This law emphasized the importance of education to the nation's defense; and, Congress provided funding that was earmarked for educational programs in the states that emphasized the improvement of instruction in science, mathematics, foreign languages, and other critical subjects in the elementary and secondary schools as well as provided scholarships and loans for students to attend colleges and universities.

With the beginning of the 1960's, the civil rights movement was born; there was an emphasis on equal rights for minorities, ending poverty, achieving racial integration of schools, and improving the education received by the "culturally and socially" disadvantaged; whereupon, Lyndon B. Johnson, the President of the United States, declared a "War on Poverty," under the umbrella of what he envisioned as the "Great Society." On August 20, 1964, the Congress passed the Economic Opportunity Act (P.L. 88-452). This law established the following national policy:

> Although the economic well-being and prosperity of the United States has progressed to a level surpassing any achieved in world history, and although these benefits are widely shared throughout the Nation, poverty continues to be to the lot of a substantial number of our people. The United States can achieve its full economic and social potential as a Nation only if every individual has the opportunity to contribute to the full extent of his capabilities and to participate in the workings of our society. It is, therefore, a policy of the United States to eliminate the paradox of poverty in the midst of plenty in this nation by opening up to everyone the opportunity for education and training, the opportunity to work, and the opportunity to live in decency and dignity. It is the purpose of this Act to strengthen, supplement and coordinate efforts in the furtherance of this policy.

With the passage of this law and policy, the Head Start Program which provided pre-school education to disadvantaged poverty-stricken children and families and other community-based programs were started. It was also under this policy that the Congress passed the all-important Elementary and Secondary Education Act (ESEA) of 1965 (P.L. 89-10). This law provided funds for a variety of compensatory educational programs for disadvantaged children in the elementary and secondary schools. In addition, Congress passed the Civil Rights Act of 1964 (P.L. 88-352) which provided that all federal programs that were supported by federal monies must be operated and administered without discrimination: Title VI of this Act, prohibited discrimination against exclusion or participation in any federally assisted program on the basis of race, color or national origin; whereas, Title VII, of this Act, prohibited employers of federally assisted programs from discriminating against any person with respect to employment opportunities, compensation, and status of employment on the basis of an individual's race, color, religion, sex, or national origin. Also, in 1972, the Congress passed the Emergency School Aid Act (ESAA) that provided federal funds to assist local school districts in voluntarily integrating their schools.

The Congress also passed the Bilingual Education act in 1968 and provided federal funds to encourage and support the education of non-English or limited-English speaking children in either their native language or English, so that they could progress effectively through the educational systems in the states. In addition, there were three laws passed by Congress to encourage the education of handicapped children in the states: the Section 504 of the Rehabilitation Act of 1973 (P.L. 93-112), the Education for All Handicapped Children Act (P.L. 94-142) in 1975, and the Americans With Disabilities Act of 1990. Section 504 of the Rehabilitation Act prohibits discrimination against or exclusion from participation in any government program receiving federal assistance solely because of a person's handicap; and, Public Law 94-142 established a new national policy stating that a "free appropriate public education . . . must be extended to handicapped children as their fundamental right." Most recent amendments to P.L. 94-142 changed its name to the Individuals with Disabilities Act (IDEA) in October 1990. The American With Disabilities Act of 1990 is a civil rights act that enlarged the scope of Section 504 of the Rehabilitation Act: it protects individuals with disabilities from discrimination by employers and state governments and their agencies. Finally, in 1981, Congress passed the Educational Consolidation and Improvement Act (ECIA) which changed the focus of federal funding for educational purposes from categorical (specific use) grants to block (non-specific use) grants to the states. This law, in essence, granted more authority to the states in regulating and managing federal funds and programs.

Governmental Commissions

Various commissions over the years, that were either appointed by the President of the United States or by members of his cabinet, especially, the U.S. Department of Education, have examined issues and issued reports that have influenced education in the states. In 1960, the President's Commission on National Goals that was issued by The American Assembly of

Columbia University on November 16, 1960 contained some important goals for education. John W. Gardner, speaking for the Commission, stated that:

> Education is essential not only to individual fulfillment but to the vitality of our national life .... Ultimately, education serves all of our purposes—liberty, justice, and all of our other aims—but the one it serves most directly is equality of opportunity. We promise such equality, and education is the instrument by which we hope to make good the promise. It is the high road of individual opportunity, the great avenue that all may travel. That is why we must renew our efforts to remove the barriers to education that still exist for disadvantaged individuals—barriers of poverty, or prejudice and of ignorance. The fulfillment of the individual must not be dependent on his color, religion, economic status or place of residence.

He presented a host of proposals calling for innovation in education, equality for women and minorities, improved guidance and testing, improvements in the curriculum (especially science and mathematics), and increase state responsibility to create minimum standards of services and support. He concluded his remarks by stating that:

> It has become fashionable to blame educators for every shortcoming of our schools, but educators cannot maintain standards of excellence in a community that cares more about a marching band and a winning basketball team than it does about teachers salaries. American education can be as good, as the American people want it to be. And no better. And in striving for excellence, we must never forget that American education has a clear mission to accomplish with every single child who walks into the school . . . Our schools must prepare all young people, whatever their talents, for the serious business of being free men and women [p. 100].

Another important commission was created by the U.S. Secretary of Education, Terrell H. Bell, on August 26, 1981 called the National Commission on Excellence in Education. The Commission was created as a result of the Secretary's concern about the perceived public concerns that something was seriously wrong with the educational systems in the nation. The Commission's charter specified that it pay particular attention to: (1) assessing the quality of teaching and learning in our nation's public and private schools, colleges, and universities; (2) comparing American schools and colleges with those of other advanced nations; (3) studying the relationship between college admissions requirements and student achievement in high school; (4) identifying educational programs which result in notable student success in college; (5) assessing the degree to which major social and educational changes in the last quarter century have affected student achievement; and (6) defining problems which must be faced and overcome if the nation is to successfully pursue the course of excellence in education. In addition, the Commission's charter directed it to pay particular attention to teenage youth, selective attention to the formative years students spend in elementary, vocational and technical programs, and to higher education.

The massive and impressive report issued by the National Commission on Excellence in Education on April 26, 1983 by its, chairman, David Pierpont Gardner, inspired a national reform movement for education in almost every, if not all, states of the nation. In most emphatic terms, the report, entitled *A Nation At Risk: The Imperative For Educational Reform*, (pp. 6-6) stated that:

> Our Nation is at risk. Our once unchallenged preeminence in commerce, industry, science, and technological innovation is being overtaken by competitors throughout the world. This report is concerned with only one of the many causes and dimensions of the problem, but it is the one that undergirds American prosperity, security, and civility. We report to the American people that while we can take justifiable pride in what our schools and colleges have historically accomplished and contributed to the United States and the well-being of its people, the educational foundations of our society are presently being eroded by a rising tide of mediocrity that threatens our very future as a Nation and a people. What was unimaginable a generation ago has begun to occur—others are matching and surpassing our educational attainments.
>
> If an unfriendly foreign power had attempted to impose on America the mediocre educational performance that exists today, we might have viewed it as an act of war. As it stands, we have allowed this to happen to ourselves. We have even squandered the gains in student achievement made in the wake of the Sputnik challenge. Moreover, we have dismantled essential support systems which helped make those gains possible. We have, in effect, been committing an act of unthinking, unilateral educational disarmament.
>
> Our society and its educational institutions seem to have lost sight of the basic purposes of schooling, and of the high expectations and disciplined effort needed to attain them. This report, the result of 18 months of study, seeks to generate reform of our educational system in fundamental ways and to renew the Nation's commitment to schools and colleges of high quality throughout the length and breadth of our land.

The Commission issued five (5) broad set of recommendations that shook up the educational establishment in the respective states and shocked the general public throughout the nation. Educational reform became the catch word and emphasis of the 1980's; most of which can be attributed directly to this highly influential report.

Another report that has had an influential effect on education in the states was the America 2000: Where School Leaders Stand that was issued in April 1991 by President George Bush and the U.S. Secretary of Education, Lamar Alexander. The report contained six major national education goals that was accompanied by twenty-one objectives with a time-line of ten years to accomplish them. The six goals were that by the year 2000: (1) all children in America will start school ready to learn; (2) the high school graduation rate will increase to at least 90 percent; (3) American students will leave grades four, eight, and twelve having demonstrated competency over challenging subject matter, including English, mathematics, science, history and geography, and every school in America will ensure that all students learn to use their minds well, so they may be prepared for responsive citizenship, further learning, and productive employment in our modern economy; (4) U.S. students will be first in the world in science and mathematics achievement; (5) every adult American will be literate and possess the knowledge and skills necessary to compete in a global economy and exercise the rights and responsibilities of citizenship; and (6) every school in America will be free of drugs and violence and offer a disciplined environment conducive to learning. These goals were the result of the collaboration of the President and State governors that began with the Charlottesville Education Summit in the Fall of 1989 and culminated at the winter meeting of the National Governor's Association meeting held in February 1990.

One of the last influential reports to be issued nationally was in 1992 by the Secretary's Commission on Achieving Necessary Skills (SCANS) which was appointed by the U.S. Secretary of Labor. The SCANS report identified the following list of skills necessary for young people to succeed in the world of work.

Workplace Competencies—Effective workers can productively use:
- Resources—knowledge about how to allocate time, money, materials, space, and staff.
- Interpersonal skills—ability to work on teams, teach others, serve customers, lead, negotiate, and work well with people from culturally diverse backgrounds.
- Information—ability to acquire and evaluate data, organize and maintain files, interpret and communicate, and use computers to process information.
- Systems—an understanding of social, organizational, and technological systems; ability to monitor and correct performance; and ability to design or improve systems.
- Technology—ability to select equipment and tools, apply technology to specific tasks, and maintain and troubleshoot equipment.

Foundation Skills—Competent workers in the high-performance workplace need:
- Basic Skills—possess reading, writing, arithmetic and mathematics, speaking, and listening skills.
- Thinking Skills—posses the ability to learn, to reason, to think creatively, to make decisions, and to solve problems.
- Personal Qualities—possess individual responsibility, self-esteem and self-management, sociability, and integrity [p.3].

The basic context of the Commission's recommendations was a set of principles put forth in an earlier report by the Commission entitled *What Work Requires of Schools*, which stated that:

- The Qualities of high performance that today characterize our most competitive companies must become the standard for the vast majority of our employers, public and private, large and small, local and global.
- The nation's schools must be transformed into high-performance organizations.
- All Americans should be entitled to multiple opportunities to learn the SCANS know-how well enough to earn a decent living.

To make this a reality we [the Commission] recommend:

1. The nation's school systems should make the SCANS foundation skills and workplace competencies explicit objectives of instruction at all levels.
2. Assessment systems should provide students and workers with a resume documenting attainment of the SCANS know how.
3. All employers, public and private, should incorporate the SCANS know-how into all their human resource development efforts.
4. The Federal Government should continue to bridge the gap between school and the high-performance workplace, by advancing the SCANS agenda.
5. Every employer in America Should create its own strategic vision around the principles of the high-performance workplace [pp. 5-6].

Regulatory Functions of the U.S. Department of Education

In 1867, the Department of Education was created by congressional law. It was passed by the House in June, 1866, and by the Senate in February, 1867, and subsequently signed into law by President Andrew Johnson on March 2, 1867. President Johnson appointed Henry Barnard as the first U.S. Commissioner of Education of this new department which was not granted cabinet level status, but was attached to the Department of Interior. The major functions of this new department under the direction of its Commissioner were:

(1) Collecting such statistics and facts as shall show the condition and progress of education in the several States and Territories; (2) Diffusing such information respecting the organization and management of schools and school systems, and methods of teaching, as shall aid the people of the United States in the establishment and maintenance of efficient school systems; and, (3) Otherwise [promoting] the cause of education throughout the country.

In 1870, there was a futile effort to develop a national system of education. U.S. Senator George F. Hoar of Massachusetts on February 25, 1870 introduced a bill proposing to create a national system of education. The bill, H.R. 1326, specifically called for a national system of compulsory education, for the appointment of a state superintendent of national schools in each state by the president of the United States, and for dividing the states into school districts along the lines of congressional districts with the appointment of a division inspector and a local superintendent of national schools within each district that was appointed by the Secretary of Interior. This bill aroused somewhat positive reactions in the northern states, but there were considerably more negative reactions in the southern states where it was argued that such a law and practice would destroy local control over education, and that it would be an insult to white Southerners and inflame racial tensions and issues. Such concerns, still exist today. Many people are concerned that federal aid means federal government control with subsequent loss of state and or local autonomy over a function that is reserved to the states by interpretation of the Tenth Amendment to the U.S. Constitution. The Hoar Bill did not receive adequate support and was never enacted by Congress (Knight, 1953)

Between 1867 and 1953, the U.S. Office of Education went through numerous name changes, and primarily performed only those duties and functions assigned to it by the original law. On April 11, 1953, the U.S. Congress with the passage of Public Law 83-13 created the U.S. Department of Health, Education, and Welfare (HEW) and the Office of Education with the Commissioner of Education as its executive officer became an integral unit of this cabinet level department. In 1979, under Public Law 96-88, the Department of Education Organization Act, passed by Congress and signed into law by President James Carter on October 17, 1979, authority was granted to establish a cabinet level U.S. Department of Education with a Secretary of Education as its executive officer. In May 1980, the U.S. Department of Education formally became operational under its first secretary, Shirley M. Hufstedler.

When President Ronald Reagan was elected in November 1980, he appointed Terrell H. Bell to serve as the Secretary of Education. President Reagan, in his first "State of the Union" address to Congress in January 1981, reaffirmed his intent to dismantle the U.S. Department of Education. In his speech, he stated that:

> . . . education is the principal responsibility of local school systems, teachers, parents, citizens boards and State governments. By eliminating the Department of Education we can . . . ensure that local needs and preferences rather than the wishes of Washington determine the education of our children.

The President's effort at eliminating the U.S. Department of Education was met with considerable debate and resistance by Congress, many others in the educational profession, and the public. The issue was finally dropped, and the U.S. Department of Education survived.

The U.S. Department of Education as a cabinet level agency of the Executive Branch of the federal government has the overall responsibility of establishing policy, administering, and coordinating many federal assistance programs relevant to education. Figure 5.1 depicts the organizational structure of the U.S. Department of Education.

The officials of the Department of Education have the authority and responsibility, as do the officials of other cabinets and agencies of the federal government, of drafting regulations, guidelines, and procedures to implement federal laws that create and fund federal programs. Once drafted, the regulations are submitted to the appropriate congressional committees for approval and are then published in the *Federal Register* and eventually are inserted into the Federal Administrative Code and carry the weight of administrative law.

States and local agencies are required to submit proposals and plans to the various departments and agencies in order to acquire federal program monies. If the proposals and plans are accepted and approved, the State or local agency enters into contract with the federal agency pledging to

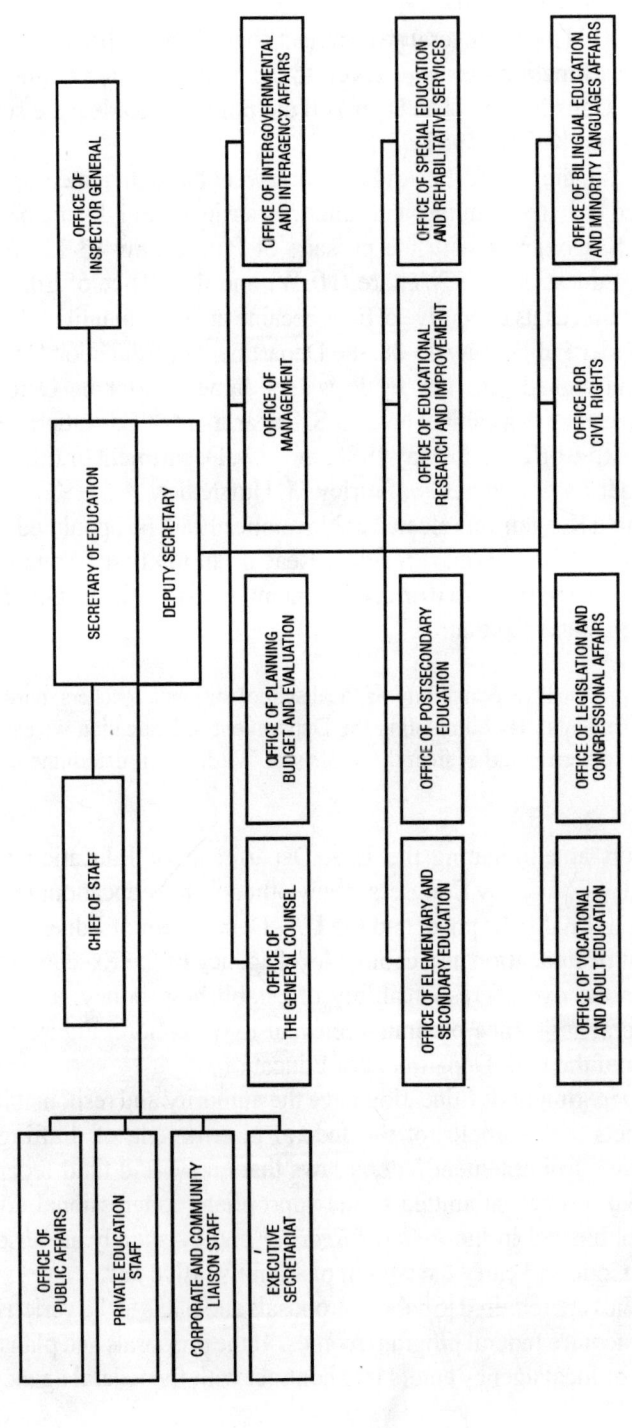

Figure 5.1. U. S. Department of Education.

comply with the federal law and agency regulations, guidelines, and procedures. The administering federal agency has the authority and responsibility to periodically perform audits to ensure that the legislation and regulations are being followed by the state or local agency receiving the federal monies.

Summary

Most lay people are not aware of the fact that education is a state function and not a function of the federal government. The focus of this chapter and book makes this fact quite explicit. It may be that the expensive nature of the education enterprise makes most people think that the "best" or most logical sources of additional revenue and assistance for education should come from the federal government. Almost every one believes that federal government involvement in and assistance to education is desirable, but they want such involvement and assistance without federal government "red tape" (regulations, etc.) and control. This rarely happens, for "he who supplies the 'gold' makes the rules." In addition, there are the rights of individuals—students, teachers, the handicapped, etc.—that are guaranteed by the Constitution of the United States that are made applicable to the states by the its Fourteenth Amendment which are enforced through the federal courts.

The limited federal government involvement in education will remain as it is, presently through: (1) protection of individuals' constitutional rights through the federal courts, (2) aid that is in the best interests of the nation; i.e., aid to provide for the general welfare and national defense through categorical aid for special purposes, (3) reports and studies issued by influential federal government commissions, and (4) rules and regulations made by various agencies of the federal government who have regulatory authority over government funded programs.

References

America 2000: Where School Leader Stand. Arlington, Va.: American Association of School Administrators.

Goals For Americans: The Report of the President's Commission on National Goals, "National Goals in Education," Chapter 3 (pp. 79-100, by John W. Gardner. Administered by The American Assembly, Columbia University, New York 27, New York, November 16, 1960 (A Spectrum Book).

Edgar W. Knight. *Readings in Educational Administration.* New York: Henry Holt and Company, 1953.

National Commission on Excellence in Education, *A Nation at Risk: The Imperative for Educational Reform.* Washington, D.C.: Superintendent of Documents, U.S. Government Printing Office.

Charles A. Quattlebaum. *Federal Educational Activities and Educational Issues Before Congress*. Washington, D.C.: United States Government Printing Office, 1952

U.S. Department of Labor, *Secretary's Commission on Achieving Necessary Skills*, 200 Constitution Avenue, N. W., Washington, D.C. 20210.

Educational Accountability in Texas

James A. Vornberg

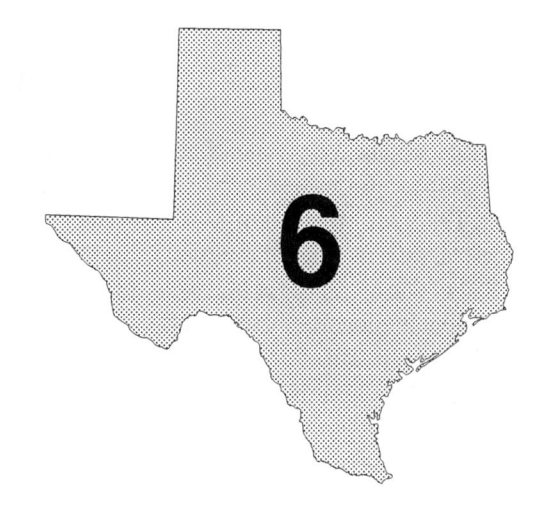

The term accountability refers to answering to those to whom one is responsible. It "expresses a relationship between the occupants of roles who control daily work in institutions and persons who possess formal power to displace them" (Browder, 1988, p. 3). In the public educational setting, this refers to answering to the citizens of the state for educational outcomes. It is an effort to introduce "quality assurance" to the learning results of students. Madaus and Stufflebeam (1984) state that accountability generally refers to individuals while program evaluation monitors educational services.

The concept of accountability does not have a clear definition, however, because it is not static. In considering education as an institution, there are many participants in the system—students, teachers, parents, administrators, board members and state policy makers. These participants create a dynamic interaction which requires various types of accountability when looking at the total picture. These include (1) input accountability—providing the tools necessary for offering quality education, (2) process accountability—the activities designed to bring about learner growth and change, and (3) product accountability—evidence of student growth in terms of knowledge, skills and attitudes resulting from the process (Texas Association of School Boards, 1974). When linked together, these three types of accountability demonstrate that the educational institution, as developed by the state, is dependent on close coordination of the efforts of many people in diverse roles. Lessinger (1973) refers to accountability in several ways: performance accountability, professional accountability, and system accountability. Of these, system accountability is the most broad since it can refer to achieving the best results possible over a wide spectrum of activity encompassing a diverse population. This is the case when educational accountability is considered for the State of Texas.

The Roots of Accountability

Accountability, when defined as being answerable for performance or outcomes, is certainly not new to administration. Although the terminology is most closely associated with the 1970s and 1980s, efforts to improve the product as a result of better management go back even before the classical or scientific period of management of the early 1900s (Madaus and Stufflebeam, 1984). The emphasis at that time was to maximize the workers' output and to provide the most efficient bureaucracy to accomplish the purpose of the organization.

In the process of organizing efficiently to produce maximum output during the Hawthorne studies, the researchers stumbled on the importance of the psycho-social needs of employees in accomplishing production. Thus, the human relations aspects of working in groups focused on motivating them to better production in the period from the mid 1920s to the 1950s.

With the midpoint of the century came a gradual shift in administrative thought from describing how managerial tasks should be accomplished to how these tasks were being accomplished. The focus of this period was on social sciences with behaviorism as the principal vehicle of study. The study of administration became more empirical in research methodology with the goal of predicting consequences of human behaviors. This effort spawned numerous studies encompassing both individual and organizational behavior, with leadership often being the center of attention. As the theorists studied complex organizations with this approach, the view that these organizations were both systems in themselves and a part of greater systems emerged as an important foundation of administrative thought. (Since the systems view of organizations developed, another view of organization, that of loose coupling, has also become important. See chapter 21 on theory).

With systems principles permeating the management process in educational administration, the concept of accountability emerged as it is currently viewed. That view is encompassed in the state educational reform movement which was most recently launched by the report in 1983 entitled *A Nation at Risk: The Imperative for Educational Reform* by the National Commission on Excellence in Education. As Finn (1986, p. 14) points out, this reform movement differs from many of the past in that it is preoccupied with results, primarily of the measurable, cognitive kind; the movement is decentralized with most activity coming from state governments; and its leadership is primarily laymen and elected officials, not professional educators.

This most recent concept of accountability no longer relies on uncorroborated testimony that administrators did their best. It now demands "ever-tighter standards and more specific expectations, especially for results received" (Browder, 1988). This generally means that performance standards are set and objective criteria are used to determine if results are achieved.

This contemporary view of accountability is made possible by the ideas which were developed in the systems thinking as applied to management. A system has become the way of describing interrelated parts which make up a whole. In the case of management, it is the allocation and coordination of the inputs involved in accomplishing any task or goal. Specifically in educational settings it is the coordination of all the inputs into the educational process which will result in an educated citizen who will contribute to society.

Thus, the educational system might be depicted as in Figure 6.1

Inputs

- Management
- Instructors
- Students
- Curriculum
- Environment
- Resource Materials
- Time
- Etc

Uncontrolled outside inputs (Problems and Conflicts)

Process

Educational System (Instructional Activity)

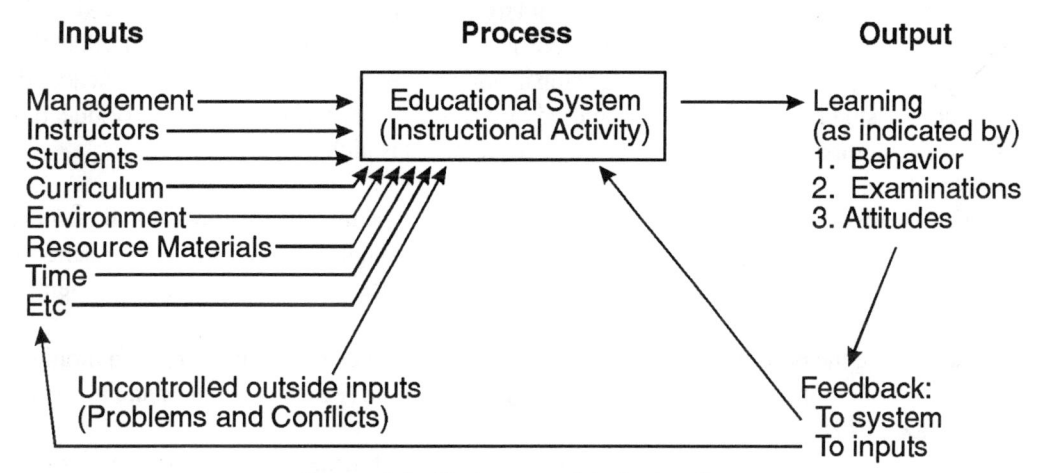

Output

Learning (as indicated by)
1. Behavior
2. Examinations
3. Attitudes

Feedback:
To system
To inputs

Figure 6.1. Systems model of education

The inputs to the system are all those resources of time, personnel, facilities, and conflicts which come together to form the educational process. As these inputs interact with each other, learning takes place on the part of the students (not to mention all others involved in the process). When measured by various means (such as testing) and if the students have learned what educators had planned for them to learn, the instructional objectives have been met. If these objectives are not met, then, the instruction was not successful. The principles of accountability would require that changes be made in the system to do a better job of meeting the objectives in the future—possibly even changes in leadership.

To develop an instructional process, a series of decisions occur. First comes systems analysis in which all the inputs—including conflicts and problems—are examined to determine their effect. At some point goals and objectives are determined. Alternative methods of reaching those goals are considered and the favored method selected. Then the system design is determined in some detail. As the design is implemented, systems management takes place on the part of the administrator and all those who help to make instruction occur. Continual adjustments are made by changing the inputs or altering the design during this management phase. These decisions are made as the result of both internal feedback while the process is ongoing and external feedback as the result of evaluations of the product (output).

With demonstrations of successful programs evidenced by favorable output there is a desire on the part of upper-level policy makers (at the state level) to extend such successes throughout the state. As the design is broadened to include more students, systems engineering is taking place. The concept of a state school system is exemplified when state-level policy makers, far removed from the local instructional process, set goals, determine inputs, and structure outcome criteria into a complex and broad system. In attempting to become more accountable for the educational process, the policy makers and executives at the state level in Texas have utilized the systems approach to administration to direct a large number of diverse people involved in the educational process. (It is important to note here that Texas state leadership in education currently has adopted a stance to move decision making to the lowest level possible, consequently site-based decision making is being promoted by the legislature and State Board of Education (SBOE). The components of this systems approach in Texas include the following:

1. identifying the goals which are to be achieved by the system and by the individual learners.
2. managing the inputs to the educational process through accreditation of the schools, certification of administrative, instructional, and service personnel, and development of curriculum.
3. monitoring the process which occurs through the feedback mechanisms of data monitoring—Public Education Information Management System (PEIMS)—and financial control (Bulletin 679).
4. assessing the outputs of the system in terms of student achievement as measured by the Texas Assessment of Academic Skills (TAAS), the optional Norm-Referenced Assessment Program for Texas (NAPT), and the Texas Academic Skills Program (TASP) and in terms of district/school accountability as demonstrated by the Academic Excellence Indicator System (AEIS).

The development of the components in the Texas systems approach to education has occurred over a long period of time. Initial efforts by the state board, legislature, and the commissioner of education have been refined numerous times. The state education reform movement which resulted in House Bill 72 passed in 1984 and modified by Senate Bill 1 passed in 1990 heavily impacted Texas' approach to accountability and redefined accountability from complying with rules to achieving results. The remainder of this chapter focuses on the components of the Texas accountability effort.

In the early 1970s, TEA adopted a planning model based on the systems approach which identifies a process used at the state level to develop programs. This model (see figure 6.2) provides the foundation for establishing programs which are designed to solve educational problems and to make the ongoing decisions necessary to implement them. Such a planning model is effective not only for the state policy makers, but also should be adopted for use by local boards and district administrators.

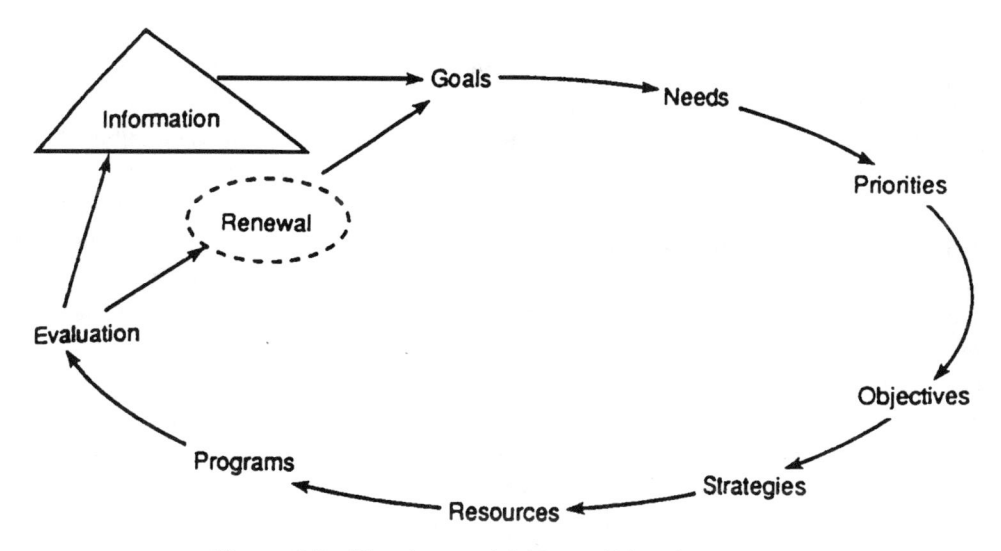

Figure 6.2. Planning model--Texas Education Agency

The Goals of the Texas System

Any well-structured system must have a vision to guide what is to be accomplished. That vision of what needs to be accomplished may have to change as the environment—particularly the demographic and economic aspects—changes. The Texas State Board of Education has recognized that Texas demographic features are changing rapidly and the state long-range plan must accommodate this change. The Texas population is second in size in the nation and the ethnic makeup of the projected 3.5 million student-age population will become proportionately more Hispanic and black. In 1986, the ethnic distribution of the first grade population was 50.5 percent white, 15.2 percent black, and 32.5 percent Hispanic. The minority-become-majority change is expected to continue through the next decade (Long Range Plan). An increasing percentage of students entering school now come from groups which have traditionally left school early. Students from disadvantaged families are expected to increase, which points out that "at-risk" students must have their special needs met. At-risk students include those who need programs extending special attention due to historical noncompletion of school, those who may learn more slowly, those who learn more rapidly, and those with special learning needs.

System Goals

These demographic changes when linked with the economic necessity of better preparing the future work force, both academically and vocationally, require that the state educational policy makers set challenging but realistic goals in their planning.

Goals were adopted originally in October 1970 by the State Board of Education (SBOE). Until the state education reform movement began, these goals were rather briefly stated in three areas: (1) Student Development, (2) Organizational Efficiency, and (3) Accountability. In 1985 the newly appointed SBOE began a process to develop not only goals but a long range plan for education. In January of 1987, the completed plan was officially adopted by the SBOE. In 1990 the SBOE again began its review of the "educational needs of the state" as stipulated by the Texas Education Code [TEC 11.26 (b)], and adopted a plan for 1990-1994 which had input from "policymakers, agency staff, specialists and researchers, practitioners, business people and other professionals, advocates, and parents" (SBOE Long Range Plan, 1990).

The SBOE's second long range plan set nine goals to characterize the state's system by quality, equity, and accountability. The SBOE's plan stipulates not only the goals and objectives but also the needs which have made the goal apparent, the actions required by the state, the service centers, the local districts, and the colleges and universities as well as the results which are expected by 1994. The nine goals address the major aspects of any system of education: student learning, curriculum and programs, personnel, organization and management, finance, parent responsibility, community and business partnerships, research, development and evaluation, and communications (see Table 6.1 for list of goals and Appendix A for full list of objectives).

TABLE 6.1
SBOE Goals for 1990-1994

1. Student Learning: All students will achieve their full educational potential.
2. Curriculum and Programs: A well-balanced and appropriate curriculum will be provided for all students.
3. Personnel: Qualified and effective personnel will be attracted and retained.
4. Organization and Management: The organization and management of all levels of the educational system will be productive, efficient, and accountable.
5. Finance: The financing of public education will be adequate, equitable, and efficient.
6. Parent Responsibility: Parents will be full partners in the education of their children.
7. Community and Business Involvement: Businesses and other members of the community will be partners in the improvement of schools.
8. Research, Development, and Evaluation: Instruction and administration will be improved through research that identifies creative and effective methods.
9. Communications: Communications among all public education interests will be consistent, timely, and effective.

As the SBOE's Long Range Plan was being developed during 1990, the Texas State Legislature was also in special session to deal with school finance issues. The result of their efforts was Senate Bill 1 which contained six goals relating to the educational system. These goals paralleled the SBOE's goals, but also were more specific in some ways. The goals include closing the gap between educationally disadvantaged students and other populations with an objective of 95 percent graduation rate of those students entering the seventh grade. Student performance is to be within national norms with a well-balanced and appropriate curriculum being provided. Qualified, effective personnel will be attracted and retained with adequate and competitive compensation. The organization of the system will be productive, efficient and accountable. Research will be utilized to improve instruction and administration. Local initiative and technology are encouraged for instructional arrangements and management techniques which will increase equity, efficiency and effectiveness of instruction and administration (TEC 2.01).

Learning Goals

Although goals one and two of the SBOE's plan and the first time goals identified by the legislature point to student performance and the curriculum to be taught in the schools, the legislature specifically directed the state board in House Bill 246 to designate the essential elements of the twelve curriculum areas, which were to be studied each year in school. These essential elements became, then, the minimum statewide learning goals for students at every grade level in Texas. When linked with adequate evaluation instruments to measure students mastering these elements, a system of individual educational accountability was created (see Chapter 11 on Curriculum and Instruction in Texas Schools).

Managing the Inputs to the System

Managing a statewide system of schools is, at first glance, an impossible task to accomplish with any degree of consistency. Yet for quality education to exist across the state, many citizens and state leaders think that is exactly what must occur. Goals have been set which identify what is to be accomplished over a five-year period. These goals identify changes in the system and specific learner outcomes. This goal orientation sets the course for the state educational system and thereby points the direction for the many subsystems. Systems theory assumes that quality inputs into the system will tend to produce better output; therefore, it is important that the resources and inputs to the educational process be controlled as much as possible so quality learning outcomes will result.

Certification of Personnel

A key component resource of the educational system is the cadre of professionals--teachers, administrators, and service personnel--who work in the schools. To insure that quality personnel are employed in educational programs, state statutes require that all teachers and other professionals be certified for their positions by the Texas Education Agency.

For an individual to become certified in Texas, one must be admitted to a teacher education program at an approved university, complete an approved course of study which meets the criteria of the Commission on Standards for the Teaching Profession, and successfully pass the Examination for the Certification of Educators in Texas (ExCET). An alternative certification program is also available for college graduates who completed their work in areas other than education. Prospective teachers qualifying under this plan complete a program with an approved *alternative certification project* including an intern year and pass the ExCET.

To be admitted to the standard teacher education program, a student with junior standing must achieve a satisfactory level of performance on a competency exam of basic skills (TASP test as of September 1989), have satisfactory academic performance (a 2.5 GPA), display good personal and social qualities, and be physically and mentally healthy. Once admitted, the student must complete the approved program which is monitored by the Texas Education Agency for meeting the Commission's standards.

The standards which must be met by approved institutions of higher education include these (TAC: Title 19, Part II, Chapter 137, Subchapter K):

1. The institution must be authorized by Texas to grant degrees of at least the baccalaureate level, accredited by the Southern Association of Colleges and Schools, and approved by the Commission on Standards for the Teaching Profession.
2. Institutional policies shall demonstrate a commitment to teacher education.
3. The institution's organizational structure shall provide a professional education unit which is administered and staffed by competent personnel with proper graduate preparation.
4. The professional education unit shall be responsible for the institution's teacher education program.
5. The institution shall provide curriculum which provides for a broad based general education, teaching specialists for instructional assignments, and a professional studies program for specific teaching roles.
6. The institution shall provide a sufficient number of faculty with appropriate preparation and experience to support the programs.
7. The institution must provide student services such as admission and retention policies, testing, counseling, advisement and professional placement.
8. Physical facility and learning resources must be accessible and adequate to achieve the objectives.
9. Adequate financial support must be provided to the programs of professional education.
10. Collaborative planning for and review of teacher education programs must be provided, including membership in a local teacher education center.
11. Evaluation of the above components must take place in a process established by the institution to include the success of its graduates, test results, and teacher appraisal, using an accountability system that includes performance of graduates and peer review of institutions and programs.

Candidates for teaching certificates complete eighteen semester hours of preparation which includes a common core of education, methodology appropriate to teaching in their chosen area, and experiences including pre-student teaching field experience and student teaching. Once the approved teacher education program is complete, the Examination for Certification of Educators in Texas (ExCET) test must be successfully passed.

The ExCET program was developed to implement Senate Bill 50, passed in 1981, requiring certification candidates to perform satisfactorily on comprehensive examinations. Structured by the SBOE, the exam tests both professional development at the appropriate level (e.g. elementary, secondary, all level) and the content specialization for the teaching area for candidates seeking initial certification. Currently certified teachers seeking additional content specialization certificate endorsements take only the content specialization test.

Persons seeking Texas certification based on a valid out-of-state certificate take both the professional development and the content specialization test. The alternative certification program available for degree holders not completing certificates during their academic preparation now requires candidates to take both the professional development and academic specialization tests.

The ExCET tests are criterion referenced, designed to "measure the candidate's knowledge and skills in relation to an established standard of competence" (*Excellence in Education,* TEA, 1987, p. 7). The tests were developed by National Evaluation Systems under contract with the Texas Education Agency. Advisory committees reviewed drafts and test objectives during their development. Content validation panels reviewed each item to ensure the item was related to content knowledge. In addition to teaching certificates, successful ExCET test scores are required to obtain a professional certificate as Learning Resources Specialist, Reading Specialist, Counselor, Educational Diagnostician, Supervisor, Mid-Management Administrator, or Superintendent.

Teacher Evaluation

Also related to personnel is the process of teacher evaluation. The reform efforts in Texas as directed by House Bill 72 required a system of teacher appraisal to be instituted. The result of this requirement was the Texas Teachers Appraisal System (TTAS). This system, instituted in the 1986-87 school year, brought the principal, as the instructional leader at the building level, into the classroom to observe and evaluate the teacher's ability to direct learning, and to conference with the teacher to improve teaching skills. The TTAS instrument is used state wide so all teachers have similar standards upon which they are evaluated. This standardized system requires that all principals and other appraisers be trained to administer the instrument equitably. Although the system is often criticized, it has undergone annual changes and has been credited with improving instruction by many people. Recent changes placed more emphasis on the performance of the students as a result of the teaching activity and sought to verify the results of the teacher's performance during the teaching process by observing the students' learning success. (See Chapter 9 for more details on TTAS.)

Accreditation

A third major component of the State's effort to manage the Texas system of schools is that of accreditation of those schools. Local school boards have a great deal of discretion in directing the administration of their districts; however, the legislature requires that the schools in a district be accredited in order to operate independently. The current process focuses on determining the effectiveness of schools to ensure that all students achieve excellence and equity in educational outcomes. As of 1994, the process is being referred to as the accountability system. Schools and districts are rated annually by the agency on the basis of the campus's performance on the Academic Excellence Indicator System—which focuses heavily on the student achievement as indicated on the Texas Assessment of Academic Skills. The ratings include exemplary, recognized, accredited (districts) or acceptable (campuses), and accredited warned (districts) or low performing (campuses). TEA uses criteria in the accreditation process such as test scores and other measures of educational effectiveness and efficiency including campus performance objectives, effective schools criteria, use of instructional technology, and efficient allocation of available resources. The commissioner, who holds the accreditation authority, may appoint a monitor, a management team, or a master, who has the power to approve or disapprove any actions by the board, superintendent or principal for districts which are warned. A district which is unaccredited for two years may be annexed to one or more adjoining districts or may be operated by the state by appointing a board of managers and superintendent to replace the board of trustees for a period of two years (TEC 21.753-.754; 21.757-.758).

Historical Background

In 1974 the TEA instituted an accreditation planning process which included the development of educational goals, a self-study and visitation, and the development and implementation of a five-year plan to improve the school. This process was linked with SBOE's goals adopted in 1970, and attempted to make schools more responsive to those goals. Prior to that date, TEA conducted audits of local districts and schools to insure compliance with the laws. In 1986 the five-year plan requirement was suspended as it did not appear to be productive for most schools. This was replaced in 1987 with the requirement for districts and campuses to develop an educational improvement plan which reflects the state reform movement, the effective school correlates, and student education performance standards. This improvement plan function is now supplemented by the Site-Based Decision Making plan which was required beginning in the 1992-93 school year. Schools which achieved specified outcomes were awarded monetary awards as part of the Texas Successful School Awards System (TSSAS).

Current Standards

Senate Bill 1 (TEC 21.7532) passed in 1990 requires that campus performance objectives be adopted annually for each academic excellence indicator with a collaborative process involving the principal, professional staff, parents and the community. Performance on indicators determines district status and campus ratings, qualification for the Texas Successful Schools Awards System, and the data reported on the family report card (as of 1994). The academic excellence indicators were adopted by the SBOE for five indicators (number in parentheses indicates requirement for exemplary/recognized categories): TAAS (90%/65%), attendance (94%), dropout rate (< 1%), and College admissions tests (70% tested; 35% over criterion score/ 55% tested, 10% above criterion score). The principal's performance appraisal is to consider achievement of the campus's objectives, performance gains, and maintenance of those gains in future years.

The Division of Accountability of the TEA does an annual review of each district and campus on the academic excellence indicators which will examine the actual performance of the district or campus and analyze subpopulations within the district or campus. Growth comparisons are made on a year-to-year basis within that school or district and not in comparison with other districts. Subgroup (i.e.: ethnic groups, disadvantaged) scores are analyzed to determine if gaps between subgroup performances are being closed. Districts with low performance levels or with a failure to narrow the gaps between subgroups become candidates for on-site visits. Criteria examined in the analysis include performance on student achievement, attendance, promotion, dropout rates, program costs or other criteria required by the SBOE. Accredited warned districts are those which do not achieve 25% passing TAAS.

The accreditation team which visits warned districts and low-performing campuses consists of peer educators who have undergone training in a program called "The Texas School Improvement Initiative." These peer educators including administrators, serve as chair and team members and have an opportunity to give feedback to schools and principals undergoing their accreditation visits. TEA accreditation staff act as facilitators to insure the integrity of the process at the campus level; at the district level the TEA staff serve as chair.

Since accreditation is based on outcomes, student performance on the AEIS indicators provide the primary evaluative criteria. Reports indicate how the district compares to the state, and the region on the TAAS performance. Performance is also indicated for subgroups in the district such as minority group and economically disadvantaged. Student attendance, student dropout rates, percentage enrolled in advanced courses, and college admission test performance are also indicators used for the 1993-94 school year.

Senate Bill 1 (TEC 11.272) provides exemptions from certain state statutes and rules for districts and campuses that are rated exemplary in this accreditation process beginning in the 1991-92 school year. This exemption is considered an enticement for districts to work toward exemplary status and recognizes that the local leadership of a district or campus may need less guidance from the state policy makers in achieving or maintaining exemplary performance.

Certain laws or rules are not included in the exemption categories including: (1) prohibitions on criminal conduct; (2) federal laws or regulations; (3) state laws or rules relating to curriculum essential elements, extracurricular activity participation, health and safety, competitive bidding, textbook selection, elementary class size limits, removal of disruptive students, suspension and expulsion, at-risk programs, pre-kindergarten programs, graduation requirements, and employee rights and benefits. The commissioner is authorized to exempt an exemplary elementary school campus from the class size limits if a written plan is submitted which outlines steps that will ensure the exemption will not harm students' academic achievement. This exemption would be in effect until the campus achievement level declines.

Monitoring the Process of Education

In any system an important feature of successful management is the ability to monitor what is taking place while the process is ongoing. Several advantages result from this ability. First, an accurate picture of what is taking place enables policy makers at all levels—the legislature, state board of education, local boards of trustees—to more effectively set policies which will impact programs. Second, a constant flow of information to the manager makes it possible to make decisions which are based on what is taking place in a timely manner. Resources may be better directed to accomplish the desired goals and objectives and in a fashion which will make the most efficient use of them. Third, operational data from all types of functions—instruction, personnel, finance, support services, facilities, etc.—enable those involved with these operations to do the best job in carrying out their roles.

To provide accurate and timely information in making a system most accountable for what is occurring, a management information system (MIS) is required. The more accurate the data which is provided by such a system and the more timely the manner in which it is available, theoretically the better the results the total system may accomplish. Texas has been making efforts to establish such a system for more than a decade. The period 1981-83 saw new statutory requirements for information which demanded that the TEA develop a comprehensive data base on student performance, finance, and personnel. Also new tasks assigned to TEA required a major increase in staff or a new way of using information with the existing staff.

Public Education Information Management System (PEIMS)

The resulting effort, adopted by SBOE in 1986, was a major development in the accountability system in Texas which is called the Public Education Information Management System or PEIMS. PEIMS was designed to overhaul the manner in which information is exchanged between local school districts and TEA. By developing this library of statewide information on the conditions and accomplishments of the local schools, TEA and the legislature may monitor what is occurring to insure compliance with the law as well as gauge the successes and failures of programs and the school systems. Also raw data is provided for educational research. Hopefully paperwork for reporting will be reduced as well as travel of TEA personnel to monitor schools and programs.

School districts submit their data via computer reports which are standardized and detailed to the TEA. By standardizing the definitions of data required in the system, confusing and sometimes contradicting sets of forms and definitions were eliminated. Training and assistance in implementing PEIMS are available from the PEIMS coordinators at regional service centers. In addition, standard edits were performed at service centers to insure the integrity of data being submitted.

Data being collected by the system increase in scope and detail as the implementation process becomes more comprehensive each year. The 1992-93 school year data inputs to the system included the following:

1. Organization Data: District name and number; campus name and number; cooperative memberships.
2. Staff data: demographics as name, sex, ethnicity, qualifications/permits, teacher performance (i.e. career ladder level), payroll information, responsibilities (i.e. students serviced).
3. Financial data: end of year financial data for the past year and the budget for the current year;
4. Student data: demographic and program participation (e.g. gifted and talented, ECIA Chapter 1, vocational education, special education, etc.); student identification number; ethnicity; date of birth; campus; grade level; eligibility for funding; student attendance and contact hours; student course schedules in grades 9-12; grade retention; and graduation data;
5. Dropout data: demographic and program data including social security or ID numbers, ethnic origin, grade level, special education indicator, sex, date of birth, socioeconomic status, and time of year of dropout. This information will help to track dropouts.
6. Student achievement test data: TAAS. This data is part of the state MIS system and is input directly by the state.
7. School facility data.

Several advantages are anticipated from the resulting products which are being realized with the implementation of PEIMS. First, open access to the data will be provided for administrators to be able to determine answers to questions of concern. Specialized reports will be able to be generated without the difficulty of requiring local districts to submit data each time. Both "off-the-shelf" products and custom applications requiring specialized processing will be available. Direct user access for building reports and answering questions will be possible. Second, the data can be returned to the local district for internal use and analysis and for comparison to other districts or schools throughout the state. Third, the Academic Excellence Indicator System

(AEIS) performance reports can be developed by disaggregating the data in the PEIMS and used by the accreditation division at TEA. Fourth, although the initial implementation of PEIMS has required additional local district effort, in the long run local district effort should be reduced by the standardized sets of data. Future requirements for data reporting should be available to TEA with no additional reports being required of local districts. More than forty forms or reports required of districts have been replaced or streamlined by PEIMS since its initiation.

Financial Accounting

Developed prior to the recent requirement for PEIMS, financial accounting in Texas has been structured in a systems mode since about 1970. The common terminology for such a system is Planning Programming Budgeting System (PPBS) or frequently shortened to "programmed budgeting." The budget line items are truly task or goal oriented. Such a system is designed to combine expenses of the educational effort into programs designed to achieve particular goals or objectives (e.g. teaching reading to primary students) rather than to combine charges that are for similar type expenditures (e.g. teacher salaries). This capability makes it possible to more critically evaluate the success of a particular program in achieving the specified goals and more critically analyze alternative programs during the process of decision making at budgeting time.

Bulletin 679, *The Financial Accounting Manual,* specifies the budgeting, accounting, and auditing procedures used in Texas school districts. Of major importance to the monitoring process are the accounting codes contained in Bulletin 679. These codes provide the basis of financial reporting to PEIMS and also enable school districts to analyze their expenditures (planned and actual) for effective decision making. As the PEIMS is more fully implemented, these codes will enable state level budgetary composites to be analyzed with respect to other data collected, such as student achievement or dropouts. With this capability, state policy makers may look at programs with increased accountability as a verifiable goal. (See Chapter 12 for more detail on financial accounting.)

Assessing the Outputs of the System

Educators have collected performance data on students for years in the form of norm referenced achievement tests such as the California Achievement Test or the Iowa Test of Basic Skills at the elementary level as well as the Scholastic Aptitude Test (SAT) or the American College Testing Program (ACT) at the high school level. These tests gave a picture of student performance in relation to other students, but were not specifically linked to a set of identified goals that were being taught. Also there was no common measurement instrument with which all students were being assessed, but rather each district was using the program which was desired by their personnel. At the secondary level, the SAT or ACT programs were optional (at a cost to the student) and usually only selected by students with post secondary educational aspirations. At best, a somewhat inadequate picture of performance when viewing the state as a whole was available.

Texas Assessment of Academic Skills

In 1979 the State Legislature mandated a testing program known as Texas Assessment of Basic Skills (TABS) designed to test students at fifth and ninth grade levels in their proficiency of basic educational skills. The TABS program preceded the state education reform movement which culminated in a special legislative session in July, 1984. This session mandated a comprehensive assessment of students using criterion-reference tests to assess minimum basic skill competencies in mathematics, reading and writing. This program known as Texas Educational Assessment of Minimum Skills (TEAMS) was criticized because the TEAMS objectives became "the curriculum" for schools to focus on until after the tests had occurred in April and that the "minimums" had become the "maximums" due to the stress placed on teachers and administrators for students to perform well. Content was sometimes being tested on the exam which had not yet been taught, due to the developmental level of some students.

In order to satisfy the legislative requirement for student assessment, to meet the SBOE's Long Range Plan objectives, and ameliorate concerns raised by the TEAMS program, the Texas Assessment of Academic Skills (TAAS) program was instituted for the period 1990-95. In the fall of 1993 the program began with testing to take place in grades 3, 4, 5, 6, 7, 8, and 10. The exit level test given at grade 10 must be successfully passed in order to graduate from a Texas high school. This program provides for a criterion measure of student achievement, but differs from TEAMS in that the scope of the content for the test has been broadened to include more instructional targets identified in the essential elements. Broad objectives have now become the focus of each section of the test, rather than the more limited set of TEAMS objectives. The more detailed instructional targets—the essential elements—which are tested will be sampled each year. Every instructional target will not be tested every year. Skills which require more rote memory work are deemphasized while greater emphasis is being placed on the student's ability to think independently, read critically, write clearly and solve problems logically. (See chapter 11 for more details on TAAS administration).

The TAAS exam given at the tenth grade level is also used as an exit level test which must be successfully passed for students to receive a high school diploma from a Texas public high school. The concepts are tested using multiple choice items for mathematics, reading and writing. The writing section also requires that a student write a first draft of a composition of a given subject. Five opportunities are available for a student to be tested for mastery while in school, once in sophomore year and two in each of the junior and senior years. In developing this test, TEA involved educators across the state to determine the appropriate learning objectives for which students had received adequate instruction. Writing skill objectives are assessed using multiple-choice items. Beginning with grade four (English version) and in grades 8 and 10, a written composition is used to assess the students' ability to synthesize the component skills of writing. This composition is graded using a focused holistic scoring process. Mathematics and reading skills are assessed using multiple-choice questions. Science and social studies skills are tested in grades 4 and 8 using both machine-scored items and performance tasks which are teacher scored and take six weeks to accomplish.

Mastery criteria for the examination is set by the State Board of Education based on field tests data, content and quality of the examination, phase-in-time, adequacy of preparation, and data-based projected pass rates. To master objectives measured by multiple choice items, usually three of four questions must be answered correctly. Scaled scores with a statistical conversion which allows for comparison of student performance on percentile ranks are being developed based on Texas norms from TAAS results. Other data are also collected which are useful in learning more about the effect of additional factors on the performance of students from districts with certain attributes. These include average daily attendance (ADA), district type (e.g. size, growth rates, urban/rural), wealth, maintenance and operation effective tax effort, ethnic composition, region of state, price differential index level, state property tax board land use categories, percentage of low-income students, district composite TEAMS or TAAS scores, operating costs per ADA, growth or decline in student population, and student density.

Norm-Referenced Testing

Senate Bill 1 passed in June 1990 required that the SBOE adopt one nationally recognized norm-referenced assessment battery to be given to each student in grades 4, 6, 8, and 10. This battery of tests must measure achievement in reading, mathematics, language arts, science, and social studies. As this program was fully implemented by the SBOE, the state adopted one norm-referenced test, the Norm-Referenced Assessment Program for Texas (NAPT), to be administered to all students in grades 3 through 11. In 1993-94 the test was made optional and the requirement is expected to be eliminated completely.

Texas Academic Skills Program (TASP)

In 1987 the Texas Legislature passed House Bill 2182 (TEC, 51.306) which mandated another program designed to ensure that all students attending public institutions of higher education in Texas have the necessary reading, writing, and mathematics skills to perform effectively in college. This mandate is known as the Texas Academic Skills Program (TASP) and is required of all students entering higher education for the first time in or after the fall of 1989. The TASP has five components: diagnostic testing, advisement, placement, remediation, and program evaluation.

The diagnostic component requires entering public college students to take the TASP test. Those students not performing above a standard set by the Texas Higher Education Coordinating Board and the State Board of Education will be provided advisement, placement, and remediation course work to improve performance on the test. Until all three sections of the test—reading, writing, and mathematics—are successfully passed, a student may not enroll in upper division courses which would give a student more than sixty hours of semester credit (junior standing) or graduate from a certificate program of more than nine hours credit or receive an associate or baccalaureate degree. Successful completion of the three sections indicates the student has the minimum skills to do advanced level college work. Students in high school may take the TASP test when they have passed the TEAMS or TAAS exit level test and have been accepted for future admittance or are concurrently enrolled in an institution of higher education.

Candidates for entrance into a teacher education program or persons seeking a certificate through an approved alternative certification program must also successfully pass the TASP test regardless of having earned college credit before fall 1989. Also persons on emergency teaching permits must pass the test in order to renew the permit. This test replaces the pre-professional skills test (PPST) which was required for teacher education program admittance. The PPST gave only a pass/fail indication, while the TASP will diagnose weak areas and permit remediation of indicated deficiencies.

The TASP test may not be used by a college or university as an admissions requirement but only as a diagnostic instrument to prescribe remediation. The only exception is in the case of upper division institutions. The individual institution may require a higher standard than the one set by the state boards. Remediation course work may not be counted toward degree requirements.

Each institution reports annually to the State Board concerning the results of the students tested and the effectiveness of remedial programs. The high school from which the students graduated is identified in the report along with performance above or below the standard which will help to establish a level of accountability which was not known prior to TASP. Individual student names are not reported.

The TASP testing is funded by the requirement that students pay the exam fee. Funding for the remediation program is accomplished by direct line item budget appropriation for each state institution by the state legislature. The amount funded was based on the number of students and past successes at each university. Generally, institutions felt the remediation program was under funded to meet the requirements of the TASP.

Academic Excellence Indicator System (AEIS)

The AEIS, which has been previously discussed, also plays an important role in assessing output for a school district due to the requirement that every district must widely disseminate the results throughout the district and, beginning in 1994, in a Family Report card produced for the parent or guardian of every student. In addition to a required written report which is distributed by the district, a hearing or public meeting must be held to review the results.

Accountability in Texas Reviewed

Accountability means to answer for the results of the educational process in Texas Schools. The accountability movement has gained momentum as a result of the systems process of management being adopted by policy makers in Texas. The goals of the system along with a delegation of responsibility for aspects of implementation have been articulated by the State Board of Education in their Long Range Plan. The SBOE has also adopted learning outcomes for students in the form of essential elements in the curriculum. Management of the ongoing processes of the system is directed from the state level by the accreditation of the schools through the AEIS and the certification and evaluation of teachers. In order to monitor what is occurring on an ongoing basis, the Public Education Information Management System (PEIMS) was initiated. The financial accounting system which includes program budgeting capability has been incorporated into the PEIMS. Finally, the citizens and policy makers can observe the results of the system at work by looking at district performance in the form of the AEIS and the performance of the students on their learning outcomes in the form of the TAAS test and the TASP examination.

A comprehensive accountability system, which has recently responded to the input of local district administrators, has been implemented in Texas. This input has been made possible by the current leadership at the state agency level. News media across the state have used the data from this accountability system to tell the schools' stories, sometimes without indicating all of the problems or details. School boards and educators will have to continue to initiate new methods to communicate the entire picture to the people.

References

Browder, Lesley H. (1973). *An Administrator's Handbook on Educational Accountability.* Arlington, VA.: American Association of School Administrators.
Browder, Lesley H. (1988). Administrative Accountability. *Encyclopedia of School Administration and Supervision.* Onyx Press.
Finn, Chester E. (February, 1986) *Unsolved Problems of the Excellence Movement.* The School Administrator, pp. 14-17.
Hosttop, Richard W. (1973) *Managing Education for Results.* ETC Publications.
Lessinger, Leon M. (Spring, 1973) Accountability: Present Forces and Future Concerns. *New Directions for Education,* Vol. 1, No. 1, pp. 1-9.
Madaus, George F., and Daniel Stufflebeam. (1984) "Educational Evaluation and Accountability." *American Behavioral Scientist,* Vol. 27, No. 5, pp. 649-672.

Texas Association of School Boards. (1974) *Accountability in Education.* Austin: Texas Association of School Boards.

Texas Education Agency. (1987) Excellence in Education. Austin: Texas Education Agency, Office of Teacher Assessment.

Texas Education Agency. (January, 1987) *1986-1990 Long Range Plan of the State Board of Education for Texas Public School Education.* Austin: State Board of Education.

Texas Education Agency. (July, 1987) *Suggested Guidelines for Campus and District Improvement Plans.* Austin: Texas Education Agency.

Texas Education Agency. (January 12, 1990) *PEIMS System Management Plan.* Austin: Texas Education Agency.

Texas Education Agency. (June 1990 Draft) *Quality, Equity, Accountability: Texas State Board of Education Long-Range Plan for Public Education,* 1990-1994. Austin: Texas Education Agency.

Texas Education Agency. (July 1990) *Implementation of Senate Bill 1.* Austin: Texas Education Agency.

Texas Education Agency. *Overview of the Accountability System for 1994 and 1995.* Austin: Texas Education Agency, January 1994.

Texas Education Agency. *Performance-Based Accreditation: A Responsible and Responsive Accountability System.* Austin: Texas Education Agency.

Legal References
TAC—Texas Administrative Code
TEC—Texas Education Code

Texas Cultural and Ethnic Groups

Launey F. Roberts, Jr.

To a great extent, American public schools reflect the society which created them. Moreover, public school settings "mirror" a vast array of such societal problems as widespread alcohol and drug abuse, violence, racism, teenage pregnancy, child abuse and neglect, the increasing numbers who live below the poverty line, and an alarming trend reflecting low expectations and low self-esteem. These problems wreak serious harm on the educative process. Increasingly, and like the nation-at-large, the various social, economic, political, educational and cultural fabrics of Texas are changing. Consequently, the diversity inherent in this "confluence of cultures" places new and even more challenging demands on schools, specifically on principals and other school administrators.

Without doubt, school administrators working in today's schools and those preparing to enter the profession must become aware of the diverse makeup of these school-communities and must assure the development of programs which provide a sound, sensitive and effective education. Likewise, development of a keen sense and understanding of the concept of culture and of the nature of human behavior within the American context is essential. Further, administrators and other school staff personnel need to possess a positive sense of self and high self-esteem.

Too frequently, teachers and administrators seem unaware of problems related to racial, cultural and/or individual differences, or these educators may even deny the existence of these problems. Gordon Allport (1958) suggested that this denial takes two forms: For those in whom prejudice is deeply ingrained, the admission of such beliefs threatens to upset their equilibrium and to bring forth disturbing thoughts; and for those who are automatically habituated to the status quo, there is an assumption that the "prevailing system of caste and discrimination (is) . . . .externally fixed." Despite the fact that such confrontations with prejudice and discrimination are, at best, unsettling and difficult tasks, facing oneself is imperative for anyone who wants to work successfully with children and others.

In a paper presented at the 1989 Convention of the University Council for Educational Administration, Barbara Jackson suggested that due to changing demographics a new emphasis on the issues of race, ethnicity, culture, and values was needed in preparation programs for school administrators. To wit, America's colors are changing. This belief holds especially true in large urban schools in which Anglos are no longer in the majority. Increasingly, then, African-Americans and Hispanics are becoming the majority in the schools of America. Jackson further suggested that these two were the populations whose needs have not been sufficiently addressed by the schools. For instance, dropout rates among these groups have continued to increase at an alarming rate; and among those who remain and graduate, many do so with few or minimal literacy skills.

The school is subjected to clamor for changes from all sectors of society. Change is a process with which the educational administrator must deal—sometimes being in the vanguard, yet always being responsive to change. Hawley (1975) pointed out that American public schools had become notorious for their ability to resist change and innovation. Yet an organization must constantly adjust to new people and to new demands upon it, if it is to thrive.

Campbell et al. (1983) suggested that inasmuch as school districts in many urban areas had become larger and more complex, a number of organizational and/or structural changes had also been made. These changes had produced a tremendous impact upon school administrators.

In a similar vein, Thomas J. Sergiovanni et al. (1988) in a report of the Educational Administration Advisory Committee to the Coordinating Board of the Texas College and University System, suggested that "leaders for tomorrow's schools need to be both pathfinders and realistic problem-solvers. Key will be their ability to set as well as follow agendas; to empower others to lead; to chart the course toward school improvement in times of uncertainty; and to inspire and bring together a diverse population of Texans in pursuit of common values and goals."

This chapter will focus on matters of race, ethnicity, culture, cultural diversity, educational equity and other societal concerns. Both students of administration and others will be introduced to current knowledge, goals and practices critical to the development of personal characteristics, behaviors, attitudes, and perspectives which can assist in effective planning, organization and development of educational programs for these varied publics or estates in their quests for equal educational opportunity in Texas schools.

Culture

Schools are perhaps the most complex of all our social inventions. Like any other formal organization, the school faces the tasks of structuring, managing, and giving direction to a complex mix of human and technical resources. The plethora of problems, challenges, and other concerns in today's schools makes it even more important that educational administrators understand the significance of culture and its relationship to education and to the development of viable programs for their varied publics.

The term "culture" appears difficult to define as a result of its many different uses. Perry and Perry (1974) for instance, defined culture as all accumulated knowledge, ideas, goals, and material objects of a society that are shared by the members of the society. Noted anthropologist William Haviland (1983) suggested that culture is "learned behavior, passed on from generation to generation by non-hereditary means." Thus, to a great extent, culture is whatever we have achieved and have transmitted as a way of life, including our beliefs, mores, taboos, norms, behaviors, and ideologies.

Educational administrators need to find ways of thinking about culture and cultural differences and of discerning the relationship of education to these and other aspects of our common society. Kimbrough and Nunnery (1988) opined that a viable approach would be to conceptualize the basic institutions of society, wherein, these institutions might be thought of as a taxonomy of the culture. Among the basic institutions to be included are: family, religion, education, economics, and politics. Essentially, people of all cultures experience and are affected in varying degrees by each of these institutions. Moreover, while the family is the most important and influential institution, education also ranks high. Education is the means by which culture is transmitted; education tends to socialize the populace into the basic values and practices of society. Although education is powerful and necessary, it nevertheless requires the support of all of the other important institutional sectors of society. Without this support, as was evidenced in the school integration efforts resulting from the 1954 *Brown v. Board of Education* decision, progress inevitably falters.

Cultural Diversity

The American experience has most often been portrayed as a "melting pot"—people of diverse ethnic, racial, and cultural backgrounds coming to the United States to share in a common search for the religions, economic, and personal freedoms which they could not find elsewhere—in short, searching for the American Dream (Glazer and Moynihan, 1970; Dawidowicz and Goldstein, 1963).

Any serious attempt to address matters of cultural diversity in our general society, and, with specific reference to Texas, as well as to determine the significance and implication these aspects have for providing equal educational opportunities requires forthright and determined exploration and understanding of the matter of race and racial differences in America. Even a cursory glance at the history of America reveals her as a nation who, from her very inception, has been an extremely "color conscious" society.

Race consciousness and its articulation in theories of race are primarily a modern phenomenon. Gossett (1965. p. 15) suggested that when European explorers in the New World "discovered" people who looked different from themselves, these "natives' challenged then-existing conceptions of the origin of the human species and raised disturbing questions as to whether all could be considered in the same "family of man." Several religious arguments also ensued over creation itself, as theories of polygenesis questioned whether God had made only one species of humanity ("monogenesis"). Essentially, this European approach posited a world view which distinguished Europeans—children of God, human beings, etc. from "others." Such world view was needed to explain why some had to be "free" and others enslaved, why some had rights to land and property while others did not. Race and the interpretation of racial differences were central factors in that world view.

Omi and Winant (1986) opined that, in America, race has been a profound determinant of one's political rights, one's location in the labor market, and indeed one's sense of "identity." They further suggested that

> the hallmark of this history has been racism, not the abstract ethos of equality; and while racial minority groups have been treated differently, all can bear witness to the tragic consequences of racial oppression. The United States has confronted each racially defined minority with a unique form of despotism and degradation. The examples are familiar: Native Americans faced genocide, African-Americans were subjected to racial slavery, Mexicans were invaded and colonized and Asians faced exclusion.

In January, 1985, the late Clarence Pendleton, then chairman of the U.S. Commission on Civil Rights, told President Reagan that "American is fast becoming a colorblind society where no special significance, rights, or privileges are accorded due to one's race" (Omi and Winant, 1986). While this idealized view of America constitutes the very essence of our democratic way of life, a view of our recent history, particularly the period from 1960 to the present, reveals a more complex and contradictory pattern of race relations far less certain and much less tranquil in many sectors of society.

Race was a significant factor in American politics during the 1960s. In the 1970s, by comparison, the racial minority movements seemed to lessen. While racial oppression did not cease, many of the advances in race relations acquired during the 1960s were institutionalized. The matter of race was dramatically revived in the 1980s, when the Reagan administration, the academic establishment, and several conservative movements joined to assault the legacy and logic of earlier movement advances and accomplishments.

Cultural Diversity In Texas

Since its earliest beginnings, long before the Spanish came and before the Anglo-American colonists achieved independence from Mexico in 1836, Texas was multicultural, multilingual and ethnically diverse. While the values and customs of the old South were somewhat prominent pioneer institutions in some areas of the state, the diverse culture of antebellum Texas reflected the influences of people from many other parts of the world.

Anglo-Americans were the largest group of settlers to migrate from the United States in the early 1800s, the first to establish settlements in what was north and southeastern Mexico and what is now the north and eastern regions of Texas. A review of the historical development of Texas during this era (Richardson et al., 1981) credits two men, Moses Austin, who planned the colonization of Texas by Anglo-Americans and his son, Stephen Fuller Austin, as the ones who executed and successfully implemented this plan. The first Anglo-American settlement was established by William Lawrence and William Hensley on the Red River at Jonesborough (Richardson et al., 1981). The second largest group of foreign-born people in Texas by 1860 were Mexican-Americans. Following the revolution in 1836, although many Mexicans served in the revolutionary cause, they were generally treated with prejudice, discrimination and racism. While other immigrants (Europeans) were provided free land and other inducements, many Mexicans' land titles were challenged and others even lost their holdings. On the other hand, while many Mexicans slowly migrated to South Texas in the 1850s, most remained on farms and ranches in the new colony. Wherever they lived, however, they held on tenaciously to their cultural heritage—their religion, their language, their customs, and their traditions. Though most were poor, some were very prominent and influential. Jose Navarro, who distinguished himself in the revolution, also participated in writing the Constitution of 1845 and later served in the Texas legislature. Santos Benavides, who later served as mayor of Laredo, rose to the rank of general in the Civil War (Richardson, 1981).

Did Africans explore Texas before the Spaniards? Some believe they did. A settlement of exceptionally dark Indians greeted Jose de Escandon at the mouth of the Rio Grande River when he led an expedition during the middle of the eighteenth century. It has been recorded that many years ago, Black men, armed with lances and shields arrived by sea. Many married local Indian women and created a new tribe. It is believed that these expeditions were probably from the Mandinka tribe in Western Africa (McDonald, 1986). Later, although most of the Black people in Texas at this time (1860) were slaves, some were free. Free Blacks lived in Texas under Spanish rule with a modicum of legal equality. More Blacks came during Mexican rule. Some Blacks even won their freedom around 1860 for their service to the revolution.

However, after the revolution, in the new republic under Anglo-American rule, Blacks could not vote or own property. Ironically, after statehood, additional restrictions were imposed on Blacks, especially with respect to punishments assessed for the conviction of crimes. In recent years, as a result of massive immigration of non-English-speaking people, of an increasing appreciation for all of America's ethnic and social groups, and of a shift in emphasis and support of education from the national level, there have been increasing demands for a new emphasis on cultural pluralism. Cultural pluralism, though, entails interaction and competition among groups, and is symbolized in the relative exercise of power. Thus advocates of this approach view the "melting pot" function of the public schools as a repressive form of imperialism. On the other hand, critics of this philosophy have suggested that public schools be replaced with private schools.

While the process of assimilation has been the unofficial national doctrine, America continues to be a pluralistic society, composed of ethnic subsocieties, as well as those of region, rural/urban residence, and social class. In assimilation, American society is likened to a melting pot, suggesting the absorption of diverse groups into the modern mass society. However, only the assimilation of certain racial groups was ever seriously questioned (Hraba, 1979, p. 61). For instance, pluralists contend that rather than fusing into one mass society, which is a physical as well as practical impossibility, ethnic groups fuse together in several melting pots, each distinct from the others. Rather than disappearing, ethnicity evolves into new forms and expressions in the course of societal modernization.

In recent years, a recognition of America's cultural diversity and the significance of the ethnic roots of its people have begun receiving increased attention. Perhaps this renewed attention stems, in part, from the incessant and increasing demands of ethnic minorities for more acceptance and recognition. It is also considered an acknowledgment by the predominant Anglo-American group, at long last, of the need to acknowledge and utilize fully all of America's human resources.

In any event, notwithstanding the predominant Anglo-American group's unwillingness to welcome American Indians, Blacks, Hispanics, Jews, Asians, and Irish Roman Catholics into the melting pot (M. Gordon, 1964, pp. 120121; Newman, 1973, p. 66; R. Schaefer, 1988, p. 39; Zangwill, 1914, pp. 204-255), attention focused on the fundamental diversity that marks the American population is also an acknowledgment of the realization that the United States is not a melting pot which molds all of our country's ethnic varieties into a single common amalgam.

As Gold et al. (1977) suggested,

> the time has come to celebrate the diversity that characterizes a country in which some three-hundred different native American Indian tribes were joined by numerous peoples from every continent and every country on this planet. Some came seeking freedom from want or oppression; some were brought here in chains as slaves. The time of arrival was equally varied, stretching over a period of three hundred years. The overwhelming feature was diversity, variety. It is high time for our schools to recognize this pluralism as a source of past, present and future richness and creativity rather than of possible division and conflict.

For the most part, the late 1960s ushered in what might be called an era of "ethnic fever." One by one, the nation's racial and ethnic minorities sought to rediscover their waning ethnicity and to reaffirm their ties to their cultural pasts. Ethnic fever had its origins in the African-American community, where Black nationalism, after a long period of inactivity, emerged with renewed force. This contagion rapidly spread to other ethnic minorities--Asians, Chicanos, Native Americans, Puerto Ricans—who comprised a loosely organized coalition under the banner of the Third World. Eventually, ethnic fever reached the "white ethnics"—Jews, Irish, Italians, Poles, and others of European ancestry. For more than thirty years, the dominant tendency among the nation's racial and ethnic minority had been toward integration into the economic, political, and cultural mainstream. Now, the pendulum seemed to be swinging back, as these groups repudiated their assimilationist tendencies. Through art, literature and politics, they sought to promote ethnic pride and solidarity and to affirm their right to a separate identity within the framework of a pluralist nation.

Following are several aspects of ethnicity which impinge on and affect day-to-day relationships between groups in American society at-large. Hraba (1979) listed the following key terms and basic assumptions which are here intended to add clarity and increased understanding of these groups.

Melting Pot Theory

The idea, formulated by Israel Zangwill around 1900, suggested that rather than cling to strictly English institutional and cultural focus, the United States could fuse both biologically and culturally all of the various stocks within it.

Assimilation

Congruent with notions of racial superiority and Manifest Destiny is the process of assimilation. According to common usage in the social services, assimilation is the process by which diverse ethnic and racial groups come to share a common culture and have equal access to opportunity in the structure of society. Vander Zanden (1972:258) further defined assimilation as "a process whereby groups with diverse ways of thinking, feeling, and acting become fused together in a social unity and a common culture." Bertrand (1967) suggested assimilation was essentially a process of fusion, in which one individual or group becomes completely accepted as part of another group. This is usually a slow and gradual process, whereby the group that is assimilated adopts the culture of the other group, becomes part of all social systems within the society, and has absolute freedom to intermart with members of other groups. Further, regardless of how many racial, ethnic, or religious groups are involved, assimilation dictates conformity to the dominant group (Newman, p. 53).

Pluralism

There are two dimensions of pluralism: cultural and structural. Cultural pluralism refers to the existence of distinct ethnic subcultures in a society which affect and make variable the way people think, feel, and act. Structural pluralism means that ethnic identity is evident in social interaction in a society and is manifest in either restrictions on social interaction or in the use of ethnic identity in open and free exchange.

Ethnocentrism

Ethnocentrism is the tendency to assume that one's culture and way of life are superior to all others. Ethnocentric persons judge other groups and cultures by the standards of their own group.

Manifest Destiny

Manifest destiny is the process by which the long-held beliefs in the superiority of early Anglo-Saxon political institutions became a belief in the innate superiority of the Anglo-Saxon branch of the Caucasian race and was directly linked to the new scientific interest in racial classification.

Ethnic Groups

Ethnic groups are differentiated from the dominant group on the basis of cultural differences such as languages, attitudes toward marriage and parenting, food habits, and other attributes. Further, ethnic groups are groups set apart from others because of their national origin or distinctive cultural patterns on the basis of a common origin or a separate subculture and which maintain a distinction between themselves and outsiders.

Racial Groups

Racial groups are these minority groups and corresponding majorities who are classified according to obvious physical differences. In the United States, skin color is one obvious difference.

Religious Groups

In the United States, Protestants outnumber all other religions, although Protestantism is divided into numerous denominations and splinter groups. Roman Catholics form the largest minority religion. Jews are placed among ethnic groups because, in their case, culture is a more important defining trait than is religious dogma.

Gender Groups

The attribute that divides dominant and subordinate groups is sex. Males are the social majority; females, although more numerous, are relegated to the position of a social minority. Women are a minority even though they do not exhibit all of the characteristics; they encounter prejudice and discrimination and are physically visible; group membership is involuntary, and many women are developing a sense of sisterhood.

Ethnic Evolution

Ethnicity is an evolving or emergent phenomenon, and groups and their relations with one another and the larger society change in the course of ethnic evolution. The continuation of ethnic pluralism in modern society is one dimension of ethnic evolution. Groups may fuse together in larger entities in the course of ethnic evolution, but this means the continuation of ethnic pluralism, not assimilation, so long as these larger groups remain distinct from each other in the larger society.

Accordingly, there are numerous assumptions of ethnic pluralism. Among these are:

1. While relatives among ethnic and racial groups in America evolve, this evolution does not necessarily bring the assimilation of these groups into a single monolithic entity.
2. As relations among ethnic groups evolve, the expression of ethnicity changes. In America, ethnic boundaries have generally grown more inclusive and less restrictive, and ethnic identity and its cultural expression have become more domestic and less foreign.
3. Reasons for the persistence of ethnicity in modern American society include the nation's tolerance for ethnic pluralism, the sociopolitical role of ethnic groups in modern society, and the psychological functions served by ethnicity.

In conclusion, while many social scientists agree that the pluralist position is an improvement on the early assimilationist view that ethnic evolution is unilinear and inevitable, not all are happy. LeVine and Campbell (1972) observed that ethnic boundaries of all sorts have been fluid throughout human history and are no more permeable today than they were in the past. As long as ethnicity either facilitates self-expression or can be used in the competition for scarce resources, it will endure for it captures and reflects the very essence of the human spirit—a desire to maintain one's individuality and identity.

Racial and Ethnic Groups In Texas: Who Are They?

Texas is indeed one of the most racially and culturally diverse states in the Union. While many racial and ethnic groups are currently represented in Texas, the most prominent ethnic minority groups are Mexican-Americans, African-Americans and Native Indian Americans. Each group has made significant contributions to the growth and development of Texas and of America. To understand better and thereby to be better able to assist in more effective educational program planning, school administrators, teachers, and others who work in Texas schools need to know about culture and cultural diversity. They need information and understanding of the varied histories, the cultures, the hopes, and the aspirations which these groups have for themselves and for their children and youth. Following is a series of brief vignettes focusing on each of the above groups.

African-Americans

Geneva Gay, in Gold, et al. (1977, p. 34) stated that "despite a wealth of a sociological, anthropological, and historical data to the contrary, some people still believe that (1) Black Americans are just Americans without a discernible past beyond their arrival upon the American scene as slaves; and (2) Blacks have no values or life-style other than those they share with the common American culture.

Highly developed kingdoms existed in various parts of Africa hundreds of years ago. The kings of the ancient empire of Ghana came to power about the year 700. However, their power tended to decline in the 1000s, and their capitol was destroyed in the western Sudan and in Kongo at the mouth of the Congo River. Also, African kingdoms of antiquity were responsible for some outstanding accomplishments in commerce, construction, agriculture, arts and crafts, and education. Blacks also helped design and build some of the great pyramids of Egypt.

Between 1200 and 1600, an African-Arabic university flourished at Timbuktu in West Africa and became famous throughout Spain, North Africa, and the Middle East. Each tribe had its own language, its own religion, and its own customs. The family was important everywhere in Black Africa.

Beginning in the late 1500s, White settlers from European nations established colonies in many African countries. Many of these European nations engaged in the slave trade, and during a four-hundred-year period, 1400 through 1800, they carried hundreds of thousands of Africans to North and South America. Gay (1977) further suggested that to understand fully the essence of Blacks' presence in the history and culture of the United States, there is a need to examine both the enculturative and the acculturative dimensions of Black life, that is, the results of the pull of the integrative forces and the push of the segregative forces operating upon Black Americans. To the extent that both of these elements are explored, a real understanding of what it means to be Black in America can be achieved. Such awareness is necessary if we are to understand the diversity and similarities of Black Americans within the context of the American diaspora. Further, plausible questions could also be raised about cultural parallels between Blacks in the United States, the Caribbean and South America, including the extent to which African retentions are noted in contemporary Black American lifestyles, and the degrees of acculturation and assimilation among Blacks in the United States. Brought to the New World as slaves, Africans reacted to situations in different ways. Their reactions were varied and essentially were a function of many interactive factors, including their particular African backgrounds, their time of arrival, their geographical location, how the plantation on which they lived was organized and operated, the numerical ratio of Whites to Blacks, and the extent of contact between Blacks and Whites, and between Blacks and Blacks.

Understandably, then, the first generation of Blacks probably felt a greater compulsion to try to transplant African customs and traditions in America than did later generations. They had no other language, religion or values. Another series of factors and circumstances which in part explain Black behavior in America is significant at this point. Blacks in the United States did not assimilate into the structure of mainstream society to the extent that Blacks did in Latin America. With respect to the different styles of cultural adaptations which emerged among different groups of Blacks in the New World, the same culturally cultivating processes—enculturation and acculturation—took place simultaneously in North and South America. Although slavery in South America was equally dehumanizing, as cruel and immoral as in the United States, some conditions did exist which created a socio-political climate generally more conducive to both the survival of African traditions—the enculturative process—and the assimilation of Africans into European customs and culture, the acculturative process. Among these conditions were the concentration of large numbers of Blacks in the same area; the constant influx of other Blacks directly from Africa, which contributed to the continuation and revitalization of African customs and traditions; the tendency to keep Black families together; the idea of inferiority of Blacks was less pervasive; and many African descendants inter-married with Europeans and Indians (especially in Brazil). Too, Blacks in the United States did not assimilate into the structure of mainstream society to the extent their Latin-American counterparts did. While most colonists abolished slavery during the 1800s, many of the economic, social, and political developments that accompanied slavery continue to present day.

Presently, more than 275 million Black Africans live on the continent of Africa. About 40 million persons of African heritage live in South America, more than 30 million in the United States, approximately 150 thousand live in Europe, and about fifty thousand live in Canada. The history of Blacks in America is the history of the American racial dilemma. For centuries, Blacks have seen themselves through the revelation and measurement of white people who have looked on them with sentiments ranging from amused contempt and pity to fear and hatred. To the Romans, slaves were merely vulgar and conquered people who were not accorded the rights and privileges of Roman citizenship. The Greeks looked upon slaves as unfortunate citizens of their plundered lands who failed to cultivate their minds and desires and were thus reduced to that lowly but necessary state. But in America, slaves were considered property and were not even considered human beings. With the Emancipation Proclamation came the vain search for freedom. For more than three centuries on this continent, Blacks have been denied equal access to education, economic security; and other societal advantages and generally have been relegated to menial levels of work or joblessness which, to a great extent, continue to result in conditions of poverty, disunion, and misery for countless millions. It should be recognized, however, that throughout their struggle, Blacks have wanted to be both Black and American, with pride in both. Blacks have always felt that their African heritage had something to offer America, as did the European ethnic cultures. Consistent with cultural pluralist thinking, African-Americans, not unlike Irish-Americans, are unique and different and are desirous of remaining that way. This diversity is America's greatness. This diversity is America!

African-Americans in Texas

African-Americans are not newcomers to Texas. As indicated earlier, some believe Africans explored America before the Spaniards came (McDonald, 1986:58). To be sure, Africans did arrive with the first Europeans and continued to grow in numbers, and today they make up about twelve percent of the state's population. Melvin M. Sance in *The Afro-American Texans* (1975, p.1) suggested the Black experience in the American environment represented a record of survival, despite bondage; a record of outstanding achievements and contributions to the American heritage, despite great odds. In the years leading up to the Texas Revolution of 1836, free Black colonists as well as Blacks who were slaves fought by the side of white colonists for the establishment of a new republic. Down through the years, Blacks have made significant contributions to the development of Texas and its greatness. Among these was William Goyens, who became one of the first rich Texans. Besides his vast land holdings, he was a blacksmith, wagon manufacturer, freight hauler, mill owner and planter. He was also a close ally and associate of Sam Houston. Following the Civil War, Norris Wright Cuney became the leader of the state's Republican Party, a position which made him the most influential Black in Texas. He wielded that influence for the cause of human rights. Later, Barbara Jordan would become one of the ablest persons to represent Texas in the U.S. Congress—the first African-American Texan to be elected to the U.S. House of Representatives.

African-Americans, Education and Equal Educational Opportunity

Contrary to the beliefs of many, a significant number of Blacks have always viewed the acquisition of an education as a means of escape from their plight, as a means of hope. Hilliard (1984) suggested that it is only our temporary loss of memory that causes us to forget that African people were brought here in chains, but were nevertheless very richly endowed. African captives were not ignorant, "savage," or "pagan." Some knew the Qur'an from memory and could write in Arabic. Some could read and write indigenous West African scripts. All were highly educated and profoundly religious, sharing in a very complex culture, a culture that had allowed survival for thousands of years. Some Africans had even made Atlantic Ocean crossings and were in America long before the time of Columbus. Others had arrived here before the time of Christ, leaving their portraits carved in stone in Mexico and their writing in other places as well. (Van Sertima, 1976; Fell, 1976).

It took an educational effort that was systematic, intensive, and unparalleled in the history of the world to erase these memories, to cloud vision, to impair hearing, and to impede the operation of the critical capacities among African-Americans. Once reference points were lost, African-Americans as a people became like a computer without a program, a spacecraft without a homing device, a dependent without a benefactor.

In order to understand what is happening to African-Americans as a people (not as a "minority" or as "poverty stricken" or as individuals) and especially what is happening to African-Americans in education, one must start at the beginning and try to grasp the whole story. There is a need to view the whole story in order to see the patterns, not the details, that give us the essence of what is happening. To fail to perceive the pattern is to raise one's susceptibility to the seductiveness of attractive but false issues. Jean Piaget calls this capacity in young children "conservation"; that is, being able to see the changes in form may not mean that there are changes in the form of African-American education, but few changes in substances.

The first thing that any educator or citizen needs who would attempt to solve our educational problems is a clear sense of history. In the latter regard, W.E.B. DuBois (1973), Bullock (1970),

Woodson (1969), Bond (1972), King (1971), Spivey (1978) and many others have given us all that we need to see certain key patterns. For example, in Bullock's *A History of Negro Education in the South* (1970), the following points were noted.

He described the educational system that was designed for slaves, noting the changes that took place following episodes such as Nat Turner's fight for freedom. The first adjustment that slaveowners far and near made after the fight was to change the nature of the educational system for the slave. The Slave Codes were set up to enhance this intellectual containment, among other things. After slavery, the Freedman's Bureau and its successor, African-American private education efforts, and publicly supported education that was inspired and initiated in the south mainly by African-Americans (DuBois, 1973), began to show remarkable results. For example, African-Americans excelled very quickly wherever literacy training was offered. The fear was not that African-Americans could not learn; the fear then and later was that they would.

Bullock picks as his next major point the 1964 Civil Rights Act, a comprehensive piece of legislation that included provisions for mechanisms that were designed to reduce inequities, including inequities in the schools. We must point out that it also took several major court cases to try to accelerate the equity process: *Hobson v. Hartsen* to outlaw the tracking system in Washington, D.C.; *Larry P. v. Wilson Riles* to outlaw the use of I.Q. testing for placing black children into classes for the mentally retarded in California; the Ann Arbor Joiner decision on black language to require educators to take black language diversity into account in the schools; *Debra P. v. Turlington* to prevent the denial of diploma to blacks who failed tests that did not match the schooling that they were offered, and many others. All these efforts were required after the Brown decision. They still are required and necessary now.

In 1968, Professor Charles V. Hamilton of Roosevelt University captured the essence of the time at the height of the upheavals of the 1960s led by African-American dissidents. His now widely quoted article appeared in the Harvard Educational Review and was titled "Race and Education: A Search for Legitimacy." His analysis was astute. While it was noted and quoted, this author does not believe that most of us comprehended the full implications of his comments. To be sure, Hamilton directed his attention to the crux of the problem. He revealed that African-Americans were looking for a liberating, meaningful, quality education and that they were questioning the capacity of the schools, all schools, to deliver such an education.

In his short article, Hamilton made many key points:

1. Hamilton said that African-American parents, students and educators in the 60s were asking questions about the education system which were fundamentally different from those that were being raised by traditional educators who were conducting the national dialogue. In effect, African-Americans were questioning the legitimacy of educational institutions while traditional educators were merely questioning the efficiency of those institutions.
2. Hamilton averred that as a result of such questioning, a tension arose between the two groups. One group saw community control of schools as the answer and thus would build

their own institutions. The other groups perceived school integration as the way and would have black and white students share in the same process, whatever it was. More significantly, however, the process itself was not questioned.
3. Hamilton further contended that African-Americans had made explicit demands about African and African-Americans' cultural awareness being given equal importance as equal as was that given verbal and computational skills. It is important to note that this notion was not a demand that cultural awareness be substituted for academic and intellectual skills, as some antagonists tried to suggest. African-Americans wanted both skills and awareness.

Then as now, a plethora of commissions were reporting on education. By the same token, the reports did not deal with the specific problems of African-Americans, even though African-Americans were then, as now, the most educationally depressed group. This insensitivity at the highest level was an integral catalyst which prompted African-Americans to believe that the schools would fail them, especially as matters stood then. Hamilton perceived the basic focus of the reports as how to do a more efficient job of the same thing which the schools had been doing. As Hamilton expressed it, institutions only became legitimate in the eyes of their people when the people believed that the institution's service was appropriate for them. At that point, they can give the institution their loyalty and allegiance. Needless to say, when African-Americans looked at the schools, they saw no payoff for themselves, especially the payoffs which they expected—academic excellence and positive self-images. It was this latter factor, especially, that the traditional experts failed to address then, just as they have failed to address it in the most recent state of reports.

To buttress his analysis, Hamilton compared the results of the reports of the National Association of African-American Educators with the Coleman Report, the African history and culture demands by students with the Civil Rights Commission's emphasis on Racial Isolation in the Schools, and the Harlem branch of the Congress on Racial Equity's demands for independent community schools with the Chicago Board of Education's Redmon Report. What he found was that Blacks and Whites are worlds apart in their definitions of the problem and in their visions of a solution. Hamilton summarized the views of 800 African-American educators as follows:

1. They wanted to control their own schools;
2. They wanted parents to be deeply involved in the schools and in a working alliance with their children's teachers;
3. They wanted to have schools that were designed for maximum positive psychological impact through the careful use of staffing patterns, holidays, group solidarity and pride, black curriculum perspectives, and evaluation criteria; and
4. They wanted appropriate curriculum and instructional materials.

Hamilton's own model for change highlighted three key points:

1. He challenged the notion that integrated education was synonymous with quality education;
2. He felt that the school in predominantly African-American communities should be the focal point for both school and community activities; and
3. He felt that schools should belong to the communities in which they were located.

It must be remembered that problems in education are inseparable from problems of the larger society. That is to say, the type of education that is offered will always fit the socio-politico-economic context. If there is oppression in the general society, the schools supported by that society will be a part of the oppression. Hilliard (1984) described the specific features of the system that were used to oppress African-Americans. Six of the steps used were the following:

1. African-American history and culture were suppressed and distorted;
2. African-American group identity was suppressed;
3. White supremacy was taught in the schools, churches, the mass media, etc.;
4. All African-American social institutions as well as the larger society's social institutions were controlled by European-Americans;
5. Systematic steps were taken to ensure that resources could not be accumulated by African-Americans; and
6. African-Americans were physically segregated from European-Americans.

The battle against the last step in the aforementioned system has been waged since 1954. The courts have ruled against segregation. Legislation and regulations have outlawed segregation, even though the present national leadership appears to be openly hostile to equity protections. Yet, five of the six features mentioned above have received little systematic attention. Apparently, it was believed that desegregation and integration alone would and could remedy all of the ills of the system. Indubitably, though, education has an active role to play in reversing all of the six mechanisms and their effects. For example, without a clear sense of history, without a clear cultural consciousness, and without a clear sense of identity, group unity and self-help, then, other than on an individual basis, are impossible to achieve. In the past, any educational effort which fostered these things was destroyed immediately.

To be sure, African-Americans have been derailed in efforts to rebuild a group capacity for rebuilding. Sometimes remedies for past injustices have been pursued; yet, ironically, these have worked against the development of a fundamental asset—namely, a strong sense of group unity. If the past two decades have taught nothing else, they should have shown us clearly that African-Americans cannot depend upon others, no matter how sympathetic, to sustain an effort that will change the basic conditions of life for the masses of African-Americans. In the final analysis, the real measure of progress will not be the condition of the few but will be the condition of the many.

It is because of these points that it is clear that Hamilton was right in 1968 and is right now. Like W.E.B. DuBois, Carter G. Woodson, and Marcus Garvey before him, Hamilton saw that it was not where one sat but rather what one received where he sat that mattered. Being miseducated in "integrated schools" was not really different from being miseducated in segregated schools. Certainly no one can condone or permit the evil system of legally and morally sanctioned segregation of schools to thrive. Yet community schools are not segregated schools unless enforced legal protections to maintain free access to housing, jobs, and schools are missing. Likewise, it would be inane to contend that simply because a school is predominantly African-American, then it is "segregated." We create and live in a fog of conceptual confusion whenever we use terms that cause us to lose sight of all the elements in the problem, especially to the extent that we subsequently accept incomplete remedies to that problem.

Again, Hamilton reminds us that "integration" as experienced in America is not necessarily synonymous with quality education. To wit, Hamilton's vision of a quality education is one wherein the school belongs to a community and wherein the school becomes the center of a myriad hosts of related community activities. To implement such a situation, then, means drawing on strength that flows out of group unity.

A review of public school education activity from around the nation over the past few decades does not give us great cause for hope (Witty, 1983). For example, the African-American principal is now a dying breed in many communities where once he/she was previously in abundance. Too, the National Teacher Examinations, among others, have been used to deny licensure to disproportionately large numbers of African-American teachers, to deny initial employment to others, to deny tenure to others, and to evaluate programs of teacher education in black colleges. Likewise, many black colleges are being threatened with the loss of accreditation or authorization to offer teacher education programs because of the test scores of their graduates. Yet no one has shown that the content of this national examination, or others, matches the content inherent in diverse teacher education programs, nor has anyone ever shown that high scores on the NTE are related to better teaching. The net result of the NTE's use is that fewer African-American teachers will be employed in the nation's schools, thus offering no guarantee that our children will learn better as a result.

Finally, it must be understood that Black people have left indelible marks on the pages of American history and continue to exert significant influence on the shaping of American culture. This reality needs to be judiciously considered as this nation begins to think about restructuring American education so that its underlying principles are more compatible with the ethnic, cultural, and social characteristics of our pluralistic society. Black Americans are indeed bicultural. As such, they share and practice some of the values, behaviors, institutions, and beliefs of the common American culture, while at the same time they engage in an alternative lifestyle resulting from Black culture. As Gay (1977: 51-55) explained:

> The realities and influence of Black American heritage, the nature of Black life, and the presence and influence of Blacks in American history and generally in American life posit several

important educational implications. First, teachers and other school personnel need to develop a better understanding of the concept of culture. Educators also need to understand that despite changes over time, the original heritages and historical experiences of ethnic groups still have significant impacts upon the lives and identification processes of members of these groups today. Students have a right to be proud of their ethnic and cultural identity. The inclusion of this element in school programs as legitimate curriculum content is fundamental to providing quality education. School leaders should understand why ethnic and cultural diversity has been a vital, catalytic force in American life and culture of the pest, how it can be so in the present and the future. Moreover, they need to learn how to use information about different ethnic groups and their cultural experiences in the process of analyzing the social, interfactional, and instructional dynamics of multiethic classrooms. Second, not only Blacks, but all students need to receive instruction in Black American heritage and culture. This content should become an integral part of the total school curriculum--that is, appropriately incorporated in all subjects and learning experiences for all students at all grade levels. Third, the heritage and experiences of Black Americans arc complex and multidimensional. A one-dimensional, single-subject approach to the study of Black American life is inadequate for the task. Fourth, to teach Black students most effectively and to implement the best multicultural education programs possible require more than curricular changes. Black students and their teachers who come from different ethnic and experiential backgrounds may look at the same situations and see different meanings to them. These behaviors stem from differing perceptions and referential codes. A fifth implication, learning style differences, is closely related to the foregoing. Black students arc likely to be more inclined toward learning in social-group settings instead of in the formal, individualistic environments generally prevalent in American schools. Undoubtedly, this predilection reflects the cultural and historical emphases of Black Americans on cooperation, communalism, and mutual aid in work situations, or what Lerone Bennett describes as 'the responsibility of each to all and all to each' (*The Shaping of Black America*, p. 136).

Among the thousands of African-Americans who have made Texas their home—some less important, others more important than those cited above—many individuals have made contributions in exploration, colonization, and the growth of Texas further under Spanish and then under Anglo control. Admittedly, over the past thirty years, the situation of African-American Texans has improved legally, socially, politically, and to a lesser degree, economically. Today, many closed doors of opportunity have opened into positions of wealth, power and prominence for them in the state and in the nation. Somewhat ironically, attitudes of the people now seem to change slower than do the laws. The trend, to be sure, is steady and unmistakable. Unlike some other ethnic groups in Texas, African-Americans were forced to abandon the heritage of their native land. Fortunately like most groups, they developed an indigenous culture in their new home; and the state and the nation are the richer for this cultural enrichment and development.

Mexican-Americans

In the early 1800s as white settlement expanded across the western frontier, Anglo settlers eventually came into contact with Hispanics in the Southwest. Thus was born a familiar story about the Southwest. Powerful Anglo settlers, imbued with the notion of Manifest Destiny (a belief that Destiny ordained their expansion all the way to the Pacific Ocean), came into contact with an established but weaker Hispanic community. The powerful group wanted, and got, the land of the weaker one. In 1830, Anglo colonists outnumbered Mexicans in what is now Texas by six to one. By 1836, Texas had so many Anglos that it eventually broke away from Mexico and sought to establish a separate republic. The historic battle at the Alamo in 1836 in what is now San Antonio was, indeed, lost by the colonists (Anglos and numerous persons of Spanish-American origin); however, six weeks later Sam Houston and his Anglo troops defeated Mexican President General Santa Anna's and ultimately achieved independence.

According to Tenorio (1977) many Tejanos (persons of Spanish-Mexican heritage) supported the new Republic of Texas. Three of them signed the Texas Declaration of Independence and one became the first Vice President of Texas. By 1845, Texas had become part of the United States. Later, in 1848, the United States launched an expansionist war against Mexico. As a result, Mexicans living north of the new border became known as Mexican-Americans. While they were given assurances of fair treatment, particularly regarding their land-holdings, they instead met with racism and suffered exposure to feelings of discrimination and denial. In many areas, these feelings are believed to have continued to the present time. Tenorio (1977) further suggested that when Americans of Spanish-Mexican-Indian heritage in 1848 sought citizenship status, they brought with them vestiges of the system of social stratification which had been imposed on them by Spanish rule of more than 300 years. Needless to say, becoming American citizens did not change this system. The original rulers who had been born in Spain were known as peninsulares. They were replaced after the Mexican Revolution (1810-1824) by the criollos (Mexicans born of Spanish parents). During the 19th century, most Mexican-Americans were mestizos (children of Spanish and Indian parents). Below this latter group in the social and economic status were the Indians, known as indios and indigenos.

On the other hand, the frontier contact between Anglos and Hispanics appears similar to that which existed between White settlers and American Indians. However, Mexican labor was incorporated into the economy of the Southwest later in the 20th century; and so Mexican-Americans—meaning Hispanos of the borderlands and immigrants from Mexico—were never excluded from the larger society to the extent that American Indians were. The evolution of Mexican-Americans is outlined on the following page in Figure 7.1.

Of the approximately 20 million persons of Spanish origin in the United States, persons of Mexican origin account for more than 12 and a half million, according to the U.S. Bureau of the Census. Therefore, Mexican-Americans, a heterogeneous group in itself, represent about 60 percent of the total population of Spanish extraction, the largest single group of Spanish Americans (Johnson, 1976:194).

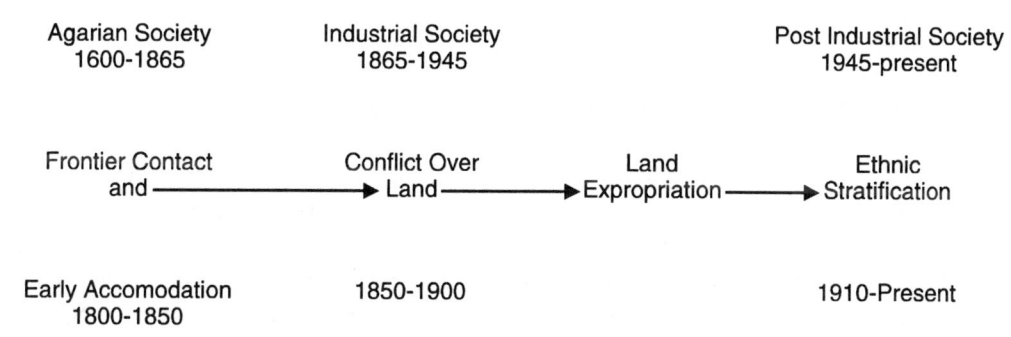

| Agrarian Society | Industrial Society | | Post Industrial Society |
| 1600-1865 | 1865-1945 | | 1945-present |

Frontier Contact and ⟶ Conflict Over Land ⟶ Land Expropriation ⟶ Ethnic Stratification

| Early Accomodation | 1850-1900 | | 1910-Present |
| 1800-1850 | | | |

Figure 7.1. Evolution of Mexican-Americans and the modernization of American society.

At the time of earliest contact, early in the 19th century, it is estimated that the Hispanic community of the Southwest numbered no more than 200,000 persons. Hraba (1979) noted that this community was composed of three economic classes: elite landlords who possessed large tracts of land and could trace their property rights back to the Spanish land grants in the New World; a large class of poor Mexican-Indian laborers; and a small number of middle class merchants, small ranchers, and farmers. Early in the 20th century, in connection with both the growth of the Southwest as an economic empire and with the Mexican Revolution (1910), the Spanish-speaking community of the Southwest was fraught with immigrants from Mexico. McWilliams (1968) estimated that fully 10 percent of the Mexican people immigrated into the United States early in this century; the vast majority of them took up work in the Southwest. This immigration pattern continues even to this day. Thus, America's second largest minority group, as Mexican-Americans are sometimes called, is unique among ethnic groups in America inasmuch as it is both indigenous and immigrant in character.

Much of the area in America's Southwest which now includes the states of Texas, California, New Mexico, Nevada, Arizona, and Colorado once was part of the Hispanic domain which originally was based in Mexico. The names of some of these states and several cities within them reflect historic Spanish and Mexican influences: Amarillo, Atascadero, Alamagordo, Los Alamos, Pueblo, San Francisco, Los Angeles and Sacramento are a few examples of these Spanish and Mexican place-names.

The Mexican-American Family Structure

Among Mexican-Americans, the family's role is significantly important and is very traditional. For one thing, the Mexican-American family is structured with the father as patriarch. Moreover, family relationships are close, and children are accorded love, warmth and attention.

Regarding adherence to ethnic values and mores, Casteneda (1974) opined that these attributes would likely vary in strength depending upon the community and family from which a child comes. Thus, values are strongest in traditional (in urban barrios and in rural colonias) where family values are almost identical with those in Mexico. On the other hand, in dualistic communities, there is some adaptation to Anglo-American values and some maintenance of traditional Mexican values. In atraditional communities, however, Mexican-American values have become amalgamated with American values.

Another significant aspect of Mexican-Americans' family structure is the continuity fostered by at least three hundred centuries of a similar culture and language. Lourdes Miranda King, in Johnson (1976, p. 199), suggested that of any single ethnic minority the Spanish-Americans have resisted "melting" by refusing to abandon their cultural and linguistic heritage. The Spanish language has persisted, despite the overwhelming attempts to assimilate forcibly the Spanish-American linguistically. Historically, however, economic, social, political, and legal pressures have been exerted in an attempt to eradicate the Spanish language from ethnic communities. As recent as the early 1970's, some southwestern states and the state of California ruled unlawful the use of Spanish as the language of instruction.

Educational Needs of Mexican-Americans

Provisions for the education of Mexican-American children must take into account the social cultural, economic and educational characteristics of the Mexican-American population. While they are represented across the economic spectrum, generally they come from poor and/or low income levels; they have a lower level of educational attainment than does the overall population; they were either born into or now live in a different cultural environment from the vast majority of students with whom they interact; in many cases they are not white by American standards but rather perceive themselves as non-black; they live within a conflict of cultural and social values—those they are expected to accept and embrace in school and those they learn at home; and, in many cases, they speak only a foreign language—Spanish.

Bilingual Education Efforts

In a recent case, the U.S. Supreme of Appeals for the 10th Circuit upheld the earlier Serna vs. Portales Municipal Schools Decision, which held bilingual-bicultural education is a right of non-English-speaking children under Title VI of the Civil Rights Act of 1964. Earlier, in a similar case, Lau et al. v. Nichols et al. the San Francisco school systems were required to provide English language instruction for approximately 1000 students of Chinese ancestry who did not speak English.

While the debate continues, these cases provide a solid legal base for enforcing the principle of special obligations to non-English-speaking children nationally via the provision of equal educational opportunity. Likewise, one can reason that the academic failures of these children are due primarily to an educational system whose practitioners have refused to intervene in the cycle of exclusion which has been their fate. As indicated in the Kerner Report, "the problem is the one who causes it, the prejudiced and biased non-disadvantaged, the 'White' people responsible for the poverty of those 'disadvantaged'."

For years, the response to this educational dilemma has been to establish English as a Second Language (ESL or ESOL) programs within schools. The object of this approach was to increase the English language skills of non English-speaking children. Studies by E. Lambert in Canada have shown that students who learn to read first in their native language have an advantage over students who must learn first in English. To be sure, the child who learns to read first in Spanish is also learning a writing system which is very regular, with close correspondence between sounds and letters. Certainly bilingual education is not a panacea for all Spanish or Mexican-American children, but it does represent a degree of hope. King (1976) continued pointing out that a well-conceived bilingual, bicultural education program will be successful only if it also takes into account cognitive styles as the Spanish-American child performs better in situations deemphasizing competitiveness and asserting cooperation, on tasks requiring visual, rather than the auditory, and with textbooks which reflect their reality.

In 1968, the U.S. Office of Education defined bilingual, bicultural education as the use of two languages, one of which is English, as mediums of instruction for the same pupil population in a well-organized program which encompasses all of the curriculum and which includes the study of history and the cultures.

Joshua Fishman (1970) listed several categories of bilingual education. These included:

1. Transitional Bilingualism, in which Spanish is used in the early grades as a remediation attempt while the student is being prepared to shift languages. This program is couched in such terms as "increasing the achievement level," "master subject matter" and/or "adjust to school"; but the program does not mention acquiring fluency and literacy in both languages. The goal is to help the children arrive at the point where they will be able to pursue a program of studies inguess-English;
2. Monoliterate Bilingualism is intermediate in orientation between transitional bilingualism and language maintenance. It stresses aural-oral skills in the native language;
3. Partial Bilingualism, which seeks fluency and literacy in both languages and restricts literacy in the mother tongue to subject matter related to the ethnic group and its cultural heritage. The mother tongue is not used in other curricular areas; and
4. Full Bilingualism, in which students develop all skills in both languages for all subjects. This is the ideal type of program, for it maintains and develops the native languages and English.

Irrespective of the selected structure, the value of a full bilingual, bicultural education program, accompanied by appropriately prepared teachers and materials, community involvement and participation, and high expectations and commitment, will achieve the desired results and outcomes.

While proponents of bilingual, bicultural approaches advocate expanding such programs, those opposed continue to question their efficacy. Recently, Rosalie Pedalino Porter (1990) in her new book, Forked Tongue: The Misleading Politics of Bilingual Education, insisted that bilingual education was not working and instead had ossified into practices that foster and prolong ethnic segregation and isolation.

In any case, administrators and teachers, as they increase in sensitivity, must understand that there is no one model of the Mexican-American. It must be equally clear, too, that negative stereotypes, often obtained from American movies and otherwise, are equally unjustified. Characterization of Mexican-Americans as lazy, indolent and lacking motivation perpetuates labeling that is erroneously applied by those who lack insight and/or understanding of the values, lifestyles, folkways, and mores of Mexican-Americans.

Native Indian Americans in Texas

Native Indian Americans, the first Americans, and likewise, the first Texans have a special uniqueness in America by virtue of being the pre-Colombian inhabitant and possessor of the American continents. Additionally, the Indian, by right of the U.S. Constitution and other national treaties and policies has a special relationship with the federal government.

Native Indian Americans, usually identified by tribe, oftentimes have been described as a unitary group. This belief and/or attitude persists for a number of reasons. There are many in America who do not realize that Indians are quite variable, and that the Native Indian American culture is not one culture but many, often at opposite ends of a continuum of human behavior. To be sure, Native Indian Americans are different, not only from non-Indians but also tremendously different among various tribal groups and subgroups.

First Dealings with Europeans

In 1528, the Karankawas were the first Texas Indians to become acquainted with the Europeans who would eventually take over their homeland. In a report titled the Indian Texans (1970) the Karankawas greeted survivors of the Narvaez expedition which was shipwrecked on an island off the Texas coast with awe and delight. Four survivors, three Spaniards and one Negro, were enslaved until they won the respect of the Indians as medicine men and traders. Eventually, these four escaped and made their way along the coast, where they were also received as healers by various tribes. This first encounter with unarmed civilized men gave the Indians the false idea of the peaceful intentions of all white men and a great respect for the magic of their religion. One of the survivors of this six-year adventure across Texas, Cabeza de Vaca, later published an account of the adventure, which is still one of the most valuable sources of information on Texas Indians of this period.

The exciting, wandering days of the Texas Indian are over. His presence in Texas is remembered in the original place names he gave to Waxahachie, Anahuac, Quitaque, Copano Quanah, Tahoka and other towns. There are also tribal names that have been applied to such places as Seminole, Comanche, Kickapoo Springs, Cherokee County, Caddo Lake, Krankaway Bay and the Creeks of Bedias, Choctaw, Kiowas, Keechi, Delaware and Shawnee.

Native Indian American people are extremely diverse and vary in life styles and languages. When the Europeans and the Native Indian Americans first came into contact, there were about 200 tribes whose customs, beliefs, value systems and languages were very complex. Much has been written which suggested that the Eastern Indian was a farmer, the Plains Indian was a buffalo hunter, the Southwest Indian was a seed-gatherer, and the Pacific Coast Indian was a fisherman. Such generalizations presented in numerous textbooks and other media are fallacious. For example, while some Eastern Indians were farmers, some were also hunters and fisherman. In another instance, the generalizations of the Southwest Indian as a seed-gatherer or dry land farmer may be true for a particular group of individuals, however, there were also skilled irrigation farmers among the Indians of the Southwest.

Native Indian Americans in Texas have left an outstanding legacy in those who now reside there. In recent decades the Native Indian American population in Texas has shown a significant increase. In 1900, the state had only 470 persons of Native American ancestry; in 1920, 2109; in 1940, 4103. The 1960 Census showed a population of 5,750 of whom 4,101 were urban and 1,649 were rural. Of all the Native American tribes which have resided in Texas, the Tiguas and Alabama-Coushattas have stayed together longer and preserved many of their customs and traditions. The one remaining Reservation in Texas is that of the Alabama Coushattas. More significantly, however, are the thousands of Native Indian Americans who, over the years, have left the reservations, secured educations, and made a place for themselves in the trades, businesses, and professions. Every major Texas city has a number of Native Indian Americans who achieved notable success. Many Texans of Mexican heritage are descended from the Mayan, Aztec and other Indian tribes who created great civilizations south of the Rio Grande river long before the Spaniards came.

Paxton (1976) further pointed out that:

1. Contemporary Native Indian American youth are often stereotyped and falsely characterized as being:
    a. romantic woodland children of nature;
    b. vanishing Americans;
    c. defeated horsemen;
    d. noble savages;
    e. ignorant heathens;
    f. drunken, lazy recipients of unearned resources,
    g. illiterate, nonintellectuals who are good only with their hands, drawing pictures, arts and crafts, music, or repetitious factory benchwork;
    h. passive, nonverbal, native aborigines;
    i. simple-minded red men who are unable to understand complex relationships; and

    j. members of a homogeneous Indian society rather than a modified multiethnic Native American society.

    Each of these stereotypes is false! They confuse the Native Indian youths when they are unable to fill these expectations, and such degrading misrepresentations must be counteracted by the discerning educator.

2. Contemporary Native Indian American youth maintain cultural, tribal, or racial identities which are uniquely different from most other Americans. Many of these ritual, ceremonial, or kinship differences may not be clearly understood by the educator, but they should be accepted as being just as valid to the Native Indian Americans as Valentine's Day, Halloween, Thanksgiving, Lent, Juneteenth and other such observances are to other Americans.

3. As are all other students, Indians are subjected hourly to numerous stimuli. These stimuli are either ego-enhancing or ego-assaultive. There is no middle ground. They are either growing and developing or their self-images as worthy human beings are being destroyed insidiously. If their cultural lifestyle is degraded as being primitive and with no meaning, educators are providing a grave disservice.

4. Contemporary Native Indian American youth, in being asked to reject their own culture, are subject to becoming as confused and as neurotic as many of their peers. Unable to fill their expected role they become maladjustive and their learning and development are inhibited.

5. Contemporary Native Indian American youth are faced with a failure expectancy whereby they are conditioned to such self-concepts as "I can't do it"; "I am not important"; or "I am not smart." This may result in an Indian adult who says "I can't compete in contemporary life."

6. Contemporary Native Indian American youth are often faced with the idea that they must be more verbal, but not too verbal; be more selfassertive, but not too much; be Indian, but a nice acculturated Indian.

7. Contemporary Native Indian American youth are also confronted with the attitude that they are being prepared to participate in an Anglo-oriented society. However, this approach is not sound as the American society is not just Anglo-oriented. The Swedish, Italian, Spanish, French, African, German, Irish, Oriental, and other cultures, as well as that of the Indians, also had a part in orienting, fashioning, and developing what we call the American society. It is a diverse, multiethnic, and modified modern society.

8. Contemporary Native Indian Americans who become educated often find themselves characterized as co-opted Indians, those who having been educated are then selected, preempted, or chosen to perform the tasks of the larger society. However, they may find themselves still not being accepted by the "larger" system. One wonders if this pseudo co-optation rather than a true co-optation—a matter tokenism.

Educational Needs of the Native Indian American

Native Indian Americans are culturally different. An appreciation for and sensitivity to these cultural differences by school leaders and other school staff personnel may be helpful in undoing some of the paternalistic, prejudicial, and presumptuous educational practices of the past. While there are exceptions, many schools that teach Native Indian Americans are subject to criticism that the curriculum is irrelevant to their needs.

While many Native Indian American parents agree that the mastery of English is important, some schools approach this problem by utilizing programs of teaching English as a second language. However, the lack of trained teachers limits this approach. Additionally, the materials often have a strong Spanish-English bias which may not be applicable for use with Native Indian Americans. Some educators resist bilingualism because they still believe in the melting pot theory, with Native Indian Americans being subjected to a one-way assimilation.

Special consideration must be given to the needs of teachers and others who work with Native Indian Americans. They need to be sensitized to the sociocultural differences which they encounter with Native Indian Americans. This is not only a problem to be addressed by teacher-training institutions, but also by administrators and supervisors who provide in-service training for teachers and generally facilitate the instructional process.

Many Native Indian American children differ from others in their level acculturation. Historically, they have learned by doing, primarily because culture and language had not been reduced to writing. Therefore, teaching approaches which failed to take into account such learning style differences tended to project Native Indian Americans as intellectually inferior and/or academically inept.

A multisensory approach which permits learning to occur in varied ways is preferred. The intent is to promote a learning environment which is responsive to students' needs. Positive learning growth promotes improved feelings and attitudes toward self, toward others, and toward learning. An enriched learning program using a multiplicity of approaches and materials should provide rewarding experiences for teachers and students. Native Indian American researchers, scholars, and educators are only now beginning to show a concerted effort to establish criteria for the selection, of varied educational materials to be used with Native Indian American students. Some suggested criteria to be utilized are as follows:

1. Is the material accurate? Does the material accurately depict Native Indian Americana as they are rather than a projection of generalized stereotypes?
2. Does the material contribute to a positive self-image of the Native Indian American? Does the experience represent an enhancing force as opposed to a degrading or ego-assaulting experience?
3. Does the material depict the Native Indian American as a person of worth, whose culture has a right to exist on an equal basis in a world of many cultures?

4. Does the material contribute to an understanding that Native Indian Americans had substantial roles of lasting impact on developing the American continents?

Finally, there are many factors which influence the learning environment of and for Native Indian Americans, including the social atmosphere of the school and the administrative practices and policies which prevail. It is reasoned that the continuation of the progress made will require the collective efforts of school boards, the community, accrediting agencies, universities, Indian parents and students and enlightened activists.

Educational Equity and Leadership

Throughout the twentieth century, researchers have addressed the matter of educational leadership from several different perspectives. In recent years, the concept of educational equity (i.e. fairness, impartiality) has been the subject of focus, although most of the research has looked at student concerns. In a recent article, McCarthy and Webb in Baptiste et al. (1990, p. 10) indicated that equity is a prerequisite of educational excellence and that they are complementary, rather than mutually exclusive concepts.

While few deny that we must have the most intelligent, creative and best qualified individuals leading our schools, the talent and abilities of ethnic minorities and women generally, have been underutilized in leadership roles. Consequently, the entire educational enterprise has suffered as a result of this shortsightedness and denial. Increasingly, the need to ensure racial, gender, and ethnic diversity and to provide appropriate role models for the diverse student populations in our schools, is becoming of paramount concern. Further, it is reasoned, to do such is both the moral and intellectual equivalent of "doing the right thing."

McCarthy and Webb (1990) further suggested that many of the problems associated with achieving gender equity in educational leadership is somewhat different from the problems faced by ethnic minorities. While women in the candidate pool have significantly increased over the past few years (women now constitute half or more of the graduate students in educational administration) a tremendous dearth of female school administrators still exists throughout the country. And, while ethnic minority men have fared better than women in securing leadership positions in school districts, the small pool of minority candidates is a matter of deep concern. Unlike women, the number of ethnic minorities, especially African-American men, is not increasing. To be sure, African-American men and women recipients of doctorates in education have declined over the past several years (Roberts and Cleveland, 1990). Minority women have experienced particular feelings of isolation as they "suffer the double bind of laboring under two negative statuses" (Yeakey et al., 1986).

Of the more than 16,000 school districts nationwide, only 3% are managed by non-White superintendents. Less than 8% of principalships are held by African-Americans, and 3% are held by Hispanics (Heller et al., 1988). In a similar vein, ethnic minority representation is only 8% in the educational administration professoriate. And, according to McCarthy et al. (1988), there are no signs that this percentage will increase in the near future.

Equity and Fairness

While continued efforts are needed to curb discriminatory practices and ensure racial and gender diversity in the educational workplace, especially in leadership roles, fundamental changes are needed in administrative preparation programs. Accordingly, preparation programs need to emphasize the identification of socialization patterns and discriminatory practices that perpetuate racial and gender stereotypes. Again, it is reasoned if educational leaders could develop greater sensitivity to equity concerns and instill such in their staff and students, systemic changes could and would occur in our schools.

Shakeshaft in Baptiste et al. (1990, p. 222) suggested that administrators need to be prepared for a world that contains men and women from a variety of cultures and races. She further suggested that if administrative preparation programs are to adequately prepare their students to deal with the issues of discrimination, bigotry and the exclusion of women and people of color, the following guidelines need to be incorporated into these programs.

1. A course on equity and schooling should be a required part of the administrative preparation curriculum. This course should include at least the following topics: personal values; conceptual, philosophical, and societal issues of equity; equity in student treatment and placement; and equity in curriculum and instructional material.
2. Existing courses in the administrative preparation sequence should be expanded to include women's and minorities' experiences in administration. Where materials are unavailable to address these, they should be developed. UCEA, ASCD, AASA and other administrative organizations should be involved in helping to prepare materials that focus on the relationships of gender and race to effective management.
3. Women and minority administrators should be brought to the classroom to discuss issues relevant to female and minority students.
4. Where possible, women students should intern with minority administrators; minority students should intern with minority administrators.
5. The number of women and minorities on faculties of educational administration should be increased.
6. Research on the styles of women and minority administrators should be supported and encouraged.
7. Workshops sponsored by UCEA and NCPEA should be developed to help professors of educational administration incorporate materials on equity into their courses.

While it has been suggested that the civil rights ruling of the 1960s and 1970s have assured equal employment and educational opportunities, and continued attention to equity concerns is no longer needed, reality suggests the contrary. The evidence from practically every sector, be it the federal, state or local level, attest to the need for eternal vigilance. A recent report written by the

House Education and Labor Committee chair accused the U.S. Department of Education of failing to enforce civil rights laws, particularly those barring race and gender discrimination (Education Committee Chief, 1989). Richards (1988) suggested that "the prospects for improvement are in the mid-1980s threatened just as much by structural factors and benign neglect as by overt discrimination" (p. 165).

Accordingly, until we begin to rethink and reconceptualize leadership in such ways that gives appropriate attention and consideration to the contributions of ethnic minorities and women, we will not significantly improve educational leadership and the appropriate delivery of educational services to the many diverse and varied school publics in Texas.

Urbanization and Population Movement

In Texas, especially in its large urban centers, Houston, Dallas, Fort Worth, San Antonio and Austin, there have been significant population growth evidenced over the last twenty years. Estimates in 1988, placed the population of Texas at 16,800,000, third largest in the nation, and more than double that of Texas in 1940. And while Texas' growth rate continues to exceed that of the national average in the early 1970s, it declined for a while in the late 1970s and early 1980s. Currently it is steadily on the upswing.

Throughout its history, Texas has depended on migration for its population growth. Currently among its many ethnic groups more than 70% are "Anglo." African-Americans comprise 12%, Native Indian Americans, less than one percent, and 21% are people speaking Spanish as a native language or with a Spanish surname (See Figure 7.2). The distribution of ethnic minorities throughout Texas has spread significantly over the past twenty years. In 1970, approximately 20 percent of the Mexican-American population, once concentrated in South Texas, was in the Dallas, Fort Worth and Houston areas.

Perhaps the most striking change of recent decades has been the altered role of ethnic minorities and women in Texas. When the situation of African-Americans, Mexican-Americans and women at the turn of the century is compared with their current circumstances, these groups have made tremendous advances. Once relegated to low-paying, common labor jobs, African-Americans, Mexican-Americans and women currently hold responsible and influential positions in business, industry, the professions and government. Other areas, such as sports and cultural activities have also been enhanced by the contributions of ethnic minorities. In a similar vein, women have been more visible. Women have outnumbered men since 1960. In the late seventies, women were elected mayor of San Antonio and Austin. Just recently, in Houston, women held seven of the top administrative positions in the city including the mayor, the police chief, the housing director, the general superintendent of schools, president of the Chamber of Commerce, president of the largest university and the director of the County Hospital District. According to news accounts, Houston probably leads the nation in the number of women holding such high and prestigious positions.

POPULATION — STATE TOTALS

1980 Population

1986 Population[E]	16,682,000
1980 Census of Population	14,229,191
Rank in State 1980/1986	
% Change 1970–80	27.1
Urban Residents	11,333,017
% Change 1970–80	27.0
Rural Residents	2,896,174
% Change 1970–80	27.3
Population Per Square Mile	54.3
Native Texans 1980 (%)[T]	67.8

Age 1980

Female (%)	50.8
Median Age	28.2
Under Age 5 (%)	8.2
Age 5–17 (%)	22.1
Age 18–64 (%)	60.1
Age 65 and Over (%)	9.6
Age 18 and Over (1980)	9,923,085
Registered Voters (3/8/88)	7,879,824

1980 Selected Ancestry Groups

Black	1,710,175
Hispanic	2,985,713
American Indian/Eskimo	40,075
Asian/Pacific Islander	120,313
English[F]	1,639,322
French[F]	152,072
German[F]	754,388
Irish[F]	572,732
Italian[F]	78,592
Polish[F]	70,688
Veterans 1980 (%)	11.9

1980 Family Characteristics

Households	4,929,267
Single Persons (Age 15+)	2,558,023
Families	3,677,865
Both Spouses Employed	1,360,111
With Children Under Age 18	1,992,484
Child. Living w/Two Parents (%)	77.9
Employed Mothers/Ages 0–5 (%)[M]	48.1
Age 3–4 in Nursery School (%)	31.6
Foreign Language in Home (%)[S]	21.8
Age 60+ Living Alone (%)	23.8

1980

School Dropouts Age 16–19 (%)	17.6
H.S. Graduates Age 25+ (%)	62.6
College Graduates Age 25+ (%)	16.9

1986

Birth Rate[R]	18.3
Death Rate[R]	7.1
Marriage Rate[R]	11.6
Divorce Rate[R]	5.9

Source: U.S. Department of Commerce, Bureau of Census/Secretary of State of Texas. Elections Division/Texas Deparment of Health, Division of Vital Statistics.

[E] Estimate.
[S] Children ages 5+ who speak a language other than English at home.
[T] Born in Texas and residing in Texas in 1980/
[R] Per 1,000 population.
[F] Those Reporting single ancestry.
[M] Employed female with children ages 0–5

Figure 7.2. Texas Population Demographics.

While to a great extent, the progress of ethnic minorities and women in Texas comes about through federal laws, public attitudes favoring change in these matters are increasing. As Texas began the decade of the eighties, a large proportion of the population was relatively well educated. In 1980, Texans had completed an average above 11.8 years of school, slightly less than the national average. More than 2.2% had attended college.

An area still in need of serious attention is the matter of wealth. There remains great disparities in the per capita income of Texans. These vast differences appear again to have racial overtones and implications. Close examination reveals for example, that some of the predominately Mexican-American communities in the Rio Grande Valley have a per capita income little more than a third of that of the city of Midland located in West Texas oil fields. Such conditions and disparities gave rise to the recent Texas Supreme Court decision in the *Edgewood vs. Kirby* lawsuit, wherein, the Texas Legislature was directed to equalize state support of education to each school district in the state.

The above conditions and circumstances bear serious and significant implications for education of the masses in Texas, especially in urban areas. Increasingly, the majority of children and youth in America's public schools, especially in urban areas, come from ethnic minority groups. Likewise, ethnic minority youngsters also constitute a majority in Texas' urban area public schools. For several reasons, many of these youngsters are educationally disadvantaged and are at-risk of school failure. During the late 1980s, researchers (Hodgkinson, 1985; Levin, 1985; McDill, Natriello, and Pallas, 1986) have called attention to the significant problem of educationally disadvantaged students within our schools, warning that unless more effective means can be found for delivering educational services to this population, not only would these students suffer personally, but there would also be severe negative consequences for our country's economic welfare and even our social and political stability.

Davis and McCaul (1990) suggested several factors and conditions that appear to have fostered the recent attention which should be of concern to school administrators, planners and researchers. Among these are:

"(1) the rapidly growing numbers of children and youth who are considered to meet the criteria for inclusion within the ''at-risk'' definition—the sheer magnitude of the problem; (2) changing socio-demographic characteristics within the United States which are presently viewed as placing increasingly larger numbers of students at risk of educational and social failure—a recognition that America is changing; (3) projected socio-demographic changes which will occur in both the school-age population and American society as a whole during the next 30 years which indicate an even greater number of at-risk students—the problem will get increasingly worse; (4) a growing, widespread dissatisfaction with the results of various past and present educational reform efforts which have targeted this population of students—failed policies and programs; and (5) a broader-based concern and approach among policymakers both in and out of the educational field to address the complex and multifaceted problems which are involved in educating at-risk students—the growing recognition that the severity and scope of the problem requires problem-solving collaboration and commitment among representatives from several professional disciplines as well as from the public at large.''

America is changing in a number of ways. Not only is its school-age population poorer, more racially diverse with many being reared by one parent, there is a large influx of immigrant children. According to Davis and McCaul (1990), in 1988 more than 2.7 million school-aged immigrants resided in the United States. Recent immigrants, primarily Hispanic, Asian and Caribbean, have settled mostly in California, Florida, New York, Texas and Massachusetts; and, as such, have drastically altered the face of public education in many cities across the country. Problems attendant to these situations are profound in addressing these problems. School leaders and policymakers consideration must be given to a broad array of concerns including factors involving society, cross-cultural relationships, parent and community involvement and empowerment, curricula and institutional concerns and the many, varied characteristics of these students, their parents and communities.

As the people of Texas enter a new and challenging era in the 1990s and beyond, the current significant progress being made in science and technology, improvements in the standard of living for many more of its inhabitants and increases in the educational opportunity for all portend important and meaningful societal changes in every sector. Although Texas has problems which remain, history has shown that many of these problems have been addressed and resolved. A free, prosperous and contented life depends upon the state's ability and commitment to solve those of the present and of the future.

References

Allport, G. (1958). The nature of prejudice. New York: Doubleday.
Baptiste, H. et al. (1990). Leadership, equity, and school effectiveness. Newbury Park: Sage Publications.
Bannett, L. (1975). The shaping of Black America. Chicago: Jotresort Publishing Company.
Bertrand, A. (1967). Basic sociology: An introduction to theory and method. New York: Appleton-Century Crofts.
Boas, F. (1938). Tag mind of primitive man. New York: The McMillan Co.
Bond, IL (1972). Black American scholars: A study of their beginnings. Detroit: Delamp.
Bullock, H. (1970). A history of Negro education in the south from 1619 to the present. New York: Praeger.
Campbell, R.F., Bridges, E. M., and Nystrand, R.O. (1983). Introduction to educational administration. Boston: Allyn and Bacon, Inc.
Casteneda, H. (1974). The structure of morality. Springfield: Thomas Publishing Co.
Davis, W. and McCaul, P. (1990). At risk children and youth: A crisis in our schools and society. Orono: Institute for the Study of At-Risk Students, University of Maine.

Dawidowicz, L. and Goldsrein, L. (1963). Politics in a pluralist democracy: Studies of voting in the 1960 election. Westport: Greenwood Press.

Dubois, W. E. B. (1973). Black reconstruction in America: An essay toward a history of the part which Black folk played in the attempt to reconstruct democracy in America, 1860-1880. New York: Athaeneum.

Education committee chief criticizes ed's civil rights enforcement record. (1898, February 17). *Education Daily*, pp. 1-2,

Fell, B. (1976). America, B.C.: Ancient settlers in the new world. New York: Quadrangle/New York Times Book Co.

Fishman, J. (1970), *Bilingual education in sociolinguistic perspective*. TESOL Quarterly, No. 4., 215-222.

Garcia, M. (1989). Mexican-Americans. New Haven: Yale University Press.

Gay, G. in Gold, et al. (1977) In praise of diversity: A resource book for multicultural education. Washington, D.C.: Teacher Corps-Association of Teacher Educators.

Glazer, N. and Moymhan, D. (1970). Beyond the melting pot. Cambridge, Mass.: MYT Press.

Gold, M. et al. (1977). In pcaisc of diversity: A resource book for multicultural education. Washington, D.C.: Teacher Corps-Association of Teacher Educators.

Gordon, M. (1964). Assimilation in American life: The role of race, religion, and national origins. New York: Oxford University Press.

Gossett, T. (1955). Race: The history of an idea in America. Schocken.

Grant, C. (1975). Sifting and winnowing. Madison: Teacher Corps Associates.

Hamilton, C. (1968). Race and education: A search for legitimacy. Cambridge: *Harvard Educational Review.*

Haviland, W. (1983). Cultural anthropology. New York: Holt Rhinehat/and Winston.

Hawley, A. (1975). Man and environment. New York: New Viewpoints—New York Times Book Co.

Heller, R.W., Conway, J.A., and Jacobson, S.L. (1988). Here's your blunt critique of administrator preparation. *Executive Educator,* 10 (9).

Hilliard, A. (1984). Pedogogy in ancient Egypt. Paper presented at the Ancient Egyptian Studies Conference. Los Angeles

Hilliard, A. (1984). Race and education: A search for legitimacy revisited. A paper presented at the Clifton M. Claye Educational Leadership Symposium at Texas Southern University, Houston, Texas.

Hodgkinson, H. (1985). All one system: Demographics of cducation—Kindergarten through graduate school. Washington, D.C.: Institute for Educational Leadership.

Horsman, R. (1981). Race and manifest destiny: The origins of American racial Anglo-Saxonism. Cambridge, Mass.: Harvard University Press.

Hrabe, J. (1979). American ethnicity. Itasca, Illinois: F. K Peacock Publishers.

Jackson, B. (1989). Race, ethnicity, culture, and values: A new emphasis needed in administrator preparation programs- An unpublished paper presented at the 1989 convention of the University Council for Educational Administration, Scottsdale, Arizona.

Johnson, H. (1976). Ethnic American minorities: A guide to media and materials. New York: R.R. Bowker Co.

Kimbrough, R. and Nunnery, M. (1988). Educational administration: An introduction. New York: Macmillan Publishing Co.

King, K (1971). Pan Africanism education: A study of race, philanthropy, and education in the southern states of Amcrican and east Africa. Oxford: Clarendon Press.

Lambert, H. (1955). Our language: The story of the words we use. New York:

Levin, H. (1985). The educationally disadvantaged: A national crisis. (The State Youth Initiatives Project, Working Paper #6). Philadelphia: Public/Private

Levine, R. and Campbell, D. (1972). Ethnocentrism: Theories of conflict, ethnic attitudes and group behavior. New York: Wiley.

Lindsey, P. and Lindsay, O. (1974). Breaking the bonds of racism. Homewood: ETC Publications.

Lourdes, Miranda King in Johnson (1976). Ethnic American minorities: A guide to media and materials. New York: R.R. Bowker, Co.

McCarthy, M. and Webb, L. in Baptiste et al. (1990). Leadership, equity, and school effectiveness. Newbury Park: Sage Publications.

McDill, E. Natriello, G. and Pappas, A. (1986). A population at risk: Potential consequences of tougher school standards for school dropouts. In G. Natriello (ed.), School Dropouts: Patterns and policies (pp. 106-147). New York: Teachers College Press.

McDonald, A. (1986). The Texas experience. College Station: Texas A and M University Press.

McWilliams, C. (1968). Noah from Mexico: The Spanish-speaking people of the United States. New York: Greenwood Press, Inc.

Newman, W. (1973). American pluralism. New York: Harper and Row, Publishers.

Omi, M. and Winant, H. (1986). Racial formation in the United States: From the 1960s to the 1980s. New York: Routledge and Kegan

Paul Perry, J. and Perry, K (1974). The social web: an introduction to sociology. San Francisco: Canfield Press.

Porter R. (1990). Forked tongue: The misleading politics of bilingual education. New York: Basic Book, Inc.

Richards, C. (1988). The search for equity in educational administration: A commentary. In N. Boyan (Ed.), Handbook of research on educational administration (pp. 159-168). New York: Longman

Richardson, R. et al. (1981). Texas: The lone star state. Englewood Cliffs: Prentice-Hall, Inc.

Roberts, L. and Cleveland, Z. (1989). African-Americans in school leadership preparation programs at UCEA member institutions: A matter of benign neglect or enlightened self-interest? An unpublished paper presented at the 1989 convention of the University Council for Educational Administration, Scottsdale, Arizona.

Rothman, Jack (1977). Issues in race and ethnic relations: Theory, research and action. Itasca, Illinois: F.E. Peacock Publishers.

Ryan, J. (1975). Cultural diversity and the American experience: Political participation among Blacks, Appalachians and Indians. Beverly Hills: Sage Publications.

Sance, M. (1975). The African-American Texans. San Antonio: Institute of Texan Cultures.

Schaefer, R. (1988). Racial and ethnic groups. Glenview, Illinois: Scott, Foresman and Co.

Sergiovanni, T.J. et al. (1987). Report of the educational administration advisory committee to the Coordinating Board of the Texas College and University System, Austin, Texas.

Shakeshaft, C. in Baptiste et al. (1990). Leadership, equity, and school effectiveness. Newbury Park: Sage Publications.

Schibles, M. (1988). School leadership preparation: A preface for action. A subcommittee report on the preparation of school administrators to the American Association of Colleges for Teacher Education, Washington, D.C.

Spivey, D. (1978). Schooling for the new slavery: Black industrial education, 1868-1915. Westport, CT: Greenwood Press.

Steinberg, S. (1981). The ethnic myth: Race, ethnicity, and class in America. New York: Atheneum.

Tenorio, A. in Gold, et al. (1977). In praise of diversity: A resource book for multicultural education. Washington, D.C.: Teacher Corps-Association of Teacher Educators.

Vander Zanden, J. (1972). American minority relations. New York: Ronald Press Company.

Van Sertima, I. (1976). They came before Columbus. New York: Ronald Press Company.

Witty, E. (1982). Prospects for Black teachers preparation, certification, and employment. Washington, D.C.: ERIC Clearinghouse on Teacher Education.

Woodson, C. (1969). The miseducation of the Negro. Washington, D.C.: The Associated Publishers.

Yeakey, C., Johnston, 0. and Adkinson, J. (1986). In pursuit of equity: A review of research on minorities and women in educational administration. *Educational Administration Quarterly*, 22, 110-149.

Young, D. (1932). American minority peoples. New York: Harper and Brothers, Co.

Zangwill, I. (1990). The melting pot: A drama in four acts. New York: The MacMillan Co.

The Politics of Education: Texas and the Nation

Frank W. Lutz

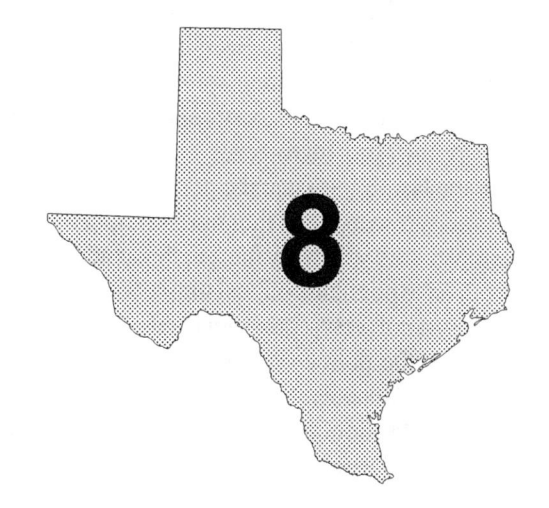

For a considerable time after the turn of the century education was held to be above mere politics and, therefore, not a "proper" arena in which politicians might play. Nor was politics a "proper" arena for school people. The corrupt "machine" politics of the late 1800s and early 1900s set the context within which that adage was operationalized. After the Civil War politics, from the federal to the local level, became a means whereby politicians bartered their causes and lobbyists hawked their wares. Whatever one wanted to get or sell to another, was available—at a price. The machine governments of the fast growing cities in the U.S. were centers of such political trade-offs. The fact that urban school districts were disseminators of large amounts of money and jobs was not lost on "machine" politicians. This was the situation when Woodrow Wilson argued, in the early 1900s, that the nation should undertake a political "reform" cleaning up corruption and leaving the administration of the public bureaucracies of government to the capable hands of the trained professionals. Public education and school administrators were fast to agree.

No less an eminent educator than George Counts was able to see the shortsightedness of that approach. He pointed out that if politics meant only the "log-rolling" and corruption of big-city machines then public education should be insulated from politics. But Counts saw much more than that to politics, and he saw the disadvantage of having education left out, and thus behind, in the political process. He tells us (1930: 181-182), "... since education must always be one of the major concerns of any advanced culture, it should be recognized as one of the central problems of politics."

Counts' caution went unheeded for more than half a century, at least so far as any formal participation was concerned. It was Eliot (1959) who rediscovered the politics of education and initiated what was to become a major thrust in educational administration for the next thirty years. Courses were added to university preparation programs, and teacher organizations and unions established offices in their state capitols and in Washington, D.C., as did other professional groups. School administrators and local school boards began to realize that either they played the game or they lost by forfeit.

In the last thirty years the politics of education has been one of the major fronts upon which programs, research and literature in education administration has advanced. While some school administrators still decry the fact that practically every educational decision is a political decision, and all have possible political implications, few would deny the reality of such a statement. There is hardly a university program in education administration without some course that specifically addresses the politics of education. At the American Educational Research Association, the Politics of Education-Special Interest Group, has grown to be one of the largest in the association. Today, any school administrator without a firm grounding in the politics of education is one bound to find trouble.

Federal Government and School Politics

The fact that the U.S. constitution fails to mention education directly and that the Tenth Amendment reserves all things not specifically mentioned in the Constitution to "the states and their people" is well known to every school administrator. That fact has been widely interpreted to mean that it is unconstitutional for the federal government to interfere in or take control of public education in the United States. It is also well understood that for two hundred years the federal government has influenced education with legislation (starting with the Land Grant Acts), by Supreme Court Decisions (perhaps the most famous of which is the *Brown v. Topeka* decision), and executive office influence from the "bully pulpit" and by cabinet level actions and decisions. Many, in fact, question whether the framers of the constitution intended there to be a "wall of separation" between public education and the federal government as the Supreme Court has decided is the case between the government and religion. Careful reading of the journal kept by James Madison during the Constitutional convention appears to indicate that there were many areas, including education, which the framers of the Constitution thought to be important to the people and considered making the responsibility of the federal government. Wisely the vast majority of these were left out of the constitution. Perhaps, however, they were not intended to be the subject of neglect by the federal government. Given the history of federal influence in public education, it seems obvious that presidents, federal legislators and judges have found ways to shape public education. The federal government by executive order, legislation or through its cabinet post, cannot establish a national education system. That fact may raise questions about the wisdom, if not the legality, of establishing national education goals or curricula. Still the federal government has and does play a role in shaping public education.

The Legislature

As noted, the Congress was always been willing to influence the direction of education or assist some favorite enterprise by aiding some aspect of education. They wanted land development in the 1700s and passed the Northwest Ordinances. About one hundred years later the Land Grant Act was passed to support agriculture and military needs through higher education. In the early 1900s, and commensurate with the rise of business influence in the U.S., the first of many vocational education support acts was passed. There were educational benefits for military veterans of the Civil War, Spanish-American, World Wars I and II, Korean, Vietnam wars and there remain today significant education benefits related to service in the military. It was not until the mid-1950s, however, that public education was to be directly aided by the federal congress. That bill was called the National Defense Education Act. The bill, like the national highway act passed shortly before it, used the excuse of the national defense and the threat of communism to justify the federal government moving directly into areas before thought to be the sole province of the individual states.

It took nearly another decade to pass an across the board federal aid public education bill. The congressional process of defeating, and finally passing that bill is instructive of the politics of getting a bill through the Congress and, in general, state legislatures as well.

The National Defense Education Act demonstrated that there was not a prohibition against the federal government directly aiding public education. Therefore, a bill to make such aid more comprehensive was introduced nearly every year in the congress. During this period an African-American representative from New York regularly added an amendment to the bill as introduced, requiring that such funds not be used in any school district practicing defacto or dejure segregation. That amendment, called the Powell Amendment, assured the bill's failure. There were both Northerners and Southern liberals in sufficient number, to vote for and to pass the unamended bill. There were enough Northern liberals (who believed in the amendment) who when added to the Southern conservatives (who did not want any federal aid to education), to pass the amendment. The amended bill was then opposed by Northern conservatives, Southern conservatives (who had voted for the amendment) and the Southern liberals (who would have voted for the original bill but would not vote for the amended bill which would deny aid to their segregated schools). The amended bill was defeated consistently. Through the process of amendment, a small group of Southern conservatives, thus, arranged to keep a bill favored by the majority of the Congress, from becoming law. Thus the will of the majority is thwarted by political maneuvering.

The above is illustrative of the floor politics that can influence the passage of any bill. In addition, there is the usual business of assigning a bill to committee, the process of getting it brought up for hearings and reporting it favorably out of committee, or reassigning it to a subcommittee committee to die. If a bill reaches the floor it is subject to floor politics, to a floor vote including leadership manipulation, and caucus politics. Both houses must pass bills in the same form, or consent to the bill of the other house, or send the bill to "conference committee" to get a bill that both houses will pass. There are several popular novels and plays that illustrate in dramatic fashion these complicated processes. The book, *Advise and Consent,* is one such book; the movie *Mr. Smith Goes to Washington,* was such a movie. Both are usually known to educational administration students and, thus, serve as useful examples.

It might be contended that the federal courts and particularly the Supreme Court have done more to actually "reform" the public schools of America than any and all other American institutions. When one looks carefully at the history of the United States, and particularly at American education, one can be convinced that all of the movement in public education has been to reemphasize the trends and structures in place since the early colonial days (see Plank 1987; and Lutz 1968). Major exceptions to this are two court decisions, one placing "a wall of separation" between government and religion, the other deciding that "separate" could not be "equal" in public schooling. Both decisions reversed long standing legal and cultural traditions in the nation and particularly in the schools (see Lutz and Mertz, 1992).

The Executive Office

There are two divergent views of the U.S. Presidency. One, held by most of the world, suggests that the President of the United States is the single most powerful person in the world and can accomplish about whatever the role incumbent chooses to accomplish. The second view is informed by experience and held by many who have occupied the "Oval Office." It describes the sense of frustration about what the incumbent intended and was unable to accomplish. That view often sees the Presidency as relatively emasculated of power by the "checks and balances" or by "grid-lock" in the structure of American government. Both views have some elements of truth. For example, Woodrow Wilson wanted to be the peace president. He pledged he would never take the nation into a war, yet he did. He was concerned about the kind of peace that would be made, and had little influence in the Treaty of Versailles. He was dedicated to the League of Nations as a peace-keeping body and could not get the U.S. Congress to ratify it. Lyndon Johnson wanted to build a "Great Society" and to be an "Education President." He got himself enmeshed in the Vietnam War, losing the war and the presidency.

Perhaps the major influence a president can effect in education is through the use of the "bully pulpit." In such a manner, Theodore Roosevelt amended the child labor laws and got the states' compulsory attendance laws extended. Ronald Reagan was probably the master of the "bully pulpit", given the medium of television. He effectively influenced public education and the people's perceptions and evaluation of its perception of the education reforms of the 1980s.

The National Role Summarized

While the federal government has no direct role in the establishment of public education and is constitutionally prohibited from establishing a national education system it has through its legislative, judicial, and executive branches, always encouraged and aided public education in ways of political interest to the federal government. Major among those areas of interest are corporate business, agriculture and the military. It is only recently that education itself has become an interest in federal politics.

State Government and School Politics

It is at the state level where the real power to govern public education resides. As noted, the tenth amendment leaves those powers not directly delegated to the federal government to the states and their people. Here, at the state level, is the center of political power in public education. When one speaks of the "inherent" right to govern local schools free from state interference, he is deluding himself. More appropriately one can refer to the "traditional privilege" to govern public education through locally elected boards. Public education is a state function governed, established, and organized by the state laws in whatever fashion the legislature decides. In most states, including Texas, that method has been, traditionally, through locally elected school boards and is largely an economic/political phenomenon. The state, wishing to avoid the major expenses entailed in public education and the blame for the subsequent taxes which would have to be levied, has also left the taxes and the responsibility at the local level. A recent change seen during the reforms of the 1980s, has been to increase the state's share of control while actually decreasing the state's proportionate share of funding for public education. This remains, in the 1990s, a matter of political contention.

Types of State Arrangements

Any state may organize public education in whatever fashion its legislature desires. These arrangements vary from Hawaii, which has but a single state district, to states, like Nevada, which organize into districts encompassing several counties, to states like Illinois which has several types of districts (i.e. elementary, secondary, comprehensive, etc,) and hundreds of local districts. Texas, depending on how one counts school districts, had 1060 Independent School Districts in 1990 (TASB 1990). That number placed Texas third in the nation in number of local school boards,—behind California and Illinois.

Some states organize education on a county basis as does Florida. Those states which organize into smaller local units often have some over-arching arrangement for cooperative local district action such as county units, intermediate units, or some sort of service units. These units provide help, service, and opportunity for cooperative purchase of goods or services. In Texas these units are called regional Education Service Centers.

One final note about the political organization of state education: in the late 80s and early 90s it has become fashionable to adopt or move toward a policy (within larger districts at least) giving some form of control to elected campus boards. The Illinois reform of 1989 gave a considerable amount to decision making power to community elected campus boards in Chicago (Illinois Senate Bill—1840, 1988). Houston I.S.D. was moving toward campus advisory boards in 1990.

There is a specific process through which any bill must pass in order to become law in any state. This is true of Texas. That process is complex not only because of the formal rules of seniority, committee structure and the rules of the legislature but, also, because of the informal rules of influence and cloakroom politics. In addition, there are "rules" for lobbying by either corporate or education interest group lobbies.

Lobbying

The first rule of lobbying is that one must obtain access. If one cannot get to see the committee chair one will not influence the chair. Any number of lobbies attempt to influence the state legislature. Often, as in Texas, an official state agency is prohibited from lobbying the legislature. While that mandate is followed "to the letter of the law," that is as far as it goes. On education matters a State Education Agency (SEA), in Texas the Texas Education Agency (TEA), is ever present in the legislative halls with "their" data, "their" interests and "their" point of view. They would be remiss if they were not. But simply because they do not press too hard or have too blatant an agenda does not mean that they do not serve their own interest while, perhaps, also serving the interest of public education. Without a great deal of distortion one could argue that the traditional interests of public education and the self-interest of a State Education Agency (SEA) is virtually congruent. That may leave the non-traditional education interests somewhat less represented. That's politics!

Whatever the interest of the particular lobby and by whatever name it calls itself, lobbying requires four essential elements to be successful: (1) honesty, (2) accurate and usable data, (3) timeliness, and (4) humbleness. Don't brag about what can be has been accomplished in the political area. Politicians know or will soon find out.

Finally, lobbying like politics is too often assumed to be an ugly word. It is not! It is the means-ends relationship of both lobbying and politics that can be ugly—not the processes themselves. If groups or individuals have a position about public policy which they believe to be moral and good, one might contend it immoral not to strongly lobby the political system in order to enact it into policy. It is, therefore, the things lobbied and the means of lobbying that are good or bad or moral or immoral. Every citizen and interest group in a democracy has a duty to lobby for public policy they believe correct—including those policies affecting public education. Professional educators and their associations are not exempt from that duty. When "professional" politicians chide professional educators for lobbying for increased support of public education they often seek the "license" to ignore public education needs. No one chides the American Medical Association for lobbying for better health care, simply because that may result in additional dollars for health care professionals. Surely the Pentagon "lobbies" for the Defense Budget. It is time professional education took a similar pro-active position. But it must be remembered to pick the right battles. Any group, which "twists arms" too often will soon become unwelcome in legislative halls.

Enacting the Law in Texas

There are 8 basic steps in getting either a House or a Senate bill enacted into law in Texas. They are as follows:

1. Convince a member of the House or Senate that your idea is worthwhile or important. Any member may file a bill as early as the Monday following the general election or as late as the 60th day of the General Session. The bills are read by caption and referred to committee. This is the easiest part of getting a proposal enacted into law.
2. Bills are then studied by the committee to which it is assigned or by one of its subcommittees. Hearings are usually held. Finally, it may be reported out with a favorable recommendation to the full House or Senate, reported out with amendment, returned to a subcommittee, or "killed" in committee. Committee chairs have a great deal of power in this process.
3. The bill then proceeds to its First Printing containing the original text, accompanying amendments and often a "fiscal note" prepared by the Legislative Budget Board. The calendar Committee then assigns the bill to one of four calendars.
4. A Second Reading of the bill is accomplished at least 24 hours after The First Reading and 24 hours after it has been on the Daily Calendar and it has been distributed to the members.
5. If the bill passes that house it is "engrossed," all committee and floor amendments are incorporated and the bill is sent to the other body—the Senate if it is a House Bill or the House if it is a Senate Bill.
6. The same procedure then is followed in the other body. The other body may concur with the bill exactly as sent to them, or they may amend it. If it is amended the bill is returned to the original body with amendments. This is called the Second Printing and must be printed and distributed 24 hours prior to the consideration by the initial body. If the amended bill is passed, in amended fashion, it is "enrolled" and signed by the Speaker of the House and the Lt. Governor and sent to the Governor.
7. If the initial body fails to concur a Conference Committee of 5 House members and 5 Senate members are appointed by the Speaker and Lt. Governor respectively. The Conference Committee tries to develop a compromise bill. The compromise bill is presented and distributed to both bodies. This printing, with side-by-side analysis of the Conference

Committee's bill together with the previous versions, is called the third Printing. If this compromise bill is passed (it is not subject to amendment) it is enrolled and sent to the governor.
8. The governor may sign or veto this as with any previous version of the bill which might reach that desk. It requires a $^2/_3$ vote of each house to over-ride a governor's veto.

Obviously it does not require all eight steps to enact every bill, only those requiring a conference committee and over-riding a governor's veto must go through the entire 8. Usually bills are enacted in a much less controversial fashion. At each step a bill may be lobbied by interested groups, both for and against.

Governor's Influence

Major education bills are, in Texas as in most states, important, costly and often controversial. Twice between 1983 and 1990 the Texas legislature struggled with major education "reform" bills. In both cases the bills were heavily lobbied, the chairs of the education committees in both houses played significant roles in shaping the final bills, and the governor (two different governors) played the major role in the final bill enacted. This strong gubernatorial role is contradictory to the usual description of the Texas governorship as "weak."

Three factors, in addition to the importance of major education bills, account for this gubernatorial anomaly. First the governor, in Texas may call for a select committee to study a problem as was the case in the major "reform" bill of 1983, H.B. 72. The appointment of a strong, prestigious, wealthy and interested chair of such a committee and the ability to conduct state wide hearings produces tremendous public interest. Second a governor may veto a bill as was the case with fiscal "reform" in 1990, or threaten to veto as with proposed revisions of the H.B. 72 bill in 1983. Finally, and related to the veto, the governor may call Special Sessions. The Governor controls the topics of these sessions and may call as many as the office sees fit, thus keeping a "part-time" legislature in session and away from their means of support almost indefinitely. The governor did that in both the 1983 and even more extensively in the 1990 "reform" bills. It appears, then, that the governor of Texas is not at all "weak" regarding major education legislation, at least not when s/he wishes to play a "strong" role. The effect is that no interest group in education can afford to ignore the governor in Texas when lobbying an education bill.

In the above paragraphs the word reform has consistently been used in quotes; a word of explanation is required. Many authors have contended that the education reforms of the 1980s, and before, were not really reform but rhetoric and reinforcement of trends long established and tried previously (Plank 1986; Lutz 1988; and Cuban 1990). Thus the term reform takes a different meaning and has been used in quotes. Some, perhaps many, may disagree with this point of view. Space here prevents pursuing the arguments supporting that position. Before the reader rejects it out of hand, however, s/he is invited to read the articles cited.

Professional Education Associations

Only passing mention has been made of the professional education associations in Texas and their potential role in education legislation. Again space prevents an extended discussion but some further attention must be provided. There are 3 teachers groups in Texas. Such "fragmented politics" (see Iannoccone 1970) prevents teachers from being as effective a lobby group as they might. It has been said that Texas teachers do not elect governors they merely defeat them. Former Governor Mark White can attest to that fact.

Other professional associations also have considerable influence in education legislation in Texas. The Texas Association of School Administrators (TASA), representing mostly superintendents, exercises a good deal of influence. Perhaps the most influential association is The Texas Association of School Boards (TASB), representing nearly 7500 elected school board members. Both organizations have a capable paid staff and together (as they usually are on important education legislation) they are a most formidable lobby. When they are joined by the two principal associations and the three teachers associations and perhaps the various parents organizations they could undoubtedly wield a "big stick." Unfortunately for public education these public education interest groups are usually "fragmented" and lose much of their potential power.

The Texas Education Agency (TEA) has previously been mentioned as an effective and omnipresent lobby in the legislative halls. The commissioner until 1990 was appointed by the 15 member elected state school board. The board, its commissioner and the TEA staff combined to have the most influence on state education public policy of any other single body, with the possible exception of the legislature. They recommend legislative policy, provide information, testify at hearings. After an education bill becomes law the State Board operationalizes it by enacting regulations which have the effect of law. The TEA staff collects data regarding compliance, analyzes it, and makes campus inspections under the direction of the commissioner. It is difficult to imagine a more powerful opportunity to influence state public education policy than provided by the State Board, the commissioner, and the TEA.

The change enacted in 1990 special session making the Commissioner of Education a governor's appointee will not likely weaken the influence. It could make the governor's hand more powerful in state public education policy and, therefore, should make the governor more politically responsible for the condition of education in Texas. Given the nature of politics, Texas governors will probably work hard at avoiding that responsibility at election time.

Politics of Local School Districts

It is the politics of local school districts which is of greatest interest to most school practitioners as it is there where most public education professionals work and are affected by public education policy.

The Concept of Local Control

The concept of local control of education has its roots in early American colonial schools. While the people do not have an inherent right to control their schools they do have a tradition which informs them otherwise. Local citizens usually think of local schools as "their" schools and often are upset when state legislatures and education agencies impose regulations which are perceived as infringements on their "right" to control "their" schools. Local control of public education, as opposed to state or national control, is uniquely American. It is interesting that in the last decade while trends in the United States have been toward less local control and more state and federal control other nations, such as Australia, have been moving toward more local control. In some ways this trend in the United States is to be lamented.

In spite of the above trend most of public education in the United States is still organized so as to permit some degree of local control. There is still approximately 15,000 local school boards in the nation and only Hawaii is organized into a single state school system. Other states use regional, county, or local school districts governed by locally elected, or appointed, school boards as a means of organizing public education.

It is assumed that in some fashion local school boards represent their local communities as they govern public education in their school districts. Two basic categories of representation can be observed; elite and arena representation. These concepts are borrowed from anthropology (Richards and Kupper, 1971) and have been applied to school boards by Lutz and Gresson (1986) and others. Elite boards think of themselves as trustees for the people. They strive to reach consensus. That consensus is usually reached in some "private fashion" and then enacted into policy in public by a unanimous vote of the board. On the other hand, arena boards think of themselves as representatives of the people. They are the "community in council." In such a fashion the range of community values can be observed in their meetings as policy decisions are made in public by debate and counter-debate. Those policy decisions are usually enacted by a non-unanimous vote.

Anyone who has watched school boards operate will recognize that the majority of school boards in the United States operate in fashion best described as more "elite" than "arena." While there is some trend for boards to move toward the arena end of the continuum, particularly as more minorities are elected to school boards, it is clear that this is still not the norm. Arena council behavior is, in fact, discomforting to both the majority of the board and the school superintendent. If school administration programs have failed superintendents in any aspect it is likely this, that most superintendents are not equipped to handle a school board which is divided in its values, its cultural origins, its aspirations for children, and its votes on school policy issues—that is, by arena council behavior.

The Superintendent-Board Relationship

By far the single most important job of the superintendent is to create and maintain a strong and positive relationship with the school board. The process of doing that will differ depending on whether the board exhibits elite or arena behavior. Either process depends on open, honest communication between the board and superintendent, and the development of mutual respect for the integrity and the ability of the each other.

Given the more usual "elite" board situation superintendents have often found a rather homogeneous board acting as trustees for a rather homogenous school population. Until the Brown Decision in 1954 school boards in some states, including Texas, operated separate school systems for African-American students, albeit without much formal representation from the African-American community. Afro-Americans are still under-represented in school boards. The vast majority of school board members have usually been male, over 40 years of age, and from the middle-class or above. Most were businessmen or professionals and members of the white race (Counts, 1927). While this historical trend has begun to change during the last twenty years it remains the dominate pattern (Spring, 1989: 160-162). Under such circumstances superintendents were advised to guide the board toward consensus, to attempt to "bind" themselves to the board as their chief initiator of policy and principal administrator of policy which had been enacted by a unanimous board. Such a board acted with the consent of an oligarchical community power structure and as trustees for the people, who they believed were less capable than they of understanding what public education ought to be. Although some superintendents, in some communities, can still survive operating in such a fashion, those situations are rapidly changing and such superintendent behavior is becoming very risky. The politics of education is changing.

Most school districts are no longer as homogeneous as they once were. Few communities are operated totally by elite oligarchical power structures. Governance in the United States, from federal to state to local, including the governance of education, is likely to be accomplished by a shifting power system best described as a polyarchy, a system of disbursed inequalities (see Dahl 1960). In such a system coalitions are built and dissolved based on the issue at hand and winners and losers change frequently. Arena boards are more usual and the politics of education is a different game. Superintendents must learn to make several recommendations with some explanation of attendant probable effects for different cultures and racial groups. Administrators must learn that no single decision can be the "best" decision for every student and that sometimes one group will win and sometimes another. Superintendents do not rise and fall with every decision. A decision "against" the superintendent is not fatal unless s/he has been educationally wrong, immoral, or unless the superintendent chooses to oppose and fight the decision, thus favoring one board coalition over another. The superintendent is the chief executive officer for the board not the chief executive officer of the board. To forget the difference is to assure serious problems when working with an arena board.

Superintendent Vulnerability

A final word about the politics of the superintendent-board relationship. Superintendents do not usually have tenure. Callahan (1962) identified the political process, when the "fate" of the superintendent rests in the hands of a lay business-oriented school board. The result he called the, "Vulnerability Thesis." According to Callahan, school superintendents are too often trained as "business managers" and operate in order to survive, making decisions based too often on economic concerns instead of educational concerns. When the superintendent opposes the business orientation of the board the superintendent becomes "vulnerable." Callahan laments that condition, blames the school board's business dominated values and argues for changing the situation. The vulnerability thesis, however, may sometimes be "used" by superintendents to excuse lack of political courage or simply poor decision making or administration.

Largely opposing that vulnerability thesis Zeigler, Kehoe and Reisman (1985) have compared the role of City Manager with the school superintendent. They find the city manager less well paid and considerably more vulnerable than the school superintendent. Zeigler (1985) bases his conclusions on a very small sample and comes close to "putting down" superintendents for self-pity.

The most realistic analysis of the situation is probably somewhere between Callahan (1962) and Zeigler (1985). People who seek the superintendency go in with their eyes open. There are risks, but there are rewards. Superintendents stand at the economic pinnacle of the public education industry. That is what the job is about, taking risks and getting paid to take them. It is political! There are risks and most superintendents willingly accept them as the "other side of the coin." All managers and leaders must take risks. It is how well the game is played that makes the difference—and understanding the "politics" of the situation reduces the risk and makes the situation more livable.

The School-Community Relationship

The school-community relationship is parallel to and second only to the superintendent-board relationship. It may be helpful to think of the superintendent as representative of the norms and values of the professional organization and the board as representative of the norms and values of the community. As the superintendent and the board work together in a close and harmonious fashion each will begin to understand the different views and positions of the other. They find common ground upon which the public schools can operate and serve the needs and values of the community while at the same time producing well educated citizens for the macro-society.

The above is not intended to suggest that the superintendent should not be concerned about the nature of the community beyond the information supplied by the school board. That would be a tragic error. As noted a board can become ingrown and "closed" in general systems terms. If the superintendent falls asleep, "in bed" with the board that has become "closed," that superintendent will be in big trouble. In similar fashion a superintendent should not get overly concerned when some board member seeks occasional and direct information about the schools. Occasionally a board member gets in trouble at election time because of poor information supplied by an unnecessarily guarded superintendent. The matter of superintendents moving into the political community and of board members seeking information directly from someone other than the superintendent is a matter of degree, discretion and conscience. Those matters are best negotiated between the superintendent and the board. When there is a problem in this area its is usually the result of poor superintendent-board relations and not the cause of those poor relationships (see Lutz & Mertz, 1992).

Political Theories of Local School Politics

As previously noted the concept of local citizen control of public education is uniquely American. It is rooted in history and tradition but not in constitutional guarantees. Although a highly prized tradition for most citizens it is, like the right to vote, not always a well used one. Actually U.S. citizens are probably the "world's worst" at utilizing their right to vote or otherwise participating in the political process, either in general or school elections. Voter turnout in national elections seldom exceeds 60% and in school elections seldom exceeds 30%. This is one reason some theories of local school politics find the governance of local school districts not very democratic.

The Continuous Participation Theory

The Continuous Participation Theory (see Zigler and Jennings, 1975) that the measure of democratic action is the extent of participation of the electorate and the consistency of that participation. As has been previously noted, participation of citizens in public school decisions, either at the polls, at board meetings, or through school committees, has been and remains extremely low. Voter turnouts in school elections seldom are above 30% and often as low as between 5% and 10%. Attendance at school board meetings is so small that it often surprises the board and superintendent to find some "uninvited" citizen in the meeting room. Such an occasion may stimulate questions among "insiders" about who the person is, the organization represented, and what they want. Even in large school districts citizen interest in the usual "run-of-the-mill" school board business is low. Attendance at board meetings is relatively small. Those who attend often are the appointed representatives of education related organizations (e.g., parent or teacher associations). Given such a condition it is not surprising that a theory which uses continuous and high citizen participation as its major criterion of democratic action sees the governance of local public education as not very democratic.

Input-Output (Systems) Theory

Easton (1965) has suggested a "systems" theory of politics. The theory proposes that citizens' demands are "inputs" to the democratic political process. The political process turns those demands into legislation and public policy. The laws and policies produced by that political process are the "outputs" of the system. When one chooses to examine the democratic nature of the political system one needs only to assess the "inputs" (citizen demands) and compare them to the "outputs" (policies enacted). If the correlation between the two is close to 1.0, if the demands of the public are commensurate with the outputs of the system, then the system is said to be democratic.

Both researchers and practitioners of public education policy generally agree that such a correlation in public education is usually considerably lower than 1.0. Specific demands of interest groups are often labeled by school boards and administrators as special or single interest demands and are to be avoided or ignored. Public education policy is presumed to be aimed at what is "good for all the kids" and school board members (school politicians) are admonished to shun representing the "special interests." Complaints are to be directed to the "administration." Thus, citizens sometimes get the perception that their elected representatives do not care, and will not or cannot do much to represent their interest, much less see to it that their demands are turned into a policy which meets their demands. Given a theory that requires that demands (inputs) are realized, in terms of satisfying policy (outputs), and given the public perception described above, it is not surprising to find that input-output theorists, such as Wirt and Kirst (1972), fail to find the governance of local public education very democratic.

The Dissatisfaction Theory

The dissatisfaction theory of American democracy (Lutz and Iannoccone, 1979) recognizes that American democracy is unique in that its citizens do not continuously participate nor do they always get specifically what they had hoped. The theory contends that a benevolent despot could grant the people what they wanted and that, although meeting the criteria of the input-output theorists, would not be democratic. Further, in a controlled communist "democracy" the people are often required to vote but not allowed to decide much of anything. While public participation is high, theoretically meeting the criterion of participation, that is surely not what is called democracy. Although both of these examples are simplistic they serve to demonstrate the problem of failing to recognize the uniqueness of the American democracy. In American democracy the people have the right to vote and the right not to vote.

Dissatisfaction theory recognizes that there is a tendency in American democracy for citizens not to bother to participate when policy is "generally alright." That is, while it is not highly and personally rewarding it is also not dissatisfying enough to motivate them to do something about it. When policy is "dissatisfying enough" (see Lutz and Wang, 1987) voters go to the polls, vote against incumbents, elect new representatives, and get policy changed; thus, the name "Dissatisfaction Theory of American Democracy." This process, it is contended, is uniquely American and is descriptive of the manner in which local school policy is usually changed. Citizens fail to participate at the polls as they are neither dissatisfied enough, nor highly and personally satisfied. As they become mildly dissatisfied and in an attempt to get satisfaction their elected representatives (the school/board) turn them away as "special interest" groups. Failing to get a satisfactory response to their specific demands they become more and more dissatisfied. They find others who are also dissatisfied, probably about other things. The single thing these groups have in common is their dissatisfaction. They are united by that dissatisfaction. They oppose incumbent board members whom they perceive as having ignored them. They coalesce around another candidate, whom they support and elect. This process is often followed by another incumbent defeat. Such political events are usually followed by superintendent turnover. Then local educational policy changes. The voters are now no longer dissatisfied enough to continue to participate and school elections again become the object of voter neglect and low voter turnout is the result. This process, dissatisfaction theorists contend, is uniquely American and describes the political process of local school governance. In such a manner local school governance is not only democratic, they contend, but it is the "grassroots" model of American democracy.

Education and Politics Revisited

In *The Last Hurrah*, O'Connor, (1956) describes the nature of American politics as he has the mayor tell the young reporter that it is not baseball that is the greatest American spectator sport but it is politics. That is the message of the dissatisfaction theory of American democracy. School people have too long been in the stands watching instead of on the field playing, participating in the game.

The American people, however, have a way of getting into the game. And they have a life time "pass!" They possess the right to vote and they will use it when they choose, not just when or if they are invited. In the American democracy the people can get what they want, eventually. They get it by voting for representatives who give them what they want. Local school boards represent, perhaps, that political process nearest to the people. Therefore, it is the grassroots model of that process. It is relatively easy for the people to get what they want in local school districts once they decide to become politically active. It could be said that if the people can get what they want—they deserve what they get in public education.

School people must become increasingly aware of these facts and the manner in which the politics of education game is played. In the game of politics of education the spectators pay the bills. The participants effect the outcome of the game. School administrators cannot afford to be spectators in that game.

References

Callahan, R. (1962). *Education and the Cult of Efficiency.* New York: Teachers College Press.

Counts, G.S. (1927). *The Social Composition of Boards of Education.* Chicago: University of Chicago Press.

Counts, G.S. (1930). *The American Road to Culture.* New York: The John Day Company.

Cuban, L. (1990). "Reforming Again, Again and Again", *The Researcher.* Vol. 19, No. 1, pp. 3-13.

Dahl, R.A. (1960). *How Governs?* New Haven, Conn.: Yale University Press.

Easton, D. (1965). *A Systems Analysis of Political Life.* New York: John Wiley.

Eliot, T.H. (1959). "Toward an understanding of public school politics", *American Political Science Review.* 52: 1032-1051.

Iannoccone, L. (1970). "Norms governing urban-state politics of education," in *Toward Improved Urban Education.* ed. F.W. Lutz, Worthington, Ohio: Charles E. Jones Publishing. pp. 233-253.

Illinois (1988). Senate Bill--1840.

Lutz, F.W. (1988). "Reforming Education in the 1980s," *The Peabody Journal of Education.* Vol. 63, No. 4, pp. 70-89.

Lutz, F.W. and Iannoccone, L. (1978). *Public Participation in Local School Districts: the Dissatisfaction Theory of American Democracy.* Lexington, Mass.: Lexington Books.

Lutz, F.W. and Gresson A. (1980). "Local School Boards as Political Councils", *Educational Studies.* Vol. 11, No. 2, pp. 125-144.

Lutz, F.W. and Wang, L.Y. (1987). "Predicting Public Dissatisfaction: A Study of School Board Member Defeat," *Educational Administration Quarterly.* Vol. 23, No. 1, pp. 65-77.

Lutz, F.W. and Mertz, C. (1992). *The Politics of School Community Relations.* New York: Teachers College Press.

Mazzoni, T.L. (1986). "Policy Making and Public School Choice in Minnesota: from conformulation to compromise", *The Peabody Journal of Education.* Vol. 63, No. 4, pp. 45-67.

O'Connor, E. (1956). *The Last Hurrah.* Boston. Mass.: Little Brown.

Plank, D.N. (1986). "The Ayes of Texas: Rhetoric, Reality and School Reform," *Politics of Education.* 13, 13-16.

Richards, A. and Kupper, A. (1971). *Councils in Action.* Cambridge, England: The University Press.

Spring, J. (1989). *American Education: and Introduction to Social and Political Aspects.* White Plains, N.Y.: Longman.

TASB (1990). Personal telephone conversation with the Texas School Board Association.

Wirt, F.M. and Kirst, M.W. (1972). *The Political Web of American Schools.* Boston: Little Brown.

Zigler, L.H. and Jennings, M.K. (1975). *Governing American Schools: Political Interaction in Local School Districts.* North Sztuate, Mass.: Duxbury Press.

Zeigler, H., Kehoe, E. and Reisman, J. (1985). *Superintendents and City Managers.* New York: Praeger.

Texas School Personnel Administration

Mike Boone

The primary goal of school personnel administration is to secure the best in human resources for the school district. In attaining that goal, personnel administrators engage in a broad range of activities which include assessing personnel needs, planning, recruiting, selecting and placing qualified school employees. It is important that the school district attract and retain not only the finest teachers, counselors, librarians and administrators, but also the most qualified secretaries, teacher's aids, cooks, bus drivers and custodians. The quality of the educational program a school district offers its students depends largely on the quality of people it employs. The personnel administrator is a very real contributor to the effectiveness of the school district.

The Personnel Function

The personnel function consists of four distinct operations. These are: planning for human resource needs; recruiting a pool of qualified applicants; selecting the best candidates from the pool to fill vacant positions; and inducting new employees into the school system. These operations are important to the success of every Texas school district, no matter what its enrollment or the size of its central office staff.

Planning for Human Resource Needs

The basic personnel operation is planning. Planning permits the school district to ask itself "Where are we now, where do we want to be and how do we get there?" Through effective planning, the school district assures that it has the right number of people, with the right skills, available when and where needed. Planning also improves the chances that the people available to the school district will be capable of performing their tasks successfully. Without planning, the school district is unable to marshall the physical, financial and human resources needed to fulfill its mission. Planning can also help the district make sure that human resource acquisition is not haphazard.

Rather than thoughtfully matching people with appropriate skills to specific needs, the district which does not take the time to plan may be forced to take whom ever is available for a position and then attempt to make the person "fit." In too many cases, the fit is inappropriate and the employee is dissatisfied and ineffective. When this happens, both the employee and the school district have lost. Good human resource planning increases the likelihood that both the school district and the employee will be winners.

The mechanics of good human resource planning are relatively simple. They include the development of a human resource inventory; the projection of enrollments over time; a review of school district goals in the light of changing needs; and the production of a human resource forecast, which becomes a mandate for the district's personnel office. The human resource inventory provides the district with important information on each of its current employees. This information includes such things as age, sex, date employed by the school district, job title, location of employment, education or training and dates completed, and certification information for professional employees. The human resources inventory enables the school district to construct a profile of each relevant job classification within the district. Projecting future enrollment patterns over an extended time is the second step in planning. Enrollment projections provide the district with data by which to estimate the number and kinds of instructional and support personnel needed in the future. The third step in planning is to review the goals of the school district. District goals serve two purposes important to personnel administration: they determine the types of programs and services to be offered students and they define the district's immediate personnel needs. Finally, the information from the other planning steps can be put together to produce a forecast of the district's human resource needs. The forecast then becomes a mandate for the district's personnel administrator as s/he sets about recruiting and selecting the types and numbers of employees indicated by the planning process.

Recruiting

The purpose of the school district's recruiting program is to identify a pool of qualified applicants for school district positions from which a selection may be made. Recruiting is a reciprocal process in that it permits the school district to identify people who possess the requisite education, training and experiences needed while at the same time advertising the features of the school district which make it an attractive place in which to work. There are a number of good sources for recruiting candidates for position with the school district. These include college and university placement officers, job fairs, referrals from current employees and contacts with professional colleagues. The most important of these sources, at least for professional personnel, are college and university placement officers. Placement officers are usually well acquainted with the candidates their institutions produce. If they are also knowledgeable about the needs of the local school district, they can be helpful in identifying a pool of likely candidates.

Recruiting An Ethnically Diverse Teaching Force

A recent study by the National Education Association indicates that, even after decades of affirmative action and aggressive recruiting by school districts, the number of minority teachers in the public schools remains low. NEA statistics reveal a nation-wide teaching cadre that is overwhelmingly white and female. Only 13.2% of all public school teachers are minorities. At the same time, overall minority enrollment in the public schools rose to 38.7%. In some states, including Texas, the percentage of minority enrollment exceeds 50%. The nation's teaching force remains remarkably homogeneous while the student body is becoming more diverse.

There are several compelling reasons for school districts to make a special effort to recruit and retain minority teachers. Huling-Austin and Cuellar (1991) suggest the following:

- **Minority students need teachers who represent strong, successful and productive role models that match their own cultural and ethnic background.**
- **Minority teachers bring additional insights and perspectives to the job of teaching.** They may be more tuned to the needs of minority students and less likely to interpret cultural differences as learning problems.
- **All students benefit from having teachers who represent today's pluralistic society.** Minority and majority students need to be exposed to other cultures as well as to their own if they are going to be comfortable interacting with others in the work place and in society.
- **An ethnically diverse teaching force can bring stability to the staffing of some schools that have traditionally experienced high teacher turnover rates.** Teachers from the same cultural and ethnic background as their students are more likely to adjust to teaching in situations with high concentrations of minority students and are likely to remain in their positions longer.

The benefits of an ethnically diverse teaching force are self-evident, especially in today's increasingly mosaic society. School districts should remain active in efforts to attract and retain qualified minority teachers.

Selection

There are four possible outcomes to the selection process as it is carried out in most school districts. (Rebore, 1992) Two of these outcomes reflect correct selection decisions and two reflect incorrect selection decisions. A correct selection decision occurs when the person selected for a position proves to be successful or when a rejected applicant would have performed poorly on the job. Incorrect selection decisions occur when a rejected applicant would have performed satisfactorily on the job or when the job performance of the person actually hired proves to be inadequate. The personnel administrator is responsible for implementing the selection process in a way that maximizes the possibility that a correct selection decision will be made. The mechanics of the selection process consists of a series of steps which begins with the generation of a job description and ends with the notification of the successful candidate. There are two critical points at which even the most thoroughly designed selection system can break down. These are the candidate interview and the reference check. If either of these steps are inadequately or carelessly done, the whole selection process will be invalidated.

An interview is a *structured* conversation designed to elicit job-related information about an applicant. It is important that both parties understand the purpose of the interview, e.g. to find the best qualified applicant for a position based on the published requirements of the job.

Interviews should be conducted by trained persons who will be able to make an informed judgment about how well the applicant matches the published job requirements and who have the authority to make the decision to hire or not hire. (Niece, 1983) A candidate's credentials should be verified and references thoroughly checked before a hiring decision is made. It is best to contact references in person, preferably by telephone. A telephone call is one of the best ways of gathering information about a candidate. Since litigation has made employers cautious in the written comments they may make about an applicant, the telephone has become an invaluable resource for verifying references.

Criminal history checks must be part of the selection process. Texas Education Code 21.917 requires that school districts obtain criminal history information about all applicants for employment. Candidates should be informed of this requirement at the time they fill out an application since the law provides that an employee be discharged if data about conviction of a felony involving moral turpitude is withheld. The law further requires school district to notify the Commissioner of Education when a certified employee is convicted of a felony or misdemeanor involving illegal conduct with a child. (Kemerer & Hairston, 1990) Criminal history checks are usually conducted through the Department of Public Safety or the Department of Corrections. Information received from the criminal history check is considered privileged information and may not be revealed to anyone other than school district or TEA officials. In addition, the National Association of State Directors of Teacher Education and Certification (NASDTEC) maintains a nation-wide data base of teachers whose certificates have been denied, revoked or suspended over the past few years. (Baas, 1990) States, but not school districts, may have access to the data base.

Induction

Induction into the school system is critical to the success of new employees. All new staff require some type of an induction program to integrate them fully into the school system, but the need is perhaps most important for new teachers. Several characteristics of the teaching profession support the need for a well thought out induction program. For example, first year teachers are expected on their first day on the job to perform as competently as those who have been teaching for several years. Teachers also tend to be isolated from their peers, which prevents any kind of natural induction from occurring through socialization. Finally, there is a "double barrier" to assistance for new teachers. Beginning teachers are reluctant to ask for help for fear of appearing incompetent and experienced teachers are hesitant to offer help for fear of being seen as interfering. As a result, the attrition rate for first year teachers approaches 30% nationwide. By the end of the second year, perhaps 50% have left the teaching ranks. This is a preventable loss of a valuable resource.

Texas is one of several states which mandates an induction program for first-year teachers. Texas Education Code 13.038 provides that all teachers entering the profession after September 1, 1987 will serve a one year induction period. During the induction year, the beginning teacher works cooperatively with a "mentor" teacher, the building principal and university faculty. The goals of the induction year are to improve the instructional performance of the first-year teacher; to increase teacher retention after the first year of professional practice; to promote the professional and personal well-being of first-year teachers; and to transmit the culture of the school system to the beginning teacher. This induction year is to be planned and directed by the local school district.

Constitutional Issues Affecting School Personnel Administration

The federal government, through legislation, executive order and court decree, has become a major determiner of employment practices in Texas school districts. The intent of much of the activity of the federal government since 1964 has been to eliminate discrimination in hiring and promotion practices because of race, color, creed, age, handicapping condition or gender. The Constitution of the State of Texas also prohibits discriminatory practices. The Equal Rights Amendment of 1972 {Article 1, Sec. 3 (a)} reads in part "Equality under the law shall not be denied or abridged because of sex, race, color, creed or national origin." Falling under the general heading of "affirmative action," federal laws and state constitutional provisions have changed the way school districts think and act when making employment decisions. Affirmative action means more than equal opportunity or nondiscrimination. Affirmative action requires school districts to be proactive in expanding employment opportunities for women and minorities, even going so far as to set goals for increasing employment of under represented groups of people.

Affirmative action is not itself a law. Rather it is an "objective reached by following a set of guidelines that insure compliance with legislation and executive orders." (Rebore, 1992, pg. 38) When a school district discriminates in hiring or promotion practices, it does not violate affirmative action. It violates the law.

There are a number of examples of federal legislation that have a direct bearing on employment practices in local school districts. Among the more important of these are:

- Title VII of the Civil Rights Act of 1964.
- The Pregnancy Discrimination Act (1978).
- The Equal Pay Act.
- The Age Discrimination and Employment Act (1967).
- Section 1981 of the Rights Act of 1866/Section 1983 of the Civil Rights Act of 1871.
- Title IX of the Education Amendments of 1972.
- Section 504 of the Rehabilitation Act of 1973.
- The Americans with Disabilities Act (1990).

Enforcement of many of these laws falls under the jurisdiction of the Equal Employment Opportunities Commission. EEOC was established by Title VII of the Civil Rights Act of 1964 to investigate allegations of discrimination in employment. The powers of the Commission were expanded in 1972 by the Equal Employment Opportunities Act. EEOC oversight extends to all private employers with fifteen or more employees, all educational institutions, all state and local governments, public and private employment agencies, labor unions with fifteen or more employees and joint labor-management committees for apprenticeships and training. Regional EEOC offices are located in Dallas, El Paso, Houston and San Antonio.

Texas law places other restrictions on the employment of personnel in the public schools. Teachers and administrators are prohibited from acting as an agent of a textbook publishing firm or from selling any kind of school supplies [T.E.C. 12.65(e)]. State law also prohibits public school employees from holding two legally incompatible offices, e.g. being a teacher and a trustee of the same school district. A teacher may, however, serve as a trustee of a neighboring school district or as a member of the governing board of a local governmental unit, such as a city council. (Kemerer & Hairston, 1990) Under the nepotism rule, school districts are prohibited from employing persons related within a proscribed degree of blood or marriage to a trustee of the school district. The method of determining these relationships was simplified in 1991 with the passage of H.B. 1345. There are two exceptions to the nepotism rule. A "grandfather" clause exempts persons who have been "continuously employed" by the school district for at least thirty days prior to the appointment of a related school trustee or at least six months prior to the election of a related school trustee. Substitute teaching does not constitute "continuous employment" for purposes of the statute. School district located in counties with fewer than 35,000 residents according to the latest census may hire substitute teacher or bus drivers who would otherwise be excluded from employment. Finally, schools may prohibit all outside employment by teachers and administrators, so long as prohibitions are applied evenly to all district employees. (Gosney v. Sonora I.S.D., 1979)

Certification and Contracts

Certification

The right to professional employment in the public schools of Texas requires the possession of an appropriate and valid certificate. Certificates are awarded upon the completion of an approved teacher or administrator preparation program through one of Texas' public or private colleges and universities. Professional educators from other states may be certified through a reciprocal agreement between Texas and the candidate's home state. Still other professionals obtain their certificates through an alternative certification program operated jointly by an independent school district, a regional service center and an institution of higher education. No one may be legally employed by a public school in Texas in any professional capacity without proper certification.

The format of teacher and administrator preparation programs is determined by the Texas legislature. In 1988, the legislature significantly altered the structure of teacher preparation programs. Senate Bill 994 required that all candidates for teacher certification possess a liberal arts degree rather than the traditional bachelor's degree in education. At the same time, course work in education was restricted to 18 semester hours. The law requires new teachers to serve an induction year supervised by a classroom teacher, a district administrator and a university supervisor. Both pre-service and practicing teachers are to be trained in the use of instructional technology and in effective teaching practices. Colleges and universities were directed to restructure their preparation programs by the fall of 1991.

Admission to a teacher preparation program requires that a student successfully complete the Pre-Professional Skills Test (PPST), generally administered at the end of the sophomore year. Graduates of teacher preparation programs must also pass an examination before the certificate is issued. Called the ExCet test, the examination is designed to measure the student's mastery of specific subject matter and instructional skills. ExCet tests are also required for certification as an administrator, guidance counselor and other professional positions.

Teachers may also be certified through an alternative method. Alternative certification was developed specifically for individuals who already possess a bachelor's degree but who have no prior teacher training. Local school districts, working cooperatively with regional service centers and institutions of higher education, may conduct alternative teacher certification programs. Candidates who meet qualifications for an alternative certification program are hired to teach in a local school district. At the same time, the candidate serves a highly structured induction year under the guidance of an experienced and competent teacher and completes classroom instruction in teaching methodology. The State Board of Education has approved an alternative certification program for school administrators which closely follows the procedures established for alternative teacher certification.

Code of Ethics

Teaching in and administering the public schools of Texas is a professional activity. A profession is defined as an occupation which possesses a distinct body of knowledge, a dedication of service to others and a code of ethics which is subscribed to by all members of the profession. The professional code of ethics to which teachers and administrators in Texas are required to adhere was developed by the Professional Practices Commission. The Code of Ethics and Standard Practices for Texas Educators describes the conduct, practices and performances expected of professional educators towards colleagues, parents, students and community. A violation of a rule of the code is considered "unprofessional conduct" and constitutes grounds for suspension or revocation of the teaching certificate. Nationally, the American Association of School Administrators (AASA), the National Association of Secondary Principals (NASSP) and the National Association of Elementary School Principals (NAESP) have established codes of ethics for members of their organizations (Kimbrough, 1985).

Contracts

Texas law provides for the employment of teachers and other professional personnel under two distinct kinds of contracts. The most commonly used type of contract is called a term contract because it provides employment with the school district for a specific period of time and is renewable at the end of that time period. The normal term contract is for one year, but depending on enrollment, districts may issue term contracts for up to five years (T.E.C. 23.28). Superintendents, principals, teachers, counselors, librarians and other professionals are eligible for a term contract (Kemerer & Hairston, 1990). A small number of school districts in Texas employ teachers under a continuing contract. (Subchapter C, Texas Education Code) Under provisions of Subchapter C, teachers may be employed for a probationary period of up to three years (extended to four years under certain circumstances). After successfully completing the probationary period, teachers are issued a continuing contract. Unlike term contracts, continuing contracts do not have to be renewed periodically, but remain in force until one of the following occurs:

- the teacher resigns or retires
- the teacher is released from employment at the end of a school year because of a necessary reduction in force (RIF)

Code of Ethics and Standard Practices for Texas Educators

Adopted by the Teachers' Professional Practices Commission
(Revised March 30, 1988)

The Texas educator should strive to create an atmosphere that will nurture to fulfillment the potential of each student.

The educator is responsible for standard practices and ethical conduct toward students, professional colleagues, parents, and the community.

The Code is intended to govern the profession, and interpretations of the Code shall be determined by the Professional Practices Commission.

The educator who conducts his affairs with conscientious concern will exemplify the highest standards of professional commitment.

PRINCIPLE I
Professional Ethical Conduct

The Texas educator should endeavor to maintain the dignity of the profession by respecting and obeying the law, demonstrating personal integrity, and exemplifying honesty.

Standards
1. The educator shall not intentionally misrepresent official policies of the school district or educational organization and shall clearly distinguish those views from his personal attitudes and opinions.
2. The educator shall honestly account for all funds committed to his charge and shall conduct his financial business with integrity.
3. The educator shall not use institutional or professional privileges for personal or partisan advantage.
4. The educator shall accept no gratuities, gifts, or favors that impair or appear to impair professional judgment.
5. The educator shall not offer any favor, service, or thing of value to obtain special advantage.
6. The educator shall not falsify records, or direct or coerce others to do so.

PRINCIPLE II
Professional Practices and Performance

The Texas educator, after qualifying in a manner established by law or regulation, shall assume responsibilities for professional teaching practices and professional performance and shall continually strive to demonstrate competence.

Standards
1. The educator shall apply for, accept, offer or assign a position or a responsibility on the basis of professional qualifications and shall adhere to the terms of a contract or appointment.
2. The educator shall possess mental health, physical stamina, and social prudence necessary to perform the duties of his professional assignment.
3. The educator shall organize instruction that seeks to accomplish objectives related to learning.
4. The educator shall continue professional growth.
5. The educator shall comply with written local school board policies, Texas Education Agency regulations, and applicable state and federal laws.

PRINCIPLE III
Ethical Conduct Toward Professional Colleagues

The Texas educator, in exemplifying ethical relations with colleagues, shall accord just and equitable treatment to all members of the profession.

Standards
1. The educator shall not reveal confidential information concerning colleagues unless disclosure serves professional purposes or is required by law.
2. The educator shall not willfully make false statements about a colleague or the school system.
3. The educator shall adhere to written local school board policies and legal statutes regarding dismissal, evaluation, and employment processes.
4. The educator shall not interfere with a colleague's exercise of political and citizenship rights and responsibilities.
5. The educator shall not discriminate against, coerce, or harass a colleague on the basis of race, color, creed, national origin, age, sex, handicap, or marital status.
6. The educator shall not intentionally deny or impede a colleague in the exercise or enjoyment of any professional right or privilege.
7. The educator shall not use coercive means or promise special treatment in order to influence professional decisions or colleagues.
8. The educator shall have the academic freedom to teach as a professional privilege, and no educator shall interfere with such privilege except as required by state and/or federal law.

PRINCIPLE IV
Ethical Conduct Toward Students

The Texas educator, in accepting a position of public trust, should measure success by the progress of each student toward realization of his potential as an effective citizen.

Standards
1. The educator shall deal considerately and justly with each student and shall seek to resolve problems including discipline according to law and school board policy
2. The educator shall not intentionally expose the student to disparagement.
3. The educator shall not reveal confidential information concerning students unless disclosure serves professional purposes or is required by law.
4. The educator shall make reasonable effort to protect the student from conditions detrimental to the following: leaning, physical health, mental health, or safety.
5. The educator shall endeavor to present facts without distortion.
6. The educator shall not unfairly exclude a student from participation in a program, deny benefits to a student, or grant an advantage to a student on the basis of race, color, sex, handicap, national origin, or marital status.
7. The educator shall not unreasonably restrain the student from independent action in the pursuit of learning or deny the student access to varying points of view.

PRINCIPLE V
Ethical Conduct Toward Parents and Community

The Texas educator, in fulfilling citizenship responsibilities in the community, should cooperate, with parents and others to improve the public schools of the community.

Standards
1. The educator shall make reasonable effort to communicate to parents information which should be revealed in the interest of the student.
2. The educator shall endeavor to understand community cultures and relate the home environment of students to the school.
3. The educator shall manifest a positive role in school public relations.

- the teacher is discharged for lawful cause as provided in the statute
- the teacher is dismissed at the end of the year for reasons described in the statute
- the teacher is returned to probationary status as prescribed in the statute

Even though the number of districts using continuing contracts is small by comparison to the number of school districts in the state, the proportion of teachers employed under a continuing contract is substantial, since many of the state's large urban school districts use this type of contract.

Adverse Actions

A certified employee's contract status with a public school district may be adversely affected under circumstances carefully prescribed by law. For teachers employed under a probationary or continuing contract these procedures are to be found in T.E.C. 13.101-116. For superintendents, principals, teachers and others employed under a term contract, procedures are spelled out in the Term Contract Nonrenewal Act (T.E.C. 21.201-21.211). A certified employee may also be dismissed during the life of a contract. Those provisions will be discussed separately.

Continuing Contracts

Provisions for terminating a probationary or continuing contract under Subchapter C differ significantly. The major difference is that the cause the district must establish for termination is more serious for a continuing, than for a probationary, contract. Probationary teachers may be terminated when in the judgment of the board of trustees "the best interests of the school district will be served thereby" (T.E.C. 13.103). The teacher must be notified of the board's intent to dismiss by April 1st of the final year of the probationary contract period and is entitled to a hearing before the board during which the reasons for termination must be explained and the teacher given an opportunity to respond to them. A request for a hearing must be submitted by the teacher following notice to nonrenew. The decision of the board is final.

A teacher employed under a continuing contract must also be notified of the intent to terminate employment and the reasons for the proposed action by April 1. The reasons for termination of a continuing contract employee at the end of a school year are spelled out in T.E.C. 13.110. They include incompetence in the performance of duties; failure to comply with reasonable requirements for improving professional performance; willful failure to pay debts; habitual use of addictive drugs, hallucinogens or alcoholic beverages; necessary reduction in force (RIF) by the school district; and "good cause," which is normally interpreted to mean failure of the teacher to meet the generally recognized, accepted standards of conduct for the profession.

Within ten days of receiving an official notice of termination the employee may submit a written request for a hearing before the board of trustees. During the hearing, the teacher has the right to be represented by counsel, to hear the evidence against him or her, to cross-examine witnesses and to present evidence in refutation. Should the board of trustees decide to proceed with the termination, the employee may appeal the decision to the Commissioner of Education for review or s/he may challenge the legality of the decision by bringing suit in the district court of the county in which the school district is located.

Term Contracts

The Term Contract Nonrenewal Act (TCNA) applies to any school district professional employee whose position requires a certificate. This includes classroom teachers, counselors, supervisors, principals and superintendents. The act requires the board of trustees of the school district to adopt written policy which covers four important matters: 1) establish a probationary period for new employees not to exceed the first two years of continuous employment with the district; 2) provide for written annual evaluations of all certified persons in its employ; 3) enumerate the reasons for which the term contract of a certified employee may be nonrenewed; and 4) describe procedures for receiving recommendations from district administrators for the nonrenewal of term contracts.

Due process procedures for employees whose term contracts are being nonrenewed are clearly described in the TCNA. After receiving the recommendation of a school district administrator for the nonrenewal of a term contract and after considering the written evaluations of the employee involved, the board "in its sole discretion" may either accept or reject the recommendation. If the board accepts the recommendations, the employee must be notified in writing of the intent to nonrenew his or her contract no later than the 60th day before the last day of instruction required in the contract. The notice of the proposed nonrenewal must clearly state the reasons for which the recommendation for nonrenewal was made.

After receiving notice of the intent to nonrenew, an employee has the right to request a hearing before the board of trustees and must submit a written request for a hearing within ten days of receipt of the notice. The hearing may be open or closed at the employee's discretion. It is the duty of the board to adopt rules for the hearing and it may appoint an impartial third party to act as a hearing officer. During the hearing, the teacher has the right to be represented by counsel, to hear the evidence against him/her, to cross-examine witnesses and to present witnesses in refutation. The decision of the board to nonrenew must be based on the evidence presented at the hearing. If the board of trustees decides to nonrenew the term contract, the employee may appeal to the Commissioner of Education. When reviewing the written record of the hearing the Commissioner may not substitute his judgment for the judgment of the board unless the decision was clearly arbitrary, capricious, unlawful or not supported by "substantial evidence." Either party may appeal the decision of the Commissioner to a district court in Travis County.

School districts will sometimes have a decision to nonrenew a term contract overturned by the Commissioner. When this occurs, the district has most likely failed to meet one of six requirements (Schulze, 1988). These include failure of the district to recognize that the TCNA applied to the employee; failure to recognize the length of time during which a teacher can be considered "probationary;" failure of the board to consider the employee's written evaluations and the reasons for nonrenewal before giving notice; an incorrectly worded notice of nonrenewal; failure of the district to present "substantial evidence" that the nonrenewal was justified; and failure to provide the employee an opportunity to remediate the deficiency given as the reason for nonrenewal when remediation was clearly appropriate.

Dismissal During a Contract

It is also possible to remove a certified employee from a position during the life of a contract. For classroom teachers employed under continuing contracts, justification for such drastic action is found in T.E.C. 13.109 and include such things as "immorality, conviction of a felony or other crime involving moral turpitude, drunkenness, repeated failure to comply with administrative directives and school board policy, physical or mental incapacity preventing performance of the contract or repeated and continuing neglect of duties."

Under TCNA teachers may be discharged in mid-contract if the reasons are sufficiently serious (Schulze, 1989). Employees may be discharged during the life of a contract for such things as conduct that poses a serious threat of physical or emotional harm to students; for violent conduct or threats of violence; for refusal to comply with directives and board policy; for misappropriation or mismanagement of school funds; or for other conduct deemed to be "inconsistent with the employer-employee relationship."

Clearly, school administrators have the authority to remove nonperforming employees from the school system regardless of the type of contract under which they are employed. The effort requires time, skill and a knowledge of the law. None of these factors, however, should prevent an ethical administrator from fulfilling his or her duty to protect the educational welfare and the physical and emotional safety of students.

Teacher Appraisal

Texas is one of several states to implement a state-wide performance appraisal system for all public classroom teachers. The Texas Teacher Appraisal System (TTAS) was implemented in 1987 following two years of intensive development. The TTAS is based on research into effective teaching practices and is structured around five "domains," four of which can be observed in the classroom. Implicit in the TTAS is the belief that effective teaching behaviors are observable and are applicable across different grade levels and subject matters. Student learning, as demonstrated by student behaviors during a lesson, is the primary indicator of effective teacher performance.

The 1993 session of the Texas Legislature drastically altered the structure and scope of TTAS. Under the new dispensation, teachers are required to have a minimum of one observation a year done by one appraiser. The observation is to be followed up with a diagnostic-prescriptive conference, during which a growth plan may be developed for any teacher whose performance is less than satisfactory. The growth plan is designed to provide the teacher opportunities to demonstrate improvement in observed teaching deficiencies. The teacher may, at his or her discretion, request observation by a second appraiser. Dates and times of classroom observations are determined by the local school district. School districts are free to continue using the TTAS appraisal instrument or to develop their own performance measures using the site-based decision-making process.

The Career Ladder incentive system for classroom teachers has also been abolished. However, the $90.00 per ADA used to fund Career Ladder will continue to be paid to local school districts. This money is to be used as salary supplements for teachers on Career Ladder as of August 31, 1993. Qualified teachers will continue to receive their supplements as long as they remain in the school district which awarded them Career Ladder status. Any qualified teacher who changed districts prior to August 31, 1993 will also continue to receive Career Ladder salary supplements. Excess funds accruing to school district are to be used to augment all teachers' salaries.

Motivation

Schools are people-oriented organizations. Teachers, counselors, librarians, diagnosticians, principals and others are the human resources schools employ to achieve their mission, the education of children and young adults. If the people who are employed in the school are not highly motivated and committed to its mission, the school cannot be successful. Schools are effective only to the extent that they are able to motivate and develop the people working in them. Maximizing the human resources available requires a consistent effort on the part of the school administrator.

There are a number of human motivation theories which are useful to administrators. Among those are Maslow's Hierarchy of Needs, McGregor's Theory X and Theory Y and Herzberg's Motivation-Hygiene Theory. Each of these theories can provide school administrators with insight into human motivation which can be applied as s/he works with teachers and others in the school setting.

The Hierarchy of Needs

Maslow (1970) conceptualized human needs as a hierarchy and suggested that satisfied and productive people must achieve each of the levels of the hierarchy to attain maximum effectiveness in their lives. Maslow described five levels of needs which individuals must satisfy. These are:

- Physiological Needs.
- Safety Needs.
- Love Needs.
- Esteem Needs.
- Self-Actualization.

Knowledge of Maslow's hierarchy can be useful to school administrators in several ways. For example, administrators can work to insure that employees receive adequate salaries which enable them to satisfy the basic physiological needs for food, clothing and shelter. Furthermore, administrators can enhance employees feelings of safety through a consistent pattern of leadership. Consistent leadership indicates to employees how they will be treated and what types of behaviors are expected of them. Employees esteem needs can be met by recognizing their achievements and by involving them in making decisions in those areas of most concern to them. Finally, employees should be provided opportunities to become self-actualized individuals. This means that administrators must provide channels for employees to assume responsibility and to expand their commitment to what Glickman (1985) calls "a cause beyond oneself." Ultimately, self-actualization will be achieved through the empowerment of individuals within the organization.

Theory X and Theory Y

McGregor (1960) argues that administrative behavior is based upon assumptions administrators make about the basic character of their subordinates. In other words, McGregor maintains that an administrator's beliefs about basic human nature influences how s/he interacts with others, how s/he administers the school on a daily basis and even impacts the organizational structure of the school itself. McGregor identifies two approaches to thinking about human nature. The first of these he calls Theory X and the second one he calls Theory Y. Administrators who hold a Theory X view of their subordinates act on a distinct set of assumptions. Among these are that the average person dislikes work and will avoid it if possible; that workers must be coerced and controlled as much as possible; and that the typical worker wants to be directed and controlled by someone in authority. Administrators who hold Theory Y views of their subordinates operate on a completely different set of assumptions. They believe that work is a normal human activity, as natural as play and rest; that the way to secure commitment of workers to the organization's goals is through rewards and recognition; and given the proper environment, workers will seek and accept responsibility.

Theory X and Theory Y are personal philosophies which structure how an administrator interacts with subordinates in the work place. Theory X is incompatible with any organization which purports to be democratic and participatory because it is based on the premise that individuals must be tightly controlled and supervised. A Theory Y administrator, however, is more likely to expand opportunities for subordinates to assume responsibility and to demonstrate leadership in achieving organizational goals. Theory Y is compatible with a collaborative style of leadership.

Satisfiers and Dissatisfiers

Herzberg (1959; 1976) has developed a two factor theory of human motivation in the work place. He calls one set of factors which contribute positively to job satisfaction "motivators." A second, more negative set of factors which can be present in the work environment and contribute to job dissatisfaction Herzberg calls "hygiene" factors. Ironically, Herzberg's research found that the elimination of hygiene factors from the work environment did not lead to job satisfaction. Workers simply regarded the removal of these factors as their due. Fortunately, both motivation and hygiene factors in the work place factors are under the control of administrators.

Motivation factors which lead to job satisfaction for employees include such things as opportunities for achievement and advancement, greater job responsibility, recognition for work well done and the possibility of professional growth. Hygiene factors which contribute to job dissatisfaction include such things as salary, working conditions, lack of job security, administrative policy, poor interpersonal relations on the job and status.

Understanding the principles of human motivation will become increasingly important to school administrators as Texas moves into full implementation of site-based decision making. Site-based decision making, which is defined as "... a process for decentralizing decisions to improve the educational outcomes at every school campus through a collaborative effort..." (TEA, 1992, pg. II-l), will place a premium on the administrator's ability to motivate professional employees and to secure commitment to the goals of the school in ways much different than traditional directive methods. Collaboration, recognition of individual and group achievements, expanded opportunities for teacher responsibility in decision making and a focus on continuous staff development and learning are the hallmarks of successful site-based decision making. Providing this style of leadership to professional staff will require administrators who are motivators and developers of people. Otherwise attempts at site-based decision making will fail.

Staff Development

Staff development is an essential concomitant to effective personnel administration. It is, as Orlich (1989) says ". . . a basic and necessary component of the continuing preparation of teachers, administrators and other staff as they extend their professional or technical knowledge" (pg. 1). The concept of staff development is broader than the idea of in-service training. In-service training tends traditionally to be job-oriented and of immediate use to an individual of specific group of individuals. On the other hand, staff development implies ongoing and consistently significant activities which are aimed at the larger issues of developing problem-solving capabilities and leadership skills. The goal of staff development is to enhance human resource potential within the organization (Orlich, 1989).

There are two general perspectives on the purpose of staff development in school districts. These are the "defects" approach and the "growth" approach (Jackson, 1971). These orientations establish the underlying vision for staff development. The defects approach to staff development is based on a negative view of human potential. From this perspective staff development is seen as an attempt to "fix" some problem or defect in teachers who are seen as incompetent or unprepared. Typically defects-oriented staff development programs are viewed by participants as arbitrarily assigned and prescriptive. This type of staff development often focuses on the simplistic or behavioral aspects of teaching and stresses the most recent in educational fads as solutions to long-standing problems. Sponsors of defects-oriented staff development perceive teachers as problems to be fixed rather than as valuable assets to be cultivated.

The growth approach to staff development is premised on the belief that teaching and learning are complex activities which no professional ever completely masters. Growth-oriented staff development becomes a vehicle through which human potential can be maximized. Participants are viewed from a humanistic rather than mechanistic perspective. Every teacher is considered to be a continuous learner who wants to be involved in decision making. Staff development itself is perceived as an on-going and imaginative process rather than as a single event.

Central to the growth approach to staff development is a positive view of adults as learners. The concept of andragogy (Knowles, 1984; 1986) is useful in capitalizing on the unique traits of adult learners. Knowles believes that adult learners differ from juvenile learners in significant ways. For example, most adults possess a high degree of self-direction. Adults also possess life experiences that form a unique knowledge base. Adults learn best by solving problems. In terms of staff development the important implications of this model of adult learning are:

- adults can benefit from planning and conducting their own learning experiences;
- life experience is the key to self-actualization for adult learners;
- the best adult learning takes place when the need to know coincides with instruction;
- adults need the opportunity to apply what they have learned; and
- adults need some independently structured options for learning.

Knowles' model of adult learning means that there are appropriate and inappropriate ways to structure staff development. Appropriately structured staff development has certain characteristics. First, participants are involved in program planning. Second, participants themselves are made a part of the instruction. Third, alternatives to planned and scheduled program components are provided and fourth, participants have an opportunity to apply what they have learned in meaningful ways. Staff development based on a clear conception of how adults learn provides an invaluable tool for the enhancement of human resources.

Creating the Staff Development Program

The goals of personnel administration and staff development converge at three points. First, staff development is designed to enhance the professional competence of all current employees. This goal is closely related to the personnel administrator's goal of providing the best quality of employee for the school district. Second, staff development is a means of developing specific skills and competencies in selected personnel who are key to the improvement of the school district. Personnel administrators also strive to provide opportunities for growth and responsibility to employees. Finally, staff development is a method of promoting the continuous growth of all personnel in ways that are meaningful both to them individually and to the school district as an organization (Rebore, 1991). To achieve these goals, staff development efforts must be carefully planned and implemented.

Planning for effective staff development is a six-step process which begins with an understanding of the goals and objectives of the school district. District goals and objectives set the direction and the parameters of staff development efforts. The second step in planning for staff development involves assessing needs. Needs assessment must occur in two areas: the needs of the district as generated by the discrepancy between where the school district wants to be as reflected in its goals and objectives and where it is now; and the felt needs of staff for both their own personal growth and the need for the improvement of specific conditions within the school. Once a needs assessment has been completed, the goals and objectives of the staff development program can be established. Program goals should be based on the assessed needs of the district and the expressed needs of the professional staff. Program design, the fourth step in planning, is a process of matching available resources with an effective program delivery method. The fifth step in creating an effective staff development program is the delivery of the instruction itself. Delivery of instruction can occur in a variety of ways which are limited only by the creativity and imagination of those responsible for the program. Evaluation is the final step in the process and it can occur in several formats, but the simplest and most direct evaluation techniques are normally the best. For example, participants can be asked to rate the individual(s) conducting the program using some established criteria. The content of the program can also be evaluated as can the way in which the program was organized and the timing and location of the program. Follow-up evaluations are also important, especially when the goal of the staff development effort is the acquisition of new skills or techniques.

Developing Instructional Staff

Even though the number of days available for staff development has been curtailed through legislation, providing professional growth opportunities for teachers remains a major concern of school administrators. Ironically, the need for staff development of school professionals has never been greater as districts move toward the adoption of state-mandated, site-based decision making. The needs of the present aside, there remain solid reasons for the continuing professional development of classroom personnel. Among the more significant of these reasons are:

- Staying abreast of skills and knowledge in a subject area
- Staying current with changes in society as a whole
- Expanding teachers' instructional repertoire
- Keeping up with changes in technology.

Staff development for classroom teachers will continue to be a major effort for most school districts. However, the payoff from time and money invested wisely in staff development will be a well-educated cadre of professional educators who are skilled in bringing about improved learning opportunities for students.

Staff Development for Administrators

All school administrators, including superintendents and central office personnel, can profit from well-planned and conducted staff development. But principals, because of the critical position they occupy in the administrative hierarchy, may especially benefit from staff development. In terms of determining effectiveness the principal is the key person in the school. For this reason the staff development needs of principals deserve special attention.

Orlich (1989) notes several reasons for directing special attention to the development of school principals. First, the principal is responsible for the successful administration of the school. It is the principal who encourages and supports teachers' efforts to improve. Moreover, it is the principal's responsibility to allocate school resources of time and money and it is the principal who serves as the "gatekeeper" of reform efforts. Second, the principal is a major determiner of how the school operates instructionally. The principal sets the climate of the school and establishes the parameters for decision making with the staff. Finally, there is strong reason to believe that the influence of the principal is the key variable in determining the academic success of students within the school. Clearly, the professional development of such a key individual cannot be ignored or left to chance.

There are many avenues of staff development for school principals. Some of these are located within the school district itself and some are provided by outside agencies such as the professional associations and the LEAD Center. Delivery of program can take place through such things as assessment centers, seminars, retreats, conferences and other formats. But no matter what format the delivery of staff development might take, the purposes and goals of principal staff development efforts remain remarkably consistent. Among the more important of these purposes are:

- Developing of new skills and techniques
- Acquiring of current information
- Becoming familiar with new programs and requirements
- Solving problems which tend to recur
- Expanding knowledge about administrative theory and practice
- Preparing for expanded job responsibilities

As principals take on more responsibility for the success of the school and work to make site-based decision making a reality, their need for training and education will expand. Those needs can best be met through a well-conceived and thoughtfully delivered staff development program.

Summary

Public school personnel administration is a broadly defined task which encompasses far more than recruiting and placing school district employees. The major goal of personnel administration is to secure and retain the very best in human resources. This requires the school personnel administrator to be able to plan for human resource needs, to effectively recruit, select and place school district employees and to understand the impact of federal law on human resource planning. The school personnel administrator must also be knowledgeable about contract and certification requirements and the fundamentals of adverse action requirements under both the Term Contract Nonrenewal Act and Subchapter C of Chapter 13 of the Texas Education Code. School personnel administrators should understand the issues surrounding the Texas Teacher Appraisal system and some of its strengths and limitations. This is especially critical now as the state enters difficult economic times and the continued existence of the Career Ladder, the reward system for the TTAS, is in question. Personnel administrators must be cognizant of theories of motivation and be able to apply these theories appropriately to increase employee satisfaction on the job. It is important that the school administrators understand the relationship between personnel administration and the staff development program of the school district. This means understanding the unique way in which adults learn. Personnel administrators must also be aware of the differences between defect-oriented and growth-oriented staff development and their impact on staff morale. Finally, the personnel administrator must have a working knowledge of the planning, implementation and evaluation of effective staff development experiences. The task is a large one. But personnel administration can be one of the most exciting and personally rewarding activities in a school district.

References

Baas, A. (1990). *Background Checks on School Personnel*. ERIC Digest No. EA 55. Eugene, Oregon: ERIC Clearinghouse on Educational Management.

Glickman, C.D. (1985). *Supervision of Instruction: A Developmental Approach*. Boston: Allyn and Bacon.

Gosney v. Sonora I.S.D., 603 F. 2nd 522 (5th Circuit, 1979): 68-69.

Herzberg, F., Mausner, B., & Snyderman, B. (1959). *The Motivation to Work*. New York: Wiley and Sons.

Herzberg, F. (1976). One more time: how do you motivate employees? Part I. *The Managerial Choice*, Homewood, HI., pp 53-60.

Herzberg, F. (1976). One more time: how do you motivate employees? Part II *The Managerial Choice*, Homewood, Ill., pp 128-36.

Huling-Austin, L. & Cuellar, E. (1991). Defining an ethnically diverse teaching force. *Teacher Education and Practice*. Fall/Winter, pp 9-12.

Jackson, P.W. (1971). Old dogs and new tricks: observations on the continuing education of teachers, in *Improving In-Service Education: Proposals and Procedures for Change*. Boston: Alyn and Bacon.

Kemerer, F.R., & Hairston, J.B. (1990). *The Educator's Guide to Texas School Law*. Austin: University of Texas Press.

Kimbrough, R.B., (1985). *Ethics: A Course of Study for Educational Leaders*. Arlington, VA: The American Association of School Administrators.

Knowles, M.S. (1984). *Andragogy in Action*. San Francisco: Jossey-Bass.

Knowles, M.S. (1986). *Using Learning Contracts: Practical Approaches to Individualizing and Structuring Learning*. San Francisco: Jossey-Bass.

McGregor, D. (1960). *The Human Side of Enterprise*. New York: McGraw-Hill.

Maslow, A.H. (1970). *Motivation and Personality*. New York: Harper and Row.

Niece, R. (1983). The interview and personnel selection: is the process valid and reliable? *The Clearinghouse*, January, pp. 232-235.

Orlich, D.C. (1989). *Staff Development: Enhancing Human Potential*. Boston: Allyn and Bacon.

Rebore, R.W. (1991). *Personnel Administration in Education: A Management Approach*. Englewood Cliffs, New Jersey: Prentice Hall.

Schulze, E.W. (1988). Why districts lose cases under the Term Contract Nonrenewal Act. *Texas School Administrator's Legal Digest*, Denton, Texas.

Schulze, E.W. (1989). Terminating an employment contract: what type of conduct justifies the firing of a school employee in mid-contract? *Texas School Administrator's Legal Digest*, Denton, Texas.

Texas Commission of Human Rights Act, Article 522 IK, *Vernon's Annotated Revised Civil Statutes of the State of Texas*, Vol. 15. St. Paul: West Publishing Company, pp. 584-598.

Texas Education Agency (1988). *Texas Teacher Appraisal System Appraiser's Manual*. Austin: The Agency.

Texas Education Agency (1992). *Resource Guide on Site Based Decision Making and District Campus Improvement*. Austin: The Agency.

Texas Education Code Chapter 12, Subchapter B, Section 12.65 (e). *Texas School Law Bulletin*, pg. 107.

Texas Education Code Chapter 13, Subchapter B, Section 13-038. *Texas School Law Bulletin*. 1992, pp. 114-115.

Texas Education Code Chapter 13, Subchapter C, Section 13. 101-116. *Texas School Law Bulletin*, 1992 pp. 118-122.

Texas Education Code Chapter 13, Subchapter B, Section 13.038, *Texas School Law Bulletin*. pg. 114-115.

Texas Education Code Chapter 21, Subchapter A, Section 21.917. *Texas School Law Bulletin*, 1992, pg. 326.

Texas Education Code Chapter 21, Subchapter G, Section 21. 201-211, *Texas School Law Bulletin*, 1992, pp. 274-276.

Texas Education Code Chapter 21, Subchapter Z, Section 21.9 17, *Texas School Law Bulletin*, pp. 326-327.

Texas Education Code Chapter 23, Subchapter B, Section 23.28. *Texas School Law Bulletin*. 1992, pg. 350.

Financing Schools in Texas

*William D. Alvarez**

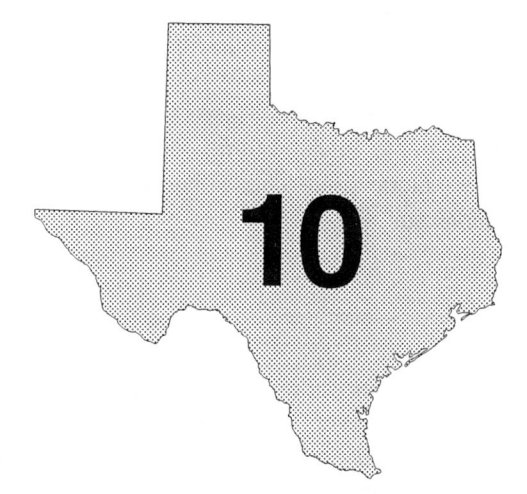

At the heart of the Texas school funding crisis is the question of distribution of wealth. The basic unit for financing public education in Texas is the local school district and the basic funding mechanism is the property tax. However, property wealth varies greatly from one district to another. The funding of public education in Texas has been marked by piecemeal attempts to make up for the disparities of the system. In so doing, Texas has perpetuated a system of inequity based upon what State District Judge Harley Clark called the "irrational accident of school district lines."

In 1875, the Texas legislature voted to allow incorporated towns and cities taxing authority for educational purposes. The following year, the new Texas Constitution established a permanent endowment, the Permanent School Fund, based largely on the value of half the land in the public domain. The revenue from this fund was apportioned to schools on a per student basis. Beginning in 1877, payments were distributed at $3.59 per student. Although, other potential sources of revenue for state education funding were available, funds from the Permanent School Fund were virtually the only actual state educational expenditure until 1915. This created the dependency upon local tax revenues by town schools.

In 1900, nearly all Texas students lived in 11,460 rural school districts. The first attempt at school equalization came in 1915, when the state legislature appropriated $1 million in school aid for rural districts that taxed at the maximum legal rate. In 1918, the legislature established a state

---

* Brian C. Stewart provided major contributions for the third edition of this chapter.
  Eugene T. Conners authored this chapter in the first and second editions. His work is used in part.

property tax to pay for textbooks and allowed the use of general revenue funds for education. To address a funding crisis the following year, Governor William P. Hobby used the 1918 provision to issue the first state general appropriation for education. Every subsequent state budget has since included an education appropriation. However, the bulk of funding of public education is provided by the local property tax which generates disparities in wealth among districts.

An opportunity has been afforded the people of Texas to accept the challenge and responsibility to use the demand for equity as a means to restructure and revitalize its schools and state. If long-term approaches rather than quick, simplistic solutions are adopted, then real progress may result.

School Finance and the State

The responsibility for providing an educational system rests with the individual states. While the federal government does become involved in educational funding in certain situations, the large majority of the funds are acquired at either the state or local level. The states' first involvement with education occurred in 17th century Massachusetts when that colony's General Court (general assembly) passed the Old Deluder Satan Act of 1647. The act provided for compulsory education of children where townships had 50 or more families. The funds to pay for this schooling were to be derived from the taxation of property.

Shortly after the passage of the Act, other New England colonies began invoking similar legislation. A general pattern toward education and school finance was developed. This model has come to be known as the New England Pattern. The New England Pattern had four basic elements. First, there was compulsory education. Second, the local township was to provide the educational program. Third, there was state supervision of schools. And fourth, education would be paid for by public funds acquired through local taxation. This pattern spread throughout the nation and set a trend in school finance—that trend being the local governance and fiscal support of education.

Ellwood P. Cubberley

The financing of public schools changed little from the 17th Century until the early 1900s when Ellwood P. Cubberley began researching how public education was funded. Cubberley was a doctoral student at Teachers College, Columbia University, at the time. His dissertation subject was the apportionment of educational funds, and the subsequent publishing of his dissertation, *School Funds and Their Apportionment*, quickly became the cornerstone of educational finance theory (Cubberley, 1906). Even though Cubberley's findings focused upon New York State school funding in the early 1900s, his observations and conclusions are applicable in Texas today. In brief, Cubberley's work made four observations:

1. There was an unequal distribution of wealth among school districts in New York.
2. As a result of this unequal distribution of wealth, the quality of education varied greatly from school district to school district.
3. No child should receive an inferior education due to the accident of where he/she lived. Consequently, Cubberley felt that educational quality should be equalized among school districts.
4. The state was the more appropriate agency to equalize educational quality.

It is important to place Cubberley's findings in historical perspective. Until this time, education was almost solely the product of local government. Over 80 percent of educational funds were supplied by the local school district with the state's contributions approaching less than 20 percent. The federal government was supplying no significant amount of funds to education.

The Evolution of the Equalization Model

Following Cubberley's findings in the early 1900s, one of the chief goals of school finance experts was to equalize education within states. Since 1910, there have been several attempts to correct educational inequality in various ways. One of the most popular and efficient ways is to utilize some variation of the equalization model as originally developed by George Strayer and Robert Haig during the 1920s.

The Strayer-Haig Equalization Model

George Strayer, a colleague of Cubberley's, and one of Strayer's associates, Robert Haig, supplied the bridge between theoretical school finance reform and the practical application of equalization. In 1933, Strayer and Haig outlined a model for equalizing educational opportunity in a state regardless of the relative wealth or lack of wealth of local school districts (Mort, 1933).

The equalizatlon model, which has come to be called the "Strayer-Haig Equalization Model," contains several basic elements. First, every school district in the state or its political subdivision would levy a uniform tax with identical assessment ratios and identical millage rates (if such a tax is the property tax). Because of the diversity of property values in a state, some school districts would be able to generate large sums of money per student while others would be able to raise only a minimum of funds. The districts would then be ranked from the poorest to the wealthiest. The amount of funds per student which the wealthiest school district was currently spending became the "minimum foundation program." In essence, every student in the state was to receive an education equal to the students who lived in the wealthiest district. Obviously, the poorer districts could not afford such an expensive education, so the state would supply the additional funds needed to bring the poorer districts up to the level of the wealthiest.

The Strayer-Haig-Mort Equalization Model

While Strayer's and Haig's development of the basic equalization model was a giant step forward in school finance reform, their model had several serious flaws when put to practical application. One of George Strayer's students at Teachers College, Columbia University, corrected some of the shortcomings in the basic equalization model. Paul Mort, known as one of the outstanding professors of educational administration, made several alterations to the basic equalization model which made its use practical and desirable. Mort found three problems with the Strayer-Haig Model. First, he recognized that very few states possessed the fiscal resources to raise all school districts' level of funding equal to that of the wealthiest. In most states, there simply were not enough funds to provide for such a costly educational program. To correct this deficiency, Mort developed the concept of the "key district." The key district is the (approximately) 80 percent wealthiest school district in the state. This key district would set the minimum foundation program instead of the wealthiest district. In this manner, the educational program would not be set unrealistically high. On the other hand, the minimum foundation program is set considerably higher than merely "average."

Secondly, Paul Mort was also a pragmatist. He realized that the wealthier school districts were frequently the most politically powerful. Few of the wealthiest districts relished the idea of having poorer school districts receiving large amounts of state aid while they received none. Consequently, the equalization model possessed some political shortcomings. Mort attempted to neutralize these political shortcomings by developing the concept of "adaptability." Adaptability is simply the state giving every school district a flat per student grant (perhaps $100 per student). In this way, wealthier school districts can no longer claim that they are receiving no state funds. The adaptability grant is given over and above the minimum foundations program which is determined by the key district.

And third, Mort, realizing that different types of educational programs have different costs, developed the "weighted pupil" concept. Programs were not to be funded at a flat per student amount since some programs may cost considerably more than others to operate. Therefore, students would be weighted to account for the increased cost of certain activities. Assume that a state can educate the average student for $3,000 per year. Also assume that students being taught through homebound instruction cost five times as much to educate. Then all homebound students would be weighted 5.0 and the homebound program would receive $15,000 per student instead of the $3,000 per student for the average program. In this manner, Paul Mort was adjusting the funding of education according to the educational needs and costs of the programs.

(In the above example, it is highly unlikely that a student would be on homebound instruction for more than a few months. Therefore, the actual cost of the homebound instruction would be considerably less than the $15,000 used in the example.)

The Strayer-Haig-Mort-Johns Equalization Model

The last major contribution to the equalization model was made by Roe L. Johns, a former student of Paul Mort's at Teachers College, Columbia University. In observing the utility of the Strayer-Haig-Mort equalization model, Johns realized that all incentive and encouragement were missing from the model. Not only were additional expenditures on education not encouraged; but, in many variations of the model, such additional expenditures were prohibited. Johns believed that every state had several "light-house" school districts. These are school districts whose communities take pride in their educational programs; these school districts are the developers of new and innovative programs; these school districts like to and want to spend additional money on education. Johns felt that prohibiting these school districts from spending additional funds was a detriment to education. Therefore, he developed the concept of "local leeway."

Within the concept of local leeway, local school districts are permitted to spend additional funds on education (if they want to but only up to a certain level). Local leeway may, for example, allow a local school district to spend up to an additional $1,000 per student on education if they wish. Although local leeway does "dis-equalize" the equalization model to some degree, it is generally felt that the educational benefits of such a concept outweigh the relatively minor inequity created by its use. However, if states elect the local leeway provision, a cap (maximum limit) must be enforced to insure that grave inequities are not created.

Legal Assaults on School Finance

Since the 1930s, there have been countless legal attempts to change school finance formulas. In general, these legal assaults have come in four waves or generations. The first wave of school finance litigation is known as the "apportionment" cases. In these court cases, taxpayers were challenging the methods by which states apportion funds back to the local school divisions. These cases were a direct result of the implementation of the equalization models. In these cases, taxpayers in wealthy districts alleged that it was unfair for the state to give their tax money to poor school districts. The taxpayers claimed that tax dollars should be spent in the local school district where the money was generated. The courts disagreed unanimously. Court after court held that states had the right to reapportion funds in an attempt to equalize educational opportunity (*Sawyer v. Gilmore*, 83 A. 673, Maine, 1912; *Miller v. Korns*, 140 N.E. 773, Ohio, 1925; *Miller v. Childers*, 238 P. 204, Oklahoma, 1924; *Dean v. Coddington*; 131 N.W. 2d 700, South Dakota, 1964). This generation of litigation ended in the early 1960s.

The second generation or wave of school finance cases concerned the "revenue" aspect of educational funding. The revenue aspect is the collecting of school funds through taxes. Ever since the development of education in this country, schools have been funded almost exclusively through the property tax. Unfortunately, the property tax is one of the most regressive taxes because it impacts on the poor much more harshly than the wealthy. The revenue cases were usually brought by poor people who claimed that the method of obtaining school funds was unfair and that educational funds should be obtained through a more equitable procedure. Although there have been literally hundreds of these cases filed throughout the United States, there are two major cases which are most commonly referenced when examining the revenue era. In 1971, a California state court, in *Serrano v. Priest* (487 P.2d 1241, 96 Cal. Rptr. 601), agreed that the method of obtaining revenue was unfair and discriminated against the poor. In 1973, the United States Supreme Court ruled in *Rodriguez v. San Antonio School District* (411 U. S. 1, 93 S. Ct. 1278, 36 L. Ed. 2d 16) that while there may be discrimination on the basis of wealth, it was a matter for the state courts and was not a federal concern. Even though the Supreme Court's decision in *Rodriguez* ended revenue litigation in federal courts, there have been many major cases at the state level with *Robinson v. Cahill* (119 N.J. Super. 40, 303 A. 2d 273, 1973) and *Edgewood Independent School District v. Kirby* (case No. 362, 516, Tex. Dist. Ct., August 27, 1987; No. 3-87190-CV, Tex. Ct. App., Austin, Dec 14, 1988 [October 2, 1989, January 22, 1991]), being two of the most notable.

The third generation of school finance cases is one which is frequently referred to as the "equal educational opportunity" cases. These cases are brought by parents claiming that their child has a "right" to an appropriate educational program regardless of its costs. Almost all cases in this era have been won by the parents. Such famous cases as *PARC v. Commonwealth of Pennsylvania* (343 F. Supp. 279, PA, 1972), *Mills v. Board of Education* (348 F. Supp. 866, D.C., 1972), *Hobson v. Hansen* (269 F. Supp. 401, 1967), and *Irving I.S.D. v. Tatro* (104 S. Ct. 3371, 1984) were concerned with the educational rights of handicapped students regardless of the costs of educating these children. The high amount of legal activity in this area had led to the passage of federal law PL 94-142 as well as various other state laws protecting the educational right of handicapped students.

The fourth wave of litigation has been referred to as the "adequacy of funding" generation of school finance litigation. These cases are the logical result of two social events. First, the high degree of inflation in the late 1970s and early 1980s and second, the reduced availability of federal and state funds to local school districts which places an extreme financial burden on most local school districts. Much of school finance literature speaks of the "partnership" of education. In theory, the federal government, state government, and local government are to be partners in the educational funding system. During the 1970s, federal and state funding to education generally increased which lessened the burden on local school districts to fund educational programs. However, changes in governmental policy drastically reduced federal funding during the 1980s. Additionally, inflation, taxpayer revolt (e.g. Proposition 13 in California), and a general apathy towards education have caused state funding of education to be less than funded in the past.

Therefore, the local education unit's percentage of funding has increased dramatically. This undesirable situation becomes even worse when it is coupled with the increased tendency of the states to meddle in the affairs of the local districts as the result of education reform. In essence, the local school district is under much more state regulation and scrutiny while receiving less money for its educational programs. The inequity of this situation has not escaped notice by local education officials. In response to these events, some local school districts have filed suits against various states alleging that the state is not "adequately" funding its share of education. These suits are an attempt to force the states to increase their share of the educational partnership. The results of these suits have yet to be seen, but one thing is becoming abundantly clear, local school officials are going to resist attempts by the state to increase regulatory control of education unless additional state funds are also provided.

School Finance and the Federal Government

The federal government's involvement in educational funding is a fairly recent phenomena. Since education is a responsibility of the individual states, the federal government must be careful when involved in school finance matters. Article 1, Section 8, of the United States Constitution (the "general welfare clause"), gives the federal government some limited authority to aid education. Traditionally, this aid has been quite small.

The first significant degree of federal funding of education occurred in 1785 with the passage of *The Ordinance of 1785* (commonly referred to as the Northwest Ordinance). The ordinance provided that the sixteenth section of every township shall be reserved "for the maintenance of public schools." The reason the sixteenth section was chosen was because it was one of the four center sections in the six-by-six (36 part) townships.

In 1862, Congress passed the *Morrill Act* which gave 30,000 acres (or its equivalent in money) to each state for each representative and senator. The lands could be sold and the proceeds could be used for education, or educational institutions could be built upon these lands; hence, the terms "landgrant colleges and universities."

The *Smith-Hughes Act* was passed in 1917 and provided funds for vocational education at the public school level. It is interesting to note that even in the early 1900s, federal funding was for purposes rather than for education in general.

After World War II, the federal government began to pour large quantities of money into education. However, such funding was always categorical in nature. This means that the funds were to be used for only specific educational purposes determined by Congress. The 1958 *National Defense Education Act* (NDEA) was passed in response to the Soviet threat made apparent by the Russian satellite Sputnik I. These funds were to be used for the areas of science, mathematics, and modern foreign languages. NDEA was an attempt to upgrade American technology through the educational process.

In 1965, Congress passed the largest appropriation to education, *The Elementary and Secondary Education Act of 1965* (ESEA). The Act is the most important measure affecting public school finance up to this time. It provided aid to public school through five categories or titles of funding:

    Title I - Underprivileged Children
    Title II - Libraries, Textbook and Media Equipment
    Title III - Supplementary Education Center
    Title IV - Educational Research
    Title V - State Department of Education

In 1975, *ESEA* was extended with several alterations. Among the additions were Title IX which was added to prohibit sex discrimination in public schools, the Buckley Amendment which was added to protect the rights of the student in school records, and several categories of the previous titles were collapsed or eliminated. ESEA was still the single most important element in federal funding of education.

In 1981, the Reagan administration put the *Education Consolidation and Improvement Act* (ECIA) into effect. Its purpose was to consolidate the various titles of funding categories into a more manageable form. In essence, federal funding fell into three groups:

    EHA Title VI-B (PL 94-142) — Special Education Funds
    Chapter I — Disadvantaged Students
    Chapter II — Consolidates Most Other ESEA Titles

Also, as part of *ECIA*, the federal government shifted much of its regulatory duties to the states. The act also provided considerably less funding to education than what had been previously enjoyed by local school districts. It is ironic that the federal government's response to the massive educational reform movements of the 1980s was to lower its level of fiscal support.

Educational Finance in Texas

Educational finance in Texas has a long and colorful history. The first major attempt to fund public education in Texas occurred in 1839 with the passage of the *Education Act of 1839*. The primary purpose of the act was to provide public lands that supported public schools (the act was used as a basis of the *Morrill Act of 1862*). In 1853, San Antonio established the first comprehensive free public school system in Texas. Like most of the rest of the country, schools were funded almost exclusively through the local property tax. Various legislation was passed from 1840 through 1861 establishing a Permanent School Fund (PSF). However, the effects of the Civil War devastated Texas' permanent school fund.

In 1869, Texans adopted the *Constitution of 1869*. The newly adopted constitution had several provisions that affected education. Twenty-five percent of the general revenue was to go to public education and all sales of public land were earmarked for the Permanent School Fund. Compulsory education was required for all children from eight to fourteen years old (children from six to eight were allowed to attend public schools but were not required to do so. Strengthening of the state education agency took place, and a provision that required local school districts to provide for school buildings with a 10-month school year supported through local property taxes was implemented as well.

From 1870 to 1970, Texas school finance evolved in much the same way as school finance in other states. Bills regulating local taxation for education purposes, state studies to determine the quality of public education in Texas, and state aid to rural education were all passed and/or amended many times during this period. In 1949, the Gilmer-Aiken Committee (which was formed by the state legislature in 1947) proposed the establishment of a "Minimum Foundation Program (MFP)." During the next year, many of the recommendations of the Gilmer-Aiken Committee were implemented. The Texas Education Agency (TEA) was created, a minimum foundation program was established (with the state funding 80 percent of the program), and the ability for local school districts to fund above the state level allowed.

In 1965, Governor John Connally appointed the Governor's Committee on Public School Education. In 1968, the committee published its report, *The Challenge and the Chance*. The report called for a complete overhaul of public education in Texas, consolidation of small school districts, a more comprehensive minimum foundation program, and increase state funding of public education. Unfortunately, the report and its recommendations were ignored by the state legislature.

In 1971, the federal district court issued its opinion in *Rodriguez v. San Antonio Independent School District*. The district court's opinion was very similar to that in *Serrano v. Priest* (the California case that began the "revenue" generation of school finance litigation). The court ruled Texas' method of funding public education to be in violation of the "equal protection" clause of the Fourteenth amendment to the United States Constitution. The court found that students in poor school districts received an inferior level of education compared to the students who lived in wealthy school districts. The court also noted that the tax rate in the poor school districts was frequently higher than the rate in wealthy districts.

Unlike the *Serrano* decision, the court found the system of funding to be in violation of the federal constitution—not the state constitution. The decision was appealed to the United States Supreme Court who, in 1973, reversed the federal district court's opinion. The Supreme Court felt that the manner in which the state chooses to fund education is a state concern and not a federal issue. (Note: the Serrano decision was unaffected by this decision since it was based on the California Constitution and not the Federal Constitution). Texas had dodged a bullet in 1973.

While there were some attempts to correct the inequities of the funding formula, during the next few years, the oil boom economy of the 1970s distracted the state legislature.

In 1983, Governor Mark White appointed the Select Committee on Public Education to investigate the status of public education in Texas. The committee, chaired by billionaire H. Ross Perot, issued a report calling for sweeping reform and changes in the Texas public school system. The report ultimately led to the passage of House Bill 72 (HB 72) in 1984 which included finance reforms (Walker & Kirby, 1986).

Edgewood v. Kirby

Local school districts were placed under great pressure as a result of HB 72. The reforms demanded much more money to be spent on education. While the state had increased its funding of education, local school districts were still bearing the brunt of the reform movement. In 1986, a suit was filed in the Travis County District Court (the court required to hear such education suits) alleging that the state system of funding was unconstitutional. The case, *Edgewood Independent School District v. Kirby* was very similar to the older *Rodriguez* case except that it alleged that the current practices violated state law (not federal law). In August, 1987, Judge Harley Clark ruled that the Texas system of financing public schools was in violation of the Texas Equal Protection Clause as well as several other state constitutional provisions and laws. Clark held that the public school students of Texas possess a "fundamental right" to education and that "equality of access to funds is the key and is one of the requirements of this fundamental right." Some of the data that led Judge Clark to his conclusions are:

There existed a range of expenditures per student unit in Texas of from $1,000 to $9,523 (a ratio of 1 to 9.5).

The 150,000 students living in the highest spending districts had more than twice as much money spent on their education as the 150,000 students living in the lowest spending districts.

The range of local tax rates ranged from $.09 to $1.55 per $100 property value. The higher rates were not paid by the higher spending school districts but rather the lower spending districts.

The average tax rate required in the 100 districts in the bottom range of wealth was more than 20 times as much as the average rate required in the 100 districts in the top range of the wealth.

Property tax bases ranged from $20,000 per student in the poorest school district to $14,000,000 per student in the wealthiest district. The state average was approximately $240,687 per student in 1989.

As a result of the gross inequities that Judge Clark found in the relative wealth of local school district and, subsequently, their funding of public education, the district court judge ruled Texas' system of financing public education to be unconstitutional and that "the current system will be set aside."

The court also felt that the use of so many small school districts in the state was one of the primary factors in the funding issue. The court concluded that "local control, as it exists in Texas, is not a compelling interest sufficient to support the state's school finance system." Judge Clark ordered the state legislature to rework the state's funding system and to create a new school system with a greatly reduced number of school districts. Needless to say, Judge Clark's opinion caught the attention of many public officials.

The case was appealed to the Court of Appeals of the Third District of Texas. In December, 1988, the Circuit Court of Appeals overturned Judge Clark's District Court's opinion in a 2 to 1 vote (No. 3-87190-CV, Tex. Ct. App., Austin, Dec. 14, 1988). The circuit court majority acknowledged that while there were great problems with the Texas school funding system, that none of these inequities were sufficiently serious to be in violation of the various state constitutional and statutory provisions on which Judge Clark based his opinion. The circuit court also concluded that the district court judge erred in finding that education constitutes a fundamental property right:

> Education, although vital, does not rise to the same level as the right to engage in freedom of speech or to exercise religion free of governmental interference, both rights which have long been recognized as fundamental and entitled to protection under both the federal and state constitutions.

On October 2, 1989, the Texas Supreme Court overturned the ruling of the Third Court of Appeals and sustained the original ruling of District Court Judge Clark. The high court did not, however, address the issue of "equal protection." Instead, the justices decided that the Texas funding system violated "fiscal neutrality" and required the state to provide the public school students of Texas "substainable equal access" to educational revenues. The court also did not specifically address the issues of consolidation or locally enriched educational programs.

As a result of the Supreme Court's ruling, the Texas legislature began a special session to address the educational funding system in February, 1990. The legislature was unable to agree on a new funding scheme during that initial special session and were called back into a second special session in April, 1990. The second session also failed to accomplish the task when the governor vetoed newly passed legislation because it used a ½ cent increase in the state's sales tax to fund the new proposals. On May 1, 1990, the legislature began a third special session to resolve the school finance crisis. Once again, the legislature passed a bill that was vetoed by Governor Clements because of an increase in state taxes to fund the revisions. The senate voted to override Clements' veto but the Texas house was unable to gather enough votes for the override.

On June 1, 1990, the court-appointed master unveiled his plan which would have taken effect if the legislature and governor did not take immediate action. The plan was quickly labeled the "Robin Hood" plan because it redistributed existing state funds from wealthy school districts to poor school districts. Throughout Texas, the people expressed their anger regarding the plan to their elected representatives. The strong public reaction forced Clements and the legislature conference committee to compromise on a new plan. The general legislature passed and Clements signed a new education finance bill that would pump an additional $528 million into the public schools by raising the state sales tax by ¼ cent.

The new educational finance bill, labeled Senate Bill 1 (SB 1), provided for numerous changes in governance as well as alterations in the school funding process. The new bill, however, did not make any significant changes in the method of funding public education. Rather, it contributed additional funds to education and created several new funding categories. Some of the highlights of Senate Bill 1 are:

- Raised the basic allotment of the foundation school program to $1,910 (1990-91) and $2,128 (1991-92).
- Altered some of the student weightings in the areas of special programs.
- Developed a second level (or tier) of state funding over and above the foundation program. The intent was to equalize funding among poor and wealthy school districts. 450 million dollars were to be allocated for this purpose. School districts that levy additional local property taxes (above $.034) would receive an additional $18.25 for each weighted student average daily attendance. The maximum tax rate compensated under this provision would be $.36 unless changed by tax code.
- The state would utilize the existing "Price Differential Index" developed by the State Board of Education (SBOE) until 1991-92 when a new "Cost Education Index" would go into effect.
- Increased funding for bilingual and vocational education students.
- Increased funding for career ladder (increase limited to $90 per student).
- Provided emergency funding for school districts in dire need of capital outlay facilities. This provision was retroactive from 1984 but would only take effect if funds were available.
- Local districts would be allowed to enrich their educational programs by increasing their local tax rate and would be provided equalized enrichment funds of up to $.37 in 1990-91 and $.48 for 1991-92 and beyond.
- $5 million was to be provided for innovative educational programs.
- $30 per student in ADA was to be provided for a technology fund.
- Provided guaranteed amounts or "grandfathering" of certain types of funds should the district experience drastic loss of ADA or be unable to attain state finance goals even though state minimum tax rates were in effect.

In July, 1990, State District Judge Scott McCown held hearings to determine if the new funding formula met the Texas Supreme Court's guidelines. Evidence presented at the hearings suggested that the new formula did little to equalize educational funding and only raised state funding levels. The following example illustrates some of the problems of the new funding scheme: At this point in time, Samnorwood ISD was ranked 165th in property wealth (only 164 districts were wealthier and 887 were poorer. Samnorwood ISD possessed approximately $340,000 of taxable property per student (97th percentile). Its tax rate was close to the state average. Yet, under the new plan, Samnorwood ISD would receive a 20 percent increase in state funding, raising its per student expenditure to about $4,138. Mercedes ISD, on the other hand, was one of Texas' poorest school districts. It had only $28,407 in taxable property per student (2,093). Mercedes ISD's tax rate was almost identical to Samnorwood's yet Mercedes ISD would only receive about a five percent increase in state funding under the new plan (to about $3,049). The inequities shown in this example illustrate the inherent problems of equity that SB 1 failed to address.

On September 25, 1990, Judge McCown ruled that the new funding formula that took four special legislative sessions and six months to pass was unconstitutional. Judge McCown, stating that Senate Bill 1 was not the dramatic structural reform that the Supreme Court saw as being required, wrote:

> The rich districts are left rich, the poor districts poor. The rich can still raise revenue through local property taxes that the poor cannot. The poor will receive funds to equalize the difference, but only up to a level of bureaucratically and legislatively determined "adequacy" not to the level of the real difference in educational opportunity.

While Judge McCown did admit that no plan can equalize the state's districts 100 percent, he also felt that the new plan used an artificial level of educational funding for equalization purposes rather than a real day-to-day operational level of expenses. Judge McCown also felt that the new plan did little to aid the poorer districts in funding school facilities. However, he did state that consolidation of school districts was not required in order to develop an acceptable formula nor did he disallow the right of wealthy school districts to "enhance" their educational programs by increasing their local tax rate over-and-above the state's requirements.

The district court allowed the newly enacted formula developed in Senate Bill 1 to be utilized until September 1, 1991 when a new finance scheme would go into effect. The legislature and the governor would have to come up with an acceptable plan or the court-appointed master's plan would go into effect on that date.

On January 22, 1991, the Supreme Court of Texas (which had taken jurisdiction on the appeal of Judge McCown's ruling) ruled unanimously in upholding the district court's unconstitutional ruling on the Senate Bill 1 funding formula. The Texas Supreme Court stated "The fundamental flaw of Senate Bill 1 lies not in any particular provisions but in its overall failure to restructure the system . . . . (SB 1) fails to provide direct and close correlation between a district's tax effort and the educational resources available to it." The court suggested consolidation of school districts as one avenue to gain greater efficiency in school finances; another suggestion was tax base consolidation. The high court said the lower court erred in not enforcing the mandate of *Edgewood I* with respect of the time deadline and reset the deadline for April 1, 1991. The deadline was later extended to April 15, 1991 with the provision that if the state legislature met the deadline with a new law to be in place by September 1, 1991, the current arrangement of finance would be allowed until September 1 (*Edgewood v. Kirby II*, Number D-0378).

In response to the Texas Supreme Court's ruling which upheld the district court's finding that Senate Bill 1 was unconstitutional, the Texas legislature passed a new school finance reform bill in April 1991. The new legislation, known as Senate Bill 351 and House Bill 2885 shifted hundreds of millions of dollars in property taxes from districts with high property values to districts with low property values. The 92-57 House vote and 21-10 Senate vote came four days before Judge McCown's deadline. The new funding system called for a minimum tax rate in each of the "educational districts" (newly devised county education districts—CEDs) to allocate $2,000 per student in 1991-92 with the amount becoming $2,800 in four years. The reform bill also added five school days to create a 180-day calendar and new state aid devoted to classroom technology.

After hearing arguments related to SB 351 and HB 2885 during the summer of 1991, Judge McCown upheld the school finance law as constitutional on August 7, 1991. Judge McCown warned the state legislature that it must abide by its commitment to fund the law fully. The state legislature passed a record two-year budget on August 13, 1991 which included $2.4 billion to pay for the new school finance plan.

Under Senate Bill 351, a number of changes came about in the way Texas funds its public school districts, changes designed to guarantee that all Texas school districts would have equal access to those funds needed to provide a good educational program. The new legislation was a dramatic departure from the way local property wealth was used to determine local school funding. The basic premise was to pool property wealth through the utilization of the newly created county education districts. Prior to Senate Bill 351, the state's richest districts, those who held 15 percent of Texas' property wealth, were not included in equalization formulas used to calculate state aid. These districts, under Senate Bill 351, were pooled with other districts with their taxes being shared. Proponents of the new finance system claimed that disparity in property wealth between rich and poor school districts which was 716-to-1 prior to Senate Bill 351 would decrease to 6-to-1 once the wealth was pooled and redistributed.

Each school district was guaranteed a basic allotment of state and local funds per student. Beyond the basic allotment, each district was guaranteed additional state monies for each penny of tax it levied above the county education district tax rate. This second tier of income could be used to enrich programs, build facilities and pay off debt (*Fiscal Notes*, 1991).

Highlights of Senate Bill 351 and House Bill 2885
Current School Finance Plan

1. Facilities

   Added facilities to Foundation School Program (FSP) through a guaranteed yield program of assistance. All facilities constructed after September 1, 1992, must meet State Board of Education (SBOE) standards in order to be financed from state and local tax funds. For the

1992-93 year only, $50 million would be set aside for emergency instructional facilities grants from SBOE. The SBOE would establish procedures and qualifications for the grants.

2. County Education Districts

    County education districts were created to include all school districts, including 31 multi-county CEDs. Each school district is in the CED where the school district was assigned in the 1990-91 Texas School Directory. If a school district is assigned to a county other than the county where the district's administrative offices are located, the district may apply to the Commissioner for reassignment, and the Commissioner shall grant the request unless a CED with greater than $280,000 value per weighted student would result. Before each regular legislative session, the LEB shall review the taxable value (SPTB value) of property in each CED and recommend changes so that no CED contains taxable value (SPTB value) in excess of $280,000 per weighted ADA.

    Each CED is an independent school district established by consolidation of local school districts within its boundaries for the limited purpose of exercising a portion of the taxing power previously authorized by the voters in those school districts and for the purpose of distributing CED revenues to the school districts.

3. Basic Allotment

    The Basic Allotment would be:

1991-92	$2,200
1992-93	$2,400
1993-94	$2,600 (or greater amount adopted by FSFBC)
1994-95	$2,800 (or greater amount adopted by FSFBC)

    A greater amount may be established each year by appropriation.

4. Technology Funds

    Technology allotments to begin in 1992-93 were included under the FSP entitlements.

1992-93	$30 per ADA
1993-94	$35 per ADA
1994-95	$40 per ADA
1995-96	$45 per ADA
1996-97	$50 per ADA (and thereafter)

    Reductions may be made before distribution.

5. Local Share of Program Cost (Tier One)

    Each CED would provide the local fund assignment (LFA-local share) of the FSP.

    LFA = TR x DPV

    where:

    DPV = Sum of the SPTB values for all school districts in the CED (for 1991-92; for 1992-93 and after, the SPTB shall determine taxable values for CEDs and each component district).

TR = Required tax rate, which is:

1991-92	$0.72
1992-93	$0.82
1993-94	$0.92
1994-95	$1.00

A CED must raise its total local share of the FSP. The funds are reallocated to school districts in the CED according to prescribed law.

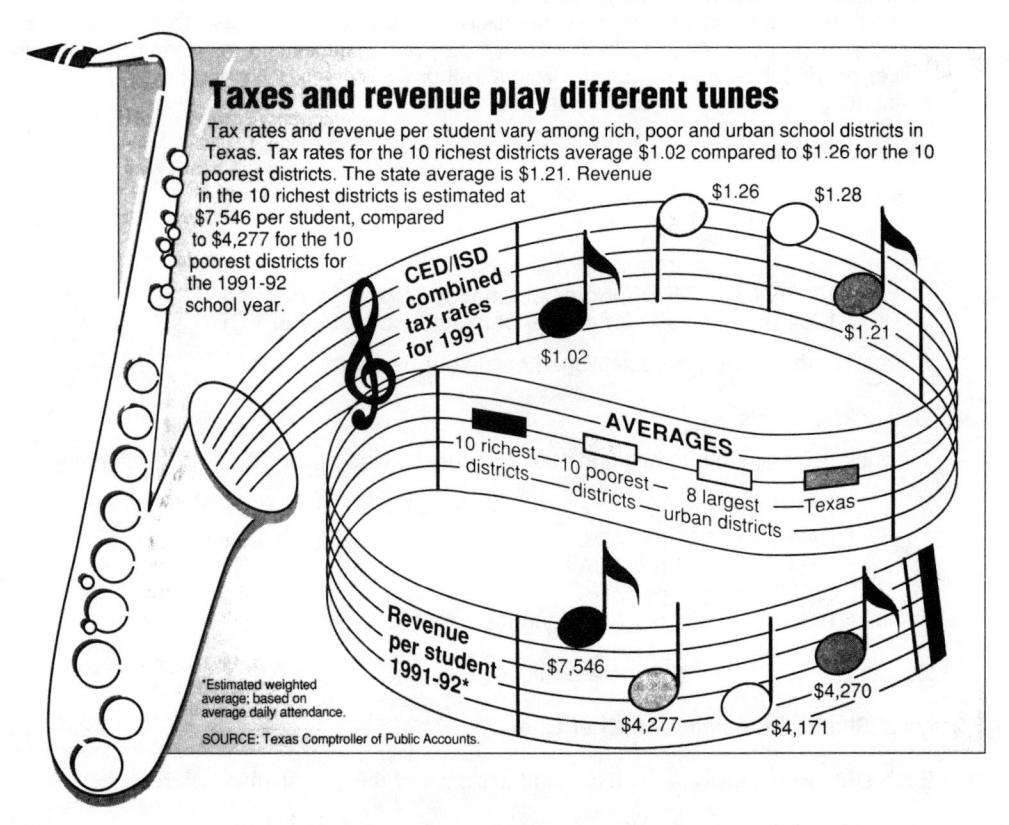

Taxes and revenue play different tunes

Tax rates and revenue per student vary among rich, poor and urban school districts in Texas. Tax rates for the 10 richest districts average $1.02 compared to $1.26 for the 10 poorest districts. The state average is $1.21. Revenue in the 10 richest districts is estimated at $7,546 per student, compared to $4,277 for the 10 poorest districts for the 1991-92 school year.

CED/ISD combined tax rates for 1991: $1.02, $1.26, $1.28, $1.21

AVERAGES
— 10 richest districts
— 10 poorest districts
— 8 largest urban districts
— Texas

Revenue per student 1991-92*: $7,546, $4,277, $4,270, $4,171

*Estimated weighted average; based on average daily attendance.

SOURCE: Texas Comptroller of Public Accounts.

Figure 10.1. Tax Rates and Revenue Per Student

6. County Education Districts Distributions
   The CED shall distribute the funds collected from its tax levy on the basis of each component district's share of the taxable value (SPTB value) of property in the CED, except that no district may receive funds in excess of its Tier One program less the ASF distribution (except as set out below).

If the amount collected by the CED exceeds the local share, the excess is retained for distribution in future years. If the amount collected is less than the local share, distributions shall be made under rules adopted by the Commissioner. For 1991-92 through 1993-94, a district that did not receive FSP funds in 1990-91 (i.e., was "budget balanced" in 1990-91) is entitled to CED collected funds above the Tier One entitlement, if the district cannot, at the maximum tax rate of $.78 per $100, maintain its 1990-91 revenue per weighted student (from local funds and the ASF distribution). The difference is received from the CED, then CED collections are distributed to other component districts according to the method indicated above.

Distribution of CED funds to school districts shall be according to schedules established by the Commissioner.

7. Guaranteed Yield Program (Tier Two)

The second tier guaranteed yield program includes funds for facilities beginning in 1993-94 (GYA-Guaranteed Yield Allotment}. The basic formula is:

GYA = (GL x WADA x DTR x 100) - LR

where:

- GL = Guaranteed level, which is:
  - 1991-92 $21.50
  - 1992-93 $22.50
  - 1993-94 $26.00
  - 1994-95 $28.00 (or greater amount set by FSFBC)
- WADA = Weighted ADA (district's total Tier One entitlement, less allotments for transportation, career ladder, technology, and 50 percent of CEI effects, divided by the Basic Allotment)
- DTR = District enrichment and facilities tax rate (total taxes levied and collected by the school district divided by SPTB value; CED collections are not counted here)
- LR = Local revenue (DTR x SPTB value)

DTR may not exceed $.45 per $100, but the FSFBC may adopt a greater amount for 1993-94 and 1994-95.

Beginning in 1993-94, ADA will be substituted for WADA if the LEB and LBB do not adopt program cost differentials and cost adjustments.

8. Revenue Limit

Imposes a revenue limit on districts. This limit is 110 percent of the district's FSP guarantee per WADA from state and local funds at a total tax rate of $.25 per $100 of SPTB taxable value of property (above the CED tax rate} as calculated for the 1994-95 year.

9. Tax Limitations

A school district may not impose a tax rate that produces a levy that exceeds the following:

```
1991-92    SPTB Value   (1/1/90) x .0078
1992-93    SPTB Value   (1/1/91) x .0068
1993-94    SPTB Value   (1/1/92) x .0058
1994-95    SPTB Value   (1/1/93) x .0050
```

A school district may impose taxes on "frozen" properties only to the extent that such taxes, when added to the taxes imposed by the CED, do not violate the constitutional limit.

A district may exceed the rate and levy limitations indicated above if the additional taxes are necessary to pay principal and interest on debt authorized prior to 4/1/91 and issued before 9/1/92 (old debt).

In order to issue "new debt," districts must demonstrate to the Attorney General a projected ability to repay the bonds, as well as any previously issued "new debt," with a tax rate not to exceed $.50 per $100 and a total tax rate not in excess of the rate limits set forth above. Once approved by the Attorney General and issued by the district, the district may levy a tax exceeding the limits (indicated above) if necessary to repay the bonds without reducing M&O expenditures. NOTE: In effect, if future value loss creates the necessity to exceed the tax rate limits in order to maintain M&O expenditures, the district may meet its "new debt" obligations. "Old Debt" obligations are not affected by the limit.

10. Rollback Tax Rate

The roll back tax rate is the sum of the district's effective maintenance tax rate, the rate of $.08 ($.08 per $100), and the district's current debt rate. For 1991, the districts effective maintenance tax rate is reduced by the rate of $.72 ($.72 per $100), or to zero, if the result would be less than zero. A district is not subject to rollback to replace a reduction in "total revenue" (not just state aid) (Walker, 1991).

Senate Bill 351 Challenged

The financing system approved in Senate Bill 351 was designed to eliminate the vast disparities between property-rich and property-poor districts by the end of the 1994-95 school year, chiefly by relying on CEDs as the mechanism to equalize revenue within county units. However, soon after the enactment of Senate Bill 351, the state faced yet another challenge to its school finance plan. The "Robin Hood" provisions of the plan were sharply questioned. A coalition of school districts and education groups urged the Texas Supreme Court to order the state to pay most of the cost of public schools and not pass the burden onto local school districts. Reservations arose over whether lawmakers had skirted a constitutional prohibition against a state property tax and that the 188 newly created county education districts were given the authority to levy and collect taxes without voter approval. On January 30, 1992, the Texas Supreme Court ruled the school financing plan (SB 351) unconstitutional. The state legislature was given until June 1, 1993, to come up with a new plan.

How school funding program stacks up

School funding in 1991-92 has a layered effect. Equalization occurs in the Tier 1 foundation level. Districts have the option of taxing at additional levels for local enrichment, though no state funds are available at Tier 3. All districts receive equal per-capita funds through the Available School Fund.

Tier 3 — Unequal Enrichment — Local Optional Enhancement

Tier 2 — Guaranteed Yield Program — State dollars | ENRICHMENT | Local dollars

Tier 1 — Foundation School Program — State dollars | FOUNDATION | Local dollars

Constitutional Fund — AVAILABLE SCHOOL FUND

Poorer districts ——— District wealth ——— Richer districts

SOURCES: Texas Comptroller of Public Accounts and Texas Education Agency.

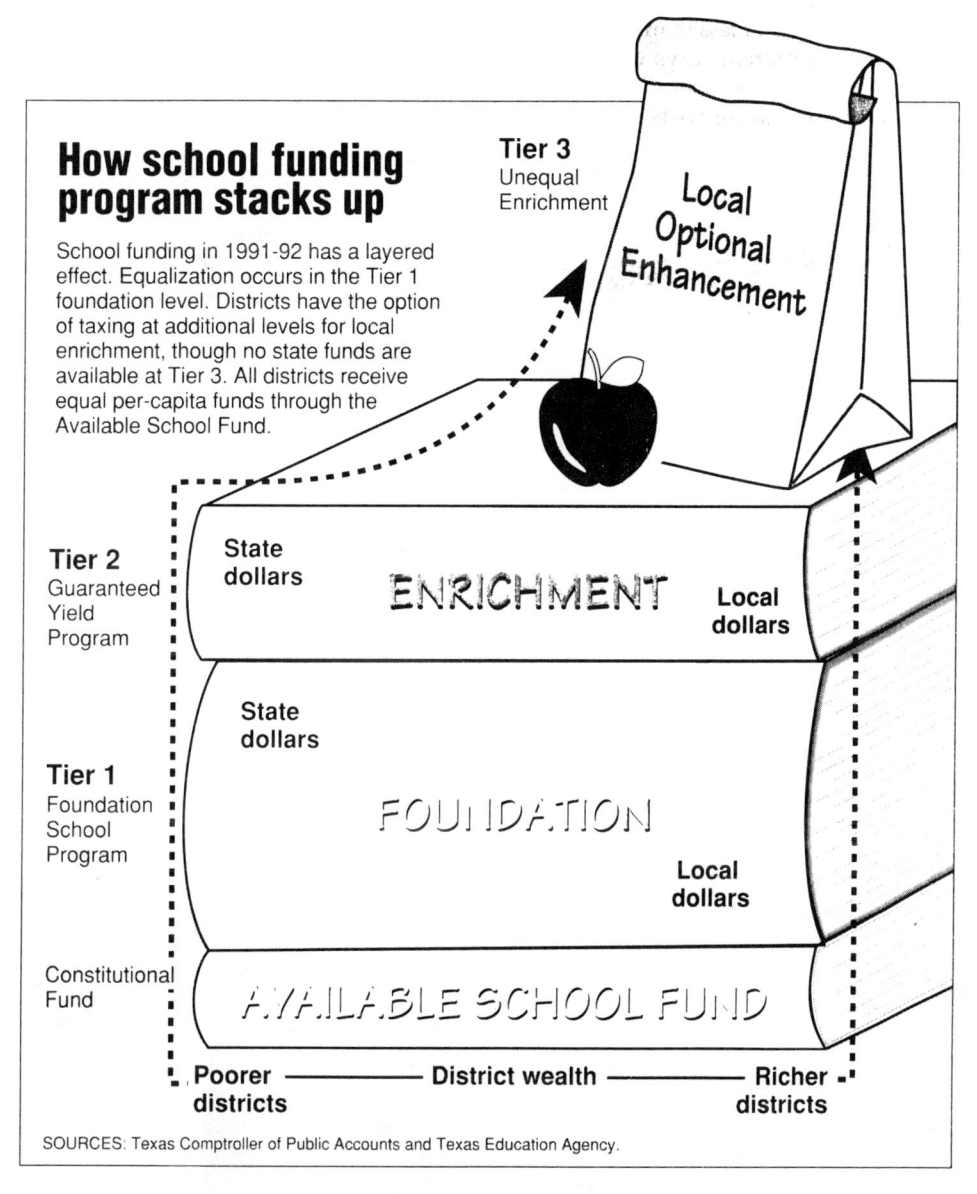

Figure 10.2. The Three Tiers of Current School Finance Plan.

With the most recent funding plan overturned on the basis that the CEDs' taxes were unconstitutional, the state once again had to develop a new method of fairly and equitably financing schools for the 3.4 million Texas public school students.

TABLE 10.1
SB 351 Shifts Revenue

	1990-91 ADA*	District wealth (per 1990-91 ADA)	1991-92 per ADA	Revenue change revenue 1991-92 (per est 91-92 ADA)
10 richest school districts				
Aliamoore	1	$10,235,361	$6,711	$-24,721
Laureles	12	9,685,439	6,711	-29,266
Kenedy County Wide	51	5,116,581	9,794	-9,827
Glen Rose	1,182	5,397,262	6,923	-4,458
Jayton-Girard	184	4,784,606	7,996	-5,194
Guthrie	84	3,836,094	8,848	-9,051
McFaddin	7	4,006,235	7,482	-3,838
Juno	2	12,863,707	6,816	-670
Iraan-Sheffield	584	3,257,728	8,122	-2,349
McMullen County	169	2,867,594	8,166	-936
10 poorest school districts				
Roma	4,610	38,541	3,690	266
Donna	7,202	38,204	4,128	671
Valley View	1,093	41,592	4,536	426
Fabens	2,182	36,640	4,491	832
Mercedes	4,683	28,152	3,941	224
Santa Rosa	1,054	27,230	4,471	301
San Elizario	1,426	29,769	4,877	1,042
Boles Home	191	27,908	4,808	-301
Progreso	1,412	24,002	5,093	1,146
Edcouch-Elsa	4,062	21,393	4,828	1,263
8 largest urban school districts				
Houston	175,977	267,444	3,928	232
Dallas	123,808	351,666	4,538	330
Fort Worth	65,374	199,385	4,069	305
Austin	60,359	286,857	4,301	-257
El Paso	57,373	119,593	3,835	210
San Antonio	56,766	110,688	4,722	648
Ysleta	47,144	83,341	4,115	517
Corpus Christi	38,716	144,333	3,843	193
STATE AVERAGE			$4,270	$315

*Average daily attendance.

SOURCES: Texas Education Agency and Texas Comptroller of Public Accounts.

Senate Bill 7
A State School Finance System Which
Meets Constitutional Standards?

"Should the quality of a student's education be so dependent upon the accident of where he/she happens to live?"

Once more, the Texas Supreme Court in January 1992 had issued to the state's policymakers the challenge of creating a school finance system which would meet constitutional standards. With the Court's ruling that SB 351 had not met constitutional standards Texas was, as many times before during the last decade, at a crossroads in its system of financing public education. The court had given state legislators until June 1993 to devise a new public school funding method. Although quite insistent on finance reform to bring about equity, the Texas Supreme Court had been less prescriptive. The state legislature has attempted five times to correct inequities in educational funding.

The first attempt was quite simple in approach: state legislators approved an increase in the state's education budget. Once the Court said no, they adopted the "Robin Hood" approach: they removed state funding from the state's wealthier school districts and redistributed the money to poorer districts. Yet, disparities still existed and the Court once more said no. The third attempt was yet an even more drastic "Robin Hood" approach: wealthy school districts were mandated to share their local revenues with the state's poorer districts. And for a third time, the Court said no. The fourth attempt occurred in November and December 1992 with Governor Ann Richards calling a Special Session of the Texas State Legislature to address the problem of Texas school finance. Presented to the state legislators was the *Richards-Bullock-Lewis school finance plan*. Central to the plan was the concept of *limited recapture* which in school finance language means taking some amount of local property tax money away from wealthy school districts and sharing it with the statewide system. However, opposition to the *recapture* concept killed all chances of passage of a constitutional school finance bill in the special session.

Reaching for the Elusive Goal

After the unsuccessful special session in November-December 1992, the Texas State Legislature convened in regular session in January 1993 knowing its immediate task was to address the public school funding issue. The Texas Supreme Court, having ruled that the 188 county education districts (CEDs) created by the state legislature two years previously for the purpose of redistributing school monies to achieve greater equity in funding among Texas public schools were unconstitutional, had threatened to cut off state education aid if the state legislature had not devised an acceptable solution by June 1, 1993.

In order to meet the June 1 deadline, any legislative action requiring voter approval had to be completed by February 20, 1993 if it was to be placed on the May 1, 1993 state ballot. After weeks of work and compromise, the Texas House approved on February 11, 1993, by the two-thirds requirement, two proposed changes in the Texas Constitution. The proposals were sent to the Texas Senate for consideration. The Texas Senate, having approved in January an earlier proposal which had met opposition in the House, faced two options: (1) request a conference committee to examine and work out the differences or (2) concur with the proposals as written. On February 15, 1993, the Texas Senate voted to approve the proposals as presented by the House.

As a result of the February 1993 legislative action, Texas voters had the opportunity to voice their opinion on the two proposed changes in the Texas Constitution on the May 1, 1993 ballot. They were:

- The constitutional amendment allowing limited redistribution of ad valorem taxes for schools, authorizing the state legislature or local districts to set a minimum tax rate in county education districts, and placing a cap on the ad valorem tax levied by a county education district.
- The constitutional amendment exempting a school district from the obligation to comply with unfunded state educational mandates.

The first proposal, if approved by the voters, would have authorized the state legislature to create county education districts (CEDs), allowing the CEDs to set tax rates of up to $1.00 per $100.00 valuation, or higher with voter approval. It would have allowed the legislature to redistribute public school funds from property-rich to property-poor school districts statewide and within counties. The amount of redistributed money would have been capped at 2.75 percent of state and local education revenue (limited recapture), amounting to $407 million at that time. The capped amount would not have taken into account revenues from the state's education trust fund, property taxes, money dedicated to textbook purchases and state contributions to retirement systems. Exactly how money would have reached individual school districts was to be determined by the enabling legislation to implement the amendments.

The second proposal, if approved by the voters, would have allowed school districts not to comply with state mandated changes that were imposed without state funding support after December 31, 1993, unless the mandates were in compliance with the Texas Constitution or federal law or if they were approved by two-thirds of the Texas House and Senate. The legislature would have been responsible for devising a system of determining whether the mandates were unfunded. If they failed to do so, then the state comptroller would be responsible to rule on individual requests from school districts. Although recognized by legislative leaders as not being the utopian solution, the proposed constitutional changes were presented as a way to keep the schools open and as an alternative to other possible solutions such as forced consolidation, a state income tax, or reinstatement of the not-so-long-ago abolished statewide property tax.

Although the compromised constitutional changes did address the current concerns of the Texas Supreme Court, the question of an equity standard still existed. The plan included limited recapture which provides a means for redistributing wealth among school districts with the hope of closing the gap between property-rich and property-poor school districts. However, the question remained: *With a state Constitution which affords little definition or flexibility, will state legislators once more take the "swift equity" approach?* Without a defined equity standard would the state's public school finance system find itself once more being subjected to other tests of constitutionality (Wright, 1992).

On May 1, 1993, Texas voters went to the polls and defeated the two proposed changes to the Texas Constitution which would have ratified the acceptability of County Education Districts (CEDs) and, to a great degree, kept the current school finance plan in place. The state legislature, then in session, moved quickly to pass new school finance legislation, Senate Bill 7 (SB 7). Senate Bill 7 eliminated the CEDs and substituted a wealth-sharing plan which impacted the 109 school districts with a wealth of greater than $280,000 per weighted ADA. The 109 school districts were allowed to lower their wealth by choosing one of five methods: consolidating their tax bases with another district(s), sending funds generated by the excess wealth to the state for redistribution, contracting with other districts to educate students, fully consolidating with other school districts, or deannexing commercial property for transfer to tax rolls of a low-wealth school district.

School districts were given to October 16, 1993, to indicate a choice which was to be approved by local election or be forced to consolidate with a property-poor school district or have taxable property removed from their tax rolls and attached to the tax rolls of a property-poor school district. Local elections resulted in most districts sending funds generated by the excess wealth to the state for redistribution. This option appeared to be the least permanent should Senate Bill 7 be declared unconstitutional.

The new plan bases funding on a $2,300 per student basic allotment, which is $100 less than provided in 1992-93. The local districts are required to levy a tax of at least 86 cents in order to receive funds from the Foundation School Program; this is 4 cents higher than required under SB 351. The new guaranteed yield provision ensures that a penny of a local district's tax effort will generate $20.55 per pupil, nearly $2 per penny less than the guaranteed yield of $22.50 provided by SB 351. Additionally, weights for special program entitlements are the same as in SB 351 except SB 7 modifies weights for special education students to encourage *inclusion* in regular classrooms. The technology allotment is also frozen at $30 per ADA instead of gradually increasing to $50 per ADA under SB 351.

Rollback provisions were modified under SB 7. A district is required to obtain voter approval if it adopts a tax rate that exceeds the sum of the district's debt service tax rate plus the rate necessary to generate the 1992-93 per student revenue by 6 cents. If voters do not approve the new rate, the rate is rolled back beneath the 6-cent limit, effective the current year.

Elements of Senate Bill 7

While there was widespread relief that the state legislature had acted (SB 7), few school districts were happy with the results. Even with the addition of 1 billion dollars to the system, the amount did not fund enrollment increases. Details of SB 7 include the following:

- School districts with wealth in excess of $280,000 per weighted student were required to select one of five options to reduce their wealth per student to $280,000. The five options were:

    Voluntary Consolidation
    Voluntary Detachment and Annexation of Property
    Voluntary Tax Base Consolidation (local election required)
    Pay to Educate Students from Other Districts (local election required)
    Purchase of Attendance Credits from the State (local election required)

- Three options in the plan (detachment and annexation, pay to educate students from other districts, and purchase of attendance credits) provide for a three-year phase-in which allows 109 budget-balanced districts to maintain their current level of spending per student. The phase-in provides for maintaining spending per student at a rate of $1,275 in the first year, and at a tax rate of $1.50 for the next two years.
- School districts which failed to exercise one of the above options would be subjected to detachment and annexation by the commissioner. For seven school districts, detachment and annexation would not reduce their wealth to $280,000. The commissioner was given the authority to order these districts consolidated if they failed to exercise an option.
- The funding elements for the plan include a two-tier system. The first tier includes a basic allotment of $2,300 at a tax rate of $0.86. The second tier is a guaranteed yield, which guarantees a district $20.55 for each penny of tax effort above the basic allotment up to the maximum rate of $1.50.
- Other provisions include changes in funding for special education, a pilot program for inclusion of special education students, and a pilot summer program for remediation.
- The bill includes accountability measures to ensure that school campuses and districts are

providing a quality education to students by requiring that certain performance measures are achieved by school campuses and districts.
- The bill includes changes in certain mandates on school districts. The teacher career ladder is repealed, but provides a grandfather clause for continuation of the stipend for teachers currently receiving career ladder funds. The reporting requirements on school districts have been streamlined, and the administrative burden on school districts is lessened. The teacher appraisal process has been improved and made less costly.
- Policy matters, as distinct from mandates, such as no pass-no play, student/teacher ratios, remain unchanged.

Senate Bill 7 Challenged

As before, litigation was filed challenging the constitutionality of SB 7 and the funding of Texas public schools. State District Judge Scott McCown on September 13, 1993 at a pretrial hearing held in Austin addressed several issues related to the *Edgewood* bench trial which was scheduled to begin in October, 1993. He dissolved a temporary restraining order blocking enforcement of the commissioner of education's rule on distribution of county education district (CED) funds and denied a motion for temporary injunction. McCown subsequently issued an order authorizing CEDs to distribute funds under the commissioner's rule and specified August 31 as the effective date of distributions.

In addition to dissolving the restraining order, McCown acted on the following:

- Denied the plaintiff's motion to strike intervention, which would have excluded from the *Edgewood* lawsuit parties asserting a constitutional right to vouchers. The court, however, invited the state to file objections to the intervention.
- Denied a motion from attorney representing Coppall, Grapevine-Colleyville, Highland Park, Plano, and Richardson ISDs (defendant-intervenors in *Edgewood*) to hold a separate trial on the *issue of adequacy* stating that he would entertain a new motion for a separate trial after the October 1993 bench trial was underway.

By the end of October, 1993, arguments had been heard in the suit, and Judge Scott McCown indicated that he would render a decision by the Christmas holidays. On December 9, 1993, State District Judge Scott McCown upheld the constitutionality of Senate Bill 7 stating it is "perhaps our last hope for establishing the system of public education our forebears believed essential to the preservation of our liberties and our rights." Judge McCown also held that the legislature failed to comply with the previous mandate to help low-wealth districts with their facility needs indicating "the state still has no equitable method of financing capital expenditures." He gave lawmakers until September 1, 1995, to develop a plan to equalize funding for school construction, or he will halt the issuance of all new school bonds in districts with high levels of property wealth. The appeal process has begun. As before in Texas school finance, the Supreme Court of Texas will make the final decision on the legislation.

Meanwhile, as of November 1993, 233 school districts, representing all areas of the state and districts of differing size and wealth, adopted resolutions to join in a lawsuit challenging that the state is not making "suitable provision" for the support and maintenance of Texas public schools. The suitable provision challenge was filed initially on October 1, 1993 on behalf of 58 school districts.

Also in November 1993, Texas voters were given the opportunity to express their desires regarding another constitutional amendment related to school finance. Amendment #4 prevents the state legislature from enacting a state income tax, except for a referendum by the public. The amendment further provides that if the public votes for an income tax, it can only be used for public education. The amendment was approved by the Texas voters.

An Elusive Goal?

1993 proved to be an interesting and complex time as Texas policymakers attempted to design a public school finance system which afforded that the *quality of a student's education NOT be dependent upon the accident of where he/she happens to live.* As expensive as public education may be, the cost to society of not educating people is much higher. Financing education at less than an adequate level is not only poor economics but could prove to be the detriment of the American way of life. As Texas moves toward the 21st century, the question of an equitable provision of public education will continue to require attention and focus. Added to this will be questions of *adequacy of state funding, concerns related to a continued reliance on ad valorem taxes to support education, vouchers, teachers' salaries, school district consolidation, as well as other issues.* The struggle to design an acceptable public school finance system should not overshadow the primary function of the public school system: educating the students of the Texas public schools.

Events in Texas School Finance

1968 Edgewood parent, Rodriguez, files suit in federal court challenging the Texas school finance system.

1971 Following the decision of a similar case adjudicated in California's state court, a three-judge Federal District Court rules that Texas' system of funding education to be in violation of the "equal protection" clause of the Fourteenth Amendment to the United States Constitution.

1973 The United States Supreme Court reverses the decision of the three-judge court ruling that state educational funding schemes are not the jurisdiction of federal courts.

1984 Edgewood Independent School District files suit against the state in state courts contending that the method of funding education discriminates against property-poor school districts.

1987 District Court Judge Harley Clark rules that the Texas method of funding education is in violation of the state's "equal protection" clause.

1988 Judge Clark's decision is reversed by the Third Court of Appeals.

1989 The Texas Supreme Court reverses the Court of Appeal decision. Thus, sustaining Judge Clark's ruling that the funding scheme was unconstitutional.

1990, February The first special legislative session fails to pass a bill.

April A second session finally passes a bill which proposes to fund education at $555 million using a ½ cent increase in the state's sales tax. Governor Clements vetoes the bill due to the tax increase.

May The state's legislature begins a third special session while a court-appointed master begins work on a plan to redistribute existing state funds to comply with the Texas Supreme Court's decision.

3rd special session passes a bill similar to the one passed in April. Clements vetoes the bill. The senate votes to override his veto but the house is unable to do so.

June With an apparent deadlock between the state legislature and the governor, the court appointed master's "Robin Hood" funding plan goes public. The concept of taking funds from wealthy school districts and redistributing them to poor school districts is not well received by the people of Texas. Threats of serious political reprisals force Governor Clements and the legislature's conference committee to compromise on a plan calling for a ¼ cent sales tax increase to fund $528 million in new education funding.

July State District Court Judge McCown begins hearings to determine if the newly passed finance plan meets constitutional requirements.

September Judge McCown rules that the new funding formula does not meet the constitutional provisions required by the Texas Supreme Court. The existing plan will stay in effect until September 1, 1991. At this time, a new plan (to be passed by the legislature and signed by the new governor) will take effect; failure of the state to come up with a new plan will force the court to accept the court-appointed master's "Robin Hood" plan.

1991, January Texas Supreme Court upholds Judge McCown's ruling and the finance system of SB 1 is declared unconstitutional with deadline given to the state legislature of April 1, 1991 to pass a satisfactory bill to be put in place by September 1, 1991. If not passed, state funds will cease to flow to local districts on April 1, 1991.

April Deadline of April 1, 1991, is extended to April 15, 1991.

McCown restores state school funding after receiving the new school finance law. Governor Ann Richards signs the bill into law only minutes before the court hearing begins. The judge says he will schedule a hearing on the new law's constitutionality as early as June.

June McCown hears arguments on the new school finance law.

	August	McCown upholds school finance law as constitutional.
		The state legislature passes a record $59.1 billion, two-year budget that includes $2.6 billion tax-and-fee bill to pay for the spending. The largest part of the budget goes to education, including $2.4 billion to pay for the new school finance plan.
	November	A coalition of school districts and education groups urges the Texas Supreme Court to order the state to pay most of the cost of public schools and not to pass the burden onto local districts.
		The Texas Supreme Court hears arguments on the new school finance law (Senate Bill 351).
1992,	**January**	The Texas Supreme Court rules the school financing plan unconstitutional. The legislature is given until June 1, 1993, to come up with a new plan.
	November	Governor Ann Richards calls a Special Session of the Texas State Legislature to once again deal with the problem of Texas school finance as the court has demanded; presenting to the state's politicians the Ann Richards-Bob Bullock-Gib Lewis school finance plan. Gridlock sets in and the politicians return home having yet to solve the problem.
1993,	**February**	Two proposed changes to the Texas Constitution pass both the House and Senate, to be voted on by citizens in May. These amendments would permit redistribution of ad valorem taxes by County Education Districts and exempt local districts from unfunded education mandates passed by the legislature. This would, in effect, make the current system of finance constitutional.
	May	Texas voters went to the polls and defeated the two proposed changes to the Texas Constitution which would have ratified the acceptability of CEDs. Legislature approves SB 7.
	July-Oct	School elections to reduce wealth as prescribed by SB 7.
	September	Pretrial hearing held in *Edgewood* lawsuit (Challenges to SB 7)
	October	*Suitable Provision* challenge filed on behalf of 58 school districts asking to intervene in *Edgewood*.
	November	Amendment #4 is approved by Texas voters.
	December	Judge Scott McCown rules SB 7 constitutional but also held that the state legislature failed to comply with the previous mandate to assist low-wealth districts with their facility needs. He gave lawmakers until September 1, 1995, to develop a plan to equalize funding for school construction or he will halt the issuance of all new school bonds in districts with high levels of property wealth.

References

Conners, Eugene T. Financing Schools in Texas. *Texas Public School Organization and Administration: 1991.* Second Edition, Dubuque, IA.: Kendall Hunt Publishing Company, 1991.

Cubberley, Ellwood P. *School Funds and Their Apportionment.* New York: Teachers College Press, 1906.

Mort, Paul and Staff. *The National Survey of School Finance: State Support for Public Education.* The American Council on Education, 1933.

Sharp, John. Texas Comptroller of Public Accounts. *Fiscal Notes.* Austin, Tx.: Issue 91:3, March 1991.

Sharp, John. Texas Comptroller of Public Accounts. *Fiscal Notes.* Austin, Tx.: Issue 91:5, May 1991.

Sharp, John. Texas Comptroller of Public Accounts. *Fiscal Notes.* Austin, Tx.: Issue 92:1, January 1992.

Sharp, John. Texas Comptroller of Public Accounts. *Fiscal Notes.* Austin, Tx.: Issue 92:4, April 1992.

Strayer, George D. and Haig, Robert M. *The Financing of Education in the State of New York.* New York: MacMillan Co., 1923.

Walker, Billy D. and Kirby, William. *School Board Member's Library: The Basics of Texas Public School Finance.* 3rd. Ed., Austin, Tx.: The Texas Association of School Boards, 1986.

Walker, Billy D. *Highlights of Senate Bill 351 and House Bill 2885 (Finance).* Austin, Tx.: The Texas Association of School Boards, July 11, 1991.

Wright, Linus. *Seminar in Educational Policy* (seminar paper). Presented March 11, 1992, East Texas State University, Commerce, Tx..

Dean v. Coddington, 131 N.W. 2d 700, South Dakota, 1964.

Edgewood Independent School District v. Kirby, Case No. 362,516, Tex. Dist. Ct., August 27, 1987; No. 3-87-190-CV, Tex. Ct. App., Austin, Dec. 14, 1988.

Hobson v. Hansen, 269 F. Supp. 401, 1967.

Irving I.S.D. v. Tatro, 104 S. Ct. 3371, 1984.

Miller v. Childers, 238 P. 204, Oklahoma, 1924. Miller v. Korns, 140 N.E. 773, Ohio, 1925.

Mills v. Board of Education, 348 F. Supp. 866, D.C., 1972.

PARC v. Commonwealth of Pennsylvania, 343 F. Supp. 279, PA, 1972. Robinson v. Cahill, 119 N.J. Super. 40, 303 A. 2d 273, 1973.

Rodriquez v. San Antonio School District, 411 U. S. 1, 93 S. Ct. 1278, 36 L. Ed. 2d 16, 1973.

Sawyer v. Gilmore, 83 A. 673, Maine, 1912.

Serrano v. Priest, 487 P. 2d 1241, 96 Cal. Rptr. 601, 1971.

Suggested Readings

Burrup, Percy E, Brimley, Vern Jr., and Garfield, Rulon R., *Financing Education in a Climate of Change*. 4th Ed., Boston: Allyn and Bacon, 1988.

Cubberley, Ellwood P. *School Funds and Their Apportionment.* New York: Teachers College Press, 1906.

Johns, Roe L., Morphet, Edgar L. and Alexander, Kern S. *The Economics and Financing of Education.* 4th Ed., Englewood Cliffs, N.J.: Prentice Hall, 1983.

Mort, Paul R. *The Measurement of Educational Need.* New York: Teachers College Press, 1924.

Mort, Paul and Staff. *The National Survey of School Finance: State Support for Public Education.* The American Council on Education, 1933.

Odden, Allan R. and Picus, Lawrence O. *School Finance: A Policy Perspective.* New York: McGraw-Hill, Inc., 1992.

Schoppmeyer, Martin W. *The Economics of Education: An Introduction.* Granville, Ohio: Trudy Know, Publisher, 1992.

Strayer, George D. and Haig, Robert M. *The Financing of Education in the State of New York.* New York: MacMillan Co., 1923.

Walker, Billy D. and Kirby, William. *School Board Member's Library: The Basis of Texas Public School Finance.* 3rd. Ed., Austin, Tx.: The Texas Association of School Boards, 1986.

Curriculum and Instruction in Texas Schools

Ross Sherman
Jerry L. Pulley

Attempts at defining and differentiating between the terms curriculum and instruction are manifold. The simplistic view of the two terms holds that curriculum is the "what" is taught, and instruction is the "how" the "what" is taught. Others have held that the terms are analogous to the Holy Trinity. That is, they are separate, yet the same.

Pinning a label on curriculum seems to be more difficult than defining instruction. Although different terms, such as methods, delivery system, techniques, procedures, strategies and pedagogy have been used to describe instruction, all of them indicate the "means" for students to learn what it is they are supposed to learn. Curriculum, however, has been defined in numerous ways. It has been viewed as "content," "courses," "subjects," "objectives," "materials," "course of study," "scope and sequence," "lesson plans," "everything that happens to students within school," "program of studies," and "the planned learning experiences for students in a school."

Since many contemporary writers appear to define curriculum as a series of planned learning experiences, the distinction between curriculum and instruction becomes rather blurred. Most hold that for purposes of analysis the two can be viewed separately, but when implemented they must function together as a singular unit.

Prior to the 1980s in the State of Texas, the curriculum was largely determined at the local level. The state did have broad discretionary powers in terms of courses to be taught and which textbooks could be selected, but the specific content to be taught was delegated to the school districts and the classrooms. A dramatic alteration occurred in 1981 when the Texas legislature decided that the K-12 students of the State could be better served through a standardized statewide curriculum that did, in fact, specify the content to be taught and learned. Texas developed a basic curriculum that would serve as the minimal, or essential elements with local options to go above and beyond the prescribed components.

House Bill 246/Chapter 75

The State of Texas leaped into the so-called "excellence in education" movement in 1981 when the 67th Texas Legislature mandated a state basic curriculum that each school district must implement. The legislation, known as House Bill 246, defined a well-balanced curriculum as including:

1. English language arts
2. other languages, to the extent possible
3. mathematics
4. science
5. health
6. physical education
7. fine arts
8. social studies
9. economics, emphasis on the free enterprise system
10. business education
11. vocational education
12. Texas and United States history as individual subjects and in reading courses.

The legislation directed the State Board of Education to designate the "essential elements" of each subject by grade level and course. Very clearly spelled out in the legislation were measures requiring the schools to stress the concepts of patriotism, the free enterprise system and the basic democratic values of the state and national heritage.

House Bill 246 (Texas Education Code #21.101) was a very brief piece of legislation. However, many contend that the Bill's brevity is also its beauty since, after providing for a general curricular intent, it instructed the State Board of Education to establish the specifics and details of the curriculum. The legislature, though not often the case, voiced a policy statement that allowed the curriculum specificities to be developed over a period of many months after considerable input from diverse groups throughout the state.

The results was a publication titled *State Board of Education Rules for Curriculum,* or *Chapter 75* of the Texas Administrative Code. It received final approval in 1984, following three years of deliberation. House Bill 246 was ultimately translated into *Chapter 75,* a 246-page state curriculum document. It is not known whether the number of pages in *Chapter 75* was intentional or coincidental.

Chapter 75 directs local boards of trustees to adopt policies which ensure that all students will participate in a well-balanced curriculum, although modifications may be made for special populations. Districts are responsible for providing teachers with adequate planning time and a climate free of interruptions so that the essential elements can be taught. Also, parents and students must be given adequate information concerning high school graduation requirements. Further, local school districts are encouraged to exceed the minimum requirements as established by the State Board of Education.

Elementary Curriculum

For grades kindergarten through six, the curriculum consists of a series of essential elements (statements of subject matter intent, or objectives) in each of the following areas:

1. English language arts
2. mathematics
3. science
4. health
5. physical education
6. fine arts (art, music, theatre arts)
7. social studies, Texas and United States history
8. other languages are encouraged but not mandated
    (If offered, the essential elements are the same as Level I languages at the high school)

Initially *Chapter 75* specified not only the subjects and content (essential elements) within each subject that is taught, but also the amount of time that was to be devoted to each subject on a daily or weekly basis. This was subsequently changed by the legislature and now prohibits the State Board of Education from designating the methodology used by the teacher or the time spent by the teacher or student on a particular task.

Junior High School Curriculum (Grades 7-8)

While the elementary curriculum specifies the various subjects that must be taught, the junior and senior high school subjects are expressed in terms of "units." For grades seven and eight, a unit is defined as a course meeting a minimum of 45 minutes per day for 180 days. For grades seven and eight, each school district must teach and each student must take:

Subjects	Units
English Language Arts (may include English as a second language)	2
Mathematics	2
Life Science (40% laboratory oriented and three weeks per semester health)	1 (or Science I)
Earth Science (40% laboratory oriented)	1 (or Science II)
Physical Education (competitive athletics may substitute)	1
Texas History/Geography (grade seven)	1
U.S. History/Citizenship (grade eight)	1
Computer Literacy (may be completed at elementary level)	0 or ½
Reading (required for students scoring below the 40th percentile or more than one year below grade level)	0, 1, or 2
Electives (selected from State approved list)	½ to 3
Total Required	12

Students who earn credits in "other languages" in grades seven and eight may use the units to satisfy the other language requirements for the high school, but must complete the total number of units required in grades nine-twelve. The same held true for students who completed courses *above* Algebra I in grades seven-eight, however, the State Board of Education later amended the rule which now allows students who complete Algebra I in grades seven-eight to be able to satisfy a portion of the high school mathematics requirement.

Some implications of the seventh and eighth grade curriculum as modified by *Chapter 75* are:

1. a decrease in the emphasis in vocational subjects and other electives for students who have some difficulty in reading. For example, 11½ of the required units are specified for students who have reading difficulties, which leaves them ½ unit for electives.
2. some difficulty has been experienced in complying with the requirement that 40% of the instructional time in science be laboratory oriented, since laboratory space and/or equipment is less than adequate in some junior high schools. Also, student conduct in a laboratory setting can be a problem.
3. some concern has been expressed about the adequacy of health instruction, since the minimum required time is six weeks per year. Furthermore, health instruction, in these cases, is usually provided by life science instructors instead of those who are certified in health education.

4. in order to implement the computer literacy requirement, school district expenditures have increased in order to purchase computers, software, and deal with the ubiquitous maintenance problem.

High School Curriculum

The courses that each school district in Texas must offer at least every other year are as follows:

1. English Language Arts—English I, II, III, IV;
2. Mathematics—Algebra I, Algebra II, Geometry and Pre-Calculus or Trigonometry or Elementary Analysis or Analytic Geometry
3. Science—Biology I, Chemistry I, Physics, Physical Science.
4. Social Studies—United States History, World History Studies, United States Government, World Geography Studies
5. Economics with an emphasis on the free enterprise system and its benefits
6. Physical Education I and II
7. Health Education
8. Fine Arts—course from two of three free arts areas (art, music, theatre arts)
9. Business Education—Typewriting, Accounting or Record Keeping, Personal Business Management
10. Vocational Education—two courses addressing separate occupational objectives (including industrial technology education) taught in the school district with provisions for contracting for additional offerings
11. Other Languages—Level I and II of another language (hardship exemption may be available)
12. Computer Science—one unit course selected from a variety of computer-related courses

As stated previously, school districts shall offer the above courses at least every other year, however, if 10 students indicate they will participate in a given course or a particular course is required for a student to graduate, the district shall teach the course.

Some implications or issues regarding the high school curriculum include:

1. Because the curriculum contained a number of courses of questionable rigor, such as, correlated language arts, fundamentals of mathematics, consumer mathematics, pre-algebra, introductory physical science and introductory biology, the State Board of Education began a phasing-out process of these courses beginning with the 1992-93

academic year. Supporting a recommendation of the Commissioner of Education, the State Board believed that the so-called remedial courses tended to isolate low-performing students and minimized expectations of them.
2. Small high schools have experienced greater difficulty in securing qualified mathematics, chemistry and physics teachers since the mathematics and science curricula have increased and these teachers have traditionally been in short supply.
3. The title of the required economics course—Economics with Emphasis on the Free Enterprise System and Its Benefits--is somewhat controversial since the title suggests that only the advantages of the free enterprise system be taught.
4. During the first few years of *Chapter 75,* high schools were fairly well standardized in offering six to seven 55 minute periods per day. The State Board of Education later provided more flexibility by allowing high schools to operate on a seven 50-minute period day if they choose to do so.

Graduation Requirements

Table 11.1 shows the graduation requirements for the "regular" high school program and the "recommended" high school program. A third program is available, advanced high school "honors" program. The honors program is the same as the recommended program except that students must complete five courses which have been designated and approved as honors courses.

Shown in Table 11.1 is the "Recommended" high school program as adopted by the State Board of Education in November, 1993. The diplomas for the four types of programs are the same, however, the academic achievement record (transcript) indicates by a particular seal which of the four programs the student pursued.

Some implications of the high school graduation requirements include:

1. With the elimination of the "remedial" type of courses from the curriculum, some contend that the more rigorous course requirements will contribute to a drop-out rate that is already considered excessive.
2. Due to the rather rigid nature of the advanced and recommended programs—very few electives—students with special interests such as journalism, science and vocational are pursuing the regular program, which allows for greater flexibility.
3. The importance the State of Texas places on football is reflected in some substitutions for physical education. Physical activity involved in drill team, marching band and cheerleading during the "fall semester" may be substituted for physical education.

TABLE 11.1
Graduation Requirements

	Regular Program	Recommended
English Language Arts	4 Units—Eng. I, II, III and IV, with options for Eng. IV	4 Units Eng. I, II, III and IV with options for Eng. IV
Mathematics	3 Units (must include Algebra I and higher)	3 Units—Algebra I, Geometry, Algebra II, or appropriate advanced mathematics I Unit—Pre-calculus (May substitute Trigonometry and either Elementary Analysis or Analytic Geometry)
Science	2 Units	4 Units may include: Physical Science, Biology I and II, Chemistry I and II, Physics I and II
Social Studies	2 ½ Units U.S. History, World History or Geography, U.S. Govt.(½)	4 Units U.S. History, World History, World Geography, U.S. Govt.(½) Economics (½)
Other Languages		3 Units from one language
Economics	½ Unit	½ Unit
Physical Education	1½ Units; substitutions available, such as athletics, marching band and cheerleading in fall semester	1½ Units; substitutions available, such as athletics, marching band, and cheerleading in fall semester
Health Education	½ Unit	½ Unit
Computer Science		1 Unit several courses as options
Fine Arts		½ Unit any approved fine arts course(s)
Electives	7 Units—21 units required	1½ Units—24 units required

Additional Provisions

Other provisions of *Chapter 75* include:

1. all Texas schools were required to fully implement *Chapter 75* during the 1985-86 school year,
2. alternative delivery systems for districts are available, such as cooperatives, contracting, technology and adjusted school week. All options, however, must be approved by the commissioner of education,
3. some correspondence courses may be used to satisfy graduation requirements, with certain limitations imposed upon the students, the districts and the universities offering the courses,
4. with the approval of the commissioner of education, experimental courses and magnet schools may be available,
5. districts may offer courses for local credit only, provided those courses are "above and beyond" the state graduation requirements,
6. under certain provisions, students may receive "credit by examination," and high school credit for college courses,
7. summer school programs, with standards parallel to those of the regular school year, are available to school districts,
8. requirements for the awarding of credit at the high school level are specified, including the regulation that the grade of 70 is minimum for awarding credit,
9. school districts are required to establish policies on promotion, retention, remediation and placement of students. In order to receive state accreditation, school districts must not only teach the essential elements, but provide evidence that essential elements are mastered.

Following the adoption of *Chapter 75* in 1984, the State Board of Education has amended the rules on several occasions. This is an indication that the state mandated curriculum is evolutionary in nature, which is as it should be.

Legislative Enactments

The State Legislature in the Spring, 1990 approved a series of programs that are having significant impact on curriculum and instruction in the State of Texas. These include the following:

1. Pre-kindergarten programs for three and four year olds who meet the State's eligibility requirements.
2. Year-round schools which provide for operating a single- or multi-track schedule which will allow groups of students and teachers to attend school and take vacations on the same schedule.

3. Public Education Development Fund to support innovative educational practices primarily on campuses where not more than 60% of the students performed satisfactorily on the TAAS. (See Table 11.2)
4. Technology fund for three purposes:
   a. to provide computers and related technologies and courses of instruction via telecommunication.
   b. to provide computers and related technologies for instruction for teachers and administrators.
   c. to measure student productivity.

TABLE 11.2
List of Innovative Programs

Innovative programs that may be approved include but are not limited to programs relating to:

1. school year restructuring
2. alternative learning environments
3. parental literacy
4. decentralization of organizational decisions
5. instructional technology
6. student and parent choice among public schools
7. child care
8. early childhood education
9. an extended school day
10. teacher and administrator development
11. continuous progress education
12. student teacher ratios below 22:1 in elementary grades
13. use of elementary school guidance counselors, social workers, and other personnel in successful dropout-prevention programs
14. career development for students
15. bilingual training
16. the generation of more effective parental involvement with the schools
17. school-age latch-key children
18. volunteer efforts with the private sector
19. coordination of school activities with community health and human services programs and other community resources
20. magnet schools
21. interdisciplinary curriculum
22. peer tutoring
23. counseling of families at-risk
24. comprehensive coordination with health and human service delivery systems

In 1994 the legislature approved several other changes and additions to programs. Under SB 7, two new opportunities to provide extended year programs for students who are likely to be retained, unless they receive additional instruction are made available: (1) A district may apply to the commissioner for a state-funded optional extended-year program of 30 days of instruction for students in kindergarten through grade 8. Teachers specially trained must provide instruction with classes limited to 12 students. Students attending at least 85 percent of the program must be promoted unless the student's parents object. Funding is limited to first grade in 1993-94 and to first and second grade in 1994-95; thereafter, funding will be provided though the foundation school program; (2) Districts may apply to the Commissioner for an alternative extended-year program for 45 days of instruction for students in kindergarten through grade 8, who would not otherwise be promoted. Funding will be provided by reducing the regular program by not more than five days and using the savings to pay for the extended instruction. Districts operating under this alternative program are not eligible for the state-funded program listed under (1) above. Attendance in an extended program is compulsory for an eligible student, but the district must provide transportation services.

A curriculum mastery plan that allows a student to advance through the curriculum as curriculum elements are mastered is to be established by the SBOE by May 31, 1995.

The Texas Advanced Placement Incentive Program is to be established and administered by TEA. It will provide financial awards to schools, teachers, and students who participate in college advanced placement (AP) courses and subsidize AP test fees to students with financial need. This program is subject to legislative appropriation.

A pilot program for the inclusion of students with disabilities in the regular classroom is established to provide those students an appropriate free public education in the least restrictive environment.

The school calendar remains at 180 school days and the Commissioner may waive up to five days for staff development. Staff development is to be "campus-based for the purposes of improving student achievement."

Curriculum Guides and Lesson Plans

While *Chapter 75* is the "official" state curriculum, two additional "official" curricula exist in most Texas schools. The first is the school district curriculum in the form of curriculum guides which are often extensions of the essential elements in *Chapter 75*. The second is the individual classroom teacher's curriculum which is manifest in the daily and/or weekly lesson plans developed by the teacher.

Curriculum guides have been found in schools for many years with varying degrees of teacher acceptance and utilization. Too often the guides were not "teacher friendly" and simply gathered dust until an accreditation visit. Some guides, however, have proven valuable to teachers willing to use them, and to school districts that stressed a standardized curriculum.

A resurgence in the development of local curriculum guides has been witnessed the past few years. This rise is mostly due to the state's insistence that guides be developed, plus the pressure on local school districts to perform well on achievement test scores, especially the TAAS test. It was believed that a unified school district curricular plan would be a boost in increasing test scores.

Curriculum guides exist in many forms. They may consist of a single subject at a particular grade level, such as, fifth grade science. Or, a curriculum guide might be written for one discipline at all levels, such as, English language arts K-12. Then again, curriculum guides may be interdisciplinary in nature.

Following a brief introduction which often contains a philosophical statement, rationale and instructions for using the guide, most curriculum guides include the following:

1. topic
2. topic's relationship to Chapter 75's essential element(s)
3. goals/objectives
4. learning activities
5. resources/materials
6. evaluation techniques

The essential elements contained within *Chapter 75* are not necessarily listed in sequence, however, the majority of curriculum guides do suggest a particular sequence. Also, curriculum guides often provide a content scope that is broader than *Chapter 75*.

If *Chapter 75* is considered the official curriculum of the state, and curriculum guides the official curriculum of the school district, then the teacher's lesson plans become the official curriculum of the classroom. While most lesson plans include the topic/objective, its relationship to the state's essential elements, learning activities, and possibly resources and evaluation techniques, a wide variation exists in the amount of detail required by the schools. The policy of some schools is simply that teachers must have a plan available when a substitute is needed, while in other schools teachers are required to develop an elaborate plan for every subject each day of the week that includes all components of a particular instructional system.

Although a consensus exists that every teacher should have an instructional plan of some type, there has been a controversy over the amount of detail that should be included in a lesson plan, and in whether or not teachers should be required to submit to building administrators their plans in advance. The controversy became rather pronounced as *Chapter 75* was being implemented. Many schools in the State were placing greater emphasis on required lesson plans—especially in the inclusion of the essential elements. The rationale behind the increased emphasis was so that the schools could document the fact that essential elements were being taught. Due, in part, to some pressure instituted by some state teacher organizations, the commissioner of education requested school administrators to use moderation in local requirements for lesson plans and documentation purposes.

It has been suggested by the preceding statements the existence of three forms of "official" curricula—*Chapter 75*, curriculum guides and lesson plans. Some educators, however, recognize an additional curriculum, sometimes called the "real" curriculum. Whereas the official curricula are really "plans," which may, or may not, be implemented in the classroom, the real curriculum consists of what the teacher has actually taught. Sometimes the official and real curricula do not match well, although it is suspected that the two curricula are more closely correlated today than in previous times since classrooms are probably monitored now to a greater degree. In addition, the implementation of uniform standardized testing (TAAS) increases the probability that curriculum alignment occurs. Curriculum alignment is the phenomena where the planned curriculum, real curriculum and the tested curriculum are in essence the same.

Curriculum mapping is a term given to a technique that can be used to analyze the amount of time actually devoted to various subject matter topics. Comparisons, therefore, can be made between the official and real curricula.

Textbooks

Texas uses a state-wide system for the adoption, purchase, distribution and use of textbooks. State statutes which address textbooks are found in the *Texas Education Code* Chapter 12.

Textbooks are adopted by the State Board of Education and are provided without cost to pupils. The term textbook is generic and includes: books, systems of instructional materials and computer software.

The State Board of Education annually appropriates funds from the available school fund for the express purpose of purchasing and distributing books for that scholastic year.

A special provision of the law authorizes that textbooks be provided for blind and visually handicapped public school students and teachers. In this instance textbooks include Braille and large type books.

Content Requirements

According to the Texas Administrative Code Chapter 81.71 all textbooks must adhere to the following content guidelines:

1. Textbooks must be free of partisan or sectarian content.
2. Textbooks must contain unbiased information that is current and accurate.
3. Textbooks must promote citizenship, free enterprise, respect for authority and individual rights.
4. Textbooks must be free of blatantly offensive language or illustrations.

5. Textbooks should treat divergent groups equitably and avoid stereotyping. Special care must be expended in the treatment of ethnic groups, roles of men and women and respect for workers.
6. Authors of textbooks must possess expertise and experience in the area.
7. Textbooks must contain illustrations that assist in the comprehension of the material.

State Adoption, Purchase, Acquisition and Custody

The State Board of Education issues Proclamations advertising for textbooks to be used in a particular school year. The proclamations are designed to articulate the following:

1. essential elements for the subject and courses.
2. general content requirements.
3. organizational sequences of material.
4. instructional materials.
5. procedures for adapting the instruction to a variety of student needs.
6. evaluation techniques.
7. requirements for teacher editions.

The proclamation also specifies the timeline for the adoption of the materials. Typically the process from the issuance of the proclamation to the utilization of the materials in the classroom entails about two to three years. For instance, a Proclamation which was issued in March, 1992 advertised for books to be used in schools beginning with the 1995-96 school year.

The State Board of Education upon the recommendation of the commissioner establishes a State Textbook Committee consisting of between seven and 15 representatives. The appointments are for one year and each person selected is experienced and possesses expertise in the fields for which adoptions are to be made for that year. In addition a majority of the members are classroom teachers, two members are not employed in public schools but are recognized as experts in the field, and at least one member is knowledgeable in the field of special education.

The textbook committee's charge is to recommend to the State Board of Education a complete list of books it approves at the various grade levels. The State Board of Education then selects and adopts a multiple list of books for use in kindergarten, elementary and secondary grades of between two and eight books.

District Procedures

During the month of April local school districts are required to report maximum attendance for each grade level for the purpose of determining the number of books to be requisitioned for that school district. The state establishes the quota of books for each subject area. The majority of the time it is on a 100% quota, that is, one book per student enrolled. Exceptions to the 100% quota are supplementary readers.

It is important to note that all textbooks remain the property of the State of Texas and the State Board of Education establishes the rules for the requisition, distribution, care, use and disposal of books. In addition, the board of trustees of the school district are designated the legal custodians of the books. The school district trustees may delegate the custodial responsibilities of books to district personnel.

Districts are required to have a printed label numbering each book on the inside cover stating that the book is the property of the state. Each district must employ some systematic accounting procedures to be able to maintain an accurate record of all books issued. In addition, annual audits of textbooks may be conducted by the district or state. Teachers are required to keep a record of all books issued. Books must be covered by the student and returned at the end of the semester/year or when the student withdraws. Each student or his parent is responsible for returning all books issued or for making financial restitution prior to being issued new books. Books may be sold to parents at the state contract price. All money accrued from such sales must be forwarded to the commissioner.

Selection Process

The selection procedures for textbooks employed by local school districts are outlined in TAC 81.153. During the month of November local school districts appoint a textbook committee consisting of between five and 15 members. Most districts then utilize some format to gather input from all teachers and other personnel who will be using the book. Typically this provides the teachers the opportunity to review the text and supplemental materials.
During this process it is important that teachers keep in mind the following criteria:

1. Does the text compliment the district's philosophy for that subject area?
2. Does the text meet the ability level and needs of the students?

Finally the district's textbook committee will recommend to the board its selection during the March board meeting.

Standardized Testing

Senate Bill 350 passed in the 66th legislature charged that the State Board of Education has a responsibility to:

Review periodically the educational needs of the state, adopt or promote plans for meeting these needs and evaluate the achievement of the educational programs.

It further stipulated that, "Beginning in 1979-80 school year and each year thereafter that the Texas Education Agency shall adopt and administer appropriate criterion referenced assessment instruments designed to assess minimum basic skills competencies in reading, writing and mathematics."

Thus, the Texas Assessment of Basic Skills (TABS) was mandated with the purpose of providing principals and teachers with information to be used in raising student achievement. In 1985-86 school year the name of the test was changed to the Texas Educational Assessment of Minimum Skills (TEAMS). Also, at this time the objectives and skills measured by the test were to be congruent with the essential elements of the curriculum as identified in the State Board of Education Rules for Curriculum.

In October of 1990 the Texas Education Agency implemented a new phase in the assessment of academic skills. The latest component in the evolution of assessment testing in Texas is the Texas Assessment of Academic Skills (TAAS). TAAS is designed to extend and expand on the TEAMS test and will be in effect from 1990-1995.

In addition to the TAAS test beginning in the 1994-1995 school year, all school districts will be administering end-of-the-course tests for grades nine through 12 for subjects as defined by the commissioner of education and the State Board of Education.

Philosophy

Standardized tests are administered according to specific directions and scored according to defined parameters (Johnson, 1977). Two classes of standardized tests include norm-referenced and criterion-referenced tests.

Norm-referenced tests are designed to include skills and achievements that are broadly taught and that do not penalize students in a specific geographical location or socioeconomic level. Students' performances on norm referenced tests are compared with other students who have taken the test and comprise the norm group. Results in the form of a raw score can be used to compute percentile norms, age norms and grade norms.

A criterion-referenced test is designed to relate items to specific objectives or levels of proficiency in skills which students have mastered. A student's performance is reported by objectives indicating whether the student has or has not mastered the objective.

Legislative Mandates

The legislative statutes which address the assessment of basic skills are found in TEC 35.023, Assessment of Academic Skills. Specifically it empowers the Texas Education Agency to adopt and implement appropriate criterion-referenced assessment instruments designed to assess student achievement in reading, writing, social studies, science, mathematics and other subject areas determined by the State Board of Education for all pupils in grades 3-8. Furthermore, all students in 10th grade are administered a secondary exit level assessment instrument designed to assess competencies in mathematics, social studies, science, and Engligh language arts.

The State Board of Education may adopt one nationally recognized norm-referenced test to be administered uniformly in the spring. The test must measure student achievement in reading, mathematics, language arts, science and social studies.

In relationship to the TAAS test the State Board of Education establishes the standard for satisfactory performance and a pupil who does not perform satisfactory on all sections of the exit level assessment will not receive a high school diploma. A student does have the opportunity to retake those sections of the test he has not passed in future administrations. In addition, the use of TAAS does not preclude local school districts from administering criterion- and/or norm-referenced assessment instruments at any grade level.

A student who has a physical or mental impairment or learning disability may be exempt from TAAS at the discretion of the Admission, Review and Dismissal Committee (ARD). The results of a student's performance on the TAAS test is confidential and may be released only to the student, parent or guardian and to school personnel directly involved with the student's educational program.

Test results, which are aggregated by district and campus, must be released to the public at a regularly scheduled meeting of the school board within a reasonable time after the results have been received.

Schools are charged with developing and providing compensatory and remedial services to:

- students who did not perform satisfactorily on any component of the secondary exit level exam.
- students whose test scores fall below a standard established by the State Board of Education.
- students who are at risk of dropping out.

The cost of preparing, administering and grading the assessment instrument is borne by each district from their compensatory aid received from the state.

Student Assessment Plan Revisions

In an attempt to clarify the issue of student assessment the Legislature established a Committee on Student Learning that was charged with recommending to the State Board of Education a comprehensive, performance-based assessment program. The committee's recommendations were subsequently submitted to and approved by the Legislative Education Board and the State Board of Education in Spring, 1992. The recommendations approved include the following:

Table 11.3
Student Assessment Transition Plan

TAAS	**1993-1994**	**1994-1995**
Performance Tasks and/or MachineScorable Items		
· Reading, Writing, Mathematics	Grades 4, 8, 10 (Exit)—Spring	Grades 4, 8, 10 (Exit)-Spring
· Science, Social Studies	Grades 4, 8—Spring	Grades 4, 8, 10 (Exit) Spring
· Computer Literacy	Grade 8	Grade 8
· End-of-Course		
·· Algebra I	High School*	High School
·· Biology I	High School*	High School
·· Computer Science	High School*	
·· 5 More Tests	High School*	
· Physical Fitness/Health	Grades 4, 8--Spring*	Grades 4, 8—Spring
· Oral Language Proficiency in a Second Language	Grades 8, High School Spanish**	Grades 4, 8, and in High School**
NAPT (Optional)		
· Reading, Mathematics	Grades 3-11—April***	Grades 3-11—April***
· Writing, Science, Social Studies		

* The first year a new test is administered will be an optional (phase-in) year. Districts may choose to participate on a trial basis.
** District may elect to participate at any or all levels (Grades 4, 8, and High School) to match the local instructional program.
*** Norm-referenced tests may be included as long as federal program evaluation regulations remain unchanged.

1. The state accountability assessment system should focus on criterion-referenced, performance-based, and developmentally appropriate assessment strategies.
2. The state accountability assessment system should be expanded to include social studies, science, computer literacy, physical fitness/health, oral proficiency in a second language, and end-of-course tests in certain high school courses.

3. The state accountability assessment system should be implemented at grades 4, 8, & 10 (exit) and provide technical assistance in using formative and diagnostic assessment to improve instructional programs.
4. The administration of the state accountability assessment system should move from the fall to the end of the instructional period.
5. The state should maintain a statewide norm-referenced assessment program in reading and mathematics for federal reporting purposes.

Table 11.3 identifies the transition plan that will be followed by the State in implementing the revised assessment plan.

Test Logistics

During the 1992-1993 school year the TAAS test will be administered to grades 3, 7, and 11 in the fall and 4, 8, 10 in the spring. In subsequent years the tests will be administered in the spring.

Each section of the TAAS test contains certain broad objectives. These objectives are consistent from grade level to grade level because they comprise a comprehensive instructional program from Grade 1 through Grade 12. The objectives are designed to assess a student's ability to think independently, read critically, write clearly and solve problems logically. Thus, the emphasis is on assessing higher level thinking skills. (See appendix for list of TAAS Instructional Targets.)

What varies in each grade level is the instructional targets or essential elements which are encompassed in that particular objective. Annually a portion of these instructional targets will be selected for assessment, however not all instructional targets will be tested each year.

Test Reporting, Analysis and Interpretation

The TAAS test is scored by an outside firm contracted to provide this service by the Texas Education Agency. Test results are reported to local school districts in a variety of forms. The standard reports include the following for each grade level tested:

1. Confidential Student Report
2. Confidential Student Label
3. Summary Report (Campus and District)
4. Demographic Performance Summaries (Campus and District)
5. Confidential List of Students' Results
6. Confidential Student Nonmastery
7. Confidential "Do Not Score" Report
8. Written Composition Analytic Information Summary Report (Campus and District)

The aggregated results allow a school district and campus to analyze the effectiveness of the school program in dispensing the essential elements. An item analysis can indicate how students performed on each objective, thus providing information on the following: organization of the curriculum, curricular areas of strengths and weaknesses, effectiveness of instructional methodology, effectiveness of test preparation.

The analysis of the individual student profile can be used to plan the appropriate instructional program for the student and to verify the student has mastered the essential elements for the grade level.

The NAPT test is also scored by an outside firm contracted to provide this service. The reports received for the NAPT test include the following:

1. Confidential Student Report
2. Confidential Student Label
3. Confidential Campus Student Roster
4. Summary Report
5. Campus/District Demographic Summary
6. Report to the School Board

The aggregate results derived from the NAPT test can be used to compare the performance of the school/grade level/subject area to the normed population. This may provide an indication of the comprehensiveness and rigor of the district's curriculum. The individual scores can be used to assess the student's performance to his peers who comprise the norm group.

The Texas Education Agency in an attempt to use the test data in a performance-based accountability system has tied the accreditation process to the TAAS test. This is based on the effective schools research premise that all students can learn and therefore should be expected to master the essential elements.

However, at issue is the use of a performance-based accountability system, a system that holds school districts, schools, administrators and teachers accountable for a product, in this case a standardized achievement test. An alternative system would hold schools accountable for the processes of education:

- curriculum that addresses the essential elements,
- instructional time allotments that adhere to state requirements,
- the use of effective schools research,
- the use of principles of instruction that promote learning.

In essence, should a school district's accreditation be based on the processes or the products of education?

TABLE 11.4
Your School Standardized Testing Plan

Goal:
Our staff will raise TAAS test scores to a minimum of 90% in all subtests and total composite areas.

Rationale:
The district is placing more emphasis on standardized test scores (Board of Education and central administration).

The state is placing more emphasis on standardized test scores (accreditation is tied to scores).

Assumptions:
TAAS is a criterion-referenced test therefore it is "OK" to teach skills covered on the test.

There is a correlation between teaching skills in format and raising test scores.
Skills taught in isolation must be applied in other areas to assure transfer and retention.

Overview:
Three Phase plan
1) Knowledge of Test Objectives
2) Test Wiseness
3) Motivation—student/teacher

Explanation:
1) Knowledge of Test Objectives
   a. the specific test objectives will be taught
   b. the test objectives will be taught daily during TAAS time
   c. the test objectives will be taught in isolation
2) Test Wiseness
   a. the objectives will be presented in TAAS format during TAAS time
3) Motivation—*"MY PERSONAL BEST"*
   a. the importance of TAAS will be stressed to students and parents
   b. students will take periodic TAAS practice tests with knowledge of results that will emphasize personal improvements

Teacher Responsibilities:
1) Be aware and teach to the TAAS objectives
2) Develop daily activities in TAAS format
3) Develop periodic TAAS review tests
4) Emphasize the importance of TAAS with student (bulletin boards, notes to parents, etc.)

Administration Responsibilities:
1) Provide staff development on test objectives and test construction
2) Public relations campaign with parents to stress importance of TAAS
3) HOLD TEACHERS ACCOUNTABLE FOR DAILY TEACHING AND PRACTICE OF TAAS OBJECTIVES

TAAS Plan for Improvement

Perhaps no other single factor in the State of Texas has as high profile or receives as much scrutiny as the TAAS test. For instance, the State uses the Academic Excellence Indicator System (AEIS) which is a performance-based accountability system for comparing school districts and schools. This system uses TAAS scores as one of the eight outcome indicators for evaluating Texas schools. Newspapers publish TAAS scores and rank school districts based on their performance. School boards use TAAS as evidence of the quality of education dispensed in the school district. Therefore it is imperative that school districts take the initiative in preparing students to be successful on TAAS.

Any program to improve TAAS scores should be based on the following assumptions:

1. TAAS is a criterion-referenced test therefore it is "OK" to teach the skills covered on the test.
2. There is a correlation between teaching skills in format and raising test scores. (Idol-Maestas, 1986)
3. Skills taught in isolation must be applied in other areas to assure transfer and retention.

Based on the preceding assumptions a systematic focused plan to improve TAAS scores would include the following components: knowledge of test objectives, test wiseness and motivation for teachers and students. (See Table 11.4.)

Alternative Assessment Models

Recently numerous states have begun to utilize alternative methods for assessing student achievement. These methods are referred to as performance-based measures and may include activities such as demonstrations, hands-on experiments, open-ended questions, computer simulations, and portfolios. The assumption is that these tasks are more indicative of the type of skills students should possess as a product of their education.

Wiggins (1992) identifies the following criteria for developing alternative assessment:

1. Assessment tasks should be, whenever possible, authentic and meaningful.
2. The set of tasks should be a valid representation that will allow generalizations about overall performance.
3. The scoring should be authentic, with credit/denial based on essential information.
4. The tasks should be valid and reliable.

Before the educational community fully embraces the concept of authentic assessment a review of the existing research is in order. A variety of researchers (Dorr-Bremme and Herman 1983, Herman and Golan 1991, Kellagham and Madaus 1991, Shepard 1991, Smith and

Rottenberg 1991) have come to the conclusion that the assessment tends to dictate what is taught. If tests are focused on minimal skills or basic skills that becomes the priority for the allocation of time and resources. When the focus of assessment is shifted to authentic tasks there is a subsequent change in teaching emphasis to reflect the test.

The problems associated with authentic assessment are those that exist in more traditional models of assuring validity. The tasks should assess the skills, abilities and concepts that they are designed to measure. Linn (1991) identified a litany of issues that must be addressed in the development of assessment tasks. These include the following:

1. **Fairness.** Does the assessment technique consider the cultural background of the student?
2. **Transfer and Generalizability.** Does the results of the assessment support a generalization concerning the student's ability?
3. **Cognitive Complexity.** Does the assessment actually assess higher level thinking?
4. **Content Quality.** Is the appropriate content selected to be assessed?
5. **Content Coverage.** Does the assessment measure the full scope of the curriculum?
6. **Cost/Efficiency.** How can assessment tasks be designed to maximize efficiency while minimizing resources (time and money)?

In conclusion as new assessment models are utilized, it is the education community's responsibility to assure that these techniques facilitate rather than impede the accomplishment of educational goals and outcomes.

Effective Schools Research

The effective schools research is a body of knowledge accumulated over the past fifteen years concerning the factors that have been identified as being associated with schools that are effectively promoting student achievement. The various findings have been adopted and provided the impetus for school improvement projects in many major urban cities and by several state departments of education (Edmonds, 1982). The effective schools research is broadly divided into four categories: leadership, instruction, environment and program.

The principal's leadership is a key to effective schools. Characteristics identified as being associated with effective principals include:

- assume an assertive instructional role (Edmonds, 1979; Brookover and Lezotte, 1979)
- provide a vision of excellence that is translated into goals and objectives (Rutherford, 1985)
- monitor classrooms frequently (Rutherford, 1985)
- intervene in a supportive manner (Rutherford, 1985)
- convey high expectations for students and staff (Rutter, 1979; Edmonds, 1979)

The second category consists of those elements of effective schools that relate to the instructional personnel. Effective teachers display the following characteristics:

- allot time equally among students (Fischer et al, 1980)
- plan for smooth transitions between activities (Brophy, 1983; Billups, 1984)
- state rules and procedures (Rutter, 1979)
- utilize behavior modification techniques effectively (Brophy, 1983)
- project a vision of excellence (Cahn, 1982)
- believe in their own efficacy (Brophy, 1979)
- make students accountable for their own learning (Rosenshine, 1983)
- communicate and teach to an objective (Rosenshine, 1979)
- demand and provide opportunities for achievement (Farrago et al, 1984)
- believe students can reach their potential (Purity and Smith, 1982; Good and Brophy, 1980)
- use the technique of overlearning (Anderson, Everston and Brophy, 1979)
- exhibit objectivity (Billups, 1979)
- use active listening (Good, 1975)
- use a student-centered style (Good, 1975; Schneider, 1981)
- innovate with a zest for learning (Schneider, 1981)

The third category is environment. Characteristics identified as promoting an environment conducive to academic achievement include:

- high academic emphasis (Brookover and Lezotte, 1979; Rutter, 1979)
- orderly school environment (Edmonds, 1979)
- parental involvement in student learning (Brookover and Lezotte, 1979)
- maximum time on task with success (Walberg, 1988)
- well-kept school plant (Edmonds, 1979)

The final category are those characteristics associated with the overall program. They include the following principles:

- high academic emphasis (Rutter, 1979)
- systematic assessment and monitoring of student progress (Edmonds, 1979; Rutter, 1979)
- emphasis on basic skills (Brookover and Lezotte, 1979)
- meaningful homework assigned (Rutter, 1979)
- regular inservice for staff (Smith and Purkey, 1982)
- lessons adjusted to student needs (Rutter, 1979)
- management of instructional time (Brophy, 1983; Berliner, 1984)
- effective grouping for instruction (Brophy, 1979; Rosenshine, 1983)

It should be noted that effective schools research has come under scrutiny concerning the nature of the research, validity of the conclusions and the impetus it is providing for educational reform. The preponderance of the research on effective schools is correlational in nature due to the inability of the researcher to manipulate the variables under study. The second concern involves the validity of the conclusions being drawn. Stedman (1987) challenges the findings of some of the more notable studies by suggesting the findings and recommendations are not substantiated by the research and that in some instances the findings are in direct contradiction to the accepted effective schools research.

Finally there is concern that the effective schools research is serving as a driving force in educational policy to mandate a narrowing of the curriculum with an undue emphasis on basic skills, uniform curriculum and standardized testing for accountability (Resinick and Resinick, 1985). In addition, it may be having a negative impact on low-income, urban schools by focusing the curriculum on lower-order test items to the exclusion of the higher-order problem solving curriculum (Meier, 1984).

Instructional Models

During the decade of the 1980s, three closely related instructional systems have made a significant impact on how students are taught in Texas. They are: direct instruction, mastery teaching, and, though not technically an instructional system, but its side effects are--the Texas Teacher Appraisal System.

Direct instruction stresses group instruction with the teacher as the central focus; time on task; teacher, rather than student choice of learning experiences; a preponderance of low-cognitive rather than high-cognitive questions with immediate feedback; and a high degree of structure.

Although some of the tenets of direct instruction were considered contrary to former instructional principles, such as frequent use of low-level questions, the attraction to direct instruction was compelling because of its research base. The research was fairly conclusive that students taught with a direct-instructional approach performed significantly higher on achievement tests. And since achievement test scores became the driving force in the State's response to the concept of accountability (albeit simplistic), it is little wonder that schools jumped on the direct instruction bandwagon. There may be limitations, however, in the research behind direct instruction. Most of the research studies were conducted at the elementary school level in the subject matter fields of reading and mathematics. Whether or not direct instruction is equally as effective and appropriate in other subject matter fields and at the high school level remains to be seen.

Another instructional system which became popular in Texas during the 1980s is known by several terms. The system, popularized by Madeline Hunter, among others, is known as mastery teaching, mastery learning, lesson cycle, or the Hunter Model. Following many of the attributes of direct instruction, the model features a guided-practice stage in which students apply a concept that was explained to them, a reteaching phase for students who did *not* master the concept, and an enrichment phase for those who *did* master the concept.

Although the Texas Education Agency has not formally advocated the mastery teaching model, it appears that many TEA personnel subscribe to its efficacy since many agency workshops for local personnel have emphasized the model to a great degree.

In implementing the mastery teaching model at the local level, it is reported that the model is utilized to a greater extent by elementary teachers than by secondary teachers.

The third entity to have impact upon instruction in the public schools of Texas is the Texas Teacher Appraisal System which was developed in response to the career ladder features H.B. 72 passed in 1984.

Although the State Board of Education clearly states that it does *not* mandate a particular instructional system, some contend that in order to receive a relatively high score on TTAS, teachers must adhere to the criteria and indicators of TTAS, which is tantamount to an instructional model. Proponents of TTAS argue, however, that the system is flexible enough to accommodate many instructional styles.

Whether or not TTAS is actually an instructional model may not be clear, but it can be assumed that it has modified instruction in Texas, at least during those times teachers are being observed.

An axiom of former years was, in general, that it was appropriate to prescribe to teachers the curriculum, but the instructional methods were left to the teachers discretion, provided an effective job was being done. Several factors, including the pressure to improve achievement test scores, the effective schools research, and the TTAS, have tended to increase the amount of time that teachers are being monitored today. This, in turn, has probably decreased the amount of freedom individual teachers have to select their instructional strategies, which means that both curricular and instructional matters are being prescribed more for teachers today. It remains to be seen whether or not these increased instructional and curricular constraints will have a positive educational influence on the students of Texas.

Gaining momentum in the late 1980s and early 1990s at national, state and local levels was another instructional model—cooperative learning. Cooperative learning, similar to what was formally called small group instruction, is considered to be an alternative to traditional, teacher-centered (directed) instruction. Students normally work in heterogeneous groups of four to six members and earn recognition, rewards, and sometimes grades based upon the work of the group (Slavin, 1983). Some research studies indicate cooperative learning has a positive effect on self-esteem, social skills and academic achievement (Slavin, 1988).

In Texas, one of the reasons for the rising popularity of cooperative learning may be the transition from the TEAMS to TAAS. Whereas the TEAMS possessed a relatively large number of lower level cognitive questions, the TAAS attempts to determine achievement with a relatively large number of higher level cognitive questions. Direct instruction, with its emphasis on memorization, seemed to work fairly well in preparing students for the TEAMS, however, instructional strategies with the potential of developing problem-solving and other higher level thinking skills are being sought in the Post-TEAMS era. Cooperative learning is one of the strategies that some believe will be beneficial in developing those skills that are useful in mastering the TAAS.

References

Anderson, L, Everstson, C. and Brophy, J. (1979). An experimental study of effective teaching in first grade reading groups. *The Elementary School Journal, 79,* 193-222.

Betliner, D. (1984). The half-full glass: a review of research on teaching. *Using What We Know About Teaching.* Alexandria, Va.: Association for Supervision and Curriculum Development.

Best, J. (1977). *Research in Education.* Englewood Cliffs: Prentice Hall.

Billups, L. and Rauth, M. (1984). The new research: how effective teachers teach. *American Educator, Summer,* 39.

Brookover, W.B. and et al. (1979). *School systems and student achievement: schools make a difference.* New York: Prager.

Brookover, W.B. and Lezotte, L.W. (1979). Changes in school characteristics coincident with changes in student achievement. East Lansing: Michigan State (Unpublished paper) ED 181 005.

Brophy, J. (1979). Classroom organization and management. *Elementary School Journal, March.*

Brophy, J. (1979). Teacher behavior and its effects. *Journal of Educational Psychology, 71,* 733-750.

Cahn, S. (1982). The art of teaching. *American Educator, Fall.*

Dorr-Bremme, D. and Herman, J. (1990). Assessing student achievement: a profile of classroom practices. Los Angeles: UCLA, Center for the Study of Evaluation.

ED-LINE News Briefs. (1987). *May.*

Edmonds, R. (1979). Effective schools for urban poor. *Educational Leadership, 37,* 15-24.

Farrar, E. et al. (1984). Effective schools programming high schools: social promotion or movement by merit. *Phi Delta Kappa, June.*

Fisher et al. (1980). Teaching behaviors, academic learning time and student achievement: an overview. *Time to Learn.* Washington, D.C.: NIE.

Good, T. (1975). *Teachers Make a Difference.* New York: Holt, Rinehart and Winston.

Good, T. and Brophy, J. (1978). *Looking in classrooms.* New York: Harper and Row.

Herman, J. and Golan, S. (1991). Effects of standardized testing on teachers and learning- another look. CSE Technical Report #334. Los Angeles: Center for the Study of Evaluation.

House Bill 246, *Texas Education Code.* (1981).

House Bill 72, *Texas Education Code.* (1984).

Idol-Maestas, L. (1986). Teaching middle school students to use a test-taking strategy. *Journal of Educational Research, 79,* 350-357.

Kellaghan, T. and Madaus. (1991). National testing: lessons for America from Europe. *Educational Leadership, 49,* 87-93.

Linn, R., Baker, E. and Dunbar, S. (1991). Complex, performance-based assessment: expectations and validation criteria. *Educational Researcher, 20,* 15-21.

Meir, D. (1984). Getting tough in schools. *Dissent, Winter,* 61-70.

Purkey, S. and Smith, M. (1982). Too soon to cheer? Synthesis of research on effective schools. *Educational Leadership,* 64-69.

Resnick, D. and Resnick, L. (1985). Standards curriculum and performance: historical comparative perspectives. *Educational Researcher, 14,* 5-20.

Rosenshine, B. (1979). Content time and direct instruction. *Research on Teaching: Concepts, Findings and Implications.* Berkley, Calif.: McCutchan.

Rosenshine, B. (1983). Teaching functions in instructional programs. *Elementary School Journal, March.*

Rutherford, W. (1985). School principals as effective leaders. *Phi Delta Kappa,* 31-34.

Rutter, M. et al. (1979). *Fifteen thousand hours: secondary schools and their effects on children.* Cambridge: Harvard University Press.

Senate Bill 1, Texas Education Code. (1990).

Shepard, L. (1991). Will national tests improve student learning? *Phi Delta Kappa,* 232-238.

Slavin, R.E. (1983). *An introduction to cooperative learning.* New York: Longman.

Slavin, R.E. (1988). Cooperative learning and student achievement. *Educational Leadership, 47,* 52-54.

Smith, M.L. and Rottenberg. (1991). Unintended consequences of external testing in elementary school. *Educational Measurement: Issues and Practice, 10,* 7-11.

Stedman, L. (1987). It's time we changed the effective schools formula. *Phi Delta Kappa, November,* 215-224.

Texas Education Agency. (1988). *State Board of Education Rules for Curriculum.* Austin, Texas.

Texas Education Agency. (1990). *Texas Assessment of Academic Skills Measurement Specifications 1990—1995.* Austin, Texas.

Texas School Law Bulletin. (1988). West Publishing Company.

Wallberg, H. (1988). Synthesis of research on time and learning. *Educational Leadership, 45,* 76-85.

Appendix

Texas Assessment of Academic Skills
Instructional Targets

Reading Objectives

DOMAIN: Reading Comprehension

Objective 1: The student will determine the meaning of words in a variety of written texts.
Objective 2: The student will identify supporting ideas in a variety of written texts.
Objective 3: The student will summarize a variety of written texts.
Objective 4: The student will perceive relationships and recognize outcomes in a variety of written texts.
Objective 5: The student will analyze information in a variety of written texts in order to make inferences and generalizations.
Objective 6: The student will recognize points of view, propaganda, and/or statements of fact and nonfact in a variety of written texts.

Mathematics Objectives

DOMAIN: Concepts

Objective 1: The student will demonstrate an understanding of number concepts.
Objective 2: The student will demonstrate an understanding of mathematical relations, functions, and other algebraic concepts.
Objective 3: The student will demonstrate an understanding of geometric properties and relationships.
Objective 4: The student will demonstrate an understanding of measurement concepts using metric and customary units.
Objective 5: The student will demonstrate an understanding of probability and statistics.

DOMAIN: Operations

Objective 6: The student will use the operation of addition to solve problems.
Objective 7: The student will use the operation of subtraction to solve problems.
Objective 8: The student will use the operation of multiplication to solve problems.
Objective 9: The student will use the operation of division to solve problems.

DOMAIN: Problem Solving

Objective 10: The student will estimate solutions to a problem situation.
Objective 11: The student will determine solution strategies and will analyze or solve problems.
Objective 12: The student will express or solve problems using mathematical representations.
Objective 13: The student will evaluate the reasonableness of a solution to a problem situation.

English Language Arts Objectives

DOMAIN: Written Communication

Objective 1: The student will respond appropriately in a written composition to the purpose/audience specified in a given topic.
Objective 2: The student will organize ideas in a written composition on a given topic.
Objective 3: The student will demonstrate control of the English language in a written composition on a given topic.
Objective 4: The student will generate a written composition that develops/supports/elaborates the central idea stated in a given topic.
Objective 5: The student will recognize appropriate sentence construction within the context of a written passage.
Objective 6: The student will recognize appropriate English usage within the context of a written passage.
Objective 7: The student will recognize appropriate spelling, capitalization, and punctuation within the context of a written passage.

Science Objectives

DOMAIN: Acquiring and Classifying Scientific Data and Information

Objective 1: The student will demonstrate the ability to acquire scientific data and/or information.
Objective 2: The student will demonstrate the ability to sequence, order and/or classify scientific data or information.

DOMAIN: Communicating and Interpreting Scientific Data and Information

Objective 3: The student will demonstrate the ability to communicate scientific data and/or information.

Objective 4: The student will demonstrate the ability to interpret scientific data and/or information.

Objective 5: The student will demonstrate the ability to make inferences, form generalized statements, and/or make predictions using scientific data and/or information.

DOMAIN: Solving Problems—Investigating

Objective 6: The student will demonstrate the ability to identify a problem, formulate an hypothesis, and design and conduct scientific investigation.

Objective 7: The student will demonstrate the ability to draw conclusions about the process(es) and/or outcome(s) of a scientific investigation.

DOMAIN: Solving Problems—Applying Knowledge

Objective 8: The student will demonstrate the ability to relate and apply scientific and technological information to daily life.

Social Studies Objectives

DOMAIN: Understanding Social Studies Concepts and Information

Objective 1: The student will demonstrate an understanding of civic values and the rights and responsibilities of American citizenship.

Objective 2: The student will demonstrate an understanding of the American and other economic systems.

Objective 3: The student will demonstrate an understanding of the American and other political systems.

Objective 4: The student will demonstrate an understanding of geographical concepts and information.

Objective 5: The student will demonstrate an understanding of historical concepts and information.

Objective 6: The student will demonstrate an understanding of sociological and cultural factors that affect human behavior.

DOMAIN: Evaluating Social Studies Concepts and Information

Objective 7: The student will demonstrate the ability to interpret social studies data.
Objective 8: The student will demonstrate the ability to analyze relationships in social studies.
Objective 9: The student will demonstrate the ability to make generalizations about and draw inferences or conclusions from social studies information.
Objective 10: The student will demonstrate the ability to use problem-solving and decision-making skills in a social studies context.

School Business Management in Texas

Kip Sullivan
Tom Huff

School Business officials facilitate the flow of funds—appropriated by official action of the majority of the school board—in, out and through schools. Educational planning requires the business administrators to weigh priorities and alternatives to achieve them. The budget is the translation of educational needs into a financial plan. Accounting in schools includes the recovery, classifying, analyzing, interpreting, and reporting data. As a result, school business administration involves a specialized knowledge of the various functions of business management. These focus on efficient and economic management of the financial affairs of schools.

Specialized tasks usually associated with the role of school business management include budget and fiscal planning, purchasing and supply management physical plant planning and constructions, maintenance and operation, transportation, insurance, food services, accounting, data processing, and office management.

This chapter examines the various economic processes involved in school business management. In Texas, monumental sums of money are spent each year for education. To insure that such public funds are utilized efficiently, procedures and practices have been developed.

This first section of this chapter, considers the accounting information available in *Bulletin 679, Financial Accounting Manual* of the Texas Education Agency. Next purchasing procedures are discussed. Third, School, Transportation in Texas is reviewed. Finally, Food Services is examined.

Educational Planning, Budgeting, Accounting under Bulletin 679

Critical demands for accurate, legal and sufficient financial information that enables the implementation of program oriented budgeting and accounting system dictated the design of such a system as encompassed by Bulletin 679. It gives to a school district the capability of resolving fiscal management concerns; facilitate uniformity of reporting financial data necessary to planning at the local, regional, and state level.

"The overall goal of accounting and financial reporting for public school districts it to provide: (1) financial information useful for making economic and educational decisions, and demonstrating accountability and stewardship; and (2) information useful for evaluating managerial and organizational performance. The basic objectives for accounting and financial reporting for public school districts are:

1. To provide financial information useful for determining and forecasting the flows balances and requirements of short-term financial resources.
2. To provide financial information useful for determining and forecasting financial condition and changes therein.
3. To provide financial information useful for monitoring performance under terms of legal, contractual and fiduciary requirements.
4. To provide information useful for planning and budgeting, and for forecasting the impact of the acquisition and allocation of resources on the achievement of operational objectives.
5. To provide information useful for evaluating managerial and organizational performance.
6. To communicate relevant information in a manner which best facilitates its use.

State Requirements for Accounting of Public School Fiscal Affairs

Bulletin 679-Public School Accounting Guide was pressed into use in Texas Public Schools, by the Texas Education Agency in the late 1960s.

The material contained in Bulletin 679 is based upon the assumption that the user have a basic knowledge and understanding of accounting principles.

The accounting codification structure represented in Bulletin 679 is a part of the enlarged program oriented budgeting and accounting system designed for public schools of Texas. "The program oriented system has been designed as a subsystem of the Educational Management Information System (EMIS) that incorporates, together with the Financial sub-system, the Personnel, Student, Curriculum and Instruction, Community Profile and Property subsystems. Program oriented financial accounting, because of the detail involved, demands and automated or electronic data processing capability. Section 11.33(b), Texas Education Code, provides a program of financial assistance for computer services to school districts of the State through regional education service centers.

Structure of Bulletin 679

For convenience of locating subject matter, the manual is divided into eight sections and three appendices. If a question arises about auditing, the reader can reference the table of contents relative to Audit. The beginning of the Audit section is identified as Aud 601, where information on the subject is found. If all changes are contained in the section all current information on Auditing will be found. The loose leaf binding and numbering procedures sequentially by section will allow timely revisions and insertion of supplemental instructions by the local education agency.

Obviously, reading through the manual will result in a general understanding of the organization and content before attempting to use the specific procedures.

The following is a listing of the sections and a general explanation of the content of each section:

ADM—The Administrative Section—numbered 001 through 009 and contains procedures for revising the manual; and contains administration instructions issued by the Texas Education Agency and the local school district.

REQ—The Requirements Section, pages 101 through 199, sets out general requirements of the state and federal regulations, statutes and accounting principles and policies that creates the basis for financial transactions relating to public schools.

BDG—The Budget Section, pages 201 through 299, gives an explanation of the objectives, principles and responsibilities for school budgeting.

ACT—The Accounting Section, pages 301 through 399, outlines the principles of fund, encumbrance and expenditure accounting.

CDE—The Accounting Code Section, pages 401 through 499, lists and gives a detailed description of the various accounting codes to be used by school districts. This section provides data necessary to proper classification of accounts and transactions.

PRC—The Accounting Procedures Section, pages 501 through 599, describes the processing of accounting documents such as requisitions, purchase orders, receiving reports, inventory requisitions, payroll documents, cash receipt, disbursements journal entries, and etc. It gives example and illustration of Accounting Journals and General Ledger and sample entries.

AUD—The Audit Section, pages 601 through 699, sets out detailed requirements for auditing public schools accounts, samples or specimen of financial statements, schedules and exhibits required for the annual audit report.

SPG—Special Program Guidelines Section, pages 701 through 799, stipulates compliance standards and regulations for the special programs.

APP–A. Appendix A—glossary, defines terms common to accounting and school operations described in the manual.

APP–B. Appendix B—Accounting code Reference Listing is a compilation of all accounting codes, but without definitions. It is intended as a quick reference to combine an account name with the correct number. The assumption is that the user will have an understanding of the proper definition. If there is doubt, refer to CDE section for proper definition.

APP–C. Appendix C—Listing of Supplies and Equipment contains criteria for discerning whether an item is a supply or is to be classified as equipment.

The principles and policies, relating to financial accounting incorporated in Bulletin 679 are official rules adopted by the State Board of Education. They set forth a basic accounting system that public schools must follow and provide uniformity in reporting at the local, regional and state level and in conformity will Generally Accepted Accounting Principles (GAAP) established by the Governmental Accounting Standards Board.

Conformity with legal requirements for reporting the operation of public schools makes necessary a system of fund accounting be instituted by each school system. The fund concept identifies a fund as an independent accounting entity with its own assets, liabilities and balances. Each school district is required to establish sufficient funds to account for all financial transactions of specific activities of a school districts operations.

Legal requirements and purposes of the various activities will determine the minimum number of funds appropriate for public school operations. The need to identify expenditures with receipts for the various separate funds makes this necessary. Funds are grouped because of similarity of purpose. Listed below are the required fund types and groups of self-balancing accounts.

1. Governmental fund types
   a. General Fund
   b. Special Revenue
   c. Debt Service
   d. Capital Projects

2. Proprietary Fund Types
   a. Enterprise Funds
   b. Internal Service Funds

3. Fiduciary Fund Types
   a. Trust Funds
   b. Agency Funds

4. Account Groups
   a. General Fixed Assets
   b. General Long Term Debt

The School District Budget

In Bulletin 679 the budget is referred to as "... a statement expressed in financial terms, which serves as management's primary tool for planning and controlling operations." C.E. Barringer, Deputy Superintendent, Finance/Supply, Temple ISD says "A budget is a picture, drawn with dollar values, which illustrates an organization's planned operation. Analysis of the picture should clearly outline the philosophy, priorities and operating mode of an organization." There are other good definitions of the budget. Regardless of how many definitions there might be, and how they developed, every school district must adopt a budget before September 1 of each year. On or before August 20 of each year the proposed budget must be presented to the Board of Trustees. The budget must be officially adopted by the majority of the local Board of Trustees before the budget may be implemented.

Upon the adoption of the budget by the Board of Trustees, a tax rate must be adopted by separate motion and action of the Board of Trustees.

The Tax Rate

At the finalization of the budget, a tax rate should be calculated that will adequately fund the total adopted budget and retire any bonded indebtedness obligation in the newly adopted budget.

If the school district has bonded indebtedness, a tax rate to meet and retire the calculated principal of the debt as well as pay the interest for the fiscal year is required. The portion of the tax rate designated to retire bonds is referred to as rate for debt service. The other portion of the tax rate is referred to as Local Maintenance Rate. The portion of the rate to retire bonds plus the maintenance portion combine to form the total tax rate.

Amended Budget Requirement

If at anytime during the fiscal year a function proves to be in jeopardy of being over expended, an amendment to that portion of the budget must be adopted prior to any over-expenditure. That is to say, such amendments shall be before the fact, must be reflected in the official minutes of the board of trustees, and may not, by law, occur after August 31.

The Official Budget

There are a number of ways that a school district may proceed in collecting and compiling data to be used in developing an official budget. The intent of this writing is not to re-hash those ways; nor will space allow such explanation.

By state law every school district in Texas is required to develop and file a budget for the fiscal year—September 1 through August 31—of all anticipated expenditures and revenues with the Texas Education Agency.

In all independent school districts, Sections 23.41 and 23.42 of the Texas Education Code, require that the president of the board of trustees is designated as the chief budget officer for the district. That designation stipulates that this person is responsible for preparing, or causes to be prepared a budget for the ensuing fiscal year. Further, the board president has the responsibility of meeting the August 20 deadline for presenting a proposed budget to the board of trustees of that district. After the local board of trustees has had an opportunity to review and make adjustments to the proposed budget, it is the duty of the president to advertize in local newspapers and post notice in designated places that a meeting will be conducted at least ten days subsequent to the posting of notice to adopt the budget. See Section 23.45, Texas Education Code for full details. The board of trustees must adopt the budget before adopting a tax rate for the tax year in which the fiscal year covered by the budget begins. Both the budget and tax rate may be adopted at the same meeting, provided it is done by two separate motions and actions, when the notice of the meeting lists both items on agenda. However, the tax rate cannot be adopted until after the budget has been adopted by a majority of board members present at the meeting.

After the budget has been adopted, a tax rate set, the board president must see that an official copy of the budget is filed with the county clerk's office in the county or counties in which the district is located and with the Texas Education Agency not later than November 1 of the budget year. See Section 23.46 of the Texas Education code.

As stated previously, the official budget covers the fiscal year September 1 through August 31 in keeping with the State of Texas fiscal year. Some programs have a funding period which differs from the State fiscal year, therefore, it is necessary that a program budget be prepared which covers a different budget time period. However, the official budget for the district shall include only the estimated expenditures and revenues occurring during the official budget period of September 1 through August 31.

Purpose of the Budget

To achieve the basic purpose of planning and controlling the district's financial operation, a comprehensive budget must be integrated with the financial accounting system to insure that objectives of planning, coordinating, evaluation and control is accomplished.

The primary objectives of the budget systems are to:

- Enhance the development of a unified system of operation and the understanding of how each educational components' activities contribute to the district's overall mission.
- Serve to communicate to all levels of management by setting forth the objectives of each component and the funds necessary to reach the stated objectives.
- Provide each component manager with financial data sufficient to perform the function and to control expenditures.
- Supply a way of measuring and directing program performance by comparing anticipated expenditures and work load against actual expenditures and work load.
- Provide historical and empirical data necessary to realistic future budget development.

Budget Principles

In order to attain satisfactory attainment of the objectives the following principles should be exercised in the preparation of the budget:

- The person responsible for performing an activity should be involved in the initial budget requests.
- Projected work load should be identified in the projected task and documented in terms of budget requests.
- Component heads should be actively involved in revisions of their budgets to insure realistic changes and allow them to modify their operations in accordance with revisions.

School administrators should be brought to the point of understanding and being involved in the planning process that they might be aware of benefits accruing from long-range financial planning. In that fashion, administrators will be able to evaluate current operations in relation to the overall or total plan for the district.

The budget should be formulated at the level at which responsibility for controlling operations is assigned. That is to say, if the principal or director has been assigned responsibility for the operations of a campus or department, responsibility for controlling and directing expenditures of that unit should belong to the person responsible for that program.

A budget message should be prepared and sent to each management member responsible for submitting prepared budget requests. The budget message should contain a statement of overall objectives for the district as well as a statement of objectives for each educational component for which the budget request is prepared.

The budget requests for expenditures should originate at the management level of each educational component and in such fashion that functional expenditures are identified according to the detail object account listed in Bulletin 679, Section BDG 202.

Official Budget Illustrations and Instructions

Procedure BDG 202 in Bulletin 679 gives an illustration for the minimum level specified for the official budget. Page 1 of BDG 202 gives examples the types of budget information required to be reported to PIEMS. Other examples of budget expenditure reports are found on subsequent pages through page 6.

Accounting Code Overview

Procedure CDE 401 of Bulletin 679 provides school districts with the required accounting code structure and definitions with the intended purpose of state-wide uniformity. Certain reports may dictate the use of certain codes. The optional codes may be used by districts to expand their capability of generating additional data for local district reports. The complete account code structure is explained in Procedure CDE 401, page 1 of Bulletin 679. (See figure 14.1.)

Fund Codes

The fund code is a mandatory three (3) digit code to be used in all financial transactions. The first digit refers to the fund group; digit two (2) refers to the specific fund; and, the third digit refers to the particular fiscal year. For example—the General Fund for fiscal year 1993 (1992-93 school year) would be 113. The first 1 indicates General Fund; the middle Local maintenance; and, the 3 is the fiscal year 1993.

The following list of funds is found in Procedure CDE 402 of Bulletin 679, pages 1-6:

10x—General Fund
11x—Local Maintenance
15x—Food Service
16x—Apprenticeship Training
18x—Co-Curricular Activity
20x through 40x—Special Revenue Fund
Fund numbers and titles have been assigned for various programs within these groups of numbers. Funds that have been designated by contract for a special purpose would be assigned a Special Revenue Fund.
50x—Debt Service Fund
60x—Capital Projects Fund
70x—Proprietary Fund types
80x—Fiduciary Fund types-Trust and Agency funds
90x—General Fixed Assets and General Long-term debt

Function Codes

The function code is a mandatory two (2) digit code used to identify the purpose of the transaction. The first digit identifies the major service area. The second digit refers to the specific function within the area. An example—21 is Instructional Administration function. Digit 2 indicates that it is an instructional related service. 1 indicates administration.

FIGURE 12.1
Accounting Code Overview

TEA-BULLETIN-679, CHANGE NO: 27   **PROCEDURE NO: CDE-401**
Date: September 10, 1992
Subject: Accounting Code Overview

Section 23.48 of the Texas Education Code requires that a standard school fiscal accounting system be adopted by each school district. The system must meet at least the minimum requirements prescribed by the State Board of Education and also be approved by the state auditor. This section further requires that a report be provided at the time that the school budget is filed, showing financial information sufficient to enable the State Board of Education to monitor the funding process, and to determine educational system costs by district, campus, and program.

The Texas Education Code, Section 21.256, requires an annual independent audit that meets the minimum requirements of the State Board of Education, as approved by the state auditor. In addition, Section 21.258 of the Code calls for an annual performance report from each school district, giving financial information related to the costs incurred by the district. The district's annual performance report may be combined with other types of reports and financial statements required by law or rule.

A major purpose of the following accounting code structure is to establish the standard school fiscal accounting system required by law. Although certain codes within the overview may be used at local option, the sequence of the codes within the structure, and the funds and chart of accounts, are to be uniformly used by all school districts in accordance with generally accepted accounting principles.

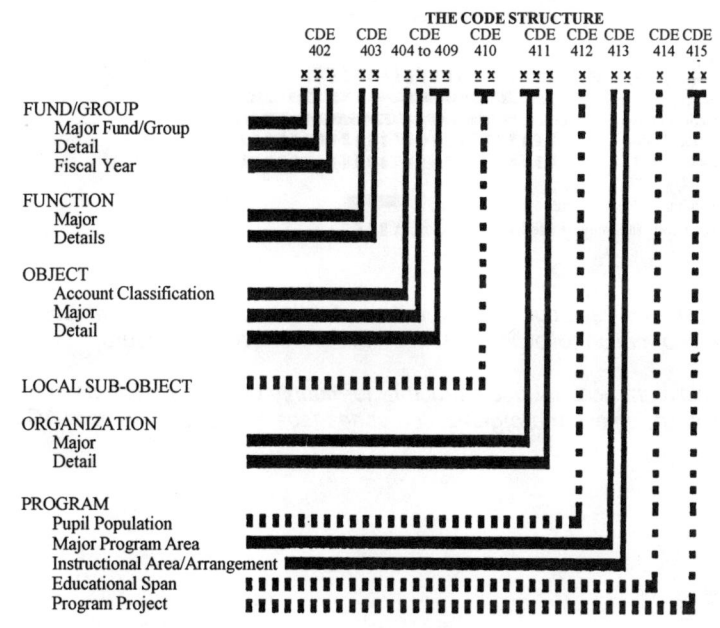

THE CODE STRUCTURE

	CDE 402	CDE 403	CDE 404 to 409	CDE 410	CDE 411	CDE 412	CDE 413	CDE 414	CDE 415
	XXX	XX	XXXX	XX	XXX	X	XX	X	XX

FUND/GROUP
  Major Fund/Group
  Detail
  Fiscal Year

FUNCTION
  Major
  Details

OBJECT
  Account Classification
  Major
  Detail

LOCAL SUB-OBJECT

ORGANIZATION
  Major
  Detail

PROGRAM
  Pupil Population
  Major Program Area
  Instructional Area/Arrangement
  Educational Span
  Program Project

Indicates a mandatory code for State reporting purposes. ▬▬
Indicates a code that may be used at local option. ▪▪▪▪▪

TEA-BULLETIN-679, CHANGE NO: 27   PROCEDURE NO: CDE-401
Date: September 10, 1992
Subject: Accounting code Overview

Effective September 1, 1993, the following code structure will take effect. The changes involve the detail level of the fund code and the conversion of the optional pupil population code into a mandatory year field.

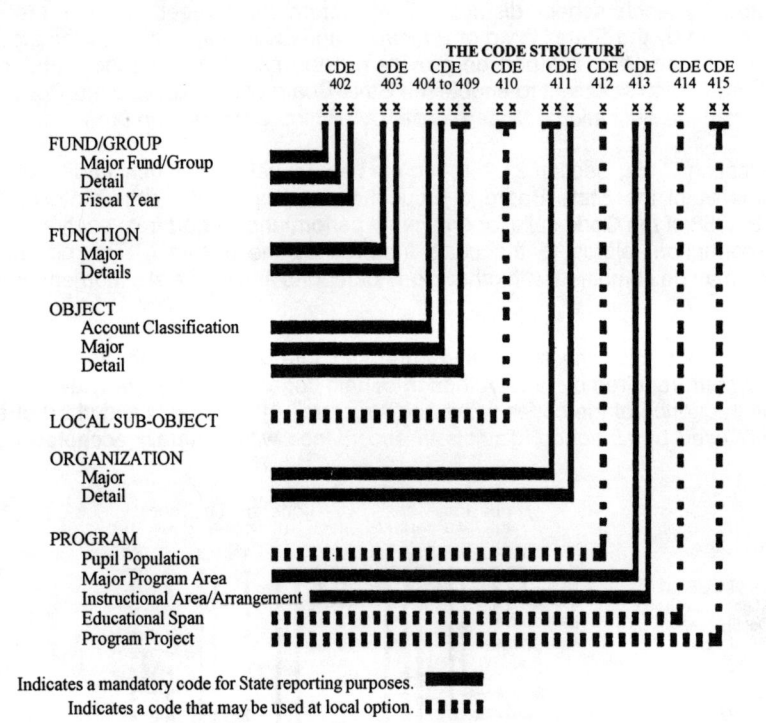

THE CODE STRUCTURE

	CDE 402	CDE 403	CDE 404 to 409	CDE 410	CDE 411	CDE 412	CDE 413	CDE 414	CDE 415
	XXX	XX	XXXX	XX	XXX	X	XX	X	XX

FUND/GROUP
  Major Fund/Group
  Detail
  Fiscal Year

FUNCTION
  Major
  Details

OBJECT
  Account Classification
  Major
  Detail

LOCAL SUB-OBJECT

ORGANIZATION
  Major
  Detail

PROGRAM
  Pupil Population
  Major Program Area
  Instructional Area/Arrangement
  Educational Span
  Program Project

Indicates a mandatory code for State reporting purposes. ▬▬▬
Indicates a code that may be used at local option. ▪ ▪ ▪ ▪ ▪

The September 1, 1993 revised code structure immediately above is for informational and planning purposes only. The information following describes the current code structure.

In regard to the minimum account code structure for county education districts, mandatory codes include the fund, function, object and organization codes (see Procedure Number ACT-323).

TEA-BULLETIN-679, CHANGE NO: 27   PROCEDURE NO: CDE-401
DATE: September 10, 1992
SUBJECT: Accounting Code Overview

BASIC SYSTEM CODE COMPOSITION:

FUND CODE--A mandatory *2* digit code, plus one digit for fiscal year, is to be used for all financial transactions to identify the fund group, specific fund, and the fiscal year. The first digit refers to the fund group, the second digit specifies the fund, and the third digit of the fund code is the last digit of the appropriate fiscal year. For example--The Special Revenue Fund for fiscal year (school year) could be coded *213*. The *3* indicates the Special Revenue Fund, the *1* specifies ESEA Chapter 1 Regular and the *3* is fiscal year 1993 (see Procedure Number CDE-402).

(Effective September 1, 1993, the third digit will no longer denote fiscal year; the fiscal year field will be moved to population served field and the population served field will no longer be used. See Appendix E for a listing of fund codes to be used for the 1993-94 school year.)

FUNCTION CODE--A mandatory *2* digit code applied to expenditures that identifies the purpose of the transaction. The first digit identifies the major service area and the second digit refers to the specific function within the area. EXAMPLE--the function "Health Service" is coded 33. The first *3* specifies Pupil Services and the second *3* is Health (see Procedure Number CDE-403).

OBJECT CODE--A mandatory *4* digit code identifying the nature and object of an account, a transaction, or a source. The first of the four digits identifies the type of account or transaction, the second digit identifies the major area, and the third and fourth digits provide further sub-classifications. For example, money received from the Federal Government for a bilingual program is recorded in account *5916*. The 5 denotes revenue, the 9 shows Federal Sources, the 1 is direct Federal, and the 6 is a bilingual project (see Procedure Numbers CDE-404 through 409).

LOCAL SUB-OBJECT CODES--A *2* digit code for optional use (see Procedure Number CDE-410).

ORGANIZATION CODE--A mandatory *3* digit code identifying the organization, i.e., High School, Middle School, Elementary School, etc., (see Procedure Number CDE-411).

PUPIL POPULATION GROUP CODE--An optional single character alphabetical code that identifies types of students for whom programs have been specifically designed (see Procedure Number CDE-412).

(Effective September 1, 1993, the pupil population group code will be replaced by fiscal year field.)

TEA-BULLETIN-679, CHANGE NO: 27   PROCEDURE NO: CDE-401
DATE: September 10, 1992
SUBJECT: Accounting Code Overview

MAJOR PROGRAM AREA CODE—A *2* digit code used to designate instructional areas and/or arrangements. The Texas Education Code, Section 23.48(d), requires a determination of costs by program. Therefore, the use of the codes designating instructional areas (10, 20, 31, 32, 50, 70, 80, 90, and 98) is mandatory for identifying costs of functions 11 and 12 for the General Fund, Special Revenue Fund, and the Governmental Expendable Trust Fund. Also, if an expenditure is clearly attributable to a broad program area in a function other than instruction, the expenditure is to be accounted for in the same manner as those for functions 11. Generic code 01 is used to account for functional expenditures not attributable to major programs areas (see Procedure Numbers CDE-413 and ACT-307).

EDUCATIONAL SPAN CODE—An optional single alphabetical character code that identifies programs/projects designed for groups or classes at various instructional levels (see Procedure Number CDE-414).

PROJECT DETAIL CODE—An optional *2* digit code that may be used by the district to further describe the program, i.e., 01 might be English I; 02 is English II, etc., (see Procedure Number CDE-415).

When classifying a transaction such as an expenditure, answering the following questions will assist in proper application of accounting codes:

(Q)	*How* and *when* is the expenditure financed?	(A)	Fund Code
(Q)	*Why* was the expenditure made?	(A)	Function Code
(Q)	*What* was purchased?	(A)	Object Code
(Q)	*Is* separate accountability required?	(A)	Local Sub-Object Code
(Q)	*Where* is the beneficiary of the expenditure located?	(A)	Organization Code
(Q)	*Who* are the students benefited?	(A)	Pupil Population Group Code
(Q)	*What* is the subject matter or differentiated instructional arrangement?	(A)	Instructional Area/ Arrangement Code
(Q)	*What* instructional level is to be charged?	(A)	Educational Span Code
(Q)	*What* other information is needed?	(A)	Project Code

EXAMPLE:

Assume that there is a program operated to provide a course in mathematics at the 11th grade level for regular students. Classes are held in one of the local high schools. The salary of the teacher is coded as follows:

FUND	FUNC.	OBJ.	SUB.	ORG.	PUPIL POP. GROUP	AREA	SPAN	PROJECT
113	11	6119	00	015	A	10	3	22

Fund code 113 is the general fund for fiscal year 1992-93. Function code 11 indicates direct classroom instruction. Object code 6119 denotes an expenditure for professional salary. The organization code 015 is the campus code for a high school. Pupil population group A is general population. Instructional area 10 is basic skills, regular. Educational Span 3 indicates the fiscal year. If this were local project number 22, that number would be assigned.

No single code can give the complete transaction information required. The fund, function, object, organization and program area codes combine to provide information and allow extraction of varying fiscal data for minimum reporting purposes required by law. In the above example, pupil population group, and project codes are used at local option.

Procedure CDE 403 of Bulletin 679 provides a list of function codes. The list of function code and titles follow:

11—Instructional
12—Instructional Computing
21—Instructional Administration
22—Instructional Resource and Media Services
23—School Administration
24—Instructional Research and Development
25—Curriculum and Personnel Development
26—Communication and Dissemination
31—Guidance and Counseling Services
32—Attendance and Social Work Services
33—Health Services
34—Pupil Transportation-Regular
35—Pupil Transportation-Exceptional
36—Co-curricular Activities
37—Food Services
41—General Administration
42—Debt Services
51—Plant Maintenance and Operation
52—Facilities Acquisition and Construction
71—Management
72—Computer Processing
73—Development
74—Interfacing (Technical Assistance)
81—Community Service

Asset Codes

Asset codes are mandatory and are recorded as debits in six categories:

I - Current Assets
    1100—Cash and Temporary Investments
    1200—Receivables
    1300—Inventories
    1400—Other Current Assets
II - Fixed Assets
    1500—Land, Building, and Equipment
III - Amounts to be Provided for Payment of Debt Principal
    1600—Amount provided
IV - Amount Available for Bond Principal
    1700—Amount available
V - Restricted Assets
    1800—Restricted or Specific Purpose Assets
VI - Other Debits
    1900—Other Debits

Each asset category has numerous accounts provided to furnish adequate detail in recording specific types of assets. Procedure CDE 404 in Bulletin 679 gives a detailed explanation of the asset codes.

Liability Codes

Procedure CDE 405 of Bulletin 679, pages 1-4, states "liabilities are recorded as credits in two (2) broad categories: (1) current liabilities, and (2) long-term debts. These are mandatory codes and accounts and must be used to assure uniformity in financial reporting..."

The first category—current liabilities—list the various accounts for payroll deductions and withholdings. Additionally, accounts due to other funds and accrued expenses are viewed as current liabilities.

The second category for liabilities is long-term and includes bonds payable and leases payable. The difference between long-term and short-term is that short-term liabilities will be liquidated during the current budget or fiscal year.

Fund Equity/Codes

Fund equity codes identify funds available at the end of the fiscal year and the use of fund equity codes is mandatory. There are four categories of equity codes.

3100-Fund Balance
3200-Invested Reserves
3300-Contributed Capital
3400-Retained Earnings

Fund Equity accounts represents funds available at the close of the fiscal year from various designated funds as reserves. A fund balance occurs when funds remain at the close of the fiscal year after all liabilities and reserves have been satisfied.

Clearing Account Codes

Procedure CDE 407 in Bulletin 679 lists and explains the clearing and encumbrance reserve accounts in some detail. These accounts are optional to the local school district.

Clearing accounts serve to be credited when proceeds are received and debited when payments are issued.

The encumbrance reserve account serves to be used to record purchase orders, contracts awarded, or any other transactions which will require eventual payment but at present time of record no liability exists.

Revenue Codes

Revenue increases the fund's ownership equity in its assets. Usually, revenues increase cash or other current assets which can be converted into cash without affecting the fund's liabilities. A revenue received must have the ability to be expended and cannot be an expenditure reimbursement.

Revenue is to be recorded in the 5000 series of accounts. Control accounts have been established in the 5000's for estimated and realized revenue in Procedure CDE 408.

The following codes are to be used to record revenues for federal, state and local sources:

5700-Revenues from local, intermediate, and out-of-state sources and transfers;
5800-State program revenues; and,
5900-Federal program revenues and nonrevenue receipts.

Specific accounts have been established to record revenues and provide for detailed accounting for the sources of all revenues received by the district.

Expenditure Codes

The recording of expenditures includes an area that is broader than just expenses. An expenditure will include expenses for goods and services received, whether paid or unpaid, and capital outlay. Accrued expenditures will be recorded in this category.

The expenditure codes listed in Procedure CDE 409 are mandatory. An expenditure is to be recorded with a debit in the accounting period it is incurred. The following are the object codes issued for recording expenditures:

6100-Payroll costs—Gross salaries or wages and benefit costs for employee services are recorded in this area. Reporting of payroll costs requires considerable detail, making necessary the use of several four (4) digit object codes.

6200-Purchased and Contracted Services—Services rendered for the school district by firms, individuals, or other organizations must be recorded in this category. Numerous areas within this category have been set-up to record the varied services with definitions provided school districts to assure uniformity of reporting.

6300-Supplies and Materials—The purchase of items to be consumer and/or used by the school district within the budget year is recorded in this category. Supplies and materials used to support the operation of facilities, classrooms, and equipment owned by the school district are generally low cost items. Even though the items may be warehoused, they are considered to be consumable within a relatively brief period of time and classified in this category of expenditures.

6400-Other Operating Expenses—Such expenditures as travel, school board member and bond elections, insurance premiums and deficits of other funds are recorded in this category. Other related expenses should be recorded in this category (6400) of expenditures.

6500-Debt Service—This category is restricted to the use of recording the expenditure to pay the principal and interest of bonds, loans, leases, and other related credit obligations.

6600-Capital Outlay—Land, Buildings, and Equipment. Expenditures recorded in this category is for the acquisition of items that fit the definition of capital outlay and considered to be a fixed asset. Various and separate object members are provided in this category to differentiate between such items as furniture, computer equipment, vehicles, audio-visual equipment, library books and others. It is mandatory that these object codes be used and that items be listed on the school district's fixed asset inventory.

6990-Other Uses—Other uses are debited in the accounting period in which a measurable fund liability is incurred. These mandatory codes should be used to record transfers of funds to other funds of the district. The transfers may include two other entities if the district is a member of a cooperative. Money expenditures for other uses within the district would also be recorded in this category.

Sub-Object Codes

Procedure CDE 410 describes local sub-object codes a two-digit number to provide accounting detail for programs and revenues where rules or law requires separate accountability. Sub-object codes are optional to the school district and provide a means to record transactions to meet local needs.

The two-digit codes are assigned at the school district's discretion. A chart of accounts should, be maintained as account numbers are developed locally. This procedure will aid the management and audit of the school district's records.

Fixed Assets

Capital expenditures are those expenditures made to acquire fixed assets. A fixed asset must be tangible in nature, have a life longer than two years, is of significant value at purchase or acquisition time, and/or may be reasonably identified and controlled through a physical inventory system. Examples of a fixed asset are: land, buildings, furniture, vehicles, and other equipment which are to be held for an extended period of time.

The accounting for fixed assets of school districts is not to include depreciation. In Procedure ACT 305 of Bulletin 679, the suggested accounting for general fixed assets is described. When equipment is depreciated, it is reduced in value over a period fiscal year. This procedure applies only to proprietary funds and nonexpendable trust and agency funds in order to measure net income and capital maintenance.

Procedures must be established to provide for adequate control of fixed assets. A system must be established to provide a method to record transfer, additions, and deletions of fixed assets. An inventory or schedule of all asset items must be maintained to help provide information for purchasing adequate insurance coverage.

When recording fixed assets at the time of acquisition, original cost is used for a basis of reporting. If documents are not available to record a fixed asset value, it is appropriate to determine a fair market value for the asset.

Fixed assets are to be recorded in recommended asset classes. The four asset classes are land, buildings and improvements, construction in progress, and furniture and equipment. When recording the cost of these assets, any related cost of acquiring or in association with acquiring an asset, is considered to be a part of the actual cost.

A physical inventory should be taken at the end of each year to verify the reliability of the inventory and maintain internal control. Any discrepancies detected by an inventory should be settled each year. A policy should be established to reconcile differences that are detected.

Procedures should be established to record disposals or retirements of fixed assets. The elimination of an asset will result in the reduction of assets and by reversing the original entry, will be deleted from inventory. Disposal can occur due to trade-in, sale of an asset item, or retirement due to obsolescence.

Fiscal Audit

Public school districts are required to have the district's accounts audited annually to comply with Section 21.256, Texas Education Code. Guidelines, in Procedure AUD 601 of Bulletin 679, have been provided to satisfy both audit requirements of state law and the Single Audit Act of 1984. This audit is to be performed in accordance with the *Financial Accounting Manual*, Bulletin 679, which is adopted by reference as a State Board of Education rule, Title 19, Texas Administrative code, Section 109.61.

The annual audit report shall be prepared and submitted to the Texas Education Agency within 120 days of the close of the fiscal year. Procedure AUD 603, Bulletin 679, contains the minimum statements, schedules, and notes in the format required by the Texas Education Agency. The school board of trustees must approve or disapprove the audit report.

The independent auditing firm that performs the audit must observe generally accepted auditing standards. The scope of the audit should encompass an examination of financial transactions, accounts, and reports, including an evaluation of compliance with applicable laws and regulations. School districts that receive Federal funds shall take measures to assure that such Federal funds are used and audited in accordance with the Special Program Guidelines (SPG) section of Bulletin 679.

The audit shall include all fund types and account groups of the school district. The auditors shall audit all programs of the district on an organization-wide basis. The independence of the auditing firm must be maintained at all times and the auditors must have a valid permit from the State Board of Public Accounting.

Optional requirements may be required by the local school district board of trustees. The audit may include statements and reports in addition to the minimum requirements. The auditors may be required to report on the efficiency of the use of resources of the school district. Also, the effectiveness may be included in the annual report if desired by the local school board.

The Division of Audits of the Texas Education Agency shall review the annual audit reports submitted by the school district. The Commissioner of Education or his designer shall notify the School Board of Trustees of the auditor's report. The audit report is public information and may be released when requested.

Purchasing Procedures

The purchasing process involves management of materials from need determination, to source identification, to shipping, to inventory, to storage, and to delivery to the appropriate location. Purchasing is an intermediate service. Supplies, equipment, and materials are bought for their educational need to teachers and students. Purchasing services is a complicated process that involves determining what is needed and the quantity and quality of products, synchronizing the time of need and the delivery time, proving the quantity needed without overspending the budgeted amount, storing what is required without overstocking inventories, keeping unsuccessful bidders happy, and satisfying school employees when recommended brands are not purchased or something interferes with the delivery of materials or equipment.

Effective school purchasing is established through a systematic purchasing organization that is operated by written procedure. This includes the adopting of purchasing policies by the Board of Education, and supplemental regulations concerning procedures established by the superintendent and business manager. Public school purchasing derives its authority from laws. Business officials are responsible to a legislative body and accountable to the voters that elect the board of trustees.

Because purchasing activities are open to public scrutiny, all such actions must be defensible to any challenge. As a result extensive record keeping must be included in the purchasing procedures. The basic components of the procedures of purchasing are essential for accountability.

Purchase Requisition

A written request and approval for the purchase of supplies, services, or equipment is the first step in determining the need and the authority necessary for the purchase. The requisition is completed by the person making the request. It is then approved by the principal/supervisor and sent to the Business Office for approval by a duly authorized administrator. The requisition should be a standard format for each of identifying information and transferring to a purchase order.

Bulletin 679, Financial Accounting Manual of the Texas Education Agency, requires a minimum of two copies for each purchase requisition. However, a five part requisition is more effective for accountability which includes the following:

1. Business office copy (white). The original copy.
2. Accounts Payable copy (green). Attached to the Accounts Payable copy of the Purchase order.
3. Receiving copy (blue) signed by the receiver, when goods are received, and returned to Accounts Payable.

4. File copy (gold) kept by Accounts Payable in purchase order number, used for quick numeric reference only.
5. Originator copy (pink) kept on location where requisition was initiated.

Requisition Routing

The following routing is normally required for purchases:

1. Requisition is initiated as a work copy approved by the principal/supervisor.
2. Requisition is typed and signed by principal/supervisor and forwarded to the Business Office.
3. Business Office date stamps the requisition and gives it to the bookkeeper for verification of appropriate budgetary account number(s) and availability of monies.
4. After proper verification the requisition is forwarded to the Purchasing Department.
5. The Purchasing Agent checks the requisition to determine if the bid item price quotation and other information are correct for generation of a purchase order.
6. The requisition is entered into the purchase order computer program as a purchase order.
7. Once the purchase order is printed, the requisition is matched with the proper purchase order and both are clipped together.
8. Purchase order signed by Purchasing Agent.
9. Purchase order and requisition mailed to vendor and copies distributed to proper locations.

The size of the school district will determine the number of specific departments needed to accomplish the above steps. Also, the computer program may be substituted for by hand work in some districts.

A requisition should be returned to the originator when any one of the following reasons is apparent:

- The requisition is not properly authorized and signed by the principal/supervisor, etc.
- The requisition is not properly typed.
- The budgetary account is overdrawn.

Purchase Order

A purchase order is written evidence of an order placed as a result of receiving a properly approved purchase requisition. It is the vehicle by which goods or services are procured in order to fill a need. The acceptance of a purchase order by a vendor effects a legally binding contract that gives the vendor the authority to ship the required goods and binds the buyer for payment upon compliance. A standard format for purchase orders is necessary for facilitating the purchasing process. Bulletin 79 recommends a five part purchase order form. The distribution process should be as follows:

Part 1 - to vendor
Part 2 - to accounting department Part 3-to receiving unit
Part 4 - to be retained by purchasing department
Part 5 - optional; may be used to notify requesting unit of purchase.

The TEA Financial Accounting Manual Bulletin 679 recommends including the following checks and balances into purchasing procedures. These will enhance internal control for the district:

1. Purchases should be based on purchase requisitions initiated by the appropriate authority.
2. Purchase orders should be approved by an appropriate authority.
3. Periodic purchasing practices review should be conducted to disclose:
    a. excessive prices paid as a result of collusion between purchaser and supplier;
    b. processing and paying of fictitious invoice or of duplicate payments;
    c. alteration of invoices
4. The preparation of a receiving report to control incoming merchandise.
5. Vendor invoices mailed directly to Accounting Department for verification with purchase order and receiving report.
6. Invoices should not be recorded as a liability until properly approved.
7. Provide adequate separation of duties.

Receiving Report

Part Two (2) of the purchase order is the instrument for reconciling the items received and ordered. Exceptions are noted on the receiving report, dated, signed, and returned to the Accounting Department of reconciliation with the invoice. The report should be completed as follows:

1. Indicate items not received
2. Signature of the person receiving the material or services

Partial shipments should be recorded on this part of the purchase order. A copy of the receiving report is made and sent to accounting. The Accounting Department will maintain a record of receipts to date per line item for all partial receipts until all items are received or the P.O. is cancelled. Once a recovery report is submitted to the Business Office, unless otherwise noted, all materials should be assumed to be in acceptable condition and payment to the vendor able to proceed.

Should a delivery be made directly to a school, or if merchandise is picked up by personnel, the district should require that a signed and dated receipt, packing list, and invoice be sent to accounting before payment is made.

Special Problems with Purchase Orders

On Approval Purchases or Free Item.

Approval purchases or free items must be ordered on the standard requisition. If the item meets the originator's approval, Purchasing will notify the vendor that it is accepted and request an invoice. Items received without a purchase order should not be accepted. If the item does not meet approval the request for returns of material form must be completed and sent to the Purchasing Agent.

This process provides Purchasing with an effective way to monitor such items. Also, the potential for being billed for an approval or free items is reduced and the possibility of being charged for shipping and handling is reduced.

Return of Material.

To return any material, a request should be sent to the Business Office on a Request for Return of Material form. If the material received is incorrect, the wrong size, the wrong color, damaged, etc., this form must be completed and sent to the business office.

This form is returned to Purchasing who makes arrangements with the vendor. Central Receiving is also contacted by Purchasing and provided a copy of the form. The procedure for returning the item, UPS, Federal Express, collect, vendor pick up, etc., is also determined.

The Purchasing Agent should be the only individual authorized to make a change, to alter, or cancel a purchase order to a vendor.

Correspondence.

All correspondence pertaining to purchase order items should be conducted by the Business Office. In order to expedite the entire process, the Business Office must be the front for all involvement with vendors. When any change in the status of a purchase occurs, or if there are questions concerning the purchase order, such information should be provided to the Business Office.

The Business Office must obtain an invoice with a purchase order number and a receiving report evidencing the item has been received before budgetary funds are expended.

Phases of Purchasing

Encumbrances.

The first phase of the purchasing process is encumbering funds. Encumbering obligates budgeted funds for the cost of goods or services until such is delivered. It in effect reserves the funds until they are needed. This can be done on a computer when the approved requisition is being converted into a purchase order. Another method of encumbering is done by hand. The purchase order is manually prepared and the account balance is correspondingly reduced.

Expenditures.

The second phase of the process is expenditures. The encumbered order becomes an account payable when goods are tendered or services rendered and invoice received. The encumbrance changes to an expenditure when this happens. In order to reduce such a liability cash must be disbursed.

Disbursements.

The final phase, disbursements results in the amount of money originally encumbered against the budget account for the amount of purchase being expended. Cash disbursements should be made by check in order to utilize internal control features.

Disbursements should be a separate function form receiving cash and of approving items for payment. Functions should be established as follows:

1. payment authorization
2. preparation of checks
3. check entry in cash disbursements journal
4. signing of checks and comparison with documents
5. check transmittal
6. reconciling bank accounts

Bids and Price Quotes

Competitive bidding is the process of at least two parties acting independently to secure the business of a third party by offering the most favorable terms and conditions. Adequate competition requires at least two responsible bidders, able to satisfy the buyer's needs to speculation and delivery, independently contending for a contract.

Texas Education Code (21.901) addresses a number of requirements for competitive bidding:

1. All proposed contracts valued at $5,000 or more for the purchase of personal property, and for the construction, maintenance, repair or renovation of any building or for materials used in such projects must be submitted to competitive bidding.
2. Notice of time and place where contracts will be let and bids opened shall be published in the county where the school is located.
3. The legal notice for bids must:
   a. describe the work
   b. state where the documents, plans, speculations, and data may be examined.
   c. state time and place for submitting bids and the time and place the bids will be publicly opened.
4. Exceptions to the regulations are provided: If a school building or equipment is destroyed or severely damaged and the school board determines a time delay would impair essential activities; if a district purchases computers and computer related equipment from the list of approved equipment prepared by the State Purchasing and General Services Commission. In addition, professional services fees such as attorney's fees or architect's fees are excluded from competitive bidding.
5. Contracts must be awarded to the lowest responsible bidder.

Bids for the selection of a bank as the school depository are subject to provisions of the Texas Education Code. Once a bank is chosen, it will serve for a term of two years. The term will commence and terminate on the fiscal year of odd-numbered years. Further information is available in Section 23.71, Subchapter E, Texas School Law Bulletin.

Price quotes lack the formality of a bid, are not required by law, and do not necessarily required board approval for implementation. It is a request for a price and may be in written or verbal form. For example a school district could have a regulation that price quotes are required for all purchases in excess of $1000 and less than $5000.

Accounting Principles and Policies (TEA-Bul-679-REQ-103)

The intent of the State Board of Education in prescribing these official rules is to cause the budgeting and financial accounting and reporting system of the public school districts to be in conformity with Generally Accepted Accounting Principles (GAAP) established by the Governmental Accounting Standards Board (GASB) and the Financial Accounting Standards Board (FASB).

The accounting system shall be organized and operated on a fund basis. It shall also provide account groups to account for general fixed assets and general long term debt of governmental fund types. The basis for accounting will be modified accrual or accrual method.

Funds shall be classified and identified on required financial statements by the terminology, provided in Procedure Number CDE-402 of Bulletin 679.

Summary

The principles of procurement apply to purchasing procedures. Such procedures must follow sound accounting principles and practices. Regulations for purchasing enhance the entire process, strengthen ethics, and control collusion. Schools deal with a broad range of materials and services. A planned, organized system for obtaining needed items requires safeguards and close scrutiny. The results will increase credibility and enhance accountability. (See glossary of terms at end of chapter).

Public School Student Transportation

Legal Basis for Transportation Services

The establishment and operation of the public school transportation program to serve school age children is a responsibility, prerogative and function of the board of trustees of the local school district. There are certain specifications imposed by the Texas Education Agency and public school law regulations for the operation of a transportation program.

Section 21.174 a and b, found in the Texas Education Code, stipulates the transportation program shall provide the most economical system for serving all eligible students residing in the school district.

Eligibility for regular students is defined in Section 16.156 (b) (d) and 21.177 (d) of the Texas Education Code. The general requirements for rider eligibility are as follows:

- the student must reside two (2) or more miles from the assigned campus of regular attendance as measured by the shortest publicly traveled route from the student's home to his or her school;
- the student must reside in the school district, or be an approved transfer student; and,
- no student is eligible for transportation reimbursement for more than 175 days of any school year.

The local school district is responsible for establishing school bus routes to serve students living in excess of two miles from their assigned school by June 1 of the current year to be operated the ensuing year, as required by Section 21.174 (b) (2) of the Texas Education Code. Each route submitted for approval to the Texas Education Agency must be described in detail using legal and/or commonly known names of streets, roads, and highways. Adjustments to approved bus routes, as well as new routes, must be submitted to the Transportation Division of the Texas Education Agency.

Requirements for Purchase and Acquisition of Buses

School buses are purchased from the successful bidding vendor awarded the contract to furnish school buses by the Texas State Purchases and General Services Commission for the stated bid period.

School districts desiring to purchase buses initiate a requisition to the State Board of Control and must comply with the following process:

- submit a requisition indicating quantity, size and desired options described by number and brief description;
- state delivery site if different from the mailing address;
- have requisition signed by the superintendent-signature verities available funds and guarantees payment of bus upon delivery;
- mail the original and one (1) copy of the completed requisition to the Texas Education Agency; and,
- for districts with more than 50 school buses, purchase buses capable of using compressed natural gas or other alternative fuel after September 1993. Bus fleets must be 50 percent capable of using such fuels in four years and 90 percent capable by September 1, 2001.

Funding of Purchased School Buses

School districts applying for transportation fund allocations must use such monies for allowable transportation expenditure only. With the exercise of proper accounting principles, transportation funds are identifiable at all times. After payment of all allowable transportation expenditures at the end of the year, any unexpended funds remaining may be retained to accumulate for future bus purchases or other transportation purposes. Transportation funds may not be used for any other purpose.

In addition to unused transportation money to pay for buses, buses may be purchased from local funds.

Method of Funding the Regular Student Transportation Program

Allocation for funding of transportation services for regular eligible bus riders is based on statistical information obtained during the first year of each biennium, which is used in established density groups for funding purposes.

In addition to the regularly approved routes to transport students residing in excess of two miles from their attending campus, school districts may qualify for special routes. If a student must encounter hazardous circumstances and conditions along their normal route to school, a special route may be approved to accommodate those students. Generally, hazardous routes are those where students must cross a heavily traveled expressway or railroad tracks.

A special request to the Transportation Division of the Texas Education Agency must be submitted to gain such a route.

When total regular transportation entitlement is determined and approved, it will become a part of the state's cost and awarded to the school district designated as Regular Transportation.

Beginning in September, and each month there after through July, the school district will receive equal monthly payments to the Regular Transportation Fund.

Establishment of Routes and Student Pickup Points

A bus route is defined as being the service provided by one bus to transport eligible bus students. All school bus routes should be measured from the last school served within the district. A student will not be expected to spend in excess of one hour each morning and each afternoon on a school bus unless the area of the school district and the location of the student's home make a longer period of time on the bus mandatory.

A complete description of each approved bus route operated by the district must be approved by the local school district board of trustees. One copy must be filed with the Transportation Division of the Texas Education Agency; and, one filed in the district office.

Pick up points must by two (2) or more miles from the assigned campus of regular attendance as measured by the shortest publicly traveled route from the student's home to the school. The student must reside in the district or be an approved transfer student. The two mile rule does not apply to students living in a hazardous area.

Local school boards have the power and perrogative to establish bus routes to serve regular student living within two (2) miles of their attending campus. However, such routes must be paid for from local funds.

Certification Requirements of School Bus Drivers-Regular Program

According to Section 85.214 of the Texas Administrative code, all drivers employed to transport school children shall:

- be at least 18 years of age;
- be properly licensed to operate a school bus;
- have undergone an annual physical examination completed of forms furnished by the Texas Education Agency which reveals the driver's physical and mental capabilities to operate a school bus safely;

- have an acceptable driving record in accordance with the standards developed jointly by the Texas Education Agency and the Department of Public Safety; and,
- be certified as having completed a state approved school bus driver's training course at least every three (3) years or possess a valid enrollment certificate.

Funding for Special Education Routes

A school district that provides special transportation services for eligible handicapped pupils is entitled to a state allocation paid on the previous year's cost-per-mile basis. The maximum rate per mile allowable shall be set by appropriation based on data gathered from the first year of each preceding biennium. Districts may use a portion of their support allocation to pay transportation costs, if necessary.

Funding, Special Features and Safety Provisions for Special Education Buses

Buses or vehicles to be used to transport special students are purchased in the same manner as buses or vehicles used in regular transportation. In addition to local and state funds, federal Public Law 94-142 monies can be used to purchase buses to transport special education students. Buses or vehicles purchased from Public Law 94-142 must be adapted to insure safety of specific handicapped students being transported as specified in the students' IEPs-individual education plans. All special modifications of equipment as well as the type of equipment chosen should be a major consideration for the safety of the children being transported.

Buses purchased with special Education funds may be used for other programs, such as field trips, only if the bus in needed to transport the children already eligible to ride a bus. At all times, the buses shall transport only eligible students for special education services.

Routes and Pick up Points for Special Education Students

Special education students are eligible for special transportation as determined by the Admission, Review, and Dismissal Committee. The ARD committee will determine the need and type of special transportation. The minutes of the meeting will reflect why special transportation is needed and the frequency of special transportation will be noted.

For a student placed by the district in a residential setting the district shall be responsible for transportation at the beginning and end of the term of school and for regularly scheduled holidays when students are expected to leave the residential campus. Transportation cost shall not exceed state approved per diem and mileage rates.

Training for School Bus Drivers of Special Education Students

As a general rule, school bus driver training requirements are the same for drivers of buses used to transport special education students as the regular program. The Program Handbook and Instructional Guide for School Bus Driver Training in Texas addresses special concerns for special education students.

In conclusion, more detailed information can and should be obtained from the Transportation Division of the Texas Education Agency.

School Food Service

One of the most important support services of school systems is the operation of food service programs. Food programs have grown from modest origins to a complex joint enterprise of the U.S. Department of Agriculture, the Texas Education Agency, and the local school system. One of the unique aspects of this expansion has been the influence of federal governmental agencies as major sponsors of the programs.

School food programs began with the realization that hungry children have definite learning impediments. The knowledge that for many students the only balanced meal of their day is the school lunch and/or breakfast has been a benchmark for the significance of food services in schools.

The National School Lunch Act of 1946 was so instrumental in the expansion of school food programs that it presently is the largest single segment of the food service industry. This act, known as P.L. 396, was passed by Congress as a security measure for the well-being and health of children as was as to encourage the consumption of domestic agricultural commodities and other foods. Further additions to federal food service legislation during the thirty years since the original passage of the law include: the Special Milk program in 1954; special assistance to low-income families for access to school lunch programs in 1961; the 1962 Nonfood Assistance Act which supported the purchase of food service equipment; the school breakfast program in 1966; and the 1970 P.L. 91-248 which emphasized free and reduced-price meals and authorized standards of eligibility.

Type A Lunch

The standard for defining a school lunch, the Type A lunch, is the basis for federal financial assistance. Federal regulations specify standard minimum portions to be served to children. These amounts may vary according to the age of pupils.

A recent modification of the Type A requirements allows secondary students an offer-versus-serve option. This provision requires schools to offer all food groups items to the student but only three of the items need be selected in order to qualify for federal reimbursement.

Local options, that do not receive federal reimbursement, include an a la carte menu, snacks, and sandwich provisions.

Free and Reduced-Price Lunch Programs

This federal legislation requires that children from low-income families be eligible for free or reduce-priced lunches and/or breakfast. The USDA annually publishes the income scale for determining family eligibility. Such ability is based on income according to the size of the family.

Donated Commodities

The USDA donates agricultural commodities to school districts based on specified value regulations. Schools are able to select, reject, or substitute from the commodities list. In some instances districts are able to receive cash in-lieu of donated commodities.

Nonfood Assistance

This program, established by the U.S. Congress enables schools to receive federal reimbursement (up to 75%) of the cost for equipment for the storage, transportation and serving of food.

Methods of Program Operation

Several options for management of food service programs are available to administrators. These include: the school operated plan; the use of food management companies; the use of food dispensing. machines.

1. *School operation.* In this plan, the school system operates the food services, employs personnel and purchases equipment.
2. *Food Management Corporations.* This plan provides a contractual agreement between the district and a food service company. Such corporations as ARA Services and Marriott Food Services are examples of firms that specialize in such agreements.
3. *Dispensing Machines/Snack Bar.* Originally designed after the Automat food system, this plan provides an agreement between a contractor and the school to provide an efficient and time saving system of food service. Recently, fast food chains and sandwich companies have entered this market for school food service.

A well organized food service program, staffed with congenial employees, serving good food, in an attractive environment can create a positive image for the school. It has been said that the one constant in any school day is that everyone, students, staff, and parents get hungry and want to eat. While the primary functions of the food service operation is to provide tasty meals at a reasonable cost, schools con use the food service as important component of the educational system. The food service program is as complex as a large restaurant. The demands for service are similar. An operation of such magnitude requires careful planning, fiscal accountability and continuous monitoring and adjustments.

Glossary

Account—descriptive heading under which are recorded financial transactions that are similar in frame of reference, purpose, object or source.

Assets—property owned by a local education agency (LEA) which has a monetary value.

Accrual Basis—accounting under which revenues are recorded when earned or when levies are made, and expenses are recorded as soon as they result liabilities, regardless of when the revenue is actually received or the payment is actually made.

Bill—statement of an amount owing for goods and/or services sold on open account.

Budgetary Accounts—accounts necessary to reflect budget operations and conditions, such as estimated revenues, appropriations, and encumbrances.

Budgetary Control—management of business affairs in accordance with an approved budget with responsibility to keep expenditures within authorized amounts.

Cash—currency, coin, checks, postal and express money orders, and banker's drafts on hand or on deposit with an official or agent designated as custodian of cash and bank deposits.

Check—bill of exchange drawn on a bank payable on demand; written order on a bank to pay on demand a specified amount of money to the order of a named person, or to the bearer out of money on deposit to the credit of the drawer.

Credit—entry into the right side of an account reflecting a decrease in an asset or a increase in a liability or fund balance; opposite of debit.

Debit—entry on the left side of an account reflecting an increase in an asset or a decrease in a liability or fund balance; opposite of credit.

Direct Expenses—elements of cost that can be obviously, easily, and conveniently identified with specific activities. (For example, materials, texts, equipment, supplies, etc.)

Encumbrance Accounting—system which involves giving recognition in the accounting budgetary control records for the issuance of purchase orders, statements, or other commitments chargeable to an appropriation in advance of any liability or payment.

Encumbrances—purchase orders, contracts, and/or other commitments which are chargeable to an appropriation and for which a part of the appropriation is reserved.

Expenditures—total charges incurred, whether paid or unpaid for current expense, capital outlay, and debt service. Fund-sum of money or other resources set aside for specific activities.

Imprest Fund—system for handling minor disbursements whereby a fixed amount of money, commonly called petty cash, is set aside for this purpose. See petty cash.

Indirect Expenses—elements of cost necessary in the provision of service which are of such nature that cannot be readily or accurately identified with specific service. (For example, custodial salaries, utility costs, etc. used for a program).

Internal Control—plan of organization under which employees' duties are so arranged and records and procedures so designed as to make it possible to exercise effective accounting control over assets, liabilities, revenues, and expenditures.

Liabilities—debt or other legal obligations arising out of transactions in the past which are payable but not necessarily due.

Overdraft—amount by which checks, drafts, or other demands for payment on the treasury or on a bank exceed the amount of credit against which they are drawn; the amount by which requisitions, purchase orders, or audited vouchers exceed the appropriation to which they are chargeable.

Petty Cash—sum of money set aside for the purpose of making change or immediate payments of comparatively small amounts for which the issuance of a formal voucher and check would be too expensive and time consuming. See Imprest Fund.

Purchase Order—document which authorized the delivery of specified merchandise or the rendering of certain services and the making of a charge for them.

Requisition—request usually from one department to the purchasing, stockroom, or other department, for specified articles or services.

References

Bulletin 679, Financial Accounting Manual, Texas Education Agency, 6th Edition.

Candoli, I. Carl, Walter G. Hack, John R. Ray, Dewey H. Stollar. *School Business Administration: A Planning Approach.* Third Edition. Allyn and Bacon, Inc. (Boston) 1984.

Hensarling, Paul R. *School Special Services.* Demand Publishing Company (Bryan) 1983.

Hentshke, Guilbert C. *School Business Administration: A Comparative Perspective,* McCutchan Publishing Corporation (Berkeley) 1986.

Public School Transportation, Texas Education Agency, Austin, Texas.

Saleme, LeRoy and Lee Robinson, "Overview and Practical Application of Bulletin 679." Texas Association of School Business Officials, 1989.

Texas Administration Code, Texas Education Agency, Austin, Texas.

Texas School Law Bulletin. Texas Education Agency, Austin, 1988.

Student Discipline

William H. Kurtz

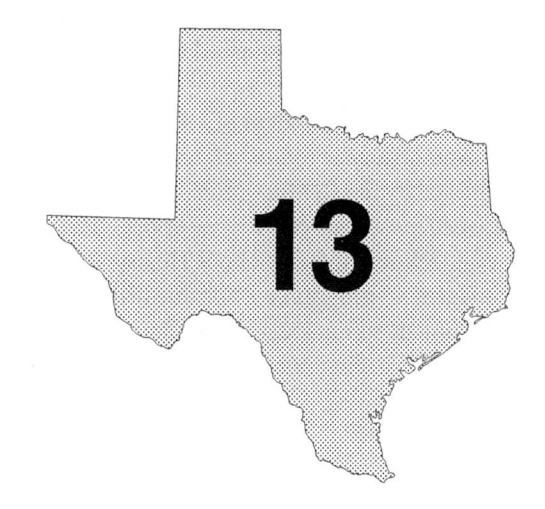

Student discipline has traditionally been the most consistently discussed problem in the public school. For most of our early history, discipline was "punishment to fit the crime" with an almost total focus on punishment. In later years, we began to spend more time trying to make discipline more of a character growth experience rather than punishment alone. At the same time, we began moving away from corporal punishment to a variety of other actions. Most recently, two actions by the state have significantly changed the way many schools approach student discipline. These actions are the passage of House Bill 72 and its amendments and the requirement for each school district to have a formal discipline management plan. Both of these actions were influenced by two national reports. These reports, *A Nation At Risk*, and *High School: A Report on Secondary Education in America*, have caused many educators and state governments to reassess their discipline management problems.

The lengthy debate among professionals, brought about by these events, has provided some clear directions that are apparent. First, school districts are interested in setting up discipline management plans that allow for local input and control. They are encouraging teachers to take an active part and to be the leading force in student discipline. Second, punishment is now clearly a means rather than a goal. (Changing student's behavior while keeping the students within the educational setting is the goal.) Finally, consistency in applying rules and regulations is a desired outcome of this process. By using seminars, group discussions and other forms of staff development, districts are achieving the consistency that they seek.

Student Rights and Responsibilities

Before an administrator can discipline students, a student conduct code must be established. Student rights and responsibilities are determined by each local district. Section 21.702 of the Texas Education Code requires that state laws and the Attorney General's Proposed Voluntary Student Code of Conduct of 1980 be used and allows district uniqueness to be added. There is no state official code of student conduct; however, each district's code of conduct must be approved by the Central Education Agency. Surprisingly, there is not a great deal of difference between most district's written codes. The vast majority were developed using a model from the Texas Association of School Boards as a part of developing the district's official discipline management program. Notable differences among the district's codes are in the use of capital punishment and in local interpretation of the written document.

The code of conduct will usually deal with the following areas:

- attendance
- class conduct
- dress codes
- student expression
- search and seizure
- controlled substance use and abuse
- school facilities use
- extra curricular activities
- expectations of students
- hazing
- vandalism and destruction of school property
- weapons and incendiary devices (fireworks).

The law also requires that students be notified as to what the rules of conduct are and as to the consequences of violating this code. Generally, districts give the rules and regulations to each student at the beginning of the school year. They are instructed to share these with their parents. Districts are required by law to have students and their parents sign acknowledgments that they have read and understand the rules and consequences.

The State of Texas has developed a unique set of regulations for dealing with handicapped students. These regulations require that the student's individual educational plan contain a statement which describes how the specific student will be handled and which rules and consequences apply and in what manner. The law requires the Admission, Review and Dismissal Committee to be involved and sets forth specific rules for suspension and expulsion in the Texas Administrative Code, section 133.28.

Enforcing the Student Code of Conduct

Due Process

The State of Texas requires that certain procedures be followed when enforcing student codes of conduct. Basic to all procedures is the concept of due process. Due process guarantees that each student will have certain rights during the disciplinary actions.

The student has a right to:

- prior notice of the charges and the proposed sanctions as to afford a reasonable opportunity for preparation;
- a full and fair hearing before the board or its designee;
- an adult representative or legal counsel;
- the opportunity to testify and to present evidence and witnesses in his or her defense; and
- the opportunity to examine the evidence presented by the school administration and to question the administration's witnesses.

This does not mean that the principal must formally follow this pattern each time a student is brought to the office to be disciplined. Normally, most infractions will be dealt with in a manner consistent with the best interest of the student and the school. Only in severe cases; chronic misbehavior; or situations where suspension, expulsion, or removal to an alternate center is contemplated, will the more formal approach be used.

The Discipline Management Plan

In Texas, enforcement procedures are a function of the district's discipline management plan. According to Texas Education Code section 21.701, Adoption and Approval of Programs, each school district shall adopt and implement a discipline management program. Before Implementation, the proposed program must be submitted to the Central Education Agency which shall review and approve or reject the program.

To be approved, a discipline management program must:

- encourage the commitment, cooperation, and involvement of school district administrators, teachers, parents, and students in the development of the program;
- encourage the use of regional education service centers to assist in developing the program and in providing training to teachers and administrators;
- require the designation of a person in each school with special training in discipline management to implement and assess the program in that school and to identify and refer appropriate students to school-community guidance programs;

- require the development of a student code of conduct that clearly describes the district's expectations with respect to student conduct, including provisions similar to the Attorney General's Proposed Voluntary Student Code of Conduct of 1980, and specifies the consequences of violating the code;
- specifically outline the responsibilities of teachers, administrators, parents, and students in the discipline management program; and
- make parental involvement an integral part of the discipline management program, requiring:

1. One or more conferences during each school year between a teacher and the parents of a student if the student is not maintaining passing grades, or achieving the expected level of performance, or presents some other problem to the teacher or in any other case the teacher considers necessary;
2. Parent training workshops for home reinforcement of study skills and specific curriculum objectives that are conducted for parents who want to participate and are based on interest indicated by parents in the community and;
3. A written statement signed by each parent that the parent understands and consents to the responsibilities outlined in the discipline management program.

Boards of education must provide for the following in the contents of the plan:

- The plan must be developed with administrators, teachers, parents, and students, and, if needed, with the assistance of the education service centers.
- The plan must contain the title of categories of the persons that have been designated as campus discipline persons, and their job duties, including the implementation and assessment of the program on that campus and referral of appropriate students to school-community guidance centers, if available, must be listed.
- A code of student conduct must be developed that, at a minimum, includes rules, procedures, and expectations related to conduct and specifies the consequences of violating the code. The school district shall explain what it will consider to be "serious" and "persistent" behavior in its discipline management program and student code of conduct. The code of student conduct shall initially be published and distributed to all administrators, teachers, parents, and students. Thereafter, the code of student conduct shall be provided for each newly employed administrator, teacher, and newly enrolled student, parent or guardian and to others upon request. The discipline management plan of each district shall provide for procedures to communicate the provisions of the code of student conduct to parents and all interested parties. Changes during the year in the code of student conduct shall be published and distributed to students in a timely manner.

- The discipline management plan shall describe the responsibilities of teachers, administrators, parents, and students.
- Parent training workshops for home reinforcement of study skills in specific curriculum objectives shall be included in the district's plan.
- The district shall provide annually for the collection of signed statements by each student's parent confirming that the parent understands and consents to the responsibilities outlined in the district's student code of conduct.

The district's discipline management plan shall specify who may serve as the student's representative, the district's hearing officer at any hearing required by the Texas Education Code, section 21.301 and section 21.3011, and shall set forth the district's notice and hearing procedures. The school district's outline of its alternative educational program shall be included in its discipline management plan.

Teachers also have state requirements within the discipline management plan. Texas Education Code section 21.705 requires that each school district shall provide, and each teacher must successfully complete, training in the discipline management program that is adopted in the district. Training may be provided through inservice work or another instructional arrangement. Also, the school district must use inservice work for reinforcing teacher training in discipline management.

The Texas Administrative code further defines the staff involvement:

- The board of trustees shall provide training in the discipline management plan of the district for each teacher, administrator, counselor, and librarian; for campus discipline personnel identified in the Texas Education Code, section 21.702(3); and for professional and support staff of alternative education programs, including school-community guidance centers. The district may include in the training other appropriate personnel such as instructional aides and bus drivers.
- The discipline management plan shall include the school district procedures for teacher training under this section. The plan shall ensure that teachers are fully informed regarding the contents of the school district's discipline management plan.
- The school district shall maintain records that document the initial discipline management training and subsequent reinforcement that each teacher receives.

Suspension

As described in the Texas Education Code section 21.301, the board of trustees of a school district may suspend a student for a period not to exceed six school days or remove a student to an alternative education program. Suspension for a total of more than six school days within a semester is considered an expulsion and may occur only as provided by 21.3011 of the code.

New, more explicit rules for suspending and expelling students have been developed and appear in Chapter 133, Texas Administrative Code, sections 133.22, 133.23, 133.24 Space does not permit a detailed discussion of these concepts, however the practitioner must be clearly aware of these provisions.

Before it may suspend a student or remove a student to an alternative education program, the board or the board's designee must determine:

- that the student's presence in the regular classroom program or at the home campus presents a danger of physical harm to the student or to other individuals; or
- that the student has engaged in serious or persistent misbehavior that violates the district's previously communicated standards of student conduct.

Before suspending a student, the board or its designee shall consider reasonable alternatives, including appropriate discipline management techniques which may include removal to an alternative education program. If the board or its designee determines that suspension is the most appropriate available alternative, the board or the board's designee is not required to precede the suspension with another disciplinary action.

If the decision to remove a student to an alternative education program is made by the board's designee, that decision may be appealed to the board. The student may be removed to the alternative education program pending appeal to the board.

A student's parent or guardian is entitled to notice, as soon as reasonably possible, of a suspension or removal of a student to an alternative education program and to an opportunity to participate in a proceeding before the board. If the board's designee suspends or removes a student to an alternative education program for three or more consecutive school days or five or more accumulative school days within a semester, the designee shall encourage the student's parent or guardian to attend a conference to discuss the designee's action and/or the student's misbehavior. Any decision of the board under this section is final and may not be appealed.

The school shall provide for the continuing education of a student who has been removed to an alternative education program. A district shall provide for one or more alternative education programs such as:

- in-school suspension;
- transfer to a different campus;
- transfer to a school-community guidance center; or
- transfer to a community-based alternative school.

If a student is suspended, the student's absence shall be considered to be an excused absence if the student satisfactorily completes the assignments for the period of suspension within a reasonable time determined by the district. A district may impose a grade adjustment on the work made up by a student who has been suspended.

The classroom teacher may effectively suspend students from class. State law says that:

- a teacher may send a student to the principal's office in order to maintain effective discipline in the classroom. The principal shall respond by employing appropriate discipline management techniques consistent with local policy.
- a teacher may remove from class a student who has been documented by the teacher to repeatedly interfere with the teacher's ability to communicate effectively with the students in the class. Not later than the third class day after the day on which the student is removed from the class, the principal shall schedule a hearing among the principal or the principal's designee, a parent or guardian of the student, the teacher, and the student. Following the hearing, and whether or not all requested parties are in attendance, after valid attempts to require their attendance, the principal shall suspend the pupil for a period consistent with local policy, not to exceed six school days, place the student in an alternative education program, or place the student back in the class. If the student is removed a second time under this section within the same semester, the student may be returned to that class only by action of the superintendent at the principal's request. If the student is removed a third or subsequent time under this subsection within the same semester, the student may be returned to that class only by action of the district's board of trustees at the request of the superintendent.

Expulsion

Expulsion means suspension of a student from school for more than six days within a semester. The term does not include removal of a student to an alternative education program.

A student may be removed from class and expelled without resort to an alternative education program under section 21.301 of the education code if the student, on school property or while attending a school sponsored or school-related activity on or off of school property:

- assaults a teacher or other individual;
- sells, gives or delivers to another person or possesses or uses or is under the influence of:
  - marijuana or a controlled substance, as defined by the Texas Controlled Substances Act (Article 4476-15, Texas Civil Statutes) or by 21 U.S.C., 801 et sea.; or
  - a dangerous drug, as defined by the Texas dangerous drug law Chapter 425, Acts of the 56th Legislature 1959 (Article 4476-14, Texas Civil Statutes);
- sells, gives, or delivers to another person an alcoholic beverage, as defined by section 1.04, Alcoholic Beverage Code, or commits a serious act or offense while under the influence of alcohol; or on more than one occasion possesses, uses, or is under the influence of an alcoholic beverage;

- possesses a firearm as defined by the section 46.01 (3), Penal Code, an illegal knife as defined by section 46.01 (6), Penal Code, a club as defined by section 46.01 (1), Penal Code, or a weapon listed as a prohibited weapon under section 46.06, Penal Code; or
- engages in conduct that contains the elements of an offense relating to abuseable glue or aerosol paint under section 4.13, Texas Controlled Substances Act (Article 4476-15, Texas Civil Statutes), or relating to volatile chemicals under Chapter 323, Acts of the 68th Legislature, Regular Session, 1983 (Article 4476-13a, Texas Civil Statutes).

A student who, after having been placed in an alternative education program under section 21.301, continues to engage in serious or persistent misbehavior that violates the district's previously communicated written standards of student conduct may be removed from class and expelled.

The board or its designee shall set a term for the expulsion.

- The expulsion may not extend beyond the end of the school year unless the conduct directly leading to the expulsion occurred during the final six-week reporting period of the school year, in which case the expulsion may extend beyond the end of the current school year but not beyond the end of the first semester of the next school year.
- A pupil who is to be expelled for the first time for possession, use, or for being under the influence of an alcoholic beverage as defined in this section, may not be expelled beyond the end of the semester, unless the conduct directly leading to the expulsion occurred during the final six-week reporting period of a semester, which may result in expulsion not to extend beyond the end of the next regular semester.

Before the expulsion, the board or its designee must provide the student a hearing at which the student is afforded appropriate due processes required by the federal constitution. If the decision to expel a student is made by the board's designee, the decision may be appealed to the board. The decision of the board may be appealed by trial de novo to a state district court of the county in which the school district's central administrative office is located.

A teacher may remove from class and recommend for expulsion a student who engages in conduct for which a student may be expelled. If a teacher recommends a student for expulsion, the board or its designee shall conduct a hearing. If the board or its designee decides not to expel the student, and the student is again recommended for expulsion by the teacher during the same school year, the hearing may be conducted only by the board.

The board or its designee shall deliver a copy of the order expelling the student to the student and the student's parent or guardian. The board or its designee shall also deliver a copy of the order to the authorized officer of the juvenile court in the county in which the student resides. The officer shall determine whether:

- a petition should be filed alleging that the student is in need of supervision or engaged in delinquent conduct; or
- the student should be referred to an appropriate state agency.

If a court orders a student who has been expelled to attend school as a condition of probation, the school district shall re-admit the student, but the student is not immune from suspension, removal to an alternative education program, or expulsion during the term of the probation.

Expulsion procedures must carefully follow the concepts of due process discussed earlier.

Alternate Educational Programs

The desire to change behaviors of problem students while they are within the school setting has caused several forms of alternate educational programs to become popular. These alternatives are extremely important to those who believe that removal from school for chronic, non-violent offenses unnecessarily interrupts the education of the student. In most of the non-violent cases, it has been demonstrated that suspension is not an effective treatment, and, in the case of unexcused absences and tardies, removal from school is exactly what the student seeks. Non-removal also helps the school financially by raising the average daily attendance upon which many funding formula calculations are based. Finally, studies show that removal from school more seriously effects the education of those students who have not had lot of academic success in the first place.

Quality is a major concern in developing the alternate educational program. A low quality program does little more than to keep kids in school, and neither causes a change in behavior or advancement in the learning process. A poor quality program may actually increase behavior problems significantly and impair the opportunity to impact the child in any way.

The Classroom Management and Discipline Program funded by the leaders of the state and housed at Southwest Texas State University has developed a set of objectives for in-school alternatives. They believe that these programs should seek to do the following:

1. Identify the real problems students have that underlie symptomatic behavior.
2. Help and encourage students to develop self-discipline.
3. Reduce the out-of-school removals for all offenses except those that clearly threaten the school's and/or community's safety.
4. Provide a place to meet the needs of problem students, while enabling the rest of the student body to participate effectively in the instructional process.
5. Accept the fact that the public schools are charged with educating all youngsters, even those with troubled backgrounds. Accordingly, educators, parents, and students must cooperate to provide a framework for educating all students.

There are several types of programs. They usually take one of the following forms.

Detention Center.

The detention center is a relatively quick and easy program to install. Characteristically, it is a room or rooms where students go before school, after lunch, after school, and/or on Saturdays. Students are required to do class work prescribed by their teachers and in many cases are subjected to intense counseling. This form is also popular as it does not require formal removal procedures or extensive due process to assign a student. It is also the lease expensive to operate.

In-School Suspension Center.

These centers are characteristically used when a student needs to be removed from the regular school environment for several days or more. If the number of days exceeds three, the action becomes a removal and must be treated as delineated under the previous section on suspension. Parent involvement is required and is an absolute necessity for the removal to be effective. This center is usually located in an isolated building on one or more of the district's campuses. There are more significant personnel and facility requirements since this center needs to isolate students from the mainstream of school life and eliminate interaction with other students as much as possible. High coordination between the center and those involved in the instructional process is required. It is also important that the atmosphere be one which will allow learning to take place and will cause students to feel that they can get sincere assistance and counsel. Easily available counseling services are also a requirement.

Stand Alone Alternative Schools.

Stand alone alternative schools are actually unique campus' within themselves. They require an organization and an administration like any other campus. However, the rules of operation will be different. These schools, which seem to be the most effective, are also the most expensive. It is possible for two or more school districts to jointly operate a campus center to save money. Proper staffing of these centers is critical. Persons who are chosen to work in these areas must be specially trained and sympathetic to problem students. Specially trained counselors are necessary and a school psychologist is a plus. The center's environment usually includes behavior modification systems, merit systems and reward systems all designed to encourage proper growth and development of the student. While delivery systems will be different, the curriculum must parallel that of the regular school programs. Most students will have an individualized program which will lead to the high school equivalency degree (GED). Close supervision, regular evaluation, flexible hours and self paced curricular offerings will also be required. Community agencies are often involved in these centers and liaison activities will be carried out by all members of the staff. Administrative requirements include significant program record keeping, extensive operational policies consistent with this special administrative practice, good documentation of everything, viable financial and program accountability measures, and dependence on a legal system of authority and operational practice.

Alternate education centers, especially the stand alone variety, are beginning to command a great deal of respect since recent research has shown that students who are not able to function in the regular school program, no matter what the reason, seem to have a chance at success in this new environment. A goal of 100% graduation is not realistic, however, the program completes the education of a significant number of students who have rejected the traditional program. Successful programs are being operated in all of the larger school districts and an increasing number of small districts are joining this trend. Two good examples in the central Texas area are the Pride Center at San Marcos CISD and W.R. Robbins School in Austin ISD. The Robbins School is a non traditional high school that concentrates its efforts on providing academic and support services to those students who are most in need. The purpose of the program is to recapture those students who have dropped out of school and to retain these students who are at risk of dropping out. The curriculum consists of a core block and electives. Several courses can be taught at the same time by a teacher who is both a coach and a facilitator. The continuous progress method of instruction allows students to progress through the curriculum at an accelerated pace as well as allowing for individual attention. The school has day and night sessions, operated as two separate schools.

The Pride school in San Marcos is directed at dropouts or those who for whatever reason cannot attend the regular sessions. The school has a nursery attached to accommodate mothers who are trying to complete their education. Programmed instruction is used as are other unique forms of instruction. Both schools were designed to fit the needs of their respective communities and have become successful alternatives to the main stream educational programs.

Implications for School Administrators

No one will question that the school administrator is responsible for the school. However, in practice, he alone is not in charge of student discipline. Teachers, parents, the school board, central office personnel, attendance officers, juvenile courts and their officers, policemen, and the various social service case workers all can have a part in disciplining students. Parents have long been seen as having the major responsibility for disciplining the child, but under present conditions, parents seem to be attempting to transfer the major responsibility to the schools. Recent legislation such as House Bill 72 has put new pressures on schools, especially teachers, to take an active part in correcting the behavior of students and at the same time require parents to be a part of the process. These events and the increasing violence in some schools are forcing an examination of the causes for acts that require discipline and a thorough examination of how the district can impact this problem.

School climate is a major determinate of how students are going to behave and, hence, a significant factor in determining the number of discipline cases. According to the recent research on "effective schools," schools that model and promote good citizenship have less discipline problems. There is also a strong link between excellent teaching and a low level of behavior problems. Other factors such as school and personal pride, student morale, and school spirit will influence the number of discipline problems.

The school principal is the key to establishing a good school climate. The principal must set the tone for and with the teaching faculty and must insure that non-teaching staff members also model positive behaviors. Positive attitudes, policies and actions are the only consistent way to keep behavior problems at a minimum.

Teachers play an integral role in the establishment of good school climate. Excellent teaching will lead to a reduction in behavior problems.

Factors which lead to excellent teaching are:

- good room arrangement
- good classroom procedures and rules
- holding students accountable for their work
- using well planned, well paced, appropriate lessons
- stopping inappropriate behavior quickly.

Positive school climate will build trust, high morale, and a spirit in students which will translate into respect for teachers, the school and each other. It is in this atmosphere that discipline problems become fewer and more solvable. It is to the administrator's own benefit to work hard to establish and maintain a positive school climate.

Another factor that school administrators must seek to improve is the interpersonal relationships among and between students and staff. There is an increasing need to emphasize these skills as our environment becomes more harsh and our personal actions more combative. Modeling good interpersonal behaviors and teaching students to use good interpersonal skills is the basis for creating a caring atmosphere. When students believe that teachers and administrators care about them, the nature and number of discipline problems will decrease markedly.

A major objective of these processes should be to get students to the point where they will discipline themselves. In a free society such as ours, self discipline must be a part of each person or self control will be lost. When self control is lost, the individual freedoms we value so highly are lost. It is more prudent to teach students self discipline than to pass numerous laws to try and to enforce. A self controlled society has much more true freedom than does any other. This concept applies to the school society as well as to society in general.

There is a small portion of any school population that will not take part in the educational process in a positive manner. This group, representing five to seven percent of the population, is alienated to the school and will not respond to normal procedures. It is the disciplining of this group that causes the most concern for teachers and administrators. For many years corporal punishment has been a popular choice, and with the truly alienated student, it has been reasonably successful. Over the last few years, the use of corporal punishment has been questioned and has been legally banned in some states. Presently, corporal punishment is legal in Texas. It is a hot topic of discussion, and several attempts have been made to make it illegal through legislation. Even if these efforts do not succeed, the continued use of corporal punishment is questionable. Ignoring the moral arguments, the legal ramifications present significant risks to teachers and administrators who choose to use it. The possibility of legal action by parents and students is increasing in Texas. There have been a number of successful law suits in recent years when school personnel were found to have used "excessive force," acted in anger, or with malice, or to have caused injury to the student. Even with a witness present, there is no guarantee against successful legal action by parents and/or students. This does present a dilemma, and the establishment of alternative centers has provided a means of punishment short of suspension or expulsion. Many are questioning the effectiveness of both of these procedures, and the debate will undoubtedly rage on for some time to come.

A final concept for administrators to consider is the psychological effects of discipline on all parties concerned. Inappropriate, ill timed and/or ill conceived disciplinary actions can create psychological problems for students. Sudden withdrawal is a common reaction to poorly chosen discipline procedures, and if this withdrawal is reinforced over time, the mind set of the student about teaching and learning can become very negative. This in turn can create more discipline problems, more strains on the teacher-student relationship, and an atmosphere where learning almost ceases. Creating a "psychologically safe" classroom should be a goal of all teachers and administrators. In order to keep the learning process manifest and students in a mode where they can be helped, a rigorous program of staff development in this arena would benefit the staff and students of many school districts.

Student Attendance

Who attends Texas' public schools? According to the latest Snapshot, published by The Texas Education Agency 3,378,318 students were enrolled in state public schools. Of this number 50 percent were white, 34 percent were Hispanic, 14 percent were African American, and the other 2 percent represented the other categories. The ages of these students ranged from less than one year to 21 years. There were approximately 400,000 handicapped students being served, covering 12 handicapping conditions. Special provisions were made for the schooling of approximately 5,500 expectant mothers. Special schools were conducted for approximately 5,000 severely handicapped students.

The composition of most of the states' 1,100 plus school districts do not reflect these averages. Some districts have as high as 99 percent minority students enrolled and some have less than one percent minority enrolled. Enrollment trends indicate that there has been a steady increase in the number of students in the Texas public schools and that this increase will continue. The central portion of the state is experiencing most of the enrollment increase, and some districts in other parts of the state are actually experiencing a decline in enrollment. Future enrollment patterns are expected to be controlled by the health of the economy and the ability of the schools and their patrons to reduce the current dropout rate of approximately 33 percent.

Attendance in public schools is mandatory. This tenet is taken for granted by most parents, and very little thought is given to enrolling their children in school. Most states have compulsory attendance laws, and at times all states have had these laws in existence. In the state of Texas, attendance laws are the basis for determining funding, services, classification, and for interpreting many mandates issued by the state legislature. Since funding is dependent on attendance, close scrutiny of attendance reporting is to be expected. These statistics are audited regularly, and when errors are found, adjustments will be made to the number of dollars the state has given a district. Often, districts have had to return dollars for which they did not qualify. In recent years, the complexity of laws governing funding is causing a large number of districts to receive less than they actually should receive. It becomes apparent that the need for a better understanding of the concepts of student attendance, and especially attendance reporting, is necessary for all members of the school staff.

Compulsory Attendance in Texas

Since the United States Supreme Court ruled in Plyler v. Doe (102 S Ct. 2382 (1982)) that undocumented or illegal alien children must be admitted to school if they otherwise meet admission requirements, the Texas statutory statement found in section 21.031 is not correct. The statute reads: "All children who are *citizens of the United States or legally admitted aliens,* and who are over the age of five years and under the age of 21 years on the first day of September of any scholastic year, shall be entitled to the benefits of the Available School Fund for that year." The Texas legislature has chosen not to change this wording; however, all school districts must abide by the ruling of the Supreme Court.

Section 21.032 of the Texas Education Code contains the specific compulsory attendance law. It was last amended by House Bill 72. It states: "Unless specifically exempted by Section 21.033 of this code or under other laws, every child in the state who is as much as six years of age, and who has not completed the academic year in which his 17th birthday occurred shall be required to attend the public schools in the district of his residence or in some other district into which he may have transferred as provided or authorized by law a minimum of 170 days of the regular school term of the district in which the child resides or to which he has been transferred."

When these two sections of statute and the court case are taken together, the interpretation is that all resident and alien children may attend school and that resident citizens must attend school between the ages of six and seventeen unless legally exempted. The slight difference caused by the use of the words "may" and "must" can create confusion when interpreting the statutes. Students of educational administration must be aware of these subtle differences and become knowledgeable of the true meanings of these statutes. In practice, most school districts simply encourage the attendance of all children and few, if any, make an attempt to distinguish between citizens and aliens until the data collection phase of enrollment.

There are several exceptions to the compulsory attendance statutes. They are found in Section 21.033 of the Texas Education Code. In general, a student may be exempted from attendance if the student is enrolled in a private or parochial school that is organized by the state; if the student is handicapped as defined in Section 21.053 of this code; if the student has a temporary physical or mental handicap that makes attendance infeasible; or if the student has been expelled in accordance with the requirements of law.

There are also exceptions that allow special classes of students to attend the public schools of Texas. These are detailed in Section 61.104 of the Texas Education Code.

In practice a Student must attend at least eighty days per semester. If the district school year is longer than 170 attendance days, by law students would be allowed to miss more than five days per semester before the minimum laws take effect as the laws are now written. Year around schools and other schedules that are different than the minimums will require a district to examine its policies to make sure they are consistent. (See Section 21.041 TEC)

A campus attendance committee is an important part of any attendance program. This committee can take appeals from parents or students, and, make decisions as to promotion, mastery of the essential elements and other issues related to attendance and learning. This relieves the principal from the burden of making the decision alone.

The School Attendance Officer

Since the State of Texas requires that non-enrolled students and non attending students be identified and reported, each district has the right to select an attendance officer. If no attendance officer is selected, the duties devolve upon the school superintendent and the peace officers of the county. The attendance officer is a paid school position; however, a superintendent or county peace officer is excluded from receiving additional compensation for these services.

The duties of the attendance officer are described in Section 21.039 of the Texas Education Code and include the power and duty to: investigate all cases of unexcused absences from school; to serve legal processes; to enforce provisions of the compulsory attendance law; to keep records of all cases; to make reports to the commissioner of education; and to proceed in juvenile court against any incorrigible student or against any recalcitrant person having parental control of a child.

The activities of the attendance officer are restricted in that he may not enter any private residence without permission of the owner or legal permission from the court; nor may he forcibly take corporal custody of any child anywhere without the permission of the parent or legal guardian except when ordered to do so by the court. The position of attendance officer is an important one. In districts of even moderate size, the officer has more than a full time job. There are no specific legal qualifications for the person who is placed in this position. It has been learned through experience that just anyone cannot be successful in this position. Some of the more significant qualities that an attendance officer should have are: a genuine interest in the welfare of children, the ability to be firm but fair, sufficient self-esteem to allow the person to deal with depressing and sometimes degenerate circumstances and not be personally affected, the ability to understand the legal processes and to carry them out in a manner acceptable to the district, and excellent interpersonal skills. Having been a peace officer of some kind is helpful, but many of these individuals lack the qualities mentioned above, especially the ability to understand the uniqueness of the student and the school's role in the community. The school administrator must carefully select this person based on a predetermined set of qualifications adapted specifically to the district and to district needs.

Truancies and Tardies

Students who are truant or tardy create the two major attendance problems faced by all schools. These are not new problems, and their persistence is testimony to the difficulty school districts have in dealing with them. The most serious problem is created by students who are either late to class or to school. Class tardies are the most prevalent problem. Since there is not a single, good way to deal with the problem, each teacher seems to select a different method of control. Some are diligent in trying to make that system work; others are not. Consequently students see the flaws in the system and are able to beat the system by exploiting the lack of consistency in applying enforcement measures. Most administrators can easily tell which teachers are in better control of the tardy situation and which are not. At the same time, administrators seem to be so frustrated that they choose to react to problems rather than seek solutions by planning and organizing. The solutions to the problem of student tardies always contain two common elements. One is consistent and constant supervision of students by teachers. The other is strong backing of teachers from all levels of administration. To impact the tardiness problem a common plan must be in force and teachers must be in position to know who is tardy, to know what rules are to be enforced, and to enforce the rules without exception. Teachers who practice the tenets of good classroom organization and control will be able to keep tardies to a minimum. Administrators must be willing to take charge of students who continually abuse the rules and to take the necessary measures to see that teachers do their part.

Most schools that are successful in keeping tardics to a minimum have a school plan that is followed by all teachers. These plans also allow the teacher to set more stringent rules when warranted and require teachers to meet acceptable levels of classroom tardies. Some of the more common techniques include: penalizing grades for excessive tardies, required attendance at a detention hall, special attendance at classes scheduled on weekends and, for serious cases, placement in in-school suspension facilities. A new version of the tardiness policy is being installed in many districts across the state. Essentially the policy is a zero tolerance policy. Halls are swept immediately after tardy bells ring, and students who are not in classrooms are taken to a special room for disciplinary purposes. In these rooms they are expected to study and do other educational activities under the very strict supervision of an specially hired faculty member. Other versions of this plan require these students to make up the time on Saturday in various types of special classes. Amazing results have been achieved in many of the schools that are using this concept. Suspension from school has not been found to be a successful solution to the problem and is not allowed under the provisions of House Bill 72.

Dealing with students who are constantly late to school provides another set of concerns. Being late to school is usually a function of parent and student attitudes. Two conditions are most prevalent: neither parent or student see the educational process as necessary; or, the parent believes in education but lacks the desire or the ability to provide the student supervision necessary to get the student to school on time.

Most of the strategies used in dealing with students who are late to class also work with students who are late to school. The difference is that these forms of punishment do not last over time. For a lasting solution to take place, both the student and the parent will need to have corrective counseling. The school can be successful in the less severe cases; however, in the more serious cases, outside professional counseling is often the better solution. The counseling process must lead to a positive commitment to the educational process on the part of the student and the parent. If this attitude cannot be changed, there is little hope that a lasting solution to chronic tardiness will be obtained.

Dealing with the truancy problem is much more difficult. Truancy, like chronic tardiness to school, is a result of students and parents who do not believe in the benefits of an education. In addition, these students and parents have developed a mind set that rationalizes their actions to the point that they don't perceive that they are doing anything wrong. Students who are chronically truant also exhibit other negative qualities. Many are regular drug users involved in many forms of petty crime, and in general are persons who refuse to be bound by society's norms or constrained by accepting its value systems. Others have emotional problems, a chronic lack of success in school, or live in conditions that destroy their self-esteem.

A revised attendance statute passed in 1993 requires students to attend at least ninety percent of the days a class is offered rather than 80 days per semester. The definitions of excused and unexcused absences previously in the Family Code are now included in the Education Code. Truancy fines are doubled and will be split between the district and the town or county of the court's jurisdiction. Truancy is now a Class C misdemeanor and the failure of a parent or guardian to attend a truancy hearing is also a Class C misdemeanor.

Strategies for dealing with the chronic truant are many. Most involve an attempt to change the behavior of the student by making basic changes in attitudes, value systems, ego systems or basic character traits. None of these systems are totally successful with all students, but all are somewhat successful with specific students. All systems require a great deal of time and a significant amount of professional counseling with psychologists or psychiatrists. School counselors have had only minimal success in this area.

When the truant student is under the tenets of the compulsory attendance laws, the school must either find a way to get the student in school or must proceed in juvenile court according to the procedures outlined in Section 4.25 of the Texas Education Code. Whether or not the case will be successful will depend on the amount and accuracy of the evidence presented by the school and the perception of the judge of the juvenile court.

Attendance Accounting

Accounting procedures are strictly controlled by state law. Subchapter D of Chapter 129 of the Texas Education Code contains the regulations. Calculations are based on what is called "average daily attendance." Average daily attendance is defined as the total number of student days of attendance divided by the number of days school was in session. As of the 1990-91 school year, the counting period will be the full academic year.

The responsibility to maintain accurate, current attendance records is given by law to superintendents, but the responsibility is passed to principals and teachers. Attendance records of students in all special programs must also be kept. Many of these special programs also require that a record of student-teacher contact hours be kept.

The actual counting of attendance has changed since the passage of House Bill 72 and its successor Senate Bill 1. In actual practice, the number of students present is determined by counting the number of students absent and subtracting this number from the current enrollment. This is done because the number present is much larger than the number absent so less recording is necessary (an average of about 94-96 percent of the students are present each day). Attendance (those absent) is recorded each day. Auditable records must be kept of each days records. District audits usually include the inspection of these records. The volume of work and the reports mandated by the state require that an attendance clerk be hired and that a computerized system of record keeping be developed.

Subchapter D contains many other rules governing attendance reporting. Some of the most pertinent are:

- When classroom instruction is departmentalized a central accounting system must be used.
- A student, who is not at school when attendance is taken, cannot be counted in attendance unless the student is participating in an approved school activity; is a Medicaid-eligible child participating in special diagnostic and screening programs; or is excused under the provisions of observing religious holy days.
- Each teacher or other employee who records attendance must certify in ink that all records are true and have been prepared, according to laws and regulations.
- Attendance for all grades shall be determined by the absences recorded in the second or fifth period. Once the time is established, it may not be changed during the school year.
- Students enrolled on a half-day basis only earn a half day of attendance.
- Students counted absent at the time official attendance is taken are counted absent all day.

- The superintendent of schools is responsible for the safe keeping of all attendance records and reports. All records must be readily available to auditors from the Texas Education Agency.
- Students who receive "excused" absences under Section 21.035 of the Texas Education Code cannot be counted for Foundation School Program purposes.

All provisions of the Family Rights and Privacy Act and the Texas Open Records Act concerning confidentiality of records apply to attendance reporting. School administrators should keep abreast of current requirements of these laws. (See end note.)

References

Kurtz, William H.; Stahl, Judy; and Furgeson, James. *Discipline Management Plans,* unpublished research report Southwest Texas State University, San Marcos, Texas, 1988.

Classroom Management and Discipline Program. *Classroom Management and Discipline Program Manual: A Modular Text.* Southwest Texas State University, San Marcos, Texas, 1987.

For information on Alternative concept schools contact: W.R. Robbins School, Wanda Flowers, Principal, 3908 Avenue B, Austin, Texas, 78751; or, Dr. John Fuller, Superintendent of Schools, San Marcos ISD, P.O. Box 1087, San Marcos, Tx. 78667-1087.

Contact Seguin High School, Alfonso Lopez, principal, Box 31, Seguin, Texas, 78156, for further information on a Zero Tolerance Tardy Policy.

Note: The technical data presented is taken from *The Texas School Law Bulletin,* and from reports and informational publications of the Texas Education Agency and are accurate as of May 1, 1992. Due to the Passage of Senate Bill 1 in the summer of 1990, and the subsequent rulings that the finance portions of the bill are unconstitutional, the student will want to continue to investigate the current validity of statements made concerning attendance reporting.

School Communication and Public Relations

Stephen Knagg

Every school district in Texas has a public image. When someone pictures a district, it's fairly easy to share in 25 words or less how they feel about that school system. If asked to explain **why** they have a specific image of a district, the task becomes much more difficult.

Texas districts are rated, consciously and subconsciously, on many factors including test scores, teacher quality, newness of schools, board politics and even the win/loss record of the football team. A district's public image therefore is omnipresent, measurable . . . and manageable.

The effective management of a school district's public image is one of the main tasks of that system's communications and public relations department.

Definition of Educational Public Relations

The National School Public Relations Association, in existence for over 50 years, defines educational public relations in the following manner:

> Educational public relations is a planned and systematic management function designed to help improve the programs and services of an educational organization. It relies on a comprehensive two-way communication process involving both internal and external publics, with a goal of stimulating a better understanding of the role, objectives, accomplishments, and needs of the organization. Educational public relations programs assist in interpreting public attitudes, identify and help shape policies and procedures in the public interest, and carry on involvement and information activities which earn public understanding and support.

The terms "systematic management function" and "public understanding and support" are the keys to a successful school communications/public relations program. While every district in Texas has a public image, the goal of an effective public relations department is to manage that image in a way which allows the public to understand, and ultimately support that district.

The Need for a Planned Public Relations Program

Public education today in Texas is under siege. Never before have educational questions and issues been so prominently displayed on the front pages of our state's and nation's newspapers. And, typically, the news isn't very good.

Whatever the problem, public educators seem to receive the blame. Teen pregnancy, drug and alcohol abuse, and lower test scores are all seen as signs that the public schools are failing. Educators must also deal with the problems of asbestos abatement, radon, and acceptable lead levels in drinking fountains. In trying to solve all of society's woes, today's teachers, administrators and trustees have found themselves having to do what people used to ask God to do!

Across our country there is an attitude of declining support for public education. Texans are asking, "What's wrong with our schools?" The perceived problems in public education are being debated from the barber shop to the floor of our state capitol.

District patrons . . . and voters are wondering what can be done to save our "failing schools." Now, as never before, school districts need to present a fair, balanced picture of their schools to their various publics. The doors of two-way communication must be flung open to allow the light of knowledge to permeate into the community.

Any effective school public relations plan must begin with the full support of that district's board of trustees. As a district's elected leaders, Texas trustees must adopt a written policy that clearly defines that district's intent to continually make effective two-way communication an ongoing district goal. Trustees must then provide superintendents with the monies and additional staff needed to begin a working program.

Mr. Edward Bernays, the recognized father of the public relations profession, believes that a school public relations planning process should involve the following: a statement of goals; a statement of research pertaining to the goals; a statement of school district reorientation that must be accomplished in light of the research and new goals; and, the timing of tactics to accomplish the goals.

Budgeting for the Public Relations Program

Texas districts vary widely in their ability to fund a school public relations program. Many smaller districts feel that they simply are not able to provide a full-time staff member to help manage their district's communication needs. Other districts commit a great deal of time and money to meet their communication needs. As a rule, all of Texas' larger districts have at least one full-time public relations professional on their staffs.

A public relations department's largest budget item, exclusive of salaries, will generally be for printing costs. Some 60-70 percent of departmental budgets will be used to print and mail newsletters and brochures. Other budget items will include production costs for slide and video presentations, funding for special district events, equipment costs, travel, and general supplies.

Programs for Smaller Districts

Many of the superintendents in Texas' smaller districts feel hamstrung because, while recognizing the vital need for an effective communications program, they also realize that the budget monies are just not there.

These districts can achieve a great deal by simply teaching their existing staffs the basics of effective school public relations. By making each of these staff members a "part of the PR Team" they can realize many of the benefits of an effective public relations program.

Smaller Texas districts may also turn to their regional service centers for help. These centers have staff members available who can provide many of the services of a full-time public relations department. Another option for smaller districts is to allow one of their teachers to teach for half of a day while concentrating on district-wide communication and public relations during the later half of the day.

Programs for Larger Districts

Larger Texas districts are often able to commit district funds for an effective communications program. Most Texas districts with over 15,000 students also have at least one full-time staff member who is given the title of coordinator or director of communications. Larger suburban districts might have several staff members in their communications department.

Budgeting for these departments varies widely from a few thousand to several hundreds of thousands of dollars per year. Average operating budgets (excluding salaries) for these departments usually fall in the range of two to three dollars per student per year.

The Public Relations Cycle

The public relations cycle is composed of four basic steps: **research, planning, communication, and evaluation.** The understanding and effective use of these steps are crucial to the success of all public relations efforts.

Research

Before an individual can begin to sell an idea to another, one must fully understand the concept. The research function can be as simple as talking to a few patrons of the school system, or as advanced as conducting a district-wide survey. Begin the research efforts by deciding what information is needed, and how the information will be used once it is gathered. This is the information age, and an amazing amount of data is valuable and accessible. Successful PR programs are started with the careful collection and sorting of this knowledge.

Planning

Because of the mind-boggling amount of information available to the public, educators must find new ways to get messages through. Audiences must be carefully targeted, and then given the information they really need. This type of action does not happen by accident. The planning process is an integral part of any public relations program. A well thought-out, written plan will allow communicators to move efficiently and effectively. The written plan is as important as the strategies of an army general or the game plan of a football team. Victory rarely comes by accident, but rather by "planning your work and then working your plan."

Communication

The communication step is where the "rubber meets the road." But many questions must first be answered. Will communication truly be two-way, allowing for audiences to share their ideas as well as to receive messages? What screens or filters will information encounter on the way to your receivers? Will past experiences, lack of confidence in the sender, racial or age bias, or a multitude of other filters color and/or distort the message? The communicator must learn to recognize and then overcome these barriers to effective communication. Once these questions are answered, the communication process may begin.

The communication tools available in the 1990s are unlimited. Desert Storm was the first war ever fought where television viewers around the world were able to watch the war as it was actually fought. The days of having to wait for a message . . . any message . . . are over. Educators must learn to harness the new technologies available to share their information. Communicators must be aware of the constant bombardment of information their potential receivers are already facing each day. All communication must be tailored to the real-life needs of the receivers. Nothing less will do.

Evaluation

Evaluation, the final step of the PR cycle, is also the most overlooked. But successful educators and communicators must be willing to learn from their experiences, both good and bad. A wise educator once said: "Good judgement comes from experience. Experience comes from bad judgement." Educators must make the time to measure the success of their efforts, both inside and outside of the classroom. Simple follow-up surveys can be extremely valuable in beginning research, and then planning the next project. This final step brings the public relations cycle full-circle.

The tumultuous times facing public educators in Texas are not going to end soon. Publics are demanding increased accountability . . . and results . . . from the schools. The effective use of this public relations cycle allows educators to hit their communication targets with regular accuracy.

Written Public Relations Plan

A written public relations plan is vital to the successful management of a district's public image. Planning saves time, money and frustration. It is also proactive rather than reactive in nature.

The public relations cycle can be used to begin the work of drafting a written PR plan. The first step in creating an effective, workable public relations plan is the surveying of the district's various publics. A variety of survey methods are available, and all will provide some type of useful research information.

Once survey results are complete, a formal goal-setting program is needed to help designate target audiences and plan messages. The best goals are measurable, obtainable, and reflect the varied needs of an individual district. The written plan to achieve these goals should be specific enough to be usable, yet flexible enough to be able to bend in the rapidly changing world of Texas public education.

Follow-up surveys are essential to the planning process. Effective public relations is measurable. Even though results are often years in coming, carefully crafted surveys and written plans are able to provide educators with helpful "snapshots" of their districts and accompanying programs.

According to the National School Public Relations Association, a district's public relations plan should balance the following four characteristics:

· **Two-way communication.** A good PR program includes listening as well as talking. Column inches of newspaper space and minutes of television or radio time are important, but public relations based on what's happening is more important.

· **For all people.** Employees, students, and teachers—the internal publics—are as important as editors, legislators and Rotarians. In fact, a well-informed internal public can serve as several thousand extra eyes, ears and mouthpieces in the community.

- **Systematic.** Use of the newspaper to the exclusion of all other media won't get the message across. Community newsletters alone won't work either. The communication specialist must systematically identify each segment of the public and decide upon the best medium to use to communicate with each—print, radio/TV, group meetings, etc.
- **Continuous.** School PR is a year-round operation. A good communications program says "good" when there's good and "problem" when there are problems.

Communicating With A District's Publics

School districts have a large group of publics who must be kept informed of district accomplishments, problems and future plans. Parents, non-parents, grandparents, business leaders and even school district employees must have up-to-date information about their schools if districts hope to receive support for their wide variety of programs and needs.

Each audience has their own information need. Senior citizens and patrons who no longer have any school-aged children at home are most often concerned with the question of rising school taxes. Parents with children in school are more interested in the educational programs and plans of a district. District employees are interested in the specifics of the operation of their districts, and if insurance rates are going up or if career ladder payments are going down. Business leaders want to know what the district is doing to effectively manage what is often the largest business in town, and how those efforts might help them in their own economic development activities.

Meeting the information needs of all of these publics is usually more than a full-time job. Public relations professionals must measure, evaluate and prioritize these needs before designing a plan of action fitting their budgets, staffs and hours available per week. This is an excellent opportunity to use community focus groups and other civic organizations to help in the establishment of the district's top PR priorities.

Most school communicators find it helpful to divide their efforts into two main target groups ... their **internal** and their **external** publics.

Internal Communications

Internal communication is focused on the employees of a district, approximately half of which are classroom teachers. Texas school districts employ a wide variety of workers to meet the needs of their students. Teachers are of obvious importance, but without the cleaners, cooks, bus drivers, secretaries, maintenance workers, and even school administrators, the teachers wouldn't be able to teach.

It is of vital importance for all school employees to realize that they are part of a larger team. These workers will never feel this esprit de corp without the availability of effective, two-way communication.

A variety of methods are being used in Texas districts to keep their employees informed of the challenges, problems and successes of their school system. Effective communication tools include:

Staff Newsletters

These publications can be produced as needed to provide current information to employees. Today's desktop publishing systems make the creation of district-wide or campus newsletters an easier undertaking. The key to success is to provide the information employees want in a concise, easy to read format.

Key Communicator Networks

Key Communicator Networks can be established allowing employees to meet face-to-face with the superintendent, assistant superintendents and trustees to share specific problem and concerns. These networks allow for immediate two-way communication which key communicators may then share with their fellow employees. One added benefit of this program is that the only cost usually involved is for coffee and donuts.

Cluster Breakfasts

Cluster Breakfasts allow for smaller groups of employees to meet with district administrators to share their ideas and concerns. A follow-up newsletter to the rest of the staff is always helpful to ensure that all employees are receiving the same information. This program is very effective in stopping rumors before they are repeated into "fact."

Staff Meetings

Regularly scheduled staff meetings can be very effective communication tools. Administrators should be careful, however, to make the time count. Staff meetings can easily cost hundreds of dollars per hour in staff time. All meetings should run from a written agenda, and be kept as brief as possible.

Special Publications

As special needs are targeted, specific newsletters, brochures and other publications may be needed to communicate a district's message. Many Texas districts are also utilizing the technological advances of our time by using computers, conference calls, audio-visual productions, videos and cable television to communicate with their employees.

External Communications

External communication targets a district's parents, students, business community and, perhaps of greatest challenge, the seventy percent of Texas households without school-aged children. All of these audiences must feel that they have a true picture of what's happening behind the classroom doors.

It is also very important for district taxpayers to feel confident that their tax dollars are being used effectively. A strong public relations effort prior to a school bond election or rollback attempt is almost always too little too late. An ongoing, carefully-planned communication program is essential to the building of public confidence and understanding.

Many communication tools are available to ensure that a district's local patrons feel that they are an informed member of the educational team:

District-Wide Newsletters

A newsletter mailed to every district patron is easily the most expensive item in any communication department's budget. Newsletters must be kept interesting, informative and timely. It is essential for this type of newsletter to carry the information that district patrons need to know, and that the writing level is easily understood by the general public.

Key Communicator Networks

Key Communicator Networks are also effective for district-wide audiences. The questions and concerns, while different than those shared by district employees, are just as vital.

School Board Meetings

Regular school board meetings can be an excellent avenue for communication to a district's publics. Information items added to the agenda allow patrons to be privy to the most current programs and accomplishments within a district. Some Texas districts have begun televising their board meetings to reach a wider audience and to increase patron participation within their school system.

News releases

School administrators may make effective use of local newspapers and other publications by regularly sharing district information with reporters through news tips, news releases and by inviting reporters to district events and meetings.

Special Publications

External audiences often need special purpose publications to meet their communication needs. Specifically targeted publications may include district maps, calendars and brochures. Again, newer technologies may be utilized to communicate with these hard to reach audiences.

Broadcast Media

No communication tool is more widely received than television programming. The majority of the American public relies on television for the bulk of their information needs, with 65 percent of the public saying that they prefer to receive their information through a television screen. While sharing a district's message via the airwaves is extremely effective, it is also exceedingly difficult. It is definitely worth the educator's while to pursue the use of television, radio broadcasts, and cable networks as valuable communication tools.

In summary, school communications must investigate every option available to reach their audiences. Today's society is constantly changing, as should educators' communication techniques. No one has time for unneeded information, and districts certainly do not have funds to waste. Both internal and external communication must be carefully targeted, planned, executed and measured.

Other Activities of the Public Relations Department

By its very nature, an effective school communications/public relations department is a busy place, normally involved in a multitude of projects and issues simultaneously. Many special projects may be coordinated through such an office, and it often seems that every activity within a district has some type of communication or public relations need. The need for careful planning and creative management becomes even more important as the number and variety of tasks increase.

Public Relations Consultant

The school public relations professional serves as the district's consultant for public affairs. It is that professional's job to measure the pulse of the community, and to help serve as the eyes and ears for the superintendent and school board. In many school systems, the communications director is a member of the superintendent's cabinet. In all cases, the PR professional should work with the administration and school board in the handling of sensitive and controversial issues, and should share the public relations impact of planned decisions and goals.

Issues Management

By managing public relations issues before they become major problems, school communicators are able to provide a valuable service. It is much easier to keep the hornets in the hive than to put the mad hornets back.

Texas school districts are faced with hundreds of issues at once, ranging all the way from drug abuse and teenaged pregnancy to radon, asbestos and lead in drinking fountains. Many of these challenges are able to be seen on the horizon for months or even years before they actually arrive on the educational scene. Other issues are much more subtle and harder to detect in advance.

Effective issues management requires a true "head-out-of-the-sand" approach by school administrators. Educators may begin to predict future issues by reading local newspapers and publications, as well as by studying national news magazines, newspapers, newscasts, and educational journals.

Bond and Rollback Elections

One very important facet of a communication department's work is realized when the district is facing a school bond election or attempt to roll back local tax rates. School systems with a working communications department are three steps ahead of the competition when district patrons head for the voting booth. Information networks have already been established, and a wide variety of extremely useful information should be readily available from departmental files.

The role of school administrators in such elections is that of "information provider." Texas educators are allowed to share what the results--positive and negative--would be of any bond or rollback election. Educators are not allowed to tell districts patrons how to vote. There is often a fine line between **informing** and **campaigning,** and Texas educators must do everything possible to avoid a conflict of interest in such situations.

Media Relations

One of a PR professional's most important daily tasks is maintaining effective media relations with local, state and even national news contacts. Many Texas districts have written board policies detailing the district's commitment to the importance of two-way communication. Most specify that the superintendent or his/her designee are responsible for serving as the district's "spokesperson." This task, in most districts, falls to the trained public relations professional.

News media relations is a never-ending job. School communicators are "on call" 24 hours per day to answer the media's questions and to provide information for reporters working on deadline. Carefully written administrative regulations are helpful in coordinating a district's media relations program.

Smart school administrators realize the need for specialized training in dealing with the media. Workshops are available whereby administrators may receive some "hands-on" experience in front of television cameras. It is this district spokesperson's role to serve as the point of contact between a school system and its many publics.

It is difficult to overemphasize the importance of effective media relations. District patrons read newspapers and watch the evening news to receive the information they need about their world. It is therefore imperative that Texas educators learn to help the news media to present a balanced, accurate picture of public education.

Crisis Communication

A well-written crisis communication plan is the first step in helping a local district to handle inevitable crisis situations. Tornadoes, kidnappings, school fires, campus violence, bus accidents, bomb threats and a multitude of other crisis situations regularly confront Texas educators. The school communicator is in a logical position to help manage these types of events.

Regular staff inservices and a written crisis communication plan are mandatory for dealing with these situations. The time to establish such a plan is well before the crisis begins. Such a plan allows a school system to be proactive rather than reactive. Once the crisis has ended, it is much easier to deal with the public relations implications if a district can show that it was prepared, organized and in charge as it "faced the fire."

Coordination of Special Programs

Many special programs fall under the organizational umbrella of the public relations department. Yearly special programs may include the coordination of school/business partnership programs, volunteer programs, senior citizen programs, and student recognition efforts. Public relations departments often handle all of a district's banquets, receptions, school dedications, and public meetings.

More and more often, school PR professionals are being called on to provide staff development activities, fund raising, teacher appreciation programs, and other morale-building activities. The coordination of these special programs can be very time consuming. School communicators must view these activities within the total context of the written public relations plan.

Summary

School public relations is an exciting, constantly changing area of Texas public education. Across the state, school superintendents, board members and school administrators are realizing that effective communication and public relations is everyone's job. That perception is also evident in the membership of the Texas School Public Relations Association whose numbers have grown by almost 300 percent during the last decade.

Texas public education is at a crossroads of sorts. The state's attention is focused on its public schools as never before. The success that educators will achieve as they work to educate the seniors of the year 2000 will be in direct relation to their ability to communicate the challenges, problems and successes of public education to their many publics.

References

Davis, B. Rodney. (1986). *School Public Relations: The Complete Book.* Arlington, VA: The National School Public Relations Association.

Bagin, Rich. (1986). *Planning Your School PR Investment.* Arlington, VA: The National School Public Relations Association.

Bagin, Rich. (1985). *Evaluating Your School PR Investment.* Arlington, VA: The National School Public Relations Association.

Wattenberg, B.J. (1984). *The Good News is the Bad News is Wrong.* New York, NY: Simon and Schuster

West, Phillip T. (1985). *Educational Public Relations.* Beverly Hills, CA: Sage Publications

Educational Facilities

Loren E. Betz
James A. Vornberg

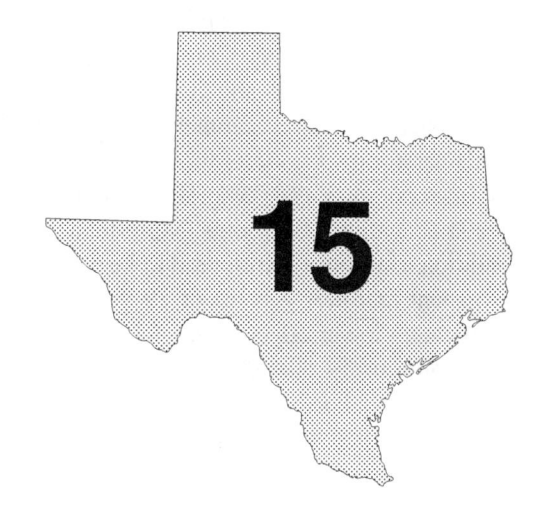

The school plant is that collection of school buildings, school sites, and fixed and moveable equipment that supports the learning activities of the school. Often referred to as the largest tool of instruction, the school plant may either enhance or detract from the educational program. A well designed facility will enhance the program by supporting the instructional design and providing a warm dynamic setting in which to conduct educational experiences. For a well designed facility to provide optimal support, effective planning must be accomplished by the school officials in conjunction with the architect. Planning must also encompass the facility's operation while it is in use.

The Texas Situation

Historically, the Texas Education Agency has not been involved in the planning, design and/or funding of public school facilities. With the reform movement in public education impacting Texas in the early 1980s, discussions related to school facility funding and policy began at the state level. Senate Bill 1 (TRS, Ch 1, Title 22, Art 717t-1) set the stage for the SBOE to make grants to school districts to meet emergency needs for acquiring, constructing, renovating or improving instructional facilities from funds appropriated for this purpose during the period of the 1991-92 school year. This action was in response to the determination of the courts in Edgewood v. Kirby that the funding scheme for Texas schools was inequitable and that the inequity of funding was apparent in the state's facilities.

In SB 1019 of the 1989 regular legislative session, the SBOE was directed to establish a statewide inventory of school facilities to be annually updated. In addition to the inventory, the act directed the SBOE to establish standards of adequacy of school facilities. A fifteen member School Facility Advisory Committee was formed and made recommendations to the SBOE relating to the inventory and the state school facility standards.

In November 1991, a summary report of the facilities inventory indicated that the average per pupil classroom space conformed to expectations, based on national standards. Portable buildings, comprising 4.05% of the facilities, were more prevalent at the elementary level and for special education classrooms. More than 96% of all rooms were rated to be in fair or good condition. Buildings were found to be generally well maintained. The average effective age of permanent facilities was about 19 years. Suburban and non-metro fast growth districts had significantly lower effective age facilities than did core urban neighboring districts. Approximately 80% of the districts had a 20:1 pupils per computer ratio.

The Schools Facilities Standards were adopted in July 1992 by the SBOE (19 TAC 61.101-61.104). All final designs approved after September 1, 1992, must comply with the standards, which address room size, construction quality, educational adequacy, and long-range planning. Minimum required room sizes indicated in table 15.1 must be met either per pupil or total room size.

TABLE 15.1
Minimum Sizes for Facilities

Room type		sq ft/pupil	sq ft/room
General Classrooms			
Pre-Kdgn		36	800
Elementary		30	700
Secondary		28	700
Specialized Classrooms			
Computer Labs:	Elem	41	900
	Second.	36	900
Science Labs:	Elem	41	900
	Middle School	50	1,000
	High School	50	1,200
Primary gymnasium for PE			
	Elementary		3,000
	Middle School		4,800
	High school		7,500
Library:		3.0 (for planned enrollment)	
	Elementary		1,400
	Middle School		2,100
	High School		2,800

The Commissioner of Education was charged to establish recommendations concerning the development of educational specifications. This charge included long-range planning for facilities to ensure educational adequacy. Local building codes must be followed where they have been adopted; where none has been adopted, the latest edition of either the Uniform Building Code or the Standard (Southern) Building Code must be met and certified by an independent certified building code consultant. The provisions of the Americans with Disabilities Act of 1990 must also be met.

The charge of state legislature to the SBOE in SB 1019 predictably has led to considerable more involvement of the Texas Education Agency in school facility planning, control of the adequacy of those plans, and funding of facilities. The TEA has named a director of school facilities and this office will provide assistance to school districts.

School District Facility Planning

Whether or not the school district facility improvement plan contributes to, or detracts from, the educational programs depends largely on the long-range planning that has taken place. Proper planning insures that the school building will serve the unique educational program of each school district the best possible way. All of the school district governing board members, administrators, teachers, and noncertificated staff should be actively involved in the ongoing development of a school plant improvement program. If the axiom of "from school program to school plant" is to be followed, local educators must be the major facilitators in identifying the specific educational program to be housed. School plant planning is an excellent way to exercise the components of site-based decision making. Although there are many others of the community and beyond the community who need to be involved in the planning process, the input of local professional educators is the key to planning school facilities that will best serve the school district and its community.

The School Survey

Developing a plan to plan is the first step. The school survey, or needs assessment, is one vehicle that local school officials may incorporate in their planning activities. The needs assessment can be a self-study or persons with expertise may be brought into the school district to assist with the study. How the needs assessment is conducted, who conducts the study, and the nature of the community involvement in the study should be controlled by the school officials, including members of the governing board. The study is, after all, ultimately the responsibility of the board of education.

Consultants from outside the district who normally conduct facility surveys include professional planners, representatives of architects and college/university professors. Each of the aforementioned types of planners will bring specific strengths and advantages to the conduct of the needs assessment. In the past there was little or no assistance with this stage of facility planning from TEA; however, the proposed planning guidelines for long-range planning and educational specifications offers some direction. It is important that school officials select professional and experienced planners who are objective, thorough, knowledgeable, and who can complete the study in a timely manner. School district administrators, teachers, service personnel, and members of the community should be prepared to contribute to a comprehensive school study to insure that it is unique to the school district.

What might be expected to be included in the contents of a school survey/needs assessment? Although the emphasis may vary from school district to school district, a facility study should have descriptions of the community, the organization of the school district, the student population, the educational program, the financial picture, and the school plant itself—including an evaluation of the physical facilities' ability to support the educational program. All of this data should present the past, the present, and most importantly, project the future. Properly conducted and periodically updated, the school facilities survey/needs assessment will be a valuable planning tool for school administrators and members of the governing board.

Recommended guidelines from TEA (1992) indicate a number of areas for consideration in planning. These include long-range planning goals, site selection process and factors, energy conservation requirements, architectural sound control, emergency management planning, and handicapped access requirements.

Educational Specifications

After the general facility needs of a school district have been determined, planners will focus on specific educational program requirements to develop educational specifications to guide the architect in the development of the actual building plans and design. These educational specifications are the responsibility of the local school officials. The scheme for the development of educational specifications can be quite complex. Everyone who will use the building should be represented in the development of educational specifications: teachers, students, secretaries, custodians, parents, cafeteria workers, bus drivers, maintenance personnel, school administrators, and members of the local board of education. Educational specifications should include the narrative descriptions and the underlying philosophy of the learning activities to be housed, the learning process requirements, the spatial relationships needed, the required kind and number of spaces, the furniture and equipment required, and any special environmental needs (Guide for Planning Educational Facilities, Council of Educational Facility Planners, International., 1992). Educators involved in the preparation of educational specifications should avoid the tendency to describe space needed only as more space than is presently available. Also, educational specifications should not be so "specific" as to handcuff the creativity of the architects.

Among areas which should be included in the specifications are the following:

Auxiliary Spaces

The term auxiliary spaces is used to describe those areas of a school plant that support instructional space. Auxiliary space includes auditoriums, cafeterias and kitchens, student commons, faculty areas, and offices (CEFPI, 1992). These spaces are often the areas of a school building that the public uses and from which the public forms its first impression of the school. Care should be taken that these areas are planned to be easily accessible, adaptable, and that the best possible impression of the school is presented.

Technology

A challenge to all school facility planners and school administration is the adaptability of the building to the changing demands of technology as it supports teaching and learning. Like the need for energy-smart school facilities alluded to in another part of this chapter, there is a need to plan and maintain school building that are technology-smart. Two potential pitfalls that should be considered with regard to technology for the schoolhouse: First, avoid being too technology-specific; technology changes and becomes obsolete rather quickly and yesterday's panacea may be found in today's cluttered storage rooms; second, keep in mind that the building will likely serve the community for fifty years and many generations of technology will have been utilized during that time. Plan for technology in a manner that will allow the building to be retrofitted with appropriate equipment and utilities with a minimum of expense and inconvenience.

The School Site

The land on which the school buildings are situated, the site, is often neglected and the contributions it might make to the educational program are not realized. The message the appearance of the building and grounds send to the public is an important one.

The school grounds should be included in the school districts long range school plant improvement program. In addition to aesthetic consideration, the school site can contribute to the educational program with playgrounds, athletic fields, community use facilities, and outdoor education facilities. Other issues relating to the school site that must be considered are security, parking, vehicle traffic, pedestrian traffic, neighbors, and cooperative arrangements between the school district and the city.

One person, preferably the principal or his representative, should be responsible to the school district for collecting and organizing the data that will become the educational specifications. The local school authorities often utilize the expertise of outside consultants in the development of written educational specifications. Appropriate educational specifications are a necessary element of educational planning that will result in school facilities that will best serve the future educational program needs of a community's children and youth.

Evaluation of the Existing School Plant

An important aspect of any long-range school plant improvement plan is the evaluation of the existing school plant. This evaluation can range from the very specific and detailed to the broad and general. In either case, this information is of great value to both building level and central office administration. How the present and existing buildings fit into future plans; the identification and prioritization of remodeling, renovation and retrofitting needs can be made; maintenance problems can be detected early; monies needed to make the necessary changes in facilities can be determined. Overall, the evaluation of existing facilities can be used for the basis of and keeping existing buildings from becoming educationally and/or structurally obsolete.

Many evaluative instruments exist to assist local school officials and consultants to objectively assess the existing school plant. One such instrument, *The Guide for School Facility Appraisal,* developed by Hawkins and Lilley, scores each component of the school plant in the areas of the school site, structural and mechanical features, plant maintainability, school building safety, educational adequacy, and the environment for education.

The concern for equity in Texas school facilities and the subsequent charge to the Texas Education Agency to oversee the comprehensive inventory the existing school buildings in Texas will undoubtedly give renewed impetus to the evaluation of existing facilities. Also the Public Education Information Management System (PEIMS) in Texas now includes school facility data in the input to the system. Almost certainly, any state funding to assist local school districts with capitol outlay expenditures will be influenced by the present condition of the school plants and the local school district efforts to maintain adequate school facilities.

Legal Requirements for School Construction

In addition to the newly adopted rules of the SBOE, Texas law directs specific requirements on school facility planning and construction which must be followed by districts. The laws are designed to protect users of the facilities and to obtain these facilities at the lowest possible costs to the taxpayer. Included among these are the following (Anderson, Goodlet, and Hunn, 1992):

A professional engineer must prepare plans for engineering services on projects in excess of $8000.

A registered architect must prepare plans and specifications for educational construction in excess of $100,000.

A board may negotiate fees with only one architect or engineer candidate at a time following initial selection based on qualifications and competence.

New structures and substantial modifications must be approved by the State Purchasing and General Services Commission for compliance with handicapped regulations prior to bid day and award.

- Bidding is required on purchasing personal property, construction or maintenance services of more than $10,000.
- Contracts for construction must be bonded (payment and performance bonds) if over $25,000 and districts may not require bonds if project is less than $25,000.

Financing School Facilities

School districts house their programs in facilities which are usually financed by borrowing funds. Most districts opt to borrow money through the issuance and sale of general obligation bonds—to be paid back from tax receipts over an extended time period. School systems in stable communities should not be in debt more than 8 to 10 percent of the fair market value of all taxable property in the district. Texas statutes control district expenditures under several laws with which districts may levy taxes. These include:

Article 2784e: Districts may issue only limited tax bonds under this law with the maximum amount available for debt being $1.00 of the $1.50 maximum tax rate per $100 assessed valuation. A few Texas districts which have not recently issued bonds are limited to using this law.

Article 2784e-1: Taking effect in 1955 as part of the Gilmer-Akin Act, this law could be adopted from 1955 to 1968. It provided $1.50 per $100 assessed valuation for local maintenance and an unlimited tax for bonded debt over and above the maintenance tax. However, a provision reduced the maximum maintenance tax as the debt/assessed valuation ratio rose above 7.5%: From 7.5% to 8.49% the Maintenance and Operations (M&O) maximum rate is $1.40; from 8.5% to 9.49% the maximum M&O rate is $1.30; and from 9.5% to 10% the maximum M&O rate is $1.20. Several districts in Texas are still bound by this statute, having never authorized by a district election, the provisions of Chapter 20 (TEC).

Chapter 20 of TEC: This law provides $1.50 per $100 assessed valuation for M&O and unlimited tax bonds without the reduction in M&O rates as the debt ratio rises. This statute, however, must be approved by a vote of the district's citizens in a proposition separate from the bond issue and is the only law that can be adopted by a district presently.

The Texas legislature has provided state guarantees for bonded indebtedness of local districts by pledging the corpus of the permanent school fund (PSF) in support of the loan. This has enabled many school districts to receive a AAA bond rating (the highest rating available) and thereby qualify for comparatively low interest rates on their bonds. Districts must apply for this guarantee at the time they prepare to sell bonds. The total amount the state will guarantee is limited to twice the corpus of the PSF. This provision in the law has saved districts much expense for interest payments in recent years.

Opening and Occupying the School Facility

Too often the planning of a school facility stops when the mortar dries and the human elements, students and faculty, occupy the facility without the benefit of a plan or the awareness of how to deal with the problems that inevitably arise. Lane (1985, p. 95) has made a number of suggestions, based on research, for opening a new school facility. These can provide a great deal of organization for the district and the program which will utilize the new facility. If possible, the principal who opens a new secondary school needs to be named to the position of principal a minimum of nine months prior to the first day of classes in the new facility. Giving the principal less time handicaps him/her in planning and preparing for the new school to open. The principal also needs to be involved in the planning of the new school prior to the architect designing it. The principal should be appointed at a time where he or she can work closely with the superintendent, board and architect in planning the design. He or she would then be developing the rationale for the designs in the new school and could communicate better with the staff, students, parents, and community about the new school. A time line should be developed by the new principal as part of the plan for opening the building. The district should appoint an employee to oversee the construction who will report to the new principal and the superintendent, thus allowing the principal to be free to plan and troubleshoot problems with construction as well as the educational program.

Whether or not the facility is new, a principal new to any building needs to become acquainted with the facilities and how many of the operating systems work. In today's technological world, some of these systems may require a specialist to operate the controls; however, some equipment must be operated by any principal or other administrator who will be present at times other staff or not. Lane and Betz (1987) developed a list of questions which are depicted in Table 15.2 which a newly appointed principal needs to have answered. While this list of questions may seem to operate on the principle of "Murphy's Law," any principal who has had a bell system go berserk or received a box of uncoded keys from a contractor, will appreciate the value of having answers to these questions. Ultimately, it is the principal's responsibility for a smooth opening and operating school, and these items are important.

Maintenance and Operations

Educational facilities require a great deal of financial resources of the district to make them capable of doing the job for which they were designed. The annual cost study done by American School & University for 1992 indicated that 9.22% of the district's current expenditures (not including transportation, capital outlay and debt service) went to provide maintenance and custodial services, energy, supplies, equipment, overhead, and outside contracts to keep school buildings going in the south central part of the US (includes Arkansas, Louisiana, New Mexico, Oklahoma and Texas). This is slightly above the national median with the cost of electricity used being about 3.9% above the national median due to air conditioning needs (see Table 15.3). Because this is a major portion of the budget requirement, it is necessary for schools to control this expense by operating an efficient and effective maintenance and operations program.

TABLE 15.2
Facility Questions for a New Principal

1. Where are the heating and air conditioning controls?
2. Where are the circuit breakers?
3. Does the school have an alarm system and how does it work?
4. Where are the water controls?
5. Is there a lawn sprinkler and how does it function?
6. Is there an outside lighting timer control and how does it operate?
7. How does the bell system operate and how can the bell schedule be changed?
8. How does the public address system operate?
9. Where are the fire alarm controls and what are the fire bell procedures?
10. What are the disaster drill procedures?
11. Where are the "as-built" drawings of the school?
12. Where are the keys secured?
13. What cleaning agents are used in the school and how are they stored?
14. How does the telephone operate?
15. Does the community share the facility during evening and weekends?
16. Who does the principal contact when something malfunctions or needs repairs.
17. Who are the custodians?
18. Are there direction manuals for the above systems? Where are they located?

Source: Lane and Betz

TABLE 15.3
Maintenance & Operations Costs

	South Central US	National
Median Dollars per student		
Payroll $ Custodial	128.81	171.18
Payroll $ Maintenance	71.20	60.21
Outside contract labor	23.44	27.55
Fuel	19.35	38.71
Electricity	78.80	78.36
Other Utilities	18.23	15.83
Equip. & Maint Supplies	49.24	38.21
Total M & 0	503.23	514.94
Total Net Current Expen.	4,761.08	5,524.11
M & O % of NCE	9.93	9.21
Salary $ Custodial	13,707.00	19,311.00
Salary $ Maintenance	20,535.00	24,799.00
M & 0 Costs; $/sq. ft.		
Custodial Payroll	.82	1.26
SF/Custodian	20,326.17	20,000.00
Fuel	.14	.25
Electricity	.54	.54
Other Utilities	.11	.10
Equip & Maint Supplies	.33	.27
Total M & 0 Costs/sq. ft.	3.25	3.64

Source: Agron. "Maintenance & Operations Cost Study," *American School and University,* April 1994, p. 31-34.

Operations

Facility operations include the necessary functions required to keep a school running on a daily basis. Housekeeping services; grounds upkeep; security of the building; safety monitoring; heating, ventilating, and air conditioning operations (HVAC); equipment servicing; electrical plant operations (including utilities); simple repairs; and assistance to the staff are generally considered to be operations functions. Although operations functions may have considerable direction from the central district office level, the individual building principal is usually responsible for giving direct supervision to custodians, security procedures and utility management for the facility. Only by having a single manager at a site can the facility operations best support the educational program.

Custodial services usually require a custodian on duty during the school day to keep the building clean in heavily used areas and for emergencies. Although one custodian per 15,000 square feet of space has been a long-used standard, actual square feet per custodian in the south central region of the US was more than 20,600 square feet in 1994 (Agron, 1994). Principals must work closely with the operations staff in the building in order to maintain adequate standards and complete all the housekeeping jobs required with the allocation of staff. Usually after school hours custodians complete the cleaning of classrooms and maintain building security. Groundskeeping services are frequently provided by a specialized grounds crew in multiple building districts. As equipment of all types become more technically sophisticated, the training of operations staff is more critical for these staff members to do their job. Low wages and high turnover of employees in the operations area frequently cause difficulty in being able to meet the school's needs. In a number of instances districts have contracted with outside firms to perform the housekeeping functions in the schools. This places the burden of recruiting, employing, training and motivating the staff on the contractor rather than the school district. A major disadvantage is that the custodian does not work for the district and sometimes motivation and stability of employees is less than desired.

Security procedures have become more important as vandalism, drugs, and violent crime have invaded the school settings, particularly in metropolitan areas. Uniformed security personnel or security aides sometimes identified by their attire are employed in many districts in addition to local police officers being assigned to a cluster of buildings in "Youth Action Centers." Social workers also may join these staff members to work closely with students in a prevention mode. Security alarms, motion detectors, and cameras have been installed and linked to a security center for monitoring the entire district. Security patrols traveling from building to building also protect students, staff and facilities. Principals within their buildings frequently use radio communications and photo IDs or security badges to help maintain security in campuses which are large. Even in small and less impacted facilities, the daily securing of doors and windows is an important security function.

Maintenance

The term maintenance is often confused with custodial functions by the uninformed. Maintenance refers to the upkeep or repair of facilities within the school site, buildings or equipment that keeps these facilities restored, as nearly as possible, to its original condition or efficiency. Maintenance is done by repair or the replacement with property of equal value or efficiency. Maintenance often requires more technical tasks because of the nature of the repair on what may be complicated equipment or a higher level or skill by the employee requiring extensive training. Maintenance requirements may be somewhat sporadic due to the timeliness of needs. Maintenance is often divided into several classifications:

Preventive maintenance involves an ongoing process of inspection and servicing of components to reduce or eliminate mechanical, physical or structural breakdown to prevent costly replacements and protect against disruptive plant failure. Good preventive maintenance programs minimize disruption of services and reduce repair costs and energy consumption costs.

Emergency maintenance is unexpected and requires an immediate response to continue to use the facility or have the support of the specific component. A high incidence of emergency maintenance may be related to poor management of the facilities and places uneven strain on the school's resources and often an undesirable effect on normal operations.

Scheduled maintenance is the result of good practices which permit changes to equipment or facilities to be done when it least disrupts normal operations. Often scheduled maintenance occurs in the summer or other vacation periods.

Replacement maintenance is conducted when components of the facility are changed out as opposed to repair of the present unit. Replacement maintenance may be scheduled or emergency in nature. A good preventative maintenance program can assist in determining replacement maintenance needs by determining the life cycle of major components and scheduling replacement requirements before the schools program is impacted negatively.

Routine maintenance refers primarily to demand maintenance conducted as the need arises but not of an emergency nature. Typically the building administrator reports routine maintenance requests in writing or by phone to the maintenance department which then arranges for their completion by the appropriate technicians.

Contract maintenance includes those maintenance tasks which require an outside person to be employed to complete the job. This requirement is necessitated by the infrequency of the job to be done, its specialized nature, and sometimes by the size of the district, i.e. a small district may contract for computer or AV equipment repairs while a large district might employ a number of skilled technicians due to the amount of equipment repairs.

Developing Maintenance Programs.

Maintenance departments usually are centralized in a district and vary in size and complexity based on the size of the district and the day-to-day requirements which occur repeatedly. Large districts may have hundreds of personnel employed while a small district may employ a single maintenance person who serves as a "jack-of-all-trades."

Maintenance programs usually are supervised by the business function of the district or may come under the direct supervision of a facilities administrator. Policies and regulations approved by the board of trustees should be developed to provide management guidance. Operating procedures will direct the flow of communications between building-level administrators and those administering the maintenance program. Budgeting is critical in effecting a satisfactory program, so adequate resources are available for the needs to be accomplished. As budgets are developed building administrators should conduct comprehensive annual inspections of their buildings and discuss needs with their staff to request adequate funds for completing needed maintenance during the next year. As funds become constrained there is a trend to place maintenance appropriations in each building's budget to be charged as the tasks are completed.

When financial constraints become most difficult on schools, there has been a tendency to take at least part of the slack up by reducing the maintenance budget. This creates what is referred to as deferred maintenance—that which is put off until another year when funds are not as tight. This is usually a false economy measure as breakdowns frequently occur causing major program impact and sometimes even more expensive costs due to increased inflation costs for components which may now have to be replaced rather than just repaired. A study by Groppel in 1988 determined that preventive maintenance allocations were less than 10% of the total maintenance budget in 65% of the Texas school districts and less than 20% of the maintenance budget in 85% of the Texas districts.

Life-cycle costing has become important in making building choices when new construction decisions are being made. In the past initial cost of construction was the primary if not only consideration in making construction choices. Today the cost of operating a facility over a twenty- or thirty-year period should be considered. Utility, maintenance and operations costs should be factors in making choices of building materials and equipment to order to best meet budget constraints. A values analysis of various materials and products, developed by adequate records of maintenance performed, as well as keeping up to date on new products for construction and maintenance can assist in making life-cycle cost decisions.

The use of computers in maintenance programs have provided a new tool to assist in management decision making as well as record keeping. By placing all maintenance records on computer files, a data base can be built to provide information for scheduling preventive maintenance tasks, maintaining inventories, making cost management decisions, and planning budgets for future years. Several commercial programs are available for this type of assistance for administrators. The preventive maintenance study by Groppel (1988) determined that this tool was being used in Texas by only 19% of school districts.

Energy Management

Costs for fuel and electricity have risen throughout the US during the last decade and it appears that they will continue to do so in the 1990s. The use of energy in Texas schools is a source of concern for school boards and administrators. The 1994 Maintenance and Operations Cost Study (Agron) indicated the south central states were spending 68 cents per square foot of building space for fuel and electricity. In order to maintain energy costs within a reasonable allocation of the total school budget, school districts must make adequate plans for controlling the cost of this resource in relation to other costs incurred.

To adequately impact a school district's energy consumption extensive planning must be done. All participants in the schools—students, teachers, administrators, support personnel—must be involved in the effort. The board of trustees must be committed by providing direction for the plan and to furnish the necessary policy decisions and fiscal support for change to occur. An energy conservation task force which can develop ideas and build support from the varied publics for educational efforts and procedural changes is usually a major factor. A manager of the energy program at both the district level and at each building is important in order to maintain direction for the program. Conservation efforts usually focus around a variety of factors:

Educational programs should be developed for both the students in the schools as well as the community in order to gain their support and to focus attention on the problem. A variety of materials are available for this factor.

Plans for individual schools should be developed to determine where energy consumption is occurring and to develop plans for reducing unnecessary usage. Mini-audits involving the building administrator, custodians, and building personnel can identify many areas using checklists. A maxi-audit involving energy engineers using computer-based models and new technological developments as thermal sensors and cameras can determine other energy loss sources. From these audits, goals can be set with specific plans for reducing the losses which are identified.

Management of these developed programs is a key to making headway in this effort. Regular recording of energy consumption levels will help to determine what is occurring and to identify possible losses which would go unnoticed normally. Recognition of schools and managers whose efforts at conserving energy have been successful by returning a portion of the funds saved for use in the educational program is an example of a management technique which supports building level cooperation in conservation efforts.

Proper maintenance of the facility's equipment and thermal shell can reduce energy losses. Improperly maintained boilers, air filters, cooling towers, and compressors all consume more energy than necessary. Poorly fitting windows and doors due to use of the facility might be changed out with newer, proper functioning ones.

Modification of existing facilities can reduce energy costs by replacing inefficient equipment with systems which make better use of energy. Examples include utilizing energy-efficient lighting systems in place of older fixtures, replacement of windows with double parted glass, or installation of an energy control system with monitors for controlling the environment.

New construction plans can be developed to take advantage of a wide variety of newer technology in construction materials and control systems. Energy-efficient insulation, computer controlled environments, installation of thermal storage and high-efficiency lighting are examples of energy-conscious designs which can be included. As demand rates are implemented by power companies, which will raise costs of electricity used during peak periods, new construction plans can significantly impact total energy costs in the years which the building is utilized.

Senate Bill 1 (TEC 21.9012) provided authorization for school districts to contract for energy conservation measures with a payback over an extended period not to exceed ten years. The arrangement may be for multiyear contracts if the annual cost of the contract does not exceed the prorated annual savings. The contractor is required to have specified energy conservation experience and the district is required to follow competitive bidding procedures in awarding the contract.

References

Agron, Joe. (April 1994). "A Clean Sweep: Maintenance and Operations Cost Study." *American School and University,* p. 31-34.

Anderson, Denise H., L. Ann Goodlet and Paul Hunn. (1992). "Texas School District Construction and Maintenance Planning Chart." *The Texas School Administrators' Legal Digest.* Denton, TX.

Council of Educational Facility Planners, International (1991). *Guide for Planning Educational Facilities.* C.E.F.P.I.

Groppel, Larry D. (1988). A Descriptive Study of Preventive Maintenance Programs in Texas School Districts. Unpublished Doctoral Dissertation, East Texas State University.

Hopkins, Mary D. (1988). A Comparative Analysis of Energy Conservation Using Schools with Differing Energy Measures. Unpublished Doctoral Dissertation, East Texas State University.

Lane, Kenneth E. (1983). Strategies for Opening and Occupying New Secondary School Facilities. Unpublished Doctoral Dissertation, East Texas State University.

Lane, Kenneth E. And Loren E. Betz. (November 1987). "'The Principal New to a School--What Questions to Ask About a Facility." *NASSP Bulletin,* Vol. 71, No. 502, p. 125.

Texas Education Agency. (November 1991). Summary Report on School Facilities Inventory Data. Resource Planning Division.

Texas Education Agency. (July 1992). School Facilities Standards and Guidelines of the Texas State Board of Education, Austin.

Dealing with Exceptional Children

Linda Avila

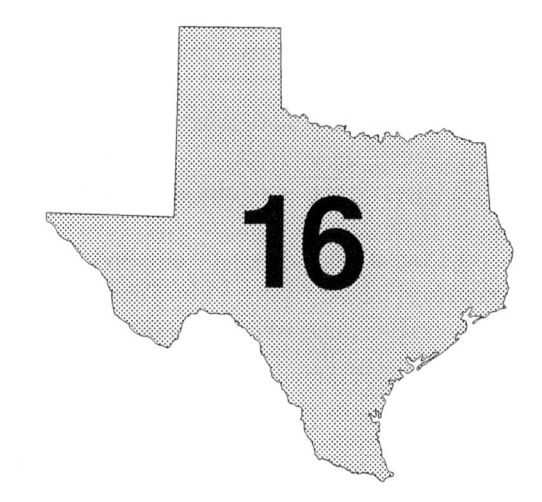

Children are unique and different from one another. Historically, some youngsters who did not fit the notions of teachers and administrators as to what constituted a "student" were excluded from public schools. As these types of children were re-introduced to the public school systems, special supplementary programs were created to serve their needs. Two broad kinds of special programs created are special education services and programs for the gifted and talented; in some states, but not in Texas, these two programs are contained under one umbrella of services for exceptional children. Current trends in these two fields reveal a movement toward integrating students receiving specialized services into the regular classrooms, in the name of heterogeneous grouping, full inclusion, detracking, and other educational terms. Integrating exceptional students into regular classes requires a full understanding of these populations and the present programs that serve them.

Special Education Programs

Federal Perspectives

Federal legislation and court action involving handicapped persons impacted education to some degree before the 1960s; however, it was not until that time that special education became a focus for federal action. This emphasis came partly as a result of advocacy group pressure; of personal commitments of President Kennedy; and of the national concern for disadvantaged school children, as expressed in the Elementary and Secondary Education Act (1965) which funded programs for economically disadvantaged students, the handicapped, and other groups with special needs. In 1968, the Handicapped Children's Early Education Act passed Congressional approval; funding was provided for model demonstration projects which served pre-school handicapped students. The 1972 Vocational Rehabilitation Act extension directed state rehabilitation agencies to grant first service priorities to those persons most severely handicapped. Hand in hand with these pieces of legislation in the 1960s and 1970s, litigation involving the handicapped increased significantly and contributed to the passage of P.L. 94-142, the Education for All Handicapped Children Act (1975).

P.L. 94-142 mandated a free appropriate public education for all handicapped children between the ages of 3 and 21 by September, 1980. Students who were unserved by the public schools and students who were most severely handicapped were those targeted as first priorities. Under P.L. 94-142:

- students are to be educated to the maximum extent possible with their non-handicapped peers (least restrictive environment or LRE).
- evaluative instruments and procedures used to determine disabilities are to be culturally and racially fair.
- due process for handicapped students and their parents/guardians is to be provided.
- individual education programs (IEP's) are to be developed for each special education student, including statements of present levels of functioning, annual goals, short-term objectives, lists of service to be provided, dates of those services, and procedures and criteria for evaluation.
- *all* children with disabilities are to be served; local districts have no choice in providing the needed services (Gallagher, 1989).

More recently, P.L. 99-457 (1986) expanded the coverage of P.L. 94-142, mandating programs for all handicapped 3-5 year olds by the 1990-91 school year and making available new grants for programs which serve the 0-2 year old handicapped population. Three year old disabled youngsters are eligible for special education services as of their third birthday, regardless of the time of the school year in which it occurs. The emphases of P.L. 99-457 in relation to the preschool handicapped population are on minimizing the risk of developmental delays by delivering services as early as possible, parent training, coordination among all agencies involved with preschool handicapped children, and the decreased use of labels. In addition, P.L. 99-457 addresses the school-aged handicapped population through the promotion of the development and use of technological advances; research and development in the area of instructional media and materials; an emphasis on providing services to members of minority groups; and a focus on vocational and life skills, particularly for drop-outs.

The newest piece of federal legislation involving students with disabilities is *The Individuals with Disabilities Education Act* (IDEA) which amended P.L. 94-142 as of October, 1990. Major changes made by IDEA include provisions that:

- two additional handicapping conditions of autism and traumatic brain injury (TBI) were added as separate categories eligible for special education services.
- the terminology for referring to handicapped students has been changed to "children with disabilities."
- new related services in the areas of therapeutic recreation, social work services, and rehabilitation counseling were added as available to students as needed.
- the IEP's of students 16 years old and older must outline needed transition services, including the responsibilities of agencies outside of the public schools. These transition services are defined as a "coordinated set of activities for a student, designed within an outcome-oriented process, which promotes movement from school to post-school activities including post-secondary education, vocational training and education, integrated employment, . . ."(Chief. State Schools Officers, 1990). In Texas, these individual transition plans are called ITP's.
- the various states in their plans for funding must include procedures for ensuring that personnel necessary to carry out the provisions of IDEA are available in sufficient numbers and qualified. Additionally continuing education for regular educators, administrators, and support personnel must be planned.

Not confined to children with disabilities, the Americans with Disabilities Act (ADA) passed in 1990 went into effect during the summer of 1992. The ADA constitutes a civil rights statute to prohibit discrimination against individuals who are disabled, who have a history of a mental or physical disability, who are regarded or perceived as disabled, or who have a relationship or association with someone with a known disability. These protections cover disabled individuals from cradle to grave and impact employment, housing, educational, and all other life-impacting opportunities. Districts not in compliance may be sued as violating the civil rights of the disabled persons involved, be they students, parents, or employees.

Cases such as the *Pennsylvania Association for Retarded Citizens* (1971) and *Mills* (1972) laid the basis for P.L. 94-142 by requiring that children with handicaps be afforded appropriate educational services. Since the implementation of P.L. 94-142, litigation important to special educators has abounded, partially in response to the rights afforded handicapped students and their parents therein. One of the most comprehensive of these, *Jose P. vs. Ambach* (1979) was actually a set of three class action suits and alleged that the Board of Education of the City of New York and the State Education Department failed to: 1) evaluate students in a timely fashion; 2) place eligible students in a timely manner; 3) develop appropriate individual education programs (IEP's); 4) provide related services;

5) make facilities appropriate and accessible; 6) educate students in the least restrictive environment; and 7) provide adequate bilingual services to handicapped students who required them. The major remedies included a 30 school-day time limit on evaluations, a 30 school-day time limit on placement, the distribution of booklets outlining parent and student rights, detailed plans to make the needed facilities accessible to the handicapped, and monthly reports to the court on progress in the implementation of the remedies. Other issues were worked out through bi-weekly meetings between defendants and plaintiffs. The impact in New York has been the overall restructuring of the school system's delivery of special education services (Fafard, Hanlon, and Bryon, 1986).

Less broad in nature, *Lora v. Board of Education* (1977) and *Larry P. v. Riles* (1979) addressed issues of serving minority students labelled as handicapped. In both instances, over-representation of ethnic minority students in special education and social segregation served as the bases of contention; remedies included the development and implementation of non-discriminatory criteria and procedures for placing students in special education settings.

Board v. Rowley (1982) represented the Supreme Court's first special education case and an attempt to fine-tune P.L. 94-142 by defining "appropriate." Although the case deals with the provision of a sign language interpreter for a child with a hearing impairment in public school, the implications are much broader. One principle established in Rowley is that schools are to provide handicapped students specially individually designed educational instruction and all related services necessary to help them benefit from that instruction. There is, however, no requirement that handicapped students be provided opportunities to reach their maximum potentials (Turnbull, 1986). Secondly, *Rowley* establishes the services outlined in the IEP based on professional judgment and parental input as "appropriate," despite legislative or regulatory mandates. For example, serving handicapped students 175 days in a year may be law or rule but could be overridden if deemed inappropriate during the IEP development. Thirdly, "appropriate" education is defined in *Rowley* as a process rather than a state of affairs, which includes the provision of related services (Turnbull, 1986).

Another special education case presented to the Supreme Court was *Irving Independent School District v. Tatro* (1984) which originated in Texas. The basic issue was the demarcation between educational services and medical services, with the school district arguing that Clean Intermittent Catheterization was a medical service and thus could not be performed by school personnel. The decision was congruent with *Espino v. Besteiro* (1981) in which a court ordered a district to air condition a mainstreamed classroom for a handicapped student who could not regulate his own body temperature. *Tatro* distinguished between medical and school health services on the basis of who was qualified to offer them; thus catheterization and other simple medical services which can be administered by a school nurse or other trained person are to be included in the IEP as related services (Vitello, 1986).

The involvement of agencies and branches of the federal government in special education since the implementation of P.L. 94-142 has been extensive. The funding provided to assist in this implementation has been minimal, running at generally less than 10% of the special education budgets of school districts. The funding aspects of I.D.E.A. provide the largest share of the limited federal funding available in support of special education; I.D.E.A. monies are distributed on a per capita basis within states. Every child being served in special education as of December 1 in each district generates a set amount of federal funding for that district, regardless of his/her handicapping condition, age, severity of impairment, or other factors. Additionally, federal monies are available through P.L. 99-457 for early childhood students and through Chapter 1 of the Education Consolidation and Improvement Act.

State Perspectives

Services for handicapped pupils have been offered in Texas for many years before the implementation of Plan A in 1971. However, Plan A, which contained the state rules and regulations governing special education within the state, reformed the services offered. Service to handicapped students not previously identified (learning disabled, for example) and the use of resource rooms in addition to other instructional arrangements previously existent were the two main thrusts of Plan A. With the advent of P.L. 94-142, the state adjusted new rules and regulations to implement the federal mandates, even though Plan A served as one of the models in the development of P.L. 94-142. These guidelines are found in the *State Board of Education Rules for the Handicapped* and are revised occasionally to meet new or changing conditions. In addition to emphasizing placement in the least restrictive environment, nondiscriminatory evaluation, due process, and the development of individualized education programs, the state board rules highlight:

- the members of basic Admission, Review, and Dismissal (ARD) committees as an administrative representative, an instructional person, and the student's parent/guardian. ARD committees for some handicapping conditions or other special circumstances may be larger and contain more required members. The decisions on ARD committees must be reached through consensus; when consensus cannot be reached, no voting occurs. The ARD committee may be reconvened within 10 school days to reconsider and try again to reach consensus.
- procedures for referring students for assessment for special education services. Responsibility for completion of the referral lies with regular education personnel.
- provisions regarding the suspension and expulsion of handicapped students. The ARD committee must meet to suspend a handicapped child for longer than six days or to remove a handicapped student to an alternative education placement for more than ten days.
- requirements for local district advisory committees to provide public participation in designing education programs for the handicapped.

The guidelines which delimit the operation of special education programs in Texas are in consonance with all provisions of P.L. 94-142, I.D.E.A., other pieces of federal legislation, and case law. H.B. 72, the major reform bill for all of education in Texas, impacted special education almost exclusively in the area of finance. Special education state funding had been available on a personnel unit basis; H.B. 72 provisions base funding on the number of full-time equivalent students receiving special education services. A weighted formula is used; students in various instructional arrangements earn various weights. For example, students who receive speech therapy only are weighted at 7.11 times the adjusted basic allotment; handicapped youngsters in a resource setting carry a weight of 2.7, while those totally in regular classrooms with consultation and monitoring are calculated with a weight of .25. A system of contact hours generates the number of full-time equivalents based on a thirty hour instructional week in each of the weighted instructional arrangement categories.

Theoretical Bases

Special education is not, and should not be, a total program different, separate and apart from the education of non-handicapped children. Special education refers to those aspects of education that are unique and/or supplementary to the regular educational program. The need for the special education services is dictated by *both* the abilities *and* disabilities of handicapped youngsters. Therefore, one of the major underpinnings of special education is an inclination to view each child as a unique individual with unique needs. This emphasis on individual differences serves as the basis for identifying students as handicapped, as well as for designing educational programs, related services, and evaluative techniques (Kirk and Gallagher, 1979).

Not only do handicapped students differ from one another, and from their non-handicapped peers, causing educational personnel to educate each child differently, but also the abilities of handicapped youngsters are inconsistent across various realms of learning. Consequently, the uneven growth in the cognitive, social, emotional, language, physical, and academic areas yield varied profiles for individual students. Even within a defined subject area, a handicapped student may do well with one skill but not with another. Consideration of these individual differences and instruction based upon them serve as part of the foundation of special education.

Setting up the environment to insure student success serves as another cornerstone of special education programs. Teachers use task analysis to outline all steps students should learn to master a skill; they watch as students work through the steps to locate any barriers which prevent further progress. Goals and objectives are set in order that the learning to be achieved will be challenging to students, though not so difficult as to foster failure. Positive reinforcement, both extrinsic and intrinsic, is built into the environment to further encourage learning and feelings of efficacy.

Classroom management becomes an important factor to a teacher of disabled students. The use of rules and procedures facilitates the perception of the classroom's being highly structured. This structure provides students with a sense of security, in that expectations are understood. Because special educators may work with individuals and small groups, clear expectations for classroom behavior help all students to proceed with their learning with or without the teacher's constant attention.

Strategies in a special education classroom may vary considerably. With some handicapped students, activities will be very concrete, with numerous models provided. Teachers may use physical, as well as verbal, cues and prompts to help students acquire skills. Methods which use more than one sense for input and/or output, particularly multisensory techniques, may be common, as teachers try to match the instruction and the demonstration of tasks mastered to the strengths and disabilities of students.

Additionally, the actual learning content may differ based on the functioning levels and the needs of students. Academic subjects and skills are common for those less severely impaired; however, many special educators teach daily living, social, motor, vocational and other skills which will help the handicapped youngsters be successful adults.

Types of Programs

The state of Texas mandates services for the same handicapping conditions as stipulated by P.L. 94-142 and IDEA. These handicapping conditions, along with some of the criteria which in part define them include:

Physically handicapped. Students who have severe orthopedic impairments and/or suffer from other health impairments as determined by a licensed physician fall into this category.
Children with audiological impairments. Based on an otological/audiological evaluation conducted by certified medical personnel, students in this group should have a serious hearing loss even after corrective medical treatment or amplification device use.
Children with visual impairments, which encompasses those students with no vision or with serious visual losses even after correction is documented by licensed optometrists or opthamologists.
Deaf-blind students, who suffer from both severe visual and hearing losses after correction. These students must meet the specific eligibility criteria as both auditorially and visually disabled.
Mentally retarded. These students must have been determined by licensed professionals using individually administered assessments to be functioning two or more standard deviations below the mean in verbal ability, non-verbal ability, and adaptive (social) behavior.
Emotionally disturbed. Students in this category must be examined by a psychologist, a psychiatrist, or a psychological associate under the direct supervision of a psychologist. The emotional disturbance must be exhibited over a long period of time and to a marked degree, adversely affecting educational performance.

Learning disabled. The criteria for this handicapping condition are numerous; not all will be cited here. In general a multi-disciplinary team must agree that a child is learning disabled by scrutinizing his/her intellectual ability (which must be above the retarded range) with his/her achievement levels as established through standardized testing. A difference in functioning of one standard deviation below ability is required; an alternative method for establishing the existence of a learning disability includes the use of work samples, observation of the student in class, and the gathering of other data.

Autistic, which includes the use of a multi-disciplinary team to determine whether or not the definition for autism and other pervasive developmental disorders found in the third edition of the Diagnostic and Statistical Manual (DSM III) is met.

Multiply handicapped, for students who have a combination of handicaps listed above and also are severely impaired in psychomotor skills, self-care, communication, cognition, and emotional/social development.

Traumatic brain injured. Because the State Board is presently defining this condition, eligibility under this category requires simply a doctor's statement that the student has suffered a traumatic brain injury and a statement indicating the educational need for special services.

Not all of the qualifications for each handicapping condition have been listed in this reference. Before participating in any procedures to label students as disabled, one should consult the *State Board of Education Rules for the Handicapped* available in all Texas school districts to learn of all the criteria to be met.

Delivery Models

The basis for determining which services will be made available to handicapped students and how those services will be made available should be the educational needs of each individual. Thus delivery models become highly idiosyncratic and individualized. A model which aids in the conceptualization of delivery methods was suggested by Deno (1972) in the form of a cascade of services:

- regular class placement on a full-time basis with no special support;
- regular classroom placement on a full-time basis with supplemental services, such as special education staff consultation with the regular classroom teacher, occupational therapy, or counseling for the student;
- part-time special class placement, which is termed "resource" placement in many areas of the country;
- full-time special classroom placement on a regular school campus;
- placement in special schools for the handicapped only;
- homebound services;
- residential placement for educational purposes;
- residential placement for custodial care for those so severely handicapped that educational services would not be of benefit.

The instructional arrangements offered in Texas are very similar to those suggested above. The main idea of such a model is to offer a variety of settings so that programs will be molded to fit children, rather than attempting to fit students into settings which are inappropriate. Deno's model also fits with the mandates of P.L. 94-142 and I.D.E.A. to provide the least restrictive environment for handicapped students. With many alternative settings available, each more confining and less normalized than the preceding one, students will be placed in the arrangements which to the maximum extent based on their handicaps afford them the most educational participation with their nondisabled peers.

One hitch in the process involves instructional arrangements for early childhood handicapped students. Because services are available at age 3 (at birth for the visually handicapped and the auditorially handicapped), some of the levels of the cascade, particularly those involving regular classroom placement, are difficult for school districts to offer. Non-handicapped students do not usually attend school until age 5; therefore, arrangements with day care centers, Headstart centers, pre-kindergarten classes, and other agencies serving young children are necessary to offer part-time placement in special education. Early childhood teachers for the handicapped, especially in small school districts, may serve wide ranges of students from several segments of the cascade, from consulting with pre-kindergarten and kindergarten teachers on students with mild handicaps to working with students who spend all of their school day in that early childhood special education class.

Related services are also available to enhance the educational offerings and to insure that students with disabilities benefit from those special educational experiences. Related services include, but are not limited to, speech therapy, occupational therapy, physical therapy, parent and/or student counseling, therapeutic recreation, career counseling, school health services, social work services, adaptive equipment, and special transportation. The related services should be written into the student's IEP as part of the program to be offered.

Personnel Considerations

Generally, four categories of personnel are available through special education programs: 1) teachers, which include speech therapists and itinerant personnel; 2) related service personnel, including occupational therapists, physical therapists, nurses, and other licensed non-educational staff members; 3) special education support personnel, among which are diagnosticians, psychologists, special education directors, and others; and 4) paraprofessionals and aides.

In Texas, teaching certification is available to perspective special education teachers on a generic basis; another option is for the teacher to earn an elementary or secondary teaching certificate and then to add special education as an endorsement, either generically or in a certain category of disability (severely emotionally disturbed, learning disabilities, mentally retarded, physically handicapped, severely/profoundly handicapped, visually handicapped, hearing impaired, speech and language therapy, or early childhood education for the handicapped).

Teachers with any type of special education certification or endorsement may be assigned to any type of special education classroom with these exceptions:

- speech therapy services may be provided only by licensed/certified speech therapists.
- teachers certified in early childhood education for the handicapped may teach only in programs of that nature.
- students with visual and auditory impairments must have available to them the services of teachers certified in those areas.

Special education aides are to be certified by the Texas Education Agency; under certain conditions, they may function under a certified teacher's supervision as a teacher in community or hospital classes, sheltered workshops, home-based instruction, residential units, or self-contained classes.

Qualifications for and duties of other special education personnel, such as special education counselors, special education directors, school psychologists, diagnosticians, and related services personnel, are listed in the *State Board of Education Rules for the Handicapped.*

A 1984 study of personnel needs conducted by the Texas Education Agency showed a teacher shortage in the area of special education in Texas. Declining enrollments in schools of education across the state, the rising incidence of children affected by parental drug abuse, and increasing numbers of school-aged children should cause this shortage to continue.

While special education teachers are expected to instruct students with differing handicaps and wide ranges of abilities, a feat which requires diverse skills, some recommendations for characteristics and/or skills which will promote the success of a special education teachers can be suggested. To promote the placement and retention of handicapped students in the least restrictive environment, special educators should be willing to become knowledgeable about the regular education system and to establish successful working relationships with regular educators. In addition to these relationships with regular educators, special education teachers must be able to establish rapport with parents which will facilitate IEP development, ARD participation, and other facets of special education processes in which parents become involved.

Special educators find themselves faced with a diversity of students; teachers who view students as individuals with strengths and weaknesses will be more able to meet the divergent needs of each child. Also special education teachers with large repertoires of instructional techniques and strategies will be better prepared to offer educational experiences which will enhance each child's abilities. The use of positive reinforcement and a caring attitude facilitate a special educator's work.

Emerging Needs

Because the offering of full educational opportunities to handicapped students is still relatively new, several issues exist which require resolution. One debate involves a court case in 1986 *(Alamo Heights ISD v. S.B.O.E.)* and the issue of extended year services (EYS), which are defined as individualized instructional programs extended beyond the regular school year for handicapped students to prevent substantial regression by those students over time periods of no school services. The concern with EYS is at a national level; students who are more severely disabled may require instructional services over long holidays or during summer vacations to prevent the loss of skills acquired during normal instructional calendars. Extended year services are not be based on specific disabilities, but on the individual needs of children; students from various handicapping conditions, such as learning disabled, mentally retarded, autistic, and others, could have extended year services built into their IEP's.

One of the most controversial segments of P.L. 94-142 deals with the least restrictive environment (LRE). For more than a decade, attempts have been made to educate students with disabilities with their non-handicapped peers to the maximum extent that each was capable. The coordination needed between regular and special educators to make LRE a reality is extensive. Attitudes toward handicapped persons, doubt about expertise and experience needed to teach disabled youngsters, the amount of support available, miscommunications, lack of time, and many other factors have hampered efforts to fully institute LRE. The state of Texas has been cited by the U.S. Department of Education as needing to concentrate efforts in making LRE become a reality in the schools of this state.

In connection with LRE, the terms of "regular education initiative" and "full inclusion" arise in the discussion of the reform movement in special education. The regular education initiative supports the maintenance of most disabled students, with the exception of those severely disabled, in the regular classroom without labels or identification. Full inclusion extends that notion by proposing that all disabled students be served in the regular classroom. Both of these ideas mean changing roles for both special and regular education teachers, more team problem-solving and teaching approaches, additional training for regular teachers in dealing with individual differences, additional training for special education teachers in consultation techniques, and, perhaps, complete restructuring of the school organization (Schattman and Benay, 1992). Whether or not these two reform ideas will alter significantly the services for disabled students is yet to be determined.

The transition of disabled individuals from public schools services to adult life, particularly in the area of work, seems to be an item of considerable debate. The concern lies in the right of disabled individuals to lead productive and dignified lives and whether the instruction offered by public schools makes this situation possible. Concurrent with this emphasis in special education to aid the transition has come the national demand for academic excellence; these two forces could conflict with one another, unless all children are viewed as individuals with differing abilities. In order for handicapped students, whether mildly or severely impaired, to occupy their niches in society, educational services must be of higher quality and make use of the full potential of each student served. The focus on the work lives of disabled individuals during and after transition calls for more vocational training which is specifically designed to meet the needs of the handicapped; through IDEA these vocational services will now be outlined in the student's individual transition plan. The ties between vocational and special education will need to be tightened; close coordination of those two programs are necessary for special education students to successfully make the jump from school to assumption of a meaningful adult role. Also the Americans with Disabilities Act will boost the necessity for meaningful transition services so that disabled individuals will be less likely to be discriminated against as they enter society as adults.

The identification of students as disabled persists as an item of discussion; much is said about assessment and its role in labeling students as needing special education. The use of intelligence tests as one determiner of eligibility for services has long been attacked and has even resulted in court cases, such as *Larry P. vs. Riles*. Biases in test scores may be the results of sex differences, socioeconomic status, cultural background, and other factors and have been documented through psychological studies. Because of these biases, groups of minority students may be over-represented in special education classes; their placement may be based on their present levels of functioning which may be hampered by environmental factors which with training can be overcome. The use of learning-process assessment procedures, which measure the quickness of a child's ability to acquire new cognitive skills with guided instruction, may provide more accurate measurements of children's potentials.

Another assessment issue arises when students of varying linguistic backgrounds are tested. It is often difficult without specific training and extensive assessment to distinguish between students whose disabilities affect their linguistic abilities and those who are learning English as a second language. These second language learners may perform poorly in classrooms and on formal measures of their ability because of limited familiarity with English. The number of assessments in other languages is limited; certified personnel with the experience to administer these are even more limited. Thus, students whose first language is something other than English are easily misdiagnosed and placed in special education classes. Once placed they continue to receive primarily English instruction, as bilingual special education teachers are rarely found in public schools. Care should be taken to assess students in their native languages to avoid this misdiagnosis.

Finally, the types of assessment to be conducted to identify students as learning disabled have been under discussion. The recent numbers of students labelled as learning disabled have substantially increased; 42.8% of all handicapped youngsters served are learning disabled (U.S. Department of Education, 1984). Claims abound that current educational definitions of learning disabilities encourage the placement in special education of many non-handicapped students who are not experiencing success in the regular educational setting. The use of assessment techniques which will distinguish learning disabilities from disadvantages in exposure to experiences which promote cognitive, academic, and linguistic growth is being investigated. The REI (regular education initiative) is an offshoot of these concerns and contends that only moderately and severely handicapped youngsters should be placed in special education classes. It is the belief of REI supporters that mildly handicapped students would be served better by remaining in the regular education program.

The due process provisions of P.L. 94-142 and I.D.E.A. which provide legal avenues to parents who perceive the services offered to be inappropriate have given rise to the issue of attorney fees resulting from hearings and/or litigation. The Handicapped Children's Protection Act of 1986 provides that districts may be required to reimburse parents for reasonable legal fees they incur, if the parents are successful in litigating their claims of inappropriate educational services. Especially in times of financial constraints, school districts may be fearful of participating in hearings or court cases involving a free appropriate education for all handicapped students, as they may find themselves paying all legal costs for both sides engaged in the action. The legal fees which can be awarded to parents are limited in that 1) they must be adjudged reasonable and comparable to costs in the community for similar legal services; 2) part of the fees may not be awarded if parents rejected a written offer by the district for prior settlement which offered services at least equivalent to what was finally granted through the hearing or court case; and 3) parents, who unreasonably prolong the controversy when the district has not procrastinated and has followed all procedural safeguards, may be denied full reimbursement.

A Look Back

- Considerable federal legislation, notably P.L. 94-142 and I.D.E.A., exist to govern the offering of special education services.
- A number of federal court cases, including some presented to the Supreme Court, clarify mandates regulating special education.
- Little federal financial support is available for special education programs.
- Texas mandates full implementation of P.L. 94-142 and I.D.E.A. in its public schools.
- Additional requirements for the operation of special education programs exist in Texas and can be found in the *State Board of Education Rules for the Handicapped.*
- State funding in Texas for special education is based on a weighted formula, with different weights for different instructional arrangements.
- Special education should be designed to meet the unique characteristics of each individual placed in services.
- Classrooms and services for the disabled should be established in such a manner to help students experience success.
- A structured environment works well with students with disabilities.
- Strategies and content used in special education classrooms may vary widely.
- Services may be delivered through a variety of models; these range from total regular classroom placement to institutionalization and support the notion of the least restrictive environment.

- Classes for students in the early childhood years are available.
- Related services are offered to insure that handicapped students benefit from their educational experiences.
- Several certification programs are available to special educators in Texas; many allow special education teachers to work with a variety of handicapping conditions.
- The issues in the field of special education include extended year services; the least restrictive environment, including the regular education initiative and full inclusion; facilitating transition to adult life, particularly in the arena of work and careers; assessment practices which lead to over-representation of minority groups; the large increase in the numbers of learning disabled students; and school districts' liabilities for attorney fees for parents who have filed complaints or litigation over the inappropriate services offered to their children with disabilities.

Gifted and Talented Programs

Federal Perspectives

The launching of Sputnik in 1957 affected federal involvement in education in many areas, one of the foremost of which is services to gifted and talented students. Following this event, several reports comparing the quantity and quality of American and Russian education emerged; all of these reports found American education inferior. Efforts to correct this imbalance included new math and science curriculum, higher academic standards, and services to gifted/talented students, the best and brightest who were believed to be the answer to America's continued need for brainpower in the scientific and technological realms.

Despite those efforts, gifted education withered until 1971 when Marland's (1972) report was issued through the U.S. Office of Education, asserting that gifted/talented students were not being adequately served. A definition of giftedness which still serves as the model was delineated in this report. This definition was refined in 1978 with P.L. 95-561, the Gifted and Talented Children Education Act, which also allotted federal dollars for gifted programs on a competitive basis. In 1981, as part of the Educational Consolidation and Improvement Act, gifted education became only one of the 27 purposes for which Chapter 2 funding may be spent at the discretion of the receiving district. The gifted federal funding was consolidated with such purposes as funding for metric education, basic skills improvement, and arts in education in the form of block grants to the states. Block grants force gifted programs to compete against programs in other areas for their share of these federal dollars.

In 1982, the U.S. Department of Education commissioned research studies resulting in a national report which emphasized basing identification procedures on the best available data, broadening the definition of giftedness, protecting the civil rights of students, and insuring that services would be offered to as many gifted students as possible.

This research, along with national concerns over the quality of education in the United States, has led to renewed interest in gifted education. The Texas Legislature has recognized the need for appropriate services for gifted/talented students and has taken action.

Texas Perspectives

H.B. 1050, as passed by the 70th Texas Legislature in 1987, mandated programs for gifted and talented students at each grade level, kindergarten through twelfth, beginning in September, 1990. These programs must be approved by the Texas Education Agency in accordance with State Board of Education rules, which allow districts flexibility to develop and implement alternatives appropriate to local needs while providing a high quality of services.

State funding for gifted/talented programs is based on a weighted formula which multiplies the number of students served in a district (not to exceed 5% of the total average daily attendance of the district); the district's per pupil adjusted basic allotment; and a weight of .12. This formula replaces a state funding system which allotted funds for gifted programs on a competitive basis with a minority of Texas school districts awarded funding. The cap on state funding, being limited to no more than 5% of the district's average daily attendance, is not to be interpreted as limiting the number of students who may be placed in a district's gifted/talented program. The *Texas State Plan and Guidelines for the Education of the Gifted/Talented* encourage school districts to include in their programs all students who meet the local criteria.

The requirements for gifted/talented programs are numerous as listed in *The Texas State Plan Guidelines for the Education of the Gifted/Talented*. A few of them include:

- a committee process for evaluating the program, using evaluation results for improving the program, refining program goals and objectives, and disseminating evaluation information to staff, local board, parents, and the community;
- placement of students by a trained committee composed of at least an administrator, a teacher, and a counselor or diagnostician;
- parental and community involvement in planning and implementing the program;
- use of differentiated learning activities and curricula, with a specific scope and sequence for content to be studied by identified students. This scope and sequence should provide for differentiation for gifted students which may be accomplished by designing interdisciplinary units, allowing for in-depth study and research, involving higher level thinking skills, and encouraging independent study;
- procedures approved by the local board for exiting students from the program and for considering transfer students for the program;
- provisions for the equitable assessment of special populations students (economically deprived, culturally different, disabled, and others);
- written parental permission for testing and placement and a process for parental appeals;

- utilization of at least 5 criteria, both objective and subjective, for identification;
- adequate staff development for teachers in the gifted program (at least 30 clock hours training initially), regular classroom teachers. principals, support staff and parents.

Theoretical Bases

Gifted/talented students are individuals and differ drastically from one another; however, some characteristics recur frequently in the research. In general, these students show advanced language and thought processes; their comprehension, vocabulary, stored information, retention, and logical abilities outstrip their peers. Although some of the characteristics of intellectually gifted children are masked in special needs students, others may be easily detected. Gifted children tend to be highly curious and inquisitive, with a need to find and understand cause-and-effect relationships. They also have the ability to handle abstractions easily, make connections and establish relationships among disparate information, and memorize and learn rapidly (VanTassel-Baska, 1989).

Early interests which are wide-ranging may be demonstrated and demand much of the gifted child's time and energy. While exhibiting much patience and diligence in pursuing his/her interests, the gifted child may have little tolerance for activities in which s/he has little interest. At an early age, the child may develop an inner control and satisfaction which may lead to divergent behavior.

Additionally, gifted students may prefer complex tasks and challenges, have a keen sense of humor, generate many solutions to a problem, demonstrate extraordinary leadership abilities, improvise with commonplace materials, and feel a sense of his/her own uniqueness, leading to loneliness.

Activities for gifted learners which are open-ended will encourage complex, abstract, and creative critical thinking skills, while again allowing students to utilize their self-directedness and independence. A focus on developing research skills will further enable talented learners to become more independent and interest-oriented. Obviously a flexible curriculum with much opportunity for student choice seems to be ideal. Other helpful strategies when working with gifted pupils include:

- encouraging the development of projects or ideas that challenge existing ideas;
- fostering the use of current knowledge, skills, ideas, and principles in new configurations to develop new forms;
- nurturing the development of self-understanding to appreciate and tolerate similarities and differences between one's self and others;
- evaluating outcomes through a variety of methods, including self-evaluation, peer evaluation, portfolio assessment, student and parent questionnaires and interviews, and other more subjective strategies.

Instruction for gifted students, generally, should not be more school work and/or harder school work; it should be different work--a chance for students to explore, create, experiment, hypothesize, and engage in other activities which will allow students to maximally utilize their capabilities.

Types of Programs

The federal definition of gifted and talented serves as the model for the definition in Texas which is included in Chapter 75 of the Texas Administrative Code:

> Gifted and talented students are those who excel consistently or who show the potential to excel in any one or combination of the following areas: general intellectual ability, specific subject matter aptitude, creative and productive thinking ability, leadership ability, ability in the visual and performing arts, and psychomotor ability. These students require educational experiences beyond those normally provided by the regular school program.

One of the first issues to be faced is the type(s) of programming to offer. Districts may choose to focus on any one, several, or all of the spheres of giftedness listed in the above definition; the programs to be implemented will impact the definition of giftedness in that particular district and, hence, the identification of students.

Using the definition above for gifted students, the range of programming is vast. For example, segregated classes, either interdisciplinary or focusing on one subject area only, and performing arts clubs are examples of programs targeting only one portion of the definition. Programs which provide many optional, voluntary achievement opportunities for students with academic talents, creative abilities, scientific capabilities, communicative gifts, artistic expertise, and musical talents are exemplary of the opposite end of the spectrum of programming possibilities. An example of such broad programs is Renzulli's revolving door concept which offers mentorships, participation in academic and other competitions, special projects, and other opportunities for students to utilize their talents as they have the time and the desire (Renzulli, Reis, and Smith, 1981).

Delivery Models

The area of gifted/talented education offers a wide range of programs and delivery models, as one would expect of a field which emphasizes individual student potential and flexibility. Regardless of the type of program(s) a district decides to offer, delivery models may vary and be combined, resulting in different configurations. Some of the most common delivery models include:

- **The pull-out model,** in which students leave their regular classrooms for a part of the school day or school week to work with the gifted/talented teacher individually or in small groups.

- **Cluster grouping.** Under this model, special and/or regular teachers work with gifted students in their regular classrooms individually and/or in small groups.
- **Acceleration,** through which students are placed in the next grade, earn credits through advanced placement or testing, experience and master academic work in shorter-than-normal time periods, and otherwise advance more quickly through the required curriculum.
- **Concurrent enrollment** in colleges and/or universities, through which students may simultaneously earn high school and college credit.
- **Self-contained** gifted classrooms.
- **Special schools or schools-within-schools** for gifted pupils only. Magnet schools serve as an example.
- **Mentorship programs** which connect gifted children with adults who have expertise in the areas of the students' interests. Generally mentorships are established on a one-to-one basis.
- **Extended programming,** such as before- and after-school activities, summer programs, camps, and Saturday schools.
- **Talent pools,** through which all students are served in the regular classroom by the gifted/talented teacher. This delivery model allows students to be identified as gifted through teacher observation and use of professional judgment as the individual child performs on specialized instructional activities along with his/her regular classmates. In Texas, the use of talent pools is permitted only in early primary grades.

Personnel Considerations

Presently, 22 universities in Texas offer coursework and training for personnel desiring to become teachers of the gifted/talented. An endorsement is available to those wishing to add it to their elementary or secondary teaching certificates; this endorsement requires 12 additional semester hours of coursework in education of the gifted/talented and a 3 hour student teaching experience. Teachers assigned to teach gifted/talented youngsters without the gifted endorsement are required to earn 30 clock hours of training in gifted education initially and then to continue their education in this area as indicated on needs assessments done each year.

When employing a teacher for gifted/talented students, administrators should look for a teacher (Maker, 1982):

- whose philosophy of gifted education complements the model established by the district;
- who is open to change, accepting, and flexible;
- who is intelligent and self-confident, has a high regard for creative and imaginative ideas, and feels a deep respect for students' abilities;
- who will be comfortable with a student-centered rather than a teacher-directed classroom and who will provide a safe environment for the expression of ideas, regardless of their merit;

- who is trained in or willing to learn individualized instruction techniques, identification or students with a variety of capabilities, and stimulation of the use of higher thinking and creative abilities;
- who is able to establish rapport with other faculty members so as to facilitate teamwork in providing services to gifted/talented students.

Emerging Needs

With the current reforms in education centering on heterogeneous grouping and with the increased use of cooperative learning strategies, some educators of the gifted/talented have been very vocal about the need for homogeneous groups for gifted students. One concern involves the exploitation of talented students in cooperative learning groups when less talented students are dependent upon the assistance of their more able peers. There is also some question as to whether or not regular classroom teachers can adequately meet all of the needs of students who are in the advanced 5% of the general student population and provide them with all of the challenges they require. Proponents of homogeneous groups for gifted students claim that research supports this practice and that without special services talented students become bored and are at risk of school failure and becoming drop-outs (O'Neil, 1990).

School districts in Texas will face several issues in the near future as they attempt to meet state mandates for services for gifted and talented students. Finding sources of funding for programs will be problematic; unless present state and federal support increases, the burden of gifted program costs will be placed on local districts. The present funding formula at the state level is claimed by districts to be inadequate; most Chapter 2 money in Texas is used for purposes other than gifted education. At the present time it seems that the majority of the funding for gifted programs is provided by local districts. In addition, the cap placed on the number of students (5% of the number of students in each district in average daily attendance) for whom state funding can be claimed may present problems to districts placing more than 5% of their students in programs for the gifted and talented.

The limit of 5% raises a concern over the definition of "giftedness" and thus the identification of gifted students. The definition chosen by a school district will determine which students are identified as gifted and which are not. The procedures for identification will be set by that definition. One problem that arises when teachers nominate students for gifted programs is that those most likely to be nominated are high achievers and amenable in class; those talented students who may cause problems in the classroom or whose academic work is not the best may go unrecognized. Other problems that occur include difficulties with the accuracy and validity of measurements used for identification and lack of formal instruments to measure certain areas of talent, like creativity and leadership.

To alleviate the difficulty in identifying students other than those with high intelligence test and academic scores, other identification methods are being suggested. These range from claims that all students are gifted in some area and that provisions should be made for every student to develop his/her own talents to the maximum extent to Renzulli's revolving door programs (Renzulli, Reis, and Smith, 1981). Provisions for students to be nominated by themselves, parents, administrators, other students, and others with knowledge of the nominees are included in the state guidelines to avoid teacher biases. Additionally staff development, also state-mandated in Texas, to heighten regular classroom teacher awareness of the characteristics of gifted/talented students and the recognition of hidden talents are helpful. Use of subjective data, samples of classroom work and special projects, observations of nominees in classroom settings, and other methods are also ways to identify gifted students who may not exhibit their talents through traditional methods.

Special problems arise when considering females, students from culturally-different backgrounds, minority students, economically disadvantaged students, disabled students, and others for gifted programs. Not only do the aforementioned difficulties connected with identifying students with talents other than academic arise; these issues are compounded because special needs students may be underachievers in the academic areas and/or screened out of contention by cultural biases in most assessment instruments. On intelligence and achievement measures, these students tend to score lower in some areas than others; their classroom performance may also be deemed average or below by teachers. Unless specific efforts are made to recognize their other-than-traditional methods, their potential may be untapped. A particularly promising technique may be in the measurement of learning potential, as in Feuerstein's (1981) research and that of others. Rather than measure what a child presently knows and can do, it may be more indicative of his/her abilities to teach specific unmastered cognitive tasks and measure how quickly students acquire those abilities; those who learn most rapidly may be gifted students. Again teacher training to increase sensitivity to students with hidden potential is a recommended practice.

At the present time, teachers in Texas may be assigned to classes for gifted/talented youngsters without special certification. However, as school districts work to implement state-mandated programs, they need more teachers for gifted programs. This fact results in increased competition among districts to acquire teachers with training and/or experience in gifted education, as districts attempt to offer high-quality services. Additionally, teachers may be asked to retrain in order to fill those gifted teacher openings. Finally, all teachers and instructional staff will need to be made aware of the characteristics of gifted children and classroom techniques to serve them in order to help with identification, particularly of those students traditionally ignored, and to provide experiences outside of the gifted/talented program which enable gifted students to utilize their abilities to their fullest during the entire school day.

A Look Back

- Federal involvement in gifted education is limited to and generally included in Chapter 2 of the Education Consolidation and Improvement Act.

- Gifted/talented education became a required program in Texas in the 1990-91 school year.
- State funding is available for gifted programs according to a weighted formula.
- Talented students vary widely; however research has generated some common characteristics.
- Instruction for gifted learners should not be **more** work or harder work; it should be **different** work.
- Most definitions of giftedness include several areas of talent: intellectual, academic, leadership, creative, psychomotor, and artistic.
- Many possibilities exist for serving gifted students: acceleration, cluster grouping, resource classes, special schools, segregated classes, mentoring programs, talent pools, and extended programming.
- In Texas no special credentials are required of teachers for the gifted/talented; however, all assigned teachers of the gifted must be trained and an endorsement on the teaching certificate is available.
- Funding of gifted programs seems to be primarily a responsibility of local school districts.
- Many programs for gifted students target certain talents, particularly academics, to the exclusion of others.
- Special needs students, such as those who are culturally different, economically disadvantaged, or handicapped, are often not identified as gifted/talented.

References

Barbe, W. B. & Renzulli, J. S. (1981). *Psychology and education of the gifted.* New York: Irvington Publishers.

Chief State Schools Officers (1990). *Summary of provisions in the 1990 amendments that are relevant to Part B.* Washington, D.C.: Chief State Schools Officers.

Davis, D. A. & Rimm, S. B. (1985). *Education of the gifted and talented.* Englewood Cliffs, NJ.: Prentice-Hall, Inc.

Deno, E. (1972). *Special education delivery: The need for reform.* The Council for Exceptional Children, Arlington, VA.

Fafard, M. B., Hanlon, R. E., & Bryon, E. A. (1986). *Jose F. v. Ambach: Progress toward compliance.* Exceptional Children, 52, 313-322.

Feuerstein, R., Miller, R., Rand, Y., & Jensen, M. R. (1981). Can evolving techniques better measure cognitive change? *The Journal of Special Education, 15,* 201-219.

Gallagher, J. J. (1985). *Teaching the gifted child.* Boston: Allyn and Bacon, Inc.

Gallagher, J. J. (1989). The impact of policies for handicapped children on future early education policy. *Phi Delta Kappan, 53,* 121-124.

Kirk, S. A. & Gallagher, J. J. (1979). *Educating exceptional children.* Boston: Houghton Mifflin Co.

Maker, J. C. (1982). *Curriculum development for the gifted.* Rockville, MD.: Aspen Systems Corporation.

Marks, W. L. & Nystrand, R. D. (1981). *Strategies for educational change: Recognizing the gifts and talents of all children.* New York: MacMillan Publishing Company, Inc.

Marland, S. P., Jr. (1972). *Education of the gifted and talented, Volume 1. Report to the Congress of the United States by the U.S. Commissioner of Education.* Washington, D.C.: U.S. Government Printing Office.

O'Neil, J. (1990, October). Issue. *ASCD Update,* p. 7.

Prasse, D. & Reschly, D. J. (1986). *Larry P.: A case of segregation, testing, or program efficacy? Exceptional Children, 52,* 333-345.

Public Law 99-457. *Amendments to the Education of the Handicapped Act,* 1986.

Renzulli, L., Reis, R. & Smith, A. (1988). *The revolving door identification model.* Mansfield, CT: Creative Learning Press.

Richert, E. S. (1986). Identification of gifted students: An update. *Roeper Review, 8,* 68-72.

Schattman, R. & Benay, J. (1992). Inclusive practices transform special education in the 1990's. *The School Administrator, 49,* 8-12.

State Board of Education Rules for the Handicapped (1990). Austin, TX: Texas Education Agency.

Texas Education Code.

The Texas State Plan and Guidelines for the Education of the Gifted/Talented (1990). Austin, TX: Texas Education Agency.

Turnbull, H. R. (1986). Appropriate education and *Rowley. Exceptional Children, 52,* 347-352.

VanTassel-Baska, J. (1989). Appropriate curriculum for gifted learners. *Educational Leadership, 48,* 13-15.

Vitello, S. J. (1986). The *Tatro* case: Who gets what and why. *Exceptional Children, 52,* 353-356.

Wood, F. H., Johnson, J. L., & Jenkins, J. R. (1986). The *Lora* case: Nonbiased referral, assessment, and placement procedures. *Exceptional Children, 52,* 323-331.

U.S. Department of Education (1984). Executive summary, Sixth annual report to Congress on the implementation of P.L. 94-142: The Education for All Handicapped Children Act. *Exceptional Children, 51,* 199-202.

Yseldyke, J. E. & Algozine, B. (1984). *Introduction to special education.* Boston: Houghton Mifflin Co.

The Challenge of Special Population Students

Carole Veir

School administrators face a diversity of challenges in the coming years. Changes on the national, state and local levels have pushed educational issues into the forefront of attention, forcing persons involved with the schools to rethink issues to meet the demands of reform, realign priorities to include GOALS 2000, and take risks to develop innovative schools and programs they did not know existed five years ago. The growing population of "at-risk" students, changing demographics, new federal thrusts, financial exigency, calls for accountability, renewed interest in vocational education, and site-based decision-making are but a few of the areas that school administrators must consider when developing programs and policies to serve schools today and prepare tomorrow's students for the diverse yet shrinking technological world that faces them.

Among the areas receiving the most attention, both today and predictably in the future, are the variety of students having special needs in the educational arena. They are also among the least understood. Although students having special needs have historically represented a minority of the Texas school enrollment, this will not be true in the future. The potential impact of these students and their needs on the school system has tremendous implications for administrators who are responsible for meeting the unique educational needs of these students.

The rapidly changing demographics of the Texas (and national) population will change the nature of the students to be served in the classroom. Administrators in charge of schools in Texas can expect an average classroom to be composed of the following:

- one teacher and 20 students
- 50% or more will need English as a Second Language

- up to 25% will have disabilities
- one in five will have been born out of wedlock
- up to 50% will come from single-parent households
- poverty level of students will be: 18%+ Anglo
                                        47%+ Black
                                        35%+ Hispanic

While these statistics are immediate and have serious implications for teaching and learning, there is more to consider that will also have a significant impact on education and the educational environment for teaching. Currently:

- 20% of all Anglo children have never seen a doctor
- 48% of all Black children have never seen a doctor
- 50%+ of all Hispanic children have never seen a doctor

and there is no new data to assure that these statistics are going to get better: in fact, the number of children who never had prenatal care or have never seen a doctor are growing.

In addition, it is important at the outset to understand the impact of a growing diverse ethnic population. At present:

- Asians are the fastest growing ethnic group nationwide
- Hispanics are the fastest growing ethnic group in Texas as well as the Southwest as a whole
- 65% of the current Hispanic population in the country is too young to vote, and that number is growing
- 17% of all school children in the U.S. 15–17 years of age come from homes where a language other than English is spoken
- the average age of Anglos is currently 33
- while the average age of Hispanics is only 22
- and for Blacks it is only 25

The current ethnic distribution in the Texas Public School System is:

- Anglo   49.50 %
- Hispanic   33.90
- African American   14.40
- Asian American   2.00
- Native American   .19

Minority enrollment in early childhood and pre-kindergarten programs is currently more than 78% in the Texas schools. This means that within less than 20 years, the voting population of this country will be dominantly Hispanic.

The question is, then, what is the impact of this on the school systems need to serve a more diverse and growing body of special needs students? If Texas education is to meet the needs of its students in the school system, it must have a life blood of multicultural content in order to be sociologically relevant, philosophically germane, and pedagogically apropos.

In addition to these statistics, by 2010 the number of teens will top the Baby Boom-fueled teen explosion of the 60s and 70s in both size and duration, cresting at 30.8 million. It is not too soon to begin preparing to meet the needs of these students in the schools—2010 is a short 15 years from now. These students will enter the school system in 3 years, and in some instances less time.

Furthermore, these teens are being exposed to adult problems at a much younger age, with rising rates of violent crime, loss of job and debt woes of parents, out-of-wedlock births soaring, substance control, increased marital splits, a dominance of working parents, AIDS, and homelessness part of their daily lessons in school and on TV. Many of them will grow up having to fend for themselves, with one in four households with kids being headed by a single parent. While parents stress getting good grades and saving money, teens major stresses are getting a job, contracting AIDS, getting divorced and not getting into college. Somewhere in this nonequation, the schools must have an impact. Already in 1992, 18% of kids 12-17 lived in poverty, up two points in just 3 years, and three points higher than the total populations. Over 105,000 juveniles were arrested in 1992 for violent crimes, up *571%* from one decade ago.

The employment outlook merits attention as well, with the swelling number of entry-level work driving down wages and increasing the competition for jobs. Not that all is gloomy—more kids are graduating from high school and going on to higher education than ever before.

Overall the implications for the Texas Public School System call for the total school environment to be put into action to meet the needs of its diverse students. Among the areas that merit attention are:

- District and School Policies and Politics
- District and School Culture and the hidden curriculum
- Student learning styles
- Languages and dialects of the school and community
- Community participation and input
- Better and more diverse counseling programs
- More appropriate and valid assessment and testing
- More diverse and meaningful instructional materials
- Formalized curriculum and course of study
- Teaching styles matched to student needs
- More diverse and creative teaching strategies
- Attitude, perceptions, belief and action adjustment on the part of the district and school staff and administration

Under the current Texas state law, Senate Bill 1, special population students are specifically addressed as one of the areas that is required to be part of the academic excellence indicator reporting process. The specific mention of the requirement to address the academic needs of this group of students in the state law is an indication of the depth of concern for the success of this particular population. In short, each of these factors and changes will each have diverse and tremendous impact on the schools in the coming decade. The constantly changing demographics in the Texas populations will continue to alter the nature and diverse needs of the school population. These changes will require more programs and personnel to deal with the special needs of these and all students.

This chapter will explore various programs in Texas designed to meet the needs of special students. Administrators must be aware of these programs, understand the parameters and interdependencies of each program, provide appropriate and effective leadership, and be cognizant of the long range educational and social implications of these educational endeavors.

Bilingual Education and English as a Second Language Programs

Federal Perspectives

Serving students with primary languages other than English and students who have English as a Second Language (ESL) is not a new challenge to our nation's schools. In a country of immigrants, the needs of non-English speaking children were faced early in our history. Even prior to the Declaration of Independence there were schools which used languages other than English. Since before 1800, German, French, Scandinavian and even some Dutch schools dotted the land. Although not bilingual in curriculum, they taught English as a subject area to non-English and limited-English speaking immigrant children. In 1840 Ohio passed legislation to provide schooling in German and English, and by 1852 several Indian tribes were operating schools in their own languages and dialects. From the colonization period until World War I, schooling which was bilingual or in languages other than English was common—school systems acknowledged the cultural and pluralistic nature of American society.

During and after World War I, however, society's sentiments shifted toward a belief in assimilation rather than pluralism, and immigrants were expected to become "Americanized," which to many meant speaking only English. Between 1917 and 1950 bilingual education was almost completely eliminated in the United States, and the study of foreign languages waned as well. Three significant events brought about a reevaluation of the prevailing attitudes: the launching of sputnik, the immigration to the United States of a flood of Cubans following Castro's takeover, and the civil rights movement of the 1960s.

Throughout the years, the federal government has provided guidance to states regarding the civil rights of diverse populations. The civil rights movements of the 1960s brought with it significant legislation that continues to oversee activities of the schools with regard to culturally and linguistically diverse students.

Title VI of the Civil Rights Act of 1964 prohibits discrimination on the basis of race, color, national origin, religion, or sex in programs receiving federal monies. The concept of Equal Educational Opportunity is closely linked to Bilingual Education and Special Language Programs. The philosophy of EEO can be traced back to the roots of our nation and are expressed in the Declaration of Independence which asserts that "all men are created equal." Additionally, the Fourteenth Amendment to the Constitution insures that persons have equal protection under the law. Thomas Jefferson at one time even proposed an EEO plan for talented students of modest means who would otherwise have little hope to achieve. This would, he asserted, bring a measure of equality of opportunity to a society where social status and access to education had so often depended on the place and parentage of birth.

EEO was defined by Coleman in his 1968 report, "Equality of Educational Opportunity," commissioned by the United States Department of Education as part of the mandates of the 1964 Civil Rights Act. Coleman cities these as components of EEO:

- Provide free education to a given level that constitutes the principal entry point to the labor force
- Provide a common curriculum for all children, regardless of background
- Provide that all children from diverse backgrounds attend the same school
- Provide equality within a given locality, since local taxes have historically meant providing the source of support for the schools

The concept of equality is still widely accepted, as well as widely discussed and disputed. This will undoubtedly continue, especially in light of the rapidly changing demographic patterns affecting the school system.

In 1968, another significant piece of federal legislation affecting education for national origin children was passed—The Bilingual Education Act (P.L. 90-247). The purpose of this act was to establish EEO for all children by a) encouraging the establishment of educational programs using bilingual educational practices, techniques and methods; b) providing financial assistance to state and local educational agencies to assist them in carrying out activities at the preschool, elementary and secondary levels designed to meet the needs of the children; and c) to demonstrate effective ways of providing limited-English speaking children instruction using their native language while achieving competence in English. All bilingual education programs funded with federal monies were to be transitional, meaning that students' first language was used as a temporary method of communication and instruction until the students could make the transition into English. Bilingual education instruction also addresses the cultural heritage of the children in the program and of other children in American society. The "use of two languages as the media of instruction" is generally agreed upon. It is the philosophy and goals that undergo discussion. Subsequent amendments have each placed more emphasis on the acquisition of English language proficiency. In addition the funding level has increased from $7.5 million in 1969-70 to a high of $167 million in the 1980-81 year, with a ceiling of $139 million being authorized in 1984.

Beginning with the 1984 Bilingual Education Act (Title II of P.L. 98-511) a number of challenges and opportunities regarding the education of limited-English proficient students were expressed. These included issues related to:

- an increasing amount of litigation
- a need to better identify students in need
- a need to better understand the needs of a diverse student population
- a better system of assessment and testing
- a better understanding of appropriate and effective instructional designs
- a need for more and diverse programs
- a need for better-trained staff and staff training
- an increase in the amount of money devoted to this area of education
- an increasing population of limited-English speaking students
- students bringing to the schools a cultural background that varies from that of the mainstream of the traditional population in the schools
- students learning primarily through their native/cognitive language and familiar cultural basis
- the segregation of students who are limited in English from the school population as a whole
- the high dropout rates prevalent among limited-English students
- the lower median years of education attained by limited-English students
- parents of limited-English students who cannot effectively participate in the educational process of their children due to their limited proficiency in English
- federal government recognition of its role in assisting equal education opportunities for these students to acquire English skills
- programmatic options available that can provide appropriate instructional alternatives for limited-English students

To address these major areas of concern the 1984 Bilingual Education Act authorized six different types of programs:

a. transitional bilingual education;
b. developmental bilingual education;

    c. special alternative English instruction;
    d. programs of academic excellence;
    e. family English literacy programs;
    f. special populations programs for preschool, special education, and gifted and talented students.

These programs have specific purposes in mind for select populations in need of assistance. Each legislative change has the intent of furthering the learning of English to enhance the concept of a productive citizenry.

A Supreme Court decision in 1974 promoted the movement, role, and responsibilities of schools in providing education to non-English speaking or limited-English speaking students. The *Lau v. Nichols* case of San Francisco addressed the needs of Chinese students in their English-speaking school environment. In this case, the public school system was found in violation of the Title VI of the Civil Rights Act of 1964 because the schools were not providing the students who were non-English speaking with instruction in the English language. The HEW Memorandum of May 25, 1970, promulgated by The Office of Civil Rights stated: "Where inability to speak and understand the English language excluded national origin minority children from effective participation in the educational program offered by a school district, the district must take affirmative steps to rectify the language deficiencies in order to open its instructional program to these students." Accordingly, and combined with the Title VI of the Civil Rights Act, the school was receiving federal funds and was held responsible for providing special instruction for non-English speaking students whose education is severely hampered by a language barrier.

To assist in providing these services, since 1969 the federal office of education has made monies available to the states. Each local educational agency with an identifiable population of students in need of services under the Act is entitled to monies, and must apply directly to the federal government for funds. Local educational agencies that choose to not apply will not receive funds. Funding allotments are based upon the numbers of students identified through testing programs. In considering the applications from local educational agencies, priority is given to applications from local education agencies which are located in various geographical regions of the United States and which propose to assist children of limited-English proficiency who have historically been underserved by programs of bilingual education. The application is also reviewed to take into consideration the relative number of such children in the schools of the local education agencies and the relative need for such programs. Local agencies that receive monies for programs under this Act must also respond to TEA requests for information related to the program, as well as the collection, aggregation, analysis, and publication of data and information on the state's population of limited-English proficient persons and the educational services provided or available to them.

Texas Perspectives: History and Growth

Education is a state responsibility. Texas has attempted to provide a uniform statewide free public school system for the children within its borders since 1905 with the passage of Senate Bill 218. The language of instruction for the students in school in Texas at the time was basically the language of the local community. However, Section 102 of Senate Bill 218 required all certified teachers to instruct in English only. The bill stated:

> It shall be the duty of every teacher in the public free schools of this state to use the English language exclusively, and to conduct all recitation and school exercises exclusively in the English language; provided that this provision shall not prevent the teaching of any other language as a branch of study, but when any other language is so taught, the use of said language shall be limited to the recitations and exercises devoted to the teaching of said language as such branch of the study.

Although bilingual education was practiced in Texas before and after this bill in Spanish, Czech, and German-speaking communities, the law did not actually take effect until 1918. The legislature reiterated its position by specifying:

> Every teacher, principal, and superintendent employed in the public schools of this state shall use the English language exclusively in the conduct of the work of the schools, and all recitations and exercises of the school shall be conducted in the English language; provided that this provision shall not prevent the teaching of Latin, Greek, French, German, Spanish, Bohemian (Czech), or other languages as branch of study in the high school grades as outlined in the state course study.

Section two of the bill went on to prescribe penalties for violating this legislation. Violations were considered misdemeanors subject to fines of $25 to $100. Teaching certification could be canceled, personnel could be removed from office, or any combination of these conditions were possible penalties.

Although not abolishing its restrictive language requirements in 1927, the Texas Legislature amended its code in what can be clearly seen as a political move: it allowed Spanish to be taught in elementary schools but not used as a medium of instruction. The law stated:

> It shall be lawful to provide textbooks for and to teach the Spanish language in elementary grades in the public free schools in counties bordering on the boundary line between the United States and the Republic of Mexico and having a city or cities of five thousand or more inhabitants according to the United States census for the year 1920.

The purpose of the amendment was stated in the Legislature's acknowledgment that the Spanish language was of inestimable value to the citizens and inhabitants of such counties and cities. It further recognized that "in order to obtain a speaking knowledge and mastery of any language ... (that instruction) be begun at the earliest possible period."

The May 25, 1970 Department of Health, Education, and Welfare memorandum, issued through the Office of Civil Rights, stipulated that school districts having more than 5 percent national origin minority students must equalize educational opportunity for the language minority students under Title VII of the Civil Rights Act of 1964. Based on this memorandum, the Uvalde Independent School District was charged with unlawful segregation of Mexican-American children in the elementary schools for failure to provide bilingual/bicultural education and for ability grouping. In evaluating the school district, the administrative law judge found that the schools were illegally segregated. As early as the 1900s "Mexican-only" schools had been established in Texas although other non-English speaking minority group students were mainstreamed. (It was not until 1974 that the Supreme Court classified Mexican-Americans as a minority or nonminority status).

The resistance to implement bilingual programs into the schools of Texas became apparent as a result of the HEW review. The review recommended that the El Paso Independent School District devise a plan that would ... include, among other things, an affirmative policy of recruiting and employing teachers who are bilingual and sensitive to cultural differences; and (provide) staff development program(s) designed to assist teachers and administrators, in redefining their role in a bilingual/bicultural district and in the development of a curriculum that does not penalize students who come to school with principal language skills in Spanish. Other Texas districts were cited for similar offenses.

Mandated bilingual education was begun in 1972. The states' current policy on language reads:

> English is the basic language of the State of Texas. Public schools are responsible for providing full opportunity for all students to become competent in speaking, reading, writing, and comprehending the English language. The legislature finds that there are large numbers of students in the state who come from environments where the primary language is other than English. Experience has shown that public school classes in which instruction is given only in English are often inadequate for the education of these students. The legislature recognized that the mastery of basic English language skills is a prerequisite for effective participation in the state's educational program. The legislature believes that bilingual education and special language programs can meet the needs of these students and facilitate their integration into the regular school curriculum. Therefore, pursuant to the policy of the state to insure equal educational opportunity to every student, and in recognition of the educational needs of students of limited English proficiency, ... to provide for the establishment of bilingual education and special language programs in the public schools and to provide supplemental financial assistance to help local school districts meet the extra costs of the program.

The statute further clarifies bilingual education and other special language programs through a 1981 amendment which provides that:

> Bilingual education or special language programs as defined by this act shall be taught in the public schools only for the purpose of assisting the learning ability of limited English proficiency students and enhance the English language.

Following the sunsetting of the State Board of Education rules for special populations, the 1992 adopted rules, Chapter 89 Adaptations for Special Populations, now provides that "... it is the policy of the State Board of Education that every student in the state who has a home language other than English and who is identified as limited English proficient shall be provided a full opportunity to participate in a special language program." It is required that each school district: a) identify limited-English proficient students based on criteria established by the State Board of Education; b) provide special language programs as integral parts of the regular program; c) seek certified teaching personnel to ensure that limited English proficient students are afforded full opportunity to master the required essential elements. The goal of bilingual education and English as Second Language programs in Texas is to enable limited-English proficient students to become competent in the comprehension, speaking, reading and composition of the English language. These programs shall be an integral part of the total school program, with content being based on the essential elements as required by Chapter 75.

Districts must conduct a home language survey for each student who is new to the district, and for students previously enrolled who were not surveyed in the past. The survey must be signed by the student's parent or guardian for students in pre-kindergarten through grade eight, or by the student in grades nine through 12. Each district is required to have a local board policy to establish and operate a Language Proficiency Assessment Committee. The district must have on file a policy and procedures for the selection, appointment, and training of the members of the language proficiency assessment committee(s). For identifying limited-English proficient students, districts shall administer an agency-approved oral language proficiency test in pre-kindergarten through grade 12, and the English reading and English language arts sections from the students assessment instrument required by the Texas Education Code in grades two through 12. For students new to the district, students must be identified as limited English proficient and entered into the required bilingual or ESL program within four weeks of their initial enrollment in the district.

There are several areas of bilingual and ESL programs that may be passed on to the administrator at the building level. These may include:

- assuring the identification and reporting of the number of students of limited-English proficiency on their campus
- monitoring program content, method of instruction mastery of essential elements, and student enrollment into programs

- appropriating facilities and space for students with other students of approximately the same age and level of educational attainment
- maintaining adequate records of student progress
- assuring home language surveys are filled out within the established timelines, signed by the parents, and in each students' folder.
- assuring the proper administration of agency-approved proficiency tests
- providing written notice of student classification and the benefits of the bilingual ESL program to parents
- checking with appropriate personnel to coordinate services if the student has a disability
- assuring that the bilingual or special language program is an integral part of the total school curriculum
- participating in the language proficiency assessment committee as required and/or requested
- offering services to students who are non-limited English proficient
- providing information for the annual performance report
- assisting in determining if summer school or extended-year programs are needed

Although administrators may be asked to assist with any or all of the above tasks, they will not have to be concerned with the responsibility of securing adequate funding for the programs to be offered. Allotments for bilingual education in pre-kindergarten through grade 5 and grade 6-12 ESL classes are provided by the state and are based on enrollment in either program. Districts may use up to 15% of their allocated funds for indirect costs, but may not exceed the program's actual share of indirect costs. A district shall use these funds, other than the indirect costs allocation, only for program and pupil evaluation, instructional materials and equipment, staff development, supplemental staff expenses, salary supplements for teachers, and other supplies required for quality instruction and small class size. The allotment may be used for reduction of class size below the state requirements or below the average class size on a campus for the affected grade level. The allotment may be used to fund an optional summer program for limited-English proficient students beyond grade one provided that the regular school year bilingual education and English as a second language requirements are met. The summer program must be in addition to the required summer program for limited-English proficient students entering kindergarten or the first grade. Districts also encouraged to use the bilingual allotment for programs designed to increase the numbers of fully certified teachers for bilingual education and/or ESL programs, and to improve the quality of the affective, linguistic and cognitive components of the bilingual education and ESL programs. Training costs for teachers and aides may include stipends, substitute pay for release time, tuition for college courses, travel expenses, and expenses for the trainers.

Theoretical Basis

Issues dealing with bilingual education and the education of language minority students (limited-English proficient) are charged with emotion and remain controversial despite their inherent need and proven positive effects. The issues that appear to be most in debate surround the types of programs that are most effective and the teaching practices that are the most beneficial to the students in the programs. As the administrator-in-charge, there is a need to be aware of the knowledge base that exists about the empirical and theoretical basis of language programs so sound policy decisions that will effect students can be made with some semblance of accuracy.

Research conducted between 1920 and 1960 led to the speculation that bilingual students were cognitively confused about language and thus were language handicapped.

These findings, along with statistics that documented that bilingual students were more often in special education classes and suffered from emotional conflicts led educators to believe that language was the basis for the students' poor academic performance. This reinforced the notion that the students' first language should be disallowed, that the student should be forced to speak only in English, thus eradicating the first language as soon as possible and eliminating the "problem."

Nearly all of this initial research was done on students who were being forced to replace their own language with that of the majority population, who were punished physically and psychologically for speaking their own language in school, or who were not being given an opportunity to acquire a second language in a transitional manner but rather by force. This situation was representative of many of the programs and attitudes of the time. Because emphasis was being placed on oral language communication skills in the classroom, these students usually failed to acquire sufficient literacy and cognitive skills to allow them to succeed in the educational environment. The crux of the problem was not the inability to learn due to bilingualism but rather the humiliating and degrading manner in which the students were treated, and the resultant loss in personal self-esteem and integrity.

Recent research on bilingual students who are in transitional and other types of appropriate programs demonstrate that bilingualism is a positive academic force for students. Both intellectual and linguistic processes are enhanced by the cognitive ability to function in two languages. Indeed, many states are reporting that bilingual students are scoring higher on some standardized tests than monolingual English students due to a greater sensitivity to linguistic meanings and expanded ability to process material more flexibly. It appears that bilingual students have a greater ability to control and manipulate language than their monolingual counterparts. In addition, cognitive abilities appear to be enhanced, a factor which has implications for academic settings and program development. These recent studies also demonstrate that students are adding the second language to their repertory of first language skill without diminishing the development of their first language. They are expanding their knowledge, as well as their linguistic and cognitive abilities, by adding another language. These findings reinforce the notion that bilingual programs in the schools have a positive effect on the academic abilities of the bilingual student. It is important then that in the beginning of their schooling experience learners continue to develop both of their languages so they may complement the development of each other. The development of another language and the accompanying literacy skills which are developed cognitively have no negative consequence for students' academic, linguistic, or cognitive development, and may indeed enhance the process.

An area that merits attention in discussing the nature of bilingualism is that of literacy-related skills. It has long been an accepted principle that the sooner and more intensely a student is exposed to English, the sooner the student will speak English and once s/he can communicate and participate in class, the problem of language is solved, because of course if s/he can talk they can write. Right? Wrong. Academic language skills are interdependent, which means they rely upon a common underlying proficiency. This proficiency can be in either language. A program, for example, that is providing Spanish instruction to develop reading skills in Spanish is not just developing those skills in Spanish, but is developing a deeper cognitive framework of conceptual and linguistic proficiency that will contribute to the development and ease of learning English. Thus the notion of developing the students cognitive language abilities in the students' first language is a strong influencing factor when determining the types of programs to implement in the schools.

This heavy reliance upon the verbal skills of the student as measured in classroom, lunchroom, playground, or other settings has been a contributing factor to the unsuccessful academic performance of many bilingual students. (It should also be noted that it makes a difference whether the students' verbal performance is assessed in an informal or formal setting). Students frequently have the ability to develop fluency in conversational language skills needed in the school environment: there is much oral stimuli in the environment from which to imitate oral speaking. However, this does little to develop the academic language skills necessary to compete or succeed in the academic environment. This is an important distinction for administrators (and teachers) to consider. The oral nature of our society (notwithstanding the power of peer influence, television, movies, etc.) provides an opportunity for students to develop a conversational vocabulary within about two years. However, to develop the vocabulary necessary to succeed linguistically in an academic setting may require five or more years. This means that although students may be able to converse, they should not be mistakenly removed from the bilingual program and placed into an all-English environment and be expected to function academically as a native English speaker does. They do not have the technical, academic proficiency of the language to compete and succeed in the classroom with native English speakers. This should be clear by the data gathered on tests that frequently label second language learners as mentally retarded or learning disabled after they have tested out of a bilingual classroom because they can "speak English." They may be able to speak conversational English, but it should be obvious that their academic language has not yet developed to the point of proficiency.

Based on this theoretical knowledge, administrators can begin to make learned policy and program decisions with regards to bilingual education. In doing so, there are four major considerations:

- programs that continue to develop academic skills in both languages will not confuse the student: students may in fact benefit from the dual language system
- students will develop oral communication skills much faster than they will develop academic skills to foster conceptual and cognitive knowledge
- conceptual development in one language assists in making input in the other language comprehensible
- opportunities to use and develop both the first and second language in meaningful settings are important variables in the growth of language skills

It is also important to consider the family and community in determining program options. These variables can have considerable influence on both the student and the school.

Types of Programs

The most recent research available reveals that in 1988-1990, there were more than 275,000 students identified as limited-English proficient, with more than 138,000 in bilingual programs and nearly 100,000 in a variety of English as a second language programs across the state. These students represented 44 different language groups. Of the students in these programs, 17% of those in bilingual programs and 20% of those in English as a second language programs (at least 37% of all students in these programs) had been retained in their grade levels for at least one school year. This data also showed that 85% of the students in special language programs were dropping out before finishing high school. There is an urgent need to understand, develop, and maintain quality special language programs throughout the state.

School districts in Texas are required to develop a local plan to meet the needs of limited-English proficient students. This plan must detail the manner in which the district will offer a special language program if they have an enrollment of 20 or more limited-English proficient students in any language in the same grade level districtwide. The programs must be offered in pre kindergarten through the elementary grades for students who speak that language. A district must provide a bilingual education program by offering either a dual language program in pre-kindergarten through the elementary grades or an approved dual language program which addresses the affective, linguistic, and cognitive needs of the limited-English proficient students. Districts can also establish bilingual education programs at grade levels in which a bilingual education program in not required. All limited-English proficient students for whom a district is not required to offer a bilingual education program must be provided an English as a second language program regardless of the students' grade levels and home language, and regardless of the number of students in need of such a program. Districts having few students in need of such programs, or with limited resources with which to provide such programs may join with other districts to provide bilingual education or ESL programs. Districts unable to provide bilingual or ESL programs may apply for a one-year waiver from the Commissioner of Education.

School districts required to offer a bilingual education or ESL program must provide each eligible student the opportunity to be enrolled in the required program at his or her grade level. The district is responsible for modifying the instruction, pacing, and materials to ensure that students have a full opportunity to master the essential elements of the required curriculum. Students participating in a bilingual education program may demonstrate their mastery of the essential elements in either their home language or English. Bilingual education programs must be full-time programs of instruction offered as an integral part of the regular education program required under Chapter 75. Bilingual programs using Spanish and English shall use state-adopted English and Spanish texts and supplementary material as curriculum tools to assist in addressing the affective linguistic, an cognitive needs of the student, in which both the students' home language and English are used for instruction. The amount of instruction in each language must be commensurate with the students' level of proficiency in both language and their level of academic achievement.

English as a second language programs must be intensive programs of instruction designed to develop proficiency in comprehension, speaking, reading, and composition in the English language. In pre-kindergarten thorough the elementary grades, instruction in English as a second language may vary from the amount of time accorded to instruction in English language arts in the regular program for nonlimited-English proficient students to total immersion in second language approaches. In grades seven through 12, instruction in English as a second language may vary from one-third of the instructional day to total immersion in second language approaches. In subjects such as art, music and physical education the limited-English proficient students shall participate with their English-speaking peers in regular classes provided in the subjects. In all other courses, English as a second language strategies, which may involve the use of the students' home language, may be provided in any of the courses or electives required for promotion or graduation to assist the student in mastering the essential elements for the required subjects. The use of ESL strategies cannot impede the awarding of credit toward meeting promotion or graduation requirements.

Delivery Models

Although each school district with an enrollment of 20 or more students of limited-English proficiency in any language classification in the same grade level is required to provide a bilingual education or special language program (ESL) program, each school district does not necessarily have to develop and establish a separate program, and the programs are to be located in the regular public schools of the district, not in separate facilities. A school district may join with any other district or districts to provide the bilingual or special language services needed for their students. Additionally, a student who resides in a district that provides no appropriate language program may be allowed to register as a nonresident in a bilingual or special language program of another district. In this case, the sending district must pay tuition to the receiving district for the services provided.

Programs for bilingual and ESL students must be located in the regular public schools of the district, and not in separate facilities. Districts may, however, concentrate the programs at a limited number of schools within the district provided that the enrollment in those schools not exceed 60% limited-English proficient students.

Personnel Considerations

In assigning teachers to provide services for bilingual and special language programs, districts must take all reasonable affirmative steps to assure that teachers are appropriately certified in accordance with the Texas Education Code concerning bilingual education and special language program teachers. Districts which are unable to secure a sufficient number of certified bilingual education and English as a second language teachers to provide the required programs must request emergency teaching permits or special assignment permits.

Teachers assigned to the bilingual education program and/or English as a second language program may receive salary supplements as authorized by the Texas Education Code. This salary supplement must be provided for in the local district policy. Districts may also compensate teachers and aides assigned to bilingual education and ESL programs for their participation in continuing education programs designed to increase their skills or lead to bilingual education or ESL certification.

In those districts unable to staff their bilingual education and ESL programs with fully certified teachers, at least 10% of their bilingual education allotment must be used for preservice and inservice training to improve the skills of the teachers who provide the instruction in the alternative bilingual education program, who provide instruction in English as a second language and/or who provide content area instruction in special classes for limited English proficient students.

It is the responsibility of the Texas Education Agency to develop bilingual education training materials for use by district and teacher training institutions in implementing bilingual education and English as a second language training. These materials shall provide a framework for training related to developmentally appropriate bilingual programs for early childhood through elementary grades; affectively, linguistically, and cognitively appropriate instruction; and developmentally appropriate programs for gifted and talented limited-English proficient students, as well as disabled limited-English proficient students.

Emerging Needs

The needs of students who are limited-English proficient are constantly changing due to various political, cultural, social, linguistic, demographic, and programmatic influences. One of the areas of emerging need that will demand attention in the coming years is that of disabled bilingual students.

Although statistics on the number of disabled bilingual students who need services are not yet definitively known, recent studies indicated the prevalence of disabled students among the LEP and bilingual populations is difficult to determine because local education agencies do not report disabling conditions by language proficiency level. In addition, the reemergence of services for students who qualify under Section 504 will compound both the identification and service issues involved with bilingual students who are disabled. However, based on traditionally accepted incidence figures, it is estimated that approximately 30,000 to 50,000 limited-English speaking students would qualify for services for students with disabilities in Texas. There is a need for the development of a systematic method for gathering data on the incidence of bilingual disabled students to enable planning for both personnel and student needs.

Another category of students who will merit more attention in the future are those students who are not proficient in either their native language or English. Given the research review regarding the need to educate children in their primary language and their language of cognitive strength, these children will need special attention, testing, methodology, and teachers to assist in determining and strengthening both languages so one language is not favored or forgotten in lieu of the other.

Perhaps the area of greatest need is that of testing. This is an area of ongoing concern to educators, parents, test developers, and policy makers alike. It is also the area that has the least readily accessible solution. In response to the lack of appropriate commercial tests on the market to meet the varying needs of the students, many school districts have chosen to make the long-term investment and commitment of developing and norming their own tests to meet the needs of the students in their locale. This is, however, a time-consuming and costly undertaking. Few districts have either the personnel or financial resources in this time of fiscal exigency to take on this type of developmental project. There is a need for assistance from both the federal and state level to afford districts the opportunity to develop tests to meet their unique needs.

A Look Back

- Administrators in the schools in Texas are facing challenging times in the years to come due to rapidly changing demography affecting the schools.
- Meeting the needs of children with special and second language needs is not a new concept in American schools.

- Although the role of the federal government has changed through the years, it has been actively involved in bilingual education efforts.
- Rapidly changing demographics, Sputnik, immigration, civil rights, and politics have played key roles in the resurgence of the bilingual education movement.
- The Bilingual Education Act was an effort by the federal government to provide leadership for second language children.
- *Lau v. Nichols* Supreme Court decision focused national attention on the needs of the limited English speaking student in the educational setting.
- The first law in Texas supporting bilingual education was enacted in 1918.
- Administrators may be asked to assist in a variety of procedures related to conducting bilingual or English as a second language programs in Texas schools.
- Issues surrounding bilingual education are often politically motivated, emotionally charged and controversial.
- Recent research in bilingual education demonstrates that both intellectual and linguistic processes are enhanced by the cognitive ability to function in two languages.
- Enrollment of 20 or more students of the same language classification in the same grade level who are limited-English proficient requires a bilingual or special language program in Texas schools; all other limited-English proficient students are served with English as a second language programs, if approved by their parents.
- School districts may cooperate to provide bilingual or English as a second language programs rather than each district establishing a separate program.
- Three areas of need that may emerge in the years ahead are disabled bilingual students, students who are not proficient in either their first or a second language, and testing of bilingual students.

Remedial and Compensatory Instruction Programs

Federal Perspectives

Compensatory and remedial programs for disadvantaged children in the schools began in 1965, during the years of dramatic social reform and civil unrest, with the passage and implementation of the Elementary and Secondary Education Act (ESEA). This act contained provisions for a large number of categorical programs developed to meet the growing needs of "disadvantaged" students eligible to be served in certain types of restricted programs in both the public and private schools. This period of federal program development, known as devolution, gave the federal government much control over the programs in an attempt to serve the students who were not being adequately serviced by other programs in the schools at the time. The major programs which will be addressed from the federal level in this section are Chapter I, Migrant

Education (a subcategory of Chapter I), tutorial services, and programs for dropout students. Many of the students are served by multiple programs and the students in these programs are likely to be dropouts before obtaining a high school diploma. It is difficult, if not impossible, to address the needs of one group of students without coming along with one or more of the other categories the student is likely to be associated with.

Chapter I was originally entitled Title I, but was retitled with the passage of the Education Consolidation and Improvement Act of 1981, when 27 programs previously separately titled under the Elementary and Secondary Education Act (ESEA) were consolidated into three basic programs. These programs became either Chapter I State Compensatory Programs, Chapter I Migrant Education, or Chapter II Block Grants (known as Discretionary Funds and used to provide programs in the areas of gifted and talented, instructional computing, guidance and counseling, pupil transportation and other such areas). Chapter I was amended in 1983 and again in 1988 (Public Law 97-35, as amended by technical amendments, PLs 98-211 and 98-312, and 100-297 in 1988). The current movement, that began in the early 1980s, is a trend towards returning much more control and responsibility of the federally assisted programs to the states. As with other federally assisted programs, districts wishing to participate must apply for the funds based on the needs identified. Chapter I funds can be used to supplement rather than supplant any nonfederal support; to demonstrate maintenance of fiscal effort from the second year preceding start-up to the first project year; to deliver services in Chapter I schools that compare equitably with similar services in non-Chapter I schools; to identify students who most need the services; and to consult with parents and children. Federal Chapter I dollars cannot supplant programs and services provided by the state educational system.

The most significant litigation to date in the area of Chapter I programs has been *Aguilar v. Felton,* a United States Supreme Court case issued on July 1, 1985. In that decision, the Supreme Court held that instructional services under Chapter I cannot be provided within religiously affiliated private schools. At the same time, however, the Supreme Court's decision left in place the statutory requirement that Chapter I services must be provided to eligible private school children on a equitable basis. The State agency is therefore required, in performing its duties under the Chapter I statute and regulations, to ensure that the local education agencies adhere to the *Felton* decision and that private school children continue to receive equitable Chapter I services. The Department of Education issued questions and answers as guidance to state commissioners of education on both August 1985 and June 1986 concerning how the Supreme Court's decision on *Aguilar v. Felton* affects the operation of Chapter I programs. Contact your district office program director or the Texas Education Agency for further guidance in this area.

Programs for migrant children are also a part of Chapter 1. Migrant children are perhaps the least understood and most at risk students in the schools. These students move frequently to follow seasonal employment opportunities and are often kept out of school for long periods of time to assist in supporting the family. Migrant children may be classified into two major categories, as either currently migratory or formerly migratory. Children who are currently migratory are those whose parent or guardian is a migratory agricultural worker or a migratory fisher and who has moved within the past 12 months from one school district to another—to enable the child, the child's guardian or a member of the child's immediate family to obtain temporary or seasonal employment in an agricultural or fishing activity. A child who is formerly migratory is one who was eligible to be counted and served as a migratory child within the past five years, but is not now a currently migratory child. They can be classified into one of six groups:

- Interstate Agricultural (currently migratory)
- Intrastate Agricultural (currently migratory)
- Formerly Migratory (agricultural)
- Interstate Fishing (currently migratory)
- Intrastate Fishing (currently migratory)
- Formerly Migratory (fishing)

To assist in tracking migratory students, a computerized national data base called the Migrant Student Record Transfer System (MSRTS) is kept in Little Rock, Arkansas. In 1987, this data base identified nearly 531,000 migrant students. Students are counted on the basis of their Full Time Equivalents (FTE) in the schools. An FTE in equal to one student in residence in the district for one full calendar year. A single FTE would be recorded if, for example, two students were in a school district for only one-half year each. In 1987, MSRTS recorded more than 441,000 FTEs. The data from this bank shows that the number of FTEs generated by migrant students declines markedly as the grade level increases. This suggests a high dropout rate for migrants. While there are more than 35,000 FTEs at the first-grade level, there are fewer than 15,000 generated at the twelfth-grade level. This represents a decline of more than 57%. Migrant students fare poorly in school and leave school ill-prepared for productive work. Opportunities for a post-secondary future are rare for migrant children. The children of migrant workers lag from six to eighteen months behind their expected grade levels for their age groups, requiring roughly three years to advance one grade level in some states, making many students older than their peers, which causes adjustment problems and tends to contribute to the dropout rate. Long working hours, lack of transportation, and isolation from the mainstream of the school and community environment all contribute to the multitude of issues needing attention for migrant students. In addition, English is often the second language for these students, another factor contributing to difficulty in testing, achievement, and adjustment in the school environment. Migrant farm workers have, on the average, no more than a sixth-grade education, and their rate of enrollment is lower than any other group of children in the country. Due to their mobility, data on achievement is difficult to gather, not done on a routine basis, and often inaccurately reflects their ability.

As with other "at-risk" students, their parents have less education, contributing to the lack of an understanding of the school system and a lack of support of the efforts of the system to assist the students in making educational progress. Migrant students do, however, have ready access to work opportunities, despite how meager the financial rewards and conditions may appear to be. This, combined with a familiar need to work, can substantially interrupt educational endeavors and aspirations. Migrant students have the lowest graduation rate of any population group identified in our public school system and the rate of completion of post-secondary educational programs is equally as grim. The dropout rate for migrant students is estimated to be twice the national average, at about 50%. Thus the cycle continues.

Funding for Chapter I and Migrant Education programs is distributed through a formula developed at the federal level that allows the individual states flexibility and latitude to control their own needs. In operating its State- or local-level programs, and may use funds received under Chapter I only to supplement and, to the extent practical, increase the level of funds that would, in the absence of such federal funds, be made available from nonfederal sources for the education of pupils participating in programs and products assisted under Chapter I, and in no case may these federal funds be used to supplant funds from non-federal sources. In order to demonstrate compliance with this subsection, no state educational agency, other than the state education agency, or local educational agency shall be required to provide services under this chapter outside the regular classroom or school program.

One of the current requirements of Chapter I monies is "comparability of services." At present, a local district may receive funds under Chapter I only if state and local funds will be used in the district to provide services for projects in areas which, taken as a whole, are at least comparable to services being offered in areas of the district which are not receiving funds under Chapter 1. Where all school attendance areas in the district are designated as project areas, the district may receive such funds only if state and local funds are used to provide services which, taken as a whole, are substantially comparable in each of the project areas. Beginning with the 1990-1991 school year, the Texas Education Agency will be requiring recipients of Chapter I funds to submit written procedures to demonstrate comparability. Procedures may include areas such as: a) districtwide salary schedule; b) a policy to ensure equivalence among schools in teachers, administrators, and auxiliary personnel; and c) a policy to ensure equivalency among schools in the provision of curriculum materials and instructional supplies. Unpredictable changes in student enrollment or personnel assignments which occur after the beginning of a school year will not be included as a factor in determining comparability of services.

In addition, Chapter I (Title I) programs also serve dropouts through compensatory education programs. In 1988, Congress enacted the Hawkins/Stafford School Improvement Act (P.L.100-297) which extensively revised Chapter I and extended it through September 30, 1993. P.L. 100-297 added two new subprograms designed to direct more resources to two previously underserved groups: preschoolers and secondary school students. This new Secondary School initiative authorizes both dropout prevention and basic skills instruction for secondary school students. This legislation, coupled with the Carl Perkins Technology Education Act that targets dropouts, provides financial incentives for serving dropout youth as well as those who are at risk of dropping out, and adults who have not completed high school. This act has provided a substantial thrust since 1968 for these students from the federal level.

As this book goes to press, Title I (Chapter I) is in the final stages of reauthorization, as part of the ESEA reauthorization package. As the current draft of the legislation is written, 1994-95 will be a transitional year. The fiscal components of the new legislation will not be in effect until 1994-95, but districts have the option of beginning to implement the programs and changes. In 1995-96, the act will be fully implemented with all of the fiscal changes.

The changes, as they are currently written in the draft legislation, contain four themes. The first could be called a "targeting emphasis." Presently, two-thirds of the campuses in the United States receive Chapter I moneys. As such, the money that is allocated is spread very sparsely among the campuses. The new legislation will provide more targeted money to schools with a high concentration of children of low-income families. These schools will receive a higher percentage of allocated money, balancing two areas of Chapter I dollars: a) 50% for basic grant funds, and b) 50% in concentration grant funds for districts with high concentrations of low income families. As a result, districts that at present only receive basic grant funds could receive less money, and districts that receive concentration grant funds could receive more money. Districts, however, must continue to qualify for the money, meaning that there must be 6500 students or more that meet the federal low-income criteria or 15% low income.

The second theme is that of "alignment." The new federal standards would require each state to identify high-goal and content-area standards, then develop assessments to determine if the receiving districts are reaching those standards. States would then have to identify how the receiving schools are moving towards attaining these standards. This requirement should not be a problem for Texas, as the state currently uses the TAAS, the AEIS, and EEs to determine individual and district standard status. The new ESEA legislation, thus including Title I, is written toward the Goal 2000 proposal, and all goals of all programs are expected to be aligned.

The third theme is "flexibility." In the proposed legislation, once the money is targeted to a district and individual campus, there will be more flexibility in the use of the funds. The eligibility for schoolwide programs can be extended. This section of the law has five new requirements:

1. the criteria of 75% would be lowered. During the first year of the new law, criteria would be 65% (94-95 or 95-96), and 50% for the second year. This lower criteria would make another 2000 campuses eligible for funding nationwide. In Texas, one-third of all campuses currently qualify;
2. schoolwide programs would not just be for Title I students, but for all students under ESEA and other federal discretionary programs yet to be announced, as well as other state programs designated in the Title I state plan;
3. the flexibility is to be implemented to assure that all students on a campus can meet the standards, whether or not they are Title I students;
4. campuses that cannot meet the 50% criteria can become "Targeted Assisted School." That is, they meet the Title I criteria but not the criteria for schoolwide projects. Eligible students

are those who are failing to meet the statewide standards and those at risk of meeting statewide standards. Concerns under this portion of the plan focus on the use of paraprofessionals to deliver Title I programs and paraprofessional training.
5. the last area is "accountability." Under the new law, the student results would be looked at more than when and how the money was spent. States would be responsible for developing strategies to monitor the standards, not the fiscal and legal compliance arena as in the past. Schoolwide programs would look at how all students met the standards, whether eligible for Title I as an individual or not. A new motivation for more money comes with the meeting of goals and standards, and the money can be used however the campus decides.

One of the purposes of the new flexibility guidelines is to transfer the federal relationship to the district and the state, rather than the campus and the state. (This appears to be rather counterproductive under the notion of Site-Based Decision Making.) The question then becomes, what is the district going to do if a campus needs improvement? This guidance would come from the district rather than the state as it now does. If a district is now successful, the state would then become involved in the process.

Texas Perspectives

There are approximately 1,500,000 special population students in Texas: more than half of those students are in compensatory and remedial education programs. The goals of remedial and compensatory programs are: a) to accelerate instruction in order to close the performance gap between identified students and other students by providing unity of purpose toward a common set of goals, and b) to empower all participants of the school community with the authority to take responsibility for building on strengths of students to achieve desired learner outcomes.

Compensatory and remedial education programs were first implemented on a uniform basis by a 1975 enactment of the legislature; the tutorial services act was first passed in 1981. Subsequent amendments have yielded much progress in the nature and development of programs for students in need of special academic assistance.

The current provisions for remedial and compensatory programs, effective June 1991, have adopted the following standards for each of the districts who participate to follow:

a. a written policy for the use of state compensatory funds that included eligibility requirements for participation in the program for students in pre-kindergarten through grade 12, a description of the program and services to be provided, and a plan to coordinate state compensatory education funds with local, federal, and other state funds;
b. an annual review of the progress of each student being served and the redirection of funds and services as necessary to ensure student learning; and

    c. an increased percentage of students mastering all three areas of the student assessment program required by the Texas Education Agency, until all students have achieved mastery.

To determine students' eligible for compensatory and remedial services, districts must use student performance data from the basic skills assessment instruments and achievement tests when designing and implementing appropriate compensatory remedial instruction. On the secondary level, students who have not performed satisfactorily on each section of the secondary exit level assessment instrument are eligible for remedial instruction. Districts must have written procedures for identifying students who might potentially be eligible to participate in a remedial or compensatory education program. Districts are required to provide a remedial and support program for any student whose achievement test score is below a standard established by the State Board of Education; or who is at risk of dropping out of school. The program for students who are at risk of dropping out of school must include an evaluative mechanism that documents the effectiveness of the program in reducing the dropout rate and in increasing achievement in each student in grade levels seven through 12 who is under 21 years of age and meets the following criteria:

    a. was not advanced from one grade level to the next two or more school years;
    b. has mathematics or reading skills that are two or more years below grade level;
    c. did not maintain an average equivalent to 70 on a scale of 100 in two or more courses during a semester, or is not maintaining such an average in two or more courses in the current semester and is not expected to graduate within four years of the date the student begins ninth grade; or
    d. did not perform satisfactorily on an assessment instrument prescribed by the state in grades seven, nine, or twelve.

In pre-kindergarten through grade level six, the following criteria apply for students who:

    a. did not perform satisfactorily on a readiness test or assessment instrument administered at the beginning of the school year;
    b. did not perform satisfactorily on an assessment instrument administered by the state in third or fifth grade;
    c. is a student of limited-English proficiency as defined by the state regulations;
    d. is sexually, physically, or psychologically abused;
    e. engages in delinquent conduct, other than a traffic offense that violates a penal law of the state or an order of a juvenile court; or
    f. is otherwise identified as at risk under rules adopted by the State Board of Education.

All of these criteria also apply to each nonhandicapped student who resides in a residential placement facility in a district in which the student's parent or legal guardian does not reside.

Tutorial services are one of the options a school district shall provide and may make available to students who are in need of such services. Texas Education Code 21.103 states that a district may require a student whose grade in a subject for a grade reporting period is lower than 70 on a scale of 100 to attend tutorials in the subject during the following reporting period as determined by the district personnel. The tutorial services may be funded from state compensatory education funds as well as other state and local funding sources. Federal funds may also be used to supplement the program in accordance with applicable laws and regulations. Each of these efforts, such as compensatory, remedial and tutorial education, to assist students while they are still enrolled in the school provides an opportunity to prevent the student from becoming a dropout statistic.

A close examination of at-risk students who are undereducated in Texas in relation to the rest of the United States gives a picture of the need to pay attention to the dropout trends in Texas. It is interesting to note that of the fifty states, Texas, California, and New York, have the largest population of children who have dropped out before receiving a high school diploma. These three states also have the largest populations, with Texas and California also having large percentages of minority students. In 1985, Texas accounted for 8.45% of the national dropout population in the United States.

The most recent research available in Texas, conducted by Intercultural Development Research Association (IDRA) in 1986, found the following to be true in Texas schools:

1. The 1985-86 attrition rate for Texas high schools was 33%;
2. One in five Texas young people (nearly half a million) age 16 to 24 were not enrolled in school and had not completed the 12th grade in 1980;
3. Three out of ten Texas dropouts (152,000) had completed fewer than nine years of schooling when they left school;
4. Attrition rates differ markedly for racial/ethnic groups in the state: 27% for Anglos, 34% for Blacks, and 45% for Hispanic youth.

IDRA found that 16% of the students tracked who were presumed dropouts had not dropped out of school. Twenty-eight percent of the students tracked were employed. Most worked at labor-intensive, minimum-wage jobs. The majority of the students tracked left school due to poor grades, marriage and/or pregnancy, or financial problems. These are startling statistics for the states most valuable asset: its youth. How can Texas more effectively deal with these statistics?

With all of the attention that is presently being focused on the at-risk, and specifically the dropout and potential dropout population, the Texas legislature felt compelled to provide specific instructions for assisting the schools with this population. House Bill 1010 was enacted by the Texas State Legislature to provide the schools with guidance in attempting to curb the dropout rate and more accurately track those students who do dropout. Section 1 of the Bill amended Section 11.205 of the Education Code to require, rather than pose as optional, that a dropout reduction program be standardized across the state. Each district is now required to designate one or more persons to serve as an at-risk coordinator. The number of coordinators required corresponds to the size of the district. These coordinators collect and disseminate data regarding dropouts in the district and coordinate the program in the district for students who are at high risk of dropping out of school. The Bill also required the development of a state clearinghouse and an Interagency Coordinating Council to coordinate efforts and distribute information on the dropout crisis. The Bill includes specific language addressing academic remediation for students at-risk of leaving school before completion, as determined by standardized test instruments.

In 1986, 39% of Texas school districts had a system for identifying dropouts; sixty-two percent of all school districts did not use a standard formula for calculating their dropout rate; and, nearly every district defined the dropout population differently. Approximately 89% of the dropout programs in Texas reported having no evaluation data. The Texas Education Agency was charged with developing a program to reduce the rate of students leaving school before completing high school. The program includes standardized statewide record keeping, documentation of school transfers by students, identification of successful dropout prevention programs, and follow-up procedures for students who drop out of school. The agency has developed a system for school districts to collect data on student dropouts. The system attempts to collect data regarding each student dropout. The agency requires each district to designate one or more employees to serve as an at-risk coordinator (Texas Education Code §11.205) to assure that each district makes progress toward reducing the dropout rate and that the appropriate data is kept.

Student/teacher ratios and length of instructional periods for compensatory and remedial programs are not prescribed by law, however, the following recommendations are made to assist districts in determining their ratios and hours:

a. level of student need;
b. specific concepts or skills to be taught;
c. grade level being served; and
d. quality and type of remedial or compensatory design.

Although in flux due to the current difficulties in resolving the issues related to state funding for education, the state funding for compensatory programs at present is based on the number of at-risk students determined by averaging the best six months' enrollment in the national school lunch program of free or reduced-price lunches for the preceding school year. Districts must participate in the National School Lunch Program to be eligible for an allotment of the state compensatory funds.

Each school district must allocate a percentage of the district's state compensatory education funds for remedial and support programs specifically for students at risk of dropping out of school. This targeted allotment shall be: a) at least equal to the state's longitudinal dropout rate, grades seven through 12, for the previous school year in any district in which the actual dropout rate in any year exceeds the state's dropout rate goal for that year, and; b) applicable to remedial and support programs for grades pre-kindergarten through 12.

Compensatory funds are to be used to improve and enhance the regular school program so that identified students can achieve success in school and meet the desired student outcomes, such as attaining grade-level proficiency, performing satisfactorily on state assessment instruments, and graduating from school. Special instruction that satisfies basic program requirements may be funded provided it is specifically designed to meet the needs of students identified for these programs and is not a standard approach to courses or subjects. The special instruction must be restructured if results show that the courses are not successful in helping students achieve the desired student outcomes. State compensatory funds may be expended for personnel, instructional materials, equipment, and supplies to the extent that such expenditures are necessary and can be justified for instructional uses for students participating in compensatory programs. Up to 15% of state compensatory education funds may be used for general administrative costs. Funds, other than those calculated for the administrative costs, cannot be used for administration, construction, building rental, or other noninstructional purposes. General administrative costs have been defined as: districtwide program administration (program directors, business managers, etc.); the program's share of plant operations (e.g. utilities); the program's share of data processing costs; the program's share of facilities costs; the program's share of other indirect costs. At least 85% of the state compensatory education funds are required to be spent on direct instruction. The direct costs of the program consist of:

a. salaries of program teachers, aides, and other staff providing direct service to students;
b. program supplies and materials;
c. program equipment or capital outlay acquisition;
d. program evaluation and testing costs for the program;
e. direct program supervision of staff providing service to students;
f. staff development for program staff;
g. program curriculum development;
h. travel of staff for staff development or supervision.

Each district must include the budget and expenditures in their annual performance report. Other state and local funds may also be used for these programs, with federal funds being used only in accordance with the supplemental, comparability and other regulations that apply to the use of federal funds for compensatory Chapter I programs.

Under the Carl Perkins Vocational Education Act, district and state eligibility for funding are determined by formula. State department vocational special needs personnel or local district vocational personnel will be able to assist. Districts use funds from the state compensatory education formula for these programs.

Theoretical Basis

Historically, students who receive Chapter I, Migrant education and services for "at-risk" children have been referred to as disadvantaged, impoverished, dropouts, deprived, lower socioeconomic, and academically handicapped. Saks writes that the economic effects of poverty and its social and psychological toll lessen the chance of academic success for many students, particularly minority students. Added to their usually lower socioeconomic status are poor school facilities, scant resources, high teacher turnover, and low expectation found in many schools in the poorer neighborhoods. These factors all contribute to the formula for continued lower performance and perpetuate the "at-risk" cycle.

These student, as Hodgkinson explains, have a typical profile. They are usually from low income or poverty settings, migrant families, families headed by a single parent (most often a female), and often from minority group backgrounds although not as likely to be from an Asian background as a Hispanic or Black. These students, for the most part, have parents who did not complete high school, are in lower paying, terminal-position jobs, and appear to be (at least on the surface) generally uninterested in their child's educational progress. Therefore, the support system for their child's academic progress is not readily apparent.

Statistically, males from the minority group are more inclined to become dropouts than females, usually leaving school to get a job that often does not last. On the other hand, when females leave school, it is usually to have a baby who is then born at risk and continues the cycle. As Gastright and Zulfi point out, some of the major influences on the growing dropout and at-risk population are drugs, alcohol, peers and role models (e.g. older siblings) who also drop out of school.

In general, at-risk students exhibit low basic academic skills, especially in the critical areas of reading and math, and in many instances English is not the dominant or native language spoken in the home. Valverde and Robertson-Courtney found that minority students have the highest dropout rate from school, begin to drop out earlier, are retained more frequently, score significantly lower on standardized tests, and have the highest attrition rate from colleges and universities. This is especially true of those from a Hispanic background. This has significant implications for Texas schools. In addition, these students tend to be referred for special education evaluation more frequently, with the majority of referrals resulting in special education placements.

Across all segments of our society, people are facing major realignments in family relationships. There is an increase in divorce rates, the number of single-parent households, and families with two working adults. For example, 55% of Puerto Rican children live in single-parent households, with the majority being headed by a female. Many attribute the increasing number of unsupervised children to comparable increases in teenage drug abuse, alcoholism, and pregnancy.

Clearly the schools cannot provide all of the services that are needed, or that will be needed to overcome these tremendous changes and shifts that are effecting the educational status of our children and putting them in the at-risk category. The problems confronting the schools are indeed very real and must be dealt with rapidly before the social changes continue to increase the number of at-risk children. Our society is becoming less Anglo and more Hispanic influenced, the very group that has the largest number of at-risk and dropout children. Immigration from Latin America and Asia accounts for one-fifth of this country's population growth in the 1980s. Minorities are growing at the fastest rates, they also have the highest dropout rates. This creates an immediate need to find solution to keep these, and all children, in school.

Types of Programs

From both the federal and state perspective, Chapter I (including Migrant Education) programs provide broad discretion for developing and implementing programs as the school district deems most valuable for the students involved. Moneys may be used to support professional and paraprofessional Chapter I staff salaries and bonuses, related nutrition, health and social services (if essential to the project and no other funds are available), staff training, instructional materials and supplies, essential equipment, identification and assessment for the purpose of selection of children who will receive services, project planning and evaluation, and reimbursements to volunteers for project-related expenses, such as transportation, babysitting, meals during service time and project-related travel. Most Chapter I and Migrant programs focus on the basic skills of mathematics, reading, and language arts development. These are the areas that hinder school progress the most for at-risk children.

Program funds may only cover the cost of essential construction when the school district has explored, but failed to obtain, other support and when the facility conforms to all federal and state standards. Programs to upgrade the entire educational program in a school may be established in eligible school attendance areas where at least 75% of the children at their school are from low-income families. Schoolwide projects must provide comprehensive assessment of educational needs of all students in the school and provide instructional programs designed to meet the special needs of all students in the school with the involvement of individuals who will be engaged in carrying out the approved plan for the school.

As with Chapter I and Migrant education programs, the purpose of state remedial and compensatory instructional programs is to provide additional instructional time on task in the identified areas of deficiency. However, with state funds, the additional time is allotted specifically to enable the student to master the essential elements for a course or subject area. The instruction and reteaching should be an integral part of the regular classroom instruction whenever the teacher determines that mastery of essential elements has not occurred. Like Chapter I programs, compensatory or remedial programs may be conducted during the regular school day as well as during other times determined by the district, and may take the form of remedial or compensatory courses, local credit courses or other locally developed courses, tutorial programs, summer school, alternative education programs, lower student-teacher ratios, for potential dropouts or pre-kindergarten and kindergarten programs for limited-English speaking or low-income families. A key to programming should be modifications in material, pacing, and instructional methodologies. Instruction should be delivered at the appropriate learning level of the student.

In addition, state funded remedial and support programs and services for students at risk of dropping out of school must include:

1. support services such as instructional material, instructional evaluation procedures, parental involvement activities, counseling, and school social work services;
2. proven models and strategies that have demonstrated statistically significant improvements in student life coping skills, and student performance such as cooperative learning, peer tutoring, computer-assisted instruction, content mastery learning, multisensory approaches, and continuous progress;
3. instructional designs that result in a reduction in class size; or
4. innovative strategies developed by the district provided a rational and program design with an evaluation component are approved by the local board of trustees and reviewed annually for program effectiveness.

Delivery Models

Many of the traditional services provided by Chapter I monies were done in pull-out settings. This model, however, has diminished in popularity through the years. In some areas, Chapter I and Migrant education personnel are assisting teachers in the classroom setting with the students needing additional attention, others are forming separate classes for students based upon the documented needs of a group of students. This is done by age level or by instructional needs, depending upon the configuration of the district program and personnel.

State compensatory and remedial programs also offer a variety of delivery methods. These include pull-out programs, teacher-assisted in-class instruction, after school programs during the regular school day, remedial courses, credit-bearing courses, one-on-one assistance, small group instruction, alternative materials and methods of instruction, and individualized progress programs. The method of delivery should be developed to best meet the needs of the students enrolled in the program and not the convenience of the personnel.

Tutorial services should reflect a small student-teacher ratio. Teacher aides may provide assistance to establish this small student-teacher ratio. Tutorial session may be before, during, after school, in the evening, on weekends. Study hall and pull-out settings are not appropriate for tutorial sessions. Students receiving instruction in a language other than English should receive tutorial services in that language in order to acquire optimum benefit. Students in special programs such as special education, compensatory education, bilingual/English as a second language, migrant, and gifted and talented programs are eligible for tutorial services, but the tutorial services cannot replace other special services provided these students under other programs. As with other special service programs, coordination of programs and program content is critical in the delivery of services.

For dropout and students at-risk of dropping out, strategies to deliver these services could include correspondence courses, magnet schools, summer schools, technological programs, alternative time schedules, day care, work-study, cooperative work programs, fifth year programs, and drug/alcohol intervention programs. Services provided in Correlated Language Arts and Fundamentals of Mathematics may also fulfill the needed support programs.

Personnel Considerations

There are no specifications from the federal level Chapter I or Migrant Education regulations in the area of personnel. Each state level agency has personnel specifically for Chapter I and Migrant Education program supervision, implementation, management, and activity funding. The number of personnel in each state agency and their specific qualifications vary according to state needs. At the local district level, there are no specifications for personnel, and each district that receives monies to conduct activities under Chapter I and Migrant Education is responsible for designating their own program director or coordinator. The number of persons assigned and the nature of their qualifications is a local district option. For state-sponsored compensatory and remedial education programs, it is required that personnel employed must meet state certification mandates. Those lacking special skills or competencies for compensatory education must be provided in-service training in the areas of need as determined by the local district. The rules also provide some guidance when stating that there shall be coordination between the regular teacher and any special teacher who provides the remediation. These personnel can consist of teachers, aides (paraprofessionals), peers, and other staff providing direct services to the students. The tutorial sessions, however, must be under the supervision of an appropriately certified teacher for each subject being remediated. Additionally, teachers selected to supervise and/or conduct tutorials should be proficient in the language of instruction. Each district is required to develop policies for personnel who provide remedial or compensatory instruction. As such, these personnel would be required to follow certification and other regulations established by state and local policy.

Personnel on a building level for any of these programs will be under the direct supervision of the building administrator. Principals are responsible for the implementation of the district plans for each of these programs at their campus level, so they may adjust the program parameters to meet the unique characteristics and circumstances of their local school environment.

Community-Based Alternative Education Programs

In an effort to provide maximum assistance to students who are at risk or who have dropped out of school, beginning June 1992, community-based programs were recognized in Texas as a viable alternative education. An organization eligible to be considered under the Texas Education Code is one that is defined as any business enterprise operated for a profit, or on a nonprofit basis, which maintains a place of business within the State of Texas or solicits business within the State of Texas. Students eligible to be enrolled in a community-based alternative education program are those between the ages of 14 and 21 who meet two or more of the state-mandated at-risk criteria as outlined previously, or who have dropped out of school for a minimum of one semester or more.

Any school district may enter into a performance-based contractual agreement to provide academic services to dropouts and identified at-risk students with a community-based organization that meets the definition and criteria outlined by the state. In operating programs for a school district, a community-based organization must meet the following standards:

- students must receive course credit upon 70% mastery of the essential elements for each course. Mastery of the essential elements must be documented and available for review by school district personnel and the state agency;
- instructional staff must possess at least a baccalaureate degree from an accredited college or university;
- enrollment and attendance must be accounted for in the manner prescribed by the state for all attendance; and
- grades, course credit data, and information on the student assessment program must be collected according to written procedures and transferred to the school district.

Districts that enter into a contractual agreement with a community-based organization must provide these services to the students:

1. textbooks;
2. transportation to the alternative education program as well as transportation to the test site for student assessment;
3. administration of the student assessment programs required by the state, and the results of the tests;
4. awarding of a diploma to a student upon successful completion of high school graduation requirements; and
5. school district personnel to monitor the performance terms of the contract.

Emerging Needs

The most critical need in the immediate future is the training of administrators to deal with special programs and populations. For administrators to effectively deal with at-risk students in any of the categories outlined, they must possess an understanding of the characteristics of these students, the programs parameters, program initiatives from both the national and state perspective, literature and research findings, and implications for the future of these students. They must be knowledgeable of the socio-economic as well as educational factors associated with this population. They should be familiar with strategies aimed at preventing learning discouragement and defeat, and know how to motivate staff and communities into action on behalf of the student. Principals must make it clear to their staff that their definition of "effective" and "successful" includes students who are at-risk and that they are willing to take the necessary steps to assure students build strong self-concepts and self-assurance. Administrators must be able to develop teacher inservice and curriculum reform into their routines. It has also been suggested that schools must become clinics where adults work together to diagnose student strengths and learning needs, prescribe creative solutions, apply treatments in teams combining variety of personalities, professional expertise, and techniques, and carefully evaluate results and redirect programs. To accomplish this formidable challenge, administrators must be educated in the area of at-risk students and their families, and truly become instructional leaders for all children.

A Look Back

- Compensatory and remedial programs from the federal level have provided assistance to the schools for over 20 years.
- Chapter I programs are intended to supplement not supplant programs funded through state and local resources.
- Migrant education, as a subcomponent of Chapter I, serves children who are mobile, provides a national data base for tracking, and has decreased migrant students' dropout rates.
- The 1988 amendment to Chapter I included initiatives for secondary students and provided additional monies for dropout and basic skill programs.
- Texas provides services with state funding for compensatory and remedial programs for students who are in need of accelerated instruction to close the performance gap.
- Compensatory and remedial programs funded at both the national and state level provide a great deal of discretion for program types and service delivery models for local school districts.
- Texas has implemented a special law to assist in curbing the dropout rate.
- The greatest need in working with educationally at-risk students is in the area of personnel training.
- Administrators must develop the mind set, the tone, environment, and attitude for working with educationally at-risk students by being instructional leaders for all children in their schools.

Senate Bill 1 and House Bill 2885 will bring new and yet undefined changes to State compensatory education programs and program successes as committees attempt to meet the needs of students on individual campuses through the use of the academic excellence indicators.

Conclusion

Building level administrators are critical influences in ensuring the academic achievement of students. Recent studies show that this is especially true for Black and low-income students. The findings also suggest that teacher perceptions of the building administrator as an instructional leader are essential to the reading and mathematics achievement of students, particularly low-achieving students. Administrators must assure that teachers acquire many of the same skills and competencies that they have in the areas of knowledge of family, socio-economic history, factors contributing to at-risk, academic strategies, etc. to effectively teach and understand the at-risk students. They also must assure that teachers are aware of the changing demographics and the educational impact of these changes on the system as a whole, and the classroom as an individual unit of instruction. Both building administrators and their teachers must know early identification techniques, alternate methods of assessment and evaluation, teaching strategies and methodologies, and material modifications that can enhance the learning ability of the student. Administrators must be able to develop and work with parents and community organizations, be willing to serve on committees and share information on successes and failures.

The changing school population will require each person involved with the schools to reevaluate their knowledge base as well as their personal convictions to face the challenges in the coming decades. As the person who sets the tone and pace of the school environment, it is critical that the administrator provide a positive outlook that gives both staff and students the opportunity to succeed with the at-risk student. This is the most critical emerging need—understanding self and students to assure a successful future for all involved.

There is no doubt that the next decade in Texas will be a challenging one for school leaders. As this book goes to press, the Texas Education Agency is gathering recommendations for a state-position paper on the redirection of the application process for the formula and discretionary programs described in this chapter in an effort to provide a more coordinated and integrated approach to the use of these funds in developing and administering successful programs for at-risk students in Texas. The redirection of funds will emphasize site-based decision-making and campus-improvement planning processes as they apply to at-risk students. Administrators are urged to stay in contact with TEA and other officials to ensure they have the most recent information upon which to develop and conduct programs for special population students.

References

Ambert, A. N. and Melendez, S. E. (1985). *Bilingual education.* New York: Garland Publishing Company.

Anderson, T. and Boyer, M. (1970). *Bilingual schooling in the United States.* Austin, TX: Southwest Educational Development Laboratory, 43-44, 63.

Baker, K. A. and deKanter, A. A. (Eds.) (1983). *Bilingual education.* Lexington, MA: Lexington Books.

Bilingual Education: The Unique Challenges These Students Pose to Educators Based upon Projected Demographics. A presentation given by Gloria Gallegos at the TCASE Regional Conference, October, 1993.

Cardenas, Robledo, and Waggoner. (1988). *Texas school dropout survey project: A summary of findings.* San Antonio, TX: Intercultural Development Research Association, Center for the Prevention and Recovery of Dropouts.

Cervantes, L. F. (1985). *The dropout-Causes and cures.* Ann Arbor, MI: The University of Michigan Press.

Conrath, Jerry. (1987). A new deal for at-risk students. *NASSP Bulletin,* 71, 84-88.

Fradd, S. H. and Tirknoff, W. J. (1987). *Bilingual education and bilingual special education, A guide for Administrators.* Boston: Little, Brown and Company.

Gastright, J. F. and Zulfi, A. (1988). *Dropout causes and characteristics: Do local findings confirm national data?* American Educational Research Association, 11-43.

Hodgkinson, H. (1988). *All one system: Demographics of education, kindergarten through graduate school.* Washington, D.C.: The Institute for Educational Leadership, Inc.

Leibowitz, A. H. (1980). *The bilingual education act: A legislative analysis.* Rosslyn, VA: National Clearinghouse for Bilingual Education.

McCarthy, M. M. and Cambron-McCabe, N. H. (1987). *Public school law: Teachers' and students' rights.* Newton, MA: Allyn and Bacon, Inc.

Migrant Education: A Consolidated View. (no date). Denver, CO: Interstate Migrant Education Council, Education Commission of the States.

Prasse, D. and Reschly, D. J. (1986). Larry P.: A case of segregation, testing, or program efficacy? *Exceptional Children,* 52, 333-345.

Public Law 98-511. Title VII, Bilingual Education Act. October 19, 1984.

Questions and Answers, 19 TAC 75.195, Alternatives to Social Promotion, and House Bill 1010. Texas Education Agency, Division of Program Planning, March 1988.

Randon, L. and Nora, A. (1988). Hispanic students: Stopping the leaks in the pipeline. *Educational Record,* 79-85.

Roos, P. D. (1984). *The handicapped limited English proficient student: A school district's obligation.* Coral Gables, FL: Miami University.

Saks, J. B. (1988). Minority achievement: A report on causes and cures for the performance gap. *Education Vital Signs,* 4, 9-12.

TEENS: Here Comes the Biggest Wave Yet. *Business Week,* April 11, 1994, pgs. 76-86.

Texas Administrative Code.

Texas Education Code.
Texas School Law Bulletin. (1988). Austin, TX: Texas Education Agency.
Valdivieso, R. (1987). A culture of concern for at-risk students. *Education Digest,* 29-31.
Valverde, L. A. and Robertson-Courtney, P. N. (1987). School efforts to reduce student dropouts. *Urban Educator,* 8, 51-58.
Vega, J. E. (1983). *Education, politics and bilingualism in Texas.* Washington, D. C.: University Press of America, Inc. 43-44.

Vocational Technical and Career Education

*Max E. Jobe**

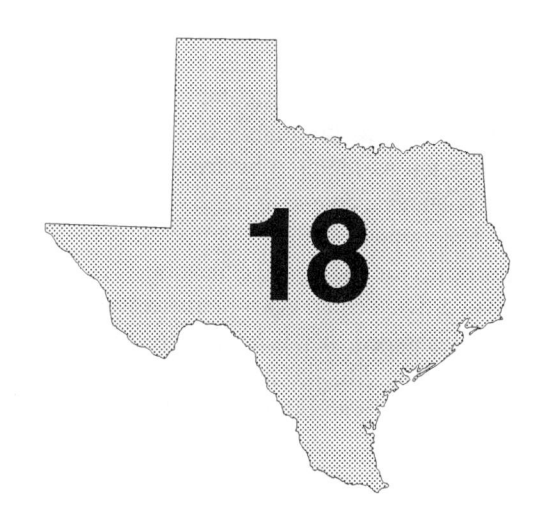

Philosophy

The history of vocational education in the United States centers around two complementary forces: the advancement of technology, and mankind's changing perceptions of himself (Thompson, 1973:27). These forces seem to be cyclical in nature, as speculation on an easier way to "the good life" leads to technological advancement, which results in more leisure time to engage in speculation and self-study, which in turn leads to further technological advancement. Each stage in the development of vocational education has been initiated by changing social conditions. The recognized disparity between "what is," the actual social condition, and "what should be," the philosophical position, seems to result in a critical technological advancement being made to fill the gap. The adjustment made by the advancement creates a new social condition, and the cycle repeats itself.

The increasing discovery that allows the technological advancement also leads to the need for a new type of education--one to ensure man's understanding of how to apply the technology. Vocational education originally emerged as the focus on man's ability to perform the physical tasks required by the new technology, and as the technology and perception cycle occurred, vocational education was shaped and directed. In short, the history of vocational education is basically a "... history of man's efforts to improve his technical competence in order to upgrade his economic position in society" (Thompson, 1973:29).

---

* Carol Z. McGnevin now at the University of Northern Colorado, authored the original text of this chapter entitled "Vocational Education" in the 1989 edition of this book. Her original work has been utilized in updating this chapter.

Differentiating between the terms "vocational education," "technical education" and "career education" is difficult. In a broad sense, vocational education is education which enables an individual to become more employable in a specific occupation. As defined by the Vocational Education Act of 1963, it included education in the areas of trades and industry, home economics, distribution, health, agriculture, and business. Individually, each of these constituted one area of the vocational program. Collectively, they constitute the complete program. Vocational education as required by federal law is preparation for occupations that require less than a baccalaureate degree.

Emerging from the 1963 Vocational Education Act and its various amendments are two main purposes for vocational education: 1) to meet local and regional needs for trained workers, and 2) to provide equal labor-market advantages for youth and adults through special programs e.g. disadvantaged, handicapped, gender minority and limited English proficiency (Thompson, 1973:307). For the most part, vocational education is concerned with the development of personal skills and attitudes, technological literacy, employability skills, occupational skills and knowledge, and career planning.

The term "technical education" connotes specific understanding or knowledge, as opposed to manipulative skill. The American Vocational Association defines technical education as:

> . . . education to earn a living in an occupation in which success is dependent largely upon technical information and understanding of the laws of science and technology as applied to modern designs, production and service (American Vocational Assoc., 1964:20).

Technical education is not clearly bounded, and vocational education is often expressed as encompassing technical education.

Although career education is rooted in the four letter word "work" it has much broader meaning and application than does vocational or technical education. Kenneth Hoyt defined career education skills "in terms of a set of general employability/adaptability skills needed by all persons in order to cope with increased rapidity of change in the occupational society" (Hoyt, 1981:14).

Historical Development

The first example of separation of academic from vocational instruction grew out of the early apprenticeship agreements of colonial America. Agreements that charged the master to teach "fundamental literacy and civic and moral responsibilities" in addition to useful employment led many masters who were unable to provide adequate non-vocational instruction ". . . to send their apprentices to evening schools for the 3 R's" (Evans, 1978:51).

In the early 19th century, the decline of apprenticeship ended vocational instruction for most American youth, as most schools' occupational instruction was limited to "the professions" and available only to the wealthy. By the 1850's, however, a few visionaries were calling for education that combined academic learning with mechanical and agricultural instruction, and in 1862, President Lincoln signed the First Morrill Act, making possible the establishment of state land-grant colleges of agriculture and engineering (Rosenberg, 1965:5). The extension of vocational education into the common schools was far more difficult because of economic considerations and the opposition of academicians until 1876, when Victor della Vos, of Moscow's Imperial Technical School of Moscow introduced his system of "instruction shops."

Featured at the 1876 Centennial Exposition in Philadelphia, the della Vos trade education program was based on four precepts: (1) analysis of the elements of the trade to be taught; (2) ordering of those elements from simple to complex; (3) use of a craftsman as teacher for group instruction; and (4) the "shop" as part of the formal school facility (Rosenberg, 1965:6).

As individualized apprenticeships were gradually disappearing because of the demand for skilled workers brought about by the Industrial Revolution, the della Vos method seemed to be exactly what was needed. New trade schools emerged, and soon the concept found its way into the public school programs as "manual training" (Rosenberg, 1965:6).

Although the della Vos system quickly became the basis for many secondary school manual training programs, manual training did not serve as the best substitute for apprenticeship needs. The primary problem was that these courses were incidental or supplementary to the primary function of the school. Thus, state and federal legislators responded to the cry for "real" vocational education by supporting "...more specific instruction in a limited number of occupational fields" (Evans, 1978:52).

During the late 1800s and early 1900s, technical institutes, trade schools, commercial and business schools and agricultural high schools began to flourish (Finch and Crunkilton, 1984:6).

The response of leading American educators was the development of the comprehensive high school, designed to serve all youth. The comprehensive high school was actually implemented in very few communities, and most secondary schools gradually drifted in the direction of emphasis on the college-bound youth.

This drift prevailed until the late 1930s, when the threat posed by the Civilian Conservation Corps and the National Youth Administration awoke the leaders of comprehensive schools to the danger of a separate school system outside their control. They responded by developing vocational programs that were to be highly effective during World War II (Evans, 1978:52). Following World War II, the drift away from vocational education began again, only to be reversed by the vocational education acts of 1963 and 1968.

Significant federal legislation in the twentieth century regarding vocational education are listed below (TEA, 1988:54-55):

1917-Smith Hughes Act—Appropriated monies for vocational education for secondary students and adults in agriculture, trades and industry, home economics and teacher training in each field.,

1929-The George-Reed Act—Provided additional funds for vocational home economics and vocational agriculture education.

1934-The George Elzey Act—Extended the provisions of the Smith-Hughes and George-Reed Acts.

1937-The George-Deen Act—Extended earlier acts to include distributive education.

1946-The George-Barden Act—Increased appropriations specified in earlier acts and increased flexibility.

1962-The Manpower Development and Training Act—Provided job training for unemployed adults.

1963-The Vocational Education Act of 1963—Extended the scope of programs to include business and office and health occupations and increased funding dramatically. The Act also authorized funds for construction of vocational education facilities.

1968-The Vocational Education Amendments of 1968—Authorized grants to help states maintain, extend, and improve existing programs and development of new programs was encouraged. There was new emphasis regarding handicapped, disadvantaged and post-secondary students and the involvement of business and industry.

1972-The Education Amendments of 1972—Created a Bureau of Occupational and Adult Education in the U.S. Office of Education.

1991-The Carl Perkins Act—Continued the emphasis of serving special needs populations by further limiting the use of Federal funds to this end.

The Vocational Education Act of 1963 reflected a change in the attitude toward vocational education. Until this point, vocational education had served the purpose of providing job skills which would afford individuals job opportunities. The Vocational Education Act of 1963 stressed that this training should provide an enrichment of the lives of people throughout their work. This attitude stemmed from a report filed by a committee designated by John F. Kennedy in 1961 to review and evaluate existing Vocational Education Acts. The panel issued a report entitled "Education for a Changing World of Work."

The conclusion of the panel was "that the vocational education programs . . . must be expanded and accelerated to train more skilled workers and to offer young people greater opportunity to develop their talents and abilities" (p. 16 of report). The panel suggested the use of the community colleges for the largest and quickest expansion of vocational education; some members thought the technical institute would be best suited for efficiency and effectiveness of vocational education.

The panel set forth three purposes of vocational education. First, it should help people enter and find a rewarding role in the workplace. Secondly, it should enable them--both economically and socially--to advance through the use of their skills. Thirdly, through the release and exercise of creative ability, their individual self-worth should increase (Wenrich, 1974:48). When these purposes were met, according to the panel, then vocational education would directly enhance the local, state, and national economic stability which sustained it.

While the Vocational Education Act of 1963 dramatically changed the purposes and scope of vocational education, the power over programs was still controlled, primarily, at a federal level. During the next five years, the states would show some independence in program development and implementation, but it wasn't until the 1970s that they accepted virtually full authority for vocational programming.

The Vocational Education Amendments of 1968, continued to focus on people and their needs. The amendments drew attention to and gave priority to people with special needs-the handicapped and the disadvantaged. While the amendments of 1968 shifted more power to the state and local units, much federal power was retained.

Texas Vocational Education

House Bill 72, enacted in 1984, directed the State Board of Education to develop both a long-range plan for public education, and a master plan for vocational education. The master plan refocused vocational education in the State of Texas. The plan is in line with the State's mission for public education and calls for all students to receive education that will enable them to live and work in a changing society. "To fulfill this mission, the plan emphasizes the need for a strong academic foundation for all students, awareness of a broad range of career opportunities, and occupationally relevant education appropriate for the Texas economy of the 21st century." (TEA, 1978:1)

The objectives of the plan for vocational education are directly tied to the goals of the Long-Range Plan for Texas Public School Education. The major thrust of the new plan is preparing students to be able to adapt to the changing environment. The plan calls for vocational education to be a supplement to academic skills, and provide the students with the opportunities to apply academic skills. All students will receive a basic academic foundation, and some students will then choose to take vocational courses. The ultimate goal is to develop an integrated curriculum exposing children as early as elementary school to the world of work and the wide range of career options available. With these principles as guidelines, the State Board of Education adopted the following definition of vocational education in Texas.

> Vocational education in Texas is designed to provide all individuals the opportunity to make informed occupational choices, determine educational needs and options, develop employability traits, and acquire marketable skills. Vocational education shall continue to be an integral part

of the total educational process. All persons should have access to high quality vocational education and necessary support services which are suited to their needs, interests, and abilities in order to benefit from such education. The vocational education system shall be accountable for high quality programs in order to ensure the most efficient use of available resources. (TEA, 1988:2)

Curriculum

The Texas State Board of Education has developed extensive guidelines for Vocational Education Programs. They are contained in the 19 TAC Chapter 75, Subchapter I. According to the Texas Education Code, 21.112(e): "all new additional and continuing vocational programs shall offer competency based instruction." Instruction must be based on the essential elements approved by the State Board of Education. A competency profile should be maintained for each student enrolled in Job Specific programs.

Vocational courses can be offered as:

Cluster course—A course designed to impart occupationally related skills that are basic to a related family of occupations.
Comprehensive course—A course designed to be exploratory in nature and provide students with a broad exposure to an entire industry.
Cooperative education course—A course designed to provide occupationally specific training. The training is planned and supervised cooperatively by the local education agency and employers. Students receive occupational and related instruction by alternating study in school with work experience in a specific occupation. A student may receive up to 3 hours credit and must be employed at an approved training station at least 15 hours per week.
Pre-employment laboratory course—A course designed to provide occupationally specific training in a school setting. The training is provided in a laboratory setting utilizing tools, equipment, and processes actually utilized in the occupation, and simulating a work environment.
Technical course—A one semester course designed to provide a concentrated focus on a specific occupational or technological area.

Subchapter I of the Texas Education Code, The Master Plan for Vocational Education (1988) identifies priorities or initiatives for vocational education in Texas. New directions for vocational education include: Principles of Technology, and "2 + 2" Programs. ("2 + 2" Programs link secondary and post-secondary courses for specific occupations. The first two years of the program would begin in high school and the last two years would be in a post-secondary institution.)

Beyond these general courses, the Plan also identifies programmatic initiatives related to twelve occupation clusters. They are:

Allied Health Cluster
Banking/Financial Cluster
Business/Office Computing Cluster
Construction Careers Cluster
Electrical/Electronics Cluster
Graphic Communications Cluster
Marketing Cluster
Merchandising Cluster
Metal Trades Cluster
Occupational Preparation Home Economics Cluster
Office Operations Cluster
Transportation Cluster

There are general and specific operational provisions and requirements for each course offered. Detailed information can be found in Chapter 75, Subchapter I of the Texas Education Code (8), The Master Plan for Vocational Education (9).

Governance

Each year the Federal Government publishes regulations for the administration of Vocational Education programs. Its primary focus is to assist the states in the delivery of quality vocational education programs through guidance (regulations) and supportive funding. The Federal Government provides money in support of the development of new programs, especially special needs populations such as the handicapped, limited English proficient, displaced homemakers, and the economically disadvantaged persons.

One of the major Federal regulations is the provision for a State Advisory Council for Vocational Education in each state. In Texas the Advisory Council serves as the group of representatives who advise the State Board of Education, the Legislature, and Governor in matters related to technical and vocational education. In addition there is a required local advisory committee to advise in the planning of the local vocational program.

The State Board of Education also serves as the State Board for Vocational Education. This organization is the State's highest ranking governing body for vocational education.

The local agencies are responsible for designing their own programs (choosing from the State published approved list of programs) of vocational education based on community need and interest. The local agency is also responsible for administering the programs, i.e. hiring of teachers, acquisition of equipment and supplies, etc., but the State provides oversight by means of periodic monitoring visits and sunset reviews.

Personnel

To teach in the vocational education program a person must have Professional Teacher Certification in a designated vocational field or be eligible for certification. In some job specific pre-employment laboratory programs such as auto mechanics, machine shop, cosmetology, etc., a person must have five years related work experience, 2 years of vocational education teaching experience (on emergency certificate) and 18 hours of college level vocational courses to become permanently certified. To teach in these same programs a person with a degree is required to have three years work experience plus the 18 hours of vocational courses to become certified. In most cases vocational teachers are required to hold a baccalaureate degree in addition to specific course requirements. Two of the goals listed in the Master Plan speak directly to vocational teachers with the skills and knowledge necessary for technological changes in their field and skills to meet varied needs of their students; the other is to develop effective methods for recruiting vocational teachers with relevant experience in business and industry.

Vocational administrators are usually chosen from the cadre of vocational teachers. Directors of Vocational Education Programs must have a Texas Supervisors Certificate in Vocational Education. This certificate requires a masters degree in education and three years teaching experience in a vocational field.

Funding

Funding for vocational education programs at the local (independent school district) level stem primarily from three sources: Federal Government, State of Texas and local community funds. Federal monies are allocated through a system of formulas developed to insure equity for all students. Funding formulas are a complex series of weighted factors multiplied by student enrollment in vocational education, special student population (e.g. handicapped, limited English speaking, academically disadvantaged) and local economic factors.

State funds for vocational education will flow to school districts on the basis of the number of contact hours generated and is weighted at 1.37 per A.D.A. contact hours as established by the State Board of Education. Local monies are allocated by the Independent School District's Board of Education based on need and commitment level. Funds used for facilities, equipment and supplies come primarily from local taxes.

Occasionally, local ISD's will apply for a "one time only" federal grant to support a specific vocational education project, or submit a proposal that has been developed cooperatively with another agency.

For more detailed information on Vocational Education Funding, see *Vocational Education and Applied Technology Funding Guidelines for School Year 1992-93,* Texas Education Agency.

Emerging Trends

The current interest in academic excellence and student proficiency in the basic skills raises some questions regarding vocational education. National studies have agreed that an essential preparation for the "world of work" is a thorough command of the basic skills in reading, writing, mathematics and science. This has placed a heavy burden on the secondary curriculum and suggests that much vocational education must be undertaken at the postsecondary level in two year colleges and technical institutes.

Further support for this philosophy is a perception that enrollment in secondary vocational courses is the "easy" way through the curriculum. In many instances "vocational education is attracting groups of students in need of basic academic skills and is unable to provide instruction to meet that need." (Lotts, 1988:307)

The attraction of vocational education to students deficient in basic skills is a "mix of perceptions of vocational education as being easy and non-academic, as simply fulfilling student expectations for their career and life roles, and as an organizational system within the schools that sorts students by background and perceived ability into curriculum areas." (Lotts, 1988:307)

The elimination of vocational education from the high school curriculum, however, may place students entering the work force upon graduation at a disadvantage. This solution also ignores the fact that many students can not or will not continue their formal education beyond high school, not to mention the large number of students that will not finish high school. The solution to this dilemma is not easy and requires the cooperative efforts of school personnel, community members and vocational educators. Strategies must be developed that would insure a blending of an academic program with a vocational program of studies.

The cycle that seems to repeat itself follows the pattern of increased emphasis on academic excellence, and a de-emphasis of the applied arts. This leads to an advanced curriculum which many students have little interest in or success with and to the establishment of separate vocational schools. Eventually there is a drift back to the comprehensive curriculum in the local high school.

The cycles tend to be directly related to the country's demand for skilled workers and paradoxically to its demands for excellence in education. Implications of the cycle are that, general education people think that vocational education is and easy course and only for those that cannot succeed in academic education, and that vocational education people feel that general educators do not truly understand the mission of vocational education, and therefore, try to minimize their influence.

The common theme in the history of vocational education to the present is diversity. There is diversity of opinion regarding the basic purpose of vocational education in the public schools; there is diversity in the quality and status, the expectations and outcomes, and the instructional approaches of the programs themselves. Much of this diversity is not bad, for differing local, district, and state needs must be met as differing needs of students must be accommodated.

In the view of the National Commission on Secondary Vocational Education, quality is the major issue in vocational education (NCSVE, 1985:23). Because of its diversity and complexity, vocational education--more perhaps than any other discipline--will need cooperation of many groups, both public and private, in and out of education in order to achieve the quality it needs. The force behind the future will have to be concern for the student, for every youngster in America has a right to the opportunity to experience the best of vocational as well as academic education. In order for that to happen, several changes will need to take place:

1. Course offerings will need to span both academic and vocational areas, with all students allowed to choose from that comprehensive set of offerings and activities.
2. Educational equity must be guaranteed by school officials, and must not be compromised to achieve a false sense of excellence.
3. An integrated curriculum must be developed that addresses the basic "academic" skills as well as general employability skills and does not restrict students' participation in vocational education courses.
4. Local school officials must take responsibility for the image of vocational education and not allow vocational programs to be a "dumping ground."
5. Schools must involve business, labor and the community, and business and labor must make an effort to work with schools to improve what goes on in the classroom.

The above ideas would offer much support to floundering vocational education programs, both statewide and on a national level.

The cost of state-of-the-art technology is staggering, as are the costs of continually training personnel to stay even with the latest advancement.

As the cost of providing quality educational programs increases, creative approaches must be sought to keep the programs alive. To accomplish this, Texas has engaged in regional planning endeavors. Regional planning brings together the best minds in business and education to plan vocational education across communities.

Cooperative planning between school districts, community college districts, technical institutes, universities and other agencies delivering vocational educational services can result in effective vocational programs. "The ultimate goal is to increase the efficiency and cost effectiveness of matching and delivery of training with jobs that are, and will be, available" (TEA, 1987:50). This reduces the duplication of expensive programs. Without this type of planning, vocational programs may suffer.

One concept that is rapidly becoming popular nationally and in Texas is the "techprep" concept. Although it is a developing concept and there is little agreement in what is tech prep, it generally refers to an articulated program between high school and a postsecondary institution. The program usually begins in the junior year of high school; includes an excellent foundation of applied academics and culminates in an associate degree. There are other versions that may start in earlier grades and some culminate in a baccalaureate degree.

With the changing role of the school in society, and the fiscal problems facing the State of Texas at this time, it is difficult to pinpoint exactly what should and shouldn't fall within the realm of the school walls. Business and industry must work cooperatively with local school districts in this end. A continued creative approach must be taken to devise a way of providing all students with the education and training necessary to be a productive citizen and fulfilled person in the 21st century.

All persons concerned about providing an educational program which will meet the needs of all students must work together to devise a system that is both fiscally and educationally sound.

References

American Vocational Association. (1964). *Definition of Terms in Vocational, Technical, and Practical Arts Education.* Washington, D.C.: American Vocational Association

American Vocational Association. (April, 1992). *Tech Prep How It's Changing Vocational Education.* Washington, D.C.: American Vocational Association.

Evans, Rupert N. and Herr, Edwin. (1978). *Foundations of Vocational Education.* Columbus, Ohio: Charles E. Merrill Publishing Co.

Finch, Curtis R. and Crunikilton. John R. (1984). *Curriculum Development in Vocational and Technical Education.* Newton, Massachusetts: Allyn and Bacon, Inc.

Hoyt, Kenneth B. Career Education (1981). *Where It Is and Where It Is Going.* Salt Lake City Utah: Olympus Publishing Company,

Keller, Franklin J. (1948). *Principles of Vocational Education.* New York, New York: D.C. Heath and Company.

Lazerson, Marvin and Grubb, W. Norton. (1974). *American Education and Vocationalism.* New York, New York: Teachers College Press.

Lotts, Linda. (1988). *"Vocational Education: Encyclopedia of School Administration and Supervision."* Phoenix, Arizona: Oryx Press.

The National Commission on Secondary Vocational Education. (1985). *The Unfinished Agenda: The Role of Vocational Education in the High School.* Columbus, Ohio: The National Center for Research in Vocational Education.

Rosenberg, Jerry M., ed. (1965). *New Conceptions of Vocational and Technical Education.* New York, New York: Teachers College Press.

Texas Education Agency. (1982). "State Board of Education Rules for Secondary Vocational Education (1982-1987)." Austin, Texas.

Texas Education Agency. (1988). *"The Master Plan for Vocational Education."* Austin, Texas: Texas

Texas Education Agency. (1987). *Career Opportunities in Texas: A Master Plan for Vocational Education.* Austin, Texas.

Texas Education Agency. (1992). *"Vocational Education and Applied Technology Funding Guidelines for School Year 1992-93."* Austin, Texas.

Thompson, John F. (1973). *Foundations of Vocational Education.* Englewood Cliffs, New Jersey: Prentice-Hall, Inc.

Wenrich, Ralph C. and Wenrich, J. Wilham. (1974). *Leadership in Administration of Vocational and Technical Education.* Columbus, Ohio: Charles E. Merrill,

Community Education

Clifford L. Whetten

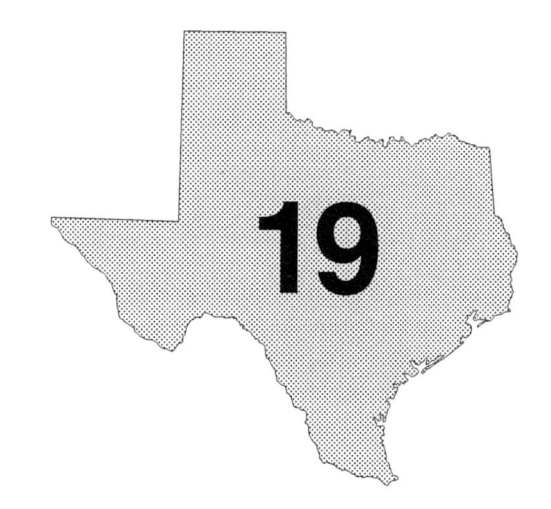

Restructuring School/Community Outreach
In the industrial society, the school, as an institution, existed largely outside the mainstream of the community. Today we understand the need for grater community involvement and integration. The restructured school will have more parents involved as participant/consumer decision makers. Schools, instead of being isolated, will be community human resource development institutions. Businesses, far from being an observer, will become a collaborator, and the school will integrate education and become the center of a learning community in which citizens of all ages engage in the continuous learning of the knowledge and skills needed for their well-being in the information society.
McCune, S. (1988)

Lifelong involvement in education becomes increasingly important as changes in society demand updated knowledge, new skills, and provide additional leisure time. People of all ages are looking for opportunities with in financial and geographic reach which will help meet their personal needs and interests for self and community improvement. Such needs and interests include leisure, social, and self-improvement skills and resources, action groups to improve communities, family participative activities, expansion of social services, cultural events, integration of community life into the basic education program and increased access and extended use of school and other public facilities. Community Education utilizes a democratic process by which people learn to identify and solve common problems, and it serves as a means for personal and group improvement.

In community after community, from Sherman to San Elizario, and from Dumas to Weslaco, Community Education since 1971 has been bringing Texas school personnel and community members together to discover that problems can be solved by mobilizing local resources under local control. A confidence that communities and schools can work together is beginning to return to public education, at a time when such confidence in local problem solving initiatives is needed most.

Defining and Describing Community Education

Because of its many dimensions, Community Education is difficult to define in just a few words. In fact, most have found it easier to describe this concept rather than to try to define it.

Community education can be described as "A school serving persons of all ages (children, youth, and adults). It provides opportunities for members of the community to plan together and use all available human and physical resources to develop their full potential. The curriculum and activities evolve from the basic wants and needs of the people served. Community Education programs provide opportunities for people to pursue academic, social, physical, recreational, cultural, health and vocational education programs." Although communities are different, each has resources that can be identified and mobilized to obtain solutions to these problems.

Inherent in the community education philosophy is the idea that education is a continuous lifelong process. The community education school opens its doors after regular school hours, on weekends and during summers, where people of all ages can gather to learn, enjoy themselves, and be involved in community problem solving efforts. Hence a multi-million dollar facility which normally lies idle most of the time, through community education, makes maximum use of the taxpayers' dollar. Programs commonly offered by community education schools include:

- defensive driving
- English as a second language
- GED high school equivalency
- adult basic education
- recreation
- academics
- wellness programs
- literacy
- staff development
- training for school personnel
- vocational training
- dropout prevention

The community education school emphasizes making what goes on in the classroom more relevant to what goes on in the students' community environment. Community resources are used to enrich and enhance the K-12 curriculum, making the school a living-learning laboratory.

In addition, through community education, new programs and state-required inservice training can be implemented. A typical community education/K-12 program might include:

- parental involvement to strengthen
- reading skills
- summer school
- K-12 enrichment
- SAT/ACT preparation
- Reading is Fundamental (RIF)
- after-school tutorials for at-risk youth
- recreation
- alternative schools
- school volunteers
- summer library
- gifted and talented program
- McGruff Safety Program
- drug/alcohol education
- latchkey programs
- school/community partnerships

Community Education As A Process for Building Learning Communities

Community education is a historically documented process for building learning communities. It has been around for a long time, but it has not been well-publicized in mainstream education circles.

Community education is both a philosophy of education and a model for systematic community development efforts. Decker and Romney (1992) state that the process has four major components:

1. Provision of diverse educational services to meet the varied learning needs of community residents of all ages;
2. Development of interagency cooperation and public-private partnerships to reduce duplication of efforts and improve effectiveness in the delivery of human services;
3. Involvement of citizens in participatory problem solving and democratic decision making; and
4. Encouragement of community improvement efforts that make the community more attractive to both current and prospective residents and business.

In the community education model (Figure 19.1), the school functions as a support center for a network of agencies and institutions committed to meeting community needs and expanding learning opportunities for all members of the community. The concept stresses broad-based community participation in problem solving and democratic decision making. The emphasis on broad-based involvement in educational reform is particularly important at a time when less than 25 percent of American households have school-age children and, therefore, often have little contact with schools. This focus on involvement is grounded in a well-known trait of human nature-people develop commitment to, and a sense of ownership in, causes, organizations, and activities for which they have some responsibility.

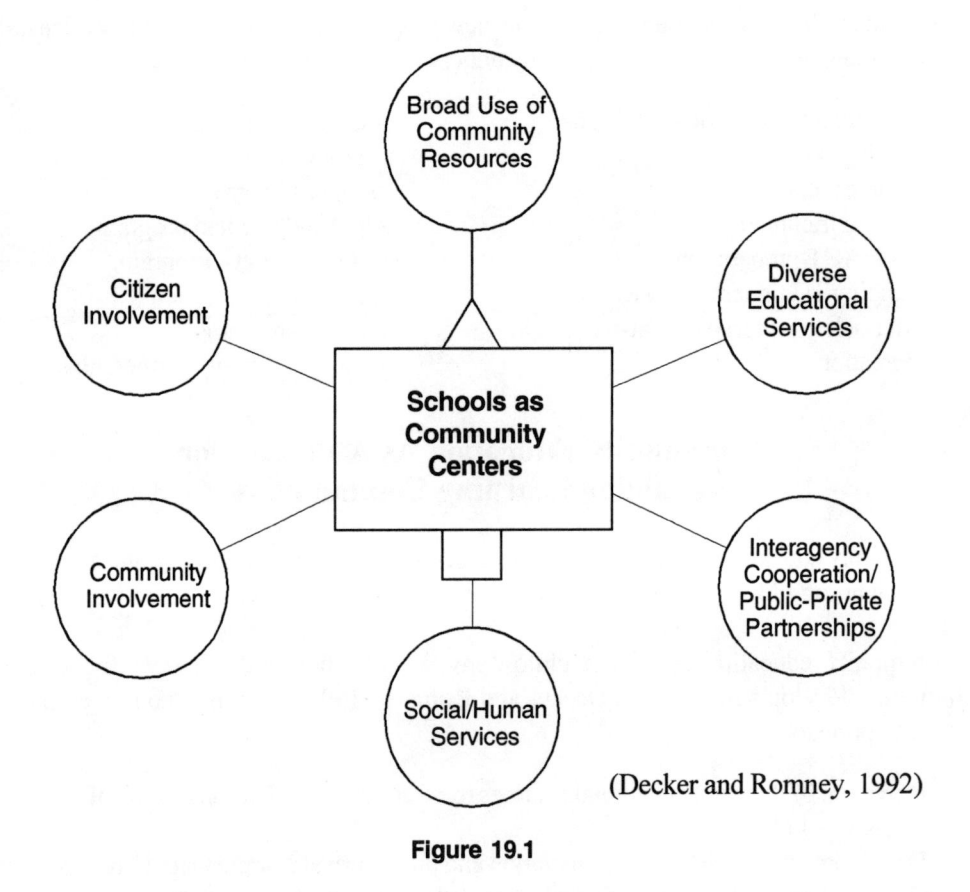

Diagram: "Schools as Community Centers" connected to: Broad Use of Community Resources, Diverse Educational Services, Interagency Cooperation/Public-Private Partnerships, Social/Human Services, Community Involvement, Citizen Involvement.

(Decker and Romney, 1992)

Figure 19.1

The School as a Learning Center for All Ages

Community education is a concept that stresses an expanded role for public education and provides a dynamic approach to individual and community improvement. Through cooperation and communication, the schools become community education schools which are operated in partnership with civic, business and lay leaders, as well as community, state and federal agencies and organizations. These community education schools offer lifelong learning and enrichment opportunities in education, recreation, social and related cultural services with the programs and activities coordinated and developed for citizens of all ages, ethnic backgrounds and socio-economic groups.

Community education schools are open the entire year, 18 hours a day or longer. They become places where people of all ages gather to learn, to enjoy themselves and to be involved in community problem solving efforts. Although activities and programs are provided through school facilities, they are not limited to the school building itself because the school extends itself into the community. Agencies, factories, businesses, and the surrounding environment become part of the learning laboratory.

The following chart contrasts the traditional school's use pattern with the community education school's:

TRADITIONAL SCHOOL VS.	COMMUNITY EDUCATION SCHOOL
children (K-12)	all ages
9 months/year	12 months/year
6-7 hours/day	12-18 hours/day
5 days/week	7 days/week
1/3 of potential	full potential
Taxpayers get ¼ return on investment in school. plus, paying for many other duplicated services	Taxpayers get full return on investment in school, plus interest through more and better organized services
	(Decker, 1990)

Community education, which provides the means for bridging the gap between the school and the community to solve individual and community problems, results in a community-centered program based upon local needs and resource, as they affect the lives of everyone.

What gives community education its individuality is an ability to mobilize the untapped physical and human resources of a community. People of all ages and backgrounds work together on the educational, cultural, vocational, recreational, and human services concerns of area residents. When community members have meaningful involvement in decisions that affect them, their support for educational experiences is enhanced. One of the greatest potentials of community education is to improve two-way communication and to build trust and understanding with the community (Whetten and Pounds, 1983).

Development of Community Education in Texas

The community education concept as described earlier, had its beginnings in Texas with the establishment of the Center for Community Education at Texas A&M University in 1971. The Center was jointly founded by Texas A&M University, Department of Educational Administration and the Charles Stewart Mort Foundation of Flint, Michigan. Seed monies were provided by the Mort Foundation, through the Center for Community Education, to local Texas school districts interested in piloting the concept

In April of 1972, the State Board of Education approved a position statement on Community Education and later designated it as one of the developmental priorities. During that same year, funding for piloting Community Education programs was initiated by the Division of Adult

Education, Texas Education Agency. In 1974, The Texas Association of School Boards indicated its support for the Community Education concept in Resolution Number 1. This was soon followed by the organization of the Texas Community Education Association.

From 1975 through June of 1987, there was continuous funding from the Texas Education Agency, Division of Adult and Community Education, for both Developmental Community Education Programs and ongoing Community Education Programs. This also included funding to the Center for Community Education at Texas A&M University to develop materials and train local community educators. Community Education received major recognition and support with the passage by the 64th Legislature of Senate Bill 350. This bill authorized Foundation School Program money for Community Education personnel at the school district level in the amount of $1.5 million annually (Whetten and Pounds, 1983).

In 1986 the Texas Community Education Advisory Council Association was organized to provide grass-roots level input and direction to Community Education. In keeping with a most basic tenet of the Community Education concept of lay citizen involvement, this newly formed association has added new vitality to the Community Education movement.

Although the recent educational reforms have resulted in a temporary loss of state funds for Community Education, such funding was around long enough for school districts to pilot the concept and learn, first-hand, that it is and can be a vehicle or method to enlarge and complement other educational programs, improve school-community relationships, reduce vandalism, increase average daily attendance and increase citizen support for bond issues and other programs. Each year more than one million Texans enroll in a Community Education class or activity.

The loss, in June of 1987, of state funding for Community Education did not have the dramatic effect which many thought it would have. In May of 1987 there were 112 Texas school districts with TEA recognized Community Education Programs, most of whom were receiving partial state funding for salaries of local Community Education Directors. At present, 120 school districts remain firmly committed to the concept, retaining their programs.

The State Board of Education has recently reaffirmed its commitment to Community Education by including a long-range plan for Adult and Community Education in its Long-Range Plan of the State Board of Education for Texas Public School Education.

Steps for Establishing a Community Education Program

Inherent in the Community Education philosophy is the idea that programs, activities and projects should be reflective of the expressed needs and interests of the community residents. There is no one model of Community Education that works in all communities. However, over the years, certain general indicators or steps, when followed, have been shown to produce effective results. The following steps are therefore offered on the basis of the author's involvement and observation over the past fifteen years in assisting communities in developing Community Education. Successful programs take from six months to one year of careful planning and preparation before actually initiating steps of implementing classes and activities.

Step I: Requesting Awareness Assistance

There are several sources available to assist school districts interested in establishing a Community Education Program. Because of the relative permanence of location and personnel, it is suggested that interested school districts contact either the Center for Community Education at Texas A&M University (409-845-2620) or Division of Adult and Community Education Programming, Texas Education Agency (512-463-9448). Both institutions have qualified personnel who will go out to the school district, free of charge, to do awareness training.

Of course, Community Education Directors from neighboring school districts are also ideal for awareness training. Most are more than anxious to help "spread the good word."

Step II: Organize a Steering Committee

This committee should not be mistaken for the Community Education Advisory Council. Its primary purpose is to conduct a feasibility study of interest in community education and plan and carry out details to initiate the process. Such a committee should be comprised of community residents and school personnel who are well known in the community and who have experience in community involvement activities. Their charge is to determine if community education is good for the community and get on with the implementation.

Step III: Organize Awareness Meetings

An in-depth understanding of the community education concept and how a community education program would affect both lay citizens and school personnel is crucial to the success of the program. All must understand the implications of adopting such a program in terms of building use, materials and equipment needed, financing and staffing.

Such awareness meetings should include, but not be limited to, the following:

- Present the concept of community education to the school system leadership.
- Have school principals discuss the concept with their school faculties and staff, emphasizing the implications of after-school use of classroom facilities and equipment.
- Meet with the local teacher's organization to develop their support for community education.
- Meet the community residents to inform them of community education and seek their support.
- Conduct a community-wide agency awareness and involvement program to inform and seek assistance from all agencies.
- Arrange for the steering committee to visit an on-going community education program.

Awareness and training films and kits are available from the Center for Community Education at Texas A&M University and the Division of Adult and Community Education Programming, Texas Education Agency.

Step IV: Secure a Commitment from the Local School Board

It is assumed that Steps I, II, and III above will have been accomplished because of the commitment of the chief administrative school officer. However, it is equally important to obtain a formal resolution in support of community education from the school board. Such a resolution serves to legitimize a program which is "different" from all other programs going on, at the school.

Step V: Hire a Director of Community Education

As early as possible in the initiation process, a director should be employed. The main responsibility of the director is the coordination of the overall project.

In order to be successful, the director should have maturity, initiative, administrative experience, be familiar with the community and be resourceful.

There is a tendency by some persons to want to employ the director on a half-time basis. If at all possible, this should not be done. When this occurs, the director usually teaches a class until 3 o'clock or is at home in the mornings, and then attempts to administer the project beginning in the late afternoon. This takes the director away from the telephone, away from personal contacts and away from the program. If community education is to be a total involvement procedure within the community, it is difficult to accomplish by a person who is assigned to other duties (Berridge, 1973).

The Director of Community Education should attend both pre- and in-service training offered by the Center for Community Education at Texas University. At such training sessions, the director will become familiar with materials, processes, and procedures for implementation of the so-called "minimum elements for a successful community education program."

Step VI: Financing Community Education

What does it cost to initiate a community education program? How much does it cost to operate programs? Where does one get the money to staff? How is the program supported over the years?

These are typical questions asked by school districts and communities wishing to initiate community education. Financing is a major concern—one which must be dealt with; however, initial planning should not be restricted because you do not have the funds "in the bank."

The key to fund raising is selling the concept of community education prior to asking for funds. A budget should be established early in the planning. However, the funding aspect should not be fully discussed until the potential of community education is explored by the community. The key is to first sell the concept—then sell the budget.

The cost of community education varies with each community and no exact figure can be quoted. In preparing a working budget, however, several categories need to be considered and decided upon. These categories are: (1) Administrative costs and (2) Programming costs.

Administrative Costs.

The proposed budget would include such entries

- *the director's salary*—usually determined by computing a teacher's base + experience + advanced degrees + a time differential + three additional months' salary.
- *part-time supervisor's wages*—an hourly wage based on the local rate paid in the community. Eater your own estimated number of hours.
- *secretarial salary*—often part-time or shared, initially, however, this usually develops into a full-time position.
- *office supplies and equipment*—projected on local needs and experience. Most can be donated.
- *telephone*—(may be in-kind) projected on local experience.
- *travel*—in-town and out-of-town budget. The director will use a car extensively and will also need to be reimbursed for out-of-town professional meetings and training.

Programming Costs.

In most communities programs are self-supporting. Fees charged participants are determined to cover instructors' costs and in some cases, a portion of the overhead costs. Instructional costs vary from subject to subject and from community to community--you will need to determine the fees to be assessed. Often times a flat fee is charged for all programs usually results in a surplus which can be used to enhance other phases of the program. As a rule of thumb, $1 per contact hour is used. The proposed budget for programming would include:

- *instructors' salaries*—computed locally—usually covered by student enrollment fees.
- *heat, air conditioning, lighting costs*—usually an in-kind contribution by the school district.
- *janitorial costs*—may be in-kind or paid from initial funds or student fees. The cost usually is derived from overtime pay.
- *rental of facilities*—no charge to community education sponsored programs. Local institutional rules and regulations must be followed in determining the types of activities acceptable.

Generally, the costs for initiating a community education program lie in the administrative or personnel area. Programming should be self-supporting (A Community Education Resource Manual, Texas A&M University, 1992,)

Funding Sources.

Until June of 1987, there had been state funding for community education to pay a portion of the local community education director's salary. However, since that time, local school districts have had to provide for the entire administrative costs of community education. Resourceful community education directors have been successful at securing funds from the following sources, to supplement both Administrative and Programming Costs:

- Foundations
- Business and Industry
- Adult Education
- Agencies
- Service Clubs
- Churches
- United Way
- Course Fees
- Local Government
- Job Training Partnership Act
- Fund Raisers

Step VII: Organize a Community Education Advisory Council

Community education espouses the idea that effective citizens organizations are important means for citizens to be able to participate and have input in those decisions which affect them. As citizens become involved, a climate of mutual respect can result in improved school-community relationships.

Advisory councils, states Nance (1975), can provide a strong link between established decision-maker and the diverse needs and wishes of the aggregate of citizens in whose interest the councils work. Councils can serve as a feedback mechanism which will ensure that citizens will be aware of changes and can analyze situations to better be able to organize programs to effectively deal with situations before they become problems. Here the concern is not merely with the appointment of a group of people to consider the implementation of various educational programs. The main goal is to establish a mechanism by which citizens will begin to analyze their situation and then determine future directions.

Responsibilities

While the ultimate responsibility for most areas of school policy is determined by state law and the board of education, community education advisory councils can and should play an important role in assessing of policies, programs, activities, and functions of the schools. They can also participate in the assessment of all kinds of needs, the establishment of priorities, and offer other advice on the resource needs of the school and the community.

Composition and Size.

The membership of each council should be representative of all facets of the community including profession, geographic location, ethnicity, gender and community groups and organizations.

The size of each council should be determined by each council at the local level. The number of representatives for each group on the council should also be determined at the local level. Optimally, a council should have a minimum official membership of fifteen (15) people and a maximum official membership of thirty (30).

Selection of Council Members and Term of Membership.

Council members should be either elected, appointed, or otherwise selected by their respective groups and any combination of these methods is acceptable. Initially, council members are usually appointed. However, once the council is ongoing either the administrative staff at the local school level, community education director or district level administrator should select or appoint council members--other than their own respective administrative representatives.

The terms of membership for council members should be structured on a "staggered" schedule. Thus, some members should serve one-year terms, while others will serve two, and possibly three-year terms. This method will ensure that there will not be complete change in council membership during any given year. However, this does not imply that a member might be denied from serving more than one term.

Council Training.

Councils should receive, from the Director, the training necessary for understanding their role in the successful implementation of the community education program.

Step VIII: Conduct a Community-wide Needs Assessment

The purpose of community education is to better utilize all resources of a community, human and material, so that individuals can improve their life circumstances and so that the total community environment can be optimized toward meeting individuals' wants and needs. The primary purpose of surveying a community is to identify the wants and needs of the people whom the community education process is intended to serve. Once the survey has been planned and conducted and the results tabulated, carefully assessed, and the needs prioritized, the community education director then works diligently to initiate those programs, in conjunction with various agencies and organizations outside the public school sector, which will best guarantee fulfilling identified wants and needs.

Surveying the community is one very valid step in the community education process. However, the director should not overlook a more important return for his/her efforts. This return deals with the positive contribution made to the new community education program, the school system, and the citizens themselves, as a result of the mechanics of surveying. Specifically, the sense of community that takes place between organizers, surveyors, and community residents suddenly emerges as a unifying force within the community. If one examines the transaction of knowledge passed from neighbor to neighbor concerning something new and exciting that is about to happen in their community when the local public schools act in cooperation with other agencies, one can quickly see a grassroots level of awareness developing towards community education.

The author believes that the results of the survey and subsequent action taken to initiate programs are secondary to the positive public relations that have been developed in the community between the sponsors of community and the local residents. Community education directors should carefully consider all phases of organizing and conducting a community-wide survey. They should constantly keep in mind that those citizens who are volunteering their time to become involved can well be the beginning of a firm foundation of support for community education as it becomes a way of life in their community (Stark, 1978).

Tips to Successful Surveying.

It should be remembered that each community must develop its own survey styles, methods, and procedures. Also, the types of surveys developed for use in one neighborhood may be entirely different from those developed for another neighborhood in the same community. Socioeconomic status, racial background, literacy, etc., are all factors which should be considered when a survey is initiated and implemented. Ten short tips for successful surveying are:

- Determine what you want to find out.
- Write and refine the questions. Be sure you ask simple, clear questions.
- Avoid the open-end questions because they are hard to tabulate.
- Test the questions on a select number of the audience you intend to sample.
- Draw the sample. The number 384 from any population will give you 95% reliability. Be sure and draw alternates.
- Train the interviewers. Have each one interview the other.
- Set a deadline to complete the survey.
- Tabulate survey results using data processing or hand tabulation.
- Report the results widely.
- Send thank you notes to all who participated.
- Act on the findings . . . surveys cannot be taken for show.

Step IX: Conduct an Assessment of Community Resources

WHY?

A major problem in today's complex and specialized society is providing a means whereby individuals and communities can identify their problems and seek practical solutions to them. A challenge in community problem solving is to achieve effective utilization of human, physical, fiscal and services resources for both individual needs and improvement of the total community. Community resources in the following areas should be identified: (1) human resources including: school, agency, business, organization personnel, and community members; (2) physical resources including: buildings, land, and equipment that might be utilized in the program; (3) fiscal resources including: budget allocations, fees, donations, grants, etc., which could be used in the program process of community education; (4) services resources including: social, health, recreational, cultural, enrichment, educational, which exist in the community.

HOW?

Information gathering forms can be completed by various organizations and individuals in the community. A personal visitation is usually the most effective method of obtaining the desired information. This gives you a chance to explain the purpose of your program and to answer any questions.

After data is compiled from the information loans, brochures and/or resource manuals can be developed for dissemination to the community. The community education coordinator can also develop, from this data, a community resources profile chart for quick reference and ease in matching resources to age levels, groups and interests (A Community Education Resource Manual, 1983).

Step X: Plan Programs and Services

Planning is a fundamental process by which people approach current and anticipated issues, with the intent of bringing change toward commonly desired outcomes. "Planning is an activity in which people engage to make the future better than the present. It is a social activity; and, therefore, it should be performed *with* people, not *for* people" (Young, 1978). The planning process is applicable to any system of program development. It provides the framework on which a group builds their programs and activities. Throughout the process, needs are identified; goals, objectives and strategies implemented; and results evaluated.

A comprehensive community education plan should make use of the human, physical and financial resources of the total community in order to allow maximum opportunity for individual and community development. Such a plan should incorporate goals and objectives which incorporate the following areas related to programming in community education:

1. Providing opportunities in cooperation with existing agencies whereby the educational, vocational, a vocational, social and cultural needs of neighborhood families and individuals of ages and backgrounds may be met on a year-round basis.
2. Maximizing the use of existing resources in providing a comprehensive community education program to the community residents.
3. Fostering the development of community cohesiveness, responsiveness and identity among the residents of the community neighborhoods so that they might establish a system of mutual support and interest in community issues and problems.
4. Developing the mutual understanding, cooperation and involvement between public schools and the community.

Step XI: Implement and Operate Programs and Services

Implementation of the preceding steps usually takes from 6 months to a year. It has been the author's observation that those who shortcut these steps, thus failing to lay a solid foundation with community support, usually end up frustrated and in other positions within a year or two.

The community education director will need to be concerned with the following areas which relate to programs and services: (1) Program planning, (2) Promotion, Publicity, Interpretation and Public Relations, (3) Recruitment and Certification of Staff, (4) General Administration, (5) Training and Supervision of Professional Staff and of Council, (6) Coordination and Cooperation With Outside Agencies, (7) Evaluation of Program, and (8) Professional

Step XII: Evaluate Programs and Services

The evaluation of community education programs and processes is a matter of determining whether or not the objectives have been met through the activities which were implemented to meet identified needs. If, for example, the needs have not been met, evaluation should tell where the process broke down, and what steps must be changed or modified to meet the objectives.

It is impossible to isolate evaluation from other community education processes. Evaluation must be an ongoing activity which permeates awareness, assessment, program development and other community education activities. As is true with community education processes, citizen involvement should be sought. The benefits of such involvement include at least the following: (1) as a result of their involvement in the evaluation process, community residents arc more likely to fill out evaluation instruments, as well as encourage others to do the same, thereby generating more valid data; (2) the evaluation process will be viewed less as a spying activity and more as a developmental process; (3) the community education philosophy, relative to citizen involvement, will not be violated; (4) there will be a greater likelihood of the community accepting and utilizing the evaluation results in modifying the community education program; and, (5) community residents will learn by taking part in the evaluation process (Nevada State Dept. of Education, 1977).

```
┌─────────────────────────────────────────────────────┐
│  GOALS                                              │
│    ↑↑   DESIGNS                                     │
│    ││    ↑↑    IMPLEMENTATION                       │
│    ││    ││     ↑                                   │
│    ││    ││     │         RESULTS                   │
│    │└────┘└─────┘            │                      │
│    └─────────────────────────┘                      │
└─────────────────────────────────────────────────────┘
```

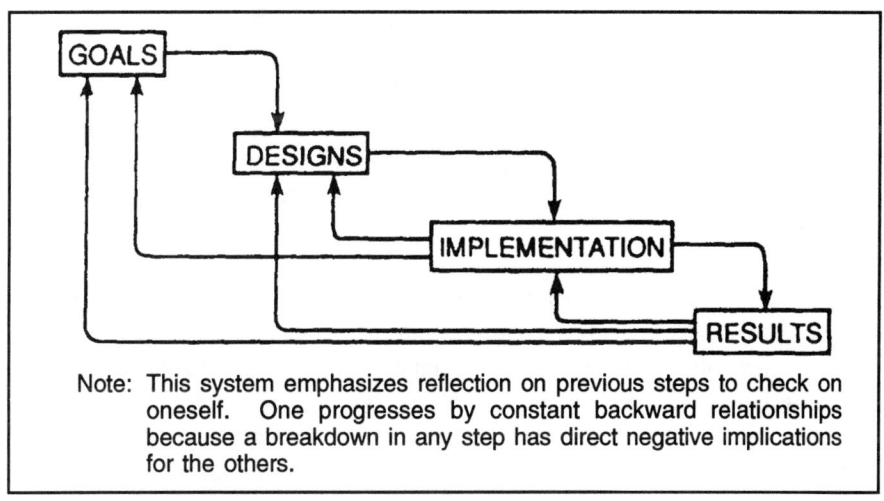

Note: This system emphasizes reflection on previous steps to check on oneself. One progresses by constant backward relationships because a breakdown in any step has direct negative implications for the others.

Figure 19.2. Process feedback system.

Santellanes, (1976) Northwest Center for Community Education, Eugene, Oregon, suggests a feedback system which will provide the community group with information relative to the impact that their efforts have on the community. This feedback system (Figure 19.2) is vital because it provides the basis for program decisions, its sophistication may vary from face-to-face conversations with community residents to periodic community attitudinal surveys. The method will depend on its applicability in any given community.

This particular model emphasizes four basic ingredients:

1. Goals: Community education coordinators should facilitate the development of goals for the community education program. This should be accomplished by a representative group of community residents interested in community improvement. Once goals are developed, a critical look should be taken at the process used in their development. The process must be evaluated to assess the extent of community involvement as well as the system used, i.e., majority vote, consensus, etc. As evaluation is a continuous process, this assessment is necessary.
2. Designs: The development of designs (activities/processes) necessary to accomplish goals is the next step. Each goal will determine the type of design most appropriate for its accomplishment. The community education coordinator should involve residents in the consideration and determination of the most appropriate course of action. Again, the process used to determine the designs must be evaluated.
3. Implementation: How are the designs to be implemented: The social climate of the community and its history will be major determinants in answering this question. Past

attempts at implementing particular designs and knowledge of the community's social climate will assist community educators and residents in their selection of an implementation strategy.
4. Results: An analytical look should be taken at the effects caused by the first three steps. Those directly affected by the intended actions should be involved in determining their effectiveness in meeting the program goals. The processes/instruments used to gather consumer reactions should also be assessed as to their effectiveness in gathering appropriate data.

If the results of a community education program are negative, an analysis of each step should be conducted. The negative results may be attributed to problems in any one of the four (4) steps. For example, a particular goal may not have been appropriate. If it was appropriate, the design (activity/process) used to accomplish it may not have been the best selection. If both the goal and design were appropriate, the implementation strategy used may not have been best suited for the target community. Finally, if all of the first three (3) steps were appropriate, the instruments/processes used to gather data may not have been relevant for gathering significant information for decisions relative to program effectiveness. An analysis of all steps (Table 19.1) will usually identify the problem and corrective measures may be taken.

Community Education and the K-12 Program

As a philosophical concept, community education transforms the idea of education from a narrow view of schooling to a much broader view of continual lifelong learning. All aspects of the community are recognized as sources in the education of people. School personnel are under increasing pressure to involve the community in the classroom. There is a greater emphasis than ever before to make what goes on in the classroom more relevant to what goes on outside the classroom.

Many community groups and individuals are being called upon to assist in supporting, developing, and implementing programs to meet the demands of educational reform. What it seems is being called for is a cooperative program of home, school and community working together.

As Decker and Decker (1988) state:

When community education is used to guide home/school/community involvement efforts, the schools are operated with a commitment to the idea that they belong to the community. Professional community educators are trained in enlisting community involvement and often provide inservice for administrators and teachers to increase their community involvement skills. Community [education] programs, based on a variety of involvement relationships and activities and community members, are the catalyst that can turn traditional schools into learning centers (p. xi).

TABLE 19.1
Process evaluation model: Questions to be answered

Goals	Designs	Implementation	Results
What are the needs and interests of the community?	What activities/ processes will accomplish goals?	What Implementation strategies are considered?	What data-gathering and analysis processes will provide significant data?
How can these needs and interests best be met?	What alternative designs are considered?	What criteria are used for strategy selection?	What data-gathering and analysis processes are considered?
What method is used in the goal-setting process?	What method(s) is used for design selection?	What selection process is used?	What data-gathering and analysis instruments are selected?
Who is involved in determining community goals?	What criteria are used for design selection?	Who is involved in the selection process?	Who is involved in the selection and data analysis process?
How are people involved in the goal setting process?	Who is involved in determining designs for goal achievement?	How are people involved in the selection process?	How are people involved in the selection and data analysis process?
	How are people involved in the design selection process?		

Decker and Decker (1988) further state that in order to accomplish the goal of greater school-community involvement in the education of youth, there needs to be a set of strategies to help them develop and nurture cooperative ventures. The following seven strategies are suggested:

1. Encourage and increase the use of community resources and volunteers to augment the educational curricula in Kindergarten through 12th grade.
2. Develop educational partnerships between the school system and schools and public and private service providers, business and industry, and civic and social service organizations.

3. Use public educational facilities as community service centers for meeting the educational, social health, cultural, and recreational needs of all ages and sectors of the community.
4. Encourage the development of an environment that fosters lifelong learning.
5. Establish community involvement processes in educational planning and decision making.
6. Provide a responsive, community-based support system for collective action among all educational and community agencies to address both current quality-of-Life issues of all citizens and specialized needs.
7. Develop a system that expedites home/school/community communication.

There is a wealth of community resources available to the perceptive classroom teacher, and these resources can enhance the classroom curriculum. Such resources are found in individuals, businesses, community agencies and organizations, and in the geography (sites) of the community. Where there is an ongoing community education program, the community education director is in an excellent position to facilitate and coordinate activities/programs utilizing these resources. Imagination is perhaps the only limit to identifying potential classroom resources.

In addition to the above mentioned resources which the perceptive teacher can use during the regular school day, in schools where there is an on-going community education program there are usually after-school programs which can also supplement the daytime program. Among others, these are: (1) Extended Day Care Services for students whose parents work and don't get home until after 5:00 o'clock, (2) Tutorial and self-help programs for At-Risk youth, (3) Enrichment Programs for the Gifted and Talented, (4) SAT Preparation Programs, and (5) Learning-to-Study Programs.

In short, a community education program goes far beyond just offering enrichment and skills training for adults in the evening. It calls for an expanded role for public education, creating within the schools, a living-learning laboratory for people of all ages.

Summary

Community education is gaining increasing acceptance throughout Texas and throughout the nation. Its ultimate value is that it can provide a community the vehicle for alternative means of achieving individual and community goals. When the total community becomes involved in identifying problems and mobilizing resources toward the solution of identified problems and needs, the ultimate value of community education becomes apparent--communities discover a reservoir of human and physical resources which can be utilized to solve community problems and concerns. While it is significant to define--a greater sense of community is enhanced when people work together to solve problems held in common.

Leaders in community education have discovered, through many years of experience, that effective community education programs have become effective because they have taken the time to carefully lay the groundwork for their program. Such planning should include the steps discussed earlier.

Community education programs are as varied as community needs and wants and are limited only by the creativity of people to plan and develop opportunities and their ability to make maximum use of agencies' and organizations' resources and human talents and skills (Decker, 1990).

. . . For today's students, we must make existing schools better and more accountable. For tomorrow's students, the next generation, we must create a New Generation of American Schools. For all of us, for the adults who think our school days are over, we've got to become a Nation of Students-recognize learning is a lifelong process. Finally, outside our schools we must cultivate communities where learning can happen.

George Bush
April 18, 1991

Resources for Technical Assistance

Some excellent resources for assisting districts interested in initiating and developing community education programs are:

Center for Community Education
College of Education
Texas A&M University
College Station, TX 77843-4226
Phone: (409) 845-2620

Adult and Community Education
Program Development
Texas Education Agency
Austin, TX 78701-1494
Phone: (512) 463-9447

National Center for Community Education
1017 Avon Street
Flint, Michigan 48503
Phone: (313) 238-0463

The Doable Dozen: A Checklist of Practical Ideas for School-Business Partnerships, 1987
National Community Education Association
801 North Fairfax Street, Suite 209
Alexandria, Virginia 22314

So You're on the Council, 1987
National Community Education Association
801 North Fairfax Street, Suite 209
Alexandria, Virginia 22314

Literacy Volunteers of America-Texas
4029 Capital of Texas Highways
South Suite 217
Austin, TX 78704-7919
Phone: 1-800-583-6000

National Community Education Association
801 North Fairfax Street, Suite 209
Alexandria, Virginia 22314
Phone: (703) 683-NCEA

Home/School/Community Involvement, 1988--Decker and Decker
American Association of School Admin.
1801 North Moore Street
Arlington, Virginia 22209-9988

Educational Restructuring and the Community Education Process,
1992-Decker and Romney
University of Virginia

School Dropouts: Patterns and Policies,
1987, Natriello
Teachers College, Columbia University
1234 Amsterdam Avenue
New York, NY 10027

Community Education: Building Learning Communities
1990-Decker and Associates
National Community Education Association
801 Fairfax Street, Suite 209
Alexandria, Virginia 22314

References

Berridge, Robert I. (1973). *The Community Education Handbook.* Midland, Michigan: Pendell Publishing Company.

Bush, George (1991). America 2000: An Education Strategy. U.S. Government Office, Washington, D.C.

Center for Community Education (1992). *Community Education Resource Manual.* Texas A&M University.

Decker, Larry E. (1990). *Community Education: Building Learning Communities.* National Community Education Association.

Decker, Larry E. and Romney, Valerie A. (1992). Educational Restructuring and the Community Education Process, pp. 7-8. University of Virginia.

Decker, Larry E. and Decker, Virginia A. (1988). *Home/School/Community Involvement.* American Association of school Administrators.

Gamble, John R. (1977). *A Process Model for Community Education Development.* Nevada Department of Education.

McCune, S. (1988). Directions for Restructuring Schools for the Future. Mid-Continent Regional Education Laboratory.

Nance, Everette E. (1978). *The Community Council: Its Organization and Function.* (8th ed., p. 20). Midland, Michigan: Pendell Publishing Company.

Santellanes, David A. (March/April 1975). "Process Evaluation in Community Education." *Community Education Journal,* p. 20-23.

Stark, Stephen L. (1978). *Conducting Community Surveys.* (3rd Ed., p. 7). Midland, Michigan: Pendell Publishing Company.

Whetten, Clifford L., and Pounds, Bill J. (1983). "Community Education: A Vehicle for Improving Education." *Texas Lone Star,* 1(6), 1, 11.

Whetten, Clifford L., (1988). "Community Education: A Vital Link to the Community." *Texas Lone Star,* 6(5), p. 16-17.

Young, Ken M. (1981). *The Basic Steps of Planning.* Community Collaborators. Charlottesville, Virginia.

Building-Level Leadership: The Principalship in Texas

Michael P. Stevens

There can be no question that the "critical attribute" with regard to school success and effectiveness is the building-level leadership. It is undeniable that the position requires enormous intellectual, emotional, and physical energy. However, being the building-level leader can, and should, be the most rewarding position in an entire school system. The position allows an unmatched opportunity to truly "make a difference" with kids.

What are the skills and behaviors that separate effective and ineffective leaders? What does an effective principal "look like?" Should the building leader be knowledgeable in all aspects of the instructional program? What about Site-Based Decision Making? This chapter will touch on these and other critical facets of being an effective principal and leader.

What Is Leadership?

Recognizing that entire courses revolve around the issues of leadership and administrative theory this discussion will be somewhat superficial, yet allow the reader to critically reflect on the skills necessary to be effective. Any discussion on leadership should start with the question—*what are the characteristics (traits and behaviors) of a true leader?* What does a leader "look like?" Is a leader judged more by her/his organizational skills and knowledge? Or is the person judged more by how (s)he treats others in the organization?

Perhaps the same skills that allow a teacher to be effective are merely carried to the principal's office. Why do students respect and work hard for a particular teacher? Most will say something to the effect—*because she cares and she will accept nothing less than the best we have to give.* In other words, the person who treats others with respect and dignity, as well as tolerating nothing less than the best a person has to give, are the ones who are most effective. People of all ages will perform well for a person who cares for them and treats them with respect.

Virtually nothing of quality is accomplished in an organization when the employees are "bossed" (Glasser, 1990). While the statement refers to students in a classroom setting, there can be no question that it also applies to the behavior in an organization. Glasser states:

> ... stimulus-response theory is wrong. When it is used to manage people, it leads to a traditional management method that I will call boss-management. Boss-management is ineffective because it relies on coercion and always results in the workers and the managers becoming adversaries. Bossing rarely leads to consistent hard work and almost never to quality work, and nowhere is this more obvious than in the schools. Managing for quality demands a new noncoercive method of management that I call lead-management.

Because of the way educators are lead, the contention above is that very little quality work is being done in our schools. People, teachers and students do not respond well to coercion and fear. The prevailing wisdom in some circles has been that managing people by "bossing" would lead to quality output in any organization. Not true. Any organization, school or industry is only as good as it's leadership. People must be led into quality (Glasser, 1990).

What are the specific traits and characteristics of an effective leader? Yukl (1989) reviews the works of R.M. Stodgill and gives us the following:

TRAITS	**SKILLS**
Adaptable to situations	Clever (intelligent)
Alert to social environment	Conceptually skilled
Ambitious and achievement oriented	Creative
Assertive	Diplomatic and tactful
Cooperative	Fluent in speaking
Decisive	Knowledgeable about group tasks
Dependable	Organized (administrative ability)
Dominant (desire to influence others)	Persuasive
Energetic	Socially skilled
Persistent	
Self-confident	
Tolerant to stress	
Willing to assume responsibility	

To clearly delineate between the concepts noted above and behaviors exhibited by effective leaders is a troublesome task. What are the affective skills and behaviors displayed by effective leaders? A partial list would include the following:

- Caring and compassionate
- Visible
- Accessible
- Uses humor
- Enthusiastic
- Personally content
- Positive self-concept
- Spontaneous
- Honesty and integrity
- Trusting
- Communication skills (verbal & nonverbal)

A close look at the skills and traits, as well as the behaviors noted, would indicate that they are the same for formal leaders and teaching staff. Effective teachers would certainly possess each of the traits and skills noted. The difference is in the way the person views her/himself and whether or not (s)he can adapt to being responsible for the entire organization, not just an integral part.

Bennis and Nanus (1985) looked in-depth at ninety effective leaders throughout the country and found the following five key skills utilized by virtually each person. They include:

1. The ability to accept people as they are, not as you would like them to be.
2. The capacity to approach relationships and problems in terms of the present rather than the past.
3. The ability to treat those who are close to you with the same courteous attention that you extend to strangers and casual acquaintances.
4. The ability to trust others, even if the risk seems great.
5. The ability to do without constant approval and recognition from others.

The difficulty in compiling lists is the tendency to prioritize what is found. In other words, to state that one behavior or skill is somehow more important than another is an unwarranted exercise. Possessing the fundamental behaviors and skills noted is likely to carry the leader through virtually any situation that might occur.

Honesty and Integrity

Among the behaviors noted earlier are those of honesty and integrity. Every survey done on leadership has concluded that honesty is one of the most critical characteristics of an effective leader (Kouzes & Posner, 1987). School boards and communities demand complete honesty. Anything less is intolerable. Consider the following:

> In every survey we conducted, honesty was selected more often than any other leadership characteristic. When you think about it, honesty is absolutely essential to leadership. After all, if we are to willingly follow someone, whether it be into battle or into the boardroom, we first want to assure ourselves that the person is worthy of our trust. We want to know that he or she is being truthful, ethical, and principled. We want to be fully confident in the integrity of our leaders. That over 80 percent of American managers want their leaders to be honest is extremely encouraging. The unfortunate news is that fewer than half of American citizens think that business executives are honest. According to a *New York Times*/CBS poll conducted in the spring of 1985, only 32 percent of the public believes that most corporate executives are honest; 55 percent think that most are not honest. There is clearly a gap between what we admire and what the public thinks it is getting. (Kouzes & Posner, 1987)

While the above refers to the business sector there is an equal lack of trust within the educational community. Whether this lack of trust is deserved is not the question--it exists. Teachers do not trust their formal leader, parents do not trust teachers, board members are not trusted by either educators or their constituents. The compelling question is—Why? Perhaps the way educators are lead causes the problems.

Rules and Policies

"Managers are people who do things right and leaders are people who do the right thing" (Bennis & Nanus, 1985). For decades managers have been in control of schools. Consequently, rules and guidelines have been developed that are supposed to cover virtually every situation that might occur. Some compelling questions might be asked with regard to rules. For example, what do rules do for an organization? Do they inhibit or promote creativity? Does an effective leader truly need a multitude of rules? Perhaps we have rules because those in leadership positions have been unwilling, or unable, to make decisions. Rules allow an organization to operate without leadership. In other words, it is conceivable that **rules are made because people in formal positions of leadership do not know how to make quality decisions.**

For example, what is done when an effective teacher wants to leave 30 minutes early once a week in order to take a graduate class? The policy states that everyone has to abide by the policy regarding the work day hours. No exceptions. What about a teacher confronted with personal problems that are not covered by any personal or professional leave policy? How about the child that has been kept home by a parent in order to take care of a younger sibling? The attendance policy clearly states that such absences are unexcused and, therefore, the student will be penalized for work not done. Is the principal going to do things right? or is (s)he going to do the right thing?

To do the *right thing* requires the leader to look past the symptom of a problem. A true leader is someone who deals with the problem itself, not just the indicators of the problem. Unfortunately, doing this requires the person to make very difficult decisions that many, not privileged to the facts of a particular situation, may attack.

Exceptions to policies are the "rule," not the exception. Rarely does a situation of any magnitude occur in a principal's office that can be easily handled with a written policy. Some of us live in a very "black-and-white" world in which we feel that virtually every situation has a simple and/or straight-forward solution.

Therefore, **people who cannot tolerate ambiguity in their lives should never consider being a school administrator.** The most concrete daily plan an administrator can make is showing up for work (Black & English, 1986). The myriad of decisions made by the building principal are, more often than not, exceptionally complex. Duke (1987) sums up the situation with the following:

> If the literature on the principalship is accurate, the role can be characterized by two trends—growing ambiguity and complexity. Ambiguity results, in part, from the fact that principals are expected to accomplish different things by different groups. It is difficult to steer a steady course through these multiple and often competing sets of expectations. And frequently, each set of expectations appears to be legitimate and reasonable. Clear choices between right and wrong are rare for principals.

Role Responsibilities

As is the case with other issues revolving around the building-level leadership, there are both formal and informal role responsibilities. To delineate exactly what is expected of a principal is virtually impossible. A look at the job description suggested by the Texas Association of School Boards found in virtually every board policy book in Texas would indicate that there is little that would be likely to occur on a campus for which a principal would not be directly responsible and accountable.

Duke (1987) lists the following key activities of a principal:

- Recruitment of talented staff members
- Carefully planned in-service education
- Informal supervision of teachers, including daily classroom visits
- Formal "clinical" supervision, including pre-observation conferences, structured classroom observation, and post-observation conferences
- Instructional support for teachers in the area of student discipline
- Coordination of school activities, with attention to minimizing the disruption of instruction
- Support for teachers in matters involving parents
- Recognition of student accomplishments

- Ensuring that teachers obtain necessary resources in a timely manner
- Coordination of school improvement and new projects
- Participation in efforts to coordinate relations between schools in the district
- Troubleshooting to determine staff and student concerns on a regular basis
- Management of "school climate"

Further the principal is asked to:

- make quality decisions that everyone will accept without question
- be an instructional leader
- attend virtually all activities associated with the school
- keep abreast of the current literature in both instruction and leadership
- maintain a positive relationship with the superintendent
- resolve all conflicts in a timely and acceptable manner
- make decisions affecting both staff and students that are beyond legal challenge
- attend and conduct staff meetings
- keep the staff apprised of "everything" that is going on in the school
- maintain a personal life that is not open to question by anyone in the community or on the staff
- establish a set of rules and guidelines for all personnel and students that will cover virtually every conceivable situation
- appraise teachers in such a manner so as not to offend anyone
- dismiss ineffective staff members
- maintain excellent personal health
- be accessible to anyone who would like to speak with the principal, and finally
- **see that every child in the school learns well what is being taught**

The job of a principal is, at times, exceptionally demanding. At first glance, a person might logically question whether or not the role is "doable."

Conflict Resolution

Because of the nature of the organization and it's mission, *conflict* among those involved is inevitable. Therefore, the principal is constantly being called upon to resolve conflict among the staff and constituents. In order to be effective people must work together well under stress, cooperate with those inside and outside the specific entity, work in close proximity with others, as well as compete with one another for reward and status (Yukl, 1989).

Being able to defuse physical confrontations among students, deal calmly and effectively with irate parents, listen to a teacher question what the principal did or did not do places the person in charge under tremendous pressure. Maintaining a calm demeanor is definitely an advantage to a building principal. There is almost no circumstance that would allow the person the option of "losing his/her cool." Even when the principal is not sure what to do in a given situation, (s)he should never let those around her/him be aware of the uncertainty. The lack of a definitive decision may cause others around to lose control of a given situation.

Formal and Informal Leaders

Ignorance of the informal power structure in any organization is very often "deadly" to the formal leader. Black and English (1986) pursue this concept with a look at "the structure that really makes the organization tick." The informal organization consists of secretaries, custodians, outsiders that are influential, etc. They refer to this informal structure as the *grapevine*. By being aware of the structure a person can be in a position to head off problems before they occur. Among their advice with regard to this extremely critical aspect of leadership is the following:

> **Split the Opposition**—Experienced school administrators facing a unique situation "shop around" for a decision maker who will give them approval if they require it. . . . The "shopper" must know who has real power and who has paper power. This knowledge is usually based on personal experience and observation.
>
> **Check the Anti's**—For every action there is a counter action. This is as true in human dynamics as physics. The street smart administrator knows that if he or she initiates an action to solve a problem, someone may take exception to it. Thus the initiative may be blocked by a "higher up" in the pyramid.
>
> **Know How High the Stakes Are**—Working the system means understanding what is important and what isn't. A school administrator who "calls in all of his or her chips" for a bucket of paint is playing "overkill." Every proposal is not of equal value or importance. One never plays an ace unless an ace is required to take the trick.

While the above is written in such a manner as to appear somewhat "cute," the advice is, however, critical to the success of any leader and the organization. The leader can often preclude some of the concern in this area by seeing that those affected in a given situation are involved.

Staff Involvement

Involving people in the process of developing the mission, decision making, goal setting, etc., has been utilized by effective leaders for centuries. Consider the following:

On Leadership

The superior leader gets things done
    with very little motion;
He imparts instruction not through many words
    but through a few deeds;
He keeps informed about everything
    but interferes hardly at all;
He is a catalyst,
    and though things wouldn't get done as well
    if he weren't there,
    when they succeed he takes no credit
    credit never leaves him.

Be still, manage things quietly,
    and keep good control over everything.

In managing the affairs of men
    let rule be entrusted
    those who meet their responsibilities
    as their very souls;
Leadership can be
    committed to that man
    who loves all people
    as he loves himself.

As for the leader at the very top,
    it is best if people barely know he exists;
Because he says very little
    his words have more value;
And when the work is done
    the people are pleased
    because they think they did it all themselves.

Lao-Tzu
6th Century B.C.

Although written over 2500 years ago, the words above tell us exactly what needs to be done in order to be effective. The concept of site-based decision making (SBDM) allows for the leader to utilize the talents of the people within the organization. People are led into making quality decisions through the art of asking appropriate questions, providing the right information, and not dictating what should be done.

With regard to this entire concept of SBDM there are several factors that should be kept in mind. First, the concept is a radical departure from past practice for a large percentage of schools. The majority of those in formal leadership positions at this time were trained as managers and, thus, they were to make virtually all decisions. Therefore, administrators and teachers alike must be trained in the art and science of sharing in the process of insuring the effectiveness of a school.

Secondly, we must keep in mind that no organization can be truly effective without a strong leader (Duke, 1987; Bennis & Nanus, 1985; Burns, 1977; et al). We should not confuse the term ''strong'' with such labels as dictatorial or autocratic. A strong leader is one who understands the role of the organization, utilizes the talents of the staff, and accepts nothing less than the best from everyone, including her/himself.

The statement has been made that the "best way to kill something good is to label it.'' We have not only labeled SBDM--it has been mandated by politicians, a true paradox. Further, a good case can be made for the fact that schools are now making bad decisions collectively (building teams), rather than individually (the principal). In order to make a quality decision an individual or group must possess one critical ingredient—**knowledge.**

Knowledge and Vision

Only within the past decade has there begun to be a true focus on instruction in schools. Until that time building administrators were more likely to be employed for the purpose of maintaining discipline. The thought at the time was that if proper discipline was maintained then learning would occur. We have found just the opposite to be true. Quality instructional programs lead to a positive atmosphere for learning and, consequently, the incidences of disciplinary problems are greatly reduced.

Vision

The term *vision* is one about which there is a multitude of literature with regard to leadership and effective schools (Duke, 1987; Sergiovanni, 1990; Bennis & Nanus, 1985). The question becomes—"How can a leader have a compelling and clear vision of an effective school if the person has no idea what an effective school looks like?" Too often formal leaders will mold a school into something they "think" is workable, paying little or no attention to the research and good practice on what is known to be true about effective schools.

For example, Carl Glickman (1991) has done extensive research and written widely on current practices and how educators do irreparable harm to students because of bad practices. How can the educational community "know" what is known about students and learning and, yet, continue to operate with the same methods and organizational structure? The answer is simple—**there is,**

and has been, a critical lack of quality leadership. There appears to be a lack of courage and conviction to do what is best for students.

The leadership of any school must be *data-driven* (Champlin, 1985). Decisions must be made on what is *known* to be true rather than what is *thought* might be appropriate. Therefore, it is incumbent on the leadership of a school to be knowledgeable. After all, the principal is referred to as the *instructional leader*. The instructional leader does not possess all the knowledge regarding the instructional program; however, there can be no question that the role of the leader is to see that learning does occur.

Involvement in Instructional Program

If instructional effectiveness and knowledge are the most critical factors related to overall school effectiveness, then what is the rationale for a building principal not becoming more involved in the instructional process? Duke (1987) contended "that many leaders unconsciously permit themselves to become absorbed in non-instructional matters because they believe they have little constructive advice to offer teachers." Excuses—such as a lack of time—are given for not working with the instructional program.

The acquisition of knowledge and skills in the instructional process presents some interesting and difficult challenges. Staff development has been an area almost totally ignored in education until the past several years. Even though schools are in the business of education—little has been to "educate" educators. Given the current structure of schools how does a principal see that the teachers and the leadership acquire knowledge?

More often than not the rationale for the lack of staff development has to do with the lack of resources (dollars). The time may have come for the educational community to decide the most appropriate places to allocate the available resources and quit complaining about the cost of staff training.

A cursory look at the issues revolving around staff development give the aspiring principal some excellent suggestions with regard to teacher training (Duke, 1987; Stevens, 1990). Further, there are a variety of ways that very worthwhile staff development can be delivered on the campus. Every group can brainstorm ways that training can be handled with little interruption to the ongoing instructional process.

When beginning the process of school improvement and staff training, questions must be asked with regard to what the staff believes about kids, what they believe about themselves, and how they will insure the training is translated into improved performance. Too often training is fragmented and concentrated with only a few and, consequently, little or no improvement occurs. The leader is charged with the responsibility of seeing that this does not take place.

Collaboration

Finally, there is an opportunity for collaboration in the area of acquiring knowledge that is not available by any other means in education. The principal should take advantage of every opportunity available to attend staff development sessions with the staff. First, this shows the staff that the leader feels that the particular training is important. Secondly, the leader learns with the staff. Learning together is rewarding and allows for appropriate discussions to occur with regard to how a particular concept might be implemented, concerns about implementation, etc. The collaboration allows the staff to develop what many consider to be exceptionally critical to any effective school—*a shared vision.*

In Retrospect

What is it really like to be a principal? Think about how many basketball games are played in a season in a high school or junior high? Attending banquets can be a pleasure. How about ARD meetings? Board meetings are, of course, always a highlight. Most principals especially enjoy three-hour PTA meetings. A principal will, more often than not, be the first one to get to work and the last one to leave. Good or bad, right or wrong, the principal is expected to attend virtually all activities associated with a particular school.

The above is not intended to scare anyone away from administration—the intent is to inform prospective administrators of the expectations associated with the position. A person entering the field must realize that, in spite of wisdom and skills, "the system can beat you down" (Black & English, 1986). However, they go on to say:

> It (the system) can erect obstacles and construct endless paper procedures with elaborate checkoff and counter checks. It can be frustrating and insensitive. Yet, every day, hundreds of school administrators in thousands of school systems make it work. They know how to 'beat' the system rather than being beaten down by it.

The person desiring to be a school administrator must ask themselves some difficult questions. What do you know about yourself? What type of person are you? How do others view you? Why are you considering being an administrator? Is your desire to be an administrator related to "making a difference?" Or is it because you are upset with someone because of your perception that you have been mistreated in the past? Are you in pursuit of power and control?

The question with regard to effective leadership has always been—**which is most important, what you know or who you are,** cognitive versus affective skills. Ponder the comments made by General Norman Schwarzkopf (Mason, 1992).

You read about how competent new leaders are. That is the wrong way to pick leaders. Leadership is a combination of competence and character. If you look at failed leaders, it is a failure of character, not competence.

In other words, what you know is not nearly as important as "who you are." People in an organization can tolerate mistakes from the leadership **if** they think that the person leading is truly trying to do the *right thing*. How many times have we heard remarks such as—"(S)he's really very knowledgeable, but his/her people skills are terrible." Leaders fail when they lose sight of the true mission of the organization and consequently, no longer trust and work well with the individuals within the organization.

Keep in mind that the people with whom everyone works within a particular organization are somewhat similar. Each has a sincere desire to have a truly effective school and to be recognized individually and collectively as professional educators *who make a difference.* By allowing those in the organization to learn and grow there will be no limit to what can be accomplished.

References

Bennis, Warren and Burt Nanus. (1985). *Leaders.* New York: Harper & Row.

Black, J.A. and Fenwick English. (1986). *What they don't tell you in school of education about school administration.* Lancaster, PA: Technomic Publishing.

Burns, James McGregor. (1978). *Leadership.* New York: Harper & Row.

Champlin, John. (1985). Remarks at Conference on School Excellence. Lubbock, TX.

Duke, Daniel L. (1987). *School leadership and instructional improvement.* New York: Random House.

Glasser, William. (1990). *The quality school: managing students without coercion.* New York: Harper & Row.

Glickman, Carl. (1991). Pretending not to know what we know. *Educational Leadership.* May, 1991.

Hanson, E. Mark. (1985). *Educational administration and organizational behavior.* Boston: Allyn & Bacon.

Kouzes, James M. and Barry Z. Posner. (1987). *The leadership challenge: how to get extraordinary things done in organizations.* San Francisco: Jossey-Bass.

Mason, Julie Cohen. (1992). Leading the way into the 21st century. *Management Review.* October, 1992.

Sergiovanni, Thomas J. (1990). *Value-added leadership: how to get extraordinary performance in schools.* New York: Harcourt Brace Jovanovich.

Stevens, Michael P. (1990). School climate and staff development: keys to school form. *NASSP Bulletin.* November, 1990.

Yukl, Gary A. (1989). *Leadership in organizations.* Englewood Cliffs, NJ: Prentice Hall.

Practical Theory in Education Administration

Frank W. Lutz

Theory, it has been said, is the most practical and useful thing one can learn. School administrators and students in school administration programs often disagree. For that matter many professors of education administration also disagree with the statement. The purpose of this chapter is to change the minds of such individuals and convince them, to paraphrase Shakespeare, "There are more things in the world than your 'philosophy' imagines." Put another way, there is more than one way to skin a cat—but some ways are better than other ways, under certain circumstances.

It is not the intent, nor is it within the scope of this chapter to tell the readers all they should know about the social sciences and the foundation they provide for the practice of education administration. There is a great deal more to know about theories in administration than can be provided here. This chapter will: (1) introduce the notion of theory in education administration, (2) provide a historical framework of such theory, (3) briefly describe the conceptual relationships of some selected theories within designated periods, and (4) illustrate a practical example demonstrating how the theory can be usefully applied.

Meaning of Theory

There are numerous definitions of theory. The American Heritage Dictionary provides two distinctively different definitions. One which is related to science and epistemology states that theory is: (1) "systematically organized knowledge applicable in a relatively wide variety of circumstance," and (2) a..."guess based on limited information or knowledge" (p. 126). This chapter rejects the latter definition as what could called an "uninformed or layman's" definition.

Theory is defined, for the purpose of this chapter, as an interrelated set of "proven" statements or hypotheses that describe, explain, account for and/or predict an empirical phenomenon. The question of epistemological "proof" will be discussed later. Additionally, there is a difference between theorizing and theory. Theorizing is concerned with hypothesis development. It does not require "proof," but it does require rigorous, empirical data collection and a relationship with some "proven" theory or theories. Theorizing is related to the concept of "Grounded Theory" (see Glaser and Strauss, 1967). It requires that the explanation or description offered is empirically observable in the "real world" and, a reasonable explanation of that phenomenon. Theorizing is not simply guessing.

History and Structure of Theory in Educational Administration

Some brief understanding that theory, or some form of non-random guessing, did not begin with the age of enlightenment is necessary to further understand that theory building and truth have not just arrived. Theory building, the search for truth, is an infinite process; however, theory building and knowing took a sharp turn with the advent of the "age of enlightenment." Such a change of direction is called a "paradigm shift," simply stated as a change in the process, the rules, the plan of scientific investigation.

In Figure 21.1, three major periods in the development of theory and science in western culture are depicted. These include (1) Pre-Positivism—the period prior to August Comte and the "age of enlightment," (2) Positivism—beginning with Comte and continuing through Bacon, Darwin, Newton, etc., and until Kuhn's 1962 publication of the Structure of Scientific Revolutions, and (3) Post-Positivism—since Kuhn, particularly such work as Chaos research. The work in education administration theory begins about the turn of the century in the period of positivism. Its movement toward a science of administration is particularly salient in the period between 1950 and the present, called in this chapter the "theory movement." Commensurate with the paradigm shift (post-Kuhn) it has been noted that theories developed in administration sometimes fail to account for empirical phenomena in organizations (e.g. one can get supplies more readily by breaking the bureaucratic rules than by following them). This has given rise to new theories (e.g. loose coupling, garbage can, etc.) in order to derive new insights and better hypotheses.

Pre-Positivism

Prior to the "age of enlightenment" knowing was a theological matter. Most knowledge was in the hands of the church and its clergy. God's "inspired word" was contained in the bible and represented ultimate truth--fairly literally stated. The earth was the center of the universe and all other things revolved around it. That is until Galileo. And Galileo faced the inquisition

```
                    MOST ED. ADMIN. THEORY
                            HERE
                             ↓
PRE-POSITIVISM ─────────→ POSITIVISM (COMTE)
(THEOLOGY)

MYSTICISM-DEDUCTIVE        WESTERN SCIENTIFIC
                           THOUGHT-INDUCTIVE

"TRUTH" IS KNOWN           TRUTH IS POSTULATED         PERIODS

Facts, data, events        * data are collected        * Classical
are organized to fit       * null hypothesis             (1890-1935)
known "truth."             * level of confidence       * Human Relations
                           * rules of data collection    (1935-1950)
                           * affect, feelings are not  * Theory Movement
                             measurable                  (1950-1980


POST POSITIVISM  →  Kuhn      CUTTING EDGE OF
PARADIGMS FAIL      Lakato    ADMIN. RESEARCH
                      ↓
                    NEW       POST-POSITIVISM          * New Movement in
                    PARADIGMS * Garbage Can              Ed. Admin. Theory
                              * Loose Coupling           (1980-present)
                              * Phenomenology
                              * Interpretive Anthropology
                              * Naturalistic Method
                              * Organizational Cultures
                              * Critical Theory
                              * Chaos Research
```

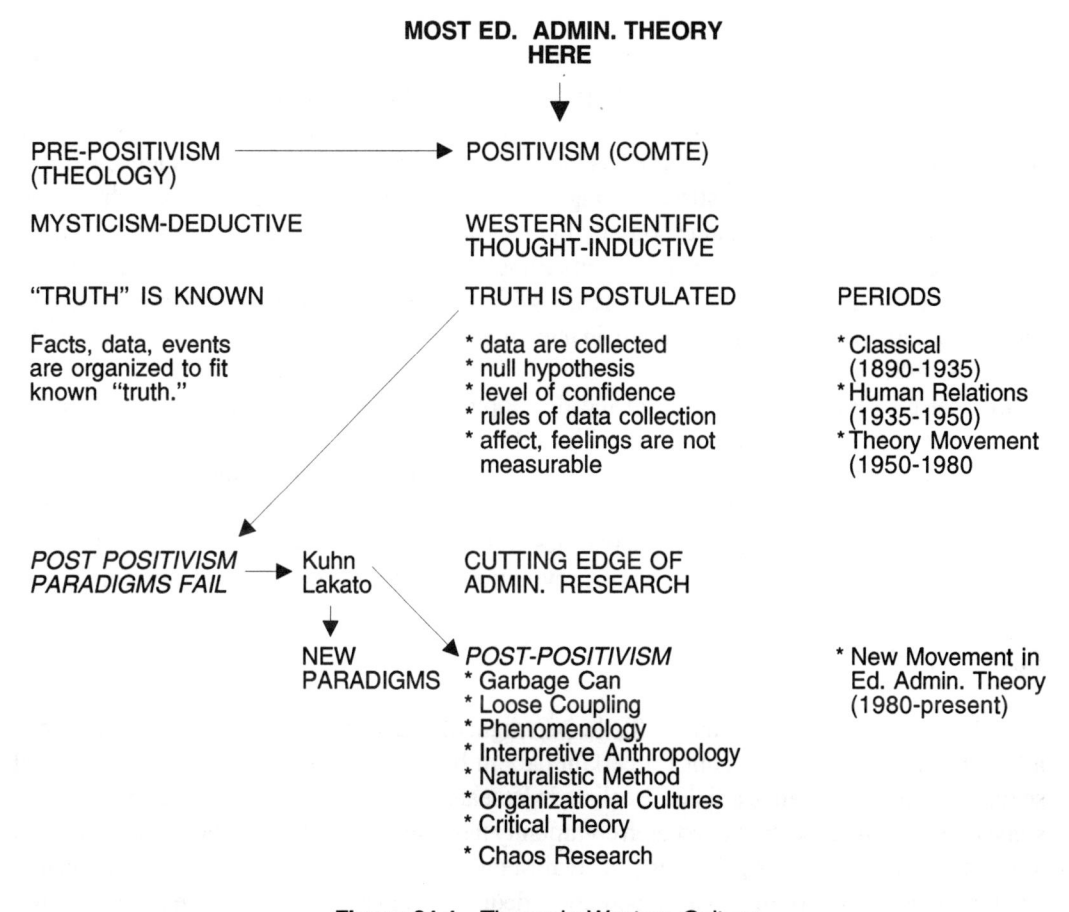

Figure 21.1. Theory in Western Culture

because of his heresy. This is not to say, however, that there was no science prior to the age of enlightenment. There was indeed! Things were studied and things were known, and it worked reasonably well. Ships navigated, calendars were produced, some medicine (even surgery) was available. It was rather that the way of knowing was different and, therefore, what was known was different because of it. Levi Strauss (1966) says that science and magic are not good and bad ways of knowing but rather different and alternative ways, each based on their own and different rules of evidence. But each is based on repeated trials and considerable data.

Logical Positivism

Dominating western scientific thought for more than a century, and theory in organization and administration since its inception and in spite of recent challenges, logical positivism defines a scientific paradigm or a way of knowing. Having its beginnings in the work of the French philosopher August Comte, it emerged as the dominating paradigm with the "Vienna Circle" ... a group of philosopher/scientists working in Vienna ... in the 1920s. It effectively challenged metaphysics as a paradigm and espoused (1) inductive reasoning, (2) observation of "sense" experience, (3) falsification (or verification failing falsification), and (4) statistical probability. Once adopted as the paradigm for the "hard" sciences, the social sciences were not far behind. Of course, education and administration, in their attempt to gain academic respectability aped its nearest kin--the social sciences.

Logical positivism with its role in the development of a body of literature in education administration has been productive, particularly during the period between 1950 and 1980, when education administration developed its own, rather respectable, body of literature. Although logical positivism has been effectively challenged, it is not dead, as noted by Phillips (1987). Still, in some ways it failed to explain some realities and to develop new hypotheses. Such failures, according to Kuhn (1962), signal scientific revolutions and the development of new paradigms.

Post-Positivism

At least since Kuhn (1962 and 1970), the paradigm of logical positivism has been under some attack for its inability to account for certain data in both the physical sciences and the social sciences. In his provocative article "Realism in Research," House (1991, p. 2) contended, "For some time now the educational research community has been in turmoil over the proper approach to practice and methodology." He argued against the slavish attachment to (1) a foundationalist epistemology, (2) use of theory as hypothetical deductive, (3) requiring absolute predictability, and (4) a human notion of causality. He further argued for a type of "scientific realism," stating that "...the standard view misconstrues the nature of science itself, even physical science, and misunderstands the nature of the real world" (p. 3). He also noted that in the social sciences, and surely in education, experimentalism is seldom if ever possible, new paradigms are required, and explanation is at least as important, if not more important, than prediction. In his conclusion, House explained,

> Scientific realism, derived in part from studying how scientists actually conduct their research, has resulted in a new conception of science and causation that has promise as a basis for educational research. . . . In the realist view, constant conjunctions are neither necessary nor sufficient. Even if one establishes such constant conjunctions, a scientific explanation is not satisfactory until one has knowledge of the underlying processes that produce them (p. 9).

As early as the 1920s Mary Parker Follett pointed out the inadequacies of a totally positivistic model when she attacked administration's complete reliance on scientific management (see Kimbrough and Nunnery, 1988, pp. 280-281). Still, the tendency to rely on the old paradigm in an effort to mock "hard science" remains in vogue in education and educational administration. Lutz (1990) suggested, however, that today post-positivism is the cutting edge of educational administration research and that researchers and practitioners in the field should take the risk of espousing different epistemologies and positing new ideas.

Rejecting the need for totally inductive thinking, "sense" observation and predictability as required elements in a scientific paradigm, post-positivism has effectively challenged the logical positivistic monologue in scientific thought in the hard sciences, social sciences and in education. Significant among those challenges in the hard sciences is the notion of linear predictability among the group of physicists, astronomers, etc., whose work comprises the "Chaos" research (see Gleick, 1987). In educational administration concepts such as loose coupling, organized anarchy, and organizational culture might be considered postpositivistic.

Paradigms and Theory in Educational Administration Research

Kuhn (1962) insists that different research paradigms are "incompatible" and one must accept and use one while rejecting the others. Lakatos (1972) takes a different view. Lakatos suggests that different paradigms can advance at the same time (not necessarily through the same research) and that different pieces of research using one or the other paradigm can be compatible and useful in understanding a single phenomena. This author accepts the Lakatos' view of "alternative" paradigms as opposed to Kuhn's position of "incompatible" and dichotomous paradigms. It surely follows that multiple theories, generated within a single paradigm, or even those emerging from "alternative" paradigms, can be useful in understanding organizational and administrative behavior. Put succinctly no single theory in educational administration is capable of explaining or predicting all administrative or organizational behavior. Present theories in the field are micro- or middle range theories. Macro theories tend to be of little use. There is not a "science" of school administration with a set of immutable "laws" nor is it likely that there ever will be (see Griffiths, 1985). Bringing theories, although incomplete, into a conceptual framework to describe, understand, or predict some portion of organizational and administrative behavior is very useful. Thus, the knowledge of theories can prove useful to practicing administrators. There is nothing as useful as a good theory. If a theory is not useful in practice then it is not a good theory. That is what Marx meant by "Theory-praxes-nexes"— the requirement that theory makes a reasonable impact on the real world.

Theory in education administration can be divided into four periods: (1) Classical (Late 1800s to Early 1930s); Human Relations (Mid 1930s to Late 1940s); Theory Movement (Early 1950s to Early 1980s); and Post-Positivistic (Mid 1980s to Present). The first three periods were nearly entirely dominated by logical positivism. That paradigm continues to be privileged; however, post-positivism has become noticeably active as a paradigm during the 80s and is perhaps the cutting edge in both theory and practice today. The remainder of this chapter will organize its presentation of theories according to these four classification periods.

The Classical Period (1890-1935)

As with other periods treated in this chapter, there are many theories and authors that will not be presented here. The choice is based on the author's perception of widely used or accepted theories and/or those of lesser "fame," but which the author believes have considerable heuristic or theory-building value. In each case, the treatment is brief and not to be taken as a full explanation. Additionally, some practical guide or exercise intended to provide an empirical/practical use of the theory-area, will be offered.

The "classical" theory period tends to treat Mankind as a machine and people as replaceable parts in that machine. Each function, role, or task is reduced to its smallest elements. This paradigm assumes that the parts equal the whole and there is one best way to do a specified job. When it is done in that specific way, then the job will be done in the most effective and efficient manner possible and everyone will "profit." However, it did not always work that way.

Bureaucracy Theory

The two dominate and long-lasting theories of this period are bureaucratic theory and scientific management. Both emerged as a natural outgrowth of the industrial revolution and both survive in the 1990s as major models for organizing and explaining organizational behavior.

Bureaucratic theory was developed by the German sociologist Max Weber. His purpose was to develop the "ideal typical" rational organizational model. Bureaucracy in its true sense is a very functional process. In Weber's "ideal typical" bureaucracy the organization is operated through: (1) a hierarchy of roles or positions with each incumbent chosen because of her/his clear ability, (2) a system of rules (of which everyone is aware and generally accepts), (3) impersonality (which treats everyone fairly), and (4) specialization (which permits everyone's particular talent and ability to be used to its fullest extent). Weber intended bureaucracy to operate a complex organization rationally, efficiently, and reliably (see Weber, 1964 and Blau, 1956).

Of course bureaucracies in real practice often do not operate in that fashion. Weber himself said the ultimate bureaucracy was an "iron cage" for humanity. People operate bureaucracies and people are not totally rational beings. They are also emotional beings. If all the favoritism, bias, greed, and hate are removed from the organization by rational and universally applied rules, then so is all the compassion, caring, forgiveness, and charity removed by the same rules.

Organizations are often dysfunctional and self-protective. If everyone in a bureaucracy is not promoted to the level of their incompetency (the Peter Principle), surely someone is. In a bureaucracy, everyone must do their job well. In a machine, a single malfunctioning twenty-five cent part can disrupt a multi-thousand dollar piece of equipment. So a single malfunctioning bureaucrat can also disrupt the entire organization. When Mankind and its organizations are treated a machines one can only expect them to function as mindless machines which sooner or later will fail and which cannot fix themselves.

Scientific Management

Scientific management was the work of Frederick Taylor (1856-1915) and was intended to provide the technological steps to correct dysfunctionalism in bureaucracies. Noticing that everything did not operate as well as expected in bureaucracies, Taylor, a mechanical engineer, studied the process of loading pig-iron onto freight cars (Taylor, 1947). From this and other studies Taylor devised a system which reduced any job to its smallest separate parts (or motions) and described the most efficient way to get that job accomplished (in the least time). Thus, was born the time-motion model of organizing a job within a bureaucracy. Taylor's scientific management was first adopted by American business as a way to cure its own ills and then by American education as a way to make common cause with the business values in American culture and local school boards (see Callahan, 1962).

Three others contributed during this period to the concepts of bureaucratic type management of complex organizations. Henri Fayol (1949), lived from 1841-1925 and developed a category of elements for administering complex organizations. Gulick, working in the early 1900s expanded Fayol's categories with Urwick (1969) to include planning, organizing, staffing, directing, coordinating, reporting, and budgeting, or the unpronounceable acronym of "POSDCoRB." One might ask if your organization has been POSDCoRBed lately? Those authors also popularized the concepts of organizational charts, line-staff administration (those who command and those who support), and span of control (the number of persons that can be reasonably supervised by a single person).

Exercise Example

It should hardly be necessary to provide examples of both the functional and dysfunctional operation of classical organizational concepts in schools. Schools are complex organizations. All of them exhibit some elements of bureaucracy. As these elements function, will they preserve human resources and allow creative activities to take place? Perhaps 80% to 90% of school functions can be taken care of in bureaucratic fashion. If the bureaucracy is functional, 80% to 90% of the tasks will require perhaps less than 15% of the resources (time, energy, etc.). That leaves at least 85% of the resources for creative activities that enhance human potential. Unfortunately almost no bureaucracy is that functional. Perhaps effective schools might simply be defined as organizations which are functional enough to deal with at least 80% of the tasks (bureaucratic tasks) using no more than 25% of the resources. As an exercise describe a familiar school in terms of its tasks (bureaucratic and non-bureaucratic), depict its organizational chart in terms of line-staff duties and its span of control, and decide if at least 75% of the resources remain (after the bureaucratic tasks are taken care of) to be spent on the non-bureaucratic needs of teaching/learning and human potential enhancing activities. If the answer is no, try to decide how that might be accomplished.

Humanistic Period (1935-1950)

Driven by a half century of the classical "man as machine" models of organization, people in the work force during the Industrial Age were desperate and unhappy. The Great Depression epitomized that while bureaucracies could organize production they could not insure everyone a profit or a job. Everything was not going well and some people saw "The Bureaucracy" run by a fairly small group of very wealthy individuals, as perhaps as evil as did Karl Marx. Something had to be done. It was clear that human beings and human organizations were more than machines.

Managing Conflict

Perhaps first and surely classic among these who recognized that something else was needed was Mary Parker Follett. Ahead of her time, both as a professional female and as an insightful observer of human organizations, Follett (1924) noted that key to any successful organization was building and maintaining a process that sustained human relationships and dealt effectively with conflict without compromise. Follett is perhaps first among women in modern administration, both in chronology and in impact. Seldom is she given the recognition in education administration which she deserves. Yet much of what is "preached" and "practiced" (albeit sometimes unfortunately distorted) grows from the writings of Follett.

Recognizing that conflict was common in human relations, she did not suggest it was something bad to be avoided, ignored, or crushed by management. Rather she regarded it as a necessary condition for movement and improvement. She saw administration as a matter of (1) maintaining direct contact among the responsible people, (2) coordination of early stages of the process, (3) reciprocal and interactive relationships among all situational factors and, (4) a continuing process, not a means-end entity (Metcalf and Urwick, 1940). She contented that compromise was a poor way to handle conflict because when two parties comprised both parties lost, and resenting that they had given up, thus, a festering, residual resentment, capable of creating new and more difficult conflict could remain. Instead Follett proposed a nearly Hegelian Dialectic process where both positions continued until they merged into a single position greater than either and more satisfying to the participants than any original position.

The Hawthorne Studies

No student of school administration can afford to be ignorant of this group of studies first conducted by Mayo and Roetheisberger and carried on and reported by Roetheisberger and Dickson (1939). Students and scholars of administration and organization were beginning to see that things occurred in organizational behavior that were not controlled by the concepts of scientific management and bureaucracy, and that could not be improved by "POSDCoRBing."

Mayo and those who worked with him were convinced that jobs meant more to workers than a mere paycheck and that something more than bureaucratic rules, technical specification, and management decisions were involved in the organizational behavior of workers. Their work remains classic in the area of the social psychology of work. George Homans (1950) in his landmark study of *Human Groups* draws on the "bankwiring" group of this Mayo-Roetheisberger set of studies, often called the "Western Electric" studies, or simply, the "Hawthorne" studies. These studies demonstrated that workers are more than cogs in a bureaucratic machine to be assembled, instructed, and supervised as parts of a well oiled machine. Workers form groups, establish norms, and respond to the organization as groups, seldom as individuals.

Participatory Decision Making

Perhaps more has been written in the education leadership in the area that might be called "democratic administration" than any other category. Some of this has been done perhaps without a clean, clear understanding of the original work of Coch and French (1948). In the article describing their research at the Harwood pajama factory those researchers describe the experimental conditions related to participative decision making or democratic administration, and its relationship to morale and resistance to change.

At Harwood, production decisions were frequently made that adversely affected the interaction patterns of workers and their paychecks. Workers were paid largely on the basis of "piece work." When patterns changed, pay went down, as new skills had to be learned. Coch and French found that when workers participated in how those decisions would be implemented, in how the decisions affected their lives, morale went up, absenteeism and turnover declined, and workers were less resistant to the change. In other words the workers did not care particularly about the change but rather about how the change affected them. Additionally, Coch and French found that it made no difference whether all workers participated (direct democracy), or their elected representatives participated for them (representative democracy). Both provided equally satisfying results when compared to no participation at all.

Based on this study school administrators have interpreted their findings to mean that employees should have input into a decision before implementing the decision, that everyone must "own a piece of the decision." Such an interpretation may lead to untenable delays in some critical decisions, or result in decisions so watered down so as to be of little value in changing school outcomes. This is not to say that the ideas of teachers, parents, business, and other citizens are worthless or not to be sought in school decision making. It is to say that not every decision can benefit from "group think" or consensus. In fact, when consensus requires compromise, then consensus violates the principles of Mary Parker Follett's process of "integration," a process greatly favored by this author.

Gretzels-Guba Model

Toward the end of the human relations period Getzels and Guba (1957) blended the concepts of the classical and human relations period into a macro-theory accounting for administrator and organization behavior. Getzels (1958) presents their work in a schematic model in one of the first attempts to produce a book on theory in educational administration. Kimbrough and Nunnery (1988), in their book in *Educational Administration*, refer to this as a systems theory. In a sense it may be, but it is somewhat different from the systems theories to be presented in this chapter.

As with most macro-theories the Getzels/Guba model describes the universe of organizational behaviors, but leaves out the numerous social science concepts that account for the rich variation among those behaviors. It is universally useful in describing behavior and at the same time useless in predicting behavior or assisting an administrator in deciding what might be done. The major concepts in the Getzels/Guba model are (1) nomothetic, or bureaucratic, concerns, and (2) idiographic, or personal, concerns. The blend of these two produce organization behavior. Most of the vast research this model generated in the 1960s and 1970s resulted in the notion that administrative behavior, in order to be helpful, was neither "nomothetic" nor "idiographic" but "transactional." Thus, successful administrators relied sometimes on bureaucratic criteria and at other times considered human criteria in making decisions, depending on the situation.

Exercise Example

Most people have experienced situations where values, honestly held, resulted in conflict. Often it is impossible to satisfy both perspectives (groups); one tends to lose, the other wins. Sometimes both give up so much that neither is satisfied. For instance, choose one such issue. Divide the class into four groups and assign two to each issue. Then have the groups "pick sides" where the opposing "side" tends to actually believe they are right and the other side wrong. Tell two groups to negotiate and compromise until each group has given up something but both can "live with the final compromise." The exercise will be more effective if the situation is real (i.e., there will be ⅓ A's, ⅓ B's, and ⅓ C's in this class. How will we decide who gets which?) Let the other two groups engage in the dialectic. They must continue until they emerge with a solution that penalizes no one, and that all agree is a better solution that the two originally proposed. Finally, bring the four groups together. Each will explain to the class their solution, why they agreed, and how they feel about what they lost and what they gained. Then explain the two different processes used in obtaining a solution. Let the class decide which process was better.

The Theory Movement (1950-1980)

Beginning in the late 1940s or early 1950s, a change took place within university programs in education administration. Stimulated by grants from the Kellogg Foundation, a group of professors of education administration formed the National Conference of Professors of Educational Administration (NCPEA) and a select group of institutions with administration doctoral programs formed a group of institutions called the University Council of Educational Administration (UCEA). Thus, began what has been termed the "theory movement" in education administration. A major influence on and leader in that movement for the past 40 years is Daniel E. Griffiths (1959). The attempt to develop a science of administration has failed and is probably impossible (Griffiths, 1985). But the existence of this chapter refutes the notion that the movement was a complete failure. Clearly a body of literature exists in the profession. Theory movement used theories from the social and behavioral sciences as the bases for hypotheses building and logical positivism as its paradigm.

Systems Theory

Some authors have labeled this entire period the "systems period" and many of the theories do use some sort of "systems" approach. Yet, one could see "POSDCoRBing" as a systems approach for planning (P) surely affected coordinating (Co) which surely is interactive in both planning and budgeting (B). So one could represent the relationship as —P—Co—B—. Surely this is a type of "systems model." But systems models are more than this, and while many theories can be represented by system-type schemata, systems theories are different and more complete than simple feedback loops.

General Systems Theory

Everything deserving consideration under the label "systems" model owes its origin to Luwig von Bertalanffy (1968). At a very rudimentary and basic level von Bertalanffy's notions of general systems deals with relatively open vs. relatively closed systems. A system is defined as an organization or organism that exchanges interactions within its specified boundaries more often that is does across its boundaries. In school a classroom is a system exchanging within its boundaries more often than with other classroom systems. However, a school can be studied as a system exchanging interactions more within than across the boundaries of the school. School districts can also be studied as systems exchanging interactions more often within the organizational boundaries but also exchanging across boundaries with its community. The more open the system, the more often it exchanges across boundaries with other systems. The more closed, the less frequently it exchanges across boundaries. A totally *closed* system does not exchange interactions and is headed toward entropy or death.

A simplistic system model could be composed of two systems. System A exchanges inputs and outputs with system B. Each may also be a subsystem of a larger system (i.e., two classrooms A & B in their environment, school 2). A's output becomes an input for B, and visa versa. The inputs received by each system are processed for meaning and implications and are used to produce and modify future outputs (i.e., Teacher A hears from teacher B about a fire drill at 9:20, so does not begin the reading lesson at 9:20 as previously planned). Such exchanges help each system survive within its environment. These elements help explain and to some extent predict the behavior of the system. Prediction, in general systems theory, is in terms of "equifinality." That is, if everything remains as it is now, some predictable state will occur at a definable time. Dickens, without intending to do so, defines equifinality and general systems when Scrooge asks if, "are these the things which must be or may be only," and is told "if these shadows remain unchanged the boy will die." But in open systems things can change. Inputs can be processed and, thus, change future outputs and future conditions. The boy did not die! Nor was the reading lesson interrupted by a fire drill!

Small Groups as Systems

Homans (1950) and (1960) sets forth what many be consider the basic work on small groups and their behavior, sometimes called "interaction theory" (Turner, 1974). Of course there are other sociologists who have contributed to the theory of how people behave in groups, however, too many to review here. For our purpose then Homans alone will do.

Homans (1950) defines the three basic elements of human behavior (in groups) as (1) activity, (2) interaction, and (3) sentiment. Activity are the things people do. Interaction is the process of one person providing a stimulus for another, and the other responding. Sentiment is the exchange of feelings. So two people can go fishing (activity). One can fall out of the boat and the other save the first person (interaction). The first person can express gratitude and the other receive it and both become friends (sentiment). The three elements are interactive. The more one increases the more likely the others increase and visa versa. These behaviors are governed in groups, by group norms, defined as behavior people expect from others, a shared sentiment, and which individuals sanction when behavior becomes too deviant. Homans' (1960) work goes quite beyond the simplistic model presented here, dealing with complicated concepts of human behavior such as justice and fair-exchange.

Relationships Between Larger Systems

In order to look at how larger social systems behave with other larger systems we turn to Loomis (1960). Again, Loomis is not the only option available, merely the choice. By larger systems is meant, for example, a metropolitan school district dealing with a large teacher union in a major city, or an influential and fundamental church in the community dealing with the school district about library book selection.

Loomis' (1960) title is informative, *Social Systems: Their Persistence and Change*. Much of American sociology has been described as conservative, that is focusing on "persistence" or status quo rather than change. In spite of the rhetoric to the contrary, American social science and public education has tended toward the preservation of the status quo. That is why real reform of education is so difficult. Loomis defines various factors that influence the manner in which one group of individuals can be predicted to behave when confronted with another group with somewhat different goals. These include the potential of the group, the group's history, its institutionalization, its perception of territoriality, and its boundary maintenance.

The potential of a social system includes those resources it can (although may not) commit to accomplishing its goal (i.e., intelligence, wealth, energy, facilities, time). The history, not only of the system itself but of other related systems in the macro-system, influences the likely success of any effort or even its undertaking. Such a condition is what is defined it is stated, "He did the right thing but at the wrong time."

Institutionalization is a type of legitimization of group activities usually by a set of laws, rules, or policies. It defines how, when, where, and under what circumstances lawful action can take place.

Territoriality is the behavior of "staking out" limits of perceived ownership by the groups. It is engaged in by all animals, including humans. Birds, fish, wolves, people, all define *their* territory in some fashion. Humans, unlike other animals, also "stake out" cognitive territories. They have rights and privileges; they "own" ideas, values, and beliefs. The "King of Siam" said, "Very soon I will fight to prove that what I do not know is so!" He was ready to fight to defend his right to believe what he was sure was wrong--but it was his belief, his "territory." And he will defend it!

Boundary maintenance is that fighting activity. It is the defense of the territory that one group perceives its "owns." We see territory in its highest relief when it becomes the object of boundary maintenance. The more "central" and precious the "territory" the more fierce the fight.

It is under these circumstances that systems engage in social intercourse with other systems. Lutz and Iannoccone (1969) merged these three system theories into a description of organizational behavior which they called simply the "Tri-systems model." It is easy to see how these three systems are more than those others sometimes called system models, and are described below as 2- and 3-factor models.

Two and Three Factor Models

We have already mentioned the Getzels and Guba model. It involved two "ideal typical" concepts along a continuum (i.e., nomothetic and idiographic) measured from high to low in some fashion. It assumed the interaction of several elements along each continuum. The result of the interaction of the two concepts resulted in "organizational behavior," the output variable which, in turn, influenced original inputs. Research using the model produced the concept of "transaction," a third factor. If the above "ideal typical" is used in Weber's sense, defining the concept in its total or extreme fashion, such an organization will operate in a 100% bureaucratic fashion. Given such a definition the organization behavior can be defined as from 1-100% of its total "ideal typical" concept (as bureaucratic) or its lack of agreement (as non-bureaucratic).

Leadership Behavior Description Questionnaire (LBDQ)

First developed for military use, the LBDQ was modified for use with school administrators (Halpin, 1956). It has two continua, which are initiation of structure (i.e., "sets deadlines") and consideration of subordinates (i.e., "listens to subordinates"). It is used to measure leadership behavior as an output. Leaders tend to be high in both initiation and consideration, but must be at least highest in initiation. Non-leaders tend to score low in both dimensions but scoring high in consideration alone will not guarantee leadership behavior.

Theory X and Y

This theory, proposed by McGregor (1960), follows the same pattern as any 2-factor theory as it explains the motivation of workers or the administrator's behavior when trying to motivate workers. Theory X assumes workers will do as little as possible and require pressure or prodding in order to get their best effort, with some clear reward if they behave "correctly." Theory Y assumes workers are self-motivated and self-actualized and will meet or exceed goals if expected to do so, and given the necessary support and encouragement to become as good as they can. Add to theory X and Y Ouchi's (1981) Theory Z (a creative combination of X and Y) and one has a three-factor model, not unlike nomothetic, idiographic, and transactional.

Blake/Mouton Grid (1964)

Developed as a means of organizational development (OD) in industry, the grid has been used by its originators to enhance leadership development. More specifically, it has been largely used with administrators to assist them in seeing the difference in the way they perceive themselves as managers as opposed to the way others see them. This information is used to create a motivation for leadership development. The originators posit a two-dimensional nine-point scale, one horizontal along a concern for people (from [9] high to [1] low) and the other vertical along a concern for production (from [9] high to [1] low). This provides a 9 x 9 or 81 cell grid where a 9.1 is very high in people concern and very low in production concern and 1.9 is very low in people concern and very high production concern. Little research has been done with the grid and no data are available on its reliability and validity (personal letter from authors, 1989). It does not take a very astute observer to see similarities between concern for people and consideration and Theory Y, and the concern for production with initiation of structure and Theory X. One might question whether dividing the continuum into nine arbitrary units, providing 81 cells is unique.

Dissatisfaction Theory

First introduced by Iannoccone and Lutz (1970) and recently applied to school community relations by Lutz and Metz (1992) this theory purports to explain and account for the local politics of education. It utilizes a systems exchange format where community dissatisfaction with schools ranges from low to high, affecting political participation (voter turnout in school elections) from low to high. Voter participation has a relationship to the likelihood of school board member incumbent defeat, from low to high. Incumbent defeat signals an increased likelihood of involuntary superintendent turnover which is often followed by hiring a new "outside" superintendent, followed by new policy and programs. Those new programs diminish dissatisfaction which again reduces voter participation. The theory has been shown to account for and to some extent predict school board and bond elections in local districts.

Total Quality Management (TQM)

Initially proposed by Deming for use in the U.S. Census Bureau in 1940, his methods were first generally accepted in post-war Japan and are now being credited for the presumed Japanese industrial superiority over the U.S. (see Mann, 1988). Recently American business has discovered TQM and, as they did with Scientific Management in the early 1900s, a "bandwagon" movement has begun (Lee, 1990). As usual, TQM now is being thrust at and willingly accepted by U.S. public education. Deming's TQM posits the following steps to TQM:

1. Control the quality of materials to be used.
2. Eliminate close and immediate supervision of workers.
3. Develop long-term loyalty/trust.
4. Break down department barriers.
5. Eliminate slogans and production targets as worker motivation.
6. Do away with specific work standards and minute accountability measures of workers.
7. Effect a pride and ownership in the quality of the total production by workers.
8. Develop "quality circles" among related workers to promote an understanding of and ability to do others' jobs.
9. Encourage workers in these "circles" to assume responsibility for the quality of the product.
10. Provide management that gives workers the resources necessary to do a quality job (including input into decisions that affect them.)

Before education is asked to adopt TQM, ask if the public and top decision makers are willing to implement all aspects of TQM? If the answer is *no,* then don't adopt a part of the process. It will fail!

Some confusion exists when attempting to operationalize TQM. TQM grew out of a postivistic, statistical method. It was first applied to the U.S. Census, a positivistic approach to human/social problems. It was born during the end of the Classical period and the beginning of the humanistic period. Its application in the U.S. and particularly in education appears as post-positive trends in theory and research are being initiated. It seeks or promotes efficiency and accountability, classical and positivistic concepts. But it abandons such classical concepts as span of control, hierarchical management, top-down communication, close supervision - replacing them with concepts more post-positive such as the emergence of institutional goals from the production process itself (loose coupling), and the responsibility for quality resting with the people who do the job (garbage can). **Warning**--administrators who use classical concepts and bureaucratic theory to insure that the organization adopts TQM in order to control quality of outputs will fail.

Many other theories from the social and behavioral sciences have been applied to school administration during this period in an effort to make school administration a "science." That goal was mistaken. It was not accomplished because it is unaccomplishable. Administration is a practice, just as medicine is a practice. That practice (in both cases) should be accomplished by professionals who possess a common body of knowledge based on the best scientific theories available. In medicine the scientific basis is the "hard sciences" such as biology, chemistry, anatomy, etc. In school administration the basis is the social and behavioral sciences such as sociology, political science, psychology, etc. To a great extent the "theory movement" in education administration accomplished its goal of amassing a body of knowledge, which has been explored only briefly in this chapter.

Exercise Example

Imagine a person who is attempting to provide leadership for a rather close-knit group of older teachers who have been at the same school, each for a minimum of 10 years. They have worked out a system of exchanges, often in violation of the bureaucratic rules. The new principal (the person trying to provide "leadership") has been hired to "shape-up" the school. "Changes must occur" at this school.

The teachers do not perceive the new principal as "considerate" nor "people oriented." Attempts to "initiate structure" are consistently rebuffed. The teachers have defined their territory and are defending their boundaries.

Divide the class into four groups, each choosing one or two theories presented in this section. Have each group attempt to "solve" the problem using concepts from their chosen theory or theories. Come together and discuss the outcomes and have each group "defend" their proposed solution.

Post-Positiveness Period (1980-Present)

Driven almost totally by a rigid logical-positivistic paradigm the "theory movement" dominated the thinking about education administration for almost half a century. But as Kuhn (1962) pointed out, paradigms fail when they stop generating fruitful hypotheses and fail to explain important observable phenomena. Then some new paradigm is offered. That event took place in education around 1980. It has not ended research using the logical positivistic paradigm, nor should it have. But it has, however, opened the field to new explanations, competitive models, and creative thinking.

Loose Coupling

Although almost everyone would agree that many organizational behaviors in public schools can be accounted for by bureaucratic theory, at least as many would now agree that everything that occurs is not controlled or accounted for by bureaucratic theory. Further, as the ideal typical bureaucracy is the "iron cage" for humanity, the fact that everything in public schooling is not bureaucratic, is probably for the best. Weick (1983) suggests the concept of loose coupling as an alternative to bureaucracy. Perhaps loosely coupled is the opposite, the antithesis, of bureaucratic or tightly coupled. In the Hegelian sense that is probably as correct as, the one requires the other.

Loosely coupled organizations behave according to the concepts of general systems theory (Weick, 1985). Therefore, it has been suggested that we did not need a new theory to account for loosely coupled behavior (Lutz, 1982). What was clearly needed, however, was a concept to call attention to the fact that school organizations often do not behave according to the rules of bureaucracy, are often unpredictable, and those unpredictable behaviors often allow the organization to survive and succeed when tight coupling would contribute to its failure and demise. Loose coupling did that.

Loosely coupled organizations:

- encourage its sub-units to maintain somewhat separate identities and individualities;
- develop only generalized organizational goals with broad parameters;
- permit sub-units to develop different goals within defined broad parameters;
- evaluate accomplishment and redistribute resources based on such goal differentiation and flexibility, sometimes through informal, rather than formal, arrangements.

Because of this loose coupling arrangement, sub-units can better respond to a varied and ever changing environment, providing greater opportunity for their survival and the survival of the larger organization. Such organizations are, however, less predictable and often experience more difficulty in effecting system-wide organizational change as the sub-units are free to resist or even subvert top-down efforts to change.

Organized Anarchy (Garbage-Can)

Weick used a sports analogy which he attributed to March when developing his loose coupling model. Cohen, March, and Olsen (1972) and March and Olsen (1976) discuss a model of "Organized Anarchy," or garbage-can model, which is similar in many ways to Weick's loose coupling. In a less known work, Padgert (1980) presents a garbage-can model which provides a kind of synthesis of loose and tighter coupling in what he calls a modified "garbage can" model. In either case the organized anarchy model suggests that organizational goals are often ill-defined and, thus, best defined in ambiguous fashion. Methods for meeting such goals are left to sub-units of the organization and the methods, and interim outcomes may even effect changes in the original goals. Thus, goals change during and because of the organizational process. Top decision makers avoid specific decisions, rather making decisions about how decisions will be made by others. They concentrate on the personnel function in order to be sure the best persons available are managing the anarchy at the various levels of the organization. It is at these levels where goals emerge and methods for meeting them are devised. This model is often recommended in professional bureaucracies where highly trained expertise is needed to meet differentiated and ambiguous goals utilizing a variety of mixed resources.

Chaos Research

This is the most radical post-positivistic theory introduced in the chapter. It is really not a theory but is better termed a research area. It grows out of the work of meteorologists such as Kurt Koreng, mathematicians such as Benait Mendelbrot, and biologists such as Michael Barnsley. Summarized by Gleick (1987) chaos research demonstrates through the multiple "hard" sciences that the law of the universe is ordered chaos rather than predictability. Natural phenomenon operate in curvilinear fashion, not in a linear one. While simultaneous linear equations are solvable, simultaneous curvilinear equations are not. Curvilinear functions are interacting in nature. Weather is unpredictable because of the interactive and curvilinear nature of the variables that affect it. A butterfly flying in Brazil may ultimately create a tornado in Texas (Lorenz, 1979).

If chaos is the universal law, then human systems, which are much more interactive than physical science systems, are even more unpredictable than physical systems. They are chaotic, but ordered. This brings to mind the notion of organized anarchy mentioned earlier and suggests some entirely new notions of human organizational behavior and school administration. One manages conflict but does not control it, much less eliminate it. One stabilizes a changing organization for short periods but does not worry about creating changes within it. The list of different ways to view human organization seems limitless, and hardly examined.

Organizational Culture

The term culture is defined in Geertz (1973) as a set of significant symbols which provide rules and recipes for how people are expected to behave and what they can expect given that behavior. Mankind and culture are inseparably linked. People shape culture but culture shapes the behavior of people.

Generally the concept of culture is applied to fairly large configurations of people (i.e., nations, states, neighborhoods, and large organizations). One can apply the concept of culture to organizations (Deal and Kennedy, 1982), schools (Smith and Keith, 1971), or even school boards (Lutz, 1975). Marshall, Mitchell, and Wirt (1989) describe the political cultures of five states and their legislatures and link that to the education politics and policies developed in those states.

By understanding the concept of culture, and its related sub-concepts, one can define, describe and to some extent predict and influence the culture's change or persistence. Non-bureaucratic means of control, communication, status, and authority become explicit. Values, beliefs, aspirations, and expectations are revealed. The rules by which the organizational-political game become known and the administrator as change agent or status quo preserver is made more tenable.

Exercise Example

Imagine an organization with absolutely unpredictable behavior. It has the usual positions of superintendent, associate superintendent for business and finance, director of public relations, assistant for personnel, secondary and elementary curriculum directors, four high school principals, four middle school and six elementary principals, all with appropriate assistants, department and grade level chairs. But it is very loosely coupled, and there is organized anarchy.

Divide into two teams each representing the roles in the organizational structure above. One team gets to make up the rules. Give the other team those rules. They now can choose to violate any of those rules if they can make up a reason to do so. They then report the organizational behavior to the first team which must try to get the second team back on their track. They issue new orders, with the same result. Play the game until one or the other team finds some type of resolution.

Suggested Readings

As suggested earlier this chapter cannot do justice to the range of theory which might guide school administration. Nor has it fully explained any one presented here. This is a brief overview of selected theory. Other books suggested for the interested student are listed.

Hailer, E.J. and Strike, K.A. (1986). *An introduction to educational administration: Social, legal and ethical perspectives.* New York: Longman.

Hoy, W.K. and Miskell, C.G. (1991). *Educational administration: Theory, research and practice* (4th Edition). New York: McGraw-Hall.

Kimbrough, R.B. and Nunnery, MY. (1988). *Educational administration: An introduction* (3rd Edition). New York: MacMillan.

Lunenburg, F.C. and Ornstein, A.C. (1991). *Educational administration: Concepts and practices.* Belmont, CA: Wadsworth.

Owens, R.G.'(1991). *Organizational behavior in education* (4th Edition). Englewood Cliffs, N.J.: Prentice Hall.

Segiovanni, T.J., Burlingame, M., Cooms, F.S., and Thurston, P.W. (1992). *Educational governance and administration* (3rd Edition). Boston: Allyn and Bacon.

References

Bertalanffy, L. von (1968). "General systems--a critical review." In Buckley, W. (Ed.) *Modern Systems Research for the Behavioral Scientist.* Chicago: Aldine.

Blake, R. R. and Mouton, J. S. (1964). *The managerial grid.* Houston, TX: Gulf.

Blau, P.M. (1956). *Bureaucracy in modern society.* New York: Random House.

Callahan, R. E. (1962). *Education and the cult of efficiency.* Chicago: Univerity of Chicago Press.

Coch, L. and French, R. P., Jr. (1948). Overcoming resistance to change. *Human Relations, 1,* 512-532.

Cohen, M. D., March, J. G., and Olsen, J. P. (1972). A garbage-can model of organizational choice. *Administrative Science Quarterly, 17,* (1), 1.

Deming, W. E. (1986). *Out of the crisis.* Cambridge, MA: MIT Center for Advanced Engineering Study.

Deal, T.E. and Kennedy, A. (1982). *Corporate cultures.* Reading, MA: Addison Wesley.

Fayol, H. (1949). *General and industrial management.* Stoars, C. (translator). London: Pitman.

Follett, M.P. (1924). *Creative experience.* New York: Longmans.

Geertz, C. (1973). *The interpretation of cultures.* New York: Basic Books.

Getzels, J.W. (1958). Administration as a social process. In *Administrative Theory in Education,* Halpin, A.W. (Ed.). New York: MacMillan, pp. 150-165.

Getzels, J.W. and Guba, E.G. (1957). Social behavior and the administration process. *School Review, 65,* 423-441.

Glaser, B. and Strauss, A.L. (1967). *The discovery of grounded theory: Strategies for qualitative research.* Chicago: Aldine.

Gleick, J. (1987). *Chaos: Making a new science.* New York: Viking.

Griffiths, D.E. (1985). *Administrative theory in transition.* Vietaria, Australia: Deakin University.

Griffiths, D.E. (1959). *Administrative theory.* New York: Appleton-Century-Crofts.

Gulick, L. and Urwick, L. (1969). *Papers on the science of administration.* Gulick, L. and Urwick, L. (Eds.). New York: Institute of Public Administration, Columbia University.

Halpin, A.W. (1956). *The leadership behavior of school superintendents.* Columbus, Ohio: College of Education, Ohio State University.

Homans, G.C. (1950). *Human groups.* New York: Harcourt, Brace, and World.

Homans, G.C. (1960). *Social behavior: its elementary form.* New York: Harcourt, Brace, and World.

Iannoccone, L. and Lutz, F.W. (1970). *Politics, power, and policy.* Columbus, Ohio: Charles Merrill.

Kimbrough, R.B. and Nunnery, M.Y. (1988). *Educational administration: An introduction* (3rd Edition). New York: MacMillan.

Kuhn, T.S. (1962). *The structure of scientific revolutions.* Chicago: The University of Chicago Press.

Lakatos, I. (1972). In *Criticism and the Growth of Knowledge,* Lakatos, I. and Musgrave, A. (Eds). Cambridge: Cambridge University Press.

Lee, C. (1990). Beyond teamwork. *Training* (June), pp. 25-32.

Levi-Strauss, C. (1966). *The savage mind.* London: Weidenfeld and Nicolson.

Loomis, C.P. (1960). *Social systems: Essays on their persistence and change.* New York: Von Norstrand.

Lorenz, K. (1979). Predictability: Does the flap of a butterfly's wings in Brazil set off a tornado in Texas? Address at the annual meeting of the American Association for the Advancement of Science, December 29, Washington, D.C.

Lutz, F.W. (1990). "Chaos in school administration." *Catalyst for Change,* (Winter) *18* (2), 8-10.

Lutz, F.W. (1982). Tightening up loose coupling in higher education. *Administrative Science Quarterly, 27* (4), 643-669.

Lutz, F.W. (1975). School boards as socio-cultural systems. In *Understanding School Boards,* Cistone, P. (Ed.). Lexington, MA: D.C. Heath.

Lutz, F.W. and Merz, C. (1992). *The politics of school community relations,* New York: Teachers College Press.

Lutz, F.W. and Iannoccone, L. (1969). *Understanding educational Organizations: A field study approach.* Columbus, OH: Charles E. Merrell.

Mann, N.R. (1988). Why it happened in Japan and not in the U.S.? *Change New Directions for Statistics and Computing, 1* (1), 8-15.

March, J.G. and Olsen, J.P. (1976). *Ambiguity and choice in Organizations.* Bergen, Norway: Universitetsforlaget.

Marshall, C., Mitchell, D., and Wirt, F. (1989). *Culture and education policy in the states.* New York: Palmer Press.

McGregor, D.M. (1960). *The human side of enterprise.* New York: McGraw-Hill.

Metcalf, H.C. and Urwick, L. (1940). *Dynamic administration: The Collected papers of Mary Parker Follett.* Metcalf, H.C. and Urwick, L. (Eds.). New York: Harper and Row.

Ouchi, W. (1981). *Theory Z: How American business can meet the Japanese challenge.* Reading, Mass.: Addison-Wesley.

Padgett, J.F. (1980). Managing garbage can hierarchies. *Administrative Science Quarterly, 25,* 583-604.

Phillips, O.C. (1987). *Philosophical science and social inquiry.* New York: Pergamon Press.

Roetheisberger, F.J. and Dickson, W.J. (1939). *Management and the worker.* Cambridge: Harvard University Press.

Smith, L.M. and Keith, P.M. (1971). *Anatomy of educational innovations: An organizational analysis.* New York: Wiley.

Taylor, F.W. (1947). *Scientific management: The principals of scientific management.* New York: Harper and Row.

Turner, J.B. (1974). *The structure of sociological theory.* Homewood, IL: Darsey Press.

Weber, M. (1964). *The theory of social and economic organization.* Henderson, A.M. and Parson, T. (translators), Parsons, T. (Ed.). New York: Free Press.

Weick, K. (1983). Administering education in loosely coupled schools. *Phi Delta Kappan, 63*(10), 673-676.

Weick, K. (1985). Sources of order in underground systems: Themes in recent organizational theory. In Yvonna S. Lindon (Ed.) *Organizational Theory and Inquiry; The Paradigm Revolution.* Beverly Hills: Sage.

Higher Education in Texas

David W. Gardner
David T. Kelly

Concerned Texans have long seen higher education as a part of the effort to achieve an educated citizenry, reflecting Mirabeau B. Lamar's well-known dictum that "It is admitted by all, that cultivated mind is the guardian genius of Democracy, and while guided and controlled by virtue, the noblest attribute of man." One critical role of colleges and universities in the total educational effort of the state, particularly that of public education from kindergarten through high school, has been in the training of teachers. However, there have been other ways in which higher education has influenced the larger education, and in recent years some of those ways have been stated in policy and law.

Background

Private Texas citizens, through their churches, were among the earliest to recognize the need for advanced learning. Present day independent institutions may be said to have had their beginnings in 1840 with the establishment of Southwestern University. Baylor University and the University of Mary Hardin-Baylor date from 1845. Five institutions serving Black citizens were established between 1873 (Wiley College) and 1894 (Texas College). A total of twenty-one independent institutions (including two junior colleges) now offering higher education to Texans had their beginnings before 1900.

The public, through its representatives, was not far behind. Texas A&M University and Prairie View A&M University were established in 1876, with Sam Houston State University

(1879) and the University of Texas (1883) following shortly thereafter. During the same period, the University of Texas Medical Branch in Galveston was rounded (1881). Three present-day junior colleges were rounded in the last two decades of the 19th century (Blinn College in 1883; Clarendon and St. Philip's Colleges in 1898).

Texans' appetites for higher education expanded throughout the twentieth century, stimulated by World War II and Korean War GI Bill recipients seeking higher education in unprecedented numbers. The peak was reached with the baby-boom generation in the mid nineteen-sixties, and enrollments began to level off somewhat in the early 1970s. The post-World War II and Korean War enrollment booms were felt particularly for their contribution to the establishment of new junior colleges, now permitted by law to be called community colleges, with the expectation of extending higher education access to all Texas citizens.

The independent senior colleges and universities multiplied steadily from 1900 until 1960 with an increase of nineteen institutions; only one has been founded since 1960. Fifteen public senior colleges and universities were created at about the same rate as the independent institutions until 1960, but after that the public institutions continued to be established at a more rapid rate resulting in the founding of nine more degree granting institutions by 1971, not including one lower division center of a university offering freshman and sophomore courses only. After 1971, one lower division center and three upper division and graduate centers were established, but no new free-standing, degree granting public institutions have been created since that date. Baylor College of Medicine and Baylor College of Dentistry were founded in 1903 and 1905, respectively, and the seven public medical, dental and allied health units now in operation (most comprising a range of different "schools") were established between 1943 and 1977.

Between 1900 and 1960, twenty-eight public junior college districts were established; between 1961 and 1971, fourteen new districts with nineteen new campuses were rounded; and since 1971, four new districts and nine new campuses of existing districts were established.

Today, public higher education in Texas includes ninety-six institutions and fourteen state agencies or service entities with an annual operating outlay of more than $4 billion and capital assets valued at nearly $7 billion. In the Fall of 1992, public colleges alone enrolled more than 800,000 students and employed more than 70,000 faculty and support staff, while independent colleges enrolled more than 89,000 students.

Seven public institutions offer programs of study in medicine and health sciences. Six of these institutions offer degrees in medicine and one in osteopathic medicine. Two of these institutions have dental schools, four have graduate schools of biomedical science, five have allied health schools and four have nursing schools. In addition, there is one College of Veterinary Medicine.

Forty-nine public community junior college districts with sixty-six campuses are dedicated to carrying out a mission prescribed by law. Community colleges enrolled nearly 400,000 students in the Fall of 1992. This represents an increase of approximately 20,000 students in just two years. Another 8,000 students were enrolled at the Texas State Technical College. Community colleges provide technical programs up to two years in length leading to associate degrees or certificates; vocational programs relating to semi-skilled and skilled occupations, general academic courses, continuing adult education, and compensatory education. The Texas State Technical College offers technical and vocational programs whose duration varies according to training objectives.

Although the number of public institutions and student enrollments in those institutions have surpassed those of the independent sector in recent years, the thirty-eight independent senior colleges and universities in Texas continue to fulfill a vital role in Texas higher education. All of the independent senior institutions offer four-year programs leading to bachelor's degrees; 20 also offer master's level programs, five have doctoral level programs, and three offer professional degrees in law. These independent institutions generally offer programs in the range of disciplines found at the public universities. However, many of the independent colleges and universities offer religion and theology programs not taught at the public institutions. Besides the senior institutions, there are an independent college of medicine, an independent college of dentistry, and three independent junior colleges offering freshman and sophomore level studies.

Governance

Independent or private institutions of higher education in Texas operate only minimally under the jurisdiction of state agencies. Of course those colleges and universities must operate in accordance with all applicable state laws, and they must comply with appropriate health and safety regulations. In order to prepare teachers for the state's schools, these institutions' teacher training programs must be approved by the Texas Education agency. Beyond such limited control and regulation, however, the independent institutions can be said to be truly independent. They are governed by boards representing their supporting constituencies, and they are free from many of the constraints that affect public institutions.

Texas public institutions of higher education are of three types: the universities (the term senior college has disappeared from use for Texas public institutions), Texas State Technical College, and the community junior colleges. The universities (and the Texas State Technical College, rounded in 1965) are "state" institutions. Texas junior (community) colleges are political subdivisions of the state; they are cooperative ventures between the state and their respective local communities, "hybrid" institutions whose evolution can be seen in their emergence from the public schools beginning in the late nineteenth century.

Public universities, the health science centers, and the technical college are creatures of the legislature. They are owned by the state and are governed by boards of public citizens who are appointed to their positions of trust by the governor and confirmed by the Senate. The duties of the governing boards are prescribed by law; they consist primarily of setting the policies by which the institutions are operated, employing the chief executive officer (and all other personnel), and overseeing the fiscal affairs and properties of the institutions.

System administrations coordinate institutional long-range planning and approve short-range institutional plans for operations and expenditures. It is also their responsibility to evaluate presidents and their institutions.

Community junior colleges are creatures of their local communities, established by vote of their constituencies under conditions prescribed by law and, since 1965, the policies of the Coordinating Board. They are governed by boards of locally elected citizens whose duties are similar to those of the public universities' boards except for one important factor: the junior college boards have taxing authority. The voters who create junior college districts and elect the members of governing boards may vote to authorize local ad valorem taxes to finance the sale of bonds for the acquisition of property and the construction of facilities and to finance certain operations and maintenance costs of the institutions. The governing boards may levy and collect such ad valorem taxes within the limits set by the voters.

Coordination of Public Higher Education

Senate Bill 145 in the 54th legislature in 1955 created a Texas Commission on Higher Education, an early effort to "establish an agency which provides additional leadership and coordinating services for senior higher education systems and their institutions and their governing boards." The Commission on Higher Education was terminated when the Coordinating Board was established in 1965 to bring order to the rapid growth that was taking place in higher education. The Board was created to address the educational needs of the state while eliminating unnecessary duplication in program offerings, faculties and physical plants. The Board is a statutory, 18-member board appointed by the governor with the advice and consent of the Senate. The Board was given authority over the role and mission and degree and certificate programs of institutions of higher education, approval authority over land purchases and the construction and rehabilitation of buildings at universities, and general supervision of the public junior colleges. In addition, the Board plays an important role in the administration of student financial aid and an influential role in the funding of higher education through its recommendations for funding formulas.

Since 1965, the legislature has given the Coordinating Board additional responsibilities. The 69th legislature, for example, transferred authority over technical-vocational programs at community colleges and the Texas State Technical College from the Texas Education Agency to the Coordinating Board and gave the Board degree program and facility approval authority over TSTC. The 70th legislature enacted many of the recommendations made by a Select Committee on Higher Education that had been created by the 69th legislature.

The 70th legislature created, by House Concurrent Resolution, a *Texas Charter for Public Higher Education,* laying out in a public policy document a comprehensive statement of goals, priorities, and policies for Texas higher education. The *Charter* (pp. 3-5) holds up the following principles to guide those responsible for the development of higher education in Texas:

- The people of Texas expect quality in all aspects of public higher education: teaching, research and public service.
- Higher education should be accessible to all those who seek and qualify for admission.
- Higher education should provide a diversity of quality educational opportunities.
- Support through adequate funding is critical if higher education is to achieve its purpose.
- The people of Texas are entitled to efficient and effective management of higher education.
- The people of Texas are entitled to capable and creative leadership in higher education.

Related legislation assigned several new responsibilities to the Board. Among these are the authority to set enrollment limits for universities, the administration of four major research programs, and the development of a statewide master plan for higher education. Of particular relevance to the larger public education system, the Board was given new responsibilities impinging on public schools and their students. Programs were mandated for improving teacher education and for the assessment of students entering higher education, with required remedial assistance to be provided for those students who are judged to need such help to succeed in college.

In keeping with the national interest in the problems of education, the legislature mandated significant changes in the way teachers are educated in Texas. In response to this legislation, the Coordinating Board adopted new policy guidelines on teacher education in December, 1987. Traditional baccalaureate degrees in education have been eliminated and the professional education component of teacher education programs has been limited to eighteen semester hours of credit. The legislation requires an induction year, that is, a supervised initial year of teaching for those entering the teaching profession. Procedures for the implementation of the induction year were completed and piloted during the 1990-91 academic year.

The legislature instructed the Coordinating Board to prescribe a diagnostic instrument to test entering college students in reading, writing and mathematics beginning in the Fall of 1989, and to prescribe minimum performance standards for the test. This assessment and testing program, the Texas Academic Skills Program (TASP), is intended to ensure that students attending public institutions have the academic skills necessary to successfully complete college work. Institutions are required to report annually on results of student testing and the effectiveness of the college's remedial and advising program. Moreover, the Coordinating Board has established guidelines with the assistance of the State Board of Education for post-secondary institutions to report student performance during the first year of enrollment after graduation from high school to the high school or community college last attended. In 1991 the TASP examination displaced the Pre-Professional Skills Test (PPST) that was previously in use for students seeking to become teachers. It is also anticipated that assessment results will be valuable to teachers and administrators in school districts, and ways are being sought to provide such information to the districts in an effective manner.

Financing

Independent institutions of higher education in Texas, as elsewhere, are financed from three principal sources: student tuition and fees, income from investments (endowments and others), and gifts and grants. (There are other, less productive sources, but they are of little significance compared to the three previously mentioned.) State and federal monies do make their way to the independent institutions, primarily in the form of student financial aid and many kinds of grants, but these institutions are dependent largely on support coming from their students and from private benefactors.

Public institutions rely heavily, but not entirely, on public support. Most of the public support comes in the form of funds appropriated by the legislature and, in the case of the junior colleges, from local ad valorem taxes. Thus, the three principal sources of support for public colleges and universities are state (and local) appropriations, student tuition and fees, and gifts and grants.

The state's support for public institutions of higher education (often called "state aid" for the community junior colleges) is appropriated by the legislature from general revenue funds each biennium. Using advisory committees appointed by the Commissioner of Higher Education, the Coordinating Board reviews, modifies and designates formulas to be used in the appropriation process. The formula system now in use has evolved slowly over the last 30 years through careful study and testing by the Coordinating Board's study committees, and acceptance by the Governor and the legislature.

The biennial formula development process takes approximately one year. At the end of this time, formula study committees make their recommendations to the Commissioner who in turn makes recommendations to the Coordinating Board. When adopted by the Board, the formulas are forwarded to the Legislative Budget Board (LBB) and the Governor's Budget Office. At that time, guidelines are developed by which appropriations requests are developed by the institutions for submission to the LBB and the Governor's Office. Following passage of appropriations bills by both houses, a Conference Committee will prepare a bill to be approved by the legislature and forwarded to the Governor for consideration.

The university formula system encompasses a variety of cost elements considered in the appropriations process, including the following: General Administration and Student Services, General Institutional Expense, Faculty Salaries, Physical Plant Operation and Maintenance, Campus Security, Instructional Administration, Departmental Operating Expense, Organized Research, and Library. Funding for the categories of Faculty Salaries, Departmental Operating Expense, and Library account for a majority of a university's appropriation. They are based on varying formula rates multiplied by student credit hours of instruction produced in the institution during a specified time called a "base period." State support (aid) for community colleges is based on Coordinating Board developed and recommended formulas which establish rates per base period contact hours for courses taught. There are formulas for both academic programs and technical and vocational training.

Public medical schools and health science centers receive appropriations from the Texas legislature based on funding requests and justifications submitted by the institutions rather than on formula calculations. Although the health science units have not been a part of the formula system in the past, a new formula procedure has been adopted by the Coordinating Board for recommendation to the legislature for use in the funding of Allied Health and Nursing programs in the health science centers and for the Nursing programs in the general academic institutions.

The formula rates and procedures used by the legislature in developing an institution's appropriation are not intended to dictate the internal operating budget for the institution. The legislature appropriates operating funds directly to the public institutions, and they have the responsibility for developing their own operating budgets based on their priorities and within the guidelines of the appropriations act.

Campus Planning

The large investment required to provide the physical facilities necessary to fulfill the educational needs of the state is addressed in the responsibilities given to the Coordinating Board by the legislature. Broadly, the Board is to monitor the planning, use, and evaluation of physical facilities. To this end, formulas for space utilization are developed for all educational and general use buildings and campuses are to develop and submit long range plans for campus development. The agency must also certify compliance with statutory building requirements for accessibility for the handicapped. All new construction costing more than $300,000 must be approved by the Coordinating Board unless specifically approved by the legislature or projects financed by nonstate funds at community colleges.

Higher Education and Public Schools

In addition to activities mentioned above which affect the public schools or their students, the Coordinating Board conducts or supports other activities that have an impact, directly or indirectly. For example, the Commissioner of Higher Education, in cooperation with the Commissioner of Education from the Texas Education Agency, has sponsored three conferences since 1986 on Teacher Education with participation by representatives of universities, community colleges, school districts, and the public. The report of the 1986 conference offers brief descriptions of cooperative projects which resulted from the conference, the 1988 conference focused on major issues facing teacher education in Texas, including primarily the impact of Senate Bill 994, and the 1990 conference gave attention to critical issues in teacher education such as alternative routes to certification and the recruitment of minority teachers.

Further, programs are conducted by the Coordinating Board to identify and assist disadvantaged and other students in seeking a college education. One such program is the Youth Opportunities Unlimited (Y.O.U.) project. Using Federal Job Training Partnership Act funds, The program brings 14 and 15-year old students, identified by their counselors as being at risk of dropping out of school, to college campuses for an 8-week summer work-study session. Participants attend classes for half days, for which they receive TEA-sanctioned credit, and are employed for half days. By the end of the summer most students are able to return home with up to $700 in savings and with improved skills in math and English. Although the program works with at-risk students, in the first years of its operations, 100% of the participants have returned to high school in the fall following the summer program. Many colleges have offered scholarships to students when they return to college.

Ninety thousand students are reached by another program called College Bound. This program, initiated by the Board in 1987 is designed to provide students with information for coping with the challenges of high school and for preparing for college and careers after college. Beginning in the eighth grade, participants in this program receive a semiannual newsletter at their home address, and each will have received ten newsletters by high school graduation. Each student is encouraged to submit questions to the College Bound Teen Board which provides an individual response to each letter.

All students in school districts with minority enrollments of at least 50% are eligible to participate. The program has been enthusiastically received. For example, in the 1987-88 academic year, over 52,000 students out of the 100,500 who were eligible registered to participate. The Coordinating Board made a commitment to these students to stay in touch with them until high school graduation. It is anticipated that as the first classes of participants approach high school graduation, the program will be broadened to include more active assistance for students in selecting colleges and applying for financial aid.

Summary

Higher education has traditionally been regarded by Texans as an important part of the education of the citizens. Public and private colleges and universities are governed by representatives of the communities and constituencies that the serve, and the support those institutions with their personal and the public funds. Colleges and universities are increasingly involved in programs that affect the public schools, and the legislature has added its concerns to those of educators and private citizens who know that the quality of life and the economy of a state depends on the education of its citizens.

Suggested Readings

"ICUT Research Foundation and Annual Statistical Supplement," Independent Colleges and Universities of Texas, Inc., Austin, Texas: September 1987.

"Fact Book on Texas Higher Education," Texas Higher Education Coordinating Board, Austin, Texas: 1989.

"Statistical Supplements," Texas Higher Education Coordinating Board, Austin, Texas: Sequential Years.

"Proceedings of the Commissioners" Conference on Teacher Education," Coordinating Board, Texas College and University System, Austin, Texas: 1986.

"Report of the Select Committee on Higher Education," February 1987.

Texas Charter for Public Higher Education, 70th Texas Legislature, 1987.

SBOE Goals and Objectives (1990-1994)

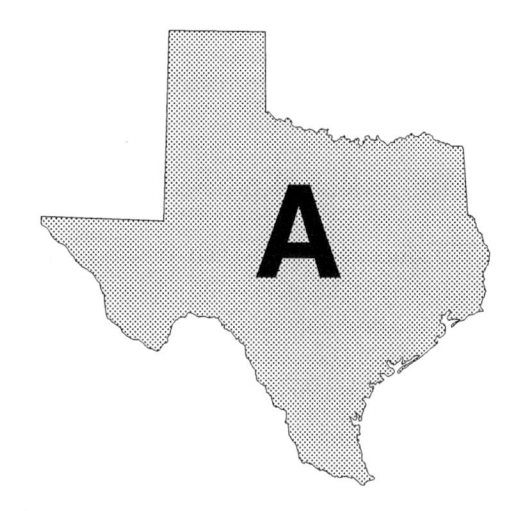

1. **Student Learning:** All students will achieve their full educational potential.
    1.1 Set increasingly challenging expectations for academic performance by all students in the Texas schools.
    1.2 Measure student learning through multiple indicators.
    1.3 Close the achievement gap between educationally disadvantaged students and other populations.
    1.4 Support the development of infants and young children through early childhood education and parenting education.
    1.5 Identify and assist slower learners to meet their learning potential.
    1.6 Through enhanced dropout prevention efforts, raise the graduation rate to 95 percent of students who enter the seventh grade.
    1.7 Identify and assist students with special needs.
    1.8 Support students' acquisition of literacy, writing, and other communications skills.
    1.9 Develop second language skills in all students.

2. **Curriculum and Programs:** A well-balanced and appropriate curriculum will be provided to all students.
    2.1 Strengthen the state curriculum, including promotion and graduation requirements.
    2.2 Increase instructional time by a lengthened school day and school year.
    2.3 Develop students' citizenship skills, self-esteem, and respect for others.
    2.4 Incorporate critical thinking and problem solving skills throughout the curriculum.
    2.5 Provide career opportunities through vocational education.
    2.6 Provide special education services to meet individual needs in the least restrictive environment.

- 2.7 Provide appropriate language and content-area instruction to limited English proficient students.
- 2.8 Provide differentiated and advanced curricula for gifted and talented students.
- 2.9 Address public health problems through the curriculum and students' health needs through appropriate programs.
- 2.10 Provide appropriate compensatory programs for students performing below standards.

3. **Personnel:** Qualified and effective personnel will be attracted and retained.
   - 3.1 Set standards for the profession and ensure that all personnel demonstrate competence in professional skills.
   - 3.2 Establish extended personnel contracts for increased instructional time and enhanced professional training.
   - 3.3 Ensure adequate and competitive compensation commensurate with responsibilities.
   - 3.4 Provide effective, professional working environments.
   - 3.5 Provide training in methods and techniques of instruction to meet students' varying abilities and learning styles.
   - 3.6 Recruit, train, and retain qualified staff in critical shortage areas.
   - 3.7 Increase the number of qualified minority teachers and administrators to reflect the ethnic composition of the state.
   - 3.8 Provide a variety of management systems to assist personnel in teaching and managing instruction.
   - 3.9 Review and refine teacher and administrator appraisal policies and procedures.

4. **Organization and Management:** The organization and management of all levels of the educational system will be productive, efficient, and accountable.
   - 4.1 Review and redefine the responsibilities of the State Board of Education, the Texas Education Agency, and regional education service centers, and reorganize to ensure efficient and effective leadership and management.
   - 4.2 Implement performance-based accreditation linked to effective schools research and attend, on a priority basis, to those districts most in need of technical assistance.
   - 4.3 Provide an efficient and effective system to ensure compliance with rule and law.
   - 4.4 Ensure that the training of school board members strengthens their abilities to direct the educational process.
   - 4.5 Coordinate statewide and local educational planning.
   - 4.6 Implement the Public Education Information Management System.
   - 4.7 Strengthen coordination among the Texas Education Agency and other state agencies, colleges and universities, employment training programs, and the private sector.
   - 4.8 Enhance local responsibility for quality educational programs.
   - 4.9 Implement methods to improve the ability of small districts to use funds efficiently and to deliver a well-balanced curriculum of high quality to all students.

4.10 Provide services at the state level to ensure effective management of the public education systems.

4.11 Implement site-based management and other systems to support campus decision making.

5. **Finance:** The financing of public education will be adequate, equitable, and efficient.
   5.1 Develop a management and financial reporting system that will provide meaningful and timely information at the state, district, and campus levels.
   5.2 Fund necessary variations in program and service costs among districts on a continuous basis.
   5.3 Establish an efficient education system in which funding supports effective programs and student progress.
   5.4 Provide adequate and equitable funding levels for education.
   5.5 Adopt efficient and effective financial and business practices.
   5.6 Provide funding to ensure adequate school facilities.
   5.7 Administer and manage the Permanent School Fund for the optimum use and benefit of public school students and public education.

6. **Parent Responsibility:** Parents will be full partners in the education of their children.
   6.1 Encourage parental participation in all facets of the school program.
   6.2 Increase interaction between school personnel and parents regarding the performance and development of students.
   6.3 Provide educational programs that strengthen parenting skills.
   6.4 Expand adult literacy programs to help parents provide educational assistance to their children.

7. **Community and Business Involvement:** Business and other members of the community will be partners in the improvement of schools.
   7.1 Seek extensive and varied participation by the private sector in public education.
   7.2 Provide adequate literacy and secondary education programs for out-of-school youths and adults.
   7.3 Encourage the full use of school resources and facilities for community and lifelong learning.
   7.4 Develop mutually beneficial partnerships between schools and community base organizations.
   7.5 Promote the establishment or expansion of school volunteer programs.
   7.6 Increase the public's awareness of the role of public education in the state's economic development.

8. **Research, Development, and Evaluation:** Instruction and administration will be improved through research that identifies creative and effective methods.
   - 8.1 Develop and sustain a comprehensive, coordinated plan for statewide educational research.
   - 8.2 Apply research results to improve all facets of public education.
   - 8.3 Institute and maintain a research clearinghouse.
   - 8.4 Develop demonstration programs and encourage local initiatives for new instructional arrangements and management techniques.
   - 8.5 Use technology to increase the equity, efficiency, and effectiveness of classroom instruction, instructional management, and administration.
   - 8.6 Establish systems of multiple measures and indicators in program and campus evaluation.
   - 8.7 Investigate options for parental choice in educational programs and school sites.

9. **Communications:** Communications among all public education interests will be consistent, timely, and effective.
   - 9.1 Communicate state education policies, needs, and performance to the Governor, the Legislature, students, parents, teachers, school administrators, and the public.
   - 9.2 Determine public perceptions of local schools and provide complete and accurate information about developments and achievements in the public school system.
   - 9.3 Establish an effective, integrated telecommunications system.
   - 9.4 Recognize outstanding achievements by students, teachers, administrators, parents, business, staff, schools, and school districts.

Field 63: Mid-Management Administrator Objectives for the ExCET

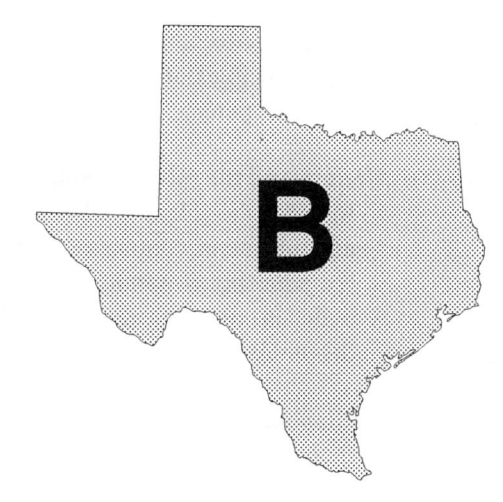

SUBAREAS

Foundations of Education
Organizational Management
Personnel Management
Instructional Management
Educational Governance, School-Community Relations, and Student Affairs

Foundations of Education

763—001 **Understand trends and issues in education.**
Includes major historical trends and factors since 1950 and current trends and issues that influence education.

763—002 **Understand principles of educational and social psychology.**
Includes major terms and concepts associated with educational psychology, factors in educational psychology related to motivation and learning, principles of motivation theories and group dynamics that can be applied to the education process.

763—003 **Understand principles of learning theories and the learning process.**
Includes major learning and instructional theories and their characteristics, significant factors that affect the learning process, the importance of the learning environment in the learning process, and the role of the mid-management administrator in making the school environment favorable to learning.

763—004 **Apply ethical principles to education practices and populations.**
Includes ethical professional practices and performance standards in education, and principles of ethical conduct toward fellow educators and administrators, students, parents, and the community.

763—005 **Understand the role of communication and communication skills in education.**
Includes the role of verbal and nonverbal communication skills in educational administration, communication techniques appropriate for accomplishing tasks in the educational administration process, and techniques used to establish and maintain communication networks in order to accomplish administrative goals and disseminate information.

763—006 **Understand major concepts of educational research.**
Includes educational research sources appropriate for various purposes, and the interpretation of educational research data.

Organizational Management

763—007 **Understand principles of organizational theory.**
Includes major organizational theories and their characteristics, concepts and procedures for implementing change, and organizational skills appropriate for various situations in a school setting.

763—008 **Understand principles and techniques of decision making.**
Includes major decision-making techniques and their characteristics, and the application of decision-making skills to various situations.

763—009 **Understand the goal-development and goal-implementation process.**
Includes steps in the goal-development process, functions of the goal-development process in educational administration, procedures for implementing goals in educational administration, and techniques for evaluating the goal-development and goal implementation process.

763—010 **Understand principles of public school finance.**
Includes federal, state, and local sources of funding and regulations that affect public school funding.

763—011 **Understand the school-budget development process.**
Includes major steps in developing a district-level or building-level budget, and budgeting principles and procedures appropriate for various situations.

763—012 **Understand building-level fiscal management**
Includes major concepts and terms associated with building-level accounting, budgeting, recordkeeping, and reporting: and appropriate techniques and applications of cost analysis.

763—013 **Understand facility planning and management.**
Includes procedures and considerations involved in facility planning and management, maintenance issues related to facility management, and safety and security procedures in facility management.

763—014 **Understand factors involved in building-level student services management.**
Includes factors involved in managing student transportation services, food services, health services, and field trips.

Personnel Management

763—015 **Apply counseling concepts, techniques, and procedures related to management.**
Includes stress management strategies and techniques, and principles and techniques of counseling appropriate for various situations.

763—016 **Apply concepts and skills associated with team management.**
Includes leadership skills associated with team management, techniques for team building, ways to involve staff in team decisions to accomplish instructional or management goals, and team management skills appropriate for various situations.

763—017 **Apply concepts and skills associated with group facilitating.**
Includes group facilitating skills and techniques and their functions, ways to facilitate effective communication among group members to accomplish tasks, and leadership and group facilitating skills appropriate for various situations.

763—018 **Identify the rights and responsibilities of teachers.**
Includes constitutional, contractual, and liability issues and federal, state, and local policies related to teacher rights and responsibilities.

763—019 **Identify procedures for recruiting, interviewing, selecting, and assigning staff.**
Includes procedures and legal guidelines for recruiting, screening, interviewing, and selecting staff; and criteria and procedures for assigning staff.

763—020 **Identify causes of and procedures for suspending, nonrenewing, and dismissing staff.**
Includes causes and procedures for suspending and dismissing staff, reasons and procedures for nonrenewing staff, and standard grievance procedures for staff.

763—021 **Understand staff development program and procedures.**
Includes types of programs and their benefits, the role of faculty and administrators in determining needs and establishing procedures, ways to evaluate programs, and the role of professional organizations.

763—022 **Analyze the relationship between administrative supervision and staff development.**
Includes competencies essential for successful administrative leadership, the role of the mid-management administrator as an instructional and administrative leader, and activities appropriate for inclusion in a continuing in-service education plan to implement.

763—023 **Understand procedures for assessing staff performance.**
Includes procedures and instruments for assessing staff performance, ways to address problems and issues related to staff performance assessment, ways in which staff assessment information can be used to formulate a plan for improvement, and techniques for communicating and disseminating staff assessment information.

Instructional Management

763—024 **Understand curriculum development and planning.**
Includes criteria and procedures for determining curriculum needs and formulating curriculum goals; ways to involve faculty, staff, and community members in curriculum planning; and procedures for developing instructional objectives and activities for accomplishing instructional objectives.

763—025 **Understand principles of curriculum design.**
Includes factors involved in designing and sequencing curricula; criteria and procedures for evaluating curriculum design and instructional materials; procedures and criteria for reviewing, selecting, and explaining the use of materials for curriculum design; and factors that can influence curriculum design.

763—026 **Identify reasons and strategies for implementing new or revised curricula.**
Includes reasons for implementing new or revised curricula; strategies for bringing about change in curricula; procedures for disseminating, promoting, and implementing new or revised curricula; and procedures for evaluating and modifying new or revised curricula.

763—027 **Understand curricular program designed to address the needs of special populations.**
Includes characteristics of curricular programs designed for special populations; ways in which curricular programs can be adapted to address the needs of special populations; procedures for designing, implementing, and monitoring curricular programs for special populations; and techniques for evaluating and revising curricular programs for special populations.

763—028 **Understand instructional management principles.**
Includes various teaching methods and their applications; factors in developing, implementing, and evaluating lessons; instructional strategies appropriate for various situations; and uses and characteristics of computers in educational instruction.

763—029 **Understand principles of program evaluation.**
Includes formative and summative program evaluations and their characteristics, methods of data collection, techniques for presenting data, and the interpretation of program evaluation data.

763—030 **Understand testing instruments and programs and their uses in curriculum evaluation.**
Includes types of standardized and nonstandardized tests and their characteristics; various measurement techniques and their uses in curriculum evaluation; testing programs used in Texas, and their functions; and the relationship between testing instruments and programs and curriculum development.

763—031 **Apply knowledge of statistical principles in testing and measurement.**
Includes concepts of validity, reliability, objectivity, standardization, and norms; and the interpretation of statistical results.

763—032 **Understand student assessment methods and programs.**
Includes methods of student assessment and their characteristics, appropriate uses of student assessment information, and techniques for communicating to parents an educational plan based on student assessment information.

Educational Governance, School-Community Relations, and Student Affairs

763—033 **Understand the organizational structure and functions of educational governance at the federal, state, and local levels.**
Includes types and functions of federal education programs, the role of the state legislature and the Texas Education Agency in determining educational policy, the regulatory functions of educational governance at the district and building-level, and the policy-making functions of educational governance at the district and building-level.

763—034 **Identify characteristics and functions of professional organizations.**
Includes national and state professional organizations and their characteristics; characteristics of national, state, and curriculum specific educational organizations; and functions of teacher unions.

763—035 **Understand factors involved in school public relations.**
Includes ways in which the media can be used to publicize school issues and activities, ways of determining and assessing local public opinion of school programs, ways in which the community can support the local school system, and ways to improve school-community public relations.

763—036 **Analyze ways to establish and maintain positive school-parent relations.**
Includes the role of the parent-teacher association, parent-teacher conferences, and booster clubs in establishing school-parent relations.

763—037 **Understand student rights and responsibilities.**
Includes constitutional issues related to student rights and responsibilities, and legislation and regulations related to student rights and responsibilities and their characteristics.

763—038 **Understand the maintenance and use of student records.**
Includes procedures for maintaining and using student records, regulations regarding access to student records, and issues of confidentiality related to maintaining and using student records.

763—039 **Analyze procedures and standards for student discipline.**
Includes appropriate and legal student disciplinary measures, functions and characteristics of behavior management strategies related to student discipline, and the influence of the learning environment on student discipline.

763—040 **Understand types, purposes, and functions of student organizations and activities.**

Includes types of student organizations and their characteristics, the purposes and functions of student organizations and activities, and regulations and procedures related to managing and supervising student organizations and activities.

763—041 **Understand school counseling and psychological services available to students.**

Includes the functions and characteristics of school counseling services, student characteristics that indicate a need for school psychological services, and procedures for referring students to counseling and psychological services.

763—042 **Understand special student populations and their needs.**

Includes programs for special needs students; types of specialists and the services they provide to special needs students; factors involved in identifying, evaluating, and placing special needs students; and the benefits of a culturally diverse student population.

763—043 **Understand causes of students' social problem and methods or referral to outside agencies.**

Includes causes and methods of referral for child abuse and other problems affecting students' well-being; causes and methods of referral for drug and alcohol abuse problems; local, county, and other student health programs and their functions; and referral procedures and selection criteria appropriate for various situations.

Field 64: Superintendent Objectives for the ExCET

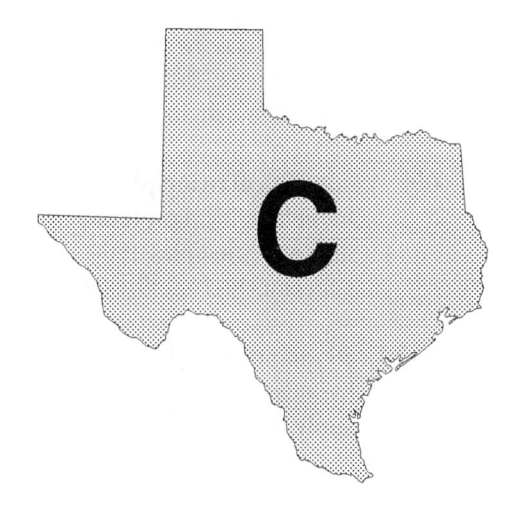

SUBAREAS

Foundations of Education
Organizational Management
Personnel Management
Curriculum and Evaluation
Educational Governance and Student Affairs

Foundations of Education

764—001 **Understand the history and philosophy of education.**
Includes major philosophies of education and their characteristics, major historical trends and factors that have influenced the development of educational philosophies and practices, and major purposes of education and their effects in the United States.

764—002 **Analyze sociological issues in education.**
Includes the influence of historical and legal factors on current sociological issues in education, the influence of current demographic trends on educational practices, and the socioeconomic factors that affect practices or issues in education.

764—003 **Understand principles of educational psychology.**
Includes major terms and concepts associated with educational psychology, factors in educational psychology related to motivation and learning, principles of motivation theories and their application to the education process, and major learning theories and their characteristics.

764—004 **Understand principles of learning theories and the learning process.**
Includes teacher and learner characteristics that affect the learning process, the importance of the learning environment in the learning process, and the role of the superintendent in making the school environment favorable to learning.

764—005 **Apply ethical principles to educational practices and populations.**
Includes ethical professional practices and performance standards used in education, and principles of the Texas Educator's Code of Ethics as they relate to fellow educators and administrators, students, parents, and the community.

764—006 **Understand the role of communication and communication skills in education.**
Includes the role of verbal, nonverbal, and written communication skills as they apply to educational administration; appropriate communication techniques for accomplishing tasks in the educational administration process; and techniques to establish and maintain communication networks to accomplish administrative goals and disseminate information.

764—007 **Interpret educational research.**
Includes the analysis of educational research data, the interpretation of educational research data for constituents, differences between experimental and nonexperimental designs in educational research, and the application of statistical terminology and principles in education.

764—008 **Understand the proposal writing process.**
Includes types and characteristics of Requests for Proposals; major sources of financial support and grants for education; steps in standard proposal writing, including program and budget audits; and methods for evaluating proposals.

Organizational Management

764—009 **Understand principles of organizational theory.**
Includes major organizational theories, their characteristics, and their relationship to various situations.

764—010 **Apply principles of organizational theory and practice.**
Includes major management models, their characteristics, and their relationship to various administrative situations.

764—011 **Understand the goal-development and goal-implementation process.**
Includes steps in the goal-development process, functions of the goal-development process in educational administration, procedures for implementing goals in educational administration, and techniques for evaluating the goal-development and goal implementation process.

764—012 **Understand theories of leadership and leadership styles.**
Includes the advantages and disadvantages of different leadership styles, and leadership styles appropriate for various situations.

764—913 **Understand the planning function.**
Includes techniques and data acquisition methods used for planning, the application of planning tools in various situations, and strategies for projecting future needs and directions.

764—014 **Understand principles of public school finance.**
Includes federal, state, and local sources of and regulations pertaining to public school funding; issues related to distribution of state monies and local taxation policies; and procedures for developing local school budgets.

764—015 **Understand the school-budget development process.**
Includes major budget development approaches, steps in developing district-level budgets, the application of budgeting principles and procedures in various situations, and steps in the budget adoption and evaluation process.

764—016 **Understand procedures for purchasing, storing, and distributing equipment and supplies.**
Includes procedures for purchasing, storing, and distributing equipment and supplies; and the influence of special problems on managing the purchase, storage, distribution, and disposal of supplies and equipment.

764—017 **Understand fiscal management.**
Includes major concepts and terms associated with internal accounting, reporting, and recordkeeping procedures; techniques and applications of cost analysis and operational efficiency; fiscal management policies related to employee benefits and other applications; applications of computer-based information processing; and principles of debt management.

764—018 **Understand principles of generating revenue.**
Includes laws and issues pertaining to taxation, bond issues, investment, and depository banking.

764—019 **Understand principles of controlling expenditures.**
Includes basic principles of debt service and insurance risk management.

764—020 **Understand facility planning and management.**
Includes procedures and considerations involved in facility planning and management, principles involved in designing and furnishing a building, maintenance and insurance issues related to facility management, and safety and security procedures in facility management.

764—021 **Understand factors involved in student services management.**
Includes factors and procedures involved in managing student transportation services, school food services, student health services, and the school calendar.

764—056 **Understand factors involved in school public relations.**
Includes ways in which the media can be used to publicize school issues and activities, ways of determining and assessing local public opinion of school programs, ways in which the community can support the local school system, and ways to improve school-community public relations.

764—057 **Analyze ways to establish effective district-wide program in school-community relations.**
Includes the roles of the parent-teacher association, parent-teacher conferences, booster clubs, civic organizations, and community advisory group in establishing school-parent relations.

764—058 **Understand principles of conducting bond election campaigns.**
Includes legal and administrative procedures for planning and conducting bond election campaigns, strategies for obtaining voter approval of bond issuance, and public relations strategies for issuing bonds.

764—059 **Understand the political environment of the school organization.**
Includes types and characteristics of community power structures within school districts, the influence of community power structures on the political environment of the school organization, and the influence of statewide political forces and interest groups.

764—060 **Understand techniques for generating or identifying community goals.**
Includes types and characteristics of community educational goals, techniques for defining and generating these goals, and the role of the superintendent in integrating school and community goals.

Personnel Management

764—022 **Understand dynamics involved in effective interpersonal relations.**
Includes major concepts related to human motivation, and major factors involved in establishing and maintaining a climate of mutual trust, respect, and concern.

764—023 **Apply concepts and skills associated with team management.**
Includes leadership skills associated with team management, techniques for team building, ways to involve personnel in team decisions to accomplish instructional or management goals, and team management skills appropriate for various situations.

764—024 **Apply concepts and skills associated with group facilitating.**
Includes group facilitating skills and techniques and their functions, ways to facilitate effective communication among group members to accomplish a task, and the application of leadership and group facilitating skills to various situations.

764—025 **Analyze the principles and procedures related to administering personnel policies.**
Includes factors involved in the development of compensation and benefit programs; and laws and regulations relating to contracts, certification, assignments, and personnel records.

764—026 **Identify procedures for recruiting, interviewing, selecting, and assigning personnel.**
Includes procedures for recruiting, interviewing, selecting, and assigning personnel; and principles of affirmative action in recruiting, selecting, and assigning personnel.

764—027 **Identify causes of and procedures for the suspension, transfer, reduction, and dismissal of personnel.**
Includes acceptable causes and procedures for suspending, reducing, and dismissing personnel; reasons and appropriate procedures for transferring personnel; and standard personnel grievance procedures.

764—028 **Analyze the rights and responsibilities of teachers.**
Includes constitutional, contractual, and liability issues, and federal, state, and local policies related to teacher rights and responsibilities.

764—029 **Identify characteristics and functions of employee organizations.**
Includes national and state employee organizations and their characteristics; characteristics of national, state, and curriculum specific educational organizations; functions of employee organizations; and the status of professional consultations in Texas.

764—030 **Understand staff development program and procedures.**
Includes types of in-service educational programs and their benefits, the role of faculty and administrators in determining needs and establishing procedures for developing in-service educational programs, ways to evaluate staff development programs, and the role of professional organizations in staff development.

764—031 **Analyze the relationship between administrative supervision and staff development.**
Includes the role of the superintendent as an instructional and administrative leader, and the implications of personnel and program evaluation for in-service programs.

764—032 **Understand procedures for assessing staff performance.**
Includes procedures and instruments for assessing staff performance, ways to address problems and issues related to staff performance assessment, ways in which staff assessment information can be used to formulate a plan for improvement, and techniques for communicating and disseminating staff assessment information.

Educational Governance and Student Affairs

764—040 **Understand the organizational structure and functions of educational governance at the federal level.**
Includes roles and responsibilities of Congress in relation to education, types and functions of federal education programs, and the role of the federal government in education.

764—041 **Understand the organizational structure and functions of educational governance at the state level in Texas.**
Includes the role of the state legislature and executive branch in determining educational policy; and the role of the State Board, the Texas Education Agency, and other state agencies in developing and implementing state educational policies.

764—042 **Understand principles of the accreditation process in Texas.**
Includes steps, standards, and criteria in the accreditation process, and ways in which the accreditation process influences curricula.

764—043 **Understand the organizational structure and functions of educational governance and accountability at the district level.**
Includes the policy-making and public relations functions of educational governance.

764—044 **Understand interrelationships between school boards and superintendents.**
Includes the roles and relationships between superintendents and school boards; the role of the school board in establishing policies, setting goals, evaluating programs, and conducting hearings; and the superintendent's role in administering school board policies and providing educational leadership.

764—045 **Understand the management of school board meetings.**
Includes issues and procedures related to establishing an agenda, standard operating procedures, functions of various personnel, and techniques and procedures for managing public participation and media coverage.

764—046 **Understand the structure and functions of the local board of education.**
Includes procedures and regulations governing the nomination and election of local board of education members, and the role of the local board of education in recruiting and hiring superintendents.

764—047 **Understand student rights and responsibilities.**
Includes constitutional issues, legislation, and regulations related to student rights and responsibilities.

764—048 **Understand the maintenance and use of student records.**
Includes procedures for maintaining and using student records, regulations regarding access to student records, and issues of confidentiality related to maintaining and using student records.

764—049 **Analyze procedures and standards for student discipline.**
Includes student disciplinary measures appropriate for various situations, functions and characteristics of behavior management strategies related to student discipline, and the influence of the learning environment on student discipline.

764—050 **Understand types, purposes, functions, and accountability of student organizations and activities.**
Includes types of student organizations and their characteristics, the purposes and functions of student organizations and activities, and regulations and procedures related to managing and supervising student organizations and activities.

764—051 **Understand school counseling and psychological services available to meet the academic and social needs of students.**
Includes functions and characteristics of school counseling and school psychological services, procedures for referring students to counseling and psychological services, and the relationship between school counseling and psychological services and social service agencies.

764—052 **Understand special student populations and their needs.**
Includes legal guidelines related to the education of special populations, types and characteristics of programs for special needs students, and factors involved in identifying, evaluating, and placing special needs students.

764—053 **Understand multicultural education and its value.**
Includes the benefits of a culturally diverse student population, instructional methods and programs for students with culturally different backgrounds, training procedures for teachers of multicultural students, and factors involved in working with various cultural groups within the community.

764—054 **Understand student assessment and reporting methods.**
Includes methods of student assessment and their characteristics, appropriate uses of student assessment information, and techniques for communicating to parents an educational plan based on student assessment information.

764—055 **Understand the identification and utilization of community resources to meet the needs of students.**
Includes types and functions of community resources used to meet the legal, social, health, and instructional needs of students (including special education students); and procedures for coordinating school and community resources.

Curriculum and Evaluation

764—033 **Understand curriculum development and planning for regular and special populations.**
Includes criteria and procedures for determining curriculum needs and formulating curriculum goals; procedures for developing instructional objectives and appropriate activities for accomplishing instructional objectives for regular and special populations; curricular programs designed for special populations and the characteristics of these programs; and techniques for evaluating and revising curricular programs for special populations.

764—034 **Understand principles of curriculum and instructional design.**
Includes factors involved in designing and sequencing curricula; criteria and procedures for evaluating curriculum design and instructional materials; factors in developing, implementing and evaluating lesson plans; and instructional strategies appropriate for various situations.

764—035 **Identify reasons and strategies for implementing new or revised curricula.**
Includes reasons for implementing new or revised curricula; strategies for bringing about change in curricula; procedures for disseminating, promoting and implementing new or revised curricula; and procedures for evaluating and modifying new or revised curricula.

764—036 **Identify state curriculum requirements.**
Includes major legislation and historical trends that have influenced the development of state curriculum requirements; recommended and mandated curriculum requirements; the relationship between state-mandated programs and federally mandated curriculum programs; and major procedures in the textbook adoption process.

764—037 **Understand principles of program evaluation.**
Includes theories and models of program evaluation and their characteristics, methods of data collection, techniques for presenting data, and the interpretation of program evaluation data.

764—038 **Understand testing instruments and programs and their uses in curriculum evaluation.**
Includes types of standardized and nonstandardized tests and their characteristics, various measurement instruments and their uses in curriculum evaluation, testing programs in Texas and their functions, and uses of testing instruments and program for curriculum development and evaluation.

764—039 **Apply knowledge of statistical principles of testing, measurement, and reporting.**
Includes concepts of validity, reliability, objectivity, standardization, and norms.

Index

A

A Nation At Risk, 84, 92
Academic Excellence Indicators, 100–101, 107
Accountability, 91–93
 system, 91
Accounting, 252–262
Accreditation by TEA
 Public School, 100–101
 Standards, Teacher Education Program, 98
ADA (average daily attendance), 294
Adequacy of Funding, 190
Administrative code, 5, 11, 13, 29
Administrative law, 9–13, 21
Administrative Theory, 92, 427–444
Admission, Review, and
 Dismissal (ARD) Committees, 327
Adverse Actions, 171
Affirmative action, 165–166
African-Americans, 119–127
Afro-Americans, 155
Aguilar v. Feltan, 363
Alexander, Lamar, 84
Allport, Gordon, 111
Alternative center, 287
American Educational Research Association, 146
American Legal System, 20
American School Districts, 31
Americans With Disabilities Act, 82
Appellate Review, 25
Arena Boards, 154
Arena, 154, 155
Article I, Section 7, 25–27,
Article I, Section 8, 7, 25, 26
Article VII, Section 1, 4, 5
Asbestos, 298, 306
Assimilation, 117
Attendance reporting, 294
Attorney General's Opinions, 12
Audio-visual presentations, 303
Auditing, 264

B

Bacon, 428
Barnard, Henry, 86
Barnsley, 444
Basic Allotment, 194, 197
Bell, Terrell H., 83, 87
Bernays, Edward, 298
Bilingual education, 348–362
Bilingual Education Act, 84, 349
Bill of Rights, 78, 81
Blake/Mouton Grid, 440
Blau, 432
Boards (see School Board Members)
Bond elections, 306
Bonds, 315
Broadcast media, 305
Brown decision, 155
Brown v. Topeka, 146
Budget, 248–251
Budget planning, 299
Building Codes, 311
Bulletin 679, 53, 245, 246, 247
Bureaucracy Theory, 432
Bureaucracy, 443
Burlingame, M., 446

C

Cabinet, superintendent's, 305
Cable television, 303, 305
Callahan, 156, 433
Carl Perkins Act, 384
Carl Perkins Vocational Education Act, 371
Case Law, 13, 19
Central Education Agency
 committees, 72
 defined, 59
Certification, 167
Commissioner of Education
 authority, 67–69

Central Education Agency, 5, 10, 12
Certification, 49, 97
Certiorari, 14
Challenges/Issues Facing Texas Schools, 44
Chaos research, 428, 431, 444
Chapter I, 363
Child Benefit Theory, 79
Child Nutrition Programs, 49
Civil Judicial Procedures, 21
Civil Law, 19
Civil Rights Act of 1871, 8, 27
Civil Rights Act of 1964, 79, 82, 349
Clark, Harley (Judge), 183, 192–195
Classical Period, 92, 432
Cluster breakfasts, 303
Coch, 435
Cochran v. Louisiana
   State Board of Education, 78
Code of conduct, 278
Code of ethics, 168, 169
Cohen, 444
Coleman Report, 124
Colonial History, 20
Commerce Clause, 25–27
Commission on Higher Education, 452
Commissioner of Education, 5, 11, 12, 48
Communication, external, 304
   filters, 300
   internal, 302, 303
Community-Based Alternative
   Education Programs, 375
Community Education, 393
   advisory councils, 402
   community needs assessments, 403
   definition, 394
   developmental in Texas, 397
   evaluation, 406
   financing, 400
   K–12, 408,
   philosophy, 393, 395
   resources, 405
   school building use, 397

   schools as community centers, 396
   scope, 394
   steps in establishing programs, 398
Compensatory education, 362–378
Complaint, 22, 23
Compulsory attendance, 290
Compulsory Education, 86
Comte, August, 428
Conflict, 434
Conflict resolution, 420
Congress, 147
Connally, John, 191
Constitution of 1869, 191
Constitutional issues, 165
Constitutional law, 6, 13
Constitutional Provisions, 6, 7, 28
Consultant, public relations, 305
Continental Congress, 25
Continuing Contracts, 171
Continuous Participation Theory, 157
Contracts, 168
Cooms, F.S., 446
Coordinating board, 112
Corporal punishment, 289
Cost Education Index, 194
Counts, George, 145, 155
County Education Districts
   (CEDs), 196, 201–207
Criminal history checks, 164
Crisis communication, 307
Cuban, 152
Cubberley, Ellwood P., 184–185
Cultural and Ethnic Groups, 111–138
Cultural diversity, 113–114
Cultural diversity in Texas, 115–119
Culture, 113, 445
Curriculum Guides/Lesson Plans, 222–223

D

Dahl, 155
Darwin, 428
Deal, 445

Debra P. v. Turlington, 123
Defendant, 14, 19–24
Definitions of theory, 427
della Vos system, 383
Deming, 441
Demographics, 345–347
Demographics of Texas, 95, 139
Desert Storm, 300
Detention center, 286
Development of American Public Schools, 2
Dickson, 434
Disabilities, 325, 329, 330
Discipline Management Plans
   board requirements, 280
   contents, 279
   staff involvement, 281
Dismissal, 173
Dissatisfaction Theory, The, 158, 441
Drug abuse, 298, 306

E
Easton, 158
Economic Opportunity Act, 81
Edgar, J.W., 74
Edgewood ISD v. Kirby,
   188, 192–196, 211, 309
Education Act of 1939, 190
Education Amendments of 1972, 384
Education for All Handicapped Children Act, 82
Education Service Centers, 150
*Education Consolidation and
   Improvement Act (ECIA)*, 82, 190
Educational Management Information System (EMIS), 246
Educational public relations, definition, 297
Effective schools, 288
Effective Schools Research, 234–235
   environment, 235
   instructional personnel, 234
   principal's leadership, 234
   program, 235

*Elementary and Secondary Education Act
   of 1965 (ESEA)*, 48, 52, 81, 190, 362
Elementary curriculum, 215
Eliot (1959), 146
Elite boards, 154–155
Emergency School Aid Act (ESAA), 82
Equal Educational Opportunity, 122, 349
Equal Employment Opportunities
   Commission, 166
Equal Protection Clause, 193
Equalization Models, 185–187
   Strayer-Haig Model, 185–186
   Strayer-Haig-Mort Model, 186–187
   Strayer-Haig-Mort-Johns Model, 187
Equity, 137
Ethnic evolution, 118
Ethnic groups, 118
Ethnically diverse, 163
Ethnocentrism, 118
Evaluation
Everson v. Board of Education, 78
ExCET, 98–99, 167
Expulsion, 283
Extended year services, 333

F
Facilities, 309–322
Facility
   evaluation, 314
   financing, 315
   opening, 316
   planning, 311
   spaces, 312
Facility inventory, state, 310
Facility standards, 310–311
Fair Labor Standards Act, 8, 26
Federal Administrative Law, 10, 13
Federal Civil Case, 19
Federal Courts, 78, 89
Federal Criminal Case, 19
Federal Government Influence, 25–27
Federal Government Involvement
   in Education, 79, 82, 91

in School Finance 189–190
Federal Judicial Law, 9
Federal Legislation, 80
Federal Register, 87
Federal Statutes, 8, 9, 28
Federal Statutory Law, 9
Financial, 183–212
First Amendment, 78, 79
Fiscal Neutrality, concept of, 193
Focus groups, 302
Follett, Mary Parker, 431, 434, 435
Food service, 273–274
Foundation School Fund
  Budget Committee, 73
Foundation School Program, 196
Fourteenth Amendment, 78, 79, 89
French, 435

G

G. I. Bill of Rights, 81
Garbage-Can, 444
Garcia v. San Antonio, 27
Gardner, David Pierpont, 83
Geertz, 445
Gender groups, 118
General Systems Theory, 437
General Welfare Clause, 25, 26, 193
George-Barden Act, 384
George-Deen Act, 384
George-Elzey Act, 384
George-Reed Act, 384
Getzels, 439
Gibbons v. Ogden, 26
Gifted and Talented characteristics, 338, 341
Gifted and Talented funding, 337, 341
Gifted and Talented legislation
  *ECIA (Education Consolidation
    and Improvement Act),* 336
  H.B. 1050, 337
  P.L. 95–561, 336
Gifted and Talented personnel
  Certification, 340
  Recommendations, 340

Shortages, 342
Training, 342
Gifted and Talented programs
  Characteristics, 338–339
  Delivery models, 339–340
  Heterogeneous grouping, 341
Gifted and Talented students and
  Cultural bias, 342
  Assessment, 342
  Identification, 341, 343
Gilmer Aiken Bill (S.B. 115), 59–62
Gleick, 431, 444
Goals, Learning, 97
  SBOE, 96
  State Legislature, 96–97
  Systems, 95–96
Governance, Local Districts, 31
Governmental Commissions, 82
Governors, 149–151
Graduation Requirements, 198–199
Great Depression, 80
Gresson, 152
Gretzels-Guba Model, 436
Griffiths, 431, 437
Guaranteed Yield, 199
Guba, 439
Gulick, 433

H

Haig, Robert, 185–187
Hailer, E. J. 445
Halpin, 440
Hawthorne Studies, 92, 434
  energy management, 321–322
  maintenance, 316, 319–320
  operations, 318
  security, 318
Hawthorne, 435
Herzberg's Motivation-Hygiene Theory, 175
Hierarchy of Needs, 175
High school curriculum, 217–218
Higher education, 449–457
  coordination, 452–453

financing, 454
governance, 451
history, 449–451
Hoar, George F., 86
Hobby, William P., 184
Hobson v. Hartsen, 123
Homans, 435, 438
Horace Mann, 4
House Bill 2885, 196–200
House Bill 72, 63–64, 94, 192, 214–220, 246, 385
House, 430
Hoy, W.K., 446
Human Relations Period, 92
Humanistic Period, 434

I

Iannoccone, 158
Idiographic, 439, 440
Imperative for Educational Reform, The, 84
In-School-Suspension, 286
Inclusion, 333
Individualized educational plans (IEP), 324, 325, 326, 331, 333
Individuals with Disabilities Act (IDEA), 82
Input-Output (Systems) Theory, 158
Instructional Models, 236–237
Interest group, 150
Interview, 164
Issues management, 306

J

Jefferson's Plan for Education, 4
Jefferson, Thomas, 3, 78
Johns, Roe L., 187
Johnson, President Andrew, 86
Judgment and Costs, 24
Judicial Law, 6, 13, 16, 29
Judicial Review, 21, 25, 27, 28
Judiciary Act of 1789, 14, 28
Junior High curriculum, 215–217

K

Keith, 445
Kennedy, 445
Key Communicator Networks
external, 304
internal, 303
Key Districts, concept of, 186
Kimbrough and Nunnery, 431
Kimbrough, R.B., 446
Kirby, Bill, 62
Kirst, 158
Koreng, 444
Kuhn, 428, 430, 431, 443

L

Lakatos, 431
Lanham Act, 81
Larger Systems, 438
Larry P. v. Wilson, 123
Lau v. Nichols, 351
Lawsuit, 9, 12, 22, 24 25
Lead, drinking fountains, 298, 306
Leadership, 415–419
Leadership Behavior Description Questionnaire, 440
Least restrictive environment (LRE), 324, 330–331, 333
Lee, 441
Legal Assaults on School Finance, 187–189
Adequacy of Funding Cases, 188–189
Apportionment Cases, 187
Equal Educational Opportunity Cases, 188
Revenue Aspect Cases, 188
Legal Basis for State Control Over Education, 3
Legal requirements
facilities construction, 314
Legislative Budget Board, 67, 73
Legislative Education Board (LEB), 64, 66, 69, 73
Legislative law, 4, 6, 8, 13
Legislative Session, 11
Lobbying, 150

Local citizen control, 157
Local Leeway, concept of, 187
Local school districts, 153
Logical Positivism, 430, 431
Long Range Plans, 96
Long-range Plan for Texas Public Schools, 385
Loomis, 438
Loose Coupling, 443
Lorenz, 444
Lunenburg, F.C., 446
Lutz and Mertz, 148
Lutz, 152, 154, 158, 431, 441, 443, 445
Lutz, 1968, 148

M
Machine politics, 145
Madison, 78
Madison, James, 146
Management Information System, 102
Manifest destiny, 118
Mann, 441
Manpower Development and Training Act, 384
Marbury v. Madison, 28
March, 444
Marrs, S.N.M., 61
Marshall, 445
Marx, 431, 434
Maslow's Hierarchy of Needs, 175
Mayo, 434
McCleskey, 3, 17–19, 29
McCollum v. Board of Education, 79
McCown, Scott (Judge), 194–196, 207
McGregor, 440
McGregor's Theory X and Theory Y, 175
Media relations, 306
Melting pot, 113
Melting Pot Theory, 115
Mendelbrot, 444
Meno, Lionel (Skip), 48, 69–70
Mertz, 157
Metcalf, 434
Metz, 441
Mexican-Americans, 128–132

bilingual education, 130
family structure, 129
Migrant education, 372
Migrant Student Record Transfer System (MSRTS}, 364
Minimum Foundation Program, 191
Miskell, C.G., 446
Mitchell, 445
Morrill Act, 80, 190, 383
Mort, Paul, 186–187
Motivation, 175
Municipal Courts, 17
Murray v. Curlett, 79

N
NAPT, 106
National Commission on Excellence in Education, 83, 84
National Conference of Professors of Educational Administration, 437
National Defense Education Act (NDEA), 81, 147, 189
National Reform Movement, 83
National School Public Relations Association, 297, 301
Native Indian Americans, 132–136
Nepotism, 39
News releases, 304
Newsletters, 303, 304
Newton, 428
Nomothetic, 439, 440
Norm reference test, 106
Northwest Ordinances, 147
Nunnery, M.Y., 446

O
O'Connor, 159
Office of the Attorney General, 12
Office of the Governor, 11
Old Deluder Satin Act, 184
Olsen, 444
Open Records Law, 12
Ordinance of 1785, 25, 80, 189

Ordinance of 1787, 80
Organization and Governance of Education, 1
Organized Anarchy, 444
Ornstein, A.C., 446
Ouchi, 440
Owens, R.G., 446

P

Padgert, 444
Paradigms, 431
Participatory Decision Making, 435
Permanent School Fund, 183, 191
Perot, H. Ross, 63, 196
Personnel, 161
   induction, 165
   planning, 162
   recruiting, 162
   selection, 164
Phillips, 430
Pierce v. Society of Sisters of the
   Holy Names of Jesus and Mary, 78
Plaintiff, 14, 19–24
Plank, 152
Planning Model, 94–95
Planning, public relations program, 298, 301
Pleadings, 21, 23
Pluralism, 117
Political Problems, 45
Politics, 145
Positivism, 428, 429, 430
Post-Positivism, 428, 443
Pregnancy, teen, 298
Pre-Positivism, 428, 429
   teacher, 99
Pre-professional Skills Test, 107
Pre-Professional Skills Test (PPST), 167
Presidency, 148
Pretrial Discovery, 23
Principal
   role responsibilities, 419

Problems of, 45
Problems, public education, 298, 306
Professional Education Associations, 153
Professional Practices Commission, 168
Property Tax, 184, 192, 196
Property Wealth, 183–184, 195, 198
Public Bureaucracies, 145
Public Education Information Management
   System (PEIMS), 53, 102–103
Public relations cycle, 300
Public Schools, 2, 4, 25
Publications, district, 303–305
Publics, district's, 301
Purchasing, 263–268

Q

Quasi-municipal Corporations, 6

R

Racial groups, 118
Radon, 298, 306
Reagan, President Ronald, 87
Reform, 152
Region Service Centers, role of, 299
   funding, 52–53
   goals & objectives, 54–55
   governance, 49–51
   history, 47
   location, 55–56
Related services, 331
Religious groups, 118
Richards and Kupper, 154
Robin Hood Plan, 193, 203
Robinson v. Cahill, 188
Rodriguez v. San Antonio ISD, 188, 191
Roetheisberger, 434
Role of the Judge, 20
Role of the Lawyers, 20
Rollback Tax Rate, 200

S

Satisfiers and Dissatisfiers, 177
S.B. 1, 94, 101, 194, 309, 322
SB 1019, 310–311
School Boards, 154, 298, 304, 305, 307
School Board Members, 149
   code of Ethics, 37
   election of, 36–38
   eligibility and Qualifications of, 35–36
   meetings, 39–40
   powers and Responsibilities, 34–35, 42
   training, 38
School-Community Relationship, 156
School Districts, 5, 6, 11–13
   Number in Texas, 32
   Organization Chart, 33
   Type, 32
School Finance, 44–45
   and the Federal Government, 189–190
   and the State, 184
School Finance Concepts
   Adaptability, 186
   Adequacy of Funding, 188
   Fiscal Neutrality, 193
   Key District, 186
   Local Leeway, 187
   Weighted Pupil, 186
School Site, 313
School Superintendent
   Evaluation, 43
   Recruitment and Appointment, 43
   Role and Responsibilities, 41–43
School-Community Relationship, 156
School Survey, 311
Scientific Management, 433
Second Morrill Act, 80
Secretary's Commission on Achieving Necessary Skills (SCANS), 85
Section 504 of the Rehabilitation Act, 82
Secular Public Schools, 4
Segiovanni, T.J., 446
Senate Bill 35I, 65, 67, 196–203

Senate Bill 1, 64, 68, 73, 198–199, 201, 348
Senate Bill 7, 206–207
Senate Education Agency, 150
Serrano v. Priest, 188, 191
Site-Based Decision Making, 415
Small Groups, 438
Smith, 445
Smith-Hughes Act, 189, 384
Societal Problems, 45
Special education delivery models, 330–331
Special education funding, 327–328
Special education identification and
   Cultural bias, 334
   Assessment, 334–335
Special education law
   Americans with Disabilities Act (ADA), 325
   H.B. 72, 328
   IDEA, 325, 327, 331, 335
   P.L. 94–140, 324, 325, 327, 331, 333, 335
   P.L. 99–457, 324
Special education litigation
   Alamo Heights ISD v. S.B.O.E., 333
   and Parent rights, 335
   Board v. Rowley, 326
   Espino v. Besteiro, 326
   Irving Independent School District v. Tatro, 326
   Larry P. v. Riles, 334
   Lora v. Board of Education, 326
   Mills, 325
   Pennsylvania Association for Retarded Citizens, 325
Special education personnel
   Aides, 332
   Certification, 331–332
   Recommendations, 332
   Types of, 331
Special education programs
   Characteristics, 328–329
   Inclusion, 333
   Transitions to work, 333–334
Special programs, 307

Specifications, educational, 312
Spring, 155
Staff development, 177, 307
   meetings, 303
Staffing, public relations department, 299
Standardized Testing, 226–233
   alternate assessment models, 233
   legislative mandates, 227–228
   philosophy, 226
   TAAS plan for improvement, 231–232
   test logistics, 228–230
   test reporting, analysis and
        interpretation, 230–231
State Administrative Law, 11
State Board, 153
State Board of Education, 5, 11, 12, 48
   early Board, 60
   of 1928, 61
   authority, 65–67, 68
State Board of Education Rules
   for the Handicapped, 327
State Department of Education, 5, 12
   authority 69–73
State Civil Case, 19
State Criminal Case, 19
State Department of Education, 5, 12
State Education Agency, 150
State Government, 1, 7, 11, 19, 26, 27
State Judicial Law, 16
State Legislature, 1, 4, 5, 8, 11, 16, 18
State of Texas Court System, 17
State of Texas, 1–5, 9, 11, 13–19, 28, 29
State Statutory Law, 9
Statutory Law, 5, 8, 9, 12, 18, 22
Stone v. Graham, 79
Strauss, Levi, 429
Strayer, George, 188–191
Strike, K. A., 445
Structure of Government, 6
Superintendent-Board Relationship, 155
Surveys, community, 301
Suspension, 281

Systems Theory, 437
Systems, 92–94
   outputs, 104

T

Tardies/truancy, 292
TASB 1990, 147
TASP, 98, 106
Tax rate, 249
Tax rollback, 306
Taylor, Frederick, 433
TEA, 309
Teacher appraisal, 173
Teaching Permits, 49
Technology, 313
Tenth Amendment, 4, 25, 27, 146, 149
Term Contracts, 172
Test scores, 297
Texas Assessment of Academic Skills
   (TAAS), 104–106, 226–233
Texas Assessment of Basic Skills
   (TABS), 104, 226–233
Texas Assessment of Minimum Skills, 105
Texas Association of
   School Administrators, 44, 153
Texas Association of School Boards, 40
Texas Constitution, 4, 9, 11, 12, 18
   authority, 59
   of 1866, '69, '71, 60
Texas Education Agency,
   5, 9–13, 29, 60, 70, 150, 153, 195
Texas Educational Assessment of
   Minimum Skills (TEAMS), 226–233
Texas Legislature, 4, 5
Texas School Districts, 32
Texas School Finance, 190–210
Texas School Finance Events, 208–210
Texas School Improvement Initiative, 101
Texas School Public Relations Association, 308
Texas State Plan and Guidelines for the
   Education of the *Gifted/Talented,* 337
Texas Supreme Court, 5, 17, 19

Textbooks, 223–226
   content requirements, 224
   district procedures, 225
   selection process, 225
   state adoption, purchase, acquisition and custody, 224–225
Theory is defined, 428
Theory Movement, 436
Theory X and Theory Y, 178, 440
Theory Z, 440
Total Quality Management, 441
Transportation, 269–272
Trial by Jury, 21, 24
Trial Courts, 14, 18
Two and Three Factor Models, 439

U
U. S. Constitution, 4, 6–8, 14, 21, 22, 27
U. S. Courts of Appeals, 14
U. S. Department of Education, 78, 82, 86–88
U. S. Supreme Court, 14, 16, 28
United States Congress, 8, 13, 14, 150
United States Constitution., 146
   Equal Protection Clause, 191
   General Welfare Clause, 189
Universal Education, 2, 4
University Council of Educational Administration, 437
Urbanization, 138
Urwick, 433, 434

V
Vocational education
   curriculum, 386
   funding, 388
   governance, 387
   history, 382
   philsophy, 381
   trends,
Vision, 423
von Bertalanffy, Luwig, 437
Vocational Education Act, 384
Vulnerability Thesis, 156

W
Wall of Separation, 146
Wang, 158
War on Poverty, 81
Weber, 432
Weick, 443
Weighted Pupil, concept of, 186
What Work Requires of Schools, 85
White, Mark, 192
Wilson, Woodrow, 145
Wirt, 160, 445
Wood, L.A., 61
Writ of Mandamus, 12, 20, 28

Z
Zeigler, Kehoe and Reisman, 156
Zorach v. Clausen, 79